Fayż Muḥammad Kātib Hazārah's

Afghan Genealogy and *Memoir of the Revolution*

Fayż Muḥammad Kātib Hazārah's
Afghan Genealogy and *Memoir of the Revolution*
Nizhādnāmah-i Afghān
and
Tazakkur al-inqilāb

Supplements to *The History of Afghanistan*

Edited and Translated by

R.D. McChesney and M.M. Khorrami

BRILL

LEIDEN • BOSTON
2019

The Library of Congress Cataloging-in-Publication Data is available online at http://catalog.loc.gov

Typeface for the Latin, Greek, and Cyrillic scripts: "Brill". See and download: brill.com/brill-typeface.

ISBN 978-90-04-39182-6 (hardback)
ISBN 978-90-04-39244-1 (e-book)

This book is printed on acid-free paper and produced in a sustainable manner.

CONTENTS

A NOTE ON TRANSLITERATION

For the most part we follow the transliteration system of *The International Journal of Middle Eastern Studies* for Persian and Arabic terms. Words that are found in either *Merriam-Webster Collegiate Dictionary*, Eleventh Edition, or *The Concise Oxford Dictionary*, Ninth Edition, are considered to be English words and are not transliterated unless part of a proper name or title. In this book these include: Afghan, Afghanistan, caravansary or caravanserai, crore (*kurūr*) Deccan, dervish, divan (or diwan), durbar, effendi, emir, emirate (or amir, amirate), farman or firman, hadith, hajj, hajji, Hanafi, fatwa, haram, harem, imam, Iran, Iraq, jihad, Kabul, kafir, khan, kelim or kilim, Lahore, lakh, madrasa or madrasah, mihrab, minaret, muezzin, mufti, mullah, munshi, Qandahar, Peshawar, Rawalpindi, sahib, seer (unit of weight), shah, Shiʿi, Shiʿism, Sufi, sultan, sultanate, Sunni, Tajik, ulema or ulama, Uzbek, Uzbekistan, wadi, zamindar.

PREFACE AND ACKNOWLEDGEMENTS

The two volumes translated here are a continuation of Fayż Muḥammad Kātib Hazārah's monumental Afghanistan history project. The two texts, *Nizhādnāmah-i Afghān*, an ethnographic-genealogical history of the peoples of Afghanistan, and *Taẕakkur al-inqilāb*, a memoir of the 1929 revolution in which the century-long Pashtūn Muḥammadzā'ī dynasty was toppled by a non-Pashtūn, the Tajik Ḥabīb Allāh Kalakānī, should be considered organic parts of the earlier-published history of his, *Sirāj al-tawārīkh*, and in terms of both style and content complement that monumental example of Afghanistan historiography.[1] We hope that this ensemble of works will serve to enrich future scholarship on Afghanistan and encourage students of Afghan history to think outside the box of colonial history. Taken together, these works offer a treasure trove of new information on economic, social, legal, political, and cultural matters including such issues as gender relations, sectarianism, tribalism, ethnic culture, minority-majority relationships, court and bureaucratic societies, military tactics, and tax and monetary policies.

Besides making available hitherto overlooked information about Afghanistan, the translations have a secondary objective as well: to contextualize and raise fundamental questions about the actual process and exigencies of historiography, i.e. how such writing is initiated and by whom, the motivation behind it—as far as that can be determined—and the immediate political ramifications and long-term consequences of the final product. Much of Fayż Muḥammad's writing was commissioned and supervised by officials—the amir and his representatives—but these two works were written for Fayż Muḥammad's own satisfaction alone and provide an opportunity to compare "official" and "unofficial" historiography. These texts remind the reader of the voice which often had to be suppressed in his commissioned and supervised writing.

It is rare in Islamicate and Persianate studies generally and in Afghan studies in particular to get a glimpse of the complex and often-changing circumstances under which a history was written; to know, in some

[1] Fayż Muḥammad Kātib Hazārah, *The History of Afghanistan: Fayż Muḥammad Kātib Hazārah's* Sirāj al-tawārīkh, Vols. 1–3 in 6 vols., edited and translated by R. D. McChesney and M. M. Khorrami, Leiden and Boston, Brill, 2013 and Vols. 3–4 in 5 vols., edited and translated by R. D. McChesney and M. M. Khorrami, Leiden and Boston, Brill, 2016 (henceforth Fayż Muḥammad, *The History*).

considerable detail, the life, career, and agonies of the historian; and have some insight into the interaction between what was written and what was going on at the same time in the writer's life. Both *Taẕakkur al-inqilāb* and *Nizhādnāmah-i Afghān* offer us just such an opportunity, providing insights, from the author's perspective, of how politicized the project of history-writing was, the kinds of rivalries that could and did emerge, and the arsenal at the author's disposal with which to counterattack and fend off efforts at appropriation.

Both works exist in Persian editions.[2] We were fortunate to be able to compare these editions with digital copies of the unicum manuscripts of both works, *Taẕakkur al-inqilāb* from the National Archives of Afghanistan in Kabul and *Nizhādnāmah-i Afghān* from the Malik Library in Tehran thanks to the work of colleagues in Afghanistan and Iran.

Twenty years ago one of the editors of this volume published a substantially reworked and annotated English translation of a Russian translation of the *Taẕakkur al-inqilāb* (Memoir of the Revolution).[3] Because the original manuscript, then held by the Afghan National Archives, was at the time (mid-1990s) inaccessible to researchers due to the civil war then engulfing the country, the only available version was the Russian translation published in 1988, towards the end of the Soviet occupation (1979–1989). In retrospect, with the original at hand, A. I. Shkirando's translation was a highly competent one. Nonetheless, translating a translation leaves a great deal to be desired. The fact that his translation raised what often seemed a slightly opaque screen of Russian between the Persian and an English rendering inevitably led to occasionally missing the point of what Fayż Muḥammad was trying to say and how he was saying it. We trust that this translation captures better the author's intent than did the 1999 publication.

---

2 Mullā Fayż Muḥammad Kātib Hazārah, *Taẕakkur al-inqilāb*, edited with introduction and notes by ʿAlī Amīrī and Dr. Ḥafīẓ Allāh Sharīʿatī, Köln: Kāveh, 2013 (henceforth Fayż Muḥammad, *Taẕakkur*) and idem, *Nizhādnāmah-i Afghān*, edited by Ḥājj Kāẓim "Yazdānī" and ʿAzīz Allāh Raḥīmī, Qum: Ismāʿīlīyan, 1372/1993 (henceforth Fayż Muḥammad, *Nizhādnāmah*).

3 R. D. McChesney, *Kabul Under Siege: Fayż Muḥammad's Account of the 1929 Uprising*, Princeton, Markus Wiener, 1999. The Russian work was Faiz Mukhammad, *Kniga upominanii o miatezhe*, translated, introduced, and annotated by A. I. Shkirando, Moscow, Nauka, 1988.

On Translating Fayż Muḥammad and Other Issues of Style

Here the translation will follow the principles adopted in the multiple volumes of Fayż Muḥammad Kātib's *The History of Afghanistan*. The author's style is followed as closely as possible while maintaining as high a degree of readability with a modern English-reading public in mind as possible. As noted in our introduction to the 2013 and 2016 publications, we diverge from Fayż Muḥammad's style in one notable way. His sentences are often extremely long and somewhat meandering. For the most part he knew where his train of thought was headed but not until one reaches the verb does the reader know for certain. These sentences often begin with an adverbial phrase indicating time ("during this time," "meanwhile," "on this same day," etc.) then introducing the topic/subject immediately followed by a relative clause often introducing another topic followed in turn by another relative clause, eventually returning to the first (and usually main) topic with a verb or gerund indicating action taken or sustained by the subject. Occasionally the sentence drifts away from what appeared to be the first and main topic and concludes with a verb indicating action taken by or against a secondary subject and never quite concluding the thought about the first topic/subject. Gerundive clauses indicate a sequence of events involving the main topic and the thought is then concluded with a perfective verb. An example from volume three of this type of sentence is the following:

> When the inter-governmental negotiations and correspondence had reached this point, His Holiness Najm al-Din Akhundzadah, who up to this time having done nothing more than advise and counsel those who had lost their way in the valley of folly and error and guide them back to the high road of the Holy Law and who, having no support from, or involvement with, officials of either [Afghan or British] government, and who, moreover, being fearful of this government and, as has been noted from time to time, having fled and settled in the mountain region of the frontier, was made aware of the secret activities and behavior of the Englishmen—for, as the [Arabic] saying goes, "a secret known to two people is as good as made public"—although they [the English] were communicating and corresponding with those people in a covert manner and, together with the son of Mulla Khalil Muhmand, focused his advice, preaching, and admonishments to prohibit vice and promote virtue on certain men like ʿAbd al-Wahid Khān, Amin Jan, Tula Khān, and Guldad, trouble-seeking and ill-natured Muhmand leaders who more than others maintained contact and corresponded with the English.

As it stands that sentence could be understood without breaking it into shorter sentences. The following eight sentences were originally one and much more difficult to follow as a single sentence.

> Today they captured Qāżī ʿAbd al-Raḥmān Khān, who from the very outset of Ḥabīb Allāh Khān [Kalakānī] and Sayyid Ḥusayn Khān's plundering and robbing had resisted them and vowed to Amān Allāh Khān that he would catch the bandits. When they learned of this, they murdered his brother and plundered the house he had in Kūh Dāman. The enmity between them grew ever more intense. When, as a result of the treachery of ministers and the disloyalty of the residents of Kabul and Chārdihī, Ḥabīb Allāh Khān and Sayyid Ḥusayn captured the capital, Qāżī ʿAbd al-Raḥmān fled to his home there and in Kūh Dāman and Kūhistān joined forces with the son of Malik Muḥammad, ʿAṭā Muḥammad. There, with the residents of Tagāb, he fought Ḥabīb Allāh Khān until they captured him in the village of Dih-i Sabz where he was hiding. By order of Ḥabīb Allāh Khān, they drew and quartered him in the Chawk while he was still alive. This monstrous infliction of the death penalty, beastly in its cruelty and inhumanity, finally convinced those who witnessed it or heard about it of the godlessness and barbarism of the Northerners.

Other slightly complicating issues in translating are punctuation and paragraphing. As is the style of all of Fayż Muḥammad's manuscripts, there is no punctuation or paragraphing. The usual sign of a completed sentence is a perfective verb followed by the conjunction *wa* (and) which together perform the same function as a period. In the print editions of both *Taẕakkur al-inqilāb* and *Nizhādnāmah-i Afghān*, the editors, Amīrī and Yazdānī and Raḥīmī respectively have added modern Persian punctuation and paragraphing but not always accurately and some of which actually confuses the intended meaning. Because accepted style for the translations obviously also requires both punctuation and paragraphing, we have altered what appears in the print editions wherever it seemed appropriate.

We have done our best to preserve Fayż Muḥammad's relatively limited range of metaphors and his ubiquitous use of repetition. His stock of metaphors generally falls into three categories: geographical ones, those derived from the body, and ones derived from clothing: mountain of adversity, valley of ignorance, highway of obedience, hand of tyranny, head of submission, ear of agreement, tongue of admonishment, foot of obedience, collar of rebelliousness, skirt of humility, sleeve of righteousness. We have also preserved his storytellers use of repetition as a memory aid. There is hardly a substantive for which a synonym is not immediately provided: "advice and counsel," "folly and error," "counseling and admonishing," activity and behavior," "troublemaking and rebelliousness," are some examples.

Here we see the influence of the oral on the written. Metaphor and repetition are the stock-in-trade of storytelling. Such rhetorical devices promote comprehension and keep the narrative thread together. Fayż Muḥammad was concerned with style for he knew his readers would be judging his style, perhaps even more than the content of what he wrote. There was also a very functionalist side to his style. He expected to be reimbursed for quantity, for number of words, lines, and pages and therefore had reason to tend towards verbosity. At one point he was told he would have to limit his output, in part because of what it was costing the government. Here we have attempted to maintain much of his often-prolix styles without, we hope, creating an unreadable text.

We have also tried to avoid bowdlerization. There are a number of places, especially in *Taẕakkur al-inqilāb* where Fayż Muḥammad quotes (or creates) some very crude language on the part of some of the officials of this brief period, or uses such language to describe certain individuals, particularly Amīr Ḥabīb Allāh Kalakānī and his brother, Ḥamīd Allāh. We have tried to find appropriately crude analogues in English.

Finally, a word needs to be said here about the index. The print editions of *Taẕakkur al-inqilāb* and *Nizhādnāmah-i Afghān*, while very helpful to producing this translation and containing tables of contents (which the manuscripts do not have), lack indexes, thereby rendering those versions less useful for reference purposes. In volumes 1–4 of *Sirāj al-tawārīkh* we keyed the index to the pagination of the 1913–15 edition of the work and to both the manuscript and the printed edition of volume 4 to allow the interested researcher to consult the original Persian. Here we key the index to the page numbers of our translation but provide page reference numbers to the print editions as well as to the unique manuscripts within the text.

Acknowledgements

We are obliged to many people and institutions for helping us bring these translations to fruition. First and foremost, we want to express our thanks to the National Endowment for the Humanities for a two-year grant in the Scholarly Editions and Translations category. For support during and after the award process we are very grateful to Lydia Medici, program officer.

At New York University, a number of people assisted in preparing the grant application and then in dealing with the minor problems that arose in the administration of it. We would like to single out Cormac Slevin, Dean Georgina Dopico, Alyson Miller, Provost Katherine Fleming, and Farooq Niazi, who helped us through the process with preparation of the proposal as well as with providing extra support for the project. To them our thanks.

To members of the Department of Middle Eastern and Islamic Studies we also wish to express our most heartfelt thanks. Professors Marion Katz and Zvi Ben-Dor Benite gave important moral support to the application and Professor Ahmed Ferhadi was unfailingly prompt in responding to questions on the Arabic in the text. Dondette Wendler, Subrina Moorley, and Shafon McNeil gave generously of their time and in some cases went well beyond the call of duty to offer invaluable assistance when potholes suddenly appeared in the generally smooth road of the grant. Special thanks as well to Dr. Guy Burak, Middle Eastern and Islamic Studies bibliographer.

For help with problems relating to the Afghan tribal information in *Nizhādnāmah-i Afghān* we would particularly like to thank Professor Robert Nichols who steered us to colonial ethnographies and censuses that helped clarify the text.

In Afghanistan, we are deeply indebted to Reza Kateb who provided us with digital images of the holograph *Tazakkur al-inqilāb* which were critical for dealing with the idiosyncrasies of the published edition. For other help with distinctively Afghan issues and terminology, we want to express our appreciation to Dr. Amin Tarzi. For all things Kabul related we deeply appreciate the unstinting help given by May Schinasi. Professor Bernard Haykel was always willing to explain the legal issues that cropped up, for which we are particularly grateful. Moreover, he and Dr. Navina Haider provided generous and delightful hospitality on the frequent trips of one of the translators to meet the other in New York. For this the former will always be thankful.

Special thanks also to colleagues at Brill Publishers who have been enormously helpful throughout the long "History of Afghanistan" project. We would like to particularly single out Nicolette van der Hoek and Wilma de Weert for their patience and encouragement.

Finally, gratitude as always to Constance McChesney for her critical readings and inexhaustible forbearance through the long process.

INTRODUCTION

On Local Sources

The world today knows the story of Afghanistan's past in large part because of the nineteenth- and twentieth-century efforts of the British Empire to secure its hold on South Asia—today's Pakistan, India, Bangladesh, Sri Lanka, and Myanmar—and the mass of documentation that resulted from those efforts. Although Afghanistan did not technically fall under British rule, its position between the area claimed by the British and, initially, the French and then an expanding Russian Empire, placed it, in British eyes, very much within its realm of strategic interests. During the nineteenth and first half of the twentieth century, until British rule in India ended in 1947, the British fought three wars (1838–42, 1879–80, and 1919) with the government of Afghanistan to protect those interests. The first resulted in a humiliating and disastrous retreat, the second in another withdrawal and abandonment of the demand that an Englishman be allowed to represent Great Britain at the Kabul court, and the third in recognition of Afghanistan's political independence from British Indian supervision, in particular its acknowledgement of the country's right to form international relationships.

There is nothing like war—its prologue and aftermath, its anticipation, execution, and then reflection about the point or pointlessness of it—to produce masses of permanent records (memoranda, intelligence reports, memoirs, newspaper articles, political analyses) for the historian to digest. For a very long time the main source of information for historians of Afghanistan has been the records produced to justify, condemn, or merely report British intentions and actions. This has given an inordinately large role to British perspectives on historical events and a correspondingly and unjustifiably small role to local interpretations. It has also privileged British discourses on the society of Afghanistan itself. Since discourses, as has been said, are "practices that systematically form the objects of which they speak"[1] one might even go so far as to say that the story or history of Afghanistan as it is generally known derives from British power—its assertion, consolidation, and expansion—and its textual legacy.

---

[1] Michel Foucault, *The Archaeology of Knowledge*, New York, Vintage-Random House, 1972, p. 49. On some of the consequences of the neglect of local sources, see Marcus Schadl. "The Man Outside: The Problem with the External Perception of Afghanistan

 | DOI:10.1163/9789004392441_002

To somewhat oversimplify the matter, the story of Afghanistan's past as produced by outsiders came to be a story of how that past meshed with the policy interests of the power under whose aegis the story was being configured. Afghanistan's history, as written in English at least, was for a long time largely a reflection of British imperial history and now, increasingly, American quasi-imperial history. One may safely say the same holds true of the comparable output of Russian writings on Afghanistan while substituting Russian sources for the English and Russian and Soviet imperial interests for those of the English and American governments. To be fair, however, Russian and Soviet scholarship has shown far more interest in indigenous writings and incorporating those writings into its scholarship than has non-Soviet and non-Russian scholarship. The indigenous version of Afghanistan's own past, even its own view of British perspectives on its past, has only recently begun to be explored in non-Russian scholarship.[2]

Yet the learned elite of the territory known today as the country of Afghanistan have long nurtured and sustained a tradition of history-writing of their own, principally in Persian (Fārsī, or Darī as Afghans today call it), whose roots and models lie in the great Arabic annals of the late ninth- early tenth-century historian, Abū Jaʿfar Muḥammad Ṭabarī, and the Persian narrative and analytic work of the eleventh-century Abū'l-Fażl Muḥammad Bayhaqī. Until recently, for many non-indigenous scholars writing on the history of Afghanistan this material—however abundant and accessible it is—might as well be locked away in some remote and closed archive for all the use that has been made of it.[3] Admittedly, without the ability to read Persian, the material is indeed inaccessible and thus, we hope, the value of a scholarly translation. In preparing these translations we also hope to serve a Persian-reading audience as well by linking the pages of the translations to the pages of the original works and providing detailed indexes to facilitate research.

---

in Historical Sources" *Asien: The German Journal on Contemporary Asia* 104, pp. 88–105 and R. D. McChesney, "Recent Work on the History of Afghanistan," *Journal of Persianate Studies* 5, pp. 64–66.

[2] Notable among contemporary scholars who have made effective use of indigenous sources are Sajjad Nejatie, "The Pearl of Pearls: A History of the Abdālī-Durrānī Confederacy and Its Transformation under Aḥmad Shāh Durr-i Durrān, Ph.D. dissertation, University of Toronto 2016; Christine Noelle(-Karimi), *State and Tribe in Nineteenth-Century Afghanistan*, Richmond, Surrey, Curzon, 1997; idem, *The Pearl in its Midst: Herat and the Mapping of Khurasan (15th–19th Centuries)*. Vienna: ÖAW 2014; and Amin Tarzi, "The Judicial State: Evolution and Centralization of the Courts in Afghanistan, 1883–96," Ph.D. dissertation, New York University, 2002.

[3] A recent work that shows some of the potential of these indigenous sources is Nile Green, ed., *Afghan History through Afghan Eyes*. Oxford: Oxford University Press, 2015.

The Author

Mullā Fayż Muḥammad "Kātib" ("The Writer") Hazārah, the author of both of the works translated here, and a major contributor to both of the appended works and perhaps even the ghost writer of one of them, was for most of his working life a mid-level employee of the Afghan government, a professional scribe turned author. He is identified in the preface of his most famous work, the monumental *Sirāj al-tawārīkh*, as Fayż Muḥammad Kātib, the son of Saʿīd Muḥammad Mughūl of the Muḥammad Khwājah Hazārahs.[4] The Muḥammad Khwājah clan lived in the western districts of Ghaznīn (present day Ghaznī) Province. Fayż Muḥammad's grandfather, Khudāydād, served as *wakīl* or legal representative of his clan in disputes with others and so the family was a locally prominent one if not the leading family of their village, Gardan-i (or Gardanah-i) Bukhārā, in Nāhwur District. Fayż Muḥammad's father, Saʿīd Muḥammad, is remembered as a fine calligrapher. Writing well was a highly marketable skill, and he passed it on to his son. It was this talent which eventually earned Fayż Muḥammad a career in government and the ability and opportunity to produce a prodigious amount of work.

Early in the course of his long government career—at least thirty-five years as he mentions at one point—and as a result of his output as secretary, copyist, and author, Fayż Muḥammad acquired the nickname "Kātib"—the Writer. Although it may not have been his first use of the pen-name, a copy he made in 1317/1899–1900 of the translation into Persian of an English manual on percussion fuses, entitled *Dar bayān-i fiyūz-hā-yi żarb-dār*, he signed as "Fayż Muḥammad Kātib."[5] (**Fig. 1**) Thereafter, whether as author or copyist, this was his *nom de plume*. He was also well-known for his religious scholarship and so his countrymen generally referred to him as "Mullā" as well.

The date of Fayż Muḥammad's birth is uncertain. Scholars who have studied his life believe that he was born sometime circa 1279 A.H.Q. (1862–63 A.D.)[6] while his family believe it was as early as 1858.[7] In any

[4] Fayz Muhammad, *The History*, vol. 1, p. 1.

[5] The colophon of an unpaginated copy [p. 100] (catalog number unknown) at the National Archives of Afghanistan (Arshīf-i millī-yi Afghānistān).

[6] See e.g. Ḥusayn ʿAlī Yazdānī (Ḥājj Kāẓim), "Sharḥ-i mukhtaṣarī az zindagī-yi Kātib," in Mullā Fayż Muḥammad Kātib Hazārah, *Sirāj al-tawārīkh*, 3 vols. in two, 3rd Edition, Tehran: Mu'assasah-i taḥqīqāt wa intishārāt-i Balkh, 1372/1993, introduction to vol. 1, p. *dū* (ii).

[7] Personal communication from Reza Kateb.

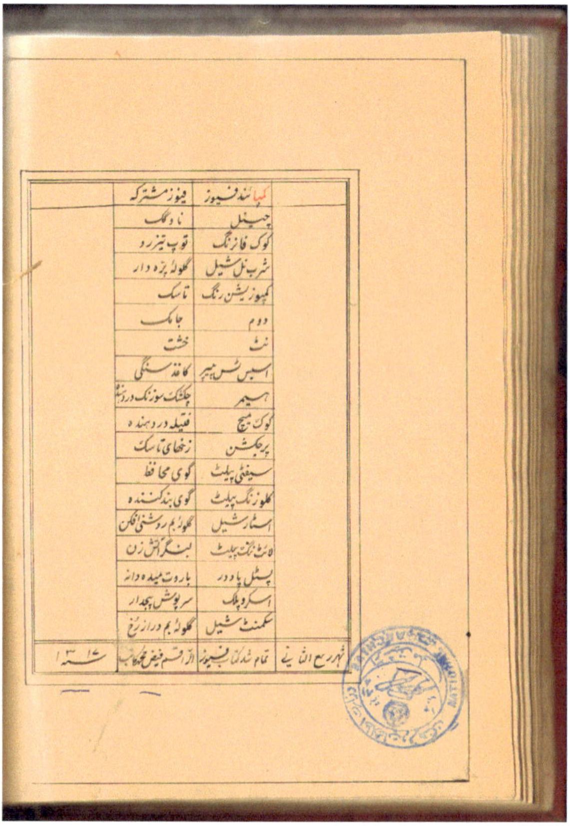

Figure 1: The colophon of *Dar bayān-i fiyūz-hā-yi żarb-dār* (Treatise on Percussion Fuses) with the nom de plume, "Fayż Muḥammad Kātib" and the date 1317/1899.

case, it was close to the end of the reign of Amīr Dūst Muḥammad Khān, the ruler of Kabul who had extended more or less permanent Afghan control over, or at least laid claim to, the regions of Qandahar, Harāt, and Turkistān south of the Oxus River and who established the Muḥammadzā'ī clan of the Durrānī-Abdālī Afghāns as the recognized legitimate heir to the Afghan emirate.[8] (Dūst Muḥammad had taken the title "Amīr" (emir) in order to prosecute a legal jihad against the Sikhs and then continued to use that title in place of "shah," the title used by his Afghan predecessors.)

[8] On Dūst Muḥammad's career see Christine Noelle, *Tribe and State in Afghanistan: The Reign of Amīr Dost Muhammad Khān (1826–1863)*, Richmond, Surrey: Curzon, 1997.

Fayż Muḥammad was born in Zard Sang, a hamlet in a subdistrict of Qarābāgh, a large town between Ghaznīn (Ghaznah or Ghaznī) and Muqur on the main Kabul-Qandahar highway. But he thought of his homeland (*waṭan, mawṭin*) as Gardan(ah)-i Bukhārā, a village northwest of Ghaznīn in Nāhwur District, Ghaznīn Province.[9] His grandfather had lived there until some local dispute forced his widow and her family, including the son who would become Fayż Muḥammad's father, to leave. It is unknown when this occurred but might well have been connected to the turmoil that arose with the invasion of Afghanistan by the East India Company's Army of the Indus in the spring of 1839. Much later, Fayż Muḥammad may have been sent back to live with an uncle in Gardan(ah)-i Bukhārā for a time during his youth. The most telling sign of his feelings for the place was the house that he built for himself in the village.[10]

To map Fayż Muḥammad's position in Afghanistan's highly particularist society one must emphasize his inherited identity as Hazārah and Imāmī (or Twelver) Shiʿi as well as his acquired elite identity as a member of the royal court and a scholar. Either the inherited religious or the ethnic or, in this case, the ethno-religious identity was sufficient to make him a fringe figure in a country where Hanafi Sunnis—Afghans, Tajiks, Uzbeks, Qirghiz, Pashahʾī, and others—made up the vast confessional majority of the country's population. Nonetheless, he achieved high status as a member of the royal court and his designated role as spokesperson and ombudsman for Hazārahs gave him a privileged voice.

The Hazārahs, almost all of whom identified themselves as Imāmī Shiʿis,[11] inhabited the central highlands of the country, the Hazārahjāt, and had a history of martial independence. However, clan rivalries, the importation of Akhbārī-Uṣūlī theological factionalism, the class or caste structure of local aristocracies of mīrs and sayyids, and the usual economic and social flashpoints of conflict over land and water rights and

[9] The Afghanistan Information Management Services 2004 electronic map of "Nawur" (i.e., Nāhwur) transliterates the name of the village as "Gardane Bakhara" [*sic*]. The Persian spelling of the village is also inconsistent so it is difficult to know whether the intent is "*gardanah*" meaning "a pass (*kūtal*) and mountain height (*bulandī-yi kūh*)" (see Afghani-Nawis, *Lughat-i ʿāmyānah-i Afghānistān*, Kabul, Maṭbaʿah-i Dawlatī, 1340/1961, s.v.) or "*gardan-i*" meaning "neck of". The rendering Bakhara is perhaps the local pronunciation of Bukhārā or just indifferent transliteration, an endemic problem in Afghan studies. In the *Historical and Political Gazetteer of Afghanistan*, ed. Ludwig W. Adamec, Graz, Austria: Akademische Druck- u. Verlagsanstalt, 1985, volume 6, "Kabul" there is an entry for "Bokhara-I-Nawar" [*sic*], p. 112, which is undoubtedly the same place, but no information is given about it.

[10] Personal communication from Reza Kateb, July 2010.

[11] The exception being the Shaykh ʿAlī Hazārahs of the Baghlān and Parwān region.

issues of personal honor worked against their common interests in confronting a hostile Sunni society and in maintaining any degree of independence from a moderately competent central government.

By the time Fayż Muḥammad grew to manhood, those who governed Kabul had long since extended their authority to the central Hazārahjāt. The Hazārah regions closest to the Kabul-Qandahar highway were long-accustomed to the reach of government tax assessors and collectors[12] although those areas were also quite ready to sever ties (and payments) to Kabul when there was political uncertainty or turmoil, as was often the case.[13] In any event, although Fayż Muḥammad was brought up in a rural environment, the central government, through its agents and involvements, was a powerful reality and a focus of opportunity as well.

As Fayż Muḥammad repeatedly emphasizes, the Hazārahjāt and the Hazārah people were not simply to be exploited for tax reasons. The inhabitants of the Hazārahjāt played a major role in the domestic economy for their production of meat, fiber, and finished goods: Flat weave carpets (kilims), a wool textile called *barak*, and cooking oil were all important products of the Hazārahjāt. One of the most memorable (and traumatic) episodes in Fayż Muḥammad's own life was linked to an abortive effort in 1922 by the Amānī government to assert its right to control the trade in one of these products, cooking oil (*rawghan*).[14]

The Hazārahjāt was also an important source of human capital in the form of unskilled labor. The seasonal requirements of subsistence agriculture freed men and women for employment in the urban centers—Qandahar, Ghaznīn, and Kabul especially. Porter, cart puller, sweeper, nightsoil remover, stable hand, and construction worker were some of the unskilled occupations filled by Hazārahs in Fayż Muḥammad's time as they are, with some exceptions, right up to the present. As for Hazārah women, those who accompanied their husbands, or were purchased from their families, could find low-paid work as servants. As Fayż Muḥammad himself notes in his description of the population of Kabul, "the domestic

[12] For a document concerning the remittance of tax arrears from the Hazārahjāt see R. D. McChesney, "A *Farman* Issued by Amīr Shir ʿAli Khān in 1877," *Journal of Asian History* 17 (1983), pp. 136–58.

[13] For the extreme turmoil created by another British invasion in 1879 and its effect on Fayż Muḥammad's life in the Qarābāgh region see Fayż Muḥammad, *The History*, vol. 1, pp. xxiii–xxvi.

[14] See ibid., vol. 4, pp. 278–79, 463–69.

servants of the people of Kabul are Hazārahs and Kāfirs (*khadamah-i ahl-i Kabul Hazārah wa Kāfirī mībāshand*)."[15]

Aside from a few exceptional cases, like the men who traveled to Iran for religious training, the Hazārahjāt did not produce noted scholars or a corps of the learned from whom government employees could be recruited. Fayż Muḥammad was one of those exceptions. In his early years, besides being home-schooled by his father in the science and art of calligraphy, Fayż Muḥammad also attended a local primary school where he memorized Qur'ān, learned some Arabic, and married his teacher's daughter. We know something of his higher education but the sequence and timing of it is still uncertain. From his own autobiographical notes, which are scattered through his writings, we can place him in the Ghaznīn region as late as October 1886 when he was in his mid-twenties and a member of an Hazārah militia.[16] It is possible that prior to this time he had made a pilgrimage to the Shiʿi holy cities of Najaf, Karbalā, and Kāẓimayn in Iraq as some of his biographers assert,[17] although he himself never mentions it, as far as we know. He does briefly provide us, in a single sentence, a glimpse of a speedy and brief educational odyssey that took him to Qandahar and Lahore and then back to Kabul by way of Pīshāwar (Peshawar) and Jalālābād.[18] This sojourn seemingly all occurred between October 1886 and April 23, 1888, if we can trust his own chronology, and suggests that, if true, he had little success at finding a teacher willing to take him on. If he did establish such a connection, he never mentions it.

---

[15] Fayż Muḥammad Kātib, *Nukhbat al-jughrāfiyah*, National Archives of Afghanistan, ms. inv. no. 69/23, unfoliated 14r. (N B. The manuscript—or the digital images of it available to us—is missing at least one and possibly more folios after folio 4. For our purposes we provisionally numbered the folios consecutively.)

[16] Fayż Muḥammad, *The History*, vol. 3, p. 522.

[17] Ḥusayn Barzagar-i Kishtalī, "Fayż Muḥammad Kātib Hazārah," *Dānishnāmah-i Adab-i Fārsī: Adab-i Fārsī dar Afghānistān*, Tehran: Sāzmān-i Chāp wa Intishārāt, Wizārat-i Farhang wa Irshād-i Islāmī, 1378/1999 pp. 790–93; Ḥusayn Nāyil "Pazhūhishī dar bāz namā-yī wa bāz shināsī-yi āsār-i Kātib." (*Majallah-i*) *Kitāb*, 1361, no. 1: 30–49 and Ḥusayn ʿAlī Yazdānī, "Sharḥ-i mukhtaṣarī az zindagī-yi Kātib" the introduction to Mullā Fayż Muḥammad Kātib Hazārah. *Sirāj al-tawārīkh*. 3 vols. in two. 3rd Edition, Tehran, Mu'assasah-i taḥqīqāt wa intishārāt-i Balkh, 1372/1993, p. 23. British sources (see Ludwig Adamec, *A Biographical Dictionary of Contemporary Afghanistan*, Graz, Austria, Akademische Druck-u. Verlagsanstalt, 1987, p. 48) even believed that he had made the pilgrimage to Mecca, by calling him "al-Hajj Mulla Fayz Muhammad" but we have no evidence of this in his own writings where he never adds the title "pilgrim (hajj, hajji)" to his name.

[18] Fayż Muḥammad, *The History*, vol. 3, p. 588. A. I. Shkirando's proposed itinerary for Fayż Muḥammad for these years, based on H. N. Gurjistānī's *Fishārdah-i zindagānī-yi Fayż Muḥammad* (n.d., n.p.?), does not account for Fayż Muḥammad's own recollections and omits the references to his militia service.

What he does mention prominently is the very important relationship he established in Kabul when he was accepted as a student by the noted Sunni scholar, Mullā (or Mawlānā) Muḥammad Sarwar Khān of the Isḥāqzāʾī, one of the Durrānī tribes. The mullah was a Qandahārī and an influential member of the court of Prince Naṣr Allāh Khān. In 1895, he was chosen to accompany the prince to England and Europe in 1895 as an advisor and counsellor. This was an episode in Afghanistan's history in which Fayż Muḥammad himself played a small part. The mullah also enjoyed the high regard of Prince Ḥabīb Allāh Khān, the eldest son of the amir, ʿAbd al-Raḥmān Khān, and it was this court network of relationships that proved fortuitous for the Hazārah scribe.

How he came to be accepted as a student by Muḥammad Sarwar Isḥāqzāʾī is unknown but the evidence Fayż Muḥammad gives provides a possible scenario.[19] In the spring of 1888, he arrived in Jalālābād, returning from his brief sojourn to India, just as the amir, ʿAbd al-Raḥmān Khān, was preparing to return to Kabul from his winter palace there. Fayż Muḥammad writes that each member of the amir's entourage (he claims it numbered 12,000 people) was given "rice, meat, oil, candles, sugar, tea, and firewood" for the week-long trip back to Kabul. One of the staff was a fellow Hazārah and near-neighbor, Jaʿfar ʿAlī Khān from Jāghūrī, who helped Fayż Muḥammad share in the bounty and may have been helpful in getting him some employment within this enormous (though probably exaggerated) complement of court servants.[20] Later, while writing the fourth volume of *Sirāj al-tawārīkh* during the period 1924–26, Fayż Muḥammad recalled that he made a trip to Peshawar in 1305, perhaps in the late summer of 1888 (1305 covered the period September 19, 1887–September 8, 1888) to buy "some souvenirs" (*ajnās-i sawghātī*)[21] for certain employees and servants of Amīr ʿAbd al-Raḥmān Khān. This begs several questions. Was he already working as a low-level servant and simply fulfilling an assignment given him by his superiors to buy these presents?

---

19 His family believe they met in Qandahar (undated personal communication from Reza Kateb) though there is some circumstantial evidence that they first met in Kabul.

20 Fayż Muḥammad, *The History*, vol. 3, p. 588. A photograph taken about this time (ca 1888) showing Amīr ʿAbd al-Raḥmān Khān and part of his staff—85 individuals can be seen—at Bustān Sarāy Palace. There were probably more beyond the frame of the photograph but certainly not "12,000." (Photo collection of R. D. McChesney.) A large military escort would have accompanied the movements of the amir and it too might have figured in Fayż Muḥammad's calculation of the size of the amir's party.

21 Ibid., vol. 4, p. 663. Mohammad Nasim Neghat, *Qāmūs-i Darī-Inglīzī: Dari-English Dictionary*. Omaha: Center for Afghan Studies, s.v., defines *sawghāt* as "a present sent or brought by a traveler" (i.e. a souvenir). ʿAbd Allah "Afghānī-Nawīs," *Lughat-i ʿAmyānah-i Fārsī-yi Afghānistān*, [Kabul], 1340/1961, s.v. simply calls it "a gift (*hadiyah*)."

Was he buying them with his own resources in hopes of using them to gain court employment? Were these gifts intended as "tuition" to secure him a place in Mullā Muḥammad Sarwar's circle of students? Or did he simply misremember what had happened some thirty-five years earlier? It seems more than a little unusual that he could have secured a government position between the time he attached himself to the amir's entourage in the spring of 1888 and his mission to buy "souvenirs" a few months later. Eventually something may turn up in his yet-undiscovered writings but for the moment the souvenir-buying trip remains a lonely piece of data without any context.

We can be fairly certain, though, that he was accepted as a student of the well-placed mullah for he names the books he studied with him. Impressed by his skill at calligraphy and perhaps by other qualifications as well, the mullah recommended him to the prince's court where, in 1893, he was appointed to be a munshi (scribe) in Prince Ḥabīb Allāh's own secretariat. In Fayż Muḥammad's own words:

> On Monday the tenth of Shaʿbān 1310/27 February 1893, the highly regarded great teacher and esteemed man of letters, Mullā Muḥammad Sarwar Khān Isḥāqzāʾī, who spent his days in service to the noble prince Sardār Naṣr Allāh Khān and also enjoyed high standing and position with the most high prince Sardār Ḥabīb Allāh Khān, speaking solicitously and discoursing eloquently, introduced the name of a servant (i.e., Fayż Muḥammad) at an assembly of felicitous opportunity and recommended him. Because he did so, the celestial-dwelling prince[22] summoned me and bestowed his favor on me. He ordered me to copy books and correspondence and honored and feted me with an annual salary of 200 rupees.

His salary, initially quite modest, would be increased over the years, but not without considerable pleading on Fayż Muḥammad's part and repeated frustrations.

Following his appointment, we know of several writing assignments that he fulfilled during Amīr ʿAbd al-Raḥmān Khān's reign.[23] In 1895 he was assigned to make copies of the letters sent home by Prince Naṣr Allāh Khān, the amir's second son, during his six months as a guest of the English government visiting Great Britain, France and Italy, making Fayż

[22] In Fayż Muḥammad, *The History*, vol. 3, p. 868, we assumed, based on their later relationship, that the prince being referred to here was Ḥabīb Allāh Khān, not Naṣr Allāh Khān, although Fayż Muḥammad did on occasion, and for additional compensation, work for Naṣr Allāh Khān, as noted already in the case of the *Nukhbat al-jughrāfiyah* commission.

[23] Ibid., vol. 1, introduction, pp. xxxi–xxxii. One work not mentioned there is the treatise on percussion fuses mentioned above.

Muḥammad in a small way a party to the trip. His copies were then posted in the market for the edification of the public.[24]

It is not certain when Ḥabīb Allāh Khān, who came to the throne on October 3, 1901, decided to commission a history of the realm nor is it immediately apparent why he chose Fayż Muḥammad as the person to write it.[25] It would seem to be something of an anomaly for a devout Shiʿi scholar to have been chosen as official spokesman for the country's past. It is as if Abraham Lincoln had commissioned Frederick Douglass to write a history of the United States. Afghanistan was and is a composite of many sectarian societies most of which were not just Sunni Muslim but also fervently anti-Shiʿi, a latent sentiment that could be ignited into physical violence at the slightest excuse, as is still the case today. Here was not only an Imāmī Shiʿi from the most disadvantaged and despised ethnic group in the country but the individual to whom had been given the enormous responsibility of determining what the nation's history would be, albeit with some controls on what he wrote. The choice could not have failed to ruffle feathers and offend sensibilities in many quarters. What was the amir thinking? On the other hand, Fayż Muḥammad's social and political marginality might well have been a recommendation in the eyes of the amir and made him a seemingly attractive choice. He was for all intents and purposes powerless, without a meaningful political constituency. The Hazārahs had been reduced by years of ethnic cleansing and displacement from their lands to a thoroughly suppressed, dispersed, and demoralized people, many living in desperate circumstances abroad in Iran, British India, and Russian Turkistān and in internal exile in Afghan Turkistān and other places. It must have been assumed that Fayż Muḥammad would serve and write as a submissive tool of the amir. He had already shown his willingness to work for the regime that had thoroughly disrupted the lives of the Hazārah people, given away their lands, enslaved many of them, and plundered their possessions in return for a salary and the status of belonging to the court society.

But Fayż Muḥammad, as it turned out, was no dutiful servant to be dictated to and manipulated at the whim of the amir and his closest advisors. Although his work was continually reviewed by members of the court elite whom the amir trusted as well as by the amir himself, Fayż Muḥammad

---

[24] Ibid., vol. 3, p. 1107.

[25] We speculated earlier (see ibid., vol. 1 introduction, p. xxxiv) that the project might have been linked to the pay raise Fayż Muḥammad received in 1897 but no other evidence has since come to hand to either modify or corroborate that date.

had his own agenda that he intended to follow in his writing. At the top of it was recording in as much detail as possible the tragic fate of the Hazārahs of Afghanistan under ʿAbd al-Raḥmān Khān and his son and successor, Ḥabīb Allāh Khān, who also happened to be Fayż Muḥammad's patron. Knowing that his own agenda was not going to be well-received, Fayż Muḥammad did his best to record the details of the state-sponsored ethnic cleansing of this large group of its own subjects while depicting the government's motives as reasonable and necessary and the Hazārahs as "evildoers" and "rebels." At the same time, he began a secret history in which he could record what he believed to be the unvarnished truth of Afghanistan's past. The whereabouts of this work, *Fayżī az fuyūżāt*, has yet to be discovered although one copy of it at least probably went to Iran in 1929 with the returning Iranian envoy, Sayyid Mahdī Farrukh, who quotes extensively from it in his own history of Afghanistan, *Tārīkh-i siyāsī-yi Afghānistān*.[26]

The royal commission for Fayż Muḥammad to produce an historical record of the country must have dated to the very outset of Ḥabīb Allāh's reign for by the beginning of 1905 Fayż Muḥammad had done the research and completed almost 1,688 pages in two complete volumes and one partially complete volume. It began with the rule of Aḥmad Shāh Durrānī (r. 1747–72), who was by this time seen as the founder of the country, and, according to the plan, was to bring the record of events down to the then-present. The first work was therefore chronologically arranged and was entitled *Tuḥfat al-Ḥabīb*—the first volume covering the Sadūzāʾī era (1747–1842), the second, the Muḥammadzāʾī period down to the end of the reign of Amīr Shayr ʿAli Khān (1842–1879), and the third, the incomplete one, covering the first half of the reign of Amīr ʿAbd al-Raḥmān who ruled from 1880–1901. Ḥusayn Nāyil, a specialist on the life and works of Fayż Muḥammad, believed that the first volume of *Tuḥfat al-Ḥabīb*, was written before 1320 (1902–03), in other words during the first year of Amīr Ḥabīb Allāh Khān's reign and that the second volume was completed in Shawwāl 1322 (December 1904).[27]

---

[26] Sayyid Mahdī Farrukh, *Tārīkh-i siyāsī-yi Afghānistān*. Qum: Iḥsānī, 1371 A.H.S. (Reprint of the first volume of the first edition, 2 vols., Tehran: Majlis, 1314/1935.)

[27] Ḥusayn Nāyil. "Pazhūhishī," pp. 30–49, pp. 32–35 for his analysis of the three volumes. The undated colophon of the first volume names Ghulām Qādir Kākarī as copyist. (See Mullā Fayż Muḥammad Kātib Hazārah, *Tuḥfat al-Ḥabīb*, 2 vols. in 1, edited by Dr. Muḥammad Sarwar Mawlāʾī, Kabul: Intishārāt-i Amīrī, 1393/2014; henceforth Fayż Muḥammad *Tuḥfat*.) Kākarī's note, vol. 1, p. 342 indicates corrections had been made by the amir and others before he made the final copy. The final copy of the second volume

However, something in the work displeased the amir and he would not allow it to be printed. It is thought that his displeasure arose from the portrayal of his great-grandfather, Amīr Dūst Muḥammad Khān (d. 1863), and he had the two completed manuscripts confiscated.[28] The third volume remained in Fayż Muḥammad's possession and stayed with the family until it was sold to the National Archives of Afghanistan sometime prior to 1982 at which time Ḥusayn Nāyil saw it and described it.[29] The suppression of *Tuḥfat al-Ḥabīb* was the first evidence of Fayż Muḥammad's independence of mind that would continually bring him into confrontation with readers who did not like what he wrote.

As far as we can tell, the suppression of *Tuḥfat al-Ḥabīb* was not connected in any way with Fayż Muḥammad's plan to memorialize Hazārah grievances. It ends a full three years before the war against the Hazārahs began. In any event, what is worth noting is that the frustrating conclusion of his work on *Tuḥfat al-Ḥabīb* would presage the problems he would

---

was made by the author himself, and the colophon, p. 911, gives the date for completion as "Shawwāl 1322" (December 1904–January 1905).

[28] Although the colophon of volume 2, in contrast to the colophon of volume 1, says nothing to indicate that the amir had reviewed it, made corrections, and then given approval for the final copying, we should probably assume that Fayż Muḥammad did not undertake the task of copying out a final version into what would be a 430-page manuscript codex without the amir's assent. The incomplete third volume is described by Nāyil as in the author's "everyday hand" indicating it had not been yet subjected to final review and corrections. This suggests that the problem for Fayż Muḥammad, the reason why Ḥabīb Allāh stopped him from writing further, may be found in the third volume. Had it been in an earlier volume, we presume he would have "corrected" it. If so, that would mean it was not an unfavorable treatment of Amīr Dūst Muḥammad Khān that roused the amir's displeasure since all the coverage of that amir is in the second volume. On the other hand, the reason for the amir's unhappiness with *Tuḥfat al-Ḥabīb* may have been much more prosaic: that Fayż Muḥammad was simply prone to be unnecessarily verbose. If he was operating under the terms of a contract similar to that of his Textbook Office employment in the 1920s where he was paid by the pages he produced of so many lines and so many words per line then it was to his advantage to be long-winded but not to the government's. Volume 1 of *Tuḥfat al-Ḥabīb* covering 95 years (1747–1842) is 567 pages in manuscript (342 pages in print). Vol. 2 covering only 38 years (1842–1880) is already 885 pages in manuscript (568 in print). (See Nāyil, *Pazhūhishī*, pp. 32–33). Ḥabīb Allāh Khān may have felt that Fayż Muḥammad would never get to his reign or complete the work at the rate he was going.

[29] Ibid., pp. 34–35. According to Adamec, *Biographical Dictionary*, p. 48, "volume four" was purchased from Fayż Muḥammad's son in 1978. This may refer to other volumes purchased or to a draft of volume four. The final version of volume four was sold by the family to the National Archives much more recently, in 2008. See Ayyub Arwin, "Kharīdārī-yi nuskhah-i khaṭṭī-yi jild-i chahārum-i *Sirāj al-tawārīkh-i Afghānistān*," BBCPersian.com, 20 October 2010.

have writing the *Sirāj al-tawārīkh*. Since that has been described in some detail elsewhere we will not repeat it here.[30]

Despite the amir's displeasure over *Tuḥfat*, he continued to have faith in Fayż Muḥammad and demanded he begin again. By 1907, the Hazārah writer had produced a new manuscript of the first and second volumes following the same format and including much of the same information as the *Tuḥfat al-Ḥabīb* but with a new name, *Sirāj al-tawārīkh*.[31]

In trying to reconstruct the whole historiographical process and its chronology, we have to grapple with the slightly puzzling information Fayż Muḥammad himself provides in a work of geography he wrote at the behest of the amir's brother the "Nā'ib al-Salṭanah" (Vice-Regent) Sardār Naṣr Allāh Khān, one of the times he worked under the sardār's aegis. He writes:

> (fol. 1v) After *Tuḥfat al-Ḥabīb* was written during the felicity-twinned time and by the order of the Lamp of the Nation and the Religion (Amīr Ḥabīb Allāh Khān) (it) was ennobled by the consideration of Nā'ib al-Salṭanah Sardār Naṣr Allāh Khān who read in that history an abbreviated compilation of the latitude and longitude of the kingdom of Afghanistan[32] and said that all geographers, because they were foreign and lacked local knowledge (*baladīyat*), similarly have only written compilations that include the celestial coordinates and have only defined (Afghanistan) in terms of the straight lines (latitude and longitude). They have not accounted for its actual characteristics and features such as the size of its population, its commerce (*māl al-tijārah*), its mines, its domesticated and wild animals, its birds, fruits, etc. as they really are. Therefore, a book should be written which would accurately represent the extent of the kingdom of Afghanistan and the part of Turkistān that belongs to it with a description of the tribes and peoples who inhabit it, the income and expenditures of the sultanate, the number of its subjects, and the extent of its productive land (*kas̱rat wa qillat-i żay'at*). Therefore, this humble sinner, Fayż Muḥammad Kātib, in response to the order issued to him (by Sardār Naṣr Allāh Khān) and at the suggestion of His Excellency, the one of greatest dignity, the Chief Judge, by whom I mean Sa'd Allāh Khān, former high governor (*nā'ib al-ḥukūmah*) of "the Abode of Victory," Harāt (Herat) undertook to compose this book and gave it the title *Nukhbat al-jughrāfīyah* (The Best Geography).

Within the work we find two references to the date it was written. On fol. 12v Fayż Muḥammad writes regarding extreme weather events, "… in the

---

[30] Fayż Muḥammad, *The History*, vol. 1, pp. xxxix–xliii and xlv–lxii; vol. 4, introduction pp. 4–26.

[31] A full analysis of the *Tuḥfat al-Ḥabīb* and a comparison and correlation of it to *Sirāj al-tawārīkh* is one of the many desiderata of the field of Afghan history.

[32] Fayż Muḥammad, *Tuḥfat*, vol. 1, pp. 28–29.

winter of 1325 (1907–08) *which is the year of writing this treatise* [emphasis added], it was so warm that water did not freeze." He then speaks of [the late] Amīr Ḥabīb Allāh Khān's ordering a flag permanently installed atop the drum house (*naqqārahkhānah*) of the Royal Arg, "after his return from India" (fol. 13v). The amir arrived back in Jalālābād from India on the 24th of Muḥarram 1325/9 March 1907[33] and issued an order regarding the flag atop the drum house in late April.[34] We can therefore date *Nukhbat al-jughrāfīyah* to a time in 1907 after April, not a particularly calm period in Fayż Muḥammad's life.

Two things are worth noting about what he says. First, he speaks of *Tuḥfat al-Ḥabīb* without alluding in any way to its fate. Not only should the unfinished project have been abandoned by 1907 (moreover the verb "was written" [*ta'līf shudah*] suggests the work had been completed), but the first two volumes of *Sirāj al-tawārīkh*, which he conspicuously fails to mention at all, ought to have been completed by then because one of the things he was charged to do later in 1907 was make and send copies of the two completed volumes of *Sirāj al-tawārīkh* to the amir in Qandahar. He had embarked on an around-the-country tour almost immediately after returning from India and had reached Qandahar on the 21st of May.[35] Secondly, although he tells us while writing the fourth volume of *Sirāj* in the 1920s what was happening to him in 1907, nowhere does he mention there anything about *Nukhbat al-jughrāfīyah*.[36] For now it remains a puzzle as to why, in 1907, he mentions *Tuḥfat al-Ḥabīb* but makes no mention of *Sirāj al-tawārīkh* and why he never refers to *Nukhbat al-jughrāfīyah* in *Sirāj al-tawārīkh*.

In 1907, with two volumes of *Sirāj al-tawārīkh* completed, covering the period 1747–1880 the task still remained to convince the amir to allow them to be published. This meant first persuading those who had been assigned to oversee the work on behalf of the amir and that was no easy task, as we have discussed elsewhere.[37]

It is important always to keep in mind that Fayż Muḥammad's ethnicity and religion continually influenced what he wrote, how he wrote it, and how those manuscripts managed to be published, or simply survived. Although his agenda and clear biases often show through, he must have known that his most critical writings, verging on the excoriating, would

---

33 Fayż Muḥammad, *The History*, vol. 4, p. 1138.
34 Ibid., vol. 4, p. 1142.
35 Ibid., vol. 4, p. 1150.
36 Ibid., vol. 4, pp. 1146, 1150.
37 See Fayż Muḥammad, *The History*, vol. 4, pp. 48.

never be printed and even those that passed muster with his reviewers, including the amir, were not guaranteed publication.[38] He would therefore take steps in the 1920s when he fell from favor to safeguard his unpublished and unpublishable writings.

More immediately, besides the problem he was having getting the two volumes of *Sirāj al-tawārīkh* approved for publication, there was the problem of the nascent constitutionalist movement in Afghanistan that Amīr Ḥabīb Allāh Khān feared and to which he reacted swiftly and violently. Fayż Muḥammad, who denied involvement, was nevertheless caught up in it and imprisoned for fifteen months, during which he did no work on the history project. He escaped relatively lightly; others suffered execution or spent up to eleven years in prison for their involvement.[39]

When he was released in early June 1910,[40] he returned to the task of convincing the amir to publish the first two volumes and to begin working on the third, the volume to be devoted to his patron's father, Amīr ʿAbd al-Raḥmān Khān. In 1913, the first two volumes were finally issued in a single quarto binding of 377 pages and eleven pages of errata. By then he also had the amir's consent for him to proceed without any oversight on the content (except the amir's of course) and he seems to have devoted himself wholly to the project for the nine years following his release from detention.

The fate of the whole project, not surprisingly, was completely dependent on the continuing support of Amīr Ḥabīb Allāh Khān. That support disappeared in the early morning hours of February 20, 1919 when an unknown assassin put a bullet in the amir's brain as he slept in his tent while on a hunting trip.[41]

For six days the succession remained unsettled as both the late amir's brother, Prince Naṣr Allāh Khān, who was wintering in Jalālābād, and his third son, Prince Amān Allāh Khān, in Kabul, were recognized as

---

38 As a way to mollify his own conscience about having to write circumspectly for the amir, Fayż Muḥammad could confide his true feelings to his secret history, *Fayżī az fuyūżāt*, as we noted above.

39 For the Constitutional Movement see ʿAbd al-Ḥayy Ḥabībī, *Junbish-i mashrūṭīyāt dar Afghānistān*. New Edition. Qum: Iḥsānī, Jawzā/Khurdād 1372 A.H.S./May–June 1993. On Fayż Muḥammad's being swept up in it, see Fayż Muḥammad, *The History*, vol. 4, pp. 8–11 and further R. D. McChesney, "'The Bottomless Inkwell': The Life and Perilous Times of Fayz Muhammad 'Kātib' Hazāra" in Nile Green, ed., *Afghan History through Afghan Eyes*, pp. 112–113. The date given there for his release from his imprisonment is incorrect. See next note.

40 Fayż Muḥammad, *The History*, vol. 4, part one, p. 10 of the introduction provides more information as well as the correct date of his release from confinement, June 7, 1910.

41 Ibid., vol. 4, p. 1393.

amir by those around them. When the latter emerged victorious, Fayż Muḥammad's position was for a time in some jeopardy. He had been with Naṣr Allāh in Jalālābād when Ḥabīb Allāh Khān was shot and he says he was forced to put his name to a list of the court staff swearing obedience to Naṣr Allāh, although he does note that at least two other staff members refused, without any apparent repercussions.[42] He also tells us that once it was clear that Amān Allāh had gained the upper hand, he himself organized and circulated a declaration of loyalty to the new amir among the court staff in Jalālābād, most of whom had signed a similar oath to Naṣr Allāh Khān only a few days earlier.[43]

Once back in Kabul, he must have faced some uncertainty about his future. The first evidence that he was still welcome at court comes from a visiting Soviet delegation that arrived in December 1919, two of whose members, I. M. Reisner and E. M. Ricks, collected information on people at court and those who attended official functions. One they identify as the "court chronicler" (*pridvornyi letopisetz*), Fayż Muḥammad. So at least by then he had re-established himself at court. The next piece of evidence we have that the new amir meant to keep him on was a farman dated 16 S̲awr 1299/June 5, 1920 addressed to Maḥmūd Khān, the son of Muḥammad Shāh Khān Bārakzāʾī, who was a court chamberlain and responsible for court records.[44] In the farman Maḥmūd Khān is informed that Fayż Muḥammad will continue to work on *Sirāj al-tawārīkh* and then will proceed "to record all the events of the Amānī era." He was then directed to make available to Fayż Muḥammad specific types of files and folders while excluding others.[45]

The period after 1920 was a busy one for Fayż Muḥammad. Between 1920 and 1924, he enjoyed the amir's goodwill and worked on completing volumes three and four of *Sirāj* while beginning research and writing on what was to be volume five of the history project, the reign of Amīr Amān Allāh Khān, to be entitled *Tārīkh-i ʿaṣr-i Amānīyah*. The year 1922 was a particularly busy one for Fayż Muḥammad in which he not only worked on those volumes of *Sirāj al-tawārīkh* but also closely collaborated with an Iranian colleague working on his own history of Afghanistan (see below).

---

42 Ibid., p. 1416.

43 Ibid., p. 1466.

44 Under Ḥabīb Allāh Khān, the office of chamberlain (*īshīk-āqāsī*) was divided into four separate offices, civil, court, foreign, and military chamberlains. Mahmud Khān would soon be promoted to the position of *yāwar* (aide-de-camp) to the amir.

45 Nāyil, "Pazhūhishī ..., p. 40. See also the register of farmans for Amīr Amān Allāh Khān at the Afghan National Archives, daftar no. 2027/221.

He was also assigned to a delegation to try and stem the smuggling of oil out of the Hazārahjāt to India and ensure that it first passed through the Kabul markets. This episode nearly cost him his life.[46]

From at least the beginning of Amīr Amān Allāh Khān's reign, Fayż Muḥammad was working in the Textbook Office (*dār al-taʾlīf*) of the Ministry of Education and continuing as court chronicler. There late in November 1923 he completed writing and then saw published a 189-page textbook on saints and sages from Adam to Jesus[47] under the auspices of his namesake Fayż Muḥammad Zakariyā (Zikriyā), then the deputy minister of education.[48] Zikriyā would become minister the next year or the year after.[49] But working with Zikriyā on the book of ancient sages seems to have earned Fayż Muḥammad the deputy minister's at least grudging respect. (It is not clear that Fayż Muḥammad had the same respect for the minister or if he did he later changed his mind. In *Taẕakkur al-inqilāb*, as we will see, Fayż Muḥammad would sharply criticize his former supporter and the by-then former education minister for his collaboration with the Kalakānī regime.)

While publishing the book on ancient sages, he continued to work on chronicling the reign of Amīr ʿAbd al-Raḥmān Khān in volume 3 of *Sirāj*, having gotten as far as the events of Shaʿbān 1317/December 1899. Meantime, according to one observer, Wolfgang Lentz, a German anthropologist working in Nūristān,[50] the typesetting of the remainder of volume three had resumed in 1924 and some pages were even printed.[51] Then, again most likely in 1924, printing suddenly stopped on the orders of the amir who also decreed that all printed copies of the third volume be confiscated

46 Fayż Muḥammad, *The History*, vol. 4, pp. 278–79, 463–69.

47 Fayż Muḥammad Kātib, *Tārīkh-i ḥukamā-yi mutaqaddimīn az hubūṭ-i Ḥażrat-i Ādam ta bi-wujūd āmadan-i Ḥażrat-i ʿĪsā*, Kabul, Wizārat-i Maʿārif, 1 Qaws 1302 (November 20, 1923). Online at the New York University Afghanistan Digital Library, http://hdl.handle.net/2333.1/vxok6dtc.

48 On this Bārakzāʾī figure see Ludwig W. Adamec, *Who's Who of Afghanistan*, Graz, Austria, Akademische Druck- u. Verlagsanstalt, 1975, pp. 135, 287 and idem, *Biographical Dictionary*, p. 207.

49 Ibid., p. 135 has him as acting minister of education in 1923 and appointed minister in March 1924. But in ibid., the British source says he was deputy minister of education in 1924 and minister from 1925–27, although the title page of Fayż Muḥammad Kātib's history of saints and sages has him as deputy minister in 1923. The most plausible dates for his tenure in office are: deputy minister (*wakīl-i wazīr*) by 1923 and minister by 1925.

50 V. A. Romodin, "Sochinenie 'Siradzh at-tavarikh' i ego istochniki," *Strany i Narody Vostoka*, vol. 26, Moscow, 1989, p. 227, citing W. Lentz, Sprachwissenscaftliche und völkerkundliche Studien in Nuristan: Deutsche im Hindukusch. Bericht der deutschen-Hindukusch-Expedition 1935 der Deutschen Forschungsgemeinschaft, Berlin, 1937, p. 257.

51 Romodin, "Sochinenie," p. 227.

and, it is generally believed, destroyed.[52] By some estimates, however, as many as 300 copies of what had been printed were salvaged from the press before they were lost.[53] It is difficult to imagine that the print run was much more than this and in any event the order to destroy the copies galvanized people to rescue them before the order could be carried out.

Despite this setback, Fayż Muḥammad never stopped writing and Zakariyā, now the minister of education, was willing to see him complete the project and so he assigned Hāshim Shāyiq Bukhārī, the head of the Textbook Office, to supervise Fayż Muḥammad's work. There is little evidence that Bukhārī exercised any censorship on what Fayż Muḥammad wrote except in one very important area, the amount of writing he was allowed to do. It is quite obvious to any reader of volume 4 that Fayż Muḥammad allots substantially fewer words to the reign of Amīr Ḥabīb Allāh Khān than to that of his father, Amīr ʿAbd al-Raḥmān Khān. Although Ḥabīb Allāh's reign was about eighty percent as long as his father's (seventeen years and four months versus twenty-one years and three months) Fayż Muḥammad only allotted a little more than half as many words (approximately 600,000 to 1,100,000) to his patron's reign. This was not his choice. He tells us the main reason the space allotted to Ḥabīb Allāh Khān's reign is so much less was primarily because of the salary stipulations in his contract for writing the conclusion to volume three and writing volume four.

Fayż Muḥammad was in the middle of writing about the events of December 1899 in volume 3 when he inserts a long digression entitled "The Author is Deprived of His Official Position in Government," writing about the disaster, as he characterizes it, that befell him in 1343/1924.[54] Due to "the slanders of opportunists" he says, among other things his supervisor at the Textbook Office of the Ministry of Education, Hāshim Shāyiq Bukhārī, ordered him to limit the number of pages to a predetermined figure (not specified by Fayż Muḥammad) and therefore limit his salary because he was paid on the basis of the number of pages he produced.[55] As a consequence, Fayż Muḥammad had to ignore the books in which farmans of Ḥabīb Allāh Khān's reign were registered and also the books registering all the decrees issued by the separate courts of Sardār

---

[52] Yazdani, "Sharḥ", p. 19. See also Mīr Ghulām Muḥammad Khān "Ghubār." "Fayż Muḥammad," *Tārīkh-i Adabiyāt-i Afghānistān*, edited by Aḥmad ʿAlī Kuhzād, et al., Kabul, 1330 (1951), p. 396.

[53] Romodin, "Sochinenie ...", p. 227.

[54] Fayż Muḥammad, *The History*, vol. 4, pp. 403–404.

[55] Ibid., vol. 4, pp. 1043, 1225, 1260, 1282, 1296.

Naṣr Allāh Khān, Prince ʿInāyat Allāh Khān, Prince Amān Allāh Khān, and Sardār ʿAbd al-Quddūs Khān, the prime minister. These separate courts were all established by decree of Amīr Ḥabib Allāh Khān in 1903.[56] This partially explains why the amount of space devoted to Ḥabīb Allāh's reign is so disproportionate to that of his father's, ʿAbd al-Raḥmān Khān.

This probably was also the moment when his research materials on Amīr Amān Allāh Khān's regime were confiscated and he was forbidden further access to the archives. And it also could well be the time when he says that his monthly salary was "terminated" after more than three decades of loyal service, although "terminated" might not be quite the right word. Later, while writing the fourth volume of *Sirāj*, he alludes to being "banned from the honor of attending and serving the Court" which suggests that the contract change had more consequences than simply the change in method of payment.[57] His explanation of his termination suggests less that he was terminated and more that the terms under which he was working were revised to his disadvantage and to his dismay. According to him, the original contract set a monthly income amount for the employees of the Textbook Office of the Ministry of Education. In the course of the month they all were required to produce a certain number

56 See ibid., vol. 4, pp. 786–88 for a discussion of the establishment of the separate decree-issuing courts. Fayż Muḥammad copied the farmans into his own notebooks and those relating to ʿAbd al-Raḥmān Khān's reign survive among his papers in the National Archives but whether those from Amīr Ḥabīb Allāh Khān's reign still exist is not clear. Since Fayż Muḥammad was constrained from using those registers because of the page-count issue it is possible he never copied their contents into his own notebooks. For some of the records of one of those courts, Prince ʿInāyat Allāh Khān's, see Saidanvar Shokhumorov. "Princely archive of court decrees: A Rare insight into the history of Afghanistan," in Francis Richard and Maria Szuppe, eds., *Écrit et culture en Asie Centrale et dans le monde Turco-Iranien, Xᵉ–XIXᵉ siècles / Writing and culture in Central Asia and the Turko-Iranian World, 10th–19th Centuries*, Paris: Association pour l'avancement des études Iraniennes. 111–26. The late Afghan historian ʿAzīz al-Dīn Wakīlī Fūfalzāʾī provides some information about the fate of ʿInāyat Allāh Khān's archive, known as *Aḥkām-i ḥużūr* (Court Decrees). In January 1929 as ʿInāyat Allāh prepared to leave Kabul for exile in Iran he gave nine volumes of his decrees to the Soviet envoy to Kabul, Leonide Stark, for safekeeping. Much later, in 1968, Wakīlī Fūfalzāʾī, part of an Afghan delegation to Moscow and Tashkent, heard that the archive existed and was safe (probably in Tashkent where it is now held at the library of Tashkent State University). On a second trip in 1980, Fūfalzāʾī again heard about the archive, this time from the then director of the (Biruni) Institute of Oriental Studies in Tashkent, Muzaffar Mukhitdinovich Khayrullaev. In 1987, a Tajik delegation came to Kabul, probably including Shokhumorov, and Fūfalzāʾī was told that the nine volumes were being published that year. See ʿAziz al-Din Wakili Fufalzāʾī, *Farhang-i Kabul-i Bāstān*, Kabul, Wizarat-i Iṭṭilāʿāt wa Farhang, 1387/2008, pp. 1035–37.) As far as is known no such publication has yet occurred. Shokhumorov died before his planned publication could take place.

57 Fayż Muḥammad, *The History*, vol. 4, pp. 402–04.

of pages with a given number of lines (15) and words per line (13–15). This was now replaced by a contract only for the pages produced with no guaranteed monthly income. (Apparently, some employees of the office had been happy to collect their monthly pay without producing the number of pages required.) So it is not quite as if Fayż Muḥammad were actually fired from his position but whatever happened, he believed it was greatly to his detriment.[58] A large part of his anger was focused on the fact that he was no longer considered a government employee (more like a contractor now) and had lost the prestige associated with that position. This may have meant being suspended from receiving the food rations that made up an increasingly important part of his compensation. Due to inflation, the in-kind part of his salary had become more valuable than the cash he received. Eventually, under these constraints, he completed the fourth volume of *Sirāj al-tawārīkh* on February 24, 1926 as the colophon of volume four indicates. From then until he began keeping a journal of the "revolution" of 1928–29 the information we have about his life is sketchy.

We know that for reasons unknown, he transferred ownership of his compound house (*ḥawīlī*) in Kabul, including all its furnishings and utensils, to three of his sons—ʿAlī Muḥammad, Walī Muḥammad, and Muḥammad Mahdī—and their mother, the daughter of Mīrzā Khān Bābā Khān on April 17, 1926.[59] We also now know that during this time he was teaching at the Ḥabībīyah Madrasah or Lycée although we do not yet know when he was first appointed there and how long he taught there. The Soviet scholar, A. I. Shkirando, who published the Russian translation of Fayż Muḥammad's *Tażakkur al-inqilāb*, was introduced to Fayż Muḥammad's life and works in 1979 by Amīr Muḥammad Aṡīr (known by then as "Dr. Asīr"), who said he had been a student in Fayż Muḥammad's "literature class" at the Ḥabībīyah School in 1927–28.[60]

It seems likely that Fayż Muḥammad also continued to work in the Textbook Office at the Ministry of Education. His patron there, Fayż Muḥammad Zikriyā, as far as we know was still minister of education

[58] Ibid.

[59] See Fayż Muḥammad, *The History*, vol. 1, pp. lxv–lxvi.

[60] Faiz Mukhammad, *Kniga upominanii o miatezhe*, Moscow, Izdatel'stvo Nauka, 1988, p. 3. See also Adamec, *A Biographical Dictionary*, p. 26 for a brief notice of "Dr. Mīr Muhammad Asir." Fayż Muḥammad would have certainly been pleased (and probably amused) by the Wikipedia entry "Habibia High School." Only two names are given under the heading "Notable Faculty." One is the late Harvard professor and Iranologist Richard N. Frye who taught there in the 1940s as cover for his assignment as an intelligence agent for the Office of Strategic Services (predecessor to the Central Intelligence Agency). The other name listed is "Faiz Muhammad Katib Hazārah."

when the revolution began and made his peace with the new amir. Although the Ministry of Trade was abolished and other ministries were forced to lay off employees (see translation of *Taẕakkur al-inqilāb* below), we have not found evidence that the Ministry of Education was abolished, nor its Textbook Office.

Fayż Muḥammad Kātib's life comes back into focus in the tumultuous events of 1928–29 that he records. In terms of his private life during that year, one important event was the impending marriage of one of his sons and his efforts to raise the money needed for the associated festivities. Another episode, and as it turned out, one critical to his physical well-being, was his assignment to a largely Qizilbāsh delegation sent to the Hazārahjāt to obtain oaths of loyalty to the new Tajik regime of Amīr Ḥabīb Allāh Khān Kalakānī. Fayż Muḥammad, probably in light of the political situation when he actually began writing this down, portrays himself as actively working to subvert the mission, to convince the uncommitted Hazārah factions not to submit written oaths of allegiance (*bay'at-nāmahs*) to Kalakānī. He says he used every opportunity to undermine the efforts of the leader of the delegation. The mission did fail but whether it was due to his efforts or not is uncertain. Ultimately, the resistant Hazārahs responded to a subsequent mission and offered their allegiance to the Tajik amir much to the disgust of Fayż Muḥammad. The failure of the delegation of which he was a member led to Fayż Muḥammad's being severely beaten along with the delegation's head and another member. The beating and its lasting effects are usually cited as the reason for his death in February 1931. Besides receiving some emergency medical assistance from the Iranian mission in Kabul, which he records, it is generally believed that he traveled to Iran over the winter of 1929–30 for further treatment. If Fayż Muḥammad received any medical treatment in Iran, its effects were short-lived. He returned to Kabul where he died the following February and was buried in the Chandawul quarter of the city. Until his death, he continued to write and both of the works translated here were either composed entirely (*Taẕakkur al-inqilāb*) or were largely revised (*Nizhādnāmah-i Afghān*) during the period after 1929.

It is also thought that it was at this time, or perhaps when the Iranian envoy to Kabul, Sayyid Mahdī Farrukh, evacuated Kabul along with other diplomats in February 1929, that some of Fayż Muḥammad's manuscripts made their way to Iran.[61] Fayż Muḥammad records his own close ties to the Iranian Legation and just as the legation's help was sought to counter

[61] See Yazdānī, "Sharḥ," pp. 32–33.

anti-Shiʿi outbreaks and for medical help when Fayż Muḥammad was beaten, it is reasonable that he turned to the legation and its head when seeking ways to safeguard his literary legacy. Sayyid Mahdī Farrukh had at his disposal a manuscript of *Fayżī az fuyūżāt* when writing his history of Afghanistan and although we can't know for certain Sayyid Mahdī Farrukh's role in this, somehow a manuscript of *Nizhādnāmah-i Afghān* found its way to the Malik Library in Tehran. There should be little question that Fayż Muḥammad looked to the Iranians to protect his work. He may also have harbored hopes that they would find ways to publish it as well.

Taẕakkur al-inqilāb

The *Taẕakkur al-inqilāb* (Memoir of the Revolution) is unique in being the only known account from an eyewitness in Kabul at the center of the revolution that began in late December 1928 and ended in October 1929. Another memoirist of the revolution, Muḥyī al-Dīn Anīs, author of *Buḥrān wa Najāt* (Crisis and Salvation) was in Kabul during the first two months but then escaped to Qandahar. Fayż Muḥammad on the other hand not only was an eyewitness in Kabul for the entire period but was also an active, if reluctant, participant in the attempts by the new administration to win over and gain the allegiance of the many constituencies that made up the Afghan body politic.

On his second attempt, a Tajik villager from an area some twenty miles north of Kabul, captured the Arg in Kabul, the seat of Afghan rulers since its construction in 1883 and took up residence there on January 18, 1929. The man's name was Ḥabīb Allāh, the son of a man named, perhaps, Hidāyat Allāh. They were Tajiks whose home town was Kalakān, located just east of the main road connecting Kabul, the capital, with the northern part of the country. The rise of this ex-soldier turned highwayman, a "mulberry-eater" as Fayż Muḥammad contemptuously refers to him, a man who had spent most of his forty-odd years struggling to make ends meet and put food on his family's table, was unheard of. Nominal, if not always actual, political power was understood to be the exclusive right of the Durrānīs, and in recent times, the exclusive privilege of the Muḥammadzāʾī clan of the Bārakzāʾī tribe, one of the larger of the southern Afghan tribes that made up the Durrānī confederation. For the previous 182 years no one but a Durrānī, first from the Sadūzāʾī clan and then from the Muḥammadzāʾī-Bārakzāʾī had ever been recognized as ruler at Kabul or even at Harāt or Qandahar. This was not just a break with tradition, it was a true political "revolution" (*inqilāb*) as Fayż Muḥammad labels it. Although his reign only lasted nine months before the *status quo ante* was restored and Ḥabīb Allāh Kalakānī and his associates were hunted down and executed, because of his ethnicity and because his revolution ended the reign of one dynastic family of the Muḥammadzāʾī and the rise of another, the Yaḥyā Khayl, that nine month revolution has cast a long shadow. Today the controversy over his brief rule from Kabul still resonates because it brings to the fore issues of ethnic and sectarian loyalties, the urban-rural divide, and fundamental questions of law and governance. Those who disparage Kalakānī's moment characterize him as a bandit and "the son of a watercarrier" (*pisar-i saqqā* or *bachchah-i saqqā* [in the vulgarized Anglicized form—Bacha Saqao]), the name that has defined him in the eyes of outsiders. To those who see him in these terms he is guilty of invoking Islam to destroy the progressive projects of the man he ousted, Amīr Amān Allāh Khān. Today, the administration of Afghanistan celebrates the memory and the policies of Amīr Amān Allāh Khān. The current president has stated "we will finish the unfinished business of Amīr Amān Allāh Khān"[62] and has named the country's highest civilian medal after him. However, to rural Afghanistan and to a substantial if not majority part of the urban population Amān Allāh's westernizing projects were deeply unpopular.

Inside Afghanistan there are other meanings attached to Kalakānī's image: he is celebrated for his achievements as a Tajik (making him a hero, if a flawed and ill-starred one, to the Tajik population today) and honored for restoring Islam, which the "infidel" Amān Allāh Khān had violated with his attempts to reform the institution of marriage, his attempts to force people to wear western clothing, his efforts to remove the veil (the *chadrī*) and mostly for the corruption of his administration. Fayż Muḥammad, urbanite and government employee that he was, nevertheless was no supporter of Amān Allāh's reforms nor was he, good Hazārah that he was, at all sympathetic with the Tajik, Amīr Ḥabīb Allāh Kalakānī.

The *Tazakkur al-inqilāb* exhibits many of the themes Fayż Muḥammad consciously emphasized or that he may have been unaware of but that seem evident to the modern-day reader. One is the entrenched corruption of government officials. After the invocation of God and the Prophet Muhammad, the preface to *Tazakkur al-inqilāb* begins with a section

---

62 Arshad Hunaryar, "Ashraf Ghanī wa rāh-i nā-tamām-i Shāh Amān Allāh; Qahrimān-i bad farjām-i naw girāʾyī," BBC Persian ServiceOnline http://www.bbc.com/persian/afghanistan-40985162 and http://www.bbc.com/persian/afghanistan-40985414.

entitled “The Reasons for the Revolution” a screed against Amīr Amān Allāh Khān and two of his officials in particular, Fayż Muḥammad’s own nemesis, Maḥmūd Beg Ṭarzī, and the Ottoman Turk, Maḥmūd Sāmī Effendi. After singling them out, he details the areas in which the government had failed: the economy had collapsed, money was devalued, crime was rampant, and justice was unattainable because of high fees and bribes that were beyond the means of ordinary people. Also, Fayż Muḥammad found reprehensible, as did most male Afghans, the amir’s interventions on behalf of women.

At the very end of this rant, apparently feeling the need to counterbalance all the negatives, Fayż Muḥammad lists the amir’s praiseworthy accomplishments, although he does not consider them the reasons for the revolution. These were the country’s full independence, the establishment of international relations (for Fayż Muḥammad the treaty with Iran and the opening of an Iranian mission in Kabul were clearly the most important of these international ties), and the efforts at industrialization.

Other currents that run through these two works as well as through his monumental *Sirāj al-tawārīkh* emerge in the autobiographical snippets that appear in both works and the judgments he offers that reveal his own perspective on the world. One is his frankness, his uninhibited reporting on matters sexual, both homo- and heterosexual. This aspect of his mindset comes out strongly in the fourth volume of *Sirāj al-tawārīkh*, which was largely unsupervised once the parameters of its composition were set down. But no less so in *Taẕakkur al-inqilāb* (pp. 71, 72, 79, 80, 83, 103) on occasion with graphic details (e.g. pp. 85–86). He also comes across as something of an egotist and self-promoter, presenting himself as a problem solver, a mediator, a justice-seeker for the victims of injustice and a chastiser of oppressors, and more of an expert in matters of Qur’ān and Islamic law than anyone else especially the “pseudo-mullahs” (*mullā-namāyān*) as he calls them.

Despite, or perhaps because of, this willingness to reveal his own stance, his own prejudices, both texts beguile the reader into thinking this is an authentic perspective, by no means representative of the general population but giving an insight into how events were interpreted and experienced by a single well-educated individual caught up in the sectarian and ethnic conflicts of the time.

The *Taẕakkur al-inqilāb*, an approximately 90,000-word (209 manuscript-page) account of the first seven months of the nine-month period of Kalakānī control of the Kabul throne was never completed. The last

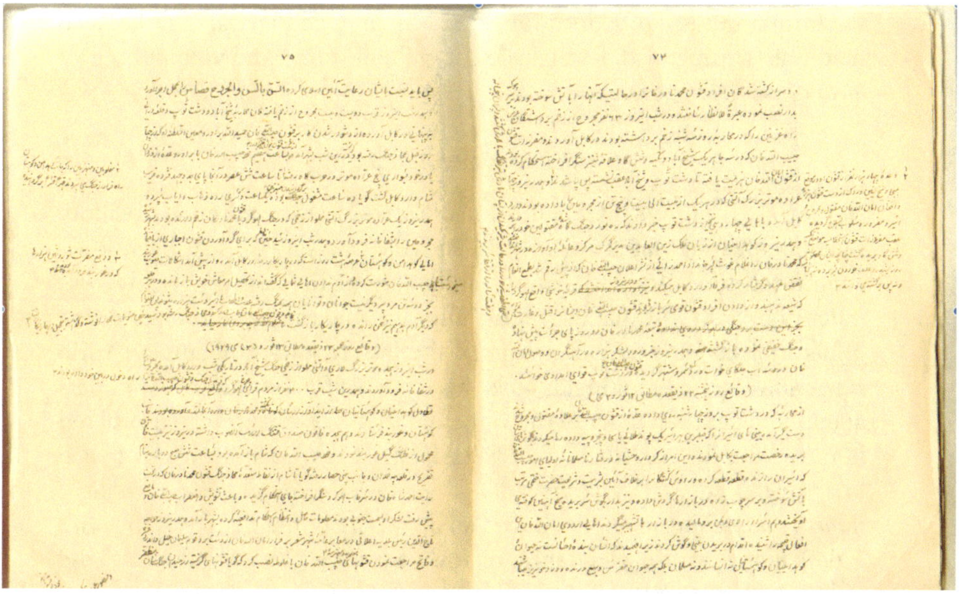

Figure 2: *Taẕakkur al-inqilāb*, pages 74–75 showing Fayż Muḥammad's edits.

entry begins "On Wednesday the twenty-second of Rabiʿ al-Awwal …" and that is all Fayż Muḥammad ever wrote. It was as if something disturbed or distracted him at that point and he never returned to the work.

It almost certainly is the case that the information in *Taẕakkur al-inqilāb* was written first in a diary which the author kept throughout the Kalakānī period. He refers more than once in the *Taẕakkur* to a "journal (*rūznāmah*)" from which the information in *Taẕakkur al-inqilāb* is derived[63] and then at least twice to the work by its name. Its structure, with the preface in which the reasons for the revolution are set out, clearly shows this as a retrospective work, a memoir, rather than a daily record. His source is his diary and in most places he simply transfers the information from one to the other. The many marginal notes show that he was repeatedly reviewing the work and adding information that was not in his journal but which he later discovered. (**Fig. 2**) Something that also suggests a retrospective work, written under the new regime of Muḥammad Nādir Shāh, is the fact that Fayż Muḥammad condemns the one-time object of his praise,[64]

63 Translation, p. 90.

64 See both the preamble, where the dedication is more pro forma, and the colophon to volume four of *Sirāj al-tawārīkh*, Fayż Muḥammad, *The History*, vol. 4, pp. 1, 1467.

the former minister of education, Fayż Muḥammad Zikriyā, the man who made his writing of the conclusion to volume three and volume four of *Sirāj al-tawārīkh* possible.

Nizhādnāmah-i Afghān

At the very beginning of volume one of *Sirāj al-tawārīkh* are the prefatory remarks of Amīr Ḥabīb Allāh Khān in which he says he had been long-committed to a plan for writing the history of the country. Yet he was much too busy with his efforts to "improve the army and the condition of his subjects" and so had delegated the task to Fayż Muḥammad Kātib Hazārah. Fayż Muḥammad adds his own self-deprecating comments about being chosen to write the work and then says that the amir ordered him to compile "a genealogy of the Afghan clans with a census of each one treated separately" (*nasab-nāmah-i ṭawā'if-i Afāghinah wa ta'dād-i nufūs-i 'alāḥaddah*) and make that an appendix to the history along with a detailed historical geography of the country.[65] Fayż Muḥammad did indeed commence the *Sirāj* with a geographical section[66] which apparently accorded with the amir's wish. However, because the full publication of *Sirāj al-tawārīkh* was interrupted a decade later by Amīr Amān Allāh Khān's order for publication to cease and for the existing printed copies to be destroyed, the printed version ended in mid-sentence on page 1240 of volume 3, and thus no tribal genealogical appendix was ever added. By the time he had put the rest of volume three and all of volume four in finished manuscript form he had decided not to include the genealogical section he had been working on for many years either because it was going to be available elsewhere, or simply because the page-limitations that he worked under forced him to give up the idea of including it in *Sirāj al-tawārīkh.*

Nonetheless, he did produce such a work and in a final form. The manuscript held by the Malik Library in Tehran, which was used for this translation, shows none of the customary marginal notes, such as those found in *Tazakkur al-inqilāb*, that would indicate Fayż Muḥammad was still revising the work. Thus it is safe to assume that when Fayż Muḥammad put the manuscript in the hands of someone he trusted, very likely the Iranian envoy, Sayyid Mahdī Farrukh, the work, by his high standards, was complete. In its forty-eight pages, there are only two small

65 Fayż Muḥammad, *The History*, vol. 1, p. 3.
66 Ibid., vol. 1, pp. 3–9.

corrections made in the margins (on pages 9 and 14) and one marginal note explaining the Pashto letter, 'ḥā' with three dots over it.[67]

There is also a note in a different hand on the first page of the manuscript that reads:

> Since I no longer have the time or patience to go forward with the publication of this book, I think it best now to present it to my deeply esteemed friend, His Excellency Ḥājj Ḥusayn Āqā-yi Malik so that if it should be deemed acceptable, it will be preserved in his National Library. 14/1/1326 (April 4, 1947).

The note is signed but the signature is illegible. (**Fig. 3**) According to the library stamp, the manuscript was added to the holdings of the Malik Library five years later on 23 Farvardīn 1331 (11 April 1952) and given the number 3730.

The *Nizhādnāmah-i Afghān* is an ethnographic snapshot in time following the format of the enormously influential early seventeenth-century work *Tārīkh-i jahānkhānī wa Makhzan-i Afghānī* or in its abbreviated form simply *Makhzan-i Afghānī.* This work established a method and a structure for explaining and describing the vastly ramified tribal society of the region bounded on the north by the Hindū Kush mountain range, on the south by the Sand Desert (Rīg or Rīgistān) to Qandahar's south, by the Indus River to the east and to the west by the ancient route connecting Kabul and Qandahar an area that contained the vast majority of Pashtūn tribes, known to outsiders as "Afghans." The *Makhzan* produced a credible origin for the tribes and a foundation story for their Islamization, however anachronistic and mythical these might have been, and provided a framework for understanding the position of any given Afghan "tribe" at the point in time of the writer. Thus Fayż Muḥammad organizes his genealogy based on seven original lineages and discusses the controversies that have arisen over the years as to the authentic "Afghan-ness" of some of them.[68]

---

[67] Fayż Muḥammad's note equates the Pashto *ḥā'* with three dots above it to the Arabic letter *t̲h̲ā'* the Persian *ṣa'* pronounced as an ess in English. Perhaps only as evidence of constant linguistic evolution, Georg Morgenstierne, in his article "Afghān. ii. The Pashto Language" in *The Encyclopaedia of Islam*, New Edition, volume 1, p. 220a, says that the *ḥā'* with three dots over it is pronounced *t̲s̲* and *d̲z̲* while the Wikipedia alphabet chart for Pashto says the pronunciation is t̲s̲ as in the word "cat̲s̲."

[68] Other sources on Afghan genealogical history that he cites are Muḥammad Taqī "Sipihr" Kāshānī "Lisān al-Mulk", *Nāsikh al-tawārīkh*; Muḥammad Qāsim Hindūshāh Astarābādī known as "Firishtah," *Tārīkh-i Firishtah*; Deputy Muḥammad Ḥayāt Khān, *Ḥayāt-i Afghān*, an Urdu work; and a textbook on Afghan history (whose title he doesn't mention) by his colleague and supervisor at the Textbook Office (Dār al-Ta'līf) of the Ministry of Education, Hāshim Shāyiq Bukhārī.

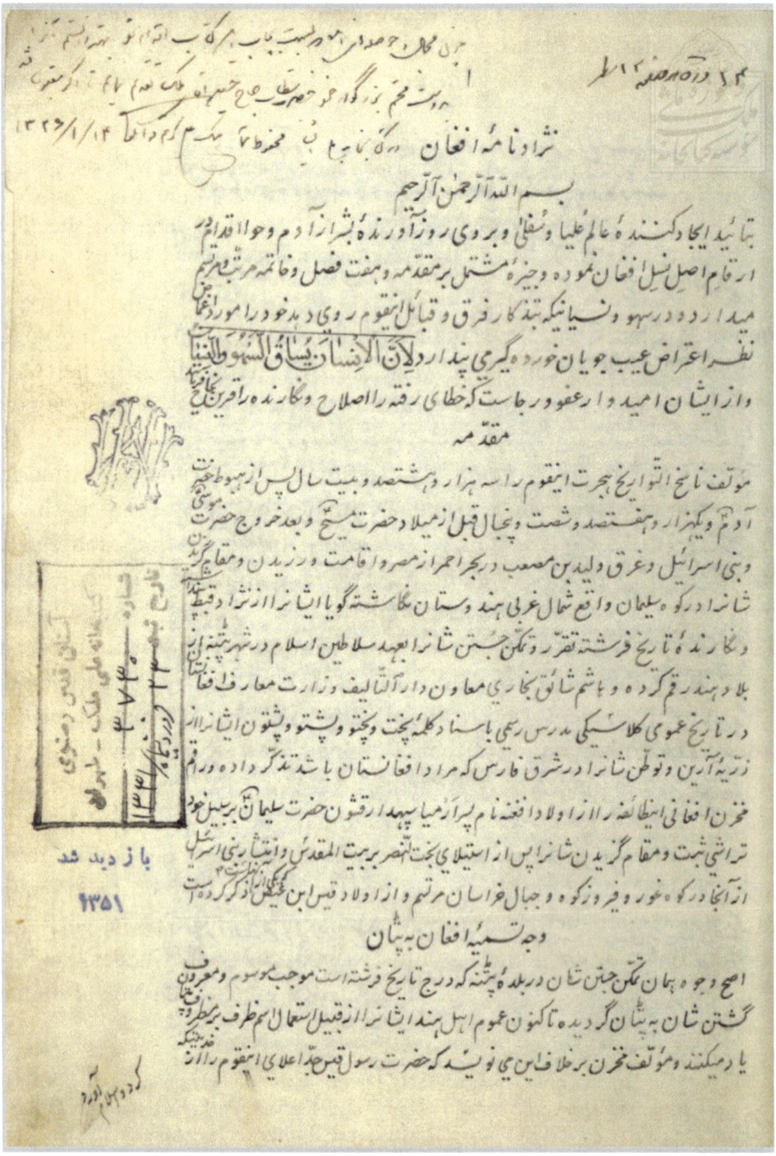

نژادنامهٔ افغان

بسم الله الرحمن الرحیم

بنا بر تأیید ایجاد کنندهٔ عالم علیا و سفلی و برروی روزآورندهٔ بشر از آدم و حوا اقدام در
ارقام اصل نسل افغان نموده وجیزهٔ مشتمل بر مقدمه و هفت فصل و خاتمه مرتب و مرتسم
میدارد و در سهو و نسیانیکه بتذکار فرق و قبائل این قوم روی دهد خود را مورد
نظر اعتراض عیب جویان خورده گیری پندارد لان الانسان یساق السهو والنسیان
و از ایشان امیدوار عفو و رجاست که خطای رفته را اصلاح و نگارنده را آفرین [illegible]

مقدمه

مؤلف تاریخ التواریخ هجرت این قوم را سه هزار و هشتصد و بیست سال پس از هبوط حضرت
آدم و یکهزار و هفتصد و شصت و پنج سال قبل از میلاد حضرت مسیح و بعد خروج حضرت موسی
و بنی اسرائیل و غرق ولید بن مصعب در بحر احمر از مصر و اقامت ورزیدن و مقام گزیدن
شان را در کوه سلیمان واقع شمال غربی هندوستان نگاشته گویا ایشان را از نژاد قبطیان
و نگارندهٔ تاریخ فرشته تقرر و تمکن جستن شان را بعهد سلاطین اسلام در شهر پتنه از
بلاد هند رقم کرده و هاشم شائق بخاری معاون دار التألیف وزارت معارف افغانستان
در تاریخ عمومی کلاسیکی مدارس رسمی باسناد کلمهٔ بخت و بختو و پشتو و پشتون ایشان را از
ذریهٔ آرین و توطن شان را در شرق فارس که مراد افغانستان باشد تذکر داده و در
مخزن افغانی این طائفه را از اولاد افغنه نام پسر ارمیا سپهدار طالوت حضرت سلیمان [illegible]
نژاد شان ثبت و مقام گزیدن شان را پس از استیلای بخت النصر بر بیت المقدس و ایشان بنی اسرائیل
از آنجا در کوه غور و فیروزکوه و جبال خراسان مرتسم و از اولاد قیس [illegible] ذکر کرده است

وجه تسمیهٔ افغان به پتان

اصح وجوه همان تمکن جستن شان در بلدهٔ پتنه که درج تاریخ فرشته است موجب موسوم و معروف
گشتن شان به پتان گردیده تاکنون عموم اهل هند ایشان را از قبیل استعمال اسم ظرف بر مظروف
یاد میکنند و مؤلف مخزن برخلاف این می نویسد که حضرت رسول قیس جد اعلای این قوم را از

Figure 3: *Nizhādnāmah-i Afghān*, page 1 with the marginal note of the unknown donor of the manuscript.

But his real concern is not so much proving or disproving the origin stories but simply to use what everyone is familiar with to structure what seems significant to him in the tribal situation of early twentieth-century Afghanistan. And the scope of his interest encompasses all the ethnic groups of Afghanistan, not just the Afghans proper as the title of his work would suggest.

For each of the distinct tribes or peoples, he first seems primarily concerned with the size of the group based on census data, that is the number of households or alternatively the number of "fighting men" the Afghan tribes in particular could muster. Secondly, he was concerned with identifying the "homeland" (*waṭan, mawṭin*) or physical location of the tribe or clan, thirdly, how its members supported themselves, and lastly, whether it was subject to British or Afghan jurisdiction. But there are a number of secondary themes that provide a narrative coherence to his catalogue. One is religion, the sectarian affiliations of each group, whether Shiʿi or Sunni, and the degree of fervor, or fanaticism, with which the group manifests its religious loyalty. Related to this is the moral standing of the tribe in Fayż Muḥammad's eyes whether the group was generally "good" or "evil." His judgments tended to be more negative than positive and it is important to note that he was writing this (although he had researched the subject for years) at a very low point in his life when he was ill and must have been contemplating his own death. This is reflected in the plaintive apology with which he introduces his chapter on the non-Afghans of Afghanistan. Commenting on the relative brevity of this section compared to the coverage of Afghan tribes, he asks to be excused for his failure to provide more detail and blames it on "physical frailty and the difficult straits caused by a lack of the food, drink, and clothing necessary for survival." He then expresses the hope that "fair-minded people will forgive him." It seems clear from this and from other remarks that the defeat of Amīr Ḥabīb Allāh Kalakānī by Nādir Khān and his brothers proved of no benefit to Fayż Muḥammad and that he spent the last two years of his life, 1929 and 1930, without paid work, and died in February 1931 an impoverished and bitter man.

Given that context, it is not surprising that his moral judgments of some Afghan tribes are harsh and we find characterizations like "in terms of their morals, [the Isḥāqzāʾī] are hardly human and are the consorts of bestiality and utter ignorance." (p. 354) (This, notwithstanding the fact that his most influential mentor Mullā Muḥammad Sarwar was from this tribe.) Of the Mulla Khayl nomads (who nearly killed him in 1922) he could say, "these are the most wicked of all Ghilzāʾī, indeed of all Afghans" (p. 377). Those he deemed more virtuous also tended to be those identified as Shiʿi as well, one of his persistent biases.

Another theme and one that runs through most of his writings is the unjust way that his own people, the Hazārahs, have been treated, a theme that those who used his work take up, as we will be seen below. Many of the Afghan tribes that he describes directly benefited from the ethnic cleansing policies of the amirs, ʿAbd al-Raḥmān Khān and his son and successor, Ḥabīb Allāh Khān, being given lands and buildings belonging to Hazārahs in historically Hazārah areas.

Not a conscious theme but one that will be evident to the reader is the fluidity and dynamic nature of Afghan tribal identity as revealed in *Nizhādnāmah-i Afghān*. There are groups who claim that they are Afghans though others reject the claim. There are those whose origins as Afghans are suspect but who are accepted as Afghans. There are those who are genealogically direct descendants of the mythic founder of all Afghans, Qays ʿAbd al-Rashīd, but who are in the process of disavowing and shedding that Afghan identity and replacing it with an urban, mercantile one. There are non-Afghans in the process of becoming Afghans though affiliation with an Afghan tribe and the reverse as well, Afghans who are becoming non-Afghans, Tajiks for example, due to their long-time living in close proximity. In Fayż Muḥammad's world, there is nothing permanent or fixed about ethnic identity.

The recent trauma of the "revolution" of "Pisar-i Saqqā" (Son of the Water Carrier), Ḥabīb Allāh Kalakānī, also provides a potent theme unifying the narrative. One feature of *Nizhādnāmah-i Afghān* is Fayż Muḥammad's profiling significant contemporary figures from a particular tribal group. What makes them significant for him is the role they played during the "revolution," either resisting or supporting Kalakānī.

Finally, the population figures presented by Fayż Muḥammad for Afghans and non-Afghans are prima facie evidence of his strongly-held belief that the political power of the Afghans (i.e. the Pashtūns) was disproportionate to their share of the population. He concludes that of a total population of 5,700,000 to 6,000,000 people within the borders of Afghanistan in the 1920s, there were no more than 300,000 households of Afghans. If we take the one place where he equates households and total number of people as indicative (in the case of the Hazārahs 650,000 households and 2,250,000 people), then the Afghan population of Afghanistan would have amounted to little more than one million people or about 15% of the whole. In his view eighty percent of the Afghans lived outside Afghanistan. Without attempting here to delve into his figures, for which we have nothing reliable to compare them with, we cite them only to show what his thinking was. He himself wished to show the reader that his numbers were from an independent census source even saying in one case that he could not provide population figures for a tribe because there was no census information available. It is somewhat ironic that he too inadvertently gave added life to the notion of Afghan paramountcy and preeminence by according Afghan tribes 76% of his ethnography (thirty-six and one-half pages of the forty-eight-page manuscript) and non-Afghans the remainder.

An invaluable and thematically rich portrayal of Afghanistan's society in the first third of the twentieth century, the *Nizhādnāmah-i Afghān*, as Fayż Muḥammad implies in his apologia, is a comprehensive account of the tribal structure of Afghanistan during his lifetime, at least as far as the Afghan tribes and clans were concerned. The non-Afghans are treated more cursorily he says. Yet we have other evidence that *Nizhādnāmah-i Afghān* was a considerably condensed version of the extensive research and writing that he had actually done on the subject. At least one and perhaps two other contemporary authors of histories of Afghanistan, both of them Iranian, incorporated his research in some fashion in their own written works and through one of them at least we have a better idea of the extent of Fayż Muḥammad's ethnographic research.

One was the Iranian envoy, Sayyid Mahdī Farrukh, who was the most likely person to have carried the manuscript of *Nizhādnāmah-i Afghān* to Iran aside from Fayż Muḥammad himself when he went for medical treatment in 1930. Farrukh was the second Iranian minister to the Afghan court, serving in Kabul from 1924 to 1929. After his return to Iran he wrote *Tārīkh-i siyāsī-yi Afghānistān* (Political History of Afghanistan) published in 1935. He included a portion of Fayż Muḥammad's secret history, the *Fayżī az fuyūżāt*, in his work and had a copy of the three published volumes of *Sirāj al-tawārīkh* at hand when he wrote his own history. How much he relied on Fayż Muḥammad's work for his ethnographic section has to be deduced from a comparison of the contents of the two and there is some evidence that his work was somewhat independent of Fayż Muḥammad's or at least had significantly different elements.

There is no doubt, however, that another Iranian had access to Fayż Muḥammad's research and writing at a point long before *Nizhādnāmah-i Afghān* was in final form or perhaps even written. The earliest known version of Fayż Muḥammad's genealogical and ethnographic research appears in the seven-volume history of Afghanistan, generally referred to as *Amān al-tawārīkh*, written by Ḥājjī Mīrzā ʿAbd al-Muḥammad "Muʾaddib al-Sulṭān" Iṣfahānī Īrānī to give him his full signifier.[69] ʿAbd al-Muḥammad "Muʾaddib al-Sulṭān" was an expatriate resident of Cairo and publisher of a Persian newspaper there called *Chihrah-numā* founded in 1904–05.

As editor of *Chihrah-numā*, ʿAbd al-Muḥammad had written a number of articles on Afghanistan and was then encouraged by colleagues, he says, to write a full history of the country.[70] What he produced in the seven volumes was more in the nature of an encyclopedia, with sections on geography, ethnography, the history of Islam up through the rise of Aḥmad Durrānī (in 1747), the kings of Afghanistan (with an entire volume devoted to ʿAbd al-Raḥmān [volume 6] and one projected for Amān Allāh Khān [volume 7][71]), an essay on poetics, and biographies of poets who had lived within the bounds of modern-day Afghanistan. Originally he had simply titled it *Tārīkh-i Afghānistān* but later renamed it *Amān al-tawārīkh* in the hope of gaining recognition and reward from Amīr Amān Allāh Khān.[72]

In 1914, ʿAbd al-Muḥammad began a correspondence with Maḥmūd Beg Ṭarzī, editor of the newspaper *Sirāj al-akhbār*, (as one editor to another) apparently hoping through Ṭarzī to gain access to Amīr Ḥabīb Allāh Khān's patronage. But the amir then had his own history project with *Sirāj al-tawārīkh* and showed no interest in what the Iranian was

---

69 For a brief and unfortunately incompletely published description of the author and his work, see R. D. McChesney. "A Little-Known Persian History of Afghanistan: the Aman al-tawarikh." In *Uzbekistan v Srednie Veka: Istoriia i Kul'tura*, edited by D. A. Alimova, et al., Tashkent: Institut Istorii, pp. 34–40.

70 *Amān al-tawārīkh*, vol. 1 pp. 6–8.

71 In the New York University manuscript (see next note), the first six volumes have 376, 799, 644, 627, 397, and 322 pages respectively. The seventh volume has only 123 pages with many left blank and has nothing about Aman Allah, a reflection of the author's disappointment with the amir and his promises.

72 A facsimile edition of *Amān al-tawārīkh* with an introduction by Dr. Sayyid Makhdum Raheen was published in Kabul by Riyāsat-i Intishārāt-i Kutub-i Bayhaqī in seven volumes (Ḥamal 1392–Mīzān 1393/March 2014–October 2015). It is a reproduction of the manuscript purchased by New York University in the 1980s from the author's son in Cairo. According to Husayn Barzagar Kishtali, "Amān al-tawārīkh," *Dānishnāmah-i Adab-i Fārsī: Adab-i Fārsī dar Afghānistān*, Tehran 1378/1999 p. 114, "all or some of the volumes were printed in Egypt under the title *Tārīkh-i mufaṣṣal-i Afghānistān*" but we have been unable to verify this. The Kabul facsimile edition is not well reproduced making it often difficult, especially with place names, to determine the diacritical markings of letters and thus how to read the name. Furthermore, at least in volume 5, words are smudged into illegibility and on one occasion two pages were omitted in the course of photographing the original. A serious researcher will need to access the finely calligraphed manuscript volumes at Fales Library and Special Collections, Bobst Library, New York University.

doing. When Amān Allāh came to the throne in 1919, ʿAbd al-Muḥammad managed to solicit an invitation from Ṭarzī to visit Kabul. He arrived in the wintry capital by way of Peshawar in late January 1922 carrying the five volumes he had written to that point.

He says he met the amir three times, once at Babur Gardens where he probably was accommodated in the haremserai building built by Amīr ʿAbd al-Raḥmān Khān but which was used by Ḥabīb Allāh Khān and Amān Allāh Khān as an official guesthouse. The amir and ʿAbd al-Muḥammad seem to have reached an agreement for the amir to sponsor the work. The terms required ʿAbd al-Muḥammad to leave the volumes he had brought with him to be copied and it may have been this that led him to an acquaintance with Fayż Muḥammad or perhaps Fayż Muḥammad sought him out when he heard of his arrival and the purpose of his journey. The two historians probably felt some rapport at first because of their similar projects and Fayż Muḥammad seems to have welcomed the acquaintance. We know that, like many other Hazārahs, he felt a special affinity for Iranians on the basis of shared religion, but his close relations with the Iranian Legation only really began to show itself with the arrival of the second Iranian envoy to an independent Afghanistan, Sayyid Mahdī Farrukh in 1924, with whom he was particularly close.[73] At the time of Farrukh's arrival Fayż Muḥammad was enjoying the fame and prestige his appointment as official chronicler for Amīr Amān Allāh Khān brought him. He had survived his unfortunate, if involuntary, backing of the amirate of Prince Naṣr Allāh Khān, and landed on his feet at the new court with his appointment in 1920 as the new amīr's official chronicler.

When ʿAbd al-Muḥammad arrived in Kabul in January 1922, he was unacquainted with either the person or the work of Fayż Muḥammad despite the fact that the three published volumes of *Sirāj al-tawārīkh* are listed among his sources in volume one of the print edition of *Amān al-tawārīkh.* When he arrived in Kabul he had not yet been introduced to the work of the Hazārah historian even though the printed edition shows

---

[73] According to Sayyid Mahdī Farrukh, *Kursī-nishīnān-i Kābul: Aḥwāl-i dawlatmardān-i Afghānistān dar rūzagār-i Amīr Amān Allāh Khān,* Tehran, Muʾassasah-i pazhūhish wa muṭālaʿāt-i farhangī, 1370/1991, pp. 252–54, the first two Iranian envoys to Afghanistan, Naṣr Allāh Khilʿatbarī "Iʿtilā al-Mulk" and Sayyid Mahdī Farrukh both reported to their superiors in Tehran on the great assistance Fayż Muḥammad Kātib could render Iran in encouraging the immigration of large numbers of Hazārahs to populate the vacant areas of Iranian Khurāsān as well as to serve as a political counterweight in Kabul to the strong pro-Turkish tendencies of the administration of Amān Allāh Khān. How that last was to be achieved is not at all evident. We don't have Khilʿatbarī's reports but we do have Farrukh's in ibid.

it in volume one in the list of sources. The reason why this is the case is because the printed facsimile is of the New York University manuscript which in turn is a revision of the volume one that ʿAbd al-Muḥammad took with him to Kabul. The revised version was written in Isfahan after his visit and, of course, after he had been introduced to and become a close acquaintance of Fayż Muḥammad. The copy of volume one now held at the National Archives (Arshīf-i Millī) in Kabul is a copy of the one he brought with him in 1922 and does not list *Sirāj al-tawārīkh* among his sources.[74]

A condition of the agreement that Amān Allāh reached with ʿAbd al-Muḥammad, as noted above, was for him to leave behind the five volumes he had brought to Kabul so that they could be copied. He did so, he admits, only with great trepidation, they being his only copies. Fayż Muḥammad was probably asked in his capacity as a munshi in the Textbook Office of the Ministry of Education to copy at least one of the volumes. The National Archives of Afghanistan today is the repository of the copy Fayż Muḥammad made of volume one of *Amān al-tawārīkh*. This is the colophon:

> The copying and writing out of this book achieved completion on Saturday, the twenty-fourth of the solar month Sunbulah 1301 equivalent to the twenty-third of Muḥarram of 1341 lunar Hijrī (15 September 1922). Fayż Muḥammad Kātib copied it. Only.

Not only did he copy at least one of the five volumes the Iṣfahānī native brought with him to Kabul, Fayż Muḥammad also contributed to the work of ʿAbd al-Muḥammad in two other important ways.

ʿAbd al-Muḥammad, well-attuned to the demands of modern publishing, sought and received a number of blurbs (*taqrīẓ* pl. *taqārīẓ*) for his book which are included in volume seven, a volume he only wrote after his Kabul sojourn. He probably collected the blurbs individually and then copied them into the end of the seventh volume (pp. 114–123) when he had returned to Iṣfahān.[75] One of the blurbs was signed by Fayż Muḥammad Kātib and dated the 21st of Ḥūt 1300 (3 March 1922) less than six weeks after ʿAbd al-Muḥammad arrived in Kabul. It is filled with somewhat restrained and perhaps not entirely sincere praise. He recommends the Iranian as "a judicious and learned man of letters, a unique great

[74] The list of sources is on pp. 16–20 of volume one in the Kabul copy; pp. 15–23 in the NYU Fales Library manuscript.

[75] Those who provided blurbs are listed in a note in Fayż Muḥammad, *The History*, vol. 1, p. lv and included the then Iranian envoy, Iʿtilā al-Mulk (Naṣr Allāh Khilʿatbarī).

and most eminently glorious scholar, Ḥājjī Mīrzā ʿAbd al-Muḥammad Khān Muʾaddib al-Sulṭān, managing editor of the incomparable journal *Chihrah-numā*;" he then praises him

> for having translated into very melodious Persian from books in French, Latin, Greek, English, German, Russian, Turkish, Arabic, and other languages all [that is known about] the rulers, governors, philosophers, scholars, savants and others who since the days of Kayūmars̱ until our own time came into existence, grew up, and passed away on the pure soil of Afghanistan and dependent Turkistān and has written this effortlessly in a way that all can easily read.[76]

He might have been a little less generous with his praise six months after writing the blurb when he finished copying the 275-page manuscript of volume one and noticed, if he hadn't known it already, that the list of the 100-plus works cited by ʿAbd al-Muḥammad as his sources did not include *Sirāj al-tawārīkh*. ʿAbd al-Muḥammad was unaware, as we've said, of the *Sirāj al-tawārīkh* when he began his project but was apparently keen to hear about it in Kabul and to include it in the revised volume when he returned to Isfahan. Whether it influenced at all his writing of volume 6, the volume to be devoted to Amīr ʿAbd al-Raḥmān Khān, remains to be seen. As the volume exists today in the print/NYU manuscript versions, volume 6 has very limited coverage of the amir's reign.

The fact that Fayż Muḥammad, along with several other officials of the Ministry of Education, were persuaded to write commendations of ʿAbd al-Muḥammad's work is another indication of Fayż Muḥammad's initial, at least, sense of gratification that this obviously important Iranian figure—we can imagine that he was unaware, at first anyway, of the lengths to which Muʾaddib al-Sulṭān had gone to get himself invited to Kabul—was interested in him and his work.

Although there is good reason to believe the Hazārah historian at first welcomed the visit of the expatriate Isfahani, as time passed his feelings seem to have changed and he connects the visitor to the problems created for him by the amir and those around him two years after ʿAbd al-Muḥammad left Kabul. At the very beginning of volume four of *Sirāj al-tawārīkh*, written sometime in 1925 when he was for all intents and purposes no longer subject to any oversight or censoring of his work, he reveals the trials he underwent at the hands of Amīr Amān Allāh Khān and writes, among other complaints,

[76] Muʾaddib al-Sulṭān, *Amān al-tawārīkh*, vol. 7, ms. Fales Library, New York University, pp. 115–16.

> … at the height of the market's activity (of writing) and in the very midst of the work, because of the efforts of some contemporaries, the tongue of the pen was hindered and the ink dried up in the well. Part of volume three still not having been printed, after being deprived of (my) salary, it was given to Mīrzā ʿAbd al-Muḥammad Khān Iṣfahānī to complete the history that he was writing.[77]

Among those "contemporaries" who caused him difficulties, we should probably include Maḥmūd Beg Ṭarzī, who may have remained resentful of the fact that Amīr Ḥabīb Allāh Khān had rejected his attempt to take over the *Sirāj al-tawārīkh* project and make it his own and perhaps saw in the Iṣfahānī, whom he had invited to Kabul, a way to frustrate Fayż Muḥammad and satisfy his own offended honor.[78]

Despite what Fayż Muḥammad said about ʿAbd al-Muḥammad being given his salary there is some evidence that Amān Allāh Khān's promises to ʿAbd al-Muḥammad were not kept and both men suffered from the amir's caprice. For one thing, on the title page of the New York University manuscript, the dedication to Amīr Amān Allāh Khān has been covered over with a piece of pasted-on paper. Moreover, in volume six, which he only began writing two years after leaving Kabul, he says (pp. 2–3) that his intentions for the book—presumably that it be a memorial to Amīr Amān Allāh Khān—turned out to be "ill-starred" and he would explain what he means by that in volume seven, which was ostensibly to cover the reign of Amīr Amān Allah Khān. But he never returns to the fate of the work. However it is very telling that volume seven, written after his Kabul stay and which he said was to be devoted to the reign of Amīr Amān Allāh Khān, is just a short (123-page) miscellany of notices of modern poets of Afghanistan from *alif* (Ulfat) to *wāw* (Walī), of contemporary poets in lands outside Afghanistan, a few pages on the Afghan administration and foreign missions in Kabul, an ode (*qaṣīdah*) composed on his departure from Cairo on his way to Afghanistan, and ten pages of blurbs of his book. Whether these things reflect promises made and broken by the Afghan amir and an honorarium withheld, Fayż Muḥammad, nonetheless, held the Iranian partly responsible for the change in his contract and his loss of salary.

The third way that Fayż Muḥammad contributed to the work of ʿAbd al-Muḥammad—and what principally concerns us here—was his allowing

77 Fayż Muḥammad, *The History*, vol. 4, p. 3.

78 On the confrontations between Ṭarzī and Fayż Muḥammad and the events leading up to them see McChesney, "The Bottomless Inkwell," pp. 112–16.

ʿAbd al-Muḥammad to include in his fifth volume the ethnographic material that he had compiled himself on the people living in Afghanistan. Since it seems probable that the five volumes ʿAbd al-Muḥammad brought to Kabul were not just any five volumes but the volumes one through five—volumes six and seven having yet to be written—he would have had to revise the fifth volume in a major way to include Fayż Muḥammad's ethnographic material. We know that he did so because the treatise appears in the fifth volume of the New York University manuscript/Kabul print edition. If the fifth volume copied in Kabul and retained there (whether it survives is unknown at this point) contains the ethnographic information then we know that it would have to have been incorporated during the four months of ʿAbd al-Muḥammad's stay in the Afghan capital.[79] However, just as the *Sirāj al-tawārīkh* is not included in ʿAbd al-Muḥammad's list of consulted works in the Kabul copy of volume, it is more than likely that the Kabul volume five, if one exists, does not contain the ethnographic section.

This was what Fayż Muḥammad had referred to at the beginning of volume one of *Sirāj al-tawārīkh* as a "genealogy" (*nasab-nāmah*) of the Afghans which he would add as an appendix to his complete work. By the time he did bring volumes three and four to completion, he had changed his mind, either because the constraints under which he wrote precluded it or because circumstances had changed. One of those circumstances was the inclusion of much of his ethnographic research in ʿAbd al-Muḥammad's *Amān al-tawārīkh*.

ʿAbd al-Muḥammad added the ethnographic section to volume 5 of *Amān*, the volume which was intended to cover Afghan history from the assassination of Nādir Shāh Afshār and the rise of Aḥmad Shāh Durrānī in 1161/1747 down to Amīr ʿAbd al-Raḥmān Khān's accession to the throne in 1297/1880, although, in fact, it only carries the chronology to the 1254/1838 siege of Herat by the Iranians. Of the 397 pages of volume 5 (of both the manuscript and facsimile edition) his ethnographic essay on the Afghan

[79] In volume six, ʿAbd al-Muḥammad says that he began writing that volume in 1342/1923–24, that is after his visit to Kabul. Volume seven includes the blurbs which had to have been written during or after his stay in Kabul. If the fifth volume was re-written then the manuscript in Kabul would represent the first edition of it. In volumes 1 and 2, the only volumes of the New York University manuscript for which there is a copyist credited, the copyists were both Iṣfahānīs, another sign, along with the inclusion of *Sirāj al-tawārīkh* in the revised bibliography, that these volumes were copied after ʿAbd al-Muḥammad's return from Kabul. A careful analysis of the two different manuscripts (Kabul and New York) as well as any other copies that come to light would help clarify the entire writing process.

peoples, which he titles simply "A Report on the Tribes, Clans, and Subclans of Afghanistan" (*Ẕikr-i qabā'il wa 'ashāyir wa ṭawā'if-i Afghānistān*) takes up almost one-third of the volume (pp. 7–132). He leaves no doubt as to whom he is indebted for the information, writing as an introduction,

> In 1340 Hijrī [in his case January–May 1922] when I made a journey to Afghanistan my only purpose for this long trip was first to pay my respects to the sublime and shining threshold of the Afghan revitalizer and the man who gave Afghanistan its independence, the wise, just, and glorious sovereign of the world of Islam and the Muslims, His Majesty Amīr Amān Allāh Khān Ghāzī, king and refuge of the Afghans, through whose kindness we succeeded in paying homage at the threshold of that embellisher of crown and throne. Secondly, my goal was to collect some historical information including an explanation of the condition of the tribes, peoples, and clans of Afghanistan, and the origin of each tribe. Praise God, all that was made easy and provided. The virtuous, learned, and distinguished Mullā Fayż Muḥammad Kātib, a fount of sublime perfections and /8/ invaluable information, made this author indebted to his artistic pen by his writings.

One hundred and twenty pages later he again acknowledges Fayż Muḥammad's assistance in writing this section:

> This was the account of the various tribes, clans, and peoples of Afghanistan which came to, and was written down by, the hand of the writer of these lines, Ḥājjī Mīrzā 'Abd al-Muḥammad Iṣfahānī Īrānī nicknamed "Mu'addib al-Sulṭān," owner of the newspaper *Chihrah-numā*, thanks to the efforts of the unique scholar, the careful and learned researcher, Fayż Muḥammad Khān, author of *Sirāj al-tawārīkh*.[80]

Between those two acknowledgements of Fayż Muḥammad's crucial involvement in the work, 'Abd al-Muḥammad cites him another ten times by name in the course of the account and then provides information on several more occasions relating to Hazārah banishment from their homelands and the appropriation of their property by Afghan tribes that would certainly have come from Fayż Muḥammad. All in all, one is left with the strong sense that 'Abd al-Muḥammad based his work almost entirely on Fayż Muḥammad's research. He does cite other sources, notably Deputy Ḥayāt Khān's *Ḥayāt-i Afghānī* which on one occasion he makes clear he was citing from Fayż Muḥammad's work.[81]

---

80 'Abd al-Muḥammad, *Amān al-tawārīkh*, pp. 7–8, 128.

81 See below, p. 421 Other sources he cites, although we can't be certain that Fayż Muḥammad did not provide them, include Khūshḥāl Khān Khatak's poetry; the *Tārīkh-i Sir John Malcolm*; Sulṭān Muḥammad Bārakzā'ī, *Tārīkh-i sulṭānī*; Khwājah Ni'mat Allāh's *Makhzan-i Afghānī*; and a work for which we have no bibliographic information, *Mukhtaṣar al-manqūl fī tārīkh-i Hazārah wa Mughūl*.

Nonetheless, ʿAbd al-Muḥammad's text bears very little resemblance to Fayż Muḥammad's *Nizhādnāmah* which makes it all the more important since it may then be understood as representing the state of Fayż Muḥammad's work on the ethnography of Afghanistan a full decade before he decided that his own work on the subject was complete.

ʿAbd al-Muḥammad's acknowledgement of his debt to Fayż Muḥammad still leaves the reader somewhat uncertain as to exactly what the contribution was. One could read it that Fayż Muḥammad gave the Iranian his own collected notes on the subject and then during the four months of ʿAbd al-Muḥammad's stay in Kabul they regularly met and Fayż Muḥammad answered any questions the Iranian might have had. ʿAbd al-Muḥammad's "Report on the tribes …" goes into such detail on the names of subsections of tribes that one is inclined to think that these were lists compiled by Fayż Muḥammad in his notebooks and handed to the visitor from Iran. The Afghan National Archives holds some of Fayż Muḥammad's notebooks that reveal something of his approach to research and may assist in recovering the process leading to the *Nizhādnāmah* manuscript now found in the Malik Library in Tehran. For example, he originally compiled information in notebooks based on region—Jalālābād, Kabul, Ghazni, Hazārahjāt, etc.—and on various subjects and personalities which he then drew on in compiling *Sirāj al-tawārīkh*. He seems to have experimented with different formats before arriving ultimately, in the case of *Sirāj al-tawārīkh* at least, at what was printed.[82]

A comparison of the two versions of this genealogical treatise shows that the basic structure of the ethnographic section of *Amān al-tawārīkh* was the same as Fayż Muḥammad's later version, the *Nizhādnāmah-i Afghān*, which in turn seems to have been drawn mainly—in terms of structure and form if not information—from Khwājah Niʿmat Allāh's oft-cited seventeenth-century genealogical history of the Afghans, *Makhzan-i Afghānī*, which Fayż Muḥammad himself cites as one of his sources, as does ʿAbd al-Muḥammad, most likely from Fayż Muḥammad.

But from the standpoint of detail, these two works differ considerably, largely because the *Nizhādnāmah* was written a decade later than the ethnography section in *Amān al-tawārīkh* and includes a description of a number of events that occurred in the intervening period. For example, it speaks of the brief reign in Kabul of "Pisar-i Saqqā" (aka Bacha-i

82 Fayż Muḥammad, *The History*, vol. 3, Appendix 1 is an example of a preliminary format for *Sirāj al-tawārīkh* based primarily on region and secondarily on chronology within the region.

Saqao, "son of the water carrier") Amīr Ḥabīb Allāh Kalakānī and refers to Muḥammad Nādir Khān of the Yaḥyā Khayl clan both as king and as still living. Therefore part of it, at least, must have been composed sometime between the last months of 1929 and February 1931, when Fayż Muḥammad passed away and two years before Muḥammad Nādir was assassinated.

Here are three random examples of the different ways in which the same tribe was reported in the two works.

In "Ẕikr-i qabāʾil:"

An account of the Bārakzāʾī tribe from which His Majesty the Amīr Ghāzī [Amān Allāh Khān] Comes

> The name Bārak (Sulaymān ibn-i ʿĪsā ibn-i Abdāl) has been mentioned above. This clan consists of 40,000 households and they live and reside in Arghastān district just south of Qandahar and along the Hīrmand (Helmand) River. They support themselves through agriculture and raising cattle and sheep.

In *Nizhādnāmah*:

The Bārakzāʾī Subdivision

> This tribe (of 43,750 households) is found in Arghastān district just south of Qandahar and along the banks of the Hīrmand [Helmand] River and in Khushk Maydān. Due to the excellent condition of the farmland, nearly everyone spends their days tilling the soil. Some [on the other hand] eke out a bare subsistence on barren ground gathering what they need only through much toil and hardship. Most also work as herders and take their flocks to summer pastures. Amīr Dūst Muḥammad Khān emerged from this ethnic group and seven of his descendants have ruled down to Amīr Amān Allāh Khān, namely: (1) Amīr Shayr ʿAlī Khān, (2) Amīr Muḥammad Afżal Khān, (3) Amīr Muḥammad Aʿẓam Khān, (4) Amīr Muḥammad Yaʿqūb Khān, (5) Amīr ʿAbd al-Raḥmān Khān, (6) Amīr Ḥabīb Allāh, and (7) Amīr Amān Allāh Khān. Because of the revolution launched by the thief, Ḥabīb Allāh, son of Amīr [Hidāyat] Allāh *saqqā* (water carrier), the reins of the emirate passed to Muḥammad Nādir Khān, a descendant of Sardār Sulṭān Muḥammad Khān, the brother of Amīr Dūst Muḥammad Khān, and he is presently the pādshāh.

In "Ẕikr-i qabāʾil:"

The Tarkalānī Tribe Better Known as Tarkānī

> The Tarkānī tribe is of the progeny of Tarkalānī, the son of Sharkhī Būn (*sic*—Sharkhbūn) as was written above. The tribe of Tarkalānī, known as

Tarkānī, was divided into four branches. The first is the Sālārzāʾī, which resides on the land of Barāwul and Chār Ming and numbers 15,000 individuals. The second, Mamūnd or Māmūnd, which is divided into two sections, the Kakāzāʾī and the Dūr Mamūnd, numbers 14,000 individuals. The third is Sūzānī which numbers 10,000 individuals and the fourth is the Ismāʿīlzāʾī which also numbers 10,000 people. These (four) live in Bājāwur District. To the west [of their territory] are the Hindū Kush mountains, to the east the mountain homeland of the Utmān Khayl, to the north [also] the Hindū Kush mountains on whose lands the people of Kāfiristān, now known as Nūristān, reside, and on the south the Kūh-i Muhmand. The Bājāwur Valley is level, open, and pristine (*ṣāf*). To the northeast it is twenty-five miles long and to the southwest twelve miles wide.

Nizhādnāmah:

The Tarkalānī Subdivision

This clan is quadripartite and numbers 15,000 households. It resides in Chār Ming, Barāwul, Nawagī, Jandūl, and Miyākulī of the Bājāwur district. After the delimitation of the border separating the English and Afghanistan by the treaty with ʿAbd al-Raḥmān Khān, the district of Bājāwur was annexed to the colonial territory of the English. It is a flat place twenty-five miles long and twelve miles wide and its area is three hundred (square) miles. Wheat is planted and the yield is good. Besides **/70/** the Tarkalānī clan group living there, north of [Bājāwur] the Siyāh Pūsh Kāfirs, new converts to Islam, live in the depths of the mountains. (Also) 5,000 of the Ṣāfī people, 37,500 Tajiks, and 5,000 Shinwār. In all, 47,500 [Tarkalānī] people are well-established on both sides of the Bājāwur River. They are English subjects and spend their time engaged in inter-tribal fighting.

From "Ẕikr-i qabāʾil:"

The Ṣāfī, better known as Ṣābī

The Ṣābī tribe is made of six subdivisions whose names are: Qandahārī, Masʿūd, Da Gurbuz, Da Dahīr, Kākī, and Daizāʾī Ḥāwī Khayl. They all consider themselves Sarah [*sic*] Banī [Sarbanī] Afghans. Sometimes they consider themselves to be [related to] the brother and son of ʿAlījānī [Ghiljāʾī?]. However, there is no doubt that the father of this tribe was one of the affiliated (*waṣlī*) successors of Shakhī, a grandson of Kharshbūn. In any case, most of them have their place on the land of Sūrkamar, one of the areas of Bājāwur located between the Tarkalānī tribe and the place of the Muhmand tribe and most villages of Swat have one or two households of them living there. A few live in Tagāb located east of Kabul and northwest of Lamqān and in Gaz east of Jalālābād.

From *Nizhādnāmah*:

The Ṣāfī Subdivision

> This clan group is in six segments: (1) Qandahārī, (2) Maswūd, (3) Gurbuz, (4) Dahīr, (5) Kākīzā'ī, and (6) Khawīzā'ī. They number 15,000 households. They consider themselves Sarbanī Afghans. Some people deem them to be [from] the brother or the offspring of Ghilzā'ī and others [consider them] affiliates [of Ghilzā'ī]. They live in Sūrkamar of Bājāwur between the homeland of the Tarkalānī tribe, the Muhmand, and the Utmān Khayl; in Lamqān and Tagāb located northeast of Kabul; and in Kunar-i Jalālābād. One or two households live in the villages of Swāt. During the uprising (coup) of the son of the water-carrier, at the instigation of Pīr Muḥammad Khān and Ghulām Muḥammad Khān, the son and grandson respectively of Mu'āẕ Allāh Khān Ṣāfī, these people came out against [the son of the water carrier] and refused to tender their obedience, instead supporting Prince 'Ināyat Allāh Khān, whose mother was from the family of Mu'āẕ Allāh Khān, the chief of the Ṣāfī tribe of Tagāb. In the hopes of having the backing of the people of Jalālābād, who sent them a message offering assistance and telling them of their [imminent] arrival with reinforcements, they fought two or three engagements with an army of the son of the water carrier, but when the Jalālābādīs did not come to help them they were both times routed. In the end, they were overwhelmed, and wiped out. 'Abd al-Ghafūr, the son of Muḥammad Shāh, from the family of Mu'āẕ Allāh, who had chosen to cast off his paternal uncle, Ghulām Muḥammad's, supervision and taken up the cause of Son of the Water Carrier in opposition to Amān Allāh Khān, eventually turned his back on the revolutionaries because of the evil deeds of the Saqqawīs. At night in secret, he was killed by the Saqqawīs, placed in a coffin, and secretly buried. He thus earned the reward of his treachery to the government whose favor and benevolence he had enjoyed for years.

Although 'Abd al-Muḥammad credits Fayż Muḥammad for his ethnography, these are clearly very different works and presumably, therefore, at a different stage of Fayż Muḥammad's research. While 'Abd al-Muḥammad generally provides some census numbers for the individual tribes, Fayż Muḥammad in the *Nizhādnāmah* gives numbers for almost all the tribes and where he doesn't include them with the entry for the tribe he tells us that they are counted with another group. The counts seem to have been site-specific and groups could be living in such close proximity that while different names signifying groups with distinct identities and discourses could be recorded, only one collective census count would be made.

Then there is the related question of the census of "fighting men." Sometimes the census count is only of fighting men and at other times both the total number of households and of the fighting men are given. Rarely, a census figure for the total population of a tribe is offered. The omission from the tribal genealogy section in *Amān al-tawārīkh* of numbers of fighting men suggests that either Fayż Muḥammad did not have those numbers to share in 1922 or was unwilling to provide them. Moreover, taking it for granted that Fayż Muḥammad was the source for the census numbers that ʿAbd al-Muḥammad provides, then he either was able to get more precise ones by the time he finished *Nizhādnāmah* or he felt it was sufficient to give ʿAbd al-Muḥammad simple estimates. When the *Amān al-tawārīkh* does give census numbers, they are almost always in round figures (40,000, 12,000, 18,000, 1,000, etc.). In one striking exception, however, as will be seen in the translation, the *Amān* gives very precise numbers. Fayż Muḥammad's numbers are in general much more precise and comprehensive.

The numbers themselves require some comment. One obvious question is: Where did Fayż Muḥammad get them? Ḥājj Kāẓim Yazdānī, who wrote an introduction and annotated the edition of *Nizhādnāmah* published in Qum in 1993 believed that many of the numbers were from tribal informants and were therefore exaggerated.[83] Yet many of the numbers have the kind of precision that suggest Fayż Muḥammad had some access at least to actual census figures compiled on both sides of the Durand Line. On the east side these might have come from the reports of English frontier officers[84] while on the Afghan side the numbers may have come from one of the many specific census surveys ordered first by Amīr ʿAbd al-Raḥmān Khān and then by his son.[85]

In addition, in *Sirāj al-tawārīkh* Fayż Muḥammad records among the many momentous events of 1893 that "the idea of a census of all the people living in the kingdom of Afghanistan emerged from the sound intellect and weighty thinking of His Majesty" and so proclamations were sent out and census-takers were appointed in every province. He then says that a full count was made and a new office, the Bureau of the Census (*Daftar-i Nufūs*) was established presumably to manage these records and conduct further censuses as required. He concludes the passage by saying, "God

83 Fayż Muḥammad, *Nizhādnāmah*, p. 22 (Yazdani introduction).

84 See for example, Robert Nichols, ed., *Colonial Reports on Pakistan's Frontier Tribal Areas*, Karachi, Ameena Saiyid, Oxford University Press, 2005, p. 56 or J. Wolfe Murray, *A Dictionary of the Pathan Tribes on the North-West Frontier of India*, Calcutta, Office of the Superintendent, Government Printing, India, 1899. Murray's *Dictionary* is mainly concerned with counting the "fighting men" in each tribal subdivision.

85 See "censuses" in the indexes to Fayż Muḥammad, *The History*. Some of these were censuses of livestock for purposes of taxation but in the later years covered by *The History* there are increasing references to censuses of people for specific and local political reasons as well as to the establishment of a Census Bureau (*daftar-i nufūs*).

willing, the number of people will be described in due course along with a geography of this kingdom and (an account of) the clans, tribes, and genealogy of the Afghans,"[86] the same promise he had made at the beginning of volume one and was never able to fulfill within the pages of *Sirāj al-tawārīkh*.

The other writer who is said to have made use of Fayż Muḥammad's ethnographic research was Sayyid Mahdī Farrukh, the second Iranian ambassador to Kabul, whose *Tārīkh-i siyāsī-yi Afghānistān* was first published in 1935, six years after he returned from Afghanistan. Yazdānī, editor of the published *Nizhādnāmah*, had this to say about Farrukh's ethnographic section:

> What is certain is that one copy of *Nizhādnāmah* was in the hands of Sayyid Mahdī Farrukh, author of *Tārīkh-i siyāsī-yi Afghānistān*, for he summarized and extracted this treatise under the heading "Afghan Tribes and Subtribes" (*Qabā'il wa ṭawā'if-i Afāghinah*) and included it in his book but, in violation of the norms of authorship and basic integrity, he makes no mention of Mullā Fayż Muḥammad.

This charge of plagiarism is difficult to either sustain or disprove. Farrukh certainly knew Fayż Muḥammad from the latter's frequent visits to the Iranian mission in Kabul in the 1920s. Fayż Muḥammad himself says he visited the legation "twice a week for eight years" and so would have been well-acquainted with Sayyid Mahdī Farrukh as well as with Farrukh's predecessor, Khilʿatbarī.[87] Moreover, Farrukh was without a doubt one of the conduits, if not the only one, for Fayż Muḥammad's manuscripts' to get to Iran. As has been noted, he certainly had in his possession Fayż Muḥammad's secret history of Afghanistan, *Fayżī az fuyūżāt*, which he borrows from in his own history.

But it is difficult to charge him with plagiarizing the *Nizhādnāmah*. In the first place, elsewhere when Sayyid Farrukh cites or quotes directly from Fayż Muḥammad he makes it clear what his source is.[88] Although he doesn't mention Fayż Muḥammad's name, he does give the titles of his books. Yazdānī is correct in saying that Farrukh does not mention Fayż Muḥammad as his source for his section on tribes. On the other hand, his work does not seem to be particularly close to Fayż Muḥammad's text, although it is possible that he did have a copy of the *Nizhādnāmah* at hand

---

[86] Fayż Muḥammad, *The History*, vol. 3, p. 876.

[87] See notes 73 and 75 above.

[88] Farrukh 1992, pp. 64 and 194–204. The publisher of the 1992 edition identifies the author as Fayż Muḥammad in a footnote.

for besides the *Fayżī az fuyūżāt* he also had a copy, at least of volumes one and two, of *Sirāj al-tawārīkh.* But if we compare some of the tribal entries, it is difficult to show that he even summarized Fayż Muḥammad's work let alone plagiarized it. He devoted less than twenty pages (in the 25-lines-per-page print edition of his *Tārīkh-i siyāsī-yi Afghānistān*) to the section as compared with 111 pages in the 20-lines-per-page print version of *Nizhādnāmah.*

For example, Farrukh on the Bārakzāʾī:

> They say that this tribe has up to 25,250 households and lives south of Qandahar and along the banks of the Hīrmand (Helmand) River at Khushk Maydān. The current emirate comes from the Muḥammadzāʾī branch of this tribe.

In a limited sense this is almost the same information found in Fayż Muḥammad's text (see above) but the number of households is quite different and the rest of the information could have been generally known and not have required borrowing it from someone else.

If we take the Pūpalzāʾī entries, the difference is more striking. First, Farrukh (p. 66):

> The Sadūzāʾī is a branch of the Pūpalzāʾī. Their [main] place of settlement is Qandahar. A section of them is found in Lūdiyānah (Ludhiana) on the banks of the Satlaj (Sutlej) River, one of the rivers of the Panjāb (Punjab); 100 households of Pūpalzāʾī live in Lahore, Peshawar, Multan, and the Dīrahjāt (Derajat). Several households live in Kirisk (Girishk), on the west side of the Hīrmand River and in Arghandāb District. They say this tribe numbers approximately 10,250 households.

Now *Nizhādnāmah*:

> *The Pūpalzāʾī*
>
> This clan, which, in terms of numbers, is equal to the Sadūzāʾī, the Sadūzāʾī being a branch of it, are mostly located in the northern mountains of Qandahar, adjacent to the Hazārahjāt. A certain number are found in Khākrīz, some in several places east of Qandahar, some in Ẕākard, Bālā Qarż, Shūr Andām, and other places south (of Qandahar); some (in) the district of Zarasht, which is one of the districts of Girishk located on the west bank of the Hīrmand River; in two locales in Garmsīr, in three places west of the lower Arghandāb [River]; and a few households in Hazārah Uruzgān where they settled when the government gave it to them. All Pūpalzāʾī are farmers and are the most noble of Afghans.

These and other examples do not show that Fayż Muḥammad was the uncredited source for Sayyid Mahdī Farrukh's section on the tribes.

Farrukh served as Iranian minister in Kabul for five years and could easily have conducted his own ethnographic research. Moreover, he cites other sources for his work. Two of them, Deputy Ḥayāt Khān's always popular *Ḥayāt-i Afghānī*, and Sulṭān Muḥammad Bārakzā'ī's *Tārīkh-i Sulṭānī*, are also cited by Fayż Muḥammad and Farrukh could have been indirectly citing them. But one of his named sources, Mounstuart Elphinstone, is not used by Fayż Muḥammad as far as it is possible to tell. At least he never mentions his name. So we should probably conclude that although Fayż Muḥammad's *Nizhādnāmah* was known to Sayyid Mahdī Farrukh and he may have made use of it—for example, he cites at one point "Afghanistan's own historians" which probably included Fayż Muḥammad—it is a little unfair to accuse him of not crediting Fayż Muḥammad when the accuser himself provides no concrete evidence. We have provided the sections on the Afghan tribes from ʿAbd al-Muḥammad's *Amān al-tawārīkh* as Appendix One and from Farrukh's *Tārīkh-i siyāsī-yi-Afghānistān* as Appendix 2 so that the interested reader might do a more thorough comparison of the two texts and perhaps find the pattern indiscernible to us that might have led Ḥājj Kāẓim Yazdānī to his conclusion concerning Farrukh's alleged intellectual debt to Fayż Muḥammad.

TAẔAKKUR AL-INQILĀB

TAẔAKKUR AL-INQILĀB

Memoir of the Revolution

1 | Praise be to God, the Merciful, the Compassionate!

Praise be to God, from whom I seek assistance for the truth of what is told and aid in recounting the circumstances of ignorant people. May God bestow prayers on the Prophet Muḥammad and his family, the best of families, and his Companions who are the best of men in virtue and perfection.

The Causes of the Revolution

The wrong-headed measures of Amīr Amān Allāh Khān and his villainous ministers in conducting political, economic, organizational, regulatory, judicial, ethical, statutory, and penal affairs invoked disgust in the general populace and dragged people from the high road of obedience and subjecthood to the black pit of despair and rebellion. This was because the actions of the amir, stemming from acquaintance, companionship, and long association with Maḥmūd Beg Ṭarzī[1] and Maḥmūd Sāmī from

[1] Maḥmūd Beg (Bīk) Ṭarzī (1865–1933) spent most of his formative years in exile, having been expelled with his family from Afghanistan in 1882. The circumstances under which he and other members of his family returned to Afghanistan will be found in Fayż Muḥammad, *The History* vol. four [see index "Maḥmūd Beg, son of Ghulām M. K. "Ṭarzī" and "Ṭarzī family"]. He only was able to finally return to Afghanistan in 1905 and was soon a leading literary and political figure close to the amir, Ḥabīb Allāh Khān. He translated and wrote numerous books but is perhaps best known as editor of the newspaper *Sirāj al-akhbār-i Afghānīyah* which was published from October 1911 until December 1918. He tried to make it a voice for reform and modernization but it only circulated among the elite and was perhaps most notable for introducing modern typography and for the effect it had outside Afghanistan. Two of his three daughters married the princes, ʿInāyat Allāh Khān and Amān Allāh Khān, the future amir. Maḥmūd Beg served as foreign minister in the 1920s and fled Afghanistan in 1929, thoroughly disenchanted with the country's prospects for entering the modern world. He died four years later of cancer, an embittered man. He was not admired by Fayż Muḥammad who had difficult relations with him. For details of his life see May Schinasi, *Afghanistan at the beginning of the twentieth century: nationalism and journalism in Afghanistan: a study of* Serâj ul-akhbâr (*1911–1918*), Naples: Istituto Universitario Orientale. Semario di Studi Asiatici, 1979, pp. 45–60; Thomas Wide, "From Patriot to Port-City Poet: Mahmud Tarzi in Istanbul," in Nile Green, ed., *Afghān History through Afghān Eyes*, pp. 161–183; and V. A. Romodin, *Ocherki po istorii i istorii kul'tury Afganistana seredina X I X -pervaia tret' X X v.*, Moscow: "Nauka," 1983, pp. 88–92, 95–109.

 | DOI:10.1163/9789004392441_003

Ḥillah [Iraq] /46/ better known as "Effendī"[2] and other army officers and instructors from Ottoman Turkey, ran counter to Islamic observances. In politics, he abandoned the path and the way of the "virtuous city" (or civilization) (*madīnah-i fāẓilah*) whose leader is mentioned in the Qurʾānic commandment "Obey God, obey the prophet and the first in authority amongst you"[3] and instead he based his policies on six types of "heathen civilizations" (*madīnah-i jāhilī*):[4] "the civilization of necessities" (*madīnah-i żarūrāt*), "the civilization of baseness" (*madīnat-i nazālat*); "the civilization of vileness" (*madīnah-i khissat*); "the civilization of niceties" (*madīnah-i karāmāt*), "the civilization of dominance" (*madīnah-i ghalābat*); and "the civilization of freedom" (*madīnah-i ḥurriyat*). On the surface, he adopted elements from each one of these and represented himself as adhering to them but in reality he was an adherent of "the civilization of depravity" (*madīnah-i fāsiqah*).[5]

In the economic sphere: He minted base coins; he introduced excessive taxes on land, on customs duties, and on commercial goods; he imposed conditions on merchants and farmers as a result of which the production of food, clothing, and other essential goods fell while it became difficult to sustain life and the misery arising from the difficulty of making a living only increased.

---

2 Maḥmūd Sāmī was an officer in the Ottoman army about whom there is much disparate information concerning his time in Afghanistan. He first arrived in Kabul in 1906 and had an up-and-down career as a military trainer. (Schinasi, *Afghanistan*, pp. 129–30.) During the reign of Amīr Amān Allāh Khān (1919–1929) he was a prominent figure. (Leon B. Poullada, *Reform and Rebellion in Afghānistān, 1919–1929: King Amanullah's Failure to Modernize a Tribal Society*, Ithaca and London, Cornell University Press, 1973, pp. 116–17.) Fayż Muḥammad calls him "the effendi, General Maḥmūd Sāmī" and places him in the circle of those who advised Amān Allāh to challenge his uncle, Naṣr Allāh Khān's, claim of the amirate in February 1919. (Fayż Muḥammad, *The History*, vol. 4, p. 1411) He wrote books on military education and training (the Afghānistān Digital Library at NYU has fifteen works by him) including one on military cookery for the War College. In 1929, he is reported to have offered his services to the Tajik, Ḥabīb Allāh Khān Kalakānī for which he was executed in 1930 for treason, when the Muḥammadzāʾī clan regained power. See Faiz Mukhammad, *Kniga upominanii o miatezhe*, translation and commentary by A. Shkirando, Moscow: Nauka, 1988, p. 258, note 2; Ludwig W. Adamec, *Who's Who of Afghanistan*, Graz, Austria: Akademische Druck-u. Verlagsanstalt, 1975, p. 185.

3 Qurʾān 4:59.

4 Fayż Muḥammad refers here to his own interpretation of al-Fārābī's *al-Madīnah al-fāḍilah* which he develops in Fayż Muḥammad, *The History*, vol. 4, pp. 1262–66. He uses the word "city (*madīnah*)" as a synonym for "civilization (*madaniyat*)" and concerns himself mostly with the classification of "unvirtuous civilizations." The terms used in that discussion are translated here as they are translated there.

5 Fayż Muḥammad is suggesting that not only could Amīr Amān Allāh Khān not be considered a member of a "virtuous civilization" but that he fell short of qualifying even for one of the "unvirtuous" civilizations.

In the administrative sphere: He issued many laws but appointed as ministers and as civil and military officials ignorant people who had never bent the knee before a teacher and had learned nothing but the degrading characteristics of ignorance. Whether because of personal agendas or because of their selfish desires /47/ they chose a path outside the Sharīʿah and government law (*qānūn*) and, taking bribes, engaged in treachery and corruption in government.

In the law and order sphere: As a result of the stupidity and ignorance
of high officials who were devoid of intellect and reason and were "friends
2 of the caravan and partners with thieves" | roads appeared as deathtraps,
byways were graveyards, and instances of murder and robbery became
more and more frequent.

In the legal and juridical sphere: Beginning with police officers and district chiefs (*ʿalāqahdārs*) all the way up to ministers, governors, high governors (*wālī, nāʾib al-ḥukūmahs*),[6] judges and the highest officers of the amirate, he established such a complicated system of appeals for plaintiffs or petitioners that the situation of the weak was worsened and those who sought justice were unable to obtain it. Anyone complaining about injustice had to send a written form to a state institution in hopes of getting redress, but, in general, that person could only expect to be frustrated. To complete the form, the plaintiff had first to work himself to the bone for several days to raise the money for a scribe and to bribe the mīrzā who was supposed to deliver the petition to the appropriate official and obtain the response. Consequently, the plaintiff would have to spend money to complete this process, money which he could get only by selling some of life's necessities /48/ or from his hard-earned income, and in the end he would receive an official written answer in which he would be told that the form should be directed either to a lower or a higher office. The unfortunate petitioner, if he still had the means, would then direct the petition from the office where he had first appealed to another one. Once he had received an unsatisfactory answer from every office, the plaintiff,

---

[6] Ever since the reign of Amīr ʿAbd al-Raḥmān Khān (1880–1901), the governors of the four major provinces—Qandahar, Harāt, Afghan Turkistān, and Qaṭaghan and Badakhshān—held the distinctive title, *nāʾib al-ḥukūmah*. Sometimes *ḥukmrān* was used instead. All other governors were simply styled *ḥākim*. Under Amīr Ḥabīb Allāh Khān, Kabul came to be administered as a distinct province, also called "Central Province," but its governor was given the unique title *wālī*. These titles remained in effect through the reign of Amīr Amān Allāh Khān (1919–29). For a map of the administrative divisions of the country at this time see Fayż Muḥammad, *Kabul Under Siege: Fayż Muḥammad's Account of the 1929 Uprising*. Translated, abridged, reworked, and annotated by R. D. McChesney. Princeton, NJ: Markus Wiener, 1999, p. xii.

in conformity with the law and with the help of the minister of court, could send the petition to the amir himself. For this he was obliged to pay an additional 11 rupees.[7] From there the petition would be sent back to the same offices that had already seen it. The course of these submissions and resubmissions could stretch out over not just half a year or even a year but up to three or four years, depending on whether it was a major or minor matter. Afterwards, the petitioner would return home in despair. Consequently, no one was ever punished nor did anyone receive what was rightfully his. Evildoers[i] thus became so audacious that they eventually shattered the authority of the amir. Then real thieves came to occupy the throne and the country's highest offices.

In the moral sphere: The founding of schools for women, the abolition of the veil, and the accompanying dishonor, violence, and fornication, instances of which the chronicler of this age and era will record one by one, were the cause of the revolution, the collapse of the regime of Amīr Amān Allāh Khān, /49/ and much of what happened to the Afghan government and nation.

Among his [laudable] accomplishments were achieving national independence, concluding treaties with the great governments of the world, establishing schools in different disciplines, acquiring various kinds of machinery, and building factories for the manufacture of high quality goods.

Here, in what follows, are set out the tragic events of the revolution in the form of a chronology and journal.

The Rebellion and Insurgency of the Tribes of the Southern Province

3 | In 1303, equivalent to 1924 on the Christian calendar, the *Niẓāmnāmah-i jazā-yi ʿumūmī*,[8] a manual on penal law translated from the Turkish of Jamāl Pāshā,[ii] a high officer from the Turkish army,[9] was printed and published

[7] According to A. I. Shkirando, editor and translator of Faiz Mukhammad, *Kniga* p. 258, note 5, the Afghan unit of currency at the beginning of the twentieth century was the silver Kābulī rupee of 60 *paysā*. In 1928, the government introduced a new silver currency in which the silver content was 47% (the old Kābulī silver rupee was 90% pure silver) and it set the exchange rate at 10% higher than the rate of exchange for the old Kābulī rupee. This would have been another source of discontent, particular among the merchants.

[8] This refers to *Niẓāmnāmah-i jazā-yi ʿumūmī* (General Penal Code) issued 17 Mīzān 1303 (23 September 1924). Available on the Afghanistan Digital Library at http://hdl.net/2333.1/pnvxokfz.

[9] Jamāl Pāshā, another fugitive from the collapsed Ottoman Empire had been a Young Turk activist with a checkered career as military commander in Syria during the Great

with corrections, emendations, and the signature of the National Council (*Hay'at-i Shūrā*[10]); a group of ulema, including Chief Justice (*qāżī al-qużāt*) ʿAbd al-Shakūr Khān,[11] Mullā ʿAbd al-Wāsiʿ Kākarī,[12] Qāżī ʿAbd al-Raḥmān Bīktūtī (Begtūtī),[13] and other scholars of the Hanafite school, and began to be enforced. Some of its articles, for example the absolute prohibition of polygamy and of child marriage, became a subject of debate for pseudo-mullahs who lacked all knowledge of the Sharīʿah. Others concerned the

---

War. He came to Afghanistan in 1920 and was granted authority by Amīr Amān Allāh Khān to reorganize the military. He was credited with forming the Model Battalion (*Qiṭʿah-i Namūnah*) of which Ḥabīb Allāh Kalakānī was a member. (See Ludwig W. Adamec, *Historical Dictionary of Afghanistan*, New Delhi: Manas Publications, 2006, p. 193 and D. A. Rustow, "D̲jemāl Pas̲h̲a," *The Encyclopaedia of Islam*, New Edition, Leiden: E. J. Brill, vol. 2. pp. 531–32.)

10 The Hay'at-i Shūrā (alternately known as Majlis-i Shūrā-yi Dawlat and Maḥfal-i Shūrā) under Amīr Amān Allāh Khān (see *Amān-i Afghān*, vol. 1, no 3, p. 1; Fayż Muḥammad, *The History*, vol. 4, p. 16; Senzil Nawid, *Religious Response to Social Change in Afghānistān, 1919–29: King Aman-Allah and the Afghān Ulama*, Costa Mesa, C A : Mazda Publishers, 1999, p. 33; and Shūrā-yi ʿAmm under Amīr Ḥabīb Allāh Khān (Fayż Muḥammad, *The History*, vol. 4, p. 597) was called Hay'at-i Shūrā under Ḥabīb Allāh Kalakānī. The title page of the *niẓāmnāmah* referred to in note 8 lists another possible variant used during Amīr Amān Allāh Khān's time, Majlis-i ʿAlī-yi Wuzarā (Supreme Council of Ministers). The institution appears under a variety of similar names in English-language publications: Consultative Assembly (Fayż Muḥammad, *The History* vol. 4, p. 19); National Consultative Assembly, (ibid., note 20); National Council (ibid., p. 597); Council of Advisers (Ludwig W. Adamec, *Afghānistān 1900–1923*, Berkeley and Los Angeles: University of California Press, 1967, p. 8); State Council (Nawid, *Religious Response* p. 33 and Poullada, *Reform and Rebellion*, p. 94); Legislative Council (Poullada, *Reform and Rebellion*, p. 161) etc. We will try to be consistent here and for Amān Allāh Khān's reign call it the National Council and for Amīr Ḥabīb Allāh Khān Kalakānī's regime, the State Council.

11 Qāżī ʿAbd al-Shakūr Khān was a Bārakzā'ī Durrānī and son of Qāżī Saʿd al-Dīn Khān, long-time high governor of Harāt under Amīr ʿAbd al-Raḥmān Khān and later chief justice himself under Amīr Ḥabīb Allāh Khān. ʿAbd al-Shakūr, when he was *qāżī* of Qandahar, was deeply involved in the forced removal of Hazārahs from their lands in the Hazārahjāt and resettlement of those lands by tribesmen from British India under both of the above amirs. For details see the index to volume 4 of Fayż Muḥammad, *The History* under ʿAbd al-Shakūr's name.

12 Mullā (or Mawlawī) ʿAbd al-Wāsiʿ Kākarī Ākhūndzādah Qandahārī, son of the noted scholar Mawlawī ʿAbd al-Ra'ūf Kākarī, was himself a prominent scholar and the author of works on judicial procedures such as *Risālah-i kulliyāt-i wa iṭṭilāʿāt-i fiqhīyah*, Kabul: Maṭbaʿah-i Ḥurūfī-yi Māshīnkhānah, 1300/1921–22, and *Tamassuk al-qużāt-i Amānīyah*, Kabul, 1300/1921–22. He was also a constitutionalist and arrested by Amīr Ḥabīb Allāh Khān along with his equally renowned brother Mawlawī ʿAbd al-Rabb. But, according to ʿAbd al-Ḥayy Ḥabībī, they were only held for a few months in light of their reputations as scholars. (See Fayż Muḥammad, *The History*, vol. 4, p. 1224 and ʿAbd al-Ḥayy Ḥabībī, *Junbish-i mashrūṭīyat dar Afghānistān*, New Edition, Qum: Iḥsānī, Jawzā/Khurdād 1372/ May–June 1993, pp. 51–55. See also Nawid, *Religious Response*, index under "Qandahari, Mawlawi ʿAbd al-Wese'" [*sic*].

13 There are numerous references to Qāżī ʿAbd al-Raḥmān Bīktūtī (Begtuti) in ibid.

paying of a fine in lieu of corporal punishment (*taʿzīr bi'l-māl*)[14] while other provisions aimed at cutting the cord of discord and conflict, ending baseless litigation and those things that led to punishments less than the canonical ones for quarrelsome[iii] and ignorant people who, out of their base natures and an absence of human dignity, considered paying a fine of two /50/ to five rupees as more onerous than being publicly humiliated, were all listed in the *niẓāmnāmah*. They were read and interpreted by pseudo-mullahs who in their deceit-filled hearts and devious minds used them at times to incite and inspire ordinary people to rebellion and sedition. Thus, due to the misbehavior, shameful acts, and prevarications of district chiefs, local governors,[iv] and military officers; the bribing of ministers, judges, and employees; the lack of accountability in cases of injustice; partisanship; denial of the rights of the deserving; imposing heavy burdens such as increasing the taxes on farmlands and doubling customs duties; [the increasing incidence of] highway robbery; forcible military conscription by lottery; etc., etc., [because of all this] many subjects' dissatisfaction with the government intensified.

At this very moment, a man from the Mangal tribe laid claim to the fiancée of another to whom he said he was betrothed, declaring that he had been engaged to her in childhood with her father acting as her guardian. The conflict between the two parties brought them before the governor, Amr al-Dīn Khān, and the *qāżī*, Mullā ʿAbd Allāh. With the consent of the fiancée, Amr al-Dīn Khān /51/ rejected the man's suit, which was based on his claiming to have married her when she was still a minor, and so he returned the woman to her husband [to-be]. But the *qāżī* had taken a bribe to see that the girl was betrothed to the plaintiff and so was unhappy with the way this dispute was settled and wanted to give the woman to the plaintiff [on the basis of] the prior date [of betrothal]. He sent the governor a letter of protest, asserting that the Sharīʿah had been violated. The governor, however, paid no attention to his technical proofs and so Mullā ʿAbd Allāh, who was bent on lighting the fire of rebellion, seized the opportunity to kindle the flames of hatred and vengeance. He encouraged and urged the plaintiff, who had lost the case, to appeal to the sense of Afghan honor of the tribal leaders and succeeded in himself lighting the flames of *fitnah* in accordance with his own personal desire.[v]
4 | With appeals, incitements and promises of Paradise for true-believing Muslims, Mullā ʿAbd Allāh "Lang" (the Lame), adducing [proofs from] the

[14] Joseph Schacht, *Introduction to Islamic Law*, Oxford: Oxford University Press, 1964, p. 88.

Clear Religion and the unassailable Holy Law, succeeded in raising all the tribes of the Southern Province against the government.[15] The war lasted for a year and two months. About 14,000 people were killed and the cost to the government was 3 crore (30 million) rupees.[vi] The honor of many people was violated and weakness[vii] was introduced into Islamic society. Thanks to this war, the only things which lead to anyone remembering the name of Amīr Amān Allāh Khān and those killed as well as a "beautiful recollection" of Mullā ʿAbd Allāh are the monument to "Knowledge and Ignorance"[16] with the names of the slain army officers carved on it and the Victory Arch[17] at Pamqān [with the names also carved on it.] Other than that nothing was accomplished (and no one was satisfied).

The Emergence of Ḥabīb Allāh,[18] Son of Hidāyat Allāh[19] the Water Carrier, and Sayyid Ḥusayn

Ḥabīb Allāh was a member of an infantry regiment called the "Model Battalion" (*Qiṭʿah-yi namūnah*) formed and trained by Jamāl Pāshā, who,

[15] This was the so-called "Khost Rebellion" of 1924 involving the Ghilzāʾī, Mangal, and Jadrān (Zadrān) of the Southern Province. Its causes were many. According to A. I. Shkirando, the Russian editor and translator of *Tazakkur al-inqilāb* into Russian, the fundamental reason behind the uprising was widespread tribal resentment at the tax and customs policies of the government. (See Faiz Mukhammad, *Kniga upominanii* p. 259, note 9.) Others have seen the root causes in the amir's social reforms, especially those relating to women and marriage; the enforcement of conscription; the requirement for government-issued identification cards, and the high salaries paid to foreigners as advisors and contractors. (See Poullada, *Reform and Rebellion*, index under "Khost Revolt;"; Nawid, *Religious Response*, p. 100; and Ludwig W. Adamec, *Afghānistān's Foreign Affairs to the Mid-Twentieth Century*, Tucson, Arizona: University of Arizona Press, 1974, pp. 86–90.)

[16] For a description of the monument see May Schinasi, *Kabul: A History, 1773–1948*, translated by R. D. McChesney, Leiden and Boston: Brill, 2016, p. 141 and for a photograph, Nancy Hatch Wolfe with Ahmad Ali Kohzad, *An Historical Guide to Kabul*, Kabul: Afghān Tourist Organization, 1965, between pp. 64–65.

[17] The Victory Arch at Paghman (Pamqān) was built to commemorate the 1919 War of Independence against the British. (Wolfe, *An Historical Guide*, p. 131.)

[18] Throughout this work, Ḥabīb Allāh Kalakānī is frequently and, as the work progresses, increasingly referred to as "Son of the Water Carrier." Sometimes, too, his brother, Ḥamīd Allāh, is also called "Son of the Water Carrier" occasionally distinguished as "younger Son of the Water Carrier." It is worth noting that Fayż Muḥammad never uses the term "*bachchah*" for "son" the form by which Ḥabīb Allāh Khān (Bachchah-i Saqqā or Bacha-i Saqao) is almost universally named in later, either intentionally or unconsciously derogatory, treatments of his brief regime. Fayż Muḥammad uses the more conventional word for son, *pisar*, in the form "Pisar-i Saqqā."

[19] The name of Ḥabīb Allāh's father appears in various forms. Fayż Muḥammad himself shows confusion. On p. 22 of the manuscript he first wrote "Amīn Allāh" then crossed that out and wrote in "Amīr Allāh" but here uses "Hidāyat Allāh." (In the *Nizhādnāmah* section of this book, he calls him "Amīr Allāh" see p. 352) Later sources add to the confusion. Adamec, *Afghānistān's Foreign Affairs*, p. 65 chose "Amīn Allāh" without indicating a

having been defeated by the English army in ʿArab Iraq, had come to Kabul in hopes of getting the Afghan government to support the Turkish government. He served the government in fighting the Mangal tribe and the people of the Southern Province /52/ mentioned above. Afterwards, with all the other soldiers of this regiment, some of whom had been chosen by lottery (*qurʿah*) to perform military service, [Ḥabīb Allāh] was demobilized and went back to his home in the village of Kalakān in Kūh Dāman. He had no means of providing a living for himself and his wife and deemed the occupations by which the people of Kūh Dāman customarily earned their livelihoods such as selling grapes and firewood to be beneath him. Most live on dried mulberries and rarely see bread made from wheat. So instead he turned his attention to highway robbery and thievery. He was joined by like-minded individuals, men like Sayyid Ḥusayn Chārīkārī, Malik Muḥsin of Sarā Khwājah[20] and others, twenty-four men in all, and they began killing and robbing Muslims. For three years they lived in caves in the mountains and in upland areas, spending trying days committing robberies and anxious nights in fear of government punishment.

During this time, afraid of falling into government hands, Ḥabīb Allāh fled to Pīshāwar (Peshawar) where he made a living selling tea and thieving. After the British police arrested and jailed an accomplice of his, Aʿẓam Maydānī, Ḥabīb Allāh, fearing arrest himself, fled Peshawar for Tal and Tūtagī. There he stayed for some time in poverty as a petty thief. Then, when he had become known there as a thief, Ḥabīb Allāh returned
5 to Kalakān and Kūh Dāman. Fearing arrest, | he left his own home and joined a group of fellow thieves, who were spending their days and nights moving from place to place. /53/ Always hungry and apprehensive, they continued their banditry, consuming their ill-gotten gains and spilling the blood of the defenseless. By turning over part of the spoils taken from the people to the district chief and the governor of Kūh Dāman and Kūhistān,

---

source. The online *Aryānā* encyclopaedia in the entry on Ḥabīb Allāh citing a variety of sources adds the names Aḥmad Allāh, ʿAbd al-Raḥmān, Imām al-Dīn, and Karīm Allāh as the name of the father. The name "Karīm Allāh" also appeared as early as 1958 in a Peshawar newspaper, as Shkirando noted (Faiz Mukhammad, *Kniga upominanii*, p. 261, note 42). Shkirando strongly believed that "Hidāyat Allāh" was the correct name, perhaps based on Fayż Muḥammad's using it in the heading here. Mostly, the father's name is given as *saqqā* in Persian (i.e., "water carrier") and "Saqqaw" or "Saqao" in other languages.

20 The editor of the Russian translation, A. I. Shkirando, (Faiz Mukhammad 1983, p. 259, note 10) says that "both Muḥyī al-Dīn Anīs in *Buḥrān wa najāt* and M. G. M. Ghubar in *Afghānistān dar masīr-i tārīkh* inform us that Malik Muḥsin came not from Sarāy Khwājah but from Kalakān and was called Malik Muḥsin-i Kalakānī."

he gradually earned their friendship and stopped fearing arrest. Meanwhile Amān Allāh Khān's personal representative (*wakīl*), Muḥammad Walī Khān, even gave him a guarantee of personal safety as well as money, guns, and ammunition, and so made him feel utterly secure.

Thus it was that these two individuals, Sayyid Ḥusayn and Ḥabīb Allāh, continued to plunder the people with impunity. They made themselves notorious and sowed terror among the populace in regions near and far. Even Kābulī merchants, who carried karakul, carpets, and Russian goods from Turkistān to Kabul, were forced to buy certificates of safe passage. Afraid that their goods would be plundered, the merchants paid for these documents but also showed them to the government. The government eventually sent contingents of cavalry and infantry to detain Ḥabīb Allāh and his confederates. But because he had a guarantees of personal safety from the governor, the district chief, and the amir's own *wakīl*, at first no serious efforts were made to arrest them. But as they grew stronger, clashes occurred with government forces. Several men were killed, but no one was captured. Afterwards, word spread far and wide of the government's weakness and the staunchness of [Ḥabīb Allāh's band] in fighting the government.

Amān Allāh Khān was angered and sent Aḥmad ʿAlī Khān, the son of ʿAbd al-Wāḥid Khān Lūdī, to capture the bandit. Aḥmad ʿAlī had been envoy to Germany[viii] and upon returning home was appointed mayor of Kabul. In just two weeks as mayor, he had tried to force everyone—the powerful and weak, the noble and the meek, shopkeepers and artisans, men and women—to wear official dress [that is the clothing decreed by the government] and European hats for which the offended citizenry began to raise their hands to God and pray for the downfall of Amīr Amān Allāh Khān's regime.[21] /54/

At this very time, the infamous desperados Ḥabīb Allāh and Sayyid Ḥusayn intensified their attacks and robberies and murdered the governor of Chārīkār, Ghulām Ghaws̱ Khān, and a district chief. The government now sent a contingent to arrest them made up of cavalry and infantry along with a cannon. But the bandits went into hiding in the mountains and the dispatched force accomplished nothing. Aḥmad ʿAlī Khān, who had been governor of Kūh Dāman and Kūhistān prior to his departure for Germany and had distinguished himself there by his despotic rule,

[21] For more information on the erratic career of Aḥmad ʿAlī Khān Lūdī(n) see Ludwig W. Adamec, *Who's Who*, p. 109 and idem, *A Biographical Dictionary of Contemporary Afghānistān*, Graz, Austria: Akademische Druck-u. Verlagsanstalt 1987, p. 95.

immediately after arriving at the citadel of Jabal al-Sirāj sent for Ḥabīb
6 Allāh and | Sayyid Ḥusayn whom he knew from his days as governor. He gave them guarantees of personal safety, confirmed by oaths on the Qur'ān, promised them appointments as deputy field marshals (*nā'ib sālār*s),[22] presented each of them with 3,000 rupees in cash, and promised to give each of the rebels who had marauded with them seven-shot rifles with ammunition.

After Amān Allāh Khān dispatched from Kabul the promised money, weapons, and a signed farman naming them deputy field marshals, as well as guarantees of personal safety written in his own hand, they announced that they would go to Kabul. But to verify the sincerity of the amir's intentions, they left for Chārīkār, which is situated eighteen *kurūh*s[23] north of Kabul, and there they tied up the telephone operator in the telephone office and rang up Amān Allāh Khān. Son of the Water Carrier pretended to be Mayor Aḥmad ʿAlī Khān, and, asking for instructions, said, "Now that I've reached agreement with Son of the Water Carrier and have him in custody, what should I do?" Amīr Amān Allāh Khān ordered him to kill the thief and cut off his head. Still pretending to be Aḥmad ʿAlī Khān, (Ḥabīb Allāh) then asked the amir, "Given the agreement that /55/ has been concluded, how can I kill him?" After hearing him out, Amīr Amān Allāh Khān replied, "True, he has made an agreement with you, but not with me. Don't let him live!" Alerted now to the amir's true intentions towards him, Son of the Water Carrier did not hang up but instead

---

22 Shkirando, who provides an excellent glossary of technical terms, translated *nā'ib sālār* as "deputy commander-in-chief" (*pomoshchnik glavnokomanduiushchego*) and says that the *nā'ib sālār* served as chief of staff at army headquarters. (Faiz Mukhammad, *Kniga upominanii*, p. 259, notes 14 and 272.) However, we believe the term "deputy field marshal" is more in keeping with Afghan usage, "field marshal" (*sipahsālār*) being the highest military rank. The term commander-in-chief would always apply to the amir.

23 Fayż Muḥammad uses *kurūh* as his unit of long measurement. The *kurūh* was equivalent to the *kos* used in India where it was approximately 2.5 miles. Today, the distance by road from Kabul to Chārīkār is 38 miles which would make the kuruh equivalent to 2.1 miles if Fayż Muḥammad's distance of 18 kuruhs is correct. In September 1907, Amīr Ḥabīb Allāh Khān, apparently influenced by his trip to India that spring and his great admiration for Mughal administrative practices ordered a surveyor to lay out mile-posts (*kurūh*-posts, actually, comparable to the kos-minars of India) beginning with No. 1 at the main gate of the Arg. Mile-post 20, which would have been 19 kuruhs from Kabul was to be at the Chārīkār Bridge which nearly corresponds to Fayż Muḥammad's distance of 18 kuruhs but if correct would reduce the length of the *kurūh* to 2.0 miles. (Fayż Muḥammad, *The History*, vol. 4, pp. 1158–59 for Amīr Ḥabīb Allāh Khān's *kurūh*-posts project.) Perhaps when the distance was actually surveyed the *kurūh*-post location would have changed. In any event without further information we will consider the kuruh to be equivalent to two miles which agrees with Irfan Habib's findings about the Mughal kuruh. (See Irfan Habib, *An Atlas of Mughal India*, Delhi: Oxford University Press, 1982, p. xiii.)

revealed his actual identity and then cursed the amir's wife and warned him that one of these days he would attack Kabul and said, "I will soon come and then you'll find out what's what." This brazen assertion and the agreements which the amir's *wakīl*, Muḥammad Walī Khān, and other ministers and influential people of Kabul, as well as various adventurers serving as ministers, had made with Son of the Water Carrier infuriated Amān Allāh Khān who was unaware of the treason of some of his ministers. He ended the conversation by hurling the telephone onto the table.

Meanwhile, because an uprising of the Shinwārī and all the tribes of the Eastern Province was imminent, the amir had sent the president of the National Council, Shayr Aḥmad Khān,[24] and the foreign minister, Ghulām Ṣiddīq Khān,[25] to Jalālābād to extinguish the flames of revolution. Ghulām Ṣiddīq Khān, however, presented himself to the rebels as a friend and suggested that they take him into custody [to make it appear that he was not conspiring with them] and then attack Jalālābād and make an attempt on the life of Shayr Aḥmad Khān.[26] As he suggested, they attacked Jalālābād, and plundered government buildings, which were all outside the city, looting them and burning a large part to the ground.

In comparison to the uprising of the Jalālābād tribes, the amir considered the rebellion of Son of the Water Carrier to be a minor thing, even of no consequence. Therefore he concentrated his efforts on raising tribal and regular army forces to send to Jalālābād. Day and night he applied
7 himself to this effort while only hearing of | the growing strength of the eastern insurgents and the extent of their looting and destruction. This went on until he realized the difficulty of the situation and so appointed the former high governor of Kabul (Province) and his brother-in-law, ʿAlī

[24] On Shayr Aḥmad Khān Muḥammadzāʾī see Adamec, *Who's Who*, p. 241 ("Shir Ahmad, Sardar") and Adamec, *A Bibliographic Dictionary*, p. 207 ("Zikria, Shir Ahmad"). He was the son of Sardār Fatḥ Muḥammad Khān, son of Sardār Zakariyā (or more commonly Zikriyā) son of Sulṭān Muḥammad son of Sardār Pāyandah Khān. See Adamec, *Who's Who*, Tables 33–40 on the extensive Zikriya or Zakariyā family.

[25] Ghulām Ṣiddīq Khān was a member of the powerful Charkhī family and a son of Amīr ʿAbd al-Raḥmān Khān's top military figure, Field Marshal Ghulām Ḥaydar Khān Charkhī. (See Adamec, *Who's Who*, pp. 151–52.)

[26] Shkirando believed that Fayż Muḥammad's account was not to be taken at face value. According to the *Amān-i Afghān* of December 9, 1928, he writes, "the following charge was given to the foreign minister: to prevent the spread of the rebellion among the tribes; to win the nomadic tribes to the side of the crown; and to conduct diplomatic talks with the leaders of the tribes in rebellion." For his source, he cites a press compilation, *Biulleten' Pressy Srednego Vostoka*, Tashkent, 1929–30, special edition nos. 4–5 [12–13], pp. 58–59.) According to him, a ten-day truce was at first agreed to but within a few days, fighting had resumed around Jalālābād. It was after this that ʿAlī Aḥmad Khān (or Jān) Lūynāb was sent.

Aḥmad Khān [Lūynāb], to supreme command of the Southern and Eastern Provinces and ordered him to leave for Jalālābād on the twelfth of Qaws (3 December) with artillery, /56/ regular troops, tribal detachments, and an adequate treasury. After arriving there, using every trick he knew and every means at his disposal, ʿAlī Aḥmad Khān managed to quench the flames of *fitnah*. Shayr Aḥmad Khān and Ghulām Ṣiddīq Khān, now discharged from the commission given to them, returned to Kabul.

Ḥabīb Allāh and Sayyid Ḥusayn's [First] Assault on Kabul

After the appointment and departure of ʿAlī Aḥmad Khān for Jalālābād, at the very moment that a tribal army including tribes of the Southern Province; men from Lahūgard; from the Mangal, Jājī, Chamkanī, Ṣabarī, Muqbil, Wazīrī, and Aḥmadzāʾī tribes; tribes from the Western Province, from Maydān, Wardak, Ghaznīn, Hazārah-i Bihsūd; people from the Northern Province, from Panjshayr, Nijrāb, Tagāb, Sāl-i Awlang [Salang], Rīzah-i Kūhistān, and Ghūrband; [people from] Pamqān, Chahārdihī, and other places surrounding Kabul; and the regular army reserves and Mazārī, Qandahārī, Harātī, and Qaṭaghanī [regular] forces which had entered Kabul one after another was in the process of collecting rifles and ammunition and setting out for Jalālābād, suddenly and without warning Ḥabīb Allāh and Sayyid Ḥusayn attacked Kabul.

It happened this way. After reaching agreement with Aḥmad ʿAlī Khān and following the telephone conversation with Amīr Amān Allāh Khān mentioned above, both Ḥabīb Allāh and Sayyid Ḥusayn returned to Jabal al-Sirāj from Chārīkār with a group of the rebels who always accompanied them and there surrounded and besieged Aḥmad ʿAlī Khān for eighteen days and nights. Aḥmad ʿAlī Khān and the squadrons of cavalry from the amir's personal guard and infantry eventually agreed to surrender the citadel of Jabal al-Sirāj peacefully. After obtaining a guarantee of safe passage and having handed over to the bandits all of the government funds in the town along with eighteen /57/ machine guns, heavy artillery ("fort-smashers"), and some of their rifles, they escaped back to Kabul. The insurgents were now much emboldened, having taken possession of the amir's citadel [at Jabal al-Sirāj] and having acquired a considerable amount of money and weaponry. So they began preparations for an attack on Kabul itself, assembling tribal contingents ostensibly for the campaign to Jalālābād.

Several ministers and influential Kābulī figures urged Son of the Water Carrier on and even told him the best time to attack. On Friday, the 22nd

8 of Qaws 1307/14 December 1928, some 2,000 men, | 200 of whom were armed with rifles and the rest [only] with sticks and axes, the majority bareheaded and barefoot, entered Qalʿah-i Murād Beg, on the northern slopes of the Kūh-i Kūtal not far from the village of Khirs Khānah (House of Bears), renamed Khayr Khānah (House of Benevolence) by the late Amīr Ḥabīb Allāh Khān, a victim of assassination. Unlike the first name, this second name is not particularly apropos because one often meets thieves and highway robbers here who are in fact just like bears. Pseudo-mullahs were also there, who are anything but religious and are devoid of any legal knowledge but really are wolves dressed in sheep's clothing and harbor nothing but evil intentions towards people. Having declared that without the participation of an amir an attack on Kabul would not be legal according to the laws of the Sharīʿah and therefore if anyone perished his blood would be reckoned as shed in vain, these mullahs recited the Friday prayer and the *khuṭbah*[27] in the name of Amīr Ḥabīb Allāh [Kalakānī], and so lent support to his insurgency. *Marginalia:*[28] Instead of taking revenge on this man who was already guilty of murdering 400 innocent people, in violation of the Sharīʿah they named him amir and embarked on this impious and unjust course. [End of marginal note.]

Shouting "Four Friends!" (*chahār yār*)[29] they passed through the village of Dih-i Kapak[ix] at 3:00 P.M. and around 3:15 reached the Bāgh-i Bālā park and the British Legation.[30] The insurgents occupied the Bāgh-i Bālā palace,

27 Again, it is worth citing Shkirando here (Faiż Mukhammad 1988, p. 259, note 17). He writes, "For the full text of the *fatwā* issued by the mullahs and ulema of the Northern Province against Amān Allāh Khān on 28 December 1928 see I. M. Reisner, *Afghānistān: s kartami i skhemami*, Moscow: Izdatel'stvo Kommunisticheskoi Akademii, 1929, pp. 259–260. There is a very curious detail in Sayyid Bahādur Ẓafar Kākākhayl's book, *Afghānistān da tārīkh pe rana ke*. He writes that on the eve of the promulgation of the fatwa, Son of the Water Carrier sent a message to Sayyid Ḥusayn whom he considered his main rival. 'To overthrow Amān Allāh Khān, it is essential that one of us proclaim himself claimant to the throne and obtain an oath of allegiance from the people. Since you descend from sayyids and are thus from the Prophet, you should be amīr and I will swear allegiance to you.' Further on, Sayyid Bahādur Ẓafar Kākākhayl tells us that Sayyid Ḥusayn, like other people not imagining that things would happen so fast, refused and declared that he had no claims on the allegiance of Son of the Water Carrier. (Sayyid Bahādur Shāh Ẓafar Kākākhayl, *Pukhtana da tārīkh pa rana ke*, Peshawar, n.d.?, p. 1086.)"

28 The Amīrī/Sharīʿatī edition incorporates into the text the many marginal notes added by Fayż Muḥammad without identifying them as such. Since they help us understand how the work was actually written yet do pertain to particular places in the text we include them in the place in the text indicated by Fayż Muḥammad but identify them as marginalia.

29 "Four Friends" refers to the first four caliphs. "Four Friends!" or "O, Four Friends" (*yā chahār yār*) was a Sunni battle cry.

30 According to I. M. Reisner (*Afghanistan*, Moscow, 1929, p. 236), as cited by Shkirando, at this time British airplanes were dropping leaflets on Kabul which appealed to "the

which was formerly the summer residence of Amīr ʿAbd al-Raḥmān Khān and at that time [December 1928] was a military hospital /58/ for the amir's personal guard and the residence of a Turkish physician, Bahjet Beg. After disarming the guards there and the gatekeepers at the British Legation, they stationed their own guards and told the inhabitants of the legation that they were the guests of the nation. They sent the other guards home after taking their weapons.

At the invitation of traitorous ministers; Ḥażrat-i Shūr Bāzār;[31] Sardār Muḥammad ʿUs̱mān;[32] other influential Kabul figures; Muḥammad Walī Khān, Amān Allāh's *wakīl*, and others who had advised [Kalakānī] on the best time of attack and assured the insurgents of their support, the mutineers, without[x] hindrance, like a son-in-law going into the home of his father-in-law, entered the house of the late prime minister, ʿAbd al-Quddūs Khān.[33] At this time the War College was housed there and

---

friendly, courageous, pious Afghan people" and also threatened direct intervention. "Oh, friendly, courageous, pious Afghan people! You know that Britain has long been a friend and well-wisher of Afghanistan and the Afghan people and has always looked with favor on their advancement and enlightenment. Up to now, Britain has had no intention of interfering in your internal affairs—as long as its mission in Kabul and its consulates in Jalālābād and Qandahar have remained safe and secure, the safeguarding and respecting of all missions being supported by all sacred traditions, by the esteemed laws of Islam and by international conventions. However, if any violent action is taken against British officials or consulate or legation buildings on your part, that is on the part of the Afghan people, then we give you fair warning that the British government will adopt all measures necessary to compensate for any loss sustained by its officials and property." (For a British account of the air operations of the Royal Air Force over Kabul in December 1928 and January 1929 see Anne Baker and Air Chief Marshal Sir Ronald Ivelaw-Chapman, *Wings over Kabul: The First Airlift*, London: William Kimber, 1975. There is no mention there of leafletting Kabul.)

31 Ḥażrat-i Shūr Bāzār was a title held by the head of the Mujaddidī family, a Naqshbandī confraternity in Kabul and a powerful political force which traced its spiritual lineage to the 17th-century Shaykh Aḥmad of Sirhind, India who was called *mujaddid-i s̱ānī* (the "second renewer" [of the faith]) whence the family name. At this time the Ḥażrat-i Shūr (Shor) Bazaar was Muḥammad Ṣādiq Gul Āqā, son of Qayyūm Jān Āqā and nephew of Shāh Āqā, holder of the title until 1925. Muḥammad Ṣādiq (Gul Āqā) inherited it then in lieu of his half-brother, Fażl ʿUmar (Shayr Āqā) who was in exile at the time. They both figure prominently in the *Tazakkur al-inqilāb*. See also Adamec, *Who's Who*, pp. 141 ("Fazl ʿUmar, Nūr ul-mashayekh") and 220 ("Sadiq Agha Mujaddidi, or Gul Agha"). When Fayż Muḥammad speaks (slightingly) of the *ḥażrats* he is referring to this family and to the heads of other local spiritual centers like Chārbāgh, just northwest of Jalālābād, and Haddah, six miles south of Jalālābād. He is not referring to religious scholars for whom he uses the word ulema.

32 On Sardār Muḥammad ʿUs̱mān Khān, son of Sardār Muḥammad ʿUmar Khān, see Adamec, *Who's Who*, pp. 260–61. He would be executed by Son of the Water Carrier.

33 On Sardār ʿAbd al-Quddūs Khān (d. 1928) "Iʿtimād al-Dawlah," son of Sardār Sulṭān Muḥammad, see especially the indexes to Fayż Muḥammad, *The History*, vols. 3, 4; also Adamec, *Who's Who*, pp. 100–01.

instruction was conducted under the direction of Ismāʿīl Ḥaqqī Beg and other Turkish officers. The insurgents also gained entry into the house and fortress tower of Shahrārā,[34] site of the Ḥabībīyah School, where instruction was under the direction of another Turk, Shawkat Beg.[xi]

Mīr Bachchah, a son of Muḥammad Akbar Khān, along with a small contingent, put up a brave resistance as far as the reservoir in Dih Afghānān where water from Pamqān is stored and a unit of mounted police who were being trained by the Turk, Shawkat Beg, and were barracked in a building in the garden-estate (*bāgh*) belonging to the late Amīr Shayr ʿAlī Khān, located southeast of the Ḥabībīyah School, organized a defense and stopped the insurgents from gaining entry into the city.

Tumult now reigned. Amīr Amān Allāh Khān, who had been kept in the dark by the deceit of his own traitorous ministers and appointees, learned what was happening. He kept his head and ordered that weapons be distributed to the people of the city and tribesmen who had come from surrounding areas to the city and had yet to set out for Jalālābād to deal with the Shinwārī uprising.

9 | The whole city was filled with the thunder of artillery and gunfire. (But only the cavalry of the amir's personal mounted guard [*risālah-i shāhī*] and a few soldiers turned out to fight. The rest were unhappy at the behavior of their officers who were appropriating their rations and leaving them to starve. Believing [their commanders] were the ones to blame for their problems [rather than the rebels] they were firing their weapons [only] into the air.)[xii] /59/ At this very moment, Her Highness, Amān Allāh Khān's mother,[35] unveiled, went among the men who were taking rifles from the arsenal of the Arg. With terror-stricken heart, she called them all her sons and tried to inspire them to fight back. Although 50,000 rifles and a huge number of cartridges were given out from the government arsenal to the residents of the capital and Chahārdihī and to tribal militias, unfortunately, due to the aversion people felt [for the government] because of the actions of traitorous and corrupt ministers and officials, except for the loss of rifles and ammunition, [this distribution] had absolutely no effect. Moreover, part of the militia from the Wazīrī, Mangal, and Aḥmadzāʾī tribes opened fire from Kūh-i Āsmāʾī and other positions on Amīr Amān Allāh's own regular troops.

---

[34] On this palace built by the Amīr ʿAbd al-Raḥmān Khān see Schinasi, *Kabul: A History*, pp. 74–75.

[35] This was ʿUlyā Ḥażrat, Sirāj al-Khawātīn, Sarwar Sulṭān, the daughter of Shayr Dil Khān "Lūynāb" Bārakzāʾī.

Ghulām Ghawṣ,[36] son of Malik Jahāndād Aḥmadzāʾī who had rebelled against the late Amīr Ḥabīb Allāh Khān and was killed on his orders,[37] took more than 300 rifles. Then, having gone to Khūst, he rose in opposition to the government. Other tribes acted in a similar way because they found it not difficult at all to make off with these rifles and cartridges [from the arsenal] without an invoice (*siyāhah*) or having it recorded in a register.

Convinced that the residents of Kabul and Chahārdihī—his last hope for support—had also turned their backs on him, Amīr Amān Allāh now became truly frightened. These were the same hypocritical people who used to express their allegiance when he and his ministers gave lofty speeches. But because of his inexperience, Amīr Amān Allāh Khān thought them to be his supporters. Four days after Ḥabīb Allāh and Sayyid Ḥusayn's assault on Kabul began, Amān Allāh sent his mother, wife, sister, and small children, and all the government's jewels by plane to Qandahar.

The fighting dragged on for twelve days and eleven nights without letup. Rifles and ammunition from the arsenals at Kulūlah-i Pushtah and Bāgh-i Bālā fell into the hands of the Kūh Dāmanīs, Kūhistānīs, and other rebels and the bulk of the weaponry stockpiled since ʿAbd al-Raḥmān's time and meant for defending against foreign enemies was cast to the wind. During the fighting, Ḥabīb Allāh was wounded in the shoulder by fragments of an aerial bomb. This time, without achieving his goal, **/60/** he returned to Kūh Dāman. He and his colleagues, wielding the pencil of shamelessness, ignorance, and dishonor, having done things like defecating on books of the various sciences, even Islamic religious books, cutting off the heads of the dead and taking them away, and so forth and so on, wrote a shameful page in the history of Afghanistan and then left. Thankfully, however, Europeans who were in Kabul at that moment and were eyewitnesses to the events and recorded the details in their journals will disseminate these reports, which will be a souvenir of the ignorance and
10 ungodliness of the people of Afghanistan | and that will be a lesson for mankind.

---

[36] Ghulām Ghawṣ is identified in Adamec, *Who's Who*, pp. 142–43 as "Ghaus-ud-din" and similarly in Poullada, *Reform and Rebellion*, pp. 174–75, 183.

[37] On Malik Jahāndād's tempestuous relations with Amīr Ḥabīb Allāh Khān (Muḥammadzāʾī) see index to Fayż Muḥammad, *The History* vol. 4, under Jahāndād Khān's name.

Anyway, [Ḥabīb Allāh][38] returned to Qalʿah-i Murād Beg while Amīr Amān Allāh Khān reinforced strategic places with regular army soldiers, tribal units, and artillery as far as Khayr Khānah Pass, all linked together. He would regularly send orders for the troops to go to Kūh Dāman and eliminate the enemy and in this fashion the war dragged on. Although 18-pound guns were fired from a hill located inside Shayrpūr and planes dropped bombs on Qalʿah-i Murād Beg and other positions of the Kūh Dāmanīs nothing good came of it and then came Son of the Water Carrier's second assault on the city and [this time] its conquest.

Son of the Water Carrier's Second Assault and His Entry into Kabul

The fighting went on day and night without a break until Sunday the first of Shaʿbān 1307[xiii] by the solar calendar corresponding to 27 Dalw and 13 January 1929.[xiv] The disloyalty of the regular and tribal forces and of the residents of Kabul and Chahārdihī, who were alienated from the government and so had wasted lakhs of rifles and ammunition by firing aimlessly into the air, and also the fact that the planes were not bombing crucial sites caused Amīr Amān Allāh Khān to give up hope of achieving victory and, overwhelmed by fear of having to surrender to Son of the Water Carrier and be taken prisoner, having no other recourse, during the early morning hours of Monday, the second of Shaʿbān corresponding to 14 January he abdicated and turned the reins of government over to his elder brother, ʿInāyat Allāh Khān. /61/ At nine o'clock that morning, 24 Jady, the second of Shaʿbān/14 January, taking 100 lakhs of rupees (10 million) worth of Russian and British gold pounds, Amān Allāh Khān fled towards Qandahar with Maḥmūd Ṭarzī; Ghulām Ṣiddīq, the foreign minister; the minister of court, Muḥammad Yaʿqūb; the *wakīl* to the minister of the interior, ʿAbd al-Aḥad Khān;[39] and six rifle-carrying soldiers of the Risālah-i Shāhī (the royal mounted bodyguard) in a convoy of five vehicles. After his departure, at one o'clock in the afternoon, while battles were raging around the Khayr Khānah Pass and the positions controlled by government forces were disappearing, ʿInāyat Allāh invited residents of Kabul and represen-

---

[38] Shkirando, citing Anis n.d. p. 89 relates, "On 9 Jadı/30 December, a government communiqué was issued which put a price of 40,000 Afghānīs on the heads of Son of the Water Carrier and Sayyid Ḥusayn and 4,000 on the heads of their colleagues. (See Faiz Mukhammad, *Kniga upominanii*, p. 260, note 23.)

[39] On ʿAbd al-Aḥad, son of Qāżī Ghulām, a Ghilzāʾī of the Ismāʿīl Khayl tribe and also known as a Wardak, see Adamec, *Who's Who*, p. 93 and idem, *A Biographical Dictionary*, p. 196, "Wardak, Abdul Ahad."

tatives of the army and the tribal militias to Dilkushā Palace to accept their oaths of allegiance. But these people had assembled, not to fight, but just to get free money, rifles, and ammunition. The ceremony lasted about two hours during which oaths were given and received and the testament (*waṣiyat-nāmah*) from Amīr Amān Allāh Khān was read out. In all fairness, he had done a great deal for the government, nation, and country of Afghanistan and for whose efforts tears of regret were now shed. Afterwards, [ʿInāyat Allāh Khān] dispatched the cunning and duplicitous Ḥażrat-i Shūr Bāzār, **/62/** who was the very essence of corruption and an inciter of vengeance and hatred, along with Sardār Muḥammad ʿUs̱mān Khān, and two or three of the so-called mullahs who were instigators of insurrection, to those infamous thieves, Son of the Water Carrier and Sayyid Ḥusayn.

Marginalia: Both Ḥażrat-i Shūr Bāzār and Sardār Muḥammad ʿUs̱mān Khān were alienated from [Amīr Amān Allāh Khān]. After the Southern Province campaign during the month of Sunbulah (August/September) Ḥażrat-i Shūr Bāzār and Qāżī ʿAbd al-Raḥmān, his disciple, had been arrested and imprisoned in harsh conditions for attempting to provoke an anti-government uprising among the tribes of that province while Mullā [i.e. Qāżī] ʿAbd al-Raḥmān and four of his sons, sons-in-law, and nephews were put to death.) [End of marginal note.]

These two or three pseudo-mullahs now were supposed to deliver the following message:

> Now that Amān Allāh Khān, whom you accused of godlessness, has left and
> 11 all the people | of Kabul, whether ordinary folk or well-to-do, strong or weak, military or civilian, have come to the city and sworn oaths of allegiance to me and set me on the amīrid throne and since I am a Muslim and you also consider me a true Muslim, therefore the reasons for bloodshed should have vanished. If you truly fought and shed blood in the name of religion and not for the sake of enmity and the kindling of hatred between Muslims, then you must return the blade of confrontation to its sheath, end the bloodshed, and recognize the amirate of Islāmism.

On the way to meet with Son of the Water Carrier and Sayyid Ḥusayn (the delegation) **/63/** notified military units and tribal groups who were manning the defenses that Amīr Amān Allāh Khān had left for Qandahar and transferred the amirate to ʿInāyat Allāh Khān. They called on the soldiers to cease all military action, informing them that they were on their way to see Ḥabīb Allāh, Son of the Water Carrier, and Sayyid Ḥusayn. "If Sayyid Ḥusayn and Ḥabīb Allāh agree, they said, then we will escort them to Amīr ʿInāyat Allāh Khān and end the war and the bloodshed. You also should stop fighting and observe the truce." Hearing these duplicitous words, many of the soldiers abandoned their positions and headed for the city while only a very small number held on until they could get a better idea of the situation.

Having reached the two individuals whom they were actually supporting [i.e. Son of the Water Carrier and Sayyid Ḥusayn], the envoys immediately delivered the contents of Amīr Amān (*sic*-ʿInāyat) Allāh Khān's message and then declared,

> in light of the fact that Ḥabīb Allāh ascended the throne on the first of Rajab while ʿInāyat Allāh's accession corresponds to the second of Shaʿbān, therefore you, not ʿInāyat Allāh Khān, are the rightful amir. If (ʿInāyat Allāh) does not declare his allegiance (to you) and swear an oath, then according to the Sharīʿah he is a rebel and his blood may be shed and would not be subject to retaliation (*mahdūr al-dam*).

Son of the Water Carrier and Sayyid Ḥusayn rejoiced when they heard ʿInāyat Allāh Khān's emissaries and the fatwa of the pseudo-mullahs—who were, after all, their own accomplices—and seeing their wishes about to be fulfilled ordered their followers to march to Kabul. (Along the way) they collected rifles, cannons, and munitions from the deserted positions and towards sunset on that same day—Monday—twenty-eight armed men, accompanied by a group of unarmed Kūh Dāmanīs dressed in rags, passed through the village of Dih Afghānān and burst into the capital shouting "Four Friends" and firing rifles and machine guns into the air, as if they were at a wedding. The residents of the city, offended by the wicked behavior of ministers and provoked by the oppression of the mayor, Aḥmad ʿAlī Khān, were already inclined against Amān Allāh Khān. **/64/** The huge quantity of rifles and bullets which had been distributed to them were not used and they did not fire them even once [against the force of Son of the Water Carrier] and as a result the followers of Ḥabīb Allāh and Sayyid Ḥusayn gained control of the city.

Ḥabīb Allāh, along with ʿInāyat Allāh Khān's envoys—his honored guests—entered Bāgh-i Bālā palace and Sayyid Ḥusayn made a tour of the
12 city. | Seeing that the situation was calm, that the 'commands and prohibitions' were being observed and everyone was submissive and obedient, he joined Ḥabīb Allāh at Bāgh-i Bālā that evening. Towards evening of the very first day of his reign, ʿInāyat Allāh Khān was barricaded inside the Royal Arg with several ministers. Because of the excessive shooting that went on for a full day and night between his own people and the enemy, he could not go out to see anyone nor could anyone come to visit him.

On Tuesday, 3 Shaʿbān, corresponding to 15 January, the people of Chahārdihī; a majority of the residents of Kabul; Sardār Ḥayāt Allāh Khān[40] and Muḥammad Kabīr Khān,[41] sons of the late Amīr Ḥabīb Allāh Khān; and other sardārs who only the day before had vowed allegiance to ʿInāyat Allāh Khān, as well as a few others who had not yet made any promise to [ʿInāyat Allāh Khān], some in fear of being robbed and murdered, but most in a happy frame of mind, all now headed group after group to Bāgh-i Bālā with gifts and presents for Amīr Ḥabīb Allāh. After congratulating him on his accession to the throne, they would then return home. That same afternoon when all matters in the city were now subject to the will of Ḥabīb Allāh and the wishes of Ḥażrat-i Shūr Bāzār, Sardār Muḥammad ʿUs̱mān Khān, and other traitorous ministers and the unfaithful people of Kabul, the *ḥażrat* and Muḥammad ʿUs̱mān Khān went to ʿInāyat Allāh Khān and related their observations and information about Ḥabīb Allāh and Sayyid Ḥusayn. They made him despair of keeping the amirate but even more, they badly frightened him.

On Wednesday, while the amir's forces and the Kūh Dāmanīs were still exchanging fire, and eighty stalwart Hazārahs from Bihsūd were defending the Qalʿah-i Buland fortress and arsenal in Kulūlah Pushtah, the populace came to declare its allegiance to Amīr Ḥabīb Allāh. On this day, the following people were given the honor of meeting with Amīr Ḥabīb Allāh and swore allegiance to him: the president of the /65/ (National) Council, Shayr Aḥmad Khān; the minister of education, Fayż Muḥammad Khān;[42] the former minister of trade, ʿAbd al-Hādī Khān; the minister of finance, Mīr Hāshim Khān; Sardār Amīn Allāh Khān and Muḥammad ʿUmar Khān, sons of Amīr ʿAbd al-Raḥmān Khān, as well as a number of deputy ministers and heads of state institutions. That afternoon, while

[40] Ḥayāt Allāh Khān was the second son of Amīr Ḥabīb Allāh Khān and would be executed by Son of the Water Carrier. For the most complete information on his life see the index to Fayż Muḥammad, *The History*, vol. 4 "Ḥayāt Allāh K., Prince." See also Adamec, *Who's Who*, p. 161 and idem, *Historical Dictionary of Afghānistān*, Third Edition, New Delhi: Manas Publications, p. 155.

[41] For Prince Muḥammad Kabīr Khān see Fayż Muḥammad, *The History*, vol. 4, index and Adamec, *Who's Who*, p. 197, "Muḥammad Kabir Jan, Siraj."

[42] As mentioned earlier, Fayż Muḥammad Zikriyā, was for a time the protector and patron of his namesake, Fayż Muḥammad Kātib, in the difficult years after the latter was fired as official court historian by Amīr Amān Allāh Khān. See the introduction to Fayż Muḥammad, *The History*, vol. 1, pp. lxii–lxv and vol. 4, pp. 1, 3 for Fayż Muḥammad Kātib's own expressions of appreciation. By this time, though, he does not treat the ex-minister quite so kindly. For more on Fayż Muhamad Zikriyā see Adamec, *Who's Who*, pp. 135–36 ("Faiz Muḥammad, Zakaria") and idem, *Biographical Dictionary*, p. 207 ("Zikria, Sardār Faiz Muḥammad").

Sayyid Ḥusayn was at the home of Nūr al-Dīn Khān, son of Qāżī Quṭb al-Dīn Jawānshayrī of the Qizilbāsh and having tea, the gate (securing the quarter) of Chandāwul was opened to the Kūhistānīs because of the adamant demands of certain Kūhistānī khans.

At sunset the town crier announced on the first day of the beginning [of the new regime] that all shops were to open and anyone caught looting would be shot. However, right on the heels of the town crier, the Kūhistānīs entered homes and plundered whatever came to hand. In fact until the last days of Ramażān, they continued these kinds of activities. Moreover, they kidnapped married women, unmarried girls, and young boys nearing puberty, at night slept with them and made them dance.

13 On Wednesday, 4 Shaʿbān, corresponding to | 16 January, representatives of the Qizilbāsh, fearing the tyranny of the Kūhistānīs, also went to Bāgh-i Bālā and offered their allegiance to Amīr Ḥabīb Allāh. During this time, fruitless fighting was still going on as well as discussions about forcing ʿInāyat Allāh Khān to abdicate the amirate and vacate the Arg. Then Ḥażrat-i Shūr Bāzār, Sardār Muḥammad ʿUs̱mān Khān, and some treacherous ministers forced ʿInāyat Allāh Khān into relinquishing the amirate and leaving the palace. Only the son of ʿAbd al-Rashīd Khān Muḥammadzāʾī, Ghulām Dastagīr Khān, who held the post of warden (*qalʿah-bīkī*) [of the Arg], **/66/** and the minister of war, ʿAbd al-ʿAzīz Khān,[43] son of Muḥammad Allāh Khān Bārakzāʾī, who were not "partners with the thieves" while pretending to be "friends of the caravan," refused to take part in this contemptible plot against the authority of Amān Allāh Khān and ʿInāyat Allāh Khān, and aimed at the fall of the family of Amīr ʿAbd al-Raḥmān Khān.

ʿInāyat Allāh's Abdication and His Departure from the Palace

The absence of loyalty of the people of Kabul and the treachery of Ḥażrat-i [Shūr Bāzār], Sardār Muḥammad ʿUs̱mān Khān, Muḥammad Walī Khān, and other traitorous followers of Satan who scurried about trying to get (ʿInāyat Allāh Khān) to abdicate and leave the Arg frightened ʿInāyat Allāh Khān and hastened his abdication. Playing the role of intermediary between ʿInāyat Allāh Khān, Son of the Water Carrier. and Sayyid Ḥusayn, Ḥażrat-i Shūr Bāzār, using the Noble Qurʾān as intercessor, while

[43] For ʿAbd al-ʿAzīz, son of Mazullah [*sic*] Khān and the nephew of Queen ʿUlyā Ḥażrat, the most powerful wife of Amīr Ḥabīb Allāh Khān and the mother of Amān Allāh Khān, see Adamec, *Who's Who*, p. 93.

remaining outwardly still amiable and friendly, but in actuality a complete hypocrite, advised ʿInāyat Allāh Khān to abdicate and abandon the Arg, which was full of money, equipment, and firearms accumulated over generations and could have been defended for a long time from the forces of the villainous evildoers. Consequently, his demands for 300,000 rupees and [permission] to go with his family to Qandahar or some other place by way of Peshawar and the Panjāb were accepted by Ḥabīb Allāh, Son of the Water Carrier. Both sides then wrote their pact in a Glorious Qurʾān and on Wednesday, Son of the Water Carrier sent a farman granting safe passage to ʿInāyat Allāh Khān by the hand of Ḥażrat-i Shūr Bāzār and also permitted his retainers to accompany him. With tears in his eyes, ʿInāyat Allāh Khān said goodbye to the wives of his late father and to his brothers and sisters who were in the Arg. To each of them and their mothers he gave some twenty-five pounds sterling so that they could live for a few days, though in miserable circumstances, and not starve to death. He also distributed money to the soldiers of the royal guard /67/ and other defenders of the Arg.

At night on Thursday, the fifth of Shaʿbān 1347 A.H./17 January, with his own hand he wrote details of his agreement and of his abdication. It said:

14 My brother, Ḥabīb Allāh Khān! | It is known to all that I have no wish to be pādshāh. After the death of my father, I relinquished any claim to the throne. Despite the fact that it was easy and I had the means when Amān Allāh Khān himself abdicated kingship, again I had no desire of becoming pādshāh. I was compelled to do so only at the insistence of the virtuous and influential leaders ("those who loose and bind") of the capital who linked my accession to the throne with the prosperity of the people and the strengthening of Islam, indicating that it was my duty. And due to my own perspective on the situation, I accepted their arguments. But now, when I see that the issue comes down to the shedding of the blood of Muslims, I have decided to relinquish [authority] and abdicate from the amirate of Afghanistan and give you my oath of allegiance like other true believing Muslims. Today in the Arg, along with me, the following distinguished people have pledged their allegiance to you: Muḥammad Walī Khān,[44]

[44] On Muḥammad Walī Khān see Adamec, *Who's Who*, p. 262 under "Wali Muhammad" [*sic*]. This is another courtier with whom Fayż Muḥammad Kātib had had amiable relations. (Fayż Muḥammad, *The History*, vol. 4, pp. 1266, 1271, 1288 for instances where Muḥammad Walī Khān as chief of court pages and with access to Amīr Ḥabīb Allāh Khān had performed services for Fayż Muḥammad which the latter, in gratitude, had recorded in the pages of his chronicle.)

ʿAbd al-ʿAzīz Khān,[45] Muḥammad Sarwar Khān,[46] Ghulām Ḥaydar Khān,[47] Aḥmad ʿAlī Khān [Lūdīn],[48] Ghulām Dastagīr Khān,[49] ʿAbd al-Ghiyāṣ Khān,[50] ʿAṭā al-Ḥaqq Khān,[51] Muḥammad Amān Khān, Muḥammad Amīn Khān,[52] Muḥammad Isḥāq Khān,[53] Sayyid Qāsim Khān,[54] ʿAbd al-Wahhāb Khān [Ṭarzī],[55] ʿAbd al-Tawwāb Khān [Ṭarzī],[56] Shāh Maḥmūd Khān,[57] [58]Sayyid ʿAbd Allāh Khān, Sulṭān Muḥammad Khān, Sayyid Aḥmad Khān, Mīr ʿAlī Aḥmad Khān, and Muḥammad Akram Khān. [Their] oath of allegiance to me is now nullified and like me, they are giving you their oath of fealty on the following conditions:

---

45 See above, note 134.

46 It is not clear which of the many Muḥammad Sarwar Khāns active at this time is the one named here.

47 This would appear to be Mīrzā Ghulām Ḥaydar Khān Wardakī although it is by no means certain. See Adamec *Who's Who*, p. 146 ("Ghulām Haidar, Mīrzā, Wardaki").

48 See above, note 112.

49 Unidentified.

50 This could be either the brother of the late prime minister and founder of the Iʿtimādī (Etemadi) family, Sardār ʿAbd al-Quddūs Khān "Iʿtimād al-Dawlah" or the son of "Abdul Majid" (but which ʿAbd al-Majīd?) or none of the above. For the former see Adamec, *Who's Who*, p. 95 ("Abdul Ghias, Sardar. Muḥammadzāʾī"); for the latter, idem, *A Biographical Dictionary*, p. 5 ("Abdul Ghias, born 1880").

51 ʿAṭā al-Ḥaqq was the brother of Shayr Jān, Ḥabīb Allāh Kalakānī's minister of court, and General Muḥammad Ṣādiq Khān, both leading officials of the Kalakānī government. Their father was a prominent Kūh Dāmanī. See Adamec, *Who's Who*, p. 126 ("Ata-ul-Haqq").

52 This would seem to be the same Muḥammad Amīn in ibid., p. 195 who died in prison in 1933.

53 Tentatively, this appears to be the same Muḥammad Isḥāq Khān as in ibid., p. 167 ("Ishaq Khān, Muhammad").

54 There is some confusion over Sayyid Qāsim Khān or alternatively Mīr Qāsim Khān between the accounts of Adamec, *Who's Who*, p. 231 and Ḥabībī, *Junbish*, p. 48. Ḥabībī identifies one man but refers to him by both names in the course of his entry and calls him the son of Sayyid Ghulām Muḥammad Chahārbāghī and the son-in-law of Maḥmūd Ṭarzī in the caption to his picture on p. 49. Adamec (or the British sources from which he derived his information such as the *Biographies of Chiefs, Sardars, and Others in Afghānistān* [Calcutta: Foreign Office, 1882] and the subsequent publications of *Who is Who in Afghānistān* in 1914, 1920, 1922, and 1940) believed there were two different men, Sayyid Qāsim, son of Aḥmad Shāh Kahan [*sic*] a Kābulī sayyid and son-in-law of Maḥmūd Ṭarzī and Mīr Sayyid Qāsim, a "Sayyid of Chārbāgh." It seems unlikely that these were different men.

55 On ʿAbd al-Wahhāb Khān son of Maḥmūd Beg Ṭarzī see Adamec, *A Biographical Dictionary*, p. 189 ("Tarzi, Abdul Wahhab").

56 On ʿAbd al-Tawwāb Khān son of Maḥmūd Beg Ṭarzī see ibid. ("Ṭarzī, Abdul Tawwab").

57 Shāh Maḥmūd was a brother of Muḥammad Nādir Khān, Shāh Walī Khān, and Muḥammad Hāshim Khān. Unlike his brothers, he was in Kabul when the revolution broke out and opted to cooperate, at least for a short time, with the Kalakānī regime. See ibid., pp. 234–35.

58 The last five names cannot be identified with any certainty at this point. All apparently were in the Arg with ʿInāyat Allāh Khān at the time he wrote the terms for his abdication.

> First, safety must be guaranteed for me, my immediate family, those attached to my household and other members of my extended family (*ahl-i bayt*), as well as the above-named persons, and to all officers, soldiers, and those who work here in the Arg on my behalf, and to my dependents. My personal property and belongings should also be safeguarded.
>
> Second, I /68/ myself and my dependents are going to Qandahar or abroad. An airplane must be put at my disposal to deliver us to Qandahar.
>
> Thirdly, permission should be given to Muḥammad Walī Khān, ʿAbd al-ʿAzīz Khān, and Aḥmad ʿAlī Khān to go with me.
>
> Fourthly, permission should be granted within a month's time to those high-ranking officials listed above who wish to go abroad with their families.
>
> Fifthly, up until the time when an airplane is readied for my departure, I will be in the Arg. After my being driven to the airplane and my physical departure, the Arg will be vacated for you.

Thursday night. 5 Shaʿbān 1347 A.H. (17 January 1929) ʿInāyat Allāh[59]

After this agreement was written and delivered, the artillery and small arms fire ceased.

On Friday night, 6 Shaʿbān 1347 corresponding to 18 January 1929, the minister of war, ʿAbd al-ʿAzīz Khān; ʿAbd al-Ḥabīb Khān;[60] the amir's *wakīl*, Muḥammad Walī Khān; and the mayor of Kabul, Aḥmad ʿAlī Khān [Lūdīn], swore oaths on the Qurʾān and conveyed the text of these oaths [to Amīr Ḥabīb Allāh Khān] by the hand of the deceitful and despicable Ḥażrat (-i Shūr Bāzār).

15 We, the undersigned, ʿAbd al-ʿAzīz, |, ʿAbd al-Ḥabīb, Muḥammad Walī, and Aḥmad ʿAlī swear to Amīr Ḥabīb Allāh Khān on the Qurʾān that we will never act against him or the authority of the amir nor will we incite insurgency or corruption against Amīr Ḥabīb Allāh Khān and we will live like all citizens of Afghanistan under the protection of the Islamic government. Friday night, 6 Shaʿbān 1347. [Signed] ʿAbd al-ʿAzīz, Aḥmad ʿAlī, ʿAbd al-Ḥabīb, Muḥammad Walī.

ʿInāyat Allāh Khān Vacates the Arg

On Friday, the eighteenth of January 1929, corresponding to the twenty-eighth of Jady 1307 at eleven o'clock in the morning, at the request of

---

[59] The document is also given in Baker and Ivelaw-Chapman, *Wings over Kabul*, pp. 134–35.

[60] ʿAbd al-Ḥabīb, son of ʿAbd al-Wahhāb, son of Sardār Mīr Afżal Khān, was a chamberlain to Sardār ʿInāyat Allāh Khān. (Fayż Muḥammad, *The History*, vol. 4, p. 75.)

Son of the Water Carrier, two British (Bālūn)[61] aircraft /69/ landed in Kabul. At 1:00 P.M. ʿInāyat Allāh Khān, with his immediate family and relatives as well as ʿAbd al-ʿAzīz Khān and Aḥmad ʿAlī Khān, took off for Peshawar.[62] As for the sons of Maḥmūd Ṭarzī—ʿAbd al-Wahhāb and ʿAbd al-Tawwāb—as well as several of the sons and daughters of ʿInāyat Allāh Khān, the "Bālūn" did not have room for them and they were put off until another day.

That evening, Son of the Water Carrier sent Sayyid Ḥusayn to take possession of the Arg while he himself went to the Bāgh-i Āqā building[63] where the provincial headquarters (of Kabul Province) and finance administration were housed. Their ignorant followers, who in the bazaars and the Pārk-i Niẓām wa Qūmāndānī (Kūtwālī)[64] engaged in oppressing and robbing members of the Hazārah, Wardak, Wazīrī, and Mangal tribal forces; the cavalrymen of the Risālah-i Shāhī [the royal bodyguard]; and looting some houses, fired their guns and rifles in celebration, terrifying the city residents who were not accustomed to such violent fusillades and the noise of rifles and cannons being fired. Wherever anyone happened to be, he quickly headed for home.

---

61 It is unclear what make of aircraft Fayż Muḥammad was trying to identify. There was a British manufacturer named "Boulton & Paul, Ltd." producing various models of aircraft in the 1920s. This name comes closest to the *bālūn* of Fayż Muḥammad. However, the only planes the Royal Air Force had available at Peshawar to ferry the evacuees were the Vickers Victoria, the Arco DH9A, and the Handley Hinaidi, none of which bear any phonetic resemblance to *bālūn*. It was the Vickers Victoria and the Handley Hinaidi that actually carried out the airlift. See Baker and Ivelaw-Chapman, *Wings over Kabul*, especially chapters 9–18.

62 According to Shkirando, on the eve of ʿInāyat Allāh Khān's departure, the former amīr distributed six-months' pay to the soldiers guarding the Arg. And although he carried away quite a bit of money and many valuable articles, when Ḥabīb Allāh Kalakānī took over, he had at his disposal 60 million rupees. (Faiz Mukhammad, *Kitāb upominanii*, pp. 260–61, note 29.

63 This was Mihmānkhānah (Guest House), a splendid building built by Ustād Walī Muḥammad Khān as a palace for Amīr ʿAbd al-Raḥmān Khān and completed in the early 1890s. See Schinasi, *Kabul: A History*, p. 72.

64 The Pārk-i Niẓām wa Qūmāndānī (or as Fayż Muḥammad parenthetically explains, the *kūtwālī* or police headquarters) is a later name applied to Bāgh-i Āqā as its purpose changed. For a full history of the development of this site over the years, see Schinasi, *Kabul: A History*, index, "Bâgh-i Âqâ" and "Mehmânkhâna/Bâgh-e Mehmânkhâna." In his use of the English word "park" here and in a reference below (p. 100), Fayż Muḥammad clearly had in mind the meaning "a space occupied by military vehicles, materials, or animals" not a place of relaxation and recreation (s.v., *Merriam-Webster's Collegiate Dictionary*, Eleventh Edition).

Sayyid Ḥusayn, standing under the dome of the Arg's drum house (*naqqārahkhānah*),[65] ordered his ignorant followers to stop firing their rifles. When they did not stop, he fired his own rifle into the chest of one of them and killed him on the spot (literally: emptied his body of its soul). The rest, witnessing this brutal and vicious act by a man who without a second thought had killed hundreds of people as well as this one individual, [now] stopped firing their guns. Entering the Arg, they treated the people who had been trapped there in the worst possible way. Despite the oaths taken on the Qur'ān, they beat, stripped, and even killed some of them and dragged the bodies out of the Arg. Among the victims were staff of the Arg, troopers from the Risālah-i Shāhī, the warden of the Arg, and others. Four soldiers of the Risālah-i Shāhī passing through the bazaar, heartsick and physically exhausted, were shot in Sar-i Chawk.[66] Similarly, these bandits disarmed, stripped, and shot dead Wazīrīs, **/70/** Mangals, Wardakīs, and Hazārahs who were members of tribal contingents whether inside or outside the city. They even dragged them from
16 their homes where they had taken refuge. | They perpetrated many dishonorable things, plundering and thieving. Despite all their assurances of devotion to Islam, these marauders perpetrated so many horrors that they made Islam the subject of condemnation by foreigners and gave it a bad name. In describing these tragic events, the writer, a Muslim, has a thousand times cursed their claims to piety and their Muslim utterances and prayed to God to send them straight to the lowest depths of Hell. Only curses come to mind when recalling the activities of this gang of rebels and thieves. Those pseudo-mullahs, who call their leader and these thieves and highway robbers "mujahideen" and "holy warriors" (*ghāzīs*),

---

[65] The Naqqārahkhānah, built by ʿAbd al-Raḥmān Khān, stood at the southwest corner of the Arg and housed the police station (*kūtwālī*). Schinasi describes it as "a monumental covered passageway to serve as the main gate of the city ... an octagonal building constructed of fired brick, decorated here and there, and topped by a dome (*gonbad*) on a circular base some eight meters in diameter." Schinasi, *Kabul: A History*, p. 80. The site it stood on was part of the former Bāgh-i Āqā.

[66] The Chār Chattah was Kabul's main covered market and was built by the Mughal governor of Kabul, ʿAlī Mardān Khān, during the reign of Emperor Shāh Jahān. It had nine sections including five plazas open to the sky spaced evenly along it and four roofed sections (*chattah*) connecting them. The main open plazas were Sar-i Chawk, Miyān-i Chawk, and Pā'īn-i Chawk (Head, Middle, and Foot of the Covered Market). It's not clear if "Miyān-i Chawk" covered the three middle plazas or just the middlemost one. (See May Schinasi, *Kaboul: de la ville historique à la vieille ville*, unpublished ms., vol. 1, p. 67 and Annexe 3 for a schematic of the whole bazaar.) The roofed structure of the market was destroyed by the British in October 1842 in retaliation for the murder of their political agent, William Macnaghten, but the plaza locations remained. (See Schinasi, *Kabul: A History*, pp. 135–37.)

ordered them to attack true Muslims who, from the time they get up in the morning until they go to bed at night, five times raise their Muslim voices to say "Allāhu Akbar" and perform the prayer and on Fridays perform it in the mosque. And one of them they even raised to the amirate. What should one call those who shed the blood of hundreds of people and set Islamic social power back a hundred years and weakened and incapacitated it? They plundered and carried off all the stored-up treasure and resources of the government which were intended to be used for the defense of national honor, national independence, and the religion.

The Pious Declarations and the Impious Actions of the Northerners

On Saturday, 7 Shaʿbān and 29 Jady, corresponding to 19 January, the sons of Maḥmūd Ṭarzī and the rest of the children and dependents of ʿInāyat Allāh arrived in Peshawar on an English airplane and from there, accompanied by ʿInāyat Allāh himself and his immediate family, all set off by train /71/ for Chaman. Then by motor car they rejoined Amān Allāh Khān in Qandahar.

Subsequently, Son of the Water Carrier; his brother Ḥamīd Allāh; Sayyid Ḥusayn, the minister of war; the field marshal, Purdil; and other thieves, each of whom had given himself a lofty title and rank, under the pretext that shooting was heard coming from this or that house or that a rifle was in this or that house, began to engage in plundering and immoral behavior. They broke into homes in groups, seized personal belongings, and dragged young boys, married women, and unmarried girls off to secluded rooms where they raped them. Every ten or twenty men would take one or two women, boys, and girls to the places where they spend the night and no one has stopped them so that up until today—Sunday, the 28th of Ramażān 1347 corresponding to 11 March 1929—this sort of thing still goes on but somewhat less than was the case during the first days and nights.

When Son of the Water Carrier left the Kabul or Central Province administrative offices [in Bāgh-i Āqā] and moved to the Royal Arg, he invited his father, who like him had spent his whole life in caves, mountains, and barren wastes hungry and in rags, to join him that evening. Finding themselves in a royal palace, they were utterly taken aback. After giving thanks to the All-High, in order to show their self-control, they decided not to eat pilau and instead, having confused the dining room and the toilet, used the white china chamberpot from Amīr Amān Allāh Khān's personal toilet that he used for urinating and defecating [for soup]

[17]

17 | and dunked their bread in the soup, thanking God after each morsel, until they had eaten their fill.

From this day forward, [Son of the Water Carrier] ignored the agreement he had concluded with ʿInāyat Allāh Khān that addressed the safety of the twenty individuals who had stayed at the palace and the safeguarding of their wealth and personal belongings. He arrested all but two or three, including ministers and high-ranking officials, ordered them imprisoned in the Arg, and confiscated their belongings and money. In addition, he threatened to kill them and [then] extorted even more money from them.

Worried that Afghans would attack from Jalālābād, Qandahar, and other regions, over the course of several days Son of the Water Carrier ferried the privy purse (*ʿayn al-māl*) and the government treasury (*bayt al-māl*) and arsenal /72/ by car to Kūh Dāman. But when he was assured that Afghans on the whole lacked the honor and bravery to resist him, he called a halt to the transfer to Kūh Dāman and Kūhistān of the national treasure and other plundered and confiscated property. Later, his partisans, from sepoys to officers, began to hunt for the wives, young daughters, and sons of reputable sardārs and other influential people. They took them by force at night and dragged them off to their rooms. By the beginning of Ramażān, they had emptied and looted 191 homes of wealthy individuals, ministers, and high-ranking officials.

Prior to 27 Shaʿbān/8 February 1929, Amīr Amān Allāh Khān's *wakīl*, Muḥammad Walī Khān, who had reached an accommodation with Son of the Water Carrier and Sayyid Ḥusayn and had given help to their supporters, asked that they arrest him along with other people. He was [then] held under house arrest at the home of the new minister of court, Shayr Aḥmad Khān.[67] His own home and belongings were not touched.

At this time, the former governor of Kabul, ʿAlī Aḥmad Khān [Lūynāb], declared himself amir in Jalālābād.

The Reign of ʿAlī Aḥmad Khān

ʿAlī Aḥmad Khān was the son of Khūshdil Khān "Lūynāb." Khūshdil Khān's father was Shayrdil Khān, who had held the post of chamberlain (*īshīk-āqāsī*) at the court of the late amir, Shayr ʿAlī Khān [r. 1863–66,

67 This seems to have been a mistake on Fayż Muḥammad's part. Although both the ms. p. 17 and the published text p. 70 have Shayr Aḥmad Khān, the new minister of court was Shayr Jān Khān.

1868–79].[68] [ʿAlī Aḥmad's] mother was the daughter of Amīr Dūst Muḥammad Khān and he was born in the holy city of Mashhad [Iran]. Because his father and mother had worked for the late Amīr Shayr ʿAlī Khān, Amīr ʿAbd al-Raḥmān Khān requested, the British government demanded, and Nāsir al-Dīn Shāh Qājār ordered that the two of them, along with two sons of Amīr Shayr ʿAlī Khān, Sardār Muḥammad Ayyūb Khān and Amīr Muḥammad Yaʿqūb Khān, leave Iran for exile in India. There /73/ [ʿAlī Aḥmad Khān] studied Urdu and English besides Afghānī [Pashto] and Persian, his mother tongue. During Amīr Ḥabīb Allāh Khān's reign, the family returned to Kabul from India thanks to Amān Allāh Khān's mother, Her Majesty (ʿUlyā Ḥażrat) Sarwar Sulṭān, the sister of
18 Khūshdil Khān, ʿAlī Aḥmad Khān's father. | Khūshdil Khān was appointed [high] governor of the Central Province while the high-paying posts of chief custodian (*farrāsh-bāshī*), governor, colonel, and high governor of Kabul were awarded to ʿAlī Aḥmad's uncles—Fayż Muḥammad Khān, Sulṭān ʿAlī Khān, Muḥammad ʿUmar Khān, and Muḥammad ʿAlī Khān. ʿAlī Aḥmad himself became "civil chamberlain" [one of whose responsibilities was road maintenance.] Towards the end of Amīr Ḥabīb Allāh Khān's reign, his father [Khūshdil Khān] was named [high] governor of Qandahar.[69]

After Fayż Muḥammad [Khān, the uncle] had been ordered bastinadoed by Sardār Naṣr Allāh Khān, they appointed him governor in Maymanah and Sulṭān ʿAlī Khān governor of Kūhistān-i Kabul. Muḥammad ʿAlī Khān remained in his former post of high governor of the Central Province; Muḥammad ʿUmar Khān, as before, held the rank of colonel and doorkeeper (*qāpūchī*) at the court of his sister—Her Highness (the Queen) while ʿAlī Aḥmad Khān continued as civil chamberlain.

After Amīr Ḥabīb Allāh Khān's assassination, ʿAlī Aḥmad's father [Khūshdil Khān], who took part in the fight for independence against the British at the beginning of Amān Allāh Khān's reign, incited an attack by the Afghans of Qandahar and its environs on the Qizilbāsh, who lived in the region and fought against the British at Chaman and Kadanī. They

---

68 In 1874, Amīr Shayr ʿAlī Khān appointed Īshīk-āqāsī Shayrdil Khān to be high governor of (Afghan) Turkistān and gave him the Pashto title "Lūy Nāb" (Great Deputy). At the same time he gave his son Khūshdil Khān the title "Kumakī Nāb" (Assistant Deputy), and his chief secretary, Mīrzā Muḥammad Ḥasan Khān, the title "Kām Nāb" (Managing Deputy). When Shayrdil Khān died, the amir transferred his title to Khūshdil Khān. (Fayż Muḥammad, *The History*, vol. 2, p. 336.) When Khūshdil Khān died during Amān Allāh Khān's reign (1919–1929), the title was inherited by ʿAlī Aḥmad. The other titles disappear.

69 Fayż Muḥammad, *The History*, vol. 4, p. 1377.

assaulted their families, including the children, and plundered their possessions. As a consequence of his instigating the Afghans, a monstrous injustice occurred. Sardār ʿAbd al-Quddūs Khān, the prime minister, who was sent to Qandahar to direct military action /74/ against the English, managed to settle the conflict. Khūshdil Khān was then recalled to Kabul where he remained in retirement until his death.

People with personal motives say that the groundwork for the annihilation of the Qizilbāsh of Qandahar was laid by the English who paid Khūshdil Khān Lūynāb a huge sum of money to perform this horrific deed. They also say that every incident and political provocation which has occurred and still occurs inside Afghanistan and on its eastern and northern borders is not connected so much with the ignorance and savagery of the people or the corruption and oppression of the government as it is with the subversive activities of the English government. [However] they ignore the fact that as a result of the rivalry which that government has with Russia, (England) considers Afghanistan an iron shield to repel any attack on [England's territories] by her rival and so that country makes considerable efforts to increase the capabilities of the country and to strengthen it, not to take an axe to her own roots by destroying that solid bulwark. Rather, if the conceptions and imaginings of those who retail these sorts of rumors and wild speculations were based on sound sources and credible facts grounded in reality then truly it would be convincing proof of the irreligiosity, stupidity, and misguidedness of Afghans, both leaders and followers.[xv] For any provocation and incitement by the English government would not seem right to Afghans with their outward, at least, profession of religiosity and Islamism. If they believe in the Sharīʿah of the Lord of Prophets or if they spend time reading the Qurʾān or listening when mullahs recite the verse "Oh believers! Take not Jews and Christians as friends; they are friends of each other. Whoso of you makes them his friends is one of them. God guides not the people of the evildoers!"[70]
19 | then they would never submit to the provocations of England, which professes Christianity.

In any case, ʿAlī Aḥmad Khān himself, having negotiated with the English, concluded /75/ a temporary truce with them [in 1919] by which the independence of Afghanistan was declared.[71] However, since some articles

---

[70] Qurʾān 5:51.

[71] On these negotiations and ʿAlī Aḥmad Khān's role see Ludwig W. Adamec, *Afghanistan 1900–1923*. Berkeley and Los Angeles: University of California Press, 1967, pp. 123–35 and for the local "color" of the negotiations (from the rather jaundiced perspective of an

of the agreement somewhat contravened the interests of the Afghan government, a few of his ill-wishers denigrated him before Amīr Amān Allāh Khān and accused him of supporting the English and taking bribes from them. He thus became the object of the amir's anger. And so, although he was having a relationship with Amīr Amān Allāh Khān's older and full sister, an order was given for him to be executed. However, at the petition of Her Majesty—(ʿAlī Aḥmad's) aunt and the mother of his lover, whom in the end he married—[the amir] pardoned him and put him under house arrest, warning him that if he left the house, he would be killed.[72]

He remained under house arrest until the Mangals and other tribes of the Southern Province rebelled [in 1924] at the instigation of Qāżī Mullā ʿAbd Allāh and ʿAbd al-Karīm Khān,[73] a son of Amīr Muḥammad Yaʿqūb Khān and grandson of Amīr Shayr ʿAlī Khān, who had fled and insinuated himself into the [tribal] society of that mountain region and laid claim to the throne, thereby making things difficult [for Amīr Amān Allāh Khān]. ʿAlī Aḥmad Khān was then sent to Jalālābād to recruit a tribal army, suppress the rebels, stop ʿAbd al-Karīm Khān, and remove Mullā ʿAbd Allāh. Using every trick and device he could think of, he managed to mobilize the tribes of the Jalālābād region. He ordered (this force) to attack the homeland of the rebels from the north and annihilate them. He also assigned the Tūrī tribe which inhabited the Kurram [Valley] and were subjects of the English, to destroy the insurrectionists. In the end, he was victorious: ʿAbd al-Karīm fled, was arrested, and detained in an English jail, where he was murdered. Mullā ʿAbd Allāh and a group of evildoers swore oaths [of obedience] on the Qurʾān and were granted safe passage to go to Kabul. But when they reached Kabul, [the mullah] was executed (literally: "attained the *yāsā*.")[74]

As a reward for his services, ʿAlī Aḥmad Khān was honored with appointment as high governor of the Central Province. Later, he went with Amīr Amān Allāh Khān on the European tour. But there /76/ he lost the amir's respect and upon his return found himself sitting at home [without a position] when the Shinwārī, nay, all the tribes of the east, raised high the

English participant) see Lieut.-General G. N. Molesworth, *Afghanistan 1919: An Account of Operations in the Third Afghan War*, New York: Asia Publishing House, 1962, pp. 87–92.

72 For more on ʿAlī Aḥmad Khān Lūynāb see Adamec, *Who's Who*, pp. 114–15 and idem, *Biographical Dictionary*, p. 96.

73 ʿAbd al-Karīm, son of Amīr Muḥammad Yaʿqūb Khān, seeking to advance his own claims to the amirate, played a role in the 1924 Mangal uprising. Adamec, *Who's Who*, p. 97.

74 The *yāsā*, Chinggis Qān's thirteenth-century law, in nineteenth-century Afghanistan had come to mean a capital crime for which the punishment was execution.

flags of insurrection against the godlessness of Amīr Amān Allāh Khān. An army led by Maḥmūd Khān aide-de-camp (*yāwar*);[75] the president of the [National] Council, Shayr Aḥmad Khān; and the foreign minister, Ghulām Ṣiddīq Khān,[76] was sent to put down the rebellion of those evildoers. But because of the double-dealing of Ghulām Ṣiddīq Khān, who feigned capture by the rebels but in reality went over to their camp and incited them to attack Jalālābād, no progress was made. Thereupon ʿAlī Aḥmad Khān was appointed high commissioner with full powers for the Eastern and
20 Southern Provinces and ordered to suppress the revolt. A week before | the first attack by the water carrier's son on Kabul, [ʿAlī Aḥmad Khān] headed for Jalālābād at the head of a large force well-equipped with arms, mountain guns, siege weapons, and armored cars. There, employing every means and every trick that he knew, he devoted himself to counseling the savage and lost-to-humanity Shinwārīs and other evildoers who were engaged in wicked activities and immoral behavior, winning them over, quenching the flames of insurgency and rebellion, and [persuading them] to take the high road of obedience to the amir. To some he gave money, to others he presented robes of honor (*khilʿat*s), and to others [only] advice. He thus succeeded in placating them and restoring peace.

Also, during the reign of [the martyred] Amīr Ḥabīb Allāh Khān, after the opening of the madrasah called "Maktab-i Ḥabībīyah" (the Ḥabībīyah Lycée, today's Habibiya High School) where new sciences and foreign languages were to be taught, Sayyid Qāsim,[77] son of Mīr Ghulām Muḥammad Chārbāghī, through flattery and toadying but also by giving assurances that he was an expert in the Sharīʿah as well as in Persian and Arabic literature, managed to obtain from the director [of Public Education], Dr. ʿAbd al-Ghanī Khān,[78] /77/ a post as an elementary-level teacher and a

---

[75] Adamec, *Who's Who*, p. 182 where he is called "Mahmud Jan." In the late 1960s Maḥmūd Khān was one of the twenty survivors of the 1929 revolution who agreed to be interviewed by Leon Poullada for his book, *Reform and Rebellion*, according to the mimeographed "Confidential Key to Informants."

[76] Adamec, *Who's Who*, pp. 151–52.

[77] For more on him see ibid., p. 231 ("Sayyid Qasim, Mir"). Adamec does not name his father but the career information is identical.

[78] Dr. ʿAbd al-Ghanī Hindī, a Hindustānī Muslim, was hired by Amīr ʿAbd al-Raḥmān Khān in 1898 to work for the government but it is unclear in what capacity. [According to Fayż Muḥammad, *The History*, vol. 4, p. 163, he was the son of Mawlawī Sawandī Khān but according to British sources (Adamec, *Who's Who*, p. 95) his father was "Maulavi Roshandil Khān."] He was instrumental in the founding of the Ḥabībīyah School but is perhaps best remembered for his role in the constitutional movement of the early 1900s. For his involvement he was arrested in 1909 and not released until 1920. On his career in Afghanistan see Fayż Muḥammad, *The History*, vol. 4, index under "ʿAbd al-Ghanī K. Panjābī Hindī, Dr." and Adamec, *Historical Dictionary*, pp. 1–2 and idem, *Who's Who*, p. 95.

small salary to go with it. During the reign of Amīr ʿAbd al-Raḥmān Khān, (Sayyid Qāsim's) father (Mīr Ghulām Muḥammad Chārbāghī), famed for his knowledge of religious matters, had been one of the professors at the Royal Madrasah (Madrasah-i Shāhī) and lived a modest life. Later, he (Sayyid Qāsim) and the doctor (ʿAbd al-Ghanī Khān), two of (the doctor's) brothers—Najaf ʿAlī and Chirāgh ʿAlī, and several other adherents of constitutionalism (*mashrūṭah-khwāhī*) were arrested and imprisoned. Seven of those arrested faced a firing squad or were blown from cannons and seventy-five others suffered various punishments and torture, the personal belongings of their families were confiscated, and members of their families were dishonored. A few of those arrested were released after a short time, some perished in prison, and the rest were [only] released [eleven years later] during the time of Amīr Amān Allāh Khān. Sayyid Qāsim, who was one of the first pardoned and freed, again thanks to flattery and fawning, began to teach once more at the Maktab-i Ḥabībīyah which Amīr Amān Allāh had re-opened. Due to a lack of knowledge [about him] by the people who held the post of minister of education—in this order: ʿAbd al-Ḥabīb Khān, son of ʿAbd al-Wahhāb Khān and grandson of Sardār Mīr Afżal Khān, the father of Amīr Shayr ʿAlī Khān's wife; Prince Ḥayāt Allāh Khān ʿAżud al-Dawlah, son of [the martyred] Amīr Ḥabīb Allāh Khān; and Muḥammad Sulaymān Khān, son of Muḥammad Āṣaf Khān and grandson of Sakhī Khān, son of Sardār Sulṭān Muḥammad Khān, who was a half-brother of Amīr Dūst Muḥammad Khān—(Sayyid Qāsim) was able to put it about that he was a teacher of the eastern sciences (*ʿulūm-i sharqīyah*) and newspapers even wrote about it. Concealing his low level of education, he was able to obtain the post of advisor to the ministry of education. But his manifest ignorance was soon discovered and he was dismissed from that position and relieved of all service in the scientific field. Amīr Amān Allāh Khān barred him from further govern-
21 ment work | and ordered him to sit with ruffians and lowlifes and to earn his own living [instead of getting it by fraud]. But hardly had a few days passed and the ink dried on this order /78/ when this schemer managed to recommend himself to the editor of *Amān-i Afghān* and gain his acquaintance. Some time later, Ghulām Ṣiddīq Khān, head munshi [of the newspaper], was appointed temporary chief secretary of the legation in Berlin, the capital of Germany, and [Sayyid Qāsim] was named temporary chief munshi in place of Ghulām Ṣiddīq Khān at the newspaper.

Until the time under discussion, he occupied this post and tried to pass himself off as a scholar. Since by birth he was from Chārbāgh, Jalālābād and his father was an eminent scholar and very highly regarded by the people of that province, Amīr Amān Allāh Khān like a "drowning man clutching at straws"[79] sent [Sayyid Qāsim] to the insurgents to advise and admonish them. But his real business became collecting money for himself from everywhere so that no matter what happened he would come out ahead. It was decided that he would act as emissary and go-between to the insurgents on behalf of ʿAlī Aḥmad Khān and would go to Kabul to reveal the cynical designs of the evildoers to Amīr Amān Allāh Khān. By order of the *wālī* [ʿAlī Aḥmad Khān] he came to Kabul by plane, remained one night and received 20,000 rupees from the amir which was supposed to make the pseudo-mullahs of the Jalālābād region happy and which they were to use to win over the evildoers there. He flew back to Jalālābād but was unable to make any progress. No one knows for what purpose that money was spent.

After ʿInāyat Allāh Khān's departure and the capture of Kabul by Son of the Water Carrier's forces, the people of the mountainous region around Jalālābād asked [ʿAlī Aḥmad Khān] to accept the duties and responsibilities of the amirate. However, being a man of foresight, he at first refused and only later, because of their insistence and his own ambition, agreed to accept it after concluding agreements with the heads of the tribes. They swore oaths [of loyalty] on the Qurʾān and he then hoisted the flag of his amirate. He then combined the regular troops who had been sent from Kabul to Jalālābād to pacify the Shinwārī and other insurgents with the Shinwārī, Khūgyānī, and other [tribal forces] in order to attack Kabul and overthrow Son of the Water Carrier. He told them to march to Samūch-hā-yi Mullā ʿUmar, Tang-i Khūrd Kabul, and /79/ Chinārī (?) and that as soon as he joined them they would attack Kabul.

At the head of a 2,000-man force of regular army soldiers and tribal fighters, ʿAlī Aḥmad Khān marched to Jagdalak and there waited in hopes of the arrival of a tribal force from the Muhmands. From Wednesday, the 11th of Shaʿbān until Tuesday, the 17th corresponding to the 23rd to the 29th of January 1929, he sent out farmans in which he proclaimed his amirate to the elders of the peoples of Kabul, Lahūgard, the Hazārahjāt, the Southern Province and other regions and called on them to join him and render their obedience. These were all written and signed in his own hand and sent by secret messengers. In the end nothing came of it and he failed to achieve what he desired. His camp was looted and he himself,

[79] The proverb is given in Arabic and is literally "the drowning man hangs on to every blade of grass" (*al-gharīq yatashabbat̲h̲u bi-kulli ḥashīshīn*).

half-naked, and in a miserable state, only managed to get away on foot
22 and barely escaped being killed. |

ʿAlī Aḥmad Khān Abandons Hope of the Throne

When ʿAlī Aḥmad Khān and his force arrived in Jagdalak and were awaiting the arrival of the Muhmand tribal forces, rumors circulated in Kabul that his attack on the city would begin in a day or two. Driven to despair by the tyranny, oppression, and degradation of the irreligious Kūhistānī and Kūh Dāmanī savages, thieves who had made themselves into sardārs and commanders; had taken women, young girls and boys to their lairs and raped and sodomized them; had imprisoned wealthy people, notables, and bazaar merchants and confiscated and stolen their property—all of this being due to [the people of Kabul's] disloyalty and ingratitude towards Amīr Amān Allāh Khān—the inhabitants of Kabul day and night spent their time in anticipation of the attack of **/80/** the forces of ʿAlī Aḥmad Khān in order to avenge themselves on the evildoers of Son of the Water Carrier, Sayyid Ḥusayn, and on the other thieves.

However, while waiting, Malik Qays of the Khūgyānī tribe broke the agreement that he had solemnly concluded with ʿAlī Aḥmad Khān and faithfully upheld to this point using as an excuse the fact that ʿAlī Aḥmad Khān had punished the Khūgyānī and had had him bastinadoed. With three or four followers Malik Qays came to see Ḥabīb Allāh, commander of thieves and son of Amīr Allāh, the water carrier. For 17,000 rupees and the post of deputy field marshal, he promised to capture ʿAlī Aḥmad Khān, shackle him in neck and leg irons and bring him to Kabul. Two or three days before Qays' arrival [in the capital], Son of the Water Carrier sent some emissaries to ʿAlī Aḥmad Khān, namely Muḥammad Mūsā Khān Muḥammadzāʾī[80] and ʿAlī Aḥmad Khān's uncle Muḥammad ʿAlī Khān, whose home he had looted and himself arrested but then quickly released with a message that said that ʿAlī Aḥmad Khān ought to renounce the amirate, come to Kabul as a subject, and place the noose of submission around the neck of obedience to the [Son of the Water Carrier's] farman. Otherwise each of his wives, one being Amīr Amān Allāh Khān's sister and the other one the sister of Gul Muḥammad Khān, the daughter of Tāj Muḥammad Khān, the aunt of the minister of education, Fayż Muḥammad Khān, and the mother of Ghulām Muḥammad Khān and Nūr Aḥmad Khān, would both be dishonored and killed. These two men reached ʿAlī

[80] Adamec, *Who's Who*, p. 203 ("Musa Khān, Muhammad").

Aḥmad Khān and delivered the message. They had yet to receive any answer from him—acceptance or refusal—when the godless Malik Qays returning from Kabul /81/ reached Tangī Khūrd Kabul, which is the location of the new Ghāzī Dam.[81] Malik Qays ordered the members of the Khūgyānī tribal force who had established themselves there with a few soldiers of the regular army to disarm the regular army men and plunder them. After some minor skirmishes, they succeeded and then headed to Khāk-i Jabbār. The plundered [regular] troops straggled obediently back
23 to Kabul. This led to the dispersal of the tribal forces | that had stopped in Chinārī and Samūch-hā-yi Mullā ʿUmar awaiting orders to attack Kabul and Son of the Water Carrier. They abandoned their field guns and ammunition where they were and [now] headed for Kabul to declare their obedience to Son of the Water Carrier. For two days after they entered Kabul, [the amir] had ranks of [his own] soldiers lined up to welcome them on the Chaman-i Ḥużūrī [the Kabul parade ground] and had the army band serenade them. Then with all due military ceremony he ordered them to enter the Arg and received them in audience. For three nights they were treated as guests and then enrolled in his regular army.

Meanwhile, when 2,000 members of a Shinwārī tribal force, who had joined ʿAlī Aḥmad Khān[xvi] and were camped on both sides of the Chashang Pass, learned of the betrayal of the Khūgyānīs and their seizing the rifles and ammunition [of the regular forces at Tangi Khurd Kabul] their misguided hearts were filled with envy and admiration for the good fortune [of the Khūgyānīs]. When they had first arrived in Jagdalak, ʿAlī Aḥmad Khān gave them a few head of cattle for their evening meal. But they were more inclined to pillaging and visions of guns and ammunition were lodged in their hearts and they refused the cattle on the grounds that they were old and emaciated. Instead, they suddenly fell upon the baggage train, disarming the regular sepoys and tearing down ʿAlī Aḥmad Khān's tent and scattering his gear on the ground. They made off with everyone's clothing, leaving them all naked. Among the pillagers, ʿAbd al-Raḥmān Khān,[82] son of ʿIṣmat Allāh Khān Ghilzāʾī, who for a long time had nurtured hatred for the government in his heart, took possession of the [English] pounds which were worth three lakhs of rupees and took them home. Two or three maliks from Lamqān spirited away ʿAlī Aḥmad

[81] The Ghāzī Dam was built under Amīr Amān Allāh and irrigated Butkhāk and its region. (See Fayż Muḥammad, *The History*, vol. 4, p. 80.)

[82] For more on him, see Adamec, *Who's Who*, p. 103 ("Abdur Rahman, Jabbar Khayl Ghilzāʾī").

Khān, two of his sons, and his personal letter writer, Mīrzā Muḥammad Ibrāhīm Khān, son of Mīrzā Āqā Jān Khān, and, out of a sense of Afghan honor, /82/ delivered them, naked and on foot, to the safekeeping of the *naqīb*[83] who had proclaimed ʿAlī Aḥmad Khān's amirate.

The *naqīb*, observing the situation and the treachery of the Khūgyānī and Shinwārī, decided to make hijrat (emigrate) to India with his family and relatives. Although the Khūgyānīs and Shinwārīs were at this time preoccupied with plunder and fighting over weapons and ammunition, still, as soon as they learned of his plans, they came to him, apologized for their actions and prevented him from leaving. The *naqīb* agreed to their request on condition that they support ʿAlī Aḥmad Khān and again they made a pact and promised to support him. But ʿAlī Aḥmad Khān, who was fully aware of the untrustworthiness and ingratitude of the Shinwārī and all the other frontier tribes, knew any promise of theirs was insubstantial and they would violate any pact. So he negotiated with them only enough to save his own life. He would not have anything to do with any covenant or agreement with those people and applied to his situation the verses of Amīr ʿAbd al-Raḥmān Khān, translated from Afghānī to Persian, who, after expanding on the wicked behavior of evil mullahs and the tribal chiefs during his life, had written down in his journal:

> Even if you work and struggle for two hundred years,
> 24 The snake, the Shinwārī, and the scorpion will never be your friends.[84] |

---

[83] This was Sayyid Ḥasan, Naqīb-Ṣāḥib of Chārbāgh, Jalālābād, one of the many Mujaddidī Naqshbandī leaders scattered around Afghanistan. See Nawid, *Religious Response*, pp. 22, 173.

[84] The "journal" being referred to here is ʿAbd al-Raḥmān Khān's memoir *Pandnāmah-i dunyā wa dīn*. The *Pandnāmah*, published in unfinished form in Kabul in 1885, was the basis for the two-volume English work, *The Life of Abdur Rahman Amīr of Afghānistān G. C. B., G. C. S. I.*, London, John Murray, 1900. (See Amin Tarzi, "The Judicial State: Evolution and Centralization of the Courts in Afghānistān, 1883–1896," Ph.D. dissertation, New York University, 2002, pp. 5–7 for the best available description of *The Life of Abdur Rahman* and its value.) The English work was quickly translated back into Persian and published in several editions in Mashhad and Bombay. Only a bit over thirty per cent of *The Life* (the first 192 pages of a total of 614 pages including 15 pages of glossary and index) can be linked to the known 140-page published edition of the *Pandnāmah*. It is certainly possible that there existed a full manuscript of the *Pandnāmah* from which *The Life* was generated. However, none has ever come to light though it is quite likely that any such manuscript would have been brought to England by the author of *The Life*, Sultan Mahomed Khān, and if so would logically have wound up at the library of Cambridge University where he was a student and where he apparently wrote *The Life*. In any event, Fayż Muḥammad, in quoting ʿAlī Aḥmad's citing the above verses, must have been referring to one of the Persian translations of the English for those verses do not appear in the 140 pages of the published version of *Pandnāmah*. In the English translation the verses are given as:

[24]

The Initiatives of Son of the Water Carrier and Sayyid Ḥusayn in Governing the Amirate

Two days after ʿInāyat Allāh Khān's departure, Son of the Water Carrier and Sayyid Ḥusayn along with a group of barbarous Kūhistānī and Kūh Dāmanī know-nothings and thieves who had given themselves high ranks and titles, now took up the reins of government. First of all, /83/ they published a proclamation regarding the status of all government employees. However, almost immediately they abrogated it by another proclamation. The ministry of trade was abolished.[85] It was the reference point and means for facilitating the import and export of goods; it controlled public expenditures in the economic sphere and thereby ensured the wealth and prosperity of the country; and it maintained [a supply of] those necessities of life for humankind such as food and clothing, etc., Similarly, he laid off employees of some ministries' offices and caused them hardship.

During these first two or three days, [the new amir] gave each sardār and notable who voluntarily came to meet him the glad tidings of a promise of one-and-a-half times their previous salary. In their stupidity they believed his promises and rejoiced. But they were all arrested, their wealth and belongings confiscated, and they were deprived of any stipend. After that, Son of the Water Carrier and his followers began to extort large sums of money from traders and wealthy people. As a result, they upset the populace and instilled fear in their hearts. He then began his initiatives in pursuit of women among which was his trying to coerce the daughters of the late Nā'ib al-Salṭanah Sardār Naṣr Allāh Khān and Prince Amīn Allāh Khān, sons of Amīr ʿAbd al-Raḥmān Khān, to marry him. He [also] discovered the register containing the names of the girls attending the Mastūrāt School[86] and ordered that each one of these girls be given as a wife to the mulberry-eaters, thieves, and ragged vagrants from Kūhistān and Kūh Dāman.

Marginalia: Using this devilish sort of "propaganda" (*parūpagān*), he was trying to encourage the thieves and wild men who were his followers to wholeheartedly support his oppression and cruelty. [End of marginal note.]

"You may try gently for hundreds of years to make friends / But it is impossible to make scorpions, snakes, and Shinwārī, friends." (*The Life*, vol. 1, p. 238.)

85 According to Shkirando, who does not mention his source, the ministries of education, health, and justice were also abolished. (See Fayż Muḥammad, *Kniga upominanii*, p. 261, note 44.

86 On the Mastūrāt School, one of the first two schools for girls opened in Afghanistan see Schinasi, *Kabul: A History*, pp. 136–37.

Each day he ordered 1,000 trays of pilau to be prepared for those who had never seen wheat bread in their lives. He paid for it with money from the government treasury that had been accumulated over fifty years of hard work and toil on the part of ordinary people and was saved for an emergency. Day and night they trucked away this wealth to Chārīkār and Jabal al-Sirāj. The Arg, once a symbol of purity, was transformed by the Kūhistānī and Kūh Dāmanī thieves into a latrine and a dunghill. /84/ Hiding behind Islamic slogans, they wrought a disaster impossible for the human mind to comprehend.

Each day the voice of the town crier could be heard: "Shops must open and anyone who is caught looting will be shot." Nonetheless, this gang of thieves would never pay for goods but would just stuff them in the bags which they always carried with them. Also, on the pretext of searching for guns in a house, these bandits would break into homes and steal money and belongings. Also, (the amir) proclaimed that if anyone had a rifle and did not turn it in, this would be a death-penalty matter or would lead to the owner's imprisonment, the forfeiture of his property, and the seizure
25 of his family. Consequently, many people suffered losses | and punishment. These thieves even stripped some fighters from the Wazīrī, Mangal, Wardak and Hazārah tribal forces and stole their weapons and the money they had for their daily needs. If they protested, (the thieves) shot and killed them.

For example, Son of the Water Carrier issued a farman permitting a group of Hazārahs[87] to return to their home regions. They had fallen on hard times and lacked even the bare minimum for subsistence. This group, which numbered some 1,500 men, then set off for home, relying on that farman. Near the Māshīnkhānah Bridge, adjacent to Qalʿah-i Hazārah, there suddenly appeared a bandit from the gang of Son of the Water Carrier who had decided to steal the clothes and shoes of those who had not already been stripped. He harshly ordered one of the victims, an Hazārah on horseback, to slowly remove his shoes and hand them over. But the Hazārah, knowing how difficult it would be for him to take off his shoes in such frigid weather and go barefoot gently asked him, "Dear brother! You say you are a Muslim and a fighter for the faith. We, too, are Muslims. So I beg you to pardon me /85/ and let me keep these old shoes. Truly, they don't belong to the government but to me." But this godless villain did not accept his humble plea, killed him with a rifle shot, and yanked off his shoes. People who witnessed this incident then captured and delivered

---

87 Originally the author wrote "an Hazārah" but then crossed it out.

the godless one to Son of the Water Carrier. Eager to show that he was a zealous follower of the Sharīʿah, he announced, "Let the law of retaliation (*qiṣāṣ*)[88] apply to this sepoy." However, there was a colonel there named Ghulām Nabī who was himself of Hazārah origin and had worked hard to reach his high rank and position. Not knowing the laws of the Sharīʿah, he turned to Son of the Water Carrier and his courtiers, inveterate miscreants and pseudo-mullahs all, and said in an obsequious manner, "One of our brothers has perished but we would not want another of our brothers to perish. Therefore we will not demand revenge." The mullahs and others present at the assembly nodded their heads in approval, affirming his declaration with cries of "well done!" although he had no kinship tie whatever with the murdered man [and thus no right of revenge]. Perhaps his relationship to him was like that of Buyūkā Bahādur or Āghūz Khān whose genealogies go back to Japheth, son of Noah.[89] [So] they freed the murderer and gave not a thought to the relatives of the victim—his wife, son, and daughter—who were his legal heirs [and thus entitled to retaliate or accept compensation]. They ignored the verse of the Qurʾān which says, "And there is (a saving of) life in *al-qiṣāṣ*, o men of understanding, that you may become the pious ones."[90] This kind of killing and bloodshed occurred frequently. One example serves here for the whole like "one seed from the *kharwār* and one fistful [of grain] from the warehouse."

Similarly, one day in Ramażān [February-March 1929], a handsome young boy living in the Andarābī Quarter[91] went to the bath with his aged white-haired father. In the bath, three or four followers and sepoys from
26 Son of the Water Carrier's gang | grabbed the boy, tore away the cloth he had tied around his waist, uncovered his buttocks, and private parts, and began to fondle him. He and his father, along with some honorable individuals who were inside the bathhouse, gathered nearly fifty men from inside and outside the bath and went with the boy and his father to Sayyid Ḥusayn to seek justice. /86/ However, one of the thieves managed to get

---

88 The right to retaliate (eye for an eye) or to accept monetary compensation for death or injury.

89 For the place of the biblical Japheth as the "blessed son" of Noah and the penultimate source of the genealogies of "kings and heroes," see B. Heller and A. Rippon, "Yāfith," *Encyclopaedia of Islam*, New Edition, volume 11, pp. 236–37. Fayż Muḥammad is saying that if the colonel had any relationship to the victim it was as remote and legendary as a line of kinship traced back to Japheth.

90 Qurʾān 2: 179.

91 The Andarābī Quarter was "on the left bank of the Kabul River at the foot of the east flank of Āsmāʾī Mountain." (Schinasi, *Kabul: A History*, p. 34.)

there first and tell his own version of what happened so that as soon as the plaintiffs arrived at Sayyid Ḥusayn's durbar, his minions pounced on them, beat them up, and dispersed the people who had come with the boy and his father and only wanted to bear witness to the vile act of those savages. Then having driven them away, they escorted the boy and his father in to see Sayyid Ḥusayn—the leader of the thieves and marauders. He admonished the culprits by cursing their fathers and then said, "You should first pay the 'beardless boys,' receive their consent and then take your pleasure. You should never possess other people's boys, girls, and wives by force." In this fashion did he placate both sides and conclude the inquiry. This is how he "properly" investigated the matter. This case is an example of just one of hundreds of similar incidents which (the Northerners) perpetrated.

Son of the Water Carrier and Sayyid Ḥusayn's Establishment of Government Departments

In matters of administration and organizing government responsibilities, they brought back the system employed by Amīr ʿAbd al-Raḥmān Khān and Amīr Ḥabīb Allāh Khān. Instead of writing numerals (*handasī*) they ordered that *siyāq* [a system using symbols or letters for numbers] be used. They referred all matters involving the rights of plaintiffs, punishment, and investigating oppression to the *qāżī*. The *Niẓāmnāmah*-i *jazā-yi ʿumūmī* (Amīr Amān Allāh Khān's penal code) was committed to the flames, despite the fact that with the exception of three or four articles, it was designed to deter litigation and to suppress immorality, and all the discarded articles were in complete conformity with Hanafi Sharīʿah. As for lawsuits without documentation, although it corresponded with the regulations and orders of Amīr Amān Allāh Khān, it was proclaimed that the judge, as was the case in the time of Amīr Amān Allāh Khān, did not have the right to hear a case if no documentary evidence was available. However, the new *qāżī* of Kabul, aware of the fact that he would not be able to take bribes if this were the case, began to process cases disregarding the absence of documents, even though he was not supposed to do so, considering the provision in the Qurʾān that says, "O Believers, when you contract a debt one upon another for a stated term, write it down and let a writer write it down between you justly"[92] as something that is only

[92] Qurʾān 2: 282.

recommended [*mustaḥabb*, that is, the commission of which is meritorious but the omission entails no negative consequences]. /87/ In doing so he did not realize that this will cause godless people to file groundless suits, people would be forced to bribe the *qāżī* and the bailiff, and so would face adversity, lose any sense of tranquility, and be deprived of the bare necessities of life.

Similarly, there were proclamations that were confirmed at sessions of the [State] Council (*Majlis-i Shūrā*) and the Islamic Regulatory Commission (*Hay'at-i Tanẓīmīyah-i Islāmīyah*), which was formed at the order of Son of the Water Carrier and at the request of the people of Kūh Dāman and Kūhistān who were completely ignorant of religious matters related to this world and the next. But not one of these edicts, which are posted in places where people congregate, is being implemented. On reading
27 these decrees people of the city and those gripped by oppression | feel heartened and with strengthened resolve proceed to demand their rights but wind up being beaten with lathi sticks and rifle butts and reduced to despair instead. In private gatherings, they even praise the unbelief and the actions of Amīr Amān Allāh Khān and with complete sincerity pray to the Lord to restore him to the throne. They believe that what they are experiencing from the Kūhistānīs is the result of their own ill-will and ingratitude towards Amīr Amān Allāh Khān. It drove them to revile the ministers, ḥażrats, and mullahs who have plunged the country into disaster, bloodshed, and thievery and it brought about the revolution which everywhere has encompassed all in its relentless strangling grip.

For example, Son of the Water Carrier issued a farman to pay the Jady (December/January) monthly salary to local teachers[93] who taught religious subjects, Islamic beliefs, and formal writing to madrasah students. Some of them received it but when others went to Malik Muḥsin, the high governor of Kabul, with their vouchers to get him to sign them, he accused them of being infidels and ordered them beaten. Some were beaten around the head, neck, and back with rifle butts /88/ while others were assaulted with rocks and sticks and [needless to say] were not paid.

I do not know how it is possible to correlate these acts with their assurances of devotion to the religion. To the contrary, it is impossible to call

[93] By using the adjective *waṭanī* to modify "teachers" (*mu'allimīn*), Fayż Muḥammad is distinguishing them from the many foreign teachers, i.e., Indian and Turkish Muslims, working in Afghanistan.

them anything but enemies and destroyers of religion, country, government, and the nation of Islam. There are no other ways to explain their barbarism and this is the only way to characterize them in writing and record them for history. It should be asked, "Should the order and farman of a self-appointed "amir" constantly bombarding the ear with the cry of "Islamism!" be accepted or not accepted? If people turn their heads away from (obeying) all the farmans and decrees signed by this [self-appointed] amir and distributed to them, should they be called rebels? Does the pure Holy Law permit them to beat up helpless people who are only asking for their rights? Does the Holy Lawgiver allow them to take possession of the treasury of the government and the wealth of the nation, which has been accumulated for the preservation of the country, the protection of the lives, wealth, and honor of the nation, and the defense of the borders against foreigners and instead force people to bear the provisions of his army—whose soldiers are in fact followers of Satan—without pay? Has the Sacred Lawgiver given them permission to tear down palaces and plunder homes? No, by God, He has not given them permission! Nonetheless, the corrupt ministers, ḥażrats, pseudo-mullahs, and other godless leaders regard this tragic situation, for which they are guilty, as permissible. Well, we will see how Almighty God will deal with the nation and with them!

In any case, Shayr Jān Khān, who during [the late] Amīr Ḥabīb Allāh Khān's reign served in a unit of cavalry at the royal stirrup [as bodyguard], was named minister of court; his brother ʿAṭā al-Ḥaqq Khān—foreign minister; the son of Muḥammad Shāh Tagābī of the Ṣāfī tribe, ʿAbd al-Ghafūr Khān—minister of the interior; Malik Muḥsin of Sarā(y) Khwājah—high
28 governor (*wālī*) of the Central Province [Kabul]; | Sayyid Ḥusayn—minister of war; Purdil Khān, the boldest of the thieves, and ʿAbd al-Wakīl Khān—field marshals; Ḥamīd Allāh, another son of the water carrier, /89/—great sardār. In similar fashion, every one of the bloodthirsty, godless, and cruel thieves, was given a military rank—general, brigadier, deputy field marshal, and colonel.

He formed the Islamic Regulatory Commission from a few wretched corrupters and in order to introduce various kinds of reforms that would ease worries of people about their property they published some baseless pronouncements. It had no more result than writing on water because all the barbaric people of Kūhistān and Kūh Dāman, who are inveterate thieves, ignored the edicts of Son of the Water Carrier and those above them. Each has acted and still acts precisely as he wishes.

The English Government Shows Favor and Extends Its Protection to Foreign Citizens

During the looting and plundering of the rebels from the North, the ambassadors of civilized countries—Italy, France, Germany, Turkey, and Iran—fearing for the fate and property of their citizens who worked in Kabul under contract to the Afghan government, as well as those employed in trade, tourism, and other areas, appealed to the government of Great Britain and requested evacuation of their families and citizens from Afghanistan. Their request received the kind approval and benevolent acceptance of the aforementioned government. First of all, women were carried very respectfully by plane from Kabul to Peshawar and then the men were taken out. The evacuation of all foreign citizens from Kabul began during the second ten days of Shaʿbān [1347] and lasted until the end of the first ten days of Ramażān [ca. 24 January–21 February].[94] All were freed from terror and feelings of helplessness and became the consorts of comfort and tranquility. After all foreign subjects had been evacuated, the minister [of England] accompanied by the envoys of Italy, France, and Germany departed Kabul by plane for Peshawar. At the French Legation only one interpreter remained and he was a Kabul resident. At the Italian Legation only a caretaker **/90/** remained behind. The German Legation was manned by a chargé d'affaires (*shārzh dāfayr*). Both (the caretaker and the chargé d'affaires) were there to resolve a number of issues and settle trade accounts. By law (*qanūn*[an]) all foreign citizens received a month's salary on contractual grounds and were sent home in an easy frame of mind.

Up to this point the reasons for the rebellion and [an account of] the revolutionaries has been written in a condensed form. From here on, the tragic events will be described in the form of a journal (*rūznāmah*) so that enlightened people of shrewd judgment and conscientious will avoid ill-fated policies in future and the chief person in authority having ascertained through examination and selection the innate characteristics of persons [to be considered for appointments] whether they possess integ-
29 rity, dignity, and honesty or perfidy, dishonesty, and treachery | will not select persons who do not come of noble birth and do not have a respectable genealogy. Then the reins of the important affairs of the community will not fall into the hands of people who do whatever they please.

94 According to Baker and Ivelaw-Chapman, *Wings over Kabul*, chapter 10, the evacuation of British women and children took place on the 23rd of December. Other women and children were airlifted along with the men in January.

The Public Appeal of Muḥammad Aslam Balūch and Raising the Banner of the Bewitched Sayyid

Muḥammad Aslam Balūch, who had been an English subject and then left [English territory] and settled in Kabul, on Friday, 12 Ramażān, [1347] corresponding to 4 Ḥūt 1307 and 21 February 1929, in light of the oppression and violence produced by Son of the Water Carrier and his Kūhistānī and Kūh Dāmanī thieves /91/ who had conquered and occupied Kabul and brought hardship and adversity on all the residents of the city whether ordinary folk or well-to-do, strong or weak, women or men, boys or girls, those who had not found a way to escape and who on the one hand were praying to God for Amīr Amān Allāh Khān and [on the other] in public and in private, in gatherings and assemblies, were cursing Son of the Water Carrier, Sayyid Ḥusayn, their army—a gang of oppressors—the pseudo-mullahs, the hypocrite Muḥammad Ṣādiq Khān;[95] the destroyer, Muḥammad ʿUs̱mān Khān; and the treacherous ministers who were the architects of his amirate and cast country, nation, sovereignty, and Islamic social power to the winds—in light of all this, [Muḥammad Aslam Balūch] wrote an appeal to the people of the city and posted it in the Chawk where people always congregated:

> O men! If you have weapons, this is good. If you don't, then buy them! The new government will give you cartridges so that you can defend yourselves and your property from assault and plundering by the tribes that have risen in support of Amīr Amān Allāh Khān and cinched the belt of resolve to exterminate those who have seized authority.

Followers of Son of the Water Carrier arrested [Muḥammad Aslam Balūch] and fined him 2,000 rupees but then, because of a lack of evidence, he was released from prison. Later, however, all the émigrés [from India] who supported Amān Allāh Khān were arrested on the charge of creating disturbances and turmoil among the people of the Panjāb and India.

Later, on Sunday, 21 Ramażān and 14 Ḥūt, corresponding to 4 March, a sayyid from Kunar broke into the home of an Iranian citizen, Żiyā Humāyūn, who had been evacuated to Peshawar with his family on an English plane. He had locked his house and sent the key to the Iranian consulate. The sayyid sacked the house and then raised a flag bearing the symbol of a mihrab and minbar in honor of Amīr Amān Allāh Khān.

---

[95] (General) Muḥammad Ṣādiq Khān was the brother of the minister of court, Shayr Jān Khān, and the foreign minister, ʿAṭā al-Ḥaqq. (Adamec, *Who's Who*, p. 221 ["Sadiq Khān, Muḥammad Ṣiddīq"]).

He then started a rumor saying, “My forebear, ʿAlī Murtażā [the Fourth Caliph and First Imam], appeared to me in a dream and told me to raise this flag.” /92/ Hearing this utterly false claim, the residents of the city came in groups to see and a hubbub arose among nobles and commoners alike. Son of the Water Carrier’s minions came to the sayyid and ordered him to take down the flag. But he refused saying, “I raised it as ordered by my esteemed ancestor and I [therefore] cannot take it down. If you can do it, go ahead.” Following this incident, a rumor spread that Son of the Water Carrier had sent the sayyid 2,000 rupees to take down the flag. But again he repeated this answer and refused to comply. Then the generous
30 hand of Son of the Water Carrier promised to give him 10,000–20,000 | rupees if he would lower the flag but he again refused. Finally, on the second of Shawwāl, corresponding to 24 Ḥūt and 14 March, the high governor, Malik Muḥsin, ordered the flag be lowered and the sayyid to be hung upside down by his heels.[xvii] His appointees violently tore down the flag, hanged the sayyid by his heels, and pinned the flag to his side. He hung there until Sayyid Ḥusayn, who was a rival of the high governor’s, summoned [the governor] and freed [Muḥammad Aslam Balūch]. He also confiscated several leaflets from him which had been circulating throughout the city and which called for people to support Amīr Amān Allāh. (24 Ramażān: The leaflets which were distributed in Kūh Dāman should be included.)[xviii]

The Slaughter of Son of the Water Carrier’s Army at Shaykhābād, Wardak

Elsewhere, Karīm Khān Wardak, who had refused to tender his obedience to Son of the Water Carrier, prepared breastworks (*sangar-hā*) in Shaykhābād and the region of Zaranay and dug trenches (*mūrchāl*) in the snow, having made up his mind to outwit Son of the Water Carrier’s 3,000–man army which had left Kabul and was headed for Ghaznīn and Qandahar under the command of the field marshal, ʿAbd al-Wakīl Khān.[96] When it reached Qalʿah-i Durrānī and [the village of] Bīnī Bādām, the army halted there in order to suppress Karīm Khān and his followers by any means and then to continue on as planned. As the saying has it “war is deception” so, jointly with the leaders of the Wazīrī and Hazārah tribes who had gathered at Shaykhābād in support of Amīr Amān Allāh Khān and had blocked the advance of Son of the Water Carrier’s force, [Karīm Khān] sent a message to the field marshal which said,

---

[96] On ʿAbd al-Wakīl Khān see ibid., p. 101 (“Abdul Wakil Nuristani”).

> We, the tribes of Wardak, consider ourselves subjects of Amīr Ḥabīb Allāh Khān. However, in view of the fact that up to this time we have yet to send him our oaths of allegiance, we are afraid that if an army comes it will shoot us down and plunder us. But if they forgive us for this oversight and accept our four conditions then we will not block passage of your victorious army. Our conditions are the following:
>
> > First: The fortress of ʿAbd al-Aḥad Khān,[97] who left for Qandahar with Amīr Amān Allāh Khān ought to be protected against looting and his people from violence.
> >
> > Second: The rifles distributed to us by Amīr Amān Allāh Khān should not be taken away.
> >
> > Third: All of us, the tribes of Wardak living on the territory up to Ghaznīn, should not be subject to looting and violence just because we have not yet sent our oaths of allegiance.
> >
> > Fourth: When your army passes through our territory, during the two day's march, forage and provisions /94/ ought to be procured for cash and at current prices and not for free or in the form of *sūrsāt* (requisitions).
>
> After your army passes through, we promise to go to Kabul with tranquil hearts and offer our oath of allegiance to the amir.

The inexperienced field marshal, who knew only how to rob and steal and had not the slightest skill in commanding armies and had spent all his life
31 in the mountains, was deceived by this message | and, reassured, ordered a force under his command numbering 1,800 men and called the Model Battalion (*Qiṭʿah-i Namūnah*) which was stationed in Qalʿah-yi Durrānī in the southern part of Maydān, to march to Shaykhābād along with 400 horsemen from the Royal Cavalry now at the disposal of Son of the Water Carrier and 800 Kūhistānī and Kūh Dāmanī infantry who had halted near the village of Bīnī Bādām. The road over which they marched was very narrow and hemmed in on both sides by snow-covered mountains and barren wastes so that the people had to walk in close formation, forced to drag their baggage, artillery, and pack animals along with them. The entire army was utterly exhausted by this march. When the vanguard had passed the fortifications at Zaranay, which is situated on the edge of the Dasht-i Tūp plain, and the rest of the force was approaching the hills which lay nearby, one of the soldiers fired at a bird. The Wardak, waiting in ambush, heard the shot, thought that they were discovered, and hurriedly opened fire. From the sides of the road and the tops of the hills a mighty fusillade thundered down. Not one soldier dared reach for his rifle and cartridges.

97 The minister of the interior, on him see above, p. 65, note 39.

They were convinced that their doom had come. Dead men and horses fell before their eyes. During the attack, /95/ the [Wardakīs] shouted to the soldiers from the Model Battalion and the residents of Chahārdihī to get away from the Kūhistānīs otherwise they would be killed. But since units of the army were all intermingled they could not do this. Many soldiers were killed and a few escaped in the direction of Lahūgard.

The men manning the breastworks (*sangars*) at this time emerged from the ground, from under the snow, and out of the forts and hurled themselves on those fleeing and pursued them as far as the pass which overlooks Lahūgard. Many more were killed and all their small arms and artillery fell into the hands of the Wardak braves and their allies. The residents of Lahūgard stripped, plundered, and shot the rest. Some of the wounded and other survivors managed to get back to their homes. Son of the Water Carrier had them arrested and beaten nearly to death and also warned them that the Day of Judgement awaited them. From that day forward, they never dared move towards Ghaznīn and are unable to go beyond Maydān until it becomes known what God's command will be. In any case, twenty cavalrymen of the royal horse survived, the rest, mostly
32 infantry, perished. |

A Letter from Muḥammad Nādir Khān to Son of the Water Carrier

During these events, ʿAbd al-ʿAzīz Khān, the Afghan minister to Tehran who had been supplanted by Sulṭān Aḥmad Khān,[98] son of Colonel Shayr Aḥmad Khān, a cartographer, was returning home when he was set upon by followers of Ḥabīb Allāh, Son of the Water Carrier, at Arghandah—this taking place during (Ḥabīb Allāh's) first assault [on Kabul] and the twelve days of fighting—and they stole from him 10,000 rupees belonging to the government which he had with him, along with his personal belongings, clothing, and furniture. On the advice of /96/ Sardār Muḥammad ʿUs̱mān Khān, the ḥażrat known as Shayr Āqā [Mujaddidī], and his brother [Gul Āqā] and also at the urging of a number of foreigners who had a personal interest, (Son of the Water Carrier) then dispatched ʿAbd al-ʿAzīz Khān to Paris to persuade Muḥammad Nādir Khān and his brothers—Shāh Walī Khān and Muḥammad Hāshim Khān—to return to Afghanistan. Muḥammad Nādir Khān's first cousin—Aḥmad Shāh Khān—was sent along with ʿAbd al-ʿAzīz. They departed on an English airplane. After they

[98] For Sulṭān Aḥmad Khān Shayrzāʾī, brother-in-law of Fayż Muḥammad Khān Zikriyā, the minister of education, see Adamec *Who's Who*, p. 248 ("Sultan Ahmad Sherzoy") and idem, *A Biographical Dictionary*, p. 177 ("Shirzoi, Sultan Ahmad").

left and also after Muḥammad Nādir Khān arrived in Bombay, Son of the Water Carrier paid his brother—Shāh Maḥmūd Khān—1,000 pounds sterling for travel expenses and ordered him to go to Muḥammad Nādir Khān and return to Kabul with him.

At that time, rumors spread that Muḥammad Nādir Khān had come to Lāhawr (Lahore) and then Peshawar from whence he had gone to Khūst in the Southern Province, Jalālābād in the Eastern Province, Qandahar, returned to the Southern Province (Khūst), and then gone back to Jalālābād. In Jalālābād he was assembling the tribes of both provinces to rout Son of the Water Carrier and the Kūhistānīs. Such stories, which were making the rounds day and night, gave rise to universal excitement. Since Son of the Water Carrier did not know[xix] that Muḥammad Nādir Khān and his brothers had reached Afghan soil, he summoned a son of [the martyred] Amīr Ḥabīb Allāh Khān, Asad Allāh Khān,[99] whose mother was Muḥammad Nādir Khān's sister, to get reliable information from him about Muḥammad Nādir Khān's arrival. But the fellow replied that he knew nothing.

At this time, Muḥammad Nādir Khān and his brother Muḥammad Hāshim Khān, having arrived in Jalālābād and joined forces with ʿAlī Aḥmad Khān, sent Son of the Water Carrier a letter [in Muḥammad Nādir's name] at the end of Ramażān which said,

> I do not doubt your courage and manliness and I express my admiration that you have succeeded in driving Amīr Amān Allāh Khān from Kabul and occupying [the throne] yourself. What concerns me is that, prompted by Afghan honor, /97/ I have arrived on this soil to put out the flames of rebellion. I have never entertained the thought of occupying the throne or any other high post. In fact, I despise such ambitions. Also, I refused the position of prime minister. Because of the youth, pride, and inexperience of the
> 33 above-mentioned Amīr [Amān Allāh Khān] and his haste | to carry out government policies based only on contradictory pronouncements related to matters of politics, defense, and protection without the most basic support, which led only to ill consequences, thoughtful people have been put in a very difficult position. As a consequence, I refused to be involved and settled in Paris. I had no wish to live in Afghanistan with its savage and ignorant people because living in this country brings only loss in this world and the next. Therefore I intended to leave and settle in another country. As for now, victorious brother, wishing only good things for you in this world and the next, I advise you to put an end to the bloodshed among Muslims and the destruction of Afghanistan because the government and the people have

[99] On Asad Allāh Khān see Adamec, *Who's Who*, pp. 122–23 ("Asadullah Khān, Sardar, Muhammadzai").

suffered a great deal and all the reserves and wealth of the country have been plundered. It is time to cease and desist and permit no further destruction of our country, government, and people, a destruction which has thrust Afghanistan back one hundred years, taken away its strength and its might and given rise to destitution and misery. We will not allow this sedition [to continue] and we will see to it that the holy principles of Sharīʿah are not further violated. God forbid that these disturbances should develop into war between the people of the East and the West, for if it does the country will turn into a battlefield of foreigners and the people of the Northern provinces, our brother and all the tribes and peoples of Afghanistan will be annihilated. [Those left alive] will have a miserable existence and will be doomed to perish. Repentance will be of no avail. They will only say, 'Would that I were dust.'[100] /98/ They will suffer deprivation and will despair of this world and the next. Taking into consideration the former losses, the illustrious Afghan tribes—Sarban, Ghurghusht, Bītan, Ghilzāʾī, Karrānī[101] and others, whose numbers total several hundred thousand courageous fighters—will not leave the reins of government to our brother. We therefore propose that he leave the throne to someone who enjoys influence among (the Afghan tribes). If our brother harbors in his heart a love for position and rank and asks for the rank of a *raʾīs* I give my guarantee that he shall have it and I will cause him no harm and will only help him achieve success.

Son of the Water Carrier, having earlier spent his life wandering the mountains and deserts, enduring hardship and suffering, and having had to quench his thirst and appetite with water and a bit of bread, and having now achieved the amirid throne, rest, relaxation, and fine food, and seeing himself as sovereign and master, preferred death to the life he had
34 led before. So in reply, he let it be known, "Until I am killed, | I will not leave this throne which I took with my own sword and which I now hold in my own strong hands."

Son of the Water Carrier's Reply [*Prepared*] *with the Advice of Muḥammad ʿUs̱mān Khān and the* [*Mujaddidī*] *Ḥażrats*

After receiving Muḥammad Nādir Khān' letter, Son of the Water Carrier summoned a number of people unhappy about the civil war and the bloodshed and who were calling for an end to the uprising. At first he had them write Muḥammad Nādir Khān [the following]:

After the arrival in Kabul of all your good advice and suggestions concerning the administration of the government, if that advice is sound and truly

[100] Qurʾān 78:40 "And the infidel will say [on the Day of Judgment], 'Woe is me. Would that I were dust.'"

[101] On these foundational tribal formations see the *Nizhādnāmah* in this volume.

> conscientious /99/ and corresponds to all the norms of the Sharīʿah and the will of the All High, it will be carried out and I will abandon this speculative business—administering the country.

Sardār Muḥammad ʿUs̱mān Khān and the two [Mujaddidī] ḥażrats who had ignited the flames of revolution as well as the venal and corrupt ministers and high-ranking officials and bureaucrats said something that the writer of these lines does not remember exactly but in the end they managed to remove Son of the Water Carrier from the path of expediency and convince him to hold to the barrenness of rejecting the idea of relinquishing the amirate. They summoned relatives of Muḥammad Nādir Khān and forced them to write him a letter which said,

> We, so-and-so, men and women, have been enjoying full health and peace of mind thanks to Amīr Ḥabīb Allāh Khān's kindness and fortunately we are living our lives in complete happiness. If you refuse the honor of being received by him then we will be threatened with destruction.

Son of the Water Carrier entrusted this letter to the two ḥażrats and told them to deliver it to Muḥammad Nādir Khān. He also instructed them to summon the people living along the route that they would take to render obedience to the amir and to propagandize against Muḥammad Nādir Khān. In addition to the three lakhs of rupees that they had deposited in the treasury of their greed for performing such tasks, they received an additional sum from Son of the Water Carrier and left. However, in view of the uprising of the people of Lahūgard, the blockading of the road against Son of the Water Carrier's forces and the outbreak of fighting, they were forced to postpone their trip.

After this letter had been written, an inventory of the possessions and belongings in the home of Muḥammad Nādir Khān was compiled on Thursday, the night of 2 Shawwāl/14 March. They then locked up his house and sealed it with sealing wax. The amir ordered that /100/ if he did not come voluntarily, they would confiscate all of his property and disgrace his family and his wife, the wife of his brother, Shāh Walī Khān, and the wife of ʿAlī Aḥmad Khān (Lūynāb), all sisters of Amīr Amān Allāh Khān and the daughters of Her Highness [ʿUlyā Ḥażrat Sarwar Sulṭān] [now] languishing in the house of a ḥażrat[102] who was renowned for his lechery.

---

[102] It is not clear which ḥażrat is meant here.

[35]

Son of the Water Carrier Sends Part of His Army to Lahūgard in Trucks

35 | On 4 Shawwāl/16 March, Son of the Water Carrier sent 129 of his bandits in seven lorries on a reconnaissance mission to Lahūgard. There the population, led by a Lahūgardī, Mīrzā Nawrūz—the manager of the building project of Dār al-Amān[103]—and Muḥammad Ṭāhir Khān, a cousin of Muḥammad Ayyūb Khān, minister of court under Amīr Amān Allāh Khān, had risen against Son of the Water Carrier, begun fighting and shedding blood, were stopping the supply of provisions to Kabul, and had blockaded the road. At Tangī Aghūjān, a narrow defile situated between Khūshī, Kulangār, and Shikār Qalʿah, they were fired on by Lahūgardīs, who had taken up positions on the two nearby hills. They drove the bandits, who suffered many casualties, back to the [military] park at Rīshkhūr, which is on the southern outskirts of Kabul. The dead and wounded were left in the trucks and not taken into Kabul lest people find out what had happened. But rumors began to spread that either that day or the next the Lahūgardīs would rise against Son of the Water Carrier and attack Kabul. The Kābulīs, driven to desperation by the violence and ignorance of the savage Kūhistānīs and Kūh Dāmanīs, waited impatiently for the attack and prayed to God to grant (the Lahūgardīs) victory.

However, /**101**/ the Lahūgardīs and the men of Wardak who had agreed together to attack Kabul via the road through Maydān, Tangī-yi Laʿl Andar, Chār Āsyā, Mūsāʾī and Bīnī Ḥiṣār, to engage Son of the Water Carrier in battle from two directions and so defeat him, like Ẕāt al-Naḥīyyīn,[104] delayed the assault on Kabul because the people of Ghaznīn, the Hazārahs, and residents of the Southern Province had not arrived. Taking advantage of this delay, Son of the Water Carrier augmented the defensive and offensive strength of his army and sent [the reinforcements] out to strengthen the forces on the two routes. He ordered a contingent with artillery sent on the road to Maydān to reinforce strategic spots between Qalʿah-i Māhtāb Bāgh and Qalʿah-i Durrānī including Qalʿah-i Qāżī, Arghandah, Maydān, and Qalʿah-i Durrānī. He reinforced Chār Āsyā and Mūsāʾī on the road to

103 On this new city planned by Amīr Amān Allāh Khān, see Schinasi, *Kabul: A History*, pp. 142–50.

104 Fayż Muḥammad is referring to the story of a pre-Islamic Arabian woman, Ẕāt al-Naḥīyyīn, daughter of Tīm Allāh Tha'labah, who sold oil for a living. One day a man named Khawwāt ibn Jubayr al-Anṣārī came to buy oil from her and found her all alone whereupon he was overcome by lust. He opened one oil sack as if to check it and had her hold it open with her hand. He then opened another sack and had her hold it. Then with both her hands engaged Khawwāt undertook to fulfill his desire.

Lahūgard with a number of tribal troops. Every day there is fighting in the direction of Maydān and Wardak but no one knows who's prevailing.

Son of the Water Carrier's Order to Disarm the People of Kabul

Frightened by rumors of an impending attack on Kabul by people from Khūst, Wardak, Ghaznīn and Lahūgard, and considering the barbaric behavior of his men towards the people of Kabul and its environs within a radius of six kuruhs, and by rumors of participation in the assault by people from Chahārdihī and Kabul itself, Son of the Water Carrier grew
36 worried | and on Tuesday 4 Shawwāl/16 March summoned the heads of the city quarters (*kalāntar*s), other leading figures, and elders to the Astūr (Stor) Palace, where the ministry of foreign affairs is now located. After repudiating the baseless rumors, he began to lavish praise on the whole populace and especially the people of Kabul for their goodwill and conscientiousness. In conclusion he revealed his real intention—disarming the people of Kabul. He said,

> If anyone has government-issue rifles with cartridges at home or just ammunition, he should hand them over to government officials without fear /**102**/ of being questioned about the rifle, which might have been stolen. People should not feel that if they hand over a rifle they will then be asked to hand over cartridges as well nor that if they hand over cartridges a rifle will be demanded and they will then be punished. I will not investigate cases of stolen or lost rifles and cartridges and will pardon people in such instances. Anyone who hands over their personal weapons will be compensated for their value in cash. This order will remain in effect for the next twenty days. At the end of that time, anyone who still has a rifle, informants report the fact, and a weapon is found in his house, he will be subject to the confiscation of all his property and personal belongings, severe punishment, and a fine of 500 rupees.

The People of Tagāb Begin Armed Resistance

The brother of Field Marshal Amīr Muḥammad Khān,[105] Pīr Muḥammad Khān,[106] the first cousin of the mother of Muʿīn al-Salṭanah[107] ʿInāyat Allāh Khān, who was the eldest son of [the martyred amir] Ḥabīb Allāh Khān,

---

105 On Amīr Muḥammad Khān Ṣāfī from Tagāb, see Adamec, *Who's Who*, p. 121.

106 Pīr Muḥammad Khān was the brother of Amīr Muḥammad Khān Ṣāfī and is mentioned in his brother's biographical entry, ibid.

107 The mother of Prince ʿInāyat Allāh Khān, ʿUlyā Jāh, "Badr al-Ḥaram" (Full Moon of the Harem) whose name was Shajāʿat was a Ṣāfī from Tagāb and the niece of Amīr Muḥammad Khān. See ibid., p. 258.

harbored a longstanding hatred for his nephew, Ghulām Muḥammad Khān,[108] whom Son of the Water Carrier had appointed governor of Tagāb. So he incited the residents of Lamqān against Son of the Water Carrier. His deputy had taken a force of one thousand infantrymen and two cannons and was now in Sarūbī—the headquarters of Son of the Water Carrier and his family during his bandit days—with the object of defending Kabul from attack by the people of Lamqān and other regions. But he now abandoned his obedience and called on the people of Tagāb to first attack Sarūbī and Gūgāmandah,[109] **/103/** rout this thousand-man force, and then attack Jabal al-Sirāj and Kūhistān. Because the main forces of Son of the Water Carrier, made up of Kūhistānīs and Kūh Dāmanīs, were in Kabul and its environs, there was a real chance of achieving victory.

The Tagābīs launched a surprise attack on Sarūbī and Gūgāmandah, as he had urged them to do. The soldiers there were taken completely by surprise and the Tagābīs gained an easy victory, capturing two cannons, small arms, military supplies, and all the soldiers' personal effects. Having scattered part of Son of the Water Carrier's army, they then returned to Band-i Sawlang. On Sunday, 5 Shawwāl, corresponding to 17 March, they readied themselves for an assault on Jamāl Āghah and attacked on the 6th[xx] defeating Son of the Water Carrier's force, capturing six field
37 pieces and 60,000 rupees. Crossing the Ghūrband River, | they ransacked the homes of some well-to-do people in Rīzah-i Kūhistān and took possession of Jamāl Āghah. They then decided to seize the citadel (Arg) in Jabal al-Sirāj and so brought the market of confrontation to a fever pitch.

Sayyid Ḥusayn and Ḥabīb Allāh's brother, Ḥamīd Allāh, who had recently conferred on themselves a number of lofty positions [and titles] including minister of war and supreme sardār (*sardār-i ʿālī*—for Ḥamīd Allāh) and, by resolution of the Islamic Regulatory Commission, the titles "vice-regent" (*nāʾib al-salṭanah*[110]—for Sayyid Ḥusayn) and "king's assistant" (*muʿīn al-salṭanah*[xxi]—for Ḥamīd Allāh[111]), having busied themselves debauching women and children, now learned about the uprising of the Tagābīs, panicked, and headed out that night with a group of their confederates by car to defend against an attack from Tagāb. Traveling as fast as the wind and as quick as scudding clouds, they reached Sih Āb and

[108] Ibid., p. 148.

[109] Sarūbī and Gūgāmandah are adjacent towns on the Kabul-Jalālābād highway thirty miles due east of Kabul.

[110] This title had first been conferred on Sardār Naṣr Allāh Khān by his brother, the late Amīr Ḥabīb Allāh Khān.

[111] This title was first given to ʿInāyat Allāh Khān by his father, the late Amīr Ḥabīb Allāh Khān.

there by telephone requested reinforcements from Kabul. On Tuesday,[xxii] 7 Shawwāl/19 March 1929, Ḥabīb Allāh dispatched two planes to Kūhistān and 3,000 villains from the North who were in Kabul and engaged in ransacking homes, breaking down doors, pulling off and selling palace mirrors, destroying government buildings and [military] parks, burning and defecating on scientific books, and assaulting women, girls, and young boys.

/**104**/ Despite the bombing and the persistence of Son of the Water Carrier's soldiers, success eluded them. The fighting lasted three or four days and was still raging when, on the advice of Sardār Muḥammad ʿUs̱mān Khān and Ḥażrat Shayr Āqā, Son of the Water Carrier sent ʿAbd al-Ghafūr Khān, son of Muḥammad Shāh Tagābī,[112] who had been a member of the National Council during Amān Allāh's reign and now [under Ḥabīb Allāh Kalakānī] is minister of the interior, to Tagāb to conclude a truce and put an end to the uprising. His brother, who had declared for Son of the Water Carrier, was killed during Amān Allāh's [last days]. Son of the Water Carrier gave him thirty [thousand] rupees with which he was supposed to bribe all the mullahs and maliks supporting the uprising and make sure they would stop their clamor. On Wednesday, 8 Shawwāl, [corresponding to] 20 March, (ʿAbd al-Ghafūr Khān) sent his convoy towards Tagāb and himself departed Kabul on the 9th. Towards evening of the 10th[xxiii] (i.e. Wednesday evening) Muʿīn al-Salṭanah Ḥamīd Allāh sent a request to Muḥammad Khān Qarābāghī for gasoline. Qarābāghī was an intimate (*muṣāḥib-i khāṣṣ*) of Ḥabīb Allāh and in charge of the motor pool.

Marginalia: (Qarābāghī) asked for a signed receipt and a purchase order so that he would have it for the day when his accounts were audited. The men Ḥamīd Allāh had sent angrily and violently demanded he provide the gasoline without a receipt. All (Qarābāghī) said was, "these three-days of rule have gone to your heads." In the middle of the night Ḥamīd Allāh reported this to his brother, Ḥabīb Allāh, and he ordered that (Qarābāghī) be killed. They then beat him to death with canes and (Ḥabīb Allāh) ordered his body thrown in the Arg moat where it stayed that night and, on the following day, was removed thanks to the intervention of a mullah. [End of marginal note.]

---

[112] Neither father nor son was included in the British *Who Is Who in Afghānistān* so therefore not in Adamec, *Who's Who*. Muḥammad Shāh Khān Ṣāfī Tagābī, the father, had served as governor of Nijrāb, Tagāb, and Āqchah and was twice the governor of Āqchah under Amīr ʿAbd al-Raḥmān Khān. See Fayż Muḥammad, *The History*, vol. 3, index under "Muḥammad Shāh Khān Tagābī" and vol. 4 index under "Muḥammad Shāh Khān Ṣāfī Tagābī."

[37–38]

Ḥabīb Allāh's Decision to Fight the Wardaks Himself

At the height of the fighting and struggle of the Tagābīs with Sayyid Ḥusayn and his men and his being besieged, people from Maydān, Jalrīz, and Sanglākh who had turned the face of obedience away from Ḥabīb Allāh and instead had come out in support of Amān Allāh Khān, reached an agreement with the people of Wardak about joint operations, attacked Ḥabīb Allāh's forces that had established themselves in Maydān and Qalʿah-i Durrānī, besieged the part that was in Qalʿah-i Durrānī, and defeated the contingent in Maydān, forcing it to escape to Arghandah.
38 The smaller units quartered in Arghandah were also | incapable of resistance and fled towards Qalʿah-i Qāżī, Chahārdihī, and Kūh Dāman.

Due to the routing of his own force and the discontented rumblings among the people of Kabul, who were praying to God to extinguish the star of his good fortune, Ḥabīb Allāh grew apprehensive and so he himself with a group of his most trusted thieves set out [for the battlefield] in five speedy trucks. They drove out of Kabul on Friday at 5:30, the 10th of Shawwāl equivalent to 22 March. At Arghandah he managed to bolster the fighting spirit of his soldiers who had fled from Maydān. They then attacked Amān Allāh Khān's supporters who were at Kūtal-i Shaykh. Ḥabīb Allāh himself as well as the rebels who had driven with him from Kabul took part in the fray. They drove Amān Allāh's backers from Kūtal-i Takht and marched into Maydān.

The battle lasted until the evening of that day. Because Ḥabīb Allāh's soldiers were along this side of the river, not far from a bridge, he himself then went back to Arghandah. He castigated the family and relatives of Sar Buland Khān's son—Muḥammad Akbar Khān—for the fact that he had supported Amān Allāh Khān and refused to give provisions to (Son of the Water Carrier's) soldiers. On the night of 9 Shawwāl, he had ordered the Kabul house (of Muḥammad Akbar Khān) confiscated. They also arrested Muḥammad Akbar himself and Son of the Water Carrier took him back to Kabul where he let it be known that he had marched as far as Shaykhābād, defeated the Wardak, and seized their women. /**106**/

Ḥabīb Allāh Orders an Army to Arghandah and Maydān

On Saturday, 11 Shawwāl equivalent to 23 March, at 8:30, Ḥabīb Allāh ordered 500 of the militiamen of Nijrāb summoned to Kabul. Several days before he had sent them towards Maydān and at this time they were lodged in the fort of Sardār Walī Muḥammad Khān, a son of Amīr Dūst Muḥammad Khān. This fort is now known as Qalʿah-i Māhtāb Bāgh. The late Amīr Ḥabīb Allāh Khān had given it the new name, having built a royal palace and laid out a garden there. [Ḥabīb Allāh] decided to recall the Nijrāb militiamen because the fighting with the Tagābīs had now gone on for some time and he was worried that the militiamen might go over to them because they were all Afghan. He disarmed them and sent them back to Kabul.

Marginalia: Sayyid ʿAbd al-Razzāq, who was arrested, as noted above, for hoisting a flag in support of Amān Allāh Khān, was freed by order of the vice-regent, Sayyid Ḥusayn, because he was a sayyid. However, he and 400 residents of Kabul then swore an oath of loyalty to Amān Allāh Khān and besides signing a written text of the oath, each one of them very clearly impressed their thumbprints on it in black ink. For this Son of the Water Carrier ordered him hanged at the Chawk along with Muḥammad ʿĪsā Khān, son of Muḥammad Isḥāq Khān Pūpalzāʾī, who was an inspector (*nāẓir*) under the high governor, ʿAlī Aḥmad [Lūynāb], and had instigated the people of Lahūgard to oppose Ḥabīb Allāh Khān and to support ʿAlī Aḥmad. Today it was ordered that their bodies remain hanging for three days. [End of marginal note.]

This same day, in the afternoon, rumors began to circulate that the people of Durnāmah, Sanjan[xxiv] and Bulāghayn,[113] had attacked the Tagābīs, defeated them, and occupied their positions. They then returned the weapons to the Nijrābīs of whom they considered themselves a part. On Sunday, 12 Shawwāl, at eight in the evening he ordered some Kūh Dāmanīs, Kūhistānīs, and residents of the villages of Dih-i Nūr, Maydān and Arghandah to cover /107/ the army rear which was then at Qalʿah-i Durrānī and Pul-i Maydān and so to prevent those who had been defeated to march towards Chahārdihī and Kūh Dāman. The order was given that they should arrest (those who had suffered defeat) and hold them there
39 or kill them but under no circumstances were they to let them get | to

[113] Bulāghayn and Durnāmah are both mentioned in Ludwig W. Adamec, *Historical and Political Gazetteer of Afghanistan*, 6 vols., Graz, Austria: Akademische Druck-u. Verlagsanstalt, 1972–85 [henceforth Adamec, *Gazetteer*], vol. 6, pp. 112 and 166 respectively. Both are also shown on Ayazi 1:1,500,000 map of Afghanistan (Ayazi Publishing, 2001) although their given position on the road east northeast out of Maḥmūd Rāqī does not seem correct. Cf. Generalnyi Shtab (General Staff) map "Chārīkār" I-42-X at 1:200,000 scale which shows no road between Maḥmūd Rāqī and Durnāmah. Although neither the *Gazetteer* nor the Ayazi map provide the location of Sanjan (according to ms. p. 39, line 18) and S-kh-n according to the print edition (p. 106, line 19), the Soviet army map does show a "Sanjan" in a likely place some twelve kilometers due east of Jabal al-Sirāj and fifteen kilometers north-northwest of Durnāmah.

Chahārdihī and Kūh Dāman and there spread fear among the people of those regions as well as among the soldiers in Kabul.

With reinforcements, Field Marshal Purdil Khān, who had become minister of war, was now certain of victory and on Sunday 12 Shawwāl, corresponding to 24 March, he subjected several forts in Maydān to artillery shelling and reduced and destroyed them and then plundered the inhabitants of the forts. As a consequence of these monstrous, barbaric, and heathen acts, the people of Maydān, Arghandah, and Sanglākh were even more committed to fighting Ḥabīb Allāh. They also drew to their cause the Tajiks living in Takānah and Jalrīz.

So, the fighting goes on every day ...

But despite the capture of Maydān, Ḥabīb Allāh's army is managing to advance neither towards Wardak nor Ghaznīn, for the Wardaks are holding fast.

Confiscation of Muḥammad Sarwar Khān Bābā's (*Property*)

On Sunday, 12 Shawwāl/24 March, Ḥabīb Allāh Khān with Muʿīn al-Salṭanah Ḥamīd Allāh Khān and the high governor, Malik Muḥsin, set off for the home of the Īshīk-āqāsī Muḥammad Sarwar Khān Bābā, whom (Ḥabīb Allāh) had already summoned during Ramażān and had wanted to arrest. But because he was seriously ill and it was expected that he would soon die he was not arrested.[xxv] Having given Ḥabīb Allāh Khān's agents 3,000 rupees and twenty-five pounds sterling and having told them that he did not have another rupee to his name, he then went home and two or three days later, he died. [Entering his home now], they broke the locks on his chests, but aside from 1,500 rupees and a few rugs and dishes, they found nothing else. (Ḥabīb Allāh) and his brother threatened and frightened Muḥammad Sarwar Khān's steward, Bī Khudā,[114] and his son, Muḥammad /108/ Ibrāhīm Khān, who is the high governor of Harāt. Having terrified him (Muḥammad Ibrāhīm Khān), (Ḥabīb Allāh Khān) finally took something from him and stopped harassing him. (Ḥabīb Allāh) found nothing worth mentioning of his treasure and buried wealth which

114 This is very strange syntax. The wording is: *Muḥammad Sarwar Khān bī khudā nāẓir-i ū*. The "*bī-khudā* may well be an epithet for Muḥammad Sarwar Khān, i.e. "the godless Muḥammad Sarwar Khān." Bī Khudā seems an unlikely name for anyone. It is possible that this phrase is simply a mistake on Fayż Muḥammad's part and there are missing words or some words have been inadvertently included. If Fayż Muḥammad had not made it clear that Muḥammad Sarwar Khān was dead before Ḥabīb Allāh came to the house one might have easily read the phrase by supplying a missing conjunction, "the godless Muḥammad Sarwar Khān and his steward ..."

is reckoned in lakhs, no crores, of rupees and gold. What happened to him and his son, about whom there is a rumor abroad in Harāt that he was killed, became an example of the following line of poetry:

> You know what happened to that ass of a person /
> He was punished and someone else took the gold.

He (Ḥabīb Allāh) gave Muḥammad Sarwar Khān's house to Khwājah Bābū Jān Khān.

On Monday, 13 Shawwāl, corresponding to 25 March, Ḥabīb Allāh Khān and his brother, Muʿīn al-Salṭanah Ḥamīd Allāh, on the pretext of going to Istālif on a pleasure outing, headed for Sih Āb in Kūh Dāman to visit Sayyid Ḥusayn who, judging by rumors among the common folk, had been seriously wounded during the fighting with the Tagābīs. They went to Sih Āb, Kūh Dāman, and visited him after which they set off for Istālif. On Tuesday evening, 14 Shawwāl, they returned (to Kabul) and sent Sayyid Ḥusayn's family who were living in the home of Muḥammad Yaʿqūb Khān,[115] Amān Allāh Khān's minister of court, to Sayyid Ḥusayn in Sih Āb. On that same Tuesday, 14 Shawwāl equivalent to 26 March, two Tagābīs were brought to the Chawk. One of them was an old man, the other was a youth. After an announcement that these two were the ringleaders of the Tagābī uprising, they were hanged and next to them a sign was posted which read, "This fate awaits anyone who dares rebel against the government."

Marginalia: They arrested, brought from Arghandah to Kabul, and imprisoned four relatives of Muḥammad Akbar Khān, son of Sar Buland Khān, who had decided to ally himself with Amān Allāh Khān, and whose house and belongings and that of his brother had been confiscated.[116] [End of marginal note.]

Also on this day, according to a radio bulletin that was broadcast worldwide, Amān Allāh Khān left Qandahar for Kabul with a tribal force made
40 up of Durrānīs, Hūtakīs, Tūkhīs, Ghilzāʾīs, and Hazārahs. |

From Lahūgard, the 500 men whom Ḥabīb Allāh Khān had forcibly impressed into service along with a group of /**109**/ his own partisans

[115] This Muḥammad Yaʿqūb Khān is the same as "Yaʿqūb Khān (Muhmand) in Adamec *Who's Who*, p. 266 and in "Household of Amīr Amanullah Khān. Early Period" where he is listed as minister of court from 1921 to 1927 (ibid., p. 287).

[116] Adamec, *Who's Who*, provides no entry for Muḥammad Akbar Khān but does have one for Sar Buland Khān (ibid., p. 224). The brother, according to Adamec, was Muḥammad Ḥasan Khān.

who had [voluntarily] joined him in brigandage and raiding arrived in Chār Āsyā with four guns [called] "mountain machine guns" and two eight-pound siege weapons (literally, "fort-smashing and rank-shattering artillery") to intimidate the people of Lahūgard and force them to render obedience. Their leader was Pīnī Beg Khān, one of the Chitrārī court pages.[117] During the late Amīr Ḥabīb Allāh Khān's reign he had risen to the rank of colonel but under Amān Allāh he lost rank and position, and with it esteem and respect, for which he harbored great resentment against the government. But since the people of Lahūgard had strengthened their sangars, the force [of Pīnī Beg] did not find it in themselves to push forward in order to achieve their objectives.

Due to the rumor that Muḥammad Nādir Khān had arrived in Charkh district with a tribal force from the Southern Province along with forces which were permanently stationed in that region, at (Pīnī Beg's) command, the ambushers and highwaymen rose and left their defensive positions and abandoned the fight. They moved from Chār Āsyā to Muḥammad Āqā (i.e. Āghah) and from there on the 14th of Shawwāl set off for Kulangār. The Lahūgardīs came out of their sangars, commenced to fight them and stopped them from advancing. Killing and wounding followed and small skirmishes still take place daily and the final outcome remains to be determined.

On the same day, 14 Shawwāl, a battle (also) started in Maydān. The forces of Ḥabīb Allāh Khān were defeated and fled as far as Arghandah and Qalʿah [-i Durrānī?] and nowhere could they find a safe haven. On the 15th of Shawwāl equivalent to 27 March, Ḥabīb Allāh Khān ordered his brother, Ḥamīd Allāh Khān, to leave Kabul for Maydān at the head of a force comprised of Panjshayrīs and a detachment of the royal guard, reinforced with fourteen siege guns. An order was given for the soldiers not to use their rifles but only the siege guns which they were supposed to emplace on the mountaintops with the aid of elephants and then use to bombard the forts: they then were to sack the forts and take their men prisoner. **/110/** At Kūtal-i Takht, they scattered the defenders with artillery fire and marched into Maydān. They then destroyed several forts, taking twenty-five men prisoner whom they delivered that night to Kabul.

The same day, some Shinwārī and Khūgyānī men who instigated the looting and destruction of government buildings in Jalālābād and vio-

---

117 Elsewhere he is called Panīn Beg. (See Adamec, *Who's Who*, p. 214.) Although Fayż Muḥammad clearly wrote Pīnī Beg, Shkirando translated it as "Panin." (See e.g., Faiz Mukhammad, *Kniga upominanii* p. 70, line 2.)

lated their firm agreements, which aroused the ire of all brave Afghan and especially the tribes of the Eastern Province, now fearing that [these tribes] would attack and murder them, on the pretext of delivering oaths of obedience to Amīr Ḥabīb Allāh Khān came to Kabul seeking refuge. After their arrival, forty proclamations with one message were sent in the
41 names of the elders of Jalālābād, who had assembled for a jirgah | with the brother of Muḥammad Nādir Khān—Muḥammad Hāshim Khān—to discuss the problem of overthrowing Ḥabīb Allāh Khān. These proclamations declared the necessity of ending the fighting and rendering obedience [to Son of the Water Carrier].

The Surprise Night Attack by Amān Allāh Khān's Supporters on the Force at Maydān

On Thursday, 16 Shawwāl, corresponding to 8 Ḥamal and 28 March, Jadrān, Wazīrī and Wardak braves who occupied positions in the hills overlooking Maydān, Qalʿah-i Durrānī, and the plain of Dasht-i Tūp and on which hills machine guns were also emplaced, attacked Ḥabīb Allāh Khān's army, killed and wounded a thousand men, captured their artillery and weapons, and carried them off to the hills. Before sunrise the remaining (fighters), who had survived the sword's edge and rifle bullets, sent to Kabul twenty-eight men—residents of Laʿl Andar and Maydān—who were neutral but were treading the path of obedience to Ḥabīb Allāh Khān and during the battle on 15 Shawwāl had been taken prisoner. /111/ [They were sent] escorted by a small number of brawny sepoys. At noon on the 16th, their faces smeared with mud and slime, they were led through the bazaars to the accompaniment of music played by the military band. This sowed fear and confusion in the hearts of the people who, depressed and driven to despair by the violence of the Kūhistānīs and Kūh Dāmanīs, had been impatiently awaiting the return of Amān Allāh Khān. (The supporters of Ḥabīb Allāh Khān) spread the rumor that they had defeated the Wardak and taken these men prisoner, "whom you see before you."

Also on this day and in the evening of Friday, 17 Shawwāl, corresponding to 9 Ḥamal and 29 March, foot and mounted soldiers set off to fight and assist the army that had been defeated by the night attack at Maydān. They continued the fight and spread a rumor that Amān Allāh Khān had taken to his heels from Qandahar, Muḥammad Nādir Khān had fled Khūst and Muḥammad Hāshim Khān, denied the support of the Afghan tribes, had also run away in despair.

[41–42]

The Outcome of the Jirgah and Assembly (Kangash) *of the People of the Eastern Province*

When the jirgah met, all the leaders and elders of the tribes of the Eastern Province spoke out against the regime of Amān Allāh Khān. As evidence that they did not recognize his authority, they told Muḥammad Hāshim Khān the following:

> On the day Amīr Ḥabīb Allāh Khān was killed, all the people of the Eastern Province, whether civilians or the military, elders of the tribes, sardārs and princes, proposed that the Nā'ib al-Salṭanah, Naṣr Allāh Khān, who knew the Qur'ān by heart and was a true Muslim, succeed to the throne and they swore oaths of allegiance to him.[118] However, Amān Allāh Khān, who had no right at all to the throne, usurped power. [Naṣr Allāh Khān] being a person of belief, decided not to be the cause of bloodshed and civil war and passed the reins of government [to Amān Allāh Khān]. And that one, by
> 42 cunning, | summoned him to Kabul and then did not allow him to leave for India or any other country. [Naṣr Allāh Khān] felt the most sincere feelings /112/ towards Amān Allāh Khān and at the time of the internecine discord declared for him and for Her Highness—his [Amān Allāh's] mother—and was like a father to him. Continuing to harbor feelings of family loyalty, Naṣr Allāh freed them from the heavy-handedness of Amīr Ḥabīb Allāh Khān and considered Amān Allāh a friend and a son. Therefore, completely unsuspecting, he came to Kabul in an easy frame of mind, escorted by bodyguards and reflected to himself, 'I have always thought well of Amān Allāh. His choosing his own servants as bodyguards for me is only an expression of his high regard and there is no cause at all for harm to come to me. As soon as I get to Kabul, pleasant and happy days will begin for me.' However, contrary to expectations, Amān Allāh Khān came to Butkhāk and ordered his arrest. A year later, on a Friday night, the first of Ramażān, Amān Allāh ordered him put to death by strangulation. After this he began to adopt policies which went directly counter to Muslim traditions. He changed the day of rest from Friday, abolished the veil, and introduced a number of other laws which were not in keeping with the Sharī'ah and offended the ulema. Imitating the Turks, who have abandoned the religion, he forced people to study the Latin alphabet and forsake the Arabic and Persian scripts in which Qur'ānic commentaries, the Qur'ān itself, and religious books and treatises are all written. And we should recognize a godless person like this who as amīr comes out against the fundamental principles of Islam?

In response to this, Muḥammad Hāshim Khān mentioned (Amān Allāh's) repentance as a legal (*shar'ī*) reason [for recognizing him] but they did

---

[118] For a detailed account of the assassination and the days following it in which Sardār Naṣr Allāh Khān and his nephew, Sardār Amān Allāh Khān, were both declared amirs, the former in Jalālābād and the latter in Kabul, see Fayż Muḥammad, *The History*, vol. 4, pp. 1393–1467.

not accept this because [they said] he had never once spoken the truth, and his "repentance" was all merely a trick to deceive believing Muslims, and so those present refused to accept his amirate.[xxvi] Then Muḥammad Hāshim Khān began to speak of the Muʿīn al-Salṭanah, ʿInāyat Allāh Khān, referring to his piety and good morals. However, those attending the jirgah, also rejected his candidacy for the throne, recalling his and Īshīk-āqāsī ʿAbd al-Ḥabīb's bad behavior[119] when ʿInāyat Allāh was prince. Then they recalled the time of ʿAbd al-Raḥmān Khān and spoke of the minarets he built using the skulls of people **/113/** and his despotic rule which [they said] did not conform to the principles of the Sharīʿah. Eventually, they concluded that no member of this family had the right to be amir and they resolved to get rid of the godless, bloodshedding, debauched ignoramus Ḥabīb Allāh Khān and then with the agreement of the representatives of all the residents of Afghanistan to unanimously raise to the amirate a person who was recognized for religiosity, known to be sincere and pure of heart, characterized by commendable virtues, and possessing good, praiseworthy qualities so that there would be tranquility and prosperity for the nation and a rebuilding of the kingdom in accordance with the clear ordinance of the Ḥażrat, the Final Seal, life would be secure, and the market of the "commands and prohibitions" of the Lord of Glory, [Prophet Muḥammad] would thrive. Having ended the discussion at this point, they made a pact and covenant, agreeing to choose a number of
43 men to send as a delegation to Ḥabīb Allāh Khān. | Through wise advice, counsel based on the Sharīʿah, and guidance based on Islamic ordinances, this delegation was to turn him from fighting, revolution, and the shedding of the blood of his religious and sectarian [i.e., Hanafi] brethren through good words and excellent guiding proofs and [to convince him] to give up the amirate and the killing and plundering of Muslims and their wealth and belongings so that to the extent that he had weakened the power of Islamic society (*quwwah-i jāmiʿah-i Islām*), scattered and dispersed it, driven everyone into conflict and bloodshed [they would persuade him] that he had done enough plundering of wealth and dishonoring the people and families of the worshippers of God and those who followed the path of righteousness and enough of destroying the fifty-years' worth of the treasure [accumulated by] the government and the nation and so

---

119 For ʿAbd al-Ḥabīb, who was exiled to India then returned and was named chamberlain and chief of staff to Prince ʿInāyat Allāh Khān, the reference to "bad behavior" concerns his involvement in the constitutionalist movement in 1909 (for which see Ḥabībī, *Junbish*, pp. 63–64).

[43]

should no longer be the provoker of profane acts and shameful doings. The delegation should reassure [Ḥabīb Allāh], Sayyid Ḥusayn, and their leading supporters and associates that they would receive high positions and everything necessary for a comfortable life. If they should agree to this, then that is what was desired. If not, they should prepare to fight with all the proud and valiant Afghan tribes—the Durrānī, Ghilzāʾī, and others—until whomever God befriends, /**114**/ his star will be in the ascendant and may the one who is in the wrong be wiped from the face of the earth.

Due to the rumor that this delegation had set out on the road to Kabul, Ḥabīb Allāh Khān who, as was mentioned above, had sent some sweets to them [as a welcoming gesture], when he learned of their arrival in Kabul, on Saturday eve, the 18th of Shawwāl,[xxvii] corresponding to the tenth of Ḥamal and 30 March, he ordered Ḥamīd Allāh Khān, Muʿīn al-Salṭanah, along with four of his closest confidants (*khāṣṣān-i muṭbatinah*)[120] and eighty-four men armed with rifles to drive out in seven Dodge (?) lorries (or seven lorries and a Dodge) (*haft mūtar-i lārī wa dāj*)[121] and welcome them.

The Events of 18[xxviii] Shawwāl [30 March 1929]

At dawn, Wazīrī, Jadrānī, Wardak, and Maydāni braves as well as other well-wishers of Amān Allāh Khān, having attacked Ḥabīb Allāh Khān's army at Maydān and Qalʿah-i Durrānī, drove some detachments into Qalʿah-i ʿAbd al-Ghanī Khān "Beg Samandī" and besieged them and defeated others and drove them off, up into the mountains of Kūh-i Qargh while most of the defeated fled to Arghandah and Qalʿah-i Qāżī. Ḥabīb Allāh Khān dispatched fresh reinforcements from Kabul to help those who had suffered defeat and to drive off the victors. Fighting raged until

120 This is the spelling that appears in both the ms. (p. 43, line 10) and the print edition (p. 114, line 4). The word is not found in Dihkhudā, *Lughatnāmah* and one wonders whether it wasn't a simple transposition of the letters of 'b' and 'ṭ' (i.e. *mubṭinah* or *mutabaṭṭinah* meaning to have insight, to get to the heart of the matter). In a footnote the editor of the print edition, ʿAlī Amīrī, defines the word as "*shikam-parast wa pur-khūr*" (gluttonous). This implies he either misread it or believed it was a case of transposed letters and saw the "b-ṭ-n" as signifying belly and thus the "shikam-parast wa pur-khūr." The Russian translator, working from the manuscript, simply translated the phrase "close individuals" preferring not to tackle the adjective.

121 The last word of the Persian phrase *haft mūtar-i lārī wa dāj* is unclear. In the context, only the word "Dodge" makes any sense to us and further on it is clearly used to identify some vehicles (see below p. 188). Dodge made trucks (lorries) at the time although whether they were being sold in India to the Afghan government remains to be seen. The reference may have been to a Dodge vehicle other than a truck and to lorries of some other make.

evening. By telephone [Ḥabīb Allāh Khān] had summoned Sayyid Ḥusayn to Kabul to confer and consult with him on an answer to the "Eastern" calls [for him to stop fighting and step down]. He entered Kabul on this day (18 Shawwāl). A welcoming party was assigned to go out to Manār-i Shahrārā[122] and when he entered the city guns were fired as if it were a wedding. Rumor spread that the people of Tagāb had rendered their obedience and taken an oath of loyalty and (the Saqqawīs) industriously circulated the rumor that there had been a victory. So it is not known what will happen on Sunday, the 19th of Shawwāl, or on the eve of the 20th [i.e., tomorrow]; who knows what the Mother of Time will give birth to? And the enemy as well as the friend, what are their plans?

/115/ *The Events of Sunday, 19 Shawwāl [31 March]*

Today an order was issued to the minister of court, Shayr Jān Khān, son of Khwājah Jān, who, like his father and grandfather before him had grown up under royal auspices as eater of the salt and partaker of the food from the table of sovereignty. He was instructed to appoint a valet
44 (*pīshkhidmat*), a tea boy, and a cook to attend the delegation | that had come from the Afghan of the Eastern Province to negotiate a truce. At two in the afternoon, they brought Karīm Khān, the leader of the Wardaks living in Tangī, to Kabul in a motorcar escorted by forty-two guards in three vehicles who were shouting "Four Friends" and making a great noise.

Karīm Khān had most recently led his tribe in cooperation with ʿAbd Allāh Khān, the brother of ʿAbd al-Aḥad Khān and son of Qāżī Ghulām Shaykhābādī; some Wazīrī muhajirs; and a group of the Jadrānī in fighting on the side of Amān Allāh Khān. They had launched a bold attack on the force which Ḥabīb Allāh Khān had sent to Ghaznīn and Qandahar and shed blood [but had been defeated]. Along with Karīm Khān, they also captured a young man who had led an advance party of Karīm Khān's force. Once in the city, they paraded them around the streets and bazaars to spread the word [of their victory]. Former allies of Amān Allāh Khān, who had initially come out against him and supported Ḥabīb Allāh Khān and the mutineers, assisting them in the assault on Kabul, but now, outraged by the behavior of this army of savages who busied themselves with looting, violence and depravity, had turned their backs on (Ḥabīb Allāh) and ardently wished for [the return of] Amān Allāh Khān, denied that

122 Manār-i Shahrārā was the round tower section of the Shahrārā Palace built by Amīr ʿAbd al-Raḥmān Khān in 1899–1900. See Schinasi, *Kabul: A History*, pp. 74–75, Figure 3 and Plate 10. The Shahrārā tower was also called Burj-i Yādgār. (See below, note 156).

Karīm Khān had been arrested and spread the rumor that another person named ʿAbd al-Karīm Khān had been detained.

In the evening, on Karīm Khān's heels, they brought another eight men alleged to be Wardakīs to the Harten Bridge.[123] Having tied their arms together with their turbans, it seems that they were only ordinary travelers whom they had picked up on the road. Shouting "Four Friends" and firing their guns, they brought them into the city. By Ḥabīb Allāh Khān's order, they and Karīm Khān were punished with imprisonment. /**116**/

This day, too, thirteen men of the Mangal tribe who were spies for Muḥammad Nādir Khān arrived in Kabul. Declaring that they had come on behalf of their tribe to express their obedience and deliver an oath of loyalty, they were accorded the honor of an audience [with Ḥabīb Allāh Khān], who presented each of them with a piece of cloth for a turban (*lungī*) or thirteen rupees, which was equivalent to the value of the cloth. Ḥabīb Allāh Khān also showed the Mangals Buddhist idols, which were found at excavations in Jalālābād and Kūhistān and placed in the museum and are [now] in a house. He showed them as evidence of the idol-worshipping and unbelief of Amān Allāh Khān. He accused Amān Allāh Khān of being an infidel in the hope that the Mangals, being ignorant, benighted and barely knowledgeable in religious matters, [although] they consider themselves devout Muslims, would spread the rumor amongst the wild tribes of the border zone of Amān Allāh's unbelief, for which there is no other evidence than this of his irreligion.

Muʿīn al-Salṭanah Ḥamīd Allāh Khān left to welcome the delegation from the Eastern Province on the eve of the 18th of Shawwāl. But disappointed when they did not arrive in Butkhāk he turned back and on the 19th of Shawwāl headed for Maydān to assist the troops under attack there and fought there until evening, spreading the rumor that his force had advanced to Takiyah situated two stages into the midst of Wardak tribal territory although [in reality] the army up to this point had not left Qalʿah-i Durrānī. On the same day, some prisoners were brought in from Tagāb, above and beyond the forty men already mentioned. Ḥabīb Allāh
45 Khān felt it would be politically expedient to release them and did so. |

[123] Named after Walther Harten, a German engineer who spent seven years in Kabul working on Amān Allāh's new capital city, Dār al-Amān. See Adamec, *Afghānistan's Foreign Affairs*, p. 74; and Schinasi, *Kabul: A History*, pp. 143, 145, 147.

The Events of 20 Shawwāl Corresponding to 1 April [*1929*]

Marginalia: In the evening of this day thirty-two ministers, notables, and high functionaries from the time of Amīr Amān Allāh Khān who were determined to deal with the evil intentions of Amīr Ḥabīb Allāh Khān were secretly arrested in order to eliminate the threat of the disturbances they were preparing. They say that due to the rumor of the [imminent] coming of Eastern men with Muḥammad Hāshim Khān, Southern men with Muḥammad Nādir Khān and people from Qandahar with Amān Allāh Khān, the Kūhistānīs have grown frightened and anxious, have consulted amongst themselves and decided to keep the thirty-two detained until such time as it is clear who is going to win and who is going to lose. In case of their own (the Kūhistānīs') side prevailing (these thirty-two) would then be freed depending on the exigencies of the time. In the event they (the Kūhistānīs) are defeated they would take all (the detainees) with them to Kūh Dāman as hostages and through exchanges would obtain for themselves salvation from repression. Also on this evening, (the Kūhistānīs) resolved through consultation to arrest Mīrākhūr Aḥmad ʿAlī, the Hazārah *wakīl*, and other leaders of that tribe who were in Kabul and partisans of Amān Allāh Khān to get them to sign an oath of loyalty to Amīr Ḥabīb Allāh Khān. [End of marginal note.]

Seven Russian planes, which arrived on the previous day to evacuate Russian, German, and Turkish citizens from Kabul, did not leave on Monday, 20 Shawwāl corresponding to 1 April, on the return flight. Word is that they delayed the flight in order to get more precise information about the internal political situation although their pretext /117/ was that the evacuees were not ready to leave.

On the evening of this day, the brother-in-law (wife's brother) of Nā'ib al-Salṭanah Sayyid Ḥusayn sent a letter to ʿAbd al-Wāsiʿ, an elegant and good-looking fellow. He is the son of Zamān al-Dīn Khān, son of Prince Ḥasan Badakhshānī. [ʿAbd al-Wāsiʿ's] father (Zamān al-Dīn Khān) served for a period as advisor to the Ministry of Foreign Affairs during Amān Allāh Khān's reign and then was promoted to governor of the Central (Kabul) Province. In the course of performing his duties as governor, he had gone to the Hazārahjāt to conduct an investigation. At the instigation of the son of Arsalāḥ[xxix] Khān Ghilzā'ī, Amīn Allāh, who was fanatical in his hatred of the Hazārahs, (Zamān al-Din Khān) transported nine Hazārah elders from Bihsūd and Dāy Zangī to Kabul and tried to have them permanently exiled to Qunduz in Qaṭaghan (Tukhāristān.) When the Mangal tribes rose in rebellion, the Hazārahs were pardoned and permitted to return home. Zamān al-Dīn, meanwhile, was named high governor of Harāt and there suddenly passed away. In the letter [of Sayyid Ḥusayn's brother-in-law], he propositioned [ʿAbd al-Wāsiʿ] wanting him for an obedient friend, meaning he wanted him for sodomy. If [ʿAbd al-Wāsiʿ] tried to refuse, he would force him into his bed of love and embracing. ʿAbd al-Wāsiʿ's mother hid him and gave Sayyid Ḥusayn's brother-in-law's letter to Zamān al-Dīn Khān's maternal uncle, Muḥammad Walī Khān, who had been *wakīl* to Amān Allāh Khān. But Muḥammad Walī Khān was frightened that he would be arrested and his property confiscated and told her not to mention his name but to give the letter to Sayyid Ḥusayn, Nāʾib al-Salṭanah, so that he perhaps would prevent this vile thing from happening and keep his brother-in-law from this act which from beginning to end is deviant and disgraceful, for who could say how such a vicious act would end? One perhaps ought to regard such things as heavenly punishment for the sins of the father [the author has in mind the anti-Hazārah activity of Zamān al-Dīn] and for Muḥammad Walī Khān's betrayal of the government. As they say, "you reap what you sow."

On this same day, Ḥabīb Allāh Khān, out of political expediency **/118/** ordered the release from prison of ʿAbd al-Karīm Khān, who had been incarcerated the day before and who was not[124] the Karīm Khān of the Wardak, famed for his bravery. [He released him] so that once they find out, perhaps his tribe will halt the bloodshed and declare their obedience. This was the result and the fruit of (his) courage and being mindful of his "salt." Otherwise, he who had killed hundreds of people would not have left him alive.

At the time of these events, Ḥabīb Allāh Khān, because of his lust for women, asked for the daughters of Nāʾib al-Salṭanah Naṣr Allāh Khān and Amīn Allāh Khān, sons of Amīr ʿAbd al-Raḥmān Khān, in marriage.
46 | But they kept rejecting him to the point where he was about to use force to compel them to accept his proposal. But then they said they were already married and hearing this, he withdrew his request. He then made an attempt at the beautiful-as-a-rose moon-faced daughter of Sardār Muḥammad ʿAlī Khān, son of Pīr Muḥammad Khān, who was Amīr Dūst Muḥammad Khān's brother. When she too refused him, he decided to take her by force. The girl resolved to kill herself rather than submit. She

[124] Both the ms. and the edited version say *na-būd*" "he was not (the Karīm Khān famed for bravery whom those opposed to Ḥabīb Allāh Khān wanted people to think had not been captured)." But, in light of the following sentence, which otherwise makes no sense, it is possible the author meant *būd*, i.e. "He was (the Karīm Khān Wardak, famed for bravery" despite what opponents of Ḥabīb Allāh Khān wanted people to think.)

took poison and thereby saved herself from the clutches of Ḥabīb Allāh Khān. Ultimately, thanks to the mercy of God, she survived.

Towards evening today (20 Shawwāl), some seventy Wardaks were brought in chains to Kabul.

Marginalia: Also on this day a certain mullah, a *muḥtasib* [enforcer of morals and rules of the marketplace], who would harass and annoy people and then take money [to stop], caused people a great deal of trouble, so at Nā'ib al-Salṭanah Sayyid Ḥusayn's order, his ear was nailed to a column to make him an object lesson. [End of marginal note.]

The Unbearable Situation Faced by the Inhabitants of Kabul and Their Resolve to Fight Ḥabīb Allāh Khān

The residents of Kabul, men and women, aristocrats and commoners alike, having been brought to utter despair by the abuse and violence of [Ḥabīb Allāh Khān's] army and by the vile and humiliating behavior of the Northern leaders who controlled **/119/** both civil and military matters, had come to believe that death was preferable to such a degrading life. Ministers of Amān Allāh Khān, his associates, and some well-to-do citizens met secretly to try and find a way to save the people of the capital, their families, and their wealth and to ensure tranquility. They agreed that each of them would hire people, pay them a fairly high monthly wage, and thus lay the groundwork to overthrow Ḥabīb Allāh Khān. At some point [their people] would suddenly attack and annihilate him. But he [Ḥabīb Allāh Khān] learned about their plans from spies and on Monday, 20 Shawwāl, corresponding to 1 April, ordered all the conspirators arrested in the night. This is recorded therefore on the margin of the previous page.[125]

At the time of these events, the proclamations and decrees of Amān Allāh Khān, who had raised the flag of his amirate in Qandahar with the backing of the Durrānī tribe, were being distributed through Gīzāb and Tamazān as far as the Hazārahjāt and Turkistān. The Hazārahs of Shaykh ʿAlī, Bāmyān, Turkmān, Surkh wa Pārsā, Dāy Zangī, Balkhāb, Bihsūd, and a number of other places not only refused to swear obedience to Ḥabīb Allāh Khān; they came out in support of Amān Allāh Khān. Residents of Shaykh ʿAlī, Surkh wa Pārsā, Turkmān, and Bāmyān prepared to attack Kūhistān and Kūh Dāman via Ghūrband and set forth [with this goal in mind.] The Hazārahs of Bihsūd assembled at Ūnay Pass, intending to

125 See supra, the marginal note immediately after the heading "The Events of 20 Shawwāl."

attack Kabul from there. The governor of Ghūrband and the Hazārahjāt, Kākā Muḥsin, informed Ḥabīb Allāh Khān what was happening. After consulting with his partisans, Ḥabīb Allāh ordered a force of a thousand men sent to the Hazārahjāt along the road through Ghūrband.

When Muḥammad Naʿīm Khān of Dāy Zangī, Nādir /**120**/ ʿAlī Khān Jāghūrī, Ghulām Nabī Khān, Suhrāb Khān, and Muḥammad Isḥāq Khān Bihsūdī, all of whom were in Kabul, learned of this, they decided not to allow a confrontation to occur between the Hazārahjāt forces and those of Ḥabīb Allāh Khān. They promised the latter to secure an oath of loyalty from the Hazārahs and to pacify them. But up to this point they had not

47 received a response [from him]. |

The Events of Tuesday, 21 Shawwāl/2 April

Marginalia: Also on this day a man named Nīk Muḥammad, who had been appointed by Ḥabīb Allāh Khān to one of the districts (*tawābiʿ*) of Ghaznīn but who had fled and come to Kabul because of the uprising of the people there in support of Amān Allāh Khān, was now executed at the order of Ḥabīb Allāh Khān. [End of marginal note.]

In the evening of this day, they arrested the *mīrākhūr* Aḥmad ʿAlī, an Hazārah from Dāy Mīrdād who for some time was the *wakīl* representing his tribe in the National Council under the presidency of Shayr Aḥmad Khān,[126] son of Fatḥ Muḥammad Khān, whose father was Sardār Zakariyā (Zikriyā) Khān. When Aḥmad ʿAlī was relieved of his position, he came to Kabul on the first of Shaʿbān corresponding to 23 Jady[xxx] and 13 January with a force of Hazārahs from Bihsūd numbering some 1,500 men. But because the road has been closed, he has had to remain in the city up until now enduring torment and deprivation from one day to the next. When he was arrested, they also detained Muḥammad Naʿīm Khān, son of Mīr Iqbāl Beg Sih Pāy, an Hazārah of Dāy Zangī, and four men from Bihsūd—Ghulām Nabī Khān, Muḥammad Ishaq Khān, Muḥammad Ḥasan Khān, son of Riżā Bakhsh Sulṭān, and Qāżī ʿAlī Khān, son of Sardār ʿAlī Khān. They were accused of having allied themselves with the brother of Amān Allāh Khān, Ḥayāt Allāh Khān; the aide-de-camp, Maḥmūd Khān; Ḥabīb Allāh Khān, deputy minister of war under Amān Allāh Khān; Mīrzā Hāshim Kūr Kashmīrī; Sulṭān Muḥammad, Amān Allāh Khān's tailor; as well as several other members of the Kabul nobility whom they arrested

[126] On Shayr Aḥmad see Adamec, *Who's Who*, p. 241. No mention is made there of his role under Kalakānī except a reference to him as "Bacha-i-Saqqau's adviser".

last night. /**121**/ These people had agreed to escape together, link up with the Hazārahs of Surkh wa Pārsā on the road to Pamqān, then, together with the Hazārah force and the army advancing from Qandahar through the Hazārahjāt, to attack Kabul. Then, having incited an uprising, they would drive Ḥabīb Allāh Khān out of Kabul.

They say that the governor of Bihsūd, Kākā Muḥsin Khān, also named by Ḥabīb Allāh Khān as governor of Dāy Zangī and Dāy Kundī, could not bring himself to go there because he was afraid of the brother of the late Mīr Aḥmad Shāh Khān, Mīr Muḥammad Ḥusayn Khān, who, on behalf of Amān Allāh Khān had taken on the governorship of Dāy Zangī and [at the present time] is still there. So (Kākā Muḥsin Khān) wrote to Nā'ib al-Salṭanah Sayyid Ḥusayn and said, "The Hazārahs who are under (Mīr Muḥammad Ḥusayn Khān's) authority refuse to submit and swear an oath of loyalty. You must send an army and also arrest the Hazārah elders who are in Kabul so that they will stop giving support to Amān Allāh Khān and [instead] express their obedience." So Sayyid Ḥusayn has ordered their arrest.

Some are saying that Amān Allāh Khān has sent six thousand rifles and a vast quantity of ammunition to Dāy Zangī and six thousand rifles to Bihsūd. Despite the fact that the population of these regions had in their time endured a great deal at the hands of Amān Allāh Khān and bore grievances against him, still they gave him their support to spite the Tajiks of the North. The Bihsūd lashkar reinforced the units already in the Ūnay Pass and reached agreement with the Hazārah tribal militias of Surkh wa Pārsā, Turkmān, Bāmyān, Balkhāb, and Shaykh 'Alī to attack Kūhistān and Kūh Dāman by way of the road through Ghūrband. Simultaneously, [the force from Bihsūd] would attack Kabul via the route through Maydān.

So on Tuesday, 21 Shawwāl, corresponding to 13 Ḥamal 1308 and 2 April
48 [1929] | rumors spread that the Hazārah tribal lashkar, with a lashkar of the Isḥāqzā'ī whose summer pastures were around Balkh, Hazārahs who had been displaced there, and Turkmāns from around Aqchah, Andkhud, and Maymanah had taken control of Mazār-i Sharīf and its environs and had seized well-wishers of Ḥabīb Allāh Khān like Mīrzā Muḥammad Qāsim Khān /**122**/ and others who themselves had arrested the high-ranking officials and army officers of that place who sided with Amān Allāh Khān and sent them to Kabul under guard. These included 'Abd al-'Azīz Khān,[127] son of the late Field Marshal Ghulām Ḥaydar Khān Charkhī and high governor [of Afghan Turkistān], Brigadier General Muḥammad Iklīl Khān, son of

127 For 'Abd al-'Azīz Khān see Adamec, *Who's Who*, p. 94 ("Abdul Aziz, born 1891").

Muḥammad Afżal Khān Darwāzī, and others. At this point they had not reached Kabul but were en route. [The Hazārah, Isḥāqzā'ī, and Turkmān force], having decided to attack Kūhistān and Kūh Dāman together, reached Ghūrband where they obliged the local population to join them and made a pact with and extracted oaths from them to attack Kūhistān and Kūh Dāman. As news of this spread, Vice-Regent Sayyid Ḥusayn set off for Chārīkār on Tuesday, resolved to defend it.

On the same day, they asked elementary school children to take up weapons and stand resolutely in support of Amīr Ḥabīb Allāh Khān. Moreover, the radio reported that Amān Allāh Khān has entered Ghaznīn at 5:30 today and was heading for Kabul. However, it is not known whether this is true or not.

The Events of Wednesday, 22 Shawwāl Corresponding to 3 April

/123/ *Marginalia*: On the eve of this day, the Wardak people who had taken refuge in the mountains in opposition to Amīr Ḥabīb Allāh Khān launched a surprise night attack on his army which had burned down several vacant qalʿahs, was marching towards Ghaznīn, and had reached the manzil of Shash Gaw. The attackers killed or wounded seven hundred soldiers and made off with their rifles and artillery. All trace of the five hundred Nijrābīs who were marching in this force was lost and there is no news about them. People say that the commander of this surprise night attack was Muʿīn al-Salṭanah ʿInāyat Allāh Khān, the elder brother of Amān Allāh Khān, now present with an army on the field of battle. [End of marginal note.] /123/

On the day following this evening, Malik Muḥammad ʿAlam Khān Shinwārī's[128] heading for Kabul with nearly 300 Shinwārīs had given rise to the rumor of a delegation coming from the people of the Eastern Province. Unbeknownst to other tribes, the malik made his way to Kabul via a secret route in order to offer his allegiance. [During the day of 22 Shawwāl] he entered Kabul. He himself was lodged in the Arg as an honored guest and his companions were put up at the school of the ministry of war [the War College]. Besides the "bazaar force" (*fawj-i bāzār*),[129] each one of his close companions was personally fed from the amir's kitchen. Immedi-

[128] On him see Adamec, *Who's Who*, p. 195.

[129] *Fawj-i bāzār* is an odd phrase and we are not quite sure what Fayż Muḥammad meant by it, perhaps that the 300 or so other Shinwārīs were left in the bazaar for security reasons and were provided with food there.

ately upon his arrival, the title "civil and military deputy field marshal" was bestowed on him.

On the evening of this day, some men from the Muḥammadzā'ī, influential Kābulīs and even Amān Allāh Khān's tailors and his baker, as well as several Bihsūd and Dāy Zangī Hazārahs who had earlier arrived in Kabul to file complaints and have their cases resolved, but, in connection with the uprising and the closing of the roads were forced to postpone their departures, only surviving from day to day with deprivation and torment, were all captured and imprisoned on the charges that they all were awaiting the return of Amān Allāh Khān and that the Hazārahs were his partisans and were giving him assistance. Some of the arrested men were ordered punished "with cane and wedge (*qayn wa fānah*)."[130] The soldiers who were ordered to round them up and take them to prison extorted from each one a sum ranging from 40 up to 500 and 1000 rupees as the bailiff's fee and confiscated the houses and belongings of some of them and created a great deal of commotion as if the Day of Resurrection
49 had come. |

The Events of Thursday, 23 Shawwāl Corresponding to 4 April

A few days earlier His Excellency, Nā'ib al-Salṭanah Sayyid Ḥusayn, left for Khwājah Sih Yārān,[131] Chārīkār to make preparations for receiving Amīr Ḥabīb Allāh Khān who had promised to arrive there on Friday. /124/ On this day, through a letter from Bābā Khān Kūhistānī, [Sayyid Ḥusayn] was notified to arrest those Hazārahs who a few days earlier had promised to obtain oaths of loyalty from the Hazārah tribes and then, having received permission from the amir, departed [for the Hazārahjāt] and had gone with one of his reliable deputies. From there [Sayyid Ḥusayn's] deputy let it be known that his return was delayed.[xxxi] Eventually, the Hazārahs found a way to be released.

Also on this day, there were [more] arrests. There were seizures of persons and extortion of money by the soldiers who were assigned to round up those who had come (to Kabul) and then had to stay as well as neighbors who had nothing to do [with either side]. They extorted 2,000 rupees from the son of the late Deputy Field Marshal Sayyid Shāh Khān in whose

130 The *fānah* (wedge) punishment is graphically described in Frank A. Martin, *Under the Absolute Amir*, London and New York, Harper and Brothers 1907, pp. 153–54.

131 In Adamec, *Gazetteer*, vol. 6, the name appears as "Khwaja Siahran Aolia" (i.e. Upper ['Ulyā] Khwājah Sih Yārān) and "Khwaja Siahran Sufla" (Lower [Sufla] Khwājah Sih Yārān).

fort a horse belonging to the Hazārah equerry (*mīrākhūr*) Aḥmad ʿAlī was found.

In Sar Chashmah they arrested oil sellers and fined them 300 rupees because a Tajik from Jalrīz alleged in a complaint that several years before they had killed his son. At the house of a Bihsūd Hazārah named Būlah who was not at home at the time, they seized 300 rupees that he had in the house. They arrested several people and confiscated their houses, real estate, and belongings for the amirate fisc. As a result of these evil deeds, terror and desperation gripped the people of the city from day to night and dusk to dawn whether they were strong or weak, rich or poor, wayfarers or residents. "Who knows God's plans?" [Ḥāfiẓ]

The Events of Friday, 24 Shawwāl, Corresponding to 5 April

On this day at the invitation of Sayyid Ḥusayn Khān, Amīr Ḥabīb Allāh Khān, along with his close associates, well-wishers, and lackeys came to Khwājah Sih Yārān to celebrate the Redbud Blossom Festival and spent the day enjoying themselves. It is said that he circulated a rumor that he had come as a guest to enjoy himself but in fact /125/ he was there to inspect the equipping of the strategic positions overlooking Kūhistān and Kūh Dāman because of the feared attack by the Shaykh ʿAlī, Bāmyān, Surkh wa Pārsā and Turkmān Hazārahs.[xxxii]

[Meantime] the Ūzbak, Mīrzā Muḥammad Qāsim Khān, the high commissioner of Mazār-i Sharīf, had plundered the officials serving Amān Allāh Khān,[xxxiii] arrested the high governor, ʿAbd al-ʿAzīz Khān; Brigadier General Muḥammad Ismāʿīl Khān; and other office-holders of Amān Allāh Khān's time and had sent them towards Kabul. The Hazārahs mentioned above [released them and] returned them from Bāmyān and together they set off for [Kūhistān and Kūh Dāman] in order to prepare an attack. [The Hazārahs] took measures to defend [those formerly arrested] and to defend against the inhabitants of Qaṭaghan and Badakhshān who at first
50 had sent oaths of obedience to Kabul | but then, learning of the malicious and indecent behavior of the soldiers and partisans of Ḥabīb Allāh Khān who behaved contrary to the ordinances and traditions of Islam and did not allow the residents of Kabul to utter a single word or to find an opportunity to save themselves from oppression and violence, had ended their obedience [to Ḥabīb Allāh Khān Kalakānī] and, expressing their sympathy for Amān Allāh Khān, had entertained the idea of rising against the oppressors. Eventually, the rumor of the Qaṭaghanī and Badakhshānī people's [withdrawing their obedience from the amir], which was circulated

by supporters of Amān Allāh Khān as propaganda for him turned out to be a lie and faded away.

Also during this time, the Shinwārīs with Malik Muḥammad ʿAlam Khān had come to the court in Kabul to offer an oath of allegiance in the hope of aid and being given weapons and ammunition for fighting and defending themselves against other tribes of the Eastern Province. Because the Shinwārī and the Khūgyānī had broken their pledge, destroyed government buildings, and pillaged and demolished[xxxiv] the city of Jalālābād, those other tribes had banished them from their society and from the great jirgah (*jirgah-i qawī*) and intended to exterminate them. [Contrary to their hopes, the amir] confiscated their horses and camels for transporting goods and forage. In addition, he demanded they give up their own rifles but they refused and remained for a while in Kabul.[xxxv] **/126/**

The Events of Saturday 25 Shawwāl, Corresponding to 6 April, Saturday

During these events, the seven Russian aircraft that had landed in Kabul to evacuate Russian, Turkish, and German nationals, as was mentioned earlier, had not been able to take off on the return flight because Nāʾib al-Salṭanah Sayyid Ḥusayn, on behalf of Ḥabīb Allāh Khān, refused to allow any more than two aircraft to leave and he did so in an extremely contemptuous and insulting manner, expressing the unhappiness of the amir and the government to the Russian officials. This was a great provocation to the Russian ambassador and (Sayyid Ḥusayn) thereby revealed the hostility towards that government of the amirate and the new government which was asserting its dominance.

Also on this day, radio broadcasts to the world from Bombay and Calcutta reported that Amān Allāh Khān marched from Qandahar on Tuesday, 14 Shawwāl.[xxxvi]

Also, on the eve of this day, Mīrzā Muḥammad Muḥsin Khān, better known as "Kākā" ("uncle"), son of Mīrzā Muḥammad Afżal Khān of the Kacharlū Qizilbāsh of Kabul, which is a Sunni tribe, entered his own house. The details of his situation are as follows: His brother, Ghulām Ḥusayn, had joined the thieves out of wickedness and taken the path of looting and was so friendly with Ḥabīb Allāh Khān and Sayyid Ḥusayn that at the time of the first assault on Kabul by those two men he had offered assistance and provided fodder. At night, when it had been very cold, he put his fortress and houses and also the qalʿahs of the people of Chahārdihī at the disposal of their partisans in order to obtain the rank of colonel. But later he was arrested and on the eve of the day Amān Allāh Khān left for

Qandahar, he was hanged at [the latter's] order. [Because of the support given by Ghulām Ḥusayn] his older brother, Kākā Muḥsin had gained the respect of Ḥabīb Allāh Khān and on the 14th of Shaʿbān, he was appointed governor of Hazārah Dāy Zangī, Dāy Kundī, and Bihsūd. In view of the
51 fact that | the brother of Mīr Aḥmad Shāh Khān, Mīr Muḥammad Ḥusayn Khān,[132] who had been named governor there in Qaws [November/December 1928] to replace ʿAbd al-Razzāq Khān Muḥammadzāʾī prior to Ḥabīb Allāh Khān's [first] assault [on Kabul] and was still there, [Kākā Muḥsin] was unable to implement a single measure and found himself under siege in his own village of Kharbīd. /127/ In the end, realizing that the Hazārahs were irreconcilably hostile to Ḥabīb Allāh Khān, with the help of the son of Shāh Nūr, a well-known Hazārah thief, he headed for Kabul via the Khirs Khānah Pass[xxxvii] and, as was stated above, arrived in the city.

Due to his arrival back in Kabul, rumors spread that the high governor of Qandahar, ʿAbd al-Karīm Khān, at Amān Allāh Khān's order, had delivered seven thousand rifles by way of Gīzāb, Tamazān, and Sih Pāy to the Hazārahs of Bihsūd and that 4,000 of them had erected fortified sangars at Ūnay Pass and 2,000 others had raised sangars at the Khirs Khānah Pass.[xxxviii] However, this rumor was completely baseless and mere propaganda. With the spread of the news, Ḥabīb Allāh Khān, knowing that it was without foundation, ordered 1,000 men sent to Lahūgard to prevent any offensive from the tribes of the Southern Province and Muḥammad Nādir Khān.[xxxix] On that same day, Saturday, Kākā Muḥsin was received by Ḥabīb Allāh Khān, told him what had happened, and was punished.

The Events of Sunday, 26 Shawwāl, Corresponding to 7 April

Due to a battle that took place on the road to Ghaznīn in the district of Shinīz, Wardak, along which road Ḥabīb Allāh Khān's army was advancing, the force was defeated and routed with many killed or wounded. By telephone, the army sought reinforcements from Kabul. A thousand men, ready to set out on the road through Sar Chashmah to the Hazārahjāt now stopped and set out in that direction, ordered to assist those who had been routed. From Kabul, an order obliged the people of Wazīrābād, that, although they had no rifles, they were to go to Sar Chashmah with knives, axes and swords and block the path of the Hazārahs, who were of

[132] Although we have no biographical information for Muḥammad Ḥusayn Khān, his brother, Mīr Aḥmad Shāh, is probably the wealthy and influential Kashmīrī profiled by Adamec, *Who's Who*, p. 189. There is much information about his financial dealings in Fayż Muḥammad, *The History*, vol. 4 see index "Aḥmad Shāh K., Mīr."

the same sect (i.e., Shiʿis). Because they were co-religionists, the Hazārahs would not kill them nor inflict either physical or material harm on them nor dishonor them. However, because of stupidity (the Northerners) were ignorant of the fact that the people of Kabul and its surroundings /128/ were fed up with the vicious behavior, the depravity, the plundering of homes, and the arrests of the weak by the Northerners who had declared that they were the upholders of religion and if anyone anywhere dared raise his voice [in protest], they would kill or imprison those people and by such simple-minded methods wanted to bring all the people of Afghanistan into obedience and subject to [their] farman.

Also on this day 300 armed men received an order to set up sangars on Tapah-i Maranjān on the east side of Kabul. From news of this and rumors in general people knew that this fortification was related to the [expected] attack on Kabul of Muḥammad Nādir Khān's brother, Muḥammad Hāshim Khān, and the tribes of the Eastern Province. Either that or it might have been due to the steady and significant reinforcement of the Shinwārī who on the first day numbered only 400 or so, but in the course of the third, fourth, fifth and succeeding days right up to this day had increased their numbers to 2,000 and still they continued to come like ants. These positions were therefore readied so that in the event the Shinwārī were harboring evil intentions towards the populace of the city
52 it might be possible to prevent them from penetrating into the city. |

Also on this day, two detainees[xl] who were accused of harboring ill intentions towards Ḥabīb Allāh[xli] Khān and been arrested at his order were beaten to death with canes in the Arg prison. The aide-de-camp (*yāwar*), Maḥmūd Khān, who was also sentenced to be caned, paid 35,000 rupees to ransom himself and was exempted from being beaten.[xlii]

Also on this day, a tribal lashkar from the Southern Province led by Muḥammad Nādir Khān, camped at the foot of the Tīrah Pass, planning to attack Kabul. Also[xliii] the Hazārah lashkar from Surkh wa Pārsā, Turkmān, Shaykh ʿAlī, Bāmyān, and Balkhāb arrived in Siyāhgird in Ghūrband.

/129/ Also on this day, Ḥabīb Allāh Khān's soldiers beat with canes and rifle butts and then threw into prison Brigadier General Muḥammad Hāshim Khān,[133] son of Muḥammad Yūsuf Khān whose father was Ḥabīb Allāh Khān, son of Khān Shīrīn Khān, son of Amīr Aṣlān Khān Jawānshayr, because he had been an officer in Amān Allāh Khān's army.

---

133 For a not particularly complimentary depiction of Muḥammad Hāshim Khān, a Qizilbāsh, see Fayż Muḥammad, *The History*, vol. 4, p. 397.

Also on this day,[xliv] to reinforce the army of Ḥabīb Allāh Khān [sent to Ghaznīn], which was disheartened and rendered desperate by the attack, and had requested help by telephone, a force of 1,350 men, equipped with six artillery pieces, was sent from Kabul.

The Events of Monday, 27 Shawwāl, Corresponding to 19 Ḥamal and 8 April

On this day Amīr Ḥabīb Allāh officially invited *kalāntar*s, elders, and Kabul notables to the Dilkushā Palace. Also among the invited were representatives of the Shinwārī and some Lahūgard residents. In their presence, he began his speech with these words:

> No one will reproach me for having taken the throne because Amān Allāh Khān turned his back on Islam, had begun to worship idols, and wanted to force all the subjects of Afghanistan to become idol worshippers. Some people, who joined with him in idol worship, at meetings and gatherings would insult, ridicule, and humiliate those who remained true to Islam and would curse their own fathers and grandfathers as stupid and cowardly. [Things continued like this] until now when, at the urging **/130/** of righteous ulema and spiritual leaders, after putting my life at risk, wandering through mountains and wastelands and engaging in thievery and living a life of deprivation, I decided to eliminate him and I achieved my goal. And now, when a large group of Muslims, their leaders, and the ulema have given oaths of obedience and I sit on the amirate throne, I will exert all my strength to defend and support Islam and the Light of the Sharīʿah, the Lord of Messengers, and provide peace and prosperity to my brother Muslims.

After uttering these words, he removed the coverings on the idols which had been found during excavations of Buddhist temples near Jalālābād, Kūh Dāman, Kūhistān and elsewhere conducted by the French [archaeologists] Monsieur [Alfred] Foucher and Monsieur [Philippe] Berthelot.
53 They took to Paris their share of the objects that they found | and the part which, by treaty and by contract, belonged to Afghanistan, they handed over to officials of the government. These idols and others found during the reigns of the late amirs, ʿAbd al-Raḥmān Khān and Ḥabīb Allāh Khān at the shrine of Khwājah Ṣafā in Kabul, at Qalʿah-i Murād Beg in Kūh Dāman, in Bagrām, Kūhistān, and other places in the Northern Province of the country were deposited by Amān Allāh Khān in the museum to establish the places where the communities of idol-worshippers of old had settled. [Ḥabīb Allāh Khān], having displayed to all present these once sacred statues, announced, "Look at what he worships! You can

see them with your own eyes." Two or three days ago, he had given the Shinwārī the opportunity to see them. They kissed his hand and said in Afghānī "We bow down before /85/ you. You are the real *pādshāh* and the enemy of idol worship."

Having arranged such an exhibition, he supposed that the idols would produce a major impression on people who had no grasp at all either of history or of religion. As a final word, he informed those present that Amān Allāh Khān had reached Ghaznīn with his army, Muḥammad Nādir Khān was in Lahūgard, and Hazārah contingents were in Ghūrband, the Ūnay Pass, and the Khirs-Khānah Pass. Then he said,

> O great people, if you know someone knowledgeable who deserves the amirate and is capable of protecting the country and the nation and you wish to choose him as amir then do so and just make me a simple sergeant, for I would rather put my head on the block than worship these idols and refuse your wish. I will be satisfied with the clothing and food to which I am accustomed /131/ and not strive for any higher position.

He was compelled to make this speech because he had received information from spies and secret informants that everyone—men, women and children—was outraged by the abuses of power, the oppression, and humiliations that they were forced to bear at the hands of high-ranking personages and soldiers of his army. Indignant at the thievery and coercion being perpetrated everywhere, all had turned their backs on him and, praying to God, impatiently awaited the return of Amān Allāh Khān whom they earlier had despised. The Most High had accepted the repentance of the people and instilled in their hearts love [for Amān Allāh Khān].

Marginalia: The residents of Kabul, accustomed to curse [the amir] behind his back, declared, "We recognize you as *pādshāh*" and he accepted [their recognition]. In the midst of the proceedings, an old man stood up and said, "We have one request of you. The ministers of Amān Allāh Khān who destroyed the nation and ruined him, you must not leave any of them alive. This especially applies to the minister of finance. If he is drawn and quartered and you give me his flesh, I will eat it with great relish." Then Ḥabīb Allāh Khān said, "I am killing them all except Maḥmūd Khān Yāwar who was prepared to kill me. Him, I will keep in prison but not kill. Regarding the oppression which has been and is being perpetrated on you, I am aware of all of it. In due course as the opportunity and the means present themselves, I [consider myself] fully accountable for your well-being." [End of marginal note.]

The Events of Tuesday, 28 Shawwāl, Corresponding to 20 Ḥamal 1308 and 9 April [1929]

On this day, in the village of Shaykhābād, on Wardak territory, a fierce battle was fought. Ḥabīb Allāh Khān's force, having decided that Amān Allāh's supporters /132/ were far stronger than they were, had telephoned Kabul for reinforcements [as mentioned above]. Just as the sun was coming up, some people who had been forcibly rounded up were hastily ordered to set out and departed. As the soldiers[xlv] began to lose hope, they kept demanding reinforcements over the telephone. After lunch, at one o'clock, Amīr Ḥabīb Allāh Khān, together with his brother, Muʿīn al-Salṭanah Ḥamīd Allāh Khān; Nā'ib al-Salṭanah Sayyid Ḥusayn; the field marshal and minister of war, Purdil Khān; and other experienced fighters set out for the battlefield in seven speedy vehicles. Along the way they plundered some villages.

54 | Also on this day, the Shinwārīs were given leave to go home except for several of their maliks including Malik Muḥammad ʿAlam Khān. Those maliks were encouraged to stay in Kabul in conjunction with certain matters of the revolution. All the others went home, their desires unfulfilled because they had come with their greedy minds set on getting rifles, cartridges, and money with which they hoped to protect themselves against the people of the Eastern Province who had taken up arms against them and the Khūgyānīs, as well as against Ḥabīb Allāh Khān. [The Easterners were angry with the Shinwārīs and Khūgyānīs] for violating the tribal covenant and pillaging Jalālābād. Not getting what they had hoped for, the Shinwārīs returned home in disappointment.

Also on this day, some one hundred old men and youths from the Wardak people, who had been detained and were said to be from Jīghatū-yi Wardak their homeland north of Ghaznīn City and west of the Sulṭān Dam[134] and touching on the lands of the Hazārahs, were led around the city and the bazaars to show people that the forces of Ḥabīb Allāh Khān had gained control over the environs of Ghaznīn as well as over Kabul and thus to deprive Amān Allāh Khān of support and disabuse [people] of any notion of the possibility of his coming to Kabul.

/133/ On this day, too, one thousand men recruited by force, were dispatched from Kabul to Ghūrband to repel the Hazārahs of Surkh wa

[134] On the Sulṭān Dam at Ghaznīn see Fayż Muḥammad, *The History*, vol. 4, pp. 260, 611, 757, 1313–14, 1355.

Pārsā, Turkmān, Shaykh ʿAlī, Bāmyān, and Yakah Awlang who, according to rumor, intended to attack Kūhistān and Kūh Dāman.[xlvi]

The Events of Wednesday, 29 Shawwāl, Corresponding to 21 Ḥamal and 10 April

On this day, at 7:30 in the morning, two Russian aircraft, which had earlier come to evacuate German and Turkish nationals to Tirmiẕ, charging each of them a fare of 430 Afghānīs (16 pounds sterling), landed again [in Kabul.]

Also on this day, two conscientious young men of Kabul were arrested. They had prepared a hand grenade intending to assassinate Ḥabīb Allāh Khān. They planned to deliver it to him in the mosque at the Friday service and blow him up. The grenade was found in their house during a search and they were arrested. Ḥabīb Allāh Khān himself was on his way to the field at Khwājah Rawāsh for gunnery practice. At twelve o'clock they arrested these two.[xlvii] One, named Ḥabīb Allāh, was the son of a carpenter, Ḥājjī ʿAbd al-Ghaffār. The other—ʿAbd al-Rasūl—was the son of an Indian steward, Khānjī Khān, who had enjoyed renown during the reign of the late Amīr ʿAbd al-Raḥmān. They were betrayed by Qārī Dūst Muḥammad Lamqānī who passed himself off as a mullah but was deeply involved in committing vile satanic deeds. He instigated them to commit the act and then, after the bomb was prepared, he reported them. When Ḥabīb Allāh and ʿAbd al-Rasūl were interrogated, they said, "Qārī Dūst Muḥammad Lamqānī encouraged and provoked us to carry out the deed and no one
55 else was involved." /134/ | From the testimony of those two, Ḥabīb Allāh Khān believed him to be the mastermind of the plot and ordered his arrest. But he was not at home. Instead he was at his shop on the ground floor of the building known as "Shirkat-i Samar"[135] sitting minding his own business. Ḥabīb Allāh Khān, who was going to the field at Khwājah Rawāsh for artillery practice, caught sight of him, beckoned him over, had him ride in the car with him, and took him to the range where he shot and killed all three. As they tied them to wooden posts, Qārī Dūst Muḥammad cried out to the amir, "Amīr-ṣāḥib, don't kill me. I've done good service for you and I will do even more." However, since the decree of fate had been handed down to kill an evil devil who pretended to be a mullah he was unable to find salvation and hurried off to his place in eternity. Oh, if only all the

135 The Shirkat-i Ṣamar was an exporter of dried fruit. See Schinasi, *Kabul: A History*, p. 139.

misguided pseudo-mullahs lighting the fires of sedition and destruction in the land could experience the kind of swift retribution that this one did!

The Events of Thursday, the First of Ẕīqaʿdah, Corresponding to 22 Ḥamal and 11 April

On this day, rumors were in the mouths of all the supporters of Amān Allāh Khān—men and women alike who represented most of the city people—that the troops of Ḥabīb Allāh Khān had suffered a crushing defeat near Ghaznīn; and it was said that[xlviii] two men—a brigadier general and a colonel, nephews of Malik Zayn al-ʿĀbidīn, director of the Central Customs Department, were severely wounded and taken prisoner; many others were also killed and captured; the rest had fled to Qalʿah-i Durrānī. The two wounded nephews of the aforementioned malik were transported to Kabul. One died the first night, while the other survived.[xlix]

Because of rumors, and also the news about the arrival of Muḥammad Nādir Khān with a large force at Khūshī in Lahūgard, at the Ministry of War they began to forcibly requisition pack animals from owners who were in hiding because no one paid them for the hire of their animals. **/135/** The requisitions were based on lists kept at the municipality. [The owners] were ordered to turn their animals over to the detachments which were heading out to relieve [the amir's] troops. No matter how much the owners loudly protested that at those times when animals were in demand and hard to find Amān Allāh Khān would pay each owner of pack animals around thirty rupees a day per head for their use and when they weren't particularly busy, ten rupees but now they won't pay any rent and even if they pay a few rupees, as soon as they reach the caravansary, the sepoys will take [those rupees] by force, no one would listen to them but would [only] try to placate them by saying "the fee for hire will be paid."

Also on this day, 300 members of the tribal lashkar from Lahūgard entered Kabul with honors and the army band playing. These were the same people who two or three days before had been forcibly assembled by Malik Muḥsin who had gone to Khūshī and Kulangār, but then found himself besieged in a fort. The day before [i.e., the last day of Shawwāl], Ḥabīb Allāh Khān himself had gone there, freed him from the tight spot he was in, and brought him to Kabul which they [the Lahūgard lashkar] now entered.

During these events, most of the Shinwārīs left Kabul, as mentioned above. Today some of those remaining were given permission to leave.
56 To Malik Muḥammad ʿAlam Khān and his companions | 15,000 rupees

were presented as a gift. A farman was given to the malik himself, who had already received from Ḥabīb Allāh Khān the rank of "civil and military deputy commander-in-chief," appointing him governor of Jalālābād.

During this time, in order to re-establish their good name, the Shinwārīs, who had destroyed and looted government buildings in Jalālābād and violated the tribal covenant, attacked the fort of Malik Muḥammad ʿAlam Khān—the mastermind of all the misery and misfortune of the Eastern Province—looting his property and destroying his fort. On receipt of this news, since all the tribes of the Eastern Province were arrayed against him and deemed him banished from tribal society, Malik Muḥammad ʿAlam Khān, fearing for his life, gave up the idea of returning home **/136/** and remained in Kabul, where he lived in constant dread, fearing punishment for his deeds.[1]

Also today two flying machines took off in the direction of Ghaznīn and Lahūgard on a reconnaissance flight. From the information they brought back it became clear that the rumors of Muḥammad Nādir Khān's force being in Khūshī and Amān Allāh Khān's army being at the manzil of Takiyah-i Wardak did not correspond with reality but were simply propaganda spread by supporters of Amān Allāh Khān.

The Events of Friday, 2[li] Ẕīqaʿdah, Corresponding to 23 Ḥamal and 12 April

Although during this month fighting and killing is forbidden, nonetheless, many Muslims of today are untrue to the religion, violating the commands of God and the Prophet and shedding blood. They spare nothing in plundering the property and wealth and making captives of their own people and families. We will see just what things they do. On this day [for example], Ḥabīb Allāh Khān, accompanied by his brother and a number of Kūhistān and Kūh Dāman notables, each one of whom does whatever he feels like doing, commits whatever deed he wants to, and are all hated because of their unbearable oppression, for which the people of Kabul pray night and day to God to bring their rule to an end, expecting the Almighty either to put an end to them or to deliver [the oppressed] to their own deaths [and so relieve them of oppression], came to the shrine of Khwājah Ṣafā,[136] which overlooks the city. In ancient times an idol temple was located there and idols were discovered here during the reign of the late Amīr Ḥabīb Allāh Khān. Afterwards, (the group) went out to

136 For a description of the shrine as it was in the 1960s see Wolfe, *A Historical Guide*, pp. 126–27.

admire the redbuds in bloom and did not attend Friday worship, but spent the day observing the buildings of the city through binoculars and target-shooting with their rifles and machine guns.

Because of the spread of rumors about the arrival of Amān Allāh Khān[lii] in the vicinity of Ghaznīn and his having surrounded the city, Purdil Khān /137/ asked for reinforcements and ammunition by telephone. Ḥabīb Allāh Khān sent [ammunition] on hired phaetons towards Ghaznīn.

At this same time, Ḥabīb Allāh secretly sent twenty-six of the thieves to assassinate Muḥammad Nādir Khān by promising them a reward. It was agreed that any one of them who brought his head or (the heads) of any one of his three brothers—Shāh Walī Khān, Muḥammad Hāshim Khān, and Shāh Maḥmūd Khān—to Kabul would be given 30,000 rupees. Who knows whether those thieves sent to carry out this despicable assignment will be successful or not? Two of them are bandits from Chahārdihī; the
57 rest are from other places. |

The Events of Saturday, 3 Ẕīqaʿdah, Corresponding to 24 Ḥamal and 13 April 1929

In the course of the past few days, contingents of Hazārahs from Shaykh ʿAlī, Bāmyān, Surkh wa Pārsā, Turkmān, Balkhāb, Yakah Awlang, Qawmābah, and Darghān,[137] who, as previously mentioned, had been proceeding along the road through Ghūrband intending to attack Kūhistān and Kūh Dāman, captured and looted Ghūrband, whose population had offered its allegiance to Ḥabīb Allāh Khān and, having received rifles and ammunition from him, had used them to fight the supporters of Amān Allāh Khān. The flames of war are still ablaze [there].

On Friday, Nā'ib al-Salṭanah Sayyid Ḥusayn Khān, headed for Chārīkār. After setting up defensive positions in Jabal al-Sirāj on the bridge at the junction of the road to Ghūrband, as well as in other strategic places, he returned to Kabul on Saturday eve.

They say that on Saturday, a letter from Amān Allāh reached Ḥabīb Allāh Khān in which he demanded that he stop the bloodshed, rebellion, and destruction of the kingdom and step down from the throne. Otherwise, in a few days he should be prepared for a fight to last until, depending on whom God befriends, (that one's) lucky star will be helped [to victory].

---

[137] Qawmābah and Darghān are sections of the Hazārahs rendered as "Kam-i-Aba" and "Darghan" in Adamec, *Historical Gazetteer* 6, pp. 76, 81–82.

Also on this day, the partisans and the army of Ḥabīb Allāh Khān stationed in Kabul began /138/ to circulate propaganda saying that Field Marshal Muḥammad Nādir Khān had been surrounded in Lahūgard.[liii]

Rumors also circulated today that not far from Ghaznīn, Hazārah detachments had attacked and pillaged the homes of those Tajiks who supported Ḥabīb Allāh Khān and also routed the Sulaymān Khayl tribe which had come out in opposition to Amān Allāh Khān.[liv]

Marginalia: Also on this day, Ḥabīb Allāh Khān officially invited and addressed elders (*kadkhudā*s) of the Afghan nomads who had recently arrived in the thickets and out-of-the-way corners of the suburbs of Kabul with their flocks and herds saying,

> My dear co-religionists (*millat*)! Amān Allāh Khān has become a kafir and the Hazārahs, whom you all know, have become the deputies and aides of the kafir. I want you Muslims to consider that you share with me [the right to take] Hazārah blood and [Hazārah] property and bring total destruction to their livelihoods.

Some of the Afghans present on hearing this utterance, began to say to each other in the market and in out-of-the-way corners, "A kafir is someone who steals, sheds blood, and is venal, not the Hazārahs. Anyone who says Hazārahs are kafirs is himself a kafir." [End of marginal note.]

The Events of Sunday, 4 Ẕīqa'dah, Corresponding to 5 Ḥamal and 14 April

On this day, news spread of an imminent oath of allegiance from the Hazārahs of Bihsūd but it was merely to forestall an army being sent by Amīr Ḥabīb Allāh Khān to the Hazārahjāt until Amān Allāh Khān's situation was improved and [the Hazārahs] could be reassured about the mullahs and Afghan tribes who oppose (Amīr Ḥabīb Allāh Khān) and not have only the Hazārahs on one front undertaking the fight against him. Their hope was that the attack would be launched simultaneously from Maydān, Ghūrband, Lahūgard, and the Eastern Province so that the Hazārahs could tighten the noose around Ḥabīb Allāh Khān in alliance with the Afghans and the other tribes supporting Amān Allāh Khān.

People all know that [Ḥabīb Allāh Khān] thinks himself the amir of Kabul by beating the drums [to signify his amirate] morning and evening but in fact he is encircled in Kabul with the residents of the city and a hireling army of some 20,000 men. /139/ There is no way to travel in any direction except to the immediate outskirts of the city and no reliable information is reaching Kabul from anywhere in the country. The mail, the telephone, and word-of-mouth communications are all cut off and the delivery of foodstuffs and fodder has also been brought to a standstill. In the event of an all-out war, (the city) cannot resist.

58 Also on this day, acting on the advice of | Kākā Muḥsin Khān Qizilbāsh, a Sunni, who on the 14th of Shaʿbān was named governor of Bihsūd and Dāy Zangī but, unable to get a pledge of obedience from the Hazārahs, had fled to Kabul, as mentioned above, the high governor, Malik Muḥsin Khān, ordered two or three of the leaders of the Hazārahs [*marginalia*: namely Muḥammad Naʿīm Khān, Hazārah from the Sih Pāy of Dāy Zangī; Fayż Muḥammad from the Muḥammad Khwājah of Ghaznīn,[138] and Colonel Ghulām Nabī Khān from Bihsūd—end of marginal note] who were forced to remain in Kabul because the roads were closed to go and extract an oath of allegiance from the Hazārahs and to persuade them they should open the roads and come down from the Ūnay Pass. But because of the arrival of the Hazārah's politically canny letter [offering allegiance for the motives mentioned above] and also the departure as noted above of Kākā Muḥsin Khān and the delegation, this did not happen.[lv] Prior to this, the decision had been made to send Kākā Muḥsin Khān there along with Mullā Mīr Āqā and Mīrzā Muḥammad Ismāʿīl Khān Shāhī Sawand.

On this same day, all the members of the clan and family of Muḥammad Nādir Khān were taken into custody. While [Muḥammad Nādir Khān] was in Paris, the former ambassador of Afghanistan to Tehran, ʿAbd al-ʿAzīz Khān, the brother of Shāh Maḥmūd Khān and son of the paternal uncle of Muḥammad Nādir Khān, Aḥmad Shāh Khān, had delivered 150,000 rupees and an invitation to return to Afghanistan sent by [Amīr Ḥabīb Allāh Khān]. But as was already mentioned, Muḥammad Nādir Khān had rejected the idea of obedience to Ḥabīb Allāh Khān and bestowal of the high post that he was offered. After writing a letter to Ḥabīb Allāh Khān telling him to give up the amirate and put an end to bloodshed, [Muḥammad Nādir Khān], appealing to the honor of the Afghan tribes of the Southern Province, encouraged them to oppose Ḥabīb Allāh Khān, urged them to rise up in support of Amān Allāh Khān, organize a lashkar, and resolve to attack Kabul.

All through the night, the sepoys **/140/** taunted [the family members and relatives of Muḥammad Nādir Khān] and, when day came, confiscated their homes and put the women under surveillance in the home of

[138] Although Fayż Muḥammad rarely, if ever, refers to himself in this remote fashion, preferring instead 'the writer' (*nawīsandah* or some variant), this is precisely his name and tribal affiliation or at least an exact namesake.

Fatḥ Muḥammad Khān.[139] Asad Allāh Khān, a son of the late Amīr Ḥabīb Allāh Khān and [*marginalia*: the nephew (sister's son) of Muḥammad Nādir Khān as well as other[lvi] detainees were taken to the Arg. Among them, the wife[140] of the brother of Muḥammad Nādir Khān, Shāh Walī Khān, who is the full sister of Amān Allāh Khān, and the wife[141] of Shāh Maḥmūd Khān who is Amān Allāh Khān's half-sister were taken from the house of the ḥażrats (of Shūr Bāzār) to the Arg, but the following day, (the amir) sent them back. God willing, all this will be recounted below.) End of marginal note.]

Also on this day, a resident of Kabul who had told the shopkeepers in the bazaar to close their shops because Amān Allāh Khān was about to attack Kabul, was arrested. Just for these few words, he was hung by the heels on the Chawk.

On this day as well, two lorries full of wounded were brought to Kabul from Wardak district and from along the road to Ghaznīn where fighting continues and were delivered to the military hospital. Without let-up, they keep sending troops and artillery towards Ghaznīn and Lahūgard. Also in Ghūrband, the business of fighting goes on and troops are being directed there.[lvii]

The Events of Monday, 5 Ẕīqaʿdah, Corresponding to 26 Ḥamal and 15 April 1929

On this day, in the dead of night, they brought more wounded from Ghaznīn, some of them moaning with pain inside the vehicles. Also during the night, Ḥabīb Allāh Khān ordered that the wives of Shāh Walī Khān, Shāh Maḥmūd Khān, and Muḥammad Nādir Khān be brought to the Arg from the house of the ḥażrats.[lviii] The first was Amān Allāh Khān's full sister;[lix] the second, a half-sister; the third, the sister of Sulaymān Khān, the son of Sardār Muḥammad Āṣaf Khān.[lx] It is not known how they were treated and whether what happened to them the night before **/141/** was repeated or they were handled with respect this time.

During the daytime, Nā'ib al-Salṭanah Sayyid Ḥusayn Khān came to the Astūr Palace, the Ministry of Foreign Affairs, which Ḥabīb Allāh Khān had assigned him for his durbar. With the army band playing in the

---

[139] Another member of the Zikriyā family. See Fayż Muḥammad, *The History*, vol. 4, index ("Fatḥ M. K., Amīn al-ʿasas") and Adamec, *Who's Who*, p. 138 and Tables 31, 39, 40.

[140] A daughter of Amīr Ḥabīb Allāh Khān, her name was Ṣafiyah "Ṣamar-i Sirāj." See Adamec, *Who's Who*, Tables 29, 62.

[141] Safūrah, another daughter of the martyred amir, see ibid., Table 28 and 68.

background, he spent a relaxing half day with a group of Kūhistānī khans, accepting their congratulations and handing out sweets.

59 | This same day, airplanes dropped leaflets on the tribes of the Eastern and Southern Provinces which proclaimed that Muḥammad Nādir Khān and his brothers were kafirs. They were prepared the day before from written notes of the mullahs of Ḥabīb Allāh's majlis (part of his entourage) and were printed by his order. No one knows what effect they will have. Here is the proclamation:

> In the name of God, the Merciful, the Compassionate! (A governmental proclamation.) May it be known to all brother Muslims in the Eastern and Southern Provinces! Information about the cowardly and treacherous activity of Field Marshal Nādir proves that he has shown himself to be an infidel acting contrary to the holy religion of Islam, a rebel against the Islamic government, and trying to create division in Islam. May God protect us from this great treason and rebellion! I, in any event, am obliged to tell you about the character of this rebel, who continually engages in treasonous behavior, and about his great sin. This is the same Nādir who was field marshal during the reign of the martyred amir, while his brothers were deputy field marshals, his father and uncle were close confidants of the amir and were on duty around his tent at Kalah Gūsh [when he was martyred]. All of Afghanistan knows what these traitors carried out vis-à-vis His Highness [the late amir] and you know even better. Later they supported Amān Allāh. /142/ In any event, the wagon of deceit does not move forward and in one or two years the name and fame of them all will be gone from Afghanistan. [As for Nādir], he made hijrat (religious emigration) to France in opposition to true Muslim hijrat [which is to a Muslim country]. But we will set this issue aside. This servant, who through God's grace was honored with the title "Servant of the Religion of the Prophet of God" never took a sip from the goblet of treason of these traitors. I have [even] thought that they were, perhaps, oppressed Muslims. Now—praise be to God—the Islamic sultanate stands on firm foundations. There should be some work in the kingdom for them and they should come from foreign soil to their own homeland. This is the same as their brother Shāh Maḥmūd, who recognizes the "promise and warning" of God and has given an oath of allegiance and on whom I bestowed a leadership position and a large sum (*marginalia*: 1,000 pounds in gold [end of marginal note]) from the Bayt al-Māl for his service to Islam. I also invited [Muḥammad Nādir Khān] himself to return with honor. But because in Europe, behaving like a kafir, he has eaten a great deal of pork which has made his bones and marrow turn black, in response to my generosity and sincerity he has refused obedience to Islam. He himself is spreading lies in the Southern Province while his brother does the same in the Eastern. But thanks to the grace of God, these devils will not be able to lead the faithful into error but will only corrupt themselves. Taking into account his and his brothers' treachery and perfidy, His Highness brings to your attention, you who are true Muslims,

> that the blood of these traitors is lawful according to the Sharīʿah. The one who wipes them out will be acknowledged as a holy warrior (*ghāzī*) and a defender of Islam and will also be entitled to the following from the court (*darbār*) of the Islamic government:
>
> 1. Anyone who brings Nādir in alive will be paid 40,000 rupees and the one who brings his head will be given 30,000 rupees and a rifle with
> 60 magazine. |
> 2. Whoever brings the three brothers in alive will get for each of them 10,000 rupees or 30,000 rupees for all three. /**143**/ Whoever brings in only one alive or brings in his head will receive 10,000 rupees and a rifle with a magazine.
>
> Through the above, we have informed you of our order and desire regarding Nādir and his brothers. With the object of preventing discord and eliminating strife, you, as true Muslims, have gained the approval of the Almighty, his Prophets, the Servant of the Religion, and the supporter of Islam and will certainly give this your due regard.
> Kabul, the Government Press.

Similar kinds of proclamations about Amān Allāh Khān in which he was accused of being an infidel were also frequently printed. But if the ulema turn their attention to the Qurʾān where it says "If you differ in anything amongst yourselves, refer it to God and His Messenger, if you believe in God and in the Last Day. This is better"[142] and to the hadiths and fatwas of the most learned scholars then they will recognize these as lies.

[Ḥabīb Allāh Khān] commissioned the director of the Afghan-German Trading Company, Muḥammad Mūsā Khān Qandahārī, and seven other Qandahārīs to assassinate Amān Allāh Khān and promised them a large reward.

Also on this day, Ḥabīb Allāh ordered the printing of a proclamation declaring the Hazārahs to be kafirs. However, on the evening of this day, several Hazārahs from Bihsūd arrived in Kabul on the path of peace bringing a message of obedience and received robes of honor. The delegation which had been assigned to obtain oaths of allegiance, as was mentioned above, was still in Kabul.

In addition to these measures, Amīr Ḥabīb Allāh Khān continues to issue decrees which he has neither the power nor the capability to implement. He repeatedly says, "I will conquer India, Bukhārā, and Russian Turkistān, and even Moscow itself and I will restore the Bukhāran amir

---

142 Qurʾān: 4:59.

to his throne."[143] He solicited a letter from the Bukhāran amir to the Turkmān tribes, both immigrants (*muhājir*s) and long-established residents who had risen against Ḥabīb Allāh Khān in Mazār-i Sharīf and its environs, and sent it to them. In it (the amir of Bukhārā) called on them not to oppose /**144**/ Amīr Ḥabīb Allāh but to aid his supporters with their money and their lives and to fight against the partisans of Amān Allāh Khān.

The Events of Tuesday, 6 Ẕīqaʿdah, Corresponding to 27 Ḥamal and 16 April 1929

On this day, at nine o'clock in the morning, an airplane took off on a reconnaissance flight to the Southern Province, which had been leafleted with pamphlets accusing Field Marshal Muḥammad Nādir Khān, of being a kafir, to find out how many people had joined his cause. [Another] plane went missing.

On this day, the wives of Muḥammad Nādir Khān and his brothers, who had been taken to the Arg and kept there for a night, were allowed to leave and were lodged at the house of the ḥażrats. It was agreed with them that if they revealed their belongings, cash, and things, then there would be no burden placed on them. They agreed to do so. The second time they were brought to the Arg, extraordinary things happened to them. Eventually, due to the unparalleled mediation of the daughter of Amīr Muḥammad Khān,[144] as will come below, they were allowed [to leave] with the veil of their chastity rent and the hijab of their modesty torn.

Also during these events, Ḥabīb Allāh Khān decided to demand in marriage the daughter of Sardār Muḥammad ʿAlī Khān, son of Sardār Pīr Muḥammad Khān, whose father was Sardār Sulṭān Muḥammad Khān, a

143 According to Shkirando, who cites no source, "the reference here is to the former Amīr of Bukhara, Sayyid ʿĀlim Khān, who in March 1921 fled to Afghanistan. He settled in Qalʿah-yi Fatḥ not far from Kabul and the Afghan government paid him a monthly subsidy. According to available information, Ḥabīb Allāh Khān [Kalakānī] was in contact with him even before the occupation of Kabul. After seizing power, he increased the Bukharan amir's subsidy several times." (See Faiz Mukhammad, *Kniga upominanii*, p. 264, note 100.)

144 This Amīr Muḥammad Khān may well have been the spiritual leader Ākhūndzādah Amīr Muḥammad Khān, "Mullah of Chaknāwur." See Adamec, *Who's Who*, p. 121 ("Amīr Muhammad Akhundzada"). His daughter, whose name is unknown, would have had a sufficient aura of sanctity, thanks to her father, to be able to negotiate credibly on behalf of the Yaḥyā Khayl women. For more on the influence of the mullah see Nawid, *Religious Response*, index ("Molla Din [*sic*] Mohammad of Chaknawur").

brother of Amīr Dūst Muḥammad Khān.[145] She was also the granddaughter
61 of Fāṭimah Sulṭān, a daughter of Amīr Dūst Muḥammad Khān. | The girl, having decided to take her own life [rather than marry the amir], drank poison but was treated and recovered. A second time Ḥabīb Allāh Khān tried to force her [to marry him] but she refused. [Then] he sent to her mother's door some soldiers for whom mercy was farsangs away. He issued an order saying, "I will drag this girl by force if necessary to [my] bed." The mother and daughter gave themselves up for dead and up until today have not agreed to go. Eventually, as will come, she was taken by force and possessed. /145/

Also on this day, three flying machines again headed towards Ghaznīn and Lahūgard where battles were raging in both places. They dropped bombs and also the pamphlets mentioned above which falsely spread the rumor that that Amān Allāh Khān had been arrested and was being taken to Kabul by plane.

Also on this day, the Hazārah formations of Abū'l-Ḥasan (Būl Ḥasan) of Bihsūd and the ʿAlā al-Dīn Hazārahs of Jāghūrī engaged Purdil Khān in battle at the manzil of Shash Gāw. Purdil Khān, Ḥabīb Allāh Khān's field marshal, had abandoned Ghaznīn to Amān Allāh Khān and then halted in Shash Gāw where he requested reinforcements, ammunition, and artillery from Ḥabīb Allāh Khān in order to advance on Ghaznīn. Purdil Khān and thirteen other men were surrounded in a fort by the Hazārahs and then, after a while, as will come, he escaped and came back to Kabul.[lxi]

Thus, on this day, 36-pound mountain guns and a great deal of ammunition were sent from Kabul to Ghaznīn. They say that Amān Allāh Khān has occupied Ghaznīn, set up his headquarters in the fort of ʿAbd al-Aḥmad Khān. He has defeated men of the Sulaymān Khayl tribe and reached Shaykh Sīn [Yāsīn] of Khawāt-i Wardak by way of the Majīd Pass where, as will come, he defeated and killed or captured contingents of Ḥabīb Allāh Khān's army.

The Events of Wednesday, 7 Ẕīqaʿdah, Corresponding to 28 Ḥamal and 17 April 1929

On this day, two airplanes took off at six o'clock heading towards the Southern Province and Ghaznīn. There are problems in and around

[145] Adamec, *Who's Who*, Table 26 has Muḥammad ʿAlī Khān as a son of Pīr Muḥammad Khān and grandson of Pāyandah Khān rather than Sulṭān Muḥammad Khān. His tables for Sulṭān Muḥammad's line show no Pīr Muḥammad Khān.

Ghūrband (for Ḥabīb Allāh) because Hazārah militias from this region are threatening Kūhistān and Kūh Dāman. Nā'ib al-Salṭanah Sayyid Ḥusayn, because of the rumor that the Hazārahs of Surkh wa Pārsā had come to Chārīkār en route /**146**/ to Kabul to offer their allegiance, himself had gone to Chārīkār [supposedly] to escort the Hazārahs with all due honor to the capital. In point of fact, he had left for Chārīkār to organize a defense against any Hazārah assault on Kūhistān.

Also on this day, at the request of Kākā Muḥsin, a greedy and vain man who aspires to rule over the entire Hazārahjāt, a farman-circular was drafted addressed to all Hazārahs. However, it remained unsigned because Sayyid Ḥusayn had left for Chārīkār.[lxii] As will be noted below, it remained unsigned.

Also on this day, the Hazārahs of Bihsūd, having obtained six thousand rifles and a farman from Amān Allāh Khān telling them to postpone their attack on Kabul for four days, sent a message to Ḥabīb Allāh Khān providing plausible reasons explaining their failure to send a written oath of allegiance and seeking forgiveness. They hoped to deceive Ḥabīb Allāh Khān with this letter and, as was stated above, this message was sent by way of the Hazārahs of Sar Chashmah. As a robe of honor, each of the seven members [of the Sar Chashmah delegation] was given a silk turban
62 woven in Kabul. | As for when they would send the oath of allegiance, the Hazārahs of Bihsūd swore to His Highness that they would bring it in ten or fifteen days. Ḥabīb Allāh Khān expressed his approval of their promise and even uttered some words of commendation about the Hazārah people, their virtues and their piety, although only the day before he had ordered a proclamation printed up accusing them of unbelief and had requested a fatwa from the mullahs anathematizing the Shi'is as apostates from the Muḥammadan community. But the issue of Islam and apostasy from the Muḥammadan community being in the hands of and dependent on the views of Ḥabīb Allāh Khān and know-nothing pseudo-mullahs is neither according to the Qur'ān nor the way of the Prophet. Into what misery have they led the people of Islam out of ignorance, pushed ordinary people to the brink of extermination, and destroyed the foundations of the enlightened, /**147**/ holy, Muḥammadan religion.

Also on this day, as a result of the worsening of the military situation in the Southern Province where Muḥammad Nādir Khān had assembled an army, Ḥabīb Allāh Khān and his associates became increasingly alarmed and began to send arms and ammunition to Lahūgard.[lxiii]

The Events of Thursday, 8 Ẕīqaʿdah, Corresponding to 29 Ḥamal and 18 April

On the basis of a false rumor of the appearance in Ghūrband of Ghulām Rasūl Khān, son of Sayf Ākhūndzādah Isḥāqzāʾī, with his own tribal lashkar and some displaced Hazārahs who were now settled in Mazār-i Sharīf, Sayyid Ḥusayn had gone to Chārīkār on Wednesday to repel the [expected] attack and defend against the Hazārahs of Shaykh ʿAlī, Bāmyān, Balkhāb, Yakah Awlang, Surkh wa Pārsā, Turkmān, and Darghān. Publicly, he had announced that he was going to Chārīkār for a written oath of allegiance that the Hazārahs of Surkh wa Pārsā were bringing. So, on this day he has not yet returned to Kabul since he is very busy there preparing its defenses.

Also on this day, despite the fact that yesterday representatives of the Bihsūd Hazārahs brought a message which said that the Hazārahs of Bihsūd and Dāy Zangī would provide an oath of allegiance in ten to fifteen days, Ḥabīb Allāh Khān having made their promise a basis for action and issued farmans of reconciliation, [now] he heard that farmans and announcements from Amān Allāh Khān from Ghaznīn had been written to those people [the Hazārahs of Bihsūd] saying they should hold off their attack on Kabul for four days and when his army reached the manzil of Shash Gāw, they would have entered Sar Chashmah and so could flank the forces /**148**/ of Ḥabīb Allāh Khān, which were en route to Ghaznīn, on two sides and engage them like Ẕāt al-Naḥiyyīn.[146] Having discovered this and thinking that the Hazārahs had sent their message [that they would bring an oath in ten or fifteen days] only to deceive him and to give him a false sense of security, Ḥabīb Allāh Khān having already dispatched a thousand men from Kabul to march to Sar Chashmah, on this day ordered [another] thousand armed and unarmed men from Maydān to go to the Hazārahjāt. In the event that the Hazārahs put up a fight, they should kill them, take the women and children as captives, and loot their houses and steal all their belongings.[lxiv] But his army, faced with a difficult situation on the road to Ghaznīn, was unable to advance towards Sar Chashmah
63 and went [instead] in the direction of Wardak. |

[146] On Ẕāt al-Naḥīyyīn see footnote 104 above.

The Events of Friday, 9 Ẕīqa'dah, Corresponding to 30 Ḥamal and 19 April

There is not a single rifle left in the government arsenal and now things have reached such a state that (Ḥabīb Allāh Khān) has given an order to take away the rifles of the police who are protecting the city and give them to unarmed recruits. In addition, a decree was issued regarding paying soldiers only after they had served for two months. An army like this, assembled by force at the tip of the bayonet, fighting without fodder or rations, and forced to go to the battlefield, which means they cannot provide for their families through day labor or farming, what will such an army eat and how will it fight? Such things give rise to feelings of despondency at the destruction and misfortune of the nation and the Islamic government and for the bloodshed and the prostration of our society. Unfortunately, because of ignorance, stupid ambition, and disobedience, Afghanistan /149/ has fallen into the hands of ignorant pseudo-mullahs who are, in fact, followers of Satan and because of whom there has befallen the people, who were dragged into war, so much misery and misfortune. Deprived of the necessary means of subsistence, people live in fear and the expectation of death. [The Northerners] have the name of the religion on their lips but both Islam and Muslims are being buried under the dirt.

On Friday, Ḥabīb Allāh Khān by telephone summoned Sayyid Ḥusayn from Chārīkār to Kabul for discussions about the worsening situation and how to organize a defense vis-à-vis the increasingly difficult situation in Ghaznīn, Lahūgard, and Khūst. He sent his brother, Ḥamīd Allāh Khān, towards Ghaznīn at the head of a force of one thousand men and also a large group of men with battle experience, equipped with artillery, rifles, other weapons, and a large supply of ammunition.[lxv] Because the partisans of Amān Allāh Khān, for example 'Aṭā Muḥammad, the son of Malik Muḥammad Kūh Dāmanī, and others in the Northern regions, attacked and pillaged Chārīkār, Sayyid Ḥusayn had gone in that direction to fight them.

In the late afternoon of this day, fifty camels loaded with weapons and ammunition were dispatched towards Ghaznīn.

Also on this day, Malik Muḥammad 'Alam Khān Shinwārī, who was guilty of the destruction of government buildings in Jalālābād, the plundering of its residents, and all the hardship which had befallen that region and for which he was expelled from his tribe, arrived in Kabul, as has already been related, and swore an oath of allegiance. However, he failed to accomplish his goal and, along with the group of his people who had accompanied him, he was sent off to Jalālābād to negotiate a truce. However, fearful of the wrath of his fellow tribesmen, he did not go there and today, instead, set off to join Field Marshal Muḥammad Nādir Khān. Apparently, he left Kabul and went to the field marshal thinking that perhaps he could escape his sins and misdeeds and not be held accountable. But this goal, which he imagines will correspond to the end [he desires], is impossible. **/150/**

The Events of Saturday, 10 Ẕīqaʿdah, Corresponding to 31 Ḥamal and 20 April

Sayyid Ḥusayn Khān departed on this day for Chārīkār to organize a defense against those forces which, as already mentioned, had arrived in Ghūrband. During his efforts at fortifying [the place], Sayyid Ḥusayn
64 assigned a group of his most trustworthy associates | to assassinate ʿAṭā Muḥammad, son of Malik Muḥammad Istālifī, whose fiancée he (Sayyid Ḥusayn) had taken as a wife. ʿAṭā Muḥammad had [already] vowed to kill Sayyid Ḥusayn. Initially Ḥabīb Allāh Khān had given the post of warden of the Arg to ʿAṭā Muḥammad and he was exceptionally proud of it. Sayyid Ḥusayn, fearing retribution, found a pretext and ordered him imprisoned. But [ʿAṭā Muḥammad] escaped to Kūh Dāman where he assembled 200–300 of the thieves. They began to attack the populace, fighting against the forces of Ḥabīb Allāh Khān and aiming to kill Sayyid Ḥusayn. At night, Sayyid Ḥusayn's trusted associates [who were assigned to assassinate ʿAṭā Muḥammad] set up an ambush near the gates of [ʿAṭā Muḥammad's] fort. When sunrise announced the death of ʿAṭā Muḥammad, suspecting nothing, he himself walked out the gate of the fort and straight into the ambush. Several bullets struck him in the stomach, chest, and forearm and he was killed. Sayyid Ḥusayn Khān, who had feared him, now stopped worrying and returned to Kabul. They transported [ʿAṭā Muḥammad's] corpse to Kabul and hung it at the Chawk—as a warning to others.

On this day, by order of Ḥabīb Allāh Khān, the Hazārah chief equerry, Aḥmad ʿAlī, and the son of Sardār ʿAbd Allāh Khān Tūkhī, whose brother, ʿAṭā Muḥammad, had raised a rebellion in Mazār-i Sharīf against Ḥabīb Allāh Khān, [both of whom had been jailed in Kabul], were hanged in Shayrpūr along with a member of the Tarakī tribe and a resident of Qandahar who had been accused, along with other leading figures, of conspiring against Ḥabīb Allāh Khān.

Marginalia: For other [detained conspirators], they have built twenty-four iron cages but have not locked them in them yet. [Ḥabīb Allāh Khān] also issued an order to hang Prince Ḥayāt Allāh /151/ ʿAżud al-Dawlah and he was led out of prison, his head bared and his hands tied, to be hanged. But through the intercession of Muḥammad Kabīr Khān and Malik Muḥsin Khān, the high governor, he was pardoned and saved from death. [End of marginal note.]

On this day, too, rumors spread that Amān Allāh Khān's army had entered Wardak and units of Ḥabīb Allāh Khān's forces, who had been holding positions on the slopes of the Kūh-i Chihil Tan, which abut the northern part of Qalʿah-i Qāżī, have retreated to the heights of Kūh-i Āsmāʾī, where they have set up guns on the summit.

Also on this day, rumors spread that 6,000 Hazārahs from Bihsūd had crossed over the Ūnay Pass and headed for Ghūrband while a contingent of Hazārahs numbering some 1,000 men has occupied positions at this pass in order to block the road to the Hazārahjāt before Ḥabīb Allāh Khān's army. Muʿīn al-Salṭanah Ḥamīd Allāh Khān, sent to bring order to the forces dispatched to Ghaznīn and the Hazārahjāt, made some recommendations and then returned to Kabul. Ḥabīb Allāh Khān's force, sent to Ghaznīn, [now] retreated and returned to Shinīz-i Wardak.

Also, the Chitrārī colonel, Pīnī Beg,[lxvi] having come to Muḥammad Nādir Khān with his men, allegedly to surrender but in fact to try and capture Muḥammad Nādir Khān, was arrested and his detachment was disarmed.[147]

The Events of Sunday, 11 Ẕīqaʿdah, Corresponding to 1 Ṣawr and 21 April 1929

On the eve of this day, a group of elders from the Sulaymān Khayl tribe arrived in Kabul hoping to obtain money, rifles, and ammunition. Although they gave an oath of allegiance and pledged obedience, they were unable to obtain what they wanted. Ḥabīb Allāh Khān summoned them and in a private conversation encouraged them to spare nothing in attacking, killing /152/ and plundering the Hazārahs, saying that they
65 support Amān Allāh Khān and are Shiʿites and kafirs. | In urging them to attack the Hazārahs and plunder and destroy their homes, crops and

[147] This Pīnī Beg is also known as Panīn Beg. Adamec, *Who's Who*, p. 214, has him coming from Afghan Turkistān when, according to the newspaper *Iṣlāḥ*, 1/8, 15 December 1929, in a biographical note about him it is reported that he had come from Chitrār (Chitral) at the age of eight at which time he was probably enrolled in the corps of court pages.

property, he said, "As *pādshāh*, I authorize you to act in this fashion. There is no need to fear any consequences because I do not consider it permissible to hold you to account for shedding [their] blood and looting [their] property and I will never question anyone about it." I don't know how much longer this revolution and the bloodshed and plundering of the people will last because of such barbaric provocation.

Also this evening, seven motor vehicles loaded with stalwart fighters left for Ghaznīn where the situation for Ḥabīb Allāh's force was very tenuous: 385 cavalrymen from the amir's guard have been taken prisoner by Amān Allāh Khān's forces; fifteen cavalrymen managed to escape and one secretly made his way to Kabul where he reported the following: two regiments, each of 300 men, had laid down their arms and surrendered to Amān Allāh Khān.

At the time of these events, Maḥmūd Khān Yāwar [again] was sentenced to death by hanging. For one lakh of rupees, he bought his way off and was pardoned. At the time of his first arrest, in order to save himself from death, he had paid three lakhs of rupees.

Also on this same day, part of Ḥabīb Allāh Khān's army, having sustained defeat at the hands of Amān Allāh Khān, arrived in Kabul towards evening. Leaders of its contingents had been requesting help by telephone. But in Kabul no one was left any more—everyone had been sent to fight Amān Allāh Khān in Lahūgard, Ghaznīn, and Ghūrband. Because of this, Ḥabīb Allāh Khān, unable to send more forces, authorized his troops to return to Qalʿah-i Durrānī, ordered them to strengthen their positions there, and not to allow the victorious advance units of Amān Allāh Khān's army to pass. **/153/** "Who knows God's plans?" (Ḥāfiẓ)

The Events of Monday, 12 Ẕīqaʿdah, Corresponding to 2 Ṣawr and 22 April

On this day, a number of soldiers who had been forcibly conscripted into Ḥabīb Allāh Khān's army, torn away from their work in the fields or from other occupations by which they managed to obtain the means of subsistence for their families, were sent to defend Lahūgard and to stave off an attack by Muḥammad Nādir Khān. The advance force [of Muḥammad Nādir Khān], led by his first cousin Aḥmad Shāh Khān and the brother of Muḥammad Nādir Khān, Shāh Maḥmūd Khān, reached Dūbandī of the village of Khūshī. Ḥabīb Allāh Khān's army, having decided that it could not put up a defense, headed back to Kabul. Ḥabīb Allāh Khān was outraged and when they arrived in the city ordered them to return their weapons and leave.[lxvii] In their stead, 1,350 men who had been forcibly pressed into service were quickly sent off around sunset towards Lahūgard by order of Nā'ib al-Salṭanah Sayyid Ḥusayn Khān.

On this day, too, Sayyid Ḥusayn Khān viciously caned six butchers.
66 Starting in Shaʿbān and up to the present | they have been selling one *pāw* at (96) *misqāls* of lamb and one and a half *pāw*[148] of (120) *misqāls* of beef with bone at a price of one Afghānī. The actual weight of the lamb amounted to 32 *misqāls* and the beef, 40 *misqāls*. Thus two-thirds of the meat, i.e. 64 *misqāls* [of lamb] and 80 *misqāls* [of beef], was bone. He ordered that fixed prices be set for one-half of a *chārak* [of lamb] and for three *pāws* of beef. He nailed all six butchers by their ears to stakes in three bustling areas of the city so that passers-by would get the message.

He also fixed the price for cooking oil (*rawghan*). Shopkeepers were buying one seer (*sīr*) of oil for thirty rupees. /**154**/ But he ordered them to buy from the dealers at twenty-five rupees per seer and sell at twenty-six. As a result, for every seer sold, the shopkeeper lost four rupees and the merchants (the dealers) lost five. They then wrote His Highness, Ḥabīb Allāh Khān, a letter in which they said that the dealers buy the oil at twenty-eight rupees per seer and shopkeepers buy it a thirty; they cannot afford the loss [if they follow Sayyid Ḥusayn Khān's dictate]. So they hoarded the oil in the bazaar and declared that it was all gone. As a consequence of such policies and administration, the entire population of the city has been brought to desperate straits in four months and thirteen days [of Ḥabīb Allāh Khān's regime]. Practically everyone has been deprived of his livelihood and the majority of salaried government officials find themselves without employment and are living from day to day in extreme hardship and expecting death. They are able neither to fight nor to flee. Moreover, in every house to which a bailiff has been sent from a police, provincial, or governmental administrative office on some matter, the bailiff uses his rifle butt to seize cash ranging from twenty to 100 to 500 rupees, even if the person has been summoned to perform some task for the government. Who knows what this will lead to? As a result of such malicious activity, day and night the people pray to God to grant them a speedy death but even this they cannot obtain. If anything, the arrests, looting, imprisonments, violence, and vile behavior are worsening.

---

148 The very smallest unit of weight is the *nukhūd*: 24 *nukhūd* = 1 *misqāl*; 24 *misqāl* = 1 *khurd*; 4 *khurd* = 1 *pāw*; 4 *pāw* = 1 *chārak* (*chahār yak*); 4 *chārak* = 1 *sīr*; 8 *sīr* = 1 *man*; 10 *man* = one Kābulī *kharwār*. This case indicates there were different *pāw* sizes for different meats.

The Events of Tuesday, 13 Ẕīqaʿdah, Corresponding to 3 Ṣawr and 23 April

This morning at 6:25 two planes took off for Lahūgard on a reconnaissance and bombing mission. They returned at 9:00.

Due to the fact that the Hazārahs, who are Shiʿis and followers of the Twelve Imams, have not [up to now] given oaths of allegiance to Amīr Ḥabīb Allāh Khān, a declaration was drafted at a session of the Islamic Regulatory Commission accusing them of unbelief. It was supposed to be published after the Hanafi ulema confirmed it. /155/ Also, the Sulaymān Khayl nomads, in accordance with an order from Amīr Ḥabīb Allāh Khān, declared jihad against the Hazārahs. Together with Malik Muḥammad ʿAlam Shinwārī and a group of his fellow tribesmen who were now in Kabul and fearing Muḥammad Hāshim Khān and the wrath of the Muhmand, Afrīdī, and other tribes because of the fact that they themselves had violated the inter-tribal covenant and had plundered and wreaked havoc on Jalālābād, and so cannot return to their own lands, decided to march to the Hazārahjāt, to launch a religious war and to kindle sedition over a large territory—as far as the borders with Iran, which is a Shiʿi
67 state. But the Islamic Regulatory Commission, fearing | a sectarian outbreak and the prolongation of war and bloodshed, would not affirm the above declaration. In support of their decision, they declared that in every country under the protection of any government, Christians, Jews, Zoroastrians, idolaters, Buddhists, Shiʿis, Sunnis, pagans, Ismāʿīlīs [and] even the seventy-three sects of Islam, live peacefully together. They submit to their governments, do not interfere in the religions [of other people], do not violate their ordinances and their tranquility, and do not inflict harm on them. Each upholds those norms of human conduct which do not contradict the holy code of his own religion. Citing these reasons, [the members of the regulatory commission] unanimously concluded that they should draw up a list of all the obscene and barbaric deeds which the amirs ʿAbd al-Raḥmān Khān, Ḥabīb Allāh Khān, and Amān Allāh Khān had inflicted on the Hazārahs. Among these were burning Hazārahs alive, buying and selling them, turning them into slaves, giving their lands to Afghans, etc. [These amirs] persecuted the Hazārahs and drove them from the country. It was proposed to send this declaration to the Hazārahs themselves so that they would stop supporting Amān Allāh Khān, because all they had ever witnessed from him was annihilation, injustice, and inhumanity.[lxviii] /156/ But regardless, the Hazārahs did not remove their hands from opposition to Ḥabīb Allāh Khān or from supporting Amān Allāh Khān and said, "We prefer a lion to devour us than a dog to befriend us."

Also on this day, in conjunction with the circulation of rumors about the defeat of Ḥabīb Allāh Khān's army and its retreat to Qalʿah-i Durrānī, [Ḥabīb Allāh Khān] himself, along with a group of devoted followers, set out in five motor vehicles for the battlefield in an attempt to bolster the morale of his troops and inspire them to fight. At night he returned to the city. In response to rumors that Muḥammad Hāshim Khān, the brother of Muḥammad Nādir Khān, was approaching the city under cover of darkness with militias from the Muhmand, Afrīdī, and other tribes of the Eastern Province, [Ḥabīb Allāh Khān] brought back to Kabul those same seven pieces of ordnance which he had earlier sent to reinforce positions in Ghaznīn and then dispatched them to Butkhāk and Tapah-i Maranjān.

Part of the army of Muḥammad Nādir Khān,[lxix] now arrived in Tangī Āghūjān, Lahūgard. Approximately 9,000 Hazārah militia along the road through Qattān ascended the slopes of the Kūh-i Pamqān and Shakar Darrah. They resolved to attack Chārīkār and Kūh Dāman so that simultaneously, from all sides, i.e. from Ghūrband, from the heights of Kūh-i Shakar Darrah, Wardak, Maydān, Chār Āsyā, Mūsāʾī, Bīnī Ḥiṣār, Butkhāk and from the heights of Kūh-i Khūrd Kabul, they would assault Kabul, Kūh Dāman and Kūhistān.

Well, whomever God helps, his star will surely ascend. /**157**/

The Events of Wednesday, 14 Ẕīqaʿdah, Corresponding to 4 S̱awr and 24 April

Today at 1:00 P.M. word spread that Muḥammad Nādir Khān's force had
68 entered the village of Tangī Āghūjān in the district of Lahūgard, | twelve kuruhs from Kabul. This news greatly disturbed Ḥabīb Allāh Khān, Sayyid Ḥusayn, and their supporters. Sayyid Ḥusayn Khān quickly set off for Lahūgard to get information. His sepoys and close subordinates, wielding their rifle butts, rousted out from their homes the owners who rented out the phaetons (buggies).[149] Due to the oppression of the army, which would take the vehicles and not pay but instead of money used their rifle butts to beat up the owners, they had concealed their vehicles along with their horses inside their homes. Now [the sepoys] dragged them, their horses, and their wagons out of their houses using their rifles as clubs. The sepoys drove the horse-drawn phaetons to Muḥammad Āghah and Chār Āsyā on

[149] Fayż Muḥammad writes the word phaeton (*fātūn*) and then immediately after it the word "buggy" in parentheses (*bagī*). (Also see ms. p. 68, line 3.).

the heels of Sayyid Ḥusayn who had left earlier. Sayyid Ḥusayn himself, on gathering information about Muḥammad Nādir Khān's force ordered the contingents that were assigned to defend against [Muḥammad Nādir Khān] to throw up breastworks at strategic places and wait there ready to fight. He then returned to the city. With a gesture of his hand he directed the sepoys who were driving the phaetons to turn around. /158/ They all returned to Kabul, arriving about sunset.

Also today, 20,000 men from the Sulaymān Khayl and Andar tribes to whom the Ḥażrat [of Shūr Bāzār] had sent a letter asking them to support Ḥabīb Allāh Khān came out in opposition to Amān Allāh Khān in Zurmat, Katawāz, and Shalgīr,[lxx] weapons in hand, and demanded ammunition from Ḥabīb Allāh Khān. The latter gave instructions to the Ministry of War to find and speedily send as many boxes as possible of the kind of ammunition that fit their rifles, so that without delay they could strike a blow at Amān Allāh Khān's army which had brought the fight to Ghaznīn and keep it from advancing further.

The Wazīrī muhajirs, the Wardaks, and Hazārahs moving through the Majid Pass entered Khawāt and cut off the rear of Ḥabīb Allāh Khān's forces who were in the villages of Takiyah and Shash Gaw and thereby closed the road for any movement by them so that no military supplies or fodder could reach them.[lxxi]

During this same time, Ḥabīb Allāh Khān ordered publication of a notice of reward for the assassination of Amān Allāh Khān. He set the reward at 160,000 rupees (equivalent to 32,000 Iranian tomans) and ordered leaflets with this announcement scattered by plane.

Also on this day, because of a false rumor about an attack by Muḥammad Nādir Khān's forces, the gate of the Arg was shut for about half an hour.

Marginalia: During the night of 14 Ẕīqaʿdah, Khwājah Tāj al-Dīn, mayor [of Kabul], and Commandant Sayyid Āqā Khān were ordered by Ḥabīb Allāh Khān to drag Bī Naẓīr, the daughter of Amīr Muḥammad Khān, son of Muḥammad ʿAlī Khān, son of Sardār Pīr Muḥammad Khān, son of Sardār Sulṭān Muḥammad Khān, the brother of Amīr Dūst Muḥammad Khān, by force from the house of her father and her grandmother, a daughter of Amīr Dūst Muḥammad Khān, and they brought her to Ḥabīb Allāh Khān, the "Servant of the Religion of the Messenger of God," at the Arg. When he first asked for her hand in marriage, [she had refused and then] when he demanded a second time she drank poison and tried to strangle herself with a cord around her throat. [Now] by force he "married" that benighted woman and took full possession of her. [End of marginal note.]

Marginalia: Also on this day, Malik Muḥsin, the high governor, who on several occasions had sent for elders of the Sulaymān Khayl and the Ghilzāʾī Andar tribes to come to Kabul in order to receive robes of honor so they would turn away from Amān Allāh Khān and choose to obey and support Ḥabīb Allāh Khān and they had sent some men to Kabul, [at this point] left Kabul for Ghaznīn, Zurmat, and Katawāz.] [End of marginal note.]

Marginalia: Also during the night of this day, in connection with the worsening situation of the troops in the Ghaznīn region, Ḥabīb Allāh Khān drove with his accomplices in ten automobiles almost as far as Shash Gaw. One of the cars, travelling ahead of the others, was captured by an advance force of Amān Allāh Khān's troops. [End of marginal note.]

The Events of Thursday, 15 Ẕīqaʿdah, Corresponding to 5 S̱awr 1308 and 25 April 1929

Also on this day, Ḥabīb Allāh Khān ordered the distribution of a declaration signed by the mullahs which authorized robbing the Qizilbāsh and murdering the Hazārahs of the city because they had not given an oath of allegiance and were supporters of Amān Allāh Khān. However, Sayyid Ḥusayn Khān blocked implementation of this evil plan, said a few words about the bad consequences /**159**/ of it, and raised a number of good arguments against it.

Also on this day, Ḥażrat-i Shūr Bāzār issued a fatwa authorizing the killing of Hazārahs who were long-time residents of Kabul. The great majority of them had been born in the city, had built their homes there, and had already lived fifty or sixty years in the capital. However, Sayyid Ḥusayn Khān did not recognize his fatwa as authoritative and admonished him saying, "When we were fighting with Amān Allāh Khān while he was still on the throne, he did not take it out on a single Kūhistānī who was in Kabul, let alone hundreds or thousands." This ḥażrat, who thinks himself a great Muslim and an influential leader of Muslims, is constantly engaged in such provocative acts. I don't know whether he has ever read the verse in the Qurʾān, "What each soul acquires, it remains with him and
69 the bearer will not bear the burden of another soul."[150] | To hell with such a person, who claims to be a Muslim and doesn't know that the blood of a thousand Hanafi Muslims that he has spilled and continues to spill are all of his faith. Thousands of homes plundered, hundreds of women and

[150] Qurʾān 6:164.

children violated—all this is a result of his fanaticism and ignorance. The All-High will punish him for this and send him to hell along with other enemies of the faith of the Prophet.

Sayyid Ḥusayn Khān, having arrived from Lahūgard, today conferred with Ḥabīb Allāh Khān until midnight and brought him up to date on the situation in the environs of Kabul where tribal formations were preparing to attack from all sides. They also discussed Ghulām Nabī [Khān Charkhī's[151]] taking control of Mazār-i Sharīf, something only they knew about. It is not known, though, what if any, decisions the two of them made. At one o'clock in the morning, Sayyid Ḥusayn Khān left for Chārīkār with his family and retainers.

Also during this time, in accordance with an order from Muḥammad Nādir Khān, a military unit of the Mangal tribe /160/ arrived in Ḥiṣārak, Lahūgard. They routed the troops of Ḥabīb Allāh Khān, who were trying to prevent the advance of Muḥammad Nādir Khān's units. Many soldiers were killed, four hundred were taken prisoner, and the rest scattered. A well-armed unit of Muḥammad Nādir Khān's army reached Ḥiṣārak in Khūrd Kabul with the aim of attacking the army of Ḥabīb Allāh Khān stationed at Butkhāk. But it turned around and withdrew without taking any action.

In response to rumors about the utter defeat of Ḥabīb Allāh Khān's forces in Chārīkār at the hands of the Hazārahs of Surkh wa Pārsā, an artillery battery was dispatched today to Kūh Dāman on the heels of Sayyid Ḥusayn who had left during the night.

In conjunction with the arrival of units of Muḥammad Nādir Khān's forces in Khurd Kabul and Chakarī Chinān, this evening all recruited formations, forcibly conscripted from the populace of Maydān and other villages, were hastily dispatched to Butkhāk before they had even had time for a meal. After the withdrawal [of Muḥammad Nādir Khān's units], mentioned above, they [the forces of Ḥabīb Allāh Khān] stood down.

The Events of Friday, 16 Ẕīqa'dah, Corresponding to 6 Ṣawr and 26 April 1929

On the eve of this day, Muḥammad Ṣiddīq Khān, a brigadier general (*ghundmishr*) during Amān Allāh Khān's time, arrived in Kabul and went to see Ḥabīb Allāh Khān. Ever since the Mangal uprising he had been stationed

[151] See Adamec, *Who's Who*, pp. 149–50.

in Khūst and its environs with the regular army garrison. He had been captured by Muḥammad Nādir Khān and escaped and came to see Ḥabīb Allāh Khān. On the basis of what he recounted, Ghulām ʿAlī, the aide and adjutant of Sayyid Ḥusayn, and other partisans of Ḥabīb Allāh Khān, put the word out that on Tuesday, the 13th of Shaʿbān a battle had taken place at Tīrah Pass /**161**/ in which Muḥammad Nādir Khān's force was routed and all his military supplies, tents, and equipment were plundered by the Afghans who were unfaithful to the alliance and disloyal to ʿAlī Aḥmad Khān, like the Shinwārīs and Khūgyānīs. It was said Muḥammad Nādir Khān himself had escaped to the Jadrān tribe and was staying there.

During these events, one night Ḥabīb Allāh Khān demanded that
70 the daughter of the late Nā'ib al-Salṭanah, Naṣr Allāh Khān, | whose mother[152]—also the mother of ʿAzīz Allāh Khān—was the daughter of Sardār Faqīr Muḥammad Khān, be forcibly brought to the Arg. He wanted to sleep with her and make her "marry" him. But she said that her own marriage had been contracted with Amān Allāh Khān. Amān Allāh Khān's prayer leader, Ḥāfiz Muḥammad Ḥasan Khān and other witnesses, who had attended the matrimonial contract ceremony, confirmed the truthfulness of what the princess said. Ḥabīb Allāh Khān warned them that if, after checking, he discovered they were lying he would punish them severely. He kept the woman with him for a night and in the morning let her go home. The next evening Sayyid Ḥusayn Khān summoned the princess to his house by force to check whether intercourse with Amān Allāh Khān had in fact occurred or not. He commanded: "Prepare a bed for her in a room behind this salon where I am sitting so that I can verify." He kept her the whole night and at dawn he sent her back home. It seems that what happened to her, to her sister, and the women and girls of the late Amīr Ḥabīb Allāh Khān's harem is a divine punishment for the way in which the girls and women of the Hazārahs were treated by Amīr ʿAbd al-Raḥmān Khān and his son Ḥabīb Allāh Khān. Now their family are receiving the punishment they well-deserve and this will be a lesson to people. /**162**/

Also on this day, as was earlier related, Hazārahs units reached the Kūh-i Qattān. After word spread that they had attacked from the Kūh-i Qattān heights and captured the Kūh Dāmanī villages of Shakar Darrah, Farzah, Ghāzah, Sarāy Khwājah, and also Chārīkār, followers of Sayyid

---

152 The daughter was Hājirah Sardār Bīgum and the mother was Bilqīs Kūkū [Koko] Jān. See Adamec, *Who's Who*, Tables 25 and 57.

Ḥusayn Khān along with the soldier-rebels who were in Kabul headed for Kūh Dāman, some running, some quick-marching, in order to defend their homes, families, and children. By evening they had all left the city.

The Events of Saturday, 17 Ẕīqaʿdah, Corresponding to 7 Ṣawr and 27 April 1929

Today an Hazārah tribal lashkar, numbered by some at 9,000 and by others at 30,000 men, attacked Farzah, Shakar Darrah, and Istālif, as already mentioned, and burned two forts. In response to rumors that they had captured (territory) as far as Chārīkār and Sarāy Khwājah, Ḥamīd Allāh Khān, the brother of Ḥabīb Allāh Khān, was sent off to Shakar Darrah. Before his arrival, Sayyid Ḥusayn Khān, who had earlier gone there, had already organized its defenses. The Hazārahs, after displaying their power and throwing fear into the Kūh Dāmanīs, withdrew. Ḥamīd Allāh Khān returned to the city and brought word that a conflict had supposedly taken place among the local population over rhubarb farms. But now it is settled and therefore there was no longer any threat from the Hazārahs.

After circulating this rumor, those people who at Ḥamīd Allāh Khān's order had been dispatched from Kabul to Kūh Dāman to defend their families and homes, returned to the capital. [At the same time], the Hazārahs descended the mountain from Shakar Darrah and arrived in Ghūrband,
71 **/163/** thus inspiring [more] fear in the Kūhistānīs and | Kūh Dāmanīs.

Sayyid Ḥusayn has compelled all remaining Northerners to assemble and head for the Western and Southern Provinces to fend off the attack of Amān Allāh Khān and Muḥammad Nādir Khān's forces. With regard to the latter, rumors were flying that he had fled to the Jadrān tribe. However, [the Northerners], fearful of the power of the Hazārahs, refused to obey Sayyid Ḥusayn Khān telling [him]:

> You forcibly dragged us into war with the government, tore us from our trades and our fields, and led us into misery and destitution. As a consequence of your vile deeds, all the people of Afghanistan, including the Hazārahs, have risen against us and are bent on destroying and annihilating us, our families and our children. Now that the Hazārahs have occupied positions in the mountains and are preparing to attack, we cannot leave our families and children to the mercy of fate and go fight the forces of Amān Allāh Khān and Muḥammad Nādir Khān.

This answer had a depressing effect on Sayyid Ḥusayn (*marginalia*: but ultimately he achieved what he wanted when the Hazārahs withdrew. [End of marginal note.])

[71]

This same day, two planes took off for Ghaznīn at Ḥabīb Allāh Khān's order but did not return.

Also today, a group of the human-like savages from Shinwār under the leadership of two or three pseudo-mullahs arrived in Kabul. Some say a thousand men came, others say four hundred and others, five hundred. They have come, supposedly, to express obedience to Ḥabīb Allāh Khān and to give an oath of allegiance, but in reality they are here for money, weapons, and ammunition. Their activities swell the pride of Malik Muḥammad ʿAlam Shinwārī, who destroyed Jalālābād and is now in Kabul. /**164**/

The Events of Sunday, 18 Ẕīqaʿdah Corresponding to 8 Ṣawr and 28 April [*1929*]

In conjunction with the rumors about the approach of Amān Allāh Khān's and Muḥammad Nādir Khān's armies, today Ḥabīb Allāh Khān[lxxii] busied himself readying weapons and preparing defenses. During these times, a large number of heavy and light artillery pieces had been emplaced [around Kabul] on the heights of Dukhtar-i Kāfir, Shāh Mardān, Āsmāʾī, Tapah-yi Maranjān, and Takht-i Shāh. In addition many earthworks and trenches had been dug and an 800-man detachment was ordered to man these positions. Imagining that his enemies were defeated, [Ḥabīb Allāh Khān] engaged in seizing, arresting, and bringing in the notables of the city and its environs.[lxxiii]

Also on this day, on the basis of a telephone message, they circulated as propaganda that the army of Amān Allāh Khān has been routed in Ghaznīn and that the victors will bring to Kabul 160 prisoners, forty motor vehicles, and 400 cans of gasoline captured in the fighting.

On this day too, another 800 of the Shinwārī tribe arrived in Kabul and joined forces with the 1,000 men who had come the day before. When he learned that another 6,000 Shinwārīs, both armed and unarmed, were moving in the direction of Kabul, Ḥabīb Allāh Khān, fearing lest they enter Kabul pretending that they are coming to offer allegiance but in fact intending to attack him, forbade them from entering the city and ordered that only a few of the maliks should present themselves at court, tender an oath of allegiance, and then return home.

Also on this day, [Amīr Ḥabīb Allāh Khān] appointed to the post of high commissioner (*riyāsat-i tanẓīmīyah*) for the Southern Province, Major General (*sic–firqahmishr*) Muḥammad Ṣiddīq Khān, whom people said had been sent by Muḥammad Nādir Khān, and he was ordered to leave [for the place of his appointment]. When people say that he was sent by Muḥammad Nādir Khān they mean that he was supposed to have said to Ḥabīb Allāh Khān: "The Afghans and Hazārahs /165/ will not leave you on the throne. It would be best if you who claim to be a sincere Muslim and who has adopted the title 'Friend of God and Servant of the Religion of the Prophet of God' put an end to the bloodshed, torment, and humiliation and prohibit the Northerners from engaging in brigandage and thievery."

People also said that Ḥabīb Allāh Khān asked for a seven-day truce, hoping to respond with a salvo from his guns after Sayyid Ḥusayn Khān returned from Kūhistān and Kūh Dāman and brought with him the army that he was supposed to be assembling. But what people imagined to actually be the case was confirmed and there was no peace.

The Events of Monday, 19 Ẕīqaʿdah, Corresponding to 9 S̱awr and 29 April

On this day at nine in the morning, they hanged a man at Sar-i Chawk, a muhājir of the Wazīrī tribe[lxxiv] and a supporter of Amān Allāh Khān. Two men were put before a firing squad and fifteen[lxxv] had their faces smeared with filth and were paraded through the bazaar. As they were led around, a herald would cry out, "Whoever opposes the *pādshāh* of Islām and the servant of the religion of God and unsheathes the blade of opposition, will be arrested and punished like this as a lesson." Then for each one they mixed half a *pāw* of salt with half a *pāw* of flour, baked it, and ordered that this would be their only food, day and night, until they died. Eventually however, due to the circulation of a rumor that Amān Allāh Khān would give every captive and prisoner one pound [sterling] and permission [to go home], they were freed.

Also on this day in contrast to yesterday, when news circulated that 160 men and forty motor vehicles had been captured, since liars have poor memories, the rumor now is that Field Marshal Purdil Khān supposedly had informed the amir yesterday by telephone that they hadn't captured any automobiles but rather two armoured cars, twenty-five cans of gasoline and /166/ 150 people.

Also they put it about that forty-five automobiles had been captured from Amān Allāh Khān and 400 cans of gasoline, that he himself had fled and his turban had fallen into the hands [of one of Ḥabīb Allāh Khān's supporters]. Ḥabīb Allāh Khān ordered drivers to bring in the captured vehicles.[lxxvi] In the end it was all lies! They also circulated the rumor that of the 150 men, 100 were shot at once—those who were Hazārahs—and the rest are in captivity.[lxxvii]

Marginalia: Also on this day they brought in about twenty prisoners from Amān Allāh Khān's army and ten lorries arrived in the dark of night filled with Ḥabīb Allāh Khān's wounded soldiers. Among the prisoners from Amān Allāh Khān's army were three Hazārahs. [End of marginal note.]

Also on this day, the high governor [of Kabul Province] Malik Muḥsin Khān who had taken robes of honor and gifts for the men of the Sulaymān Khayl, been besieged in Ghaznīn along with Field Marshal Purdil Khān, Saʿīd Khān, Ḥabīb Allāh Khān, and a brigadier general, and managed to escape the siege, now arrived in Kabul. Also, Muḥammad Nādir Khān's announcement that he was at any moment to arrive reached several places in Kabul.

The Events of Tuesday, 20 Ẕīqaʿdah, Corresponding to 10 Ṣawr and 30 April

On the eve of this day, ten large "fire" vehicles (*mūtar-i buzurg-i ātishī*)[153] arrived in Kabul from the battlefield in Ghaznīn and at ten o'clock in the morning, a single "fire" vehicle filled with wounded from the fighting in
73 Ghaznīn entered Kabul | and came to a stop at the military hospital.

Also during these events, Ḥabīb Allāh Khān one night secretly summoned Malik Muḥammad ʿAlam Shinwārī, Malik Qays Khūgyānī—both of whom had arrived in Kabul almost simultaneously—and also members of the Sulaymān Khayl tribe who had come to Kabul in the hope of obtaining gifts of money, rifles and ammunition. At the time of his discussions with them, [Ḥabīb Allāh Khān] said that **/167/** the population of the Hazārahjāt had refused to submit and had decided to support Amān Allāh Khān. Therefore they were to wage war on them and consider Hazārah blood, lands, wealth, families, and children as their own. In their turn, those savage people who were present, all ignorant and fanatical, vowed to carry out this monstrous business.

On this day they turned around and headed back to Jalālābād angry and upset at not having had their palms greased with guns and money. He gave each one twenty rupees in silver to cover travel expenses. Moreover, in the course of these discussions [Ḥabīb Allāh Khān] reminded them that when it came to the Hazārahs [not] rendering allegiance since

153 What exactly the "fire" vehicle was is uncertain. It is possible Fayż Muḥammad was referring to a Stanley Steamer, a steam car manufactured between 1912 and 1927. It seems unlikely that he was referring to a fire engine. One of the Stanley models, the Mountain Wagon would have had the capacity to haul the numbers of wounded (twenty to twenty-five) mentioned below (see p. 158).

like the Qizilbāsh they are all Shiʿis, therefore they ought to plunder the [Hazārahs] of Chandāwul, Murād Khānī, Maḥallah-i ʿAlī Riżā Khān, Chūbfurūshī and Qalʿah-i Ḥaydar Khān.[154] This declaration of Ḥabīb Allāh Khān thoroughly alarmed all Hazārahs as well as the Qizilbāsh of Kabul and of several villages, and they spent night and day trembling in fear. But who knows God's plans?

Also on this day, they murdered Qāżī ʿAbd al-Raḥmān Khān, who from the very outset of Ḥabīb Allāh Khān and Sayyid Ḥusayn Khān's days of thievery and robbery had resisted them and vowed to Amān Allāh Khān that he would catch the bandits [and deal with them]. When they learned of this, they murdered his brother and plundered his house in Kūh Dāman. The enmity between them grew ever more intense. When, as a result of the treachery of the ministers and disloyalty of the residents of Kabul and Chahārdihī, Ḥabīb Allāh Khān and Sayyid Ḥusayn captured the capital, Qāżī ʿAbd al-Raḥmān fled his home there and in Kūh Dāman and Kūhistān joined forces with ʿAṭā Muḥammad, son of Malik Muḥammad. There with the residents of Tagāb he continued his opposition until they captured him at this time in the village of Dih-i Sabz where he had taken refuge.[lxxviii] By order of Ḥabīb Allāh Khān and the high governor, they drew and quartered him at Sar-i Chawk while he was still alive. This merciless infliction of the death penalty, beastly in its cruelty and inhumanity, /168/ finally convinced those who witnessed it or heard about it of the godlessness and barbarism of the Northerners.

Also on this day, the heads [of three Hazārahs] and nineteen Hazārah prisoners from Shaykh ʿAlī, two of whom were Shiʾites and the rest Sunnis, were brought to Kabul. They nailed the severed heads, which had been scorched by fire, to wooden stakes and then paraded them along with the prisoners around the bazaars so that the people would realize what the politics of "the holy religion of Islam" consists of!

The Events of Wednesday, 21 Ẕīqaʿdah, Corresponding to 11 Ṣawr and 1 May 1929

Today the fighting with the units of the Southern Province under the command of Muḥammad Nādir Khān has already lasted three days. Last night 600 men from Ḥabīb Allāh Khān's army, having suffered defeat, arrived in
74 Kabul. They brought 50 wounded to the city. Also today | the heads of two

[154] These are all quarters of Kabul City.

dead fighters from the units under Muḥammad Nādir Khān were hung up at Sar-i Chawk after being scorched, as a lesson to onlookers.

On the eve of this day, sixty-three[lxxix] wounded men were brought to Kabul from Ghaznīn where a fierce battle had taken place on Tuesday. Units of Ḥabīb Allāh Khān's, occupying sangars in three places—Shaykhābād, Takiyah, and Shash Gaw all of which are in the district of Shinīz—having been defeated by Amān Allāh Khān's forces, retreated to Dasht-i Tūp and Shaykhābād.

Marginalia: Some of his 4,000 soldiers were killed, wounded, or taken prisoner and stripped of their weapons at Pambī, Shaykh Yāsīn, and Wardak by the Hazārah-Afghan force of Amān Allāh Khān. The rear guard that had fortified Takiyah and Shash Gaw and been cut off was surrounded and forced to spend its days eating clover and grass /169/ and unable either to advance or retreat. [End of marginal note.]

Also on this day, four large "fire" vehicles arrived in Kabul in each of which there were some twenty to twenty-five wounded men. The people of Chahārdihī were told about Dasht-i Tūp and also notified to go to the battlefield and collect their dead.

Also on this day the Kūh Dāmanīs, quoting the director of the Central Customs, Malik Zayn al-ʿĀbidīn and his family, spread word in the city that Ghulām Ghaws̱, son of Jāndād [Jahāndād] Aḥmadzāʾī, in hopes of the reward announced by Ḥabīb Allāh Khān and mentioned above, has captured Muḥammad Nādir Khān and will bring him to Kabul the following day.

On this day[lxxx] the forces of Ḥabīb Allāh Khān carried out a raid on the village of Khūshī in Lahūgard and pillaged its inhabitants. The fact that (the villagers) were Shiʿis and have not provided any recruits for the army served as the pretext. The soldiers slaughtered infants even while they were feeding at their mother's breasts and decapitated five to seven-year-old children.[lxxxi] As for the forces of Muḥammad Nādir Khān, which had been conducting insignificant fighting for two days, they now withdrew.

On this same day, rumors spread that Hazārah units have arrived in Āhangarān and the troops of Amān Allāh Khān have reached [the village] of Sih Āb-i Julgāy situated near the village of Khawāt in Wardak. The troops of Ḥabīb Allāh Khān in Dasht-i Tūp are requesting reinforcements.

The Events of Thursday, 22 Ẕīqaʿdah, Corresponding to 12 S̱awr and 2 May

During the Wednesday fighting in Dasht-i Tūp, several men from Ḥabīb Allāh Khān's units, in addition to those who were killed or wounded, were

taken prisoner. They cut off the noses and ears of those prisoners to whom they had earlier given one pound sterling in gold or thirty-five rupees and released. They then allowed them to return to Kabul. These actions by Amān Allāh Khān's supporters is a response to the brutality, which contravenes the norms of Islam, of those close to /170/ Ḥabīb Allāh Khān who chopped up prisoners who were still living into little pieces and in contravention of the norms of humanity and the Sharīʿah of the Seal of the Prophets, they burn the heads of those killed, impale them on stakes, parade them around the bazaars, and nail the decapitated head to a gibbet with iron nails. With prisoners, they smear their faces with filth and parade them around the bazaar. The followers of Amān Allāh Khān have heard of these outrages and so they have cut off noses and ears because they understand man is bound to do good, and is not an animal. The Kūhistānīs and Kūh Dāmanīs, however, are neither humans nor Muslims, but only rapacious animals, ravenous beasts, and bloodshedding thieves
75 | therefore, the principle of "… a tooth for a tooth and … a wound [for a wound] in equal measure"[155] should be upheld when dealing with them.

Also on the eve of this day, they secretly brought to Kabul some 220 wounded from the fighting at Shaykhābād, Dasht-i Tūp, and Qalʿah-yi Durrānī. The brother of Ḥabīb Allāh Khān, Muʿīn al-Salṭanah Ḥamīd Allāh Khān, four days ago, after setting off for the battlefield and the subsequent rout of his force, fled to save himself and returned to the city this evening, where he reported the defeat. At 7:30 [in the morning], Ḥabīb Allāh Khān himself headed for the battlefield with his brother and a gang of the brigands who served as his aides in five motor vehicles. [*Marginalia*: He forcibly rounded up the defeated men who had set out on the road of flight back to Kūhistān and Kūh Dāman] and until six o'clock in the afternoon he continued to make every effort [to stop their fleeing]. In the evening he returned to Kabul. He probably spent ten hours engaged in rounding up the defeated men and one hour and a few minutes in travel time to and from Kabul.

Also on this day, a large "fire" vehicle filled with men who had had been wounded in the fighting with the forces of Muḥammad Nādir Khān in Lahūgard reached the city and brought the wounded to the hospital. /171/ Also on the eve of this day, Sayyid Ḥusayn Khān returned to Kabul after eight days in Chārīkār rounding up the rest of its inhabitants for the army. He had also gone there to take care of the problems created by Hazārahs

[155] Qurʾān 5:45.

who had advanced to Ghūrband. In Kabul he consulted with Ḥabīb Allāh Khān about the situation in Ghūrband and to report that the Northerners do not want to provide recruits for the army on the grounds that there would be no one to feed the families and that in every house no one would be left with the exception of two or three old people. All the young and strong have already left to fight and their families and children are now vulnerable to raids and plundering by the Hazārahs. Having reported this, he again returned to Chārīkār.[lxxxii] But since Ḥabīb Allāh Khān had departed for the battlefield in Wardak, Sayyid Ḥusayn left him a note.

The Events of Friday, 23 Ẕīqaʿdah Corresponding to 13 Ṣawr and 3 May 1929

On the evening of this day, eighteen trucks loaded with wounded arrived from Shaykhābād where fighting is still going on and were brought to the hospital. Also this evening, approximately 400 men, Tajiks from the villages of the Charkh region of Lahūgard,[lxxxiii] were sent to Kūhistān and Ghūrband combined with Ḥabīb Allāh Khān forces. Boxes of ammunition were also shipped there in eighteen phaetons. Twenty phaetons of ammunition were also driven today to Ghūrband. Ḥabīb Allāh Khān himself, who had returned in the evening, at six o'clock in the morning headed out for Bīnī Ḥiṣār, reportedly for an outing at Qalʿahchah-i Khumdān. They say that he was studying the situation in Surkhāb in Lahūgard where the forces of Muḥammad Nādir Khān under the command of Aḥmad Shāh Khān have fortified positions with sangars in a number of places and from which they have been harassing Ḥabīb Allāh Khān, causing fear[lxxxiv] and preventing his units from advancing into the Southern Province. Having learned the facts of the situation and having given instructions for defensive measures, he returned to the city.

Today the mayor of Kabul, Khwājah Tāj al-Dīn, /172/ posted a notice in some of the busiest areas of the city, announcing the flight of Amān Allāh Khān after the defeat by the Sulaymān Khayl, Andar, and several other tribes and the return, as if they were victorious, of the defeated and routed forces[lxxxv] of Ḥabīb Allāh Khān. [The purpose of posting this notice was to show that] Ḥabīb Allāh Khān's forces had not fled the battlefield
76 in | defeat but, on the contrary, had carried the day and then simply dispersed and gone to their homes. They say that such lies and deceit can be learned only from the devil, but in their duplicity and machinations they far surpass the devil himself.

At this time, Amān Allāh Khān sent a message in a pouch with his own signature to the people of Kabul which read, "I am fully aware of the difficulties, hardships, unbearable conditions, violence, and robbery being inflicted on the oppressed populace of Kabul. God willing, in a short time I will march into the city and with the help of the All-High will rid you of these bloodthirsty brigands." He sent it by the hand of one of his sepoys, who had dressed in civilian clothing. On the way, the sepoy was stopped and searched. He threw the pouch with the letter in it on the ground and ran away. The inspectors delivered the pouch to Ḥabīb Allāh Khān who had the two sepoy-policemen and a colonel arrested, on the grounds that they had let Amān Allāh Khān's messenger escape.

Meanwhile, Ḥabīb Allāh Khān's forces[lxxxvi] attacked the locale of Charkh and pillaged it despite the fact that these people had broken off their alliance with the people of the Southern Province, provided support for the forces of Ḥabīb Allāh Khān, and recruited soldiers for his army from their own residents. [In the attack] their forts and houses were burned.[lxxxvii]

This evening thirty-six cases of ammunition were sent to Qalʿah-yi Durrānī. /173/

The Events of Saturday, 24 Ẕīqaʿdah, Corresponding to 14 Ṣawr and 4 May

Again this evening many vehicles arrived with a large number of wounded from Shaykhābād and transferred them to hospital. Ḥabīb Allāh Khān's soldiers who had suffered defeat in Shaykhābād surreptitiously have been returning in groups to the city and to Chahārdihī throughout the day. The routed Kūhistānīs and Kūh Dāmanīs went home by way of Bīktūt and Pamqān.

Besides the rumor that Sayyid Ḥusayn intended to leave for Mazār-i Sharīf and Turkistān where Ghulām Nabī Khān [Charkhī] has taken power into his own hands, it also was learned that Amān Allāh Khān had returned from Sih Āb[-i Julgāy] and Khawāt-i Wardak, Field Marshal Purdil Khān was headed for Ghaznīn with a well-armed force numbering 200 men, and Muḥammad Nādir Khān had moved to Khūst from Gardayz. In Butkhāk where the Shinwārīs had returned there was no fighting going on. Ḥabīb Allāh Khān outwardly remains calm.

The partisans of Amān Allāh Khān and Muḥammad Nādir Khān spent this day in complete despair and distress and the populace of Kabul was greatly intimidated by the assaults, humiliations, and thefts of the Northerners. On the pretext of looking for weapons they conducted searches of several homes in Rīkā Khānah and Shūr Bāzār, taunting the owners of the houses. Practically the entire populace of Kabul, brought to the brink of despair, lives day and night in fear and cannot escape and save

77 themselves. | How will this terror end and how is the All-High going to deal with it? It is all in His hands.

Marginalia: Also on this day, Ḥabīb Allāh Khān ordered the raising of the flag that indicates that he is in the Arg, while he himself, before the sun was up, /174/ was off either to Lahūgard, Butkhāk or Maydān to assess the situation and give instructions for strengthening the defenses. Again he returned to the city in the evening. [End of marginal note.]

The Events of Sunday, 25 Ẕīqaʿdah, Corresponding to 15 Ṣawr and 5 May

On the eve of this day Ḥabīb Allāh Khān consulted with Kūh Dāmanī and Kūhistānī khāns and invited high-ranking military officers and civilian officials to a meeting to discuss the difficult situation that was developing with the appearance of hostile forces heading for Kabul from the east, south, west, and north to consult with them on how to deal with it. They made suggestions for solving the problem based on what they knew.

Marginalia: As a result of the conference, they wrote a letter to Amān Allāh Khān on behalf of Ḥabīb Allāh Khān saying,

> I accused you of being a kafir; now because of the great shedding of the blood of Muslims it is I who am the kafir. If you leave the North to me and give me assurance of safe passage no more blood will be shed, there'll be no more fighting and strife and I will step down and hand over the amirate throne to you on condition that the people of the North will not be subjected to vengeful reprisals.

He sent the letter by plane at 3:00 P.M., but it had not returned by nightfall giving rise to changes of heart and strong misgivings on the part of those waiting for the news. [End of the marginal note.]

Also on this day, five hundred ponies were sent to provide transport for Sayyid Ḥusayn Khān, who planned to go to Mazār-i Sharīf by way of Qaṭaghan and he called for individuals separate from his own military force from Lahūgard and Kabul to go to Chārīkār.

Also on this day, word spread that armed tribal formations of the Eastern Province, having heard about the barbaric acts of Ḥabīb Allāh Khān and his soldiers towards the people of Kabul, drawing and quartering people alive; raping women, young girls, and young boys; charging people with crimes who had never committed even the smallest misdeed; hanging sayyids and people whose misdemeanors did not rise even to the level of discretionary punishment (*taʿzīr*); and [thus] shedding blood illegally, arrived in Tagāb out of a sense of Afghan honor /175/ and being jealous of the Hazārahs, who, despite seeing nothing good coming from the government [of the Afghans], had embarked on the path of supporting it.

Also, the Kurd Khayl and Khūd Khayl tribes took up positions on the heights overlooking Butkhāk intending to attack the forces of Ḥabīb Allāh Khān there.

As of today, it has been three days since there was any information about the situation of Muḥammad Nādir Khān and no one knows where he is because the people of Shāh Mazār, the son of Jāndād, men from Charkh, and the khwājahs of Kulangār, having heard about Ḥabīb Allāh Khān's announcement that whoever captures Muḥammad Nādir Khān will get a reward of 40,000 rupees, invited him to come. The pretext was that he would be their guest and they would obtain from him the order to attack Kabul. But knowing their cunning, he has fled either to Gardayz or to Khūst with 500 men who had arrived in Shāh Mazār. He is frustrated[lxxxvii] by the ignorance, the covenant-breaking, and godlessness of the Afghans of those regions and they say he has gone to Ghaznīn, settled problems there, made the Sulaymān Khayl become supporters of Amān Allāh Khān, and then returned to Gardayz.

Also on this day there were rumors coming in from all directions: that regular and popular forces of Afghans and Hazārahs opposed to Ḥabīb Allāh Khān, who support Amān Allāh Khān in suppressing the revolution and in improving the condition of ordinary ignorant people, /176/ are ready to do battle. This information seriously distressed Ḥabīb Allāh Khān and the Northerners.

Also people say that the Shinwārīs, each of whom has received twenty silver *'abbāsīs* as a gift from Ḥabīb Allāh Khān, were dismissed, headed home, and, dissatisfied at not having achieved their goal [of guns and more money], forcibly disarmed 300 soldiers at Butkhāk who were occupying positions there for Ḥabīb Allāh Khān. Making off with their rifles and ammunition, [the Shinwārīs] hurried to Jalālābād with the haste of scudding clouds and the speed of the wind. This affair only increased the
78 anxiety of the revolutionaries. |

The Events of Monday, 26 Ẕīqa'dah, Corresponding to 16 Ṣawr and 6 May

During the events and happenings [prior to the revolution] that have been described, the son of the late Field Marshal Ghulām Ḥaydar Khān Charkhī, Ghulām Nabī Khān, formerly the envoy to Paris, had his assignment changed and became envoy to the Moscow durbar. In the first days of the revolution, he had gone (to Moscow) but then when he heard that the regular army garrison at Mazār[-i Sharīf], made up of men from Kūhistān and Kūh Dāman, mutinied and plundered the possessions of Amān Allāh Khān's officials at the order[lxxxix] of the high commissioner, Amīr Mīrzā Muḥammad Qāsim Ūzbak, sent by Ḥabīb Allāh Khān, after which he arrested and sent to Kabul the high governor, ʿAbd al-ʿAzīz Khān, and Muḥammad Iklīl Khān, brigadier general of the regular army and some other officers who have already been mentioned, [on hearing this Ghulām Nabī] entered the territory of Afghānī Turkistān. With the backing of a tribal force from the Isḥāqzāʾī tribe under the leadership of Ghulām Rasūl Khān, son of Sayf Ākhūndzādah, and also with the help of displaced Hazārahs and Turkmān emigrants [from the Soviet Union], he gained control of Mazār, drove the traitor Mīrzā Muḥammad Qāsim to Transoxiana, arrested and imprisoned the high governor, the chief fiscal official (*mustawfī*), and other officials of Ḥabīb Allāh Khān, restored Amān Allāh Khān's officials to their former positions, and himself immediately set off for Bāmyān where he took command of the Shaykh ʿAlī, Balkhāb, Turkmān, Surkh wa Pārsā, and Yakah Awlang Hazārah tribes which /177/ had risen against Ḥabīb Allāh Khān and, in their campaign against Kūh Dāman and Kūhistān, had advanced as far as Ghūrband but then turned back. [Ghulām Nabī Khān] thus became protector and commander. This affair caused Sayyid Ḥusayn Khān to head for Chārīkār then direct his steps towards Mazār-i Sharīf, as mentioned above.

It was three or four days prior to this day, which is Monday the 26th of Ẕīqaʿdah, when tribal units of new recruits, forcibly conscripted from the Lahūgard districts of Charkh, Khūshī, Kulangār, and Surkhāb as well as contingents exhausted from the fighting in the Southern Province, summoned to Kabul with and without weapons, were sent off to Chārīkār. In addition, the units which were defeated at Ghaznīn and in the western region are returning in small groups and hiding in their homes. The situation of Ḥabīb Allāh Khān and the Northerners has considerably worsened. His forces, whose losses already amount to 7,000 dead and wounded, are exhausted with no possibility of regaining strength. Along with the people of Kabul, he now lives under siege until it becomes known how he will be able to fight all the Hazārahs and the majority of the Afghans and which path of ignorance and barbarity, devoid of all religiosity, will he embark on?

Also on this day, in the dark of night some of the forcibly conscripted units were ordered to fortify the breastworks of Māhtāb Qalʿah and

Arghandah. At ten o'clock an airplane returned carrying the letter proposing a truce and Amān Allāh Khān's response.[xc]

The Events of Tuesday, 27 Ẕīqaʿdah, Corresponding to 17 Ṣawr and 7 May

79 | These days, Ḥabīb Allāh Khān has fallen into despair because of the defeat of his forces, their being killed, wounded, and taken prisoner; the escape of surviving soldiers back to /178/ Kūh Dāman and Kūhistān via Pamqān and Bīktūt; and also because of the return to Chahārdihī of the units routed at Shaykh Yāsīn, Pambī, and Dasht-i Tūp. Secretly in the night he sent all his women—except for the daughters of Amīr Muḥammad Khān Muḥammadzāʾī whom, as was already mentioned, he had forcibly married and brought to the bed of his amusement and whom he left behind—from the Arg to the residence of the late prime minister ʿAbd al-Quddūs Khān which adjoined the north side of the Burj-i Yādgār[156] and the Shahrārā Palace.

Fearing that he and his family would be captured, [Ḥabīb Allāh Khān] had called a meeting where it was decided to send a letter to Amān Allāh Khān seeking a truce, as mentioned above. However, he did not count on the fact that after the thieves whom he leads have plundered the treasury and the arsenal built up over the course of fifty years, spilled the blood of hundreds of people, and destroyed their homes, Amān Allāh would not be able to forgive his savagery nor overlook the nation's [plundered] wealth. The moment will come when the nation will demand recompense from the mullahs and Northerners for what has been destroyed, in accordance with political law (*qānūn*) and the Sharīʿah. And in interrogating them about the necessity of defending [Islam] by destroying property and lives [the nation] will find their answer in the blood of those people and will recover their own property. By legal means (*sharʿan*) they will bring the killers of their slain and those who helped others to murder into the arena of retaliation.

Also during these recorded events, Sayyid Zayn al-ʿĀbidīn, son of Sayyid Shāhanshāh from Takānah; Ghulām Ḥabīb, son of Ghulām Ḥasan Khān

[156] The Burj-i Yādgār (Commemorative Tower) was the name of the tower section of the Shahrārā Palace built by Amīr ʿAbd al-Raḥmān Khān in 1899–1900. A plaque attached to the building in 1920 by his grandson, Amīr Amān Allāh Khān, commemorated the meeting that had taken place on that site in July 1880 at which the British agreed to withdraw all their troops from Afghanistan and recognize ʿAbd al-Raḥmān as amir. (See Schinasi, *Kabul: A History*, p. 74.).

Qizilbāsh, who had control of the territory and fort at Ūnay, and the father of the governor of Maydān, along with four Hazārahs from Sar Chashmah, who, as was already related, had brought [to Kabul] a message from the Hazārahs of Bihsūd seeking a truce, for which each one of them was given a piece of turban cloth as a "robe of honor," promised that they would bring a written an oath of allegiance from those (the Bihsūd) Hazārahs in ten or fifteen days and these men went off carrying conciliatory farmans from Ḥabīb Allāh Khān. After the promised ten or fifteen days had passed they went among the Hazārahs and heard this answer:

> We are Musalmans and devotees of the faith. Since we have already given a written oath of allegiance to Amān Allāh Khān we are legally bound to support and stand by him /179/ for if we break that covenant we will have to answer before God and the Prophet. In light of our vow, having embarked on the path of struggle, we are all prepared, from suckling babe to the frailest old man, to kill and plunder. We will fight as long as we have breath in our bodies and will sprinkle our blood in service to the religion and the government and to protect the nation and the kingdom from the assaults, murders, and captive-takings by ignorant and misguided thieves. We will never allow two riders to sit on one saddle lest we be held responsible in this world and the next.

Having said this, 12,000 Hazārahs occupied the Ūnay Pass and prepared for battle. Together they agreed:

> Although during the first decade of his reign, Amān Allāh Khān greatly oppressed us and failed to punish the Afghan nomads who destroyed our homes, killed us, threw us alive into the fire, took away our lands, and carried off our wives and daughters nor did he demand an explanation from the officials and governors who robbed us of lakhs of rupees, and for that he will be accountable to God, still, we have given our oath of allegiance and must
> 80 not betray it, like Afghans do. |

Thereupon, they unanimously adopted the following plan of action:

> If we attack Kabul by day, we will sustain heavy losses from artillery fire from the heights of Chihil Tan, Dukhtar-i Kāfir, Shāh Mardān, Āsmā'ī, Shayr Darwāzah and Takht-i Shāh which overlook Chahārdihī and we will not be able to achieve our goal. Therefore, we must surreptitiously make our way at night to the summits of Bīktūt and Quruq and hide there for a day and then when it's dark we should attack the hilltops where the guns are emplaced. As soon as we reach the lower slopes of the mountains, we will be safe from the artillery fire. Once we get ourselves up the mountains and, with the help of God, capture the guns, we will gain command over the city and Chahārdihī and thus prevail.

However, Amān Allāh Khān told the Hazārahs to wait until his own forces reached Maydān saying that their force would be overwhelming if they were united. /180/ Consequently, up until today, Tuesday, the 27th of Ẕīqaʿdah, the Hazārahs are positioned on the heights of Pamqān, Shakar Darrah and the Ūnay Pass waiting for the assault on Kabul.[xci]

Marginalia: On this day, one of Ḥabīb Allāh Khān's brigadier generals[xcii] along with another one of his officers who, two or three days before, heading for Ghaznīn had gone to Qalʿah-i Durrānī to stop the supporters of Amān Allāh Khān from attacking Kabul and were defeated, now came back to Kabul. One of them, [General] ʿUmrā Khān, was punished with a severe caning. [See below.] Ḥabīb Allāh Khān was worried by rumors about the arrival of a Hazārah tribal lashkar on this day at the Safid Khāk Pass which overlooks Arghandah and Maydān, about Muḥammad Nādir Khān's approaching from Lahūgard and Muḥammad Hāshim Khān from the Eastern Province. He was extremely concerned by word of an attack by Hazārahs in Kūhistān and ordered two thousand men to be sent to Butkhāk and a large unit to Kūhistān. On this day, they brought sixteen wounded men to hospital in Kabul from Qalʿah-i Durrānī where fighting was going on. [End of marginal note.]

Marginalia: As was revealed, Amān Allāh Khān did not agree to Ḥabīb Allāh Khān's terms. In reply, he declared,

> Although I was a Muslim you called me a kafir. For the sake of ending the bloodshed I renounced the throne. ʿInāyat Allāh Khān, to whom there was no objection, was encouraged by many officials and accepted the amirate but you forced him into exile and plundered the wealth of the country. You also published two letters and raised 41 points, none of which are credible, to prove that I am a kafir. Now I am ready to fight anyone who takes a step against the Islamic government and Muslims and I am willing to die for this cause. [End of marginal note.]

The Events of Wednesday, 28 Ẕīqaʿdah, Corresponding to 18 Ṣawr and 8 May

On the eve of this day, five officers who were in Qalʿah-yi Durrānī were recalled to Kabul, as was mentioned earlier, for fighting with and cursing Saʿīd Muḥammad Khān, the brother of the high governor, Malik Muḥsin. He was aide-de-camp to Ḥabīb Allāh Khān and held the office of warden [of the Arg]. The dispute culminated with both sides having drawn their guns. General ʿUmrā Khān, son of Malik Zayn al-ʿĀbidīn Dāʾudzāʾī, director of Central Customs, was given a caning and then imprisoned with the son of Saʿīd Shāh who held the rank of brigadier general, along with ten of his colleagues.

On this day Field Marshal Purdil Khān departed for Chārīkār.[xciii] /181/ Also today, two large trucks carrying wounded arrived in Kabul from Dasht-i Tūp and Bīnī[xciv] Bādām where fighting is going on. The casualties were admitted to the Qalʿah-i Bāqir Khān Hospital.

Elsewhere, during these recorded events, there were rumors that Ḥażrat Fażl ʿUmar, nicknamed Shayr Āqā, had arrived in Katawāz and Zurmat. After returning from Mecca and afraid of being persecuted by Amān Allāh Khān, he had settled in India and spent about two years there, having said that he had given up returning to Kabul. It is a matter of common speculation that he has come to Katawāz and Zurmat at the behest of the English officials who hope to get the Sulaymān Khayl, Andar, Tarakī and ʿAlī Khayl tribes, which had stopped fighting Amān Allāh Khān and instead decided to support him, to rise again against him and so continue the bloodshed the same way that his brothers who were in Kabul had done since the outset of the revolution. In particular, Russians and Turks [living in Kabul] whenever they meet their countrymen in the bazaars and other busy places, all are saying that this ḥażrat has come [to Katawāz and Zurmat] at the instructions of the English in order to prolong the revolution and
81 drive Amān Allāh Khān out of | the country. But people who are firm adherents of the religion, along with those who are well-acquainted with politics, reject this notion. In gatherings where news is exchanged, those who reject this notion cite two reasons. First, they say that the English, fearing a rivalry with the Russians, would like to see a stable, independent and powerful Afghanistan which would function as a buffer between India and Russia and protect English control of India from attack by the latter while preventing her interference in Indian affairs. The second reason is that the ulema and tribal maliks would not be able to act under English instruction /182/ against their own government on the pretext of strengthening the religion and spreading Islamic principles because the English are Christians whose teachings are alien to Islam. They believe it is clear that the instigators of the uprising are not the English, but the ignorant pseudo-mullahs and maliks who are neither adherents of the religion nor followers of the law of the Lord of Messengers.

Therefore, their opposition, their violation of oaths and agreements, and their killing and plundering, all confirm the fact that Ḥażrat Shayr Āqā came to Katawāz and Zurmat at the request of the Muslims of Peshawar and other [regions] to persuade the Sulaymān Khayl, Andar, and other tribes of the absolute necessity of supporting Amān Allāh Khān, overthrowing Ḥabīb Allāh Khān, and extinguishing the flames of the revolution. The Russians, Turks, and others disquieted [by his appearance] are undoubtedly mistaken in asserting that he came to Katawāz and Zurmat at the behest of the English to incite the aforementioned tribes against Amān Allāh Khān. In point of fact, he is raising the people against Ḥabīb Allāh Khān; the other view is nothing but propaganda. And because of this, once he heard about his arrival in those regions, Ḥabīb Allāh Khān has begun to persecute the brothers of the ḥażrat and has forbidden them from leaving their homes. If they come out they will be killed. **/183/**

The Sanctioning, Preparation, and Concluding of an Agreement Concerning an Alliance of the Tribes of the Eastern Province

During the events that have been described, Muḥammad Hāshim Khān, the brother of Muḥammad Nādir Khān, appealing to Afghan honor and making effective use of propaganda, inspired the Afghan tribes of the
82 Eastern Province to unite against Ḥabīb Allāh Khān. | They thereupon resolved to raise 40,000 fighters who would advance along three routes via 1) Tagāb, 2) Tangī Ghārū, and 3) Chakarī and Latahband and attack Kūh Dāman, Kūhistān, and Kabul. To pay the expenses of this tribal levy, [the tribes] collected the property taxes for this year on their farms and irrigated lands ahead of time and then set off. On this day, which is Wednesday, 28 Ẕīqaʿdah, they reached [two places], the Hāshim Khayl Bridge in Gandamak and Tagāb, and are planning to continue on to their ultimate goal.

Similarly, tribes of the Southern Province, under the banner of Muḥammad Nādir Khān, and tribes of the Western Province, under the flag of Amān Allāh Khān, have engaged in similar preparations. They have all agreed sooner or later to attack the Northern Province from four directions, that is from Maydān, Chār Āsyā, Butkhāk, Tangī Ghārū, Tagāb, Ghūrband, the Safīd Khāk Pass, from the mountains of Pamqān, Farzah, and Shakar Darrah, and from Istālif so that perhaps some progress will be made.

The Preparations of Nāʾib al-Salṭanah Sayyid Ḥusayn Khān

Having departed several days earlier for Chārīkār, by threats he dragged what was left of the population of Kūhistān, Kūh Dāman, Sanjan, Durnāmah, Bulāghayn, Ghūrband, and Panjshayr from their homes and is sending this force to Kabul as a display of military might. **/184/** Every day the people from those regions, in disorder and without weapons, are marched through the bazaars to the sound of a military band and shouting "Four Friends" inspiring terror in the hearts of the people of the city and displaying their own wickedness.

After Ghulām Nabī Khān seized power in Mazār-i Sharīf and Turkistān, Sayyid Ḥusayn Khān made plans to attack Mazār-i Sharīf via Khānābād and Andarāb. Every day he would send a request to Kabul for arms and supplies for his force. His chief secretary, Mīrzā Ghulām Qādir Khān, who had stayed behind in Kabul, each day sends off arms and materiel to Chārīkār for him. They say Sayyid Ḥusayn Khān drives back and forth to Bāmyān every day. En route to the Shibar Pass he has attacked the Shaykh ʿAlī Hazārahs and plundered and burned their homes. As for the Hazārahs of Surkh wa Pārsā and Turkmān, who are followers of the high governor of the Northern Province, he has sent his soldiers against them and they are collecting recruits there by force. As supporters of Amān Allāh Khān and enemies of Ḥabīb Allāh Khān they have cut the road over which [Ḥabīb Allāh Khān's] army has to march. The Hazārahs of Turkmān and Surkh wa Pārsā were undone by the fact that the Shaykh ʿAlī Hazārahs being Sunni placed their own recruits from the Nīk Pay clan in Ḥabīb Allāh Khān's army. Consequently, Sayyid Ḥusayn Khān was able to impose his will on them [the Turkmān and Surkh wa Pārsā Hazārahs] and demand they provide conscripts for his force.

The Events of Thursday, 29 Ẕīqaʿdah, Corresponding to 19 Ṣawr and 9 May

On this day, notices were printed and posted in all the places where people gather announcing that all residents or newcomers going outside
83 the city beyond | a two-kuruh [four-mile] limit /185/ must get a written permit from the chief of police or from one of the senior army officers. Anyone who arrives in the city must get a permit from the commander of one the regiments stationed in Bandar-i Arghandah, Chār Āsyā, Bīnī Ḥiṣār, Butkhāk, Kūtal-i Pāy Manār, Kūtal-i Khayr Khānah, or other locations near the city. Anyone who does not have an exit or entrance permit will be arrested and punished. As a result, the people of Kabul, cowed by threats and under siege, apprehensive of their fate and the loss of their property, now cannot leave even to go to Maydān, Jalrīz, Lahūgard, Khūrd Kabul, Butkhāk, Tangī Ghārū or Dih-i Sabz although these places are under the control of the present government. This measure evoked fear and confusion in their hearts. The populace, out of work and unpaid, having consumed all their reserves from the previous year, and awaiting with impatience the suppression of this revolution, see themselves on the

brink of destruction. Officials of the former government are unemployed and because there is no trade, no money, no fodder or provision for next year, they do not see any solution nor can they escape. [Moreover] they are unable to sell their possessions—carpets or china for example—for even one-half or one-third of their value. And if they do manage to sell, it doesn't amount to enough for food to last any length of time because the prices have risen so much. /186/

Also on this day, Ṣāḥibzādah ʿAbd al-Ghafūr Khān was named director of Central Customs because of the dismissal of Malik Zayn al-ʿĀbidīn Dāʾudzāʾī, whose son, General ʿUmrā Khān was arrested and imprisoned last night, as was already related. Ṣāḥibzādah ʿAbd al-Ghafūr Khān's brother, Ṣāḥibzādah ʿAbd Allāh Khān, was appointed high governor of Qaṭaghan and Badakhshān.

Also on this day, the high governor [of Kabul or Central Province], Malik Muḥsin, was punished by Muʿīn al-Salṭanah Ḥamīd Allāh Khān for stealing 40,000 rupees at the time of the confiscation of the home of the late chamberlain, Muḥammad Sarwar Khān, and also made off with a large number of valuables from the homes of the minister of foreign affairs, Ghulām Ṣiddīq Khān; the minister of court, Muḥammad Yaʿqūb Khān; the minister of war, ʿAbd al-ʿAzīz Khān; Maḥmūd Khān, the aide-de-camp; (Prince) Ḥayāt Allāh Khān ʿAżud al-Dawlah, and other persons, more than 200 in all, goods which he hid in his own house. They say Ḥamīd Allāh severely caned him and ordered that the 40,000 rupees be retrieved.

Also in the course of this day and night, several vehicles arrived in Kabul carrying wounded from Ghaznīn where fighting continues, and left
84 them at the hospital. |

The Events of Friday, 30 Ẕīqaʿdah, Corresponding to 20 Ṣawr and 10 May 1929

During these recorded events, a decree was published that all persons entering and leaving Kabul should be subject to search and interrogation. If any letters are found these must be handed over to the chief of the Kabul police, Sayyid Āqā Khān. Every letter is to be read to make sure, God forbid, that it contain no anti-government propaganda. The effects of such a decree, which intimidates people coming to Kabul as well as the residents of the city, is to curtail and inhibit the spread both of lies and well-founded rumors which interfere with the administration /187/ of government. Thus no one will know whether things are good or bad.

Below is the text of the decree, promulgated yesterday and posted in areas where people congregate. It was obtained from the Press Administration of the Ministry of Court and was intended for other governmental departments.

> This decree regarding the movement of travelers through control points, proposed by Major General Amīr Muḥammad Khān and confirmed by His Highness, has been prepared for your departments. This is the decision of the ministry:
>
> 1) Concerning those who travel beyond the city limits of Kabul:
>   a) Military officers and civilian officials have the right to pass through control points with permission from Amīr Ṣāḥib Ghāzī [Ḥabīb Allāh Khān], Na'ib al-Salṭanah [Sayyid Ḥusayn Khān], or the devoted and staunch supporter of religion and the government, Muʿīn al-Salṭanah [Ḥamīd Allāh Khān]. Civilians have the same right with permission from the minister of court, the chamberlain, the aide-de- camp to His Highness, the high governor of Kabul, or the chief of police.
>   b) Servicemen[xcv] may pass by order of the field marshal, deputy field marshal, major generals, and generals.
> 2) Concerning individuals coming into Kabul from the surrounding area:
>   a) Those civilian officials who have permission from the governor or high commissioner of the relevant provinces may pass through the checkpoints.
>   b) Servicemen may pass through control points with permission from a senior officer.
> 3) People who have a document corresponding to these terms will be able to pass through the checkpoints freely and no one should bother them. But anyone entering or leaving the city without a permit, the commander of the customs post having detained him and seized his belongings /188/ will send him to the major general who must send an investigative report to His Majesty.
> 4) Anyone who has no permit and tries to escape via a crossing [other than
> 85 at a checkpoint] must be arrested forthwith | and handed over to the major general for interrogation. He will forward a report to His Majesty.

The royal decree approving the decision of the ministry:

> The necessary information has been collected. The terms of your resolution concerning transiting checkpoints is affirmed by His Highness and you must adhere to them. Documents, obtained by travelers from officials, must be checked. If it is found that they have a proper permit, then they may pass. It is absolutely essential to examine the documents of suspicious persons. For all people either engaged in or sent on government service, special identity papers should be printed up permitting them passage into and out of the city. These papers should be distributed to the relevant departments and

> with the proper seals affixed to them should be considered [appropriate] documentation for civilians passing through checkpoints.
>
> We therefore inform you that copies of this decree should be printed and distributed. The end.

Due to the promulgation of this decree, the political savvy and the statesmanship of the major general, Amīr Muḥammad Khān; the minister of court, Shayr Jān Khān; and Amīr Ḥabīb Allāh Khān are acknowledged because the terms [of the decree] are aimed at the arrest of spies and saboteurs. However, they seem not to be aware that all the people of the city, worn down by high prices, hunger, and oppression, are on the brink of death because dealers in fodder and traders must [first] get a permit from the governor or high commissioner in order to pass through the checkpoints and then transport essential goods and foodstuffs like wheat, lamb, oil, firewood, charcoal, clothing, /189/ and other things into the city. And probably it is only possible to get a permit after paying a bribe and wasting several days. And what is more, after obtaining the permit it is still necessary to bribe the checkpoint officer otherwise, as is now common, he will charge the merchant with having contraband in his possession and then torture him half to death, after which the latter will abandon any wish to ever come to the city again. Thus it is that the people of Kabul find themselves without food and clothing and similarly there is nothing to be gained by the residents of the surrounding areas [for providing them].

For example, by order of the late amir, Ḥabīb Allāh Khān, a new road was built from Kabul to Pamqān and along its entire length shade trees were planted on both sides. He ordered that animal drovers were required to muzzle their livestock when passing by these trees to prevent damage to them. The decree that laid this down however contained only the word "road" without any qualification, which though it had no relevance to any other road or byway, by virtue of the absurdity of the decree [as written], caused much torment to the owners of animals traveling along any road. They were supposed to muzzle their donkeys, camels, and cows even in the center of the city. Anyone who [ignored this ordinance] had to pay a fine to the police of from one-half rupee up to one or two rupees to redeem their animals. This decree remained in effect until the assassination of [Amīr Ḥabīb Allāh Khān]. However, Son of the Water Carrier and his supporters don't seem to understand that spies and felons can travel
86 along secret paths by day or by night | to accomplish their ends. And no one can stop them.

Also on this day, Friday, the last day of Ẕīqaʿdah, due to rumors that Ghulām Jīlānī Khān had occupied Andarāb and Khānābād in Qaṭaghan; the high governor of that region, Mīr Bābā Ṣāḥib Chārīkārī had been killed there; fighting had started in Tagāb; the tribes of the Eastern Provinces were marching towards Kabul and the north; Muḥammad Nādir Khān had entered Lahūgard; Amān Allāh Khān's forces had entered Ghaznīn; /190/ and Deputy Field Marshal ʿAbd al-Wakīl Khān,[157] a Nūristānī convert to Islam, with his own tribe had begun to fight in Burj-i Guljān and Rižāh-i Kūhistān; on this same day, Friday, the 30th of Ẕīqaʿdah, Sayyid Ḥusayn Khān started a rumor that he was going to go to Mazār-i Sharīf although in fact, he had decided to attack the Hazārahjāt by way of Bāmyān. He has arranged things with the nomadic tribes who frequent the Hazārahjāt that they will join him at the moment of attack but now he has put things off and decided to stop in Chārīkār.

Also on this day, one thousand forced conscripts from Chahārdihī, Kabul, and other regions, set off for Chārīkār.

Marginalia: Also today, four large trucks carrying wounded from Dasht-i Tūp where fighting is going on, arrived in Kabul. There was a general among the wounded. [End of marginal note.]

The Events of Saturday, 1 Ẕīḥijjah Corresponding to 21 Ṣawr and 11 May 1929

On this day, due to the arrival of wounded the day before, a rumor spread in Kabul that Muḥammad Nādir Khān with his force and also the tribal forces of the Southern Province had arrived in Charkh, Lahūgard. Tribal elders of Lahūgard have secretly allied with him and together they are resolved to destroy Ḥabīb Allāh Khān's army by any means at hand. Having reached this agreement, Muḥammad Nādir Khān had prepared for battle and awaited the approach of Ḥabīb Allāh Khān who had ordered the Lahūgardīs to supply his army with bread while he himself advanced at the head of his forces. As his army approached the ambush laid by Muḥammad Nādir Khān's units, the latter's forces opened fire from in front and the Lahūgardīs opened fire from behind the Northerners. Most of the soldiers were killed; some were taken prisoner /191/ and all of their weapons and artillery were captured. The rest of Ḥabīb Allāh's soldiers turned and fled back the way they came. After Muḥammad Nādir Khān's troops had retired to their positions and the residents of Lahūgard who

[157] See Adamec, *Who's Who*, p. 101 ("Abdul Wakil Nuristani").

had brought bread had dispersed, Ḥabīb Allāh Khān's units managed to collect their wounded from the battlefield and send them back to Kabul.

Sayyid Ḥusayn Khān, two or three days before this, at the head of a force of 12,000 men—5,000 from Kūhistān, 5,000 Sunni Hazārahs from Surkh wa Pārsā who, blinded by fanaticism and Sunnism, had severed their ties with the Shiʿi Hazārahs and joined forces with Sayyid Ḥusayn
87 Khān, and 2,000 men from | Ghūrband—decided to attack the fort of the Hazārahs of Turkmān, who [at this moment] had set up their positions on the mountain heights. Marching as far as the Shibar Pass, home of the Shaykh ʿAlī Hazārahs, he burned some 120 forts and drove more than 15,000 sheep, donkeys, goats, and cows from their pastures before turning back. Hazārah tribal forces from Yakah Awlang, Bāmyān, Shaykh ʿAlī and Balkhāb, vowing revenge, attacked Ghūrband and routed Sayyid Ḥusayn Khān's forces. Sayyid Ḥusayn Khān now decided against campaigns either to Mazār-i Sharīf or the Hazārahjāt and remained in Chārīkār.

Also on this day, a caravan of Shinwārīs who had collected the goods of merchants in Kabul and were providing paid transport to Peshawar, due to the approach to Kabul of the force of Eastern Province tribes [under Muḥammad Hāshim Khān], now turned around and delayed their departure until Tuesday. After their return [to Kabul] it was discovered that at the time of their move towards Kabul, the Shinwārī thieves had attacked people of Surkh Rūd and Chaprahār. These latter had fought back and since the looted artillery /192/ and most of the small arms and ammunition that belonged to the government had fallen into the hands of the people of Surkh Rūd, they routed the Shinwārīs, killing and wounding about 120 of them, while the Surkh Rūdīs sustained twelve killed or wounded. Because of this, units from the Eastern Province stopped advancing on Kabul and the Shinwārī caravan was forced to return to the city. Moreover, the people of Surkh Rūd did not allow Muhmands to cross through their territory en route to the capital. Eventually, with the help of the sons of the late *naqīb*, Shaykh-i Pādshāh [of Chārbāgh] the Shinwārīs [who supported Ḥabīb Allāh Khān] were forgiven and ties of amity were reconnected. [The Surkh Rūdī situation] was the second obstacle. They say that the efforts of Muḥammad Nādir Khān's brother, Muḥammad Hāshim Khān, have been fruitless and so the attack on Kabul by units from the Eastern Province has been put off.

Also on this day, on the pretext that the residents of Chandāwul were concealing weapons in their compounds, the home of the head secretary of the treasury, Mīrzā Muḥammad Ismāʿīl, was thoroughly searched. Doors, floors, and ceilings as well as other places which seemed suspicious were ripped out but no weapons were found. Still, this caused Mīrzā Muḥammad Ismāʿīl great loss and it will cost him a substantial amount to repair the damage. Other homes which were searched were similarly vandalized. Does the religion really deem such damage done to Muslims permissible and legal?

The Events of Sunday, 2 Ẕīḥijjah, Corresponding to 22 Ṣawr and 12 May

Because of the arrival of eighty wounded men in Kabul yesterday, on this day rumors flew that Muḥammad Nādir Khān had crushed Ḥabīb Allāh Khān's forces at the village of Bīdak. These were the forces which had been sent to Lahūgard. Most were killed or wounded, taken prisoner, and disarmed. **/193/**

On this day too, rumors circulated that Sayyid Ḥusayn Khān's forces were surrounded in Kūhistān and that he himself had been wounded; that a force of Ḥabīb Allāh Khān had arrived in Jabal al-Sirāj after being
88 defeated in Qaṭaghan at Khānābād and Andarāb | when attacked by Muḥammad Raḥīm Khān, son of Sardār Muḥammad ʿUmar Khān and grandson of Amīr ʿAbd al-Raḥmān Khān; that Deputy Field Marshal ʿAbd al-Wakīl Khān had captured Fayż Ābād in Badakhshān and with units of his tribe had arrived in Farāj Ghān; that in Kūhistān, in the region of Pul-i Matak, fighting was just starting; and that tribal contingents from the Eastern Province, who, as mentioned earlier, had marched to Tagāb, had crushed the forces of Ḥabīb Allāh Khān that were there. [These stories] evoked fear among the Northerners and bolstered the spirits of the Kābulīs who were at the end of their rope from the oppression and tyranny of a crassly ignorant government.

The Events of Monday, 3 Ẕīḥijjah, Corresponding to 23 Ṣawr and 13 May

On this day, rumors were in everyone's mouth of fighting in Ghūrband and also about the fact that Sayyid Ḥusayn, after burning the homes of the Hazārahs of Turkmān and driving off their livestock, had sent to the Hazārahs ʿAbd al-Raḥmān Khān, son of Malik Dād Muḥammad Kūhistānī, the most corrupt and seditious of the people of the North; Sayyid Ṭālib Shāh Khān Ghūrbandī, a Shiʿi from a noble family; and also one other person to persuade them to submit to Ḥabīb Allāh Khān and recognize his government. Sayyid Ḥusayn Khān sent a message that said, **/194/**

> Beginning with ʿAbd al-Raḥmān Khān down to the day of Amān Allāh Khān's abdication from the throne, [the Afghans] have oppressed the Hazārahs.

> They have plundered, murdered, detained, enslaved, immolated, and dispossessed them; nevertheless, these rulers not only did not punish the Afghans, on the contrary they incited them to murder, plunder, and enslave the Hazārahs and these same rulers forcibly banished them [the Hazārahs] and made them flee to other lands. With respect to which good deed is it that his grandfather or his father or Amān Allāh himself did for you that you have become his supporters? By your failure to recognize the authority of Amīr Ḥabīb Allāh Khān, you condemn yourselves to destruction. The best thing is for you to take the path of obedience, and stop the bloodshed. Then you won't put yourselves on the brink of death and destruction.

The Hazārahs held his messengers [for a time] and then gave this response:

> According to the will of God and the Prophet and as it is written in the Qur'ān, '(As for) the male thief and the female thief, cut off the right hands of both as recompense …[158] and in the law of retaliation there is life O men
> 89 of understanding …[159] | and if anyone intentionally kills a Believer, his recompense is Hell to abide therein for eternity and the wrath of God and His curse are upon him and a great punishment is prepared for him,'[160] therefore, according to the Sharīʿah, we cannot acknowledge the authority of, nor submit to, a man who sheds blood, plunders Muslims, forces girls to the bed of intercourse and boys to sodomy, hacks living Muslims to pieces, scorches the heads of victims with fire or hangs them in the bazaar, and smears the faces of Muslims with filth and then parades them around for show to the music of a military band. And how many people has he hanged and shot? /195/ He has spent the contents of the government treasury and stores, the Bayt al-Māl, whether cash, kind, or weapons, which have been gathered for the protection of the country and the honor of the nation, on killing and plundering fellow Muslims. He has absolutely no fear of the Almighty. At the same time, misguided mullahs, relate this verse to such a person: "Obey God, obey the Prophet and the first in authority among you."[161] And they consider this verse, "Oh worshippers of Mine, who have transgressed against themselves, despair not of the mercy of God. Truly, God forgives all sins …"[162] to be proof of his innocence and purity and they do not consider that this verse coming down from God as a promise applies to Amān Allāh Khān. Is it really possible that this verse only pertains to thieves and not to all people? Therefore, we do not recognize [Ḥabīb Allāh Khān] as legally worthy of the amirate and consider ourselves obligated to defend ourselves and our property from destruction. We see ourselves as being both killer and victim, either we kill or are killed, and we will not withdraw the foot from

---

[158] Qurʾān 5:38.
[159] Qurʾān 2:179.
[160] Qurʾān 4:93.
[161] Qurʾān 4:59.
[162] Qurʾān 39:53.

> the arena of obligation to defend [ourselves] as long as we remain alive. As for ʿAbd al-Raḥmān, who is now with us, we will free him when the leader of the Hazārahs, the Mīrākhūr Aḥmad ʿAlī is released from prison in Kabul and sent to us.

But since Aḥmad ʿAlī had already been hanged, the issue of ʿAbd al-Raḥmān remained unresolved.

Also on this day, rumors spread in Kabul that 900 men from Ḥabīb Allāh Khān's army, along with artillery and armaments, were captured in Ghūrband by supporters of Amān Allāh Khān.

The Events of Tuesday, 4 Z̤īḥijjah Corresponding to 24 S̤awr and 14 May

On this day, there were rumors that 2,000 veteran troops from Ḥabīb Allāh Khān's army, famed for their skill at pillaging and bloodshed and under the command of Sayyid Ḥusayn Khān, were defeated and captured during the night by contingents from Hazārah and Afghan tribes who support Amān Allāh Khān. Their weapons, materiel, artillery, and other things left
90 behind **/196/** were also seized. |

Also during this time, two merchants who had obtained passports to go to India via Peshawar with a Shinwārī caravan, which had agreed to provide them security, set off. However, they were accused of planning to go to Kuwaytah (Quetta) with the intent of continuing from there to Qandahar and linking up with Amān Allāh Khān. For this they were arrested, at night secretly condemned to death and each shot with one bullet through the forehead.

Also on the eve of this day, General Muḥammad ʿUmar Khān and his unit were taken prisoner by troops of Amān Allāh Khān who were at Shaykh Yāsīn, Wardak. Muḥammad ʿUmar Khān, better known as "general of cavalry," was the son of Deputy Field Marshal Ghulām Nabī Khān of the Nāṣir tribe and a landlord in Kūh Dāman. Muḥammad ʿUmar Khān laid claim to the land of his father but was deprived of his inheritance and on the day the partisans of Ḥabīb Allāh Khān attacked and conquered Kabul, he committed an act of treachery, abandoning the breastworks at Khayr Khānah Pass and surrendering the regular army weapons of his unit and the government artillery to Ḥamīd Allāh Khān, the brother of Ḥabīb Allāh Khān, who carried out the attack with a force of thirty-three men. Muḥammad ʿUmar himself fled into the city. After the revolutionaries took the city, he was arrested but was released on account of his services. Eventually, he was reinstated to the rank of general and sent to the front with a force of 1,000 men where he was captured with the force under his command by the army of Amān Allāh Khān at Shaykh Yāsīn, Wardak.

On this same day, an infantry regiment with a colonel, cannons, weapons, and [other] war materiel arrived in Lahūgard and joined up with the forces of Muḥammad Nādir Khān.

During these events, the son of Malik Zayn al-ʿĀbidīn Dāʾudzāʾī, General ʿUmrā Khān, who had been sent to fight the enemy in Ghaznīn, was recalled to Kabul and arrested after the execution of his fellow tribesman, Qāżī ʿAbd al-Raḥmān Khān, who was killed by being hacked to pieces while still alive. (See above p. 157) The general had changed his allegiance and sent a letter to Amān Allāh Khān indicating his obedience but the letter had fallen into the hands of Field Marshal Purdil Khān. /197/ The Dāʾudzāʾī tribe nourished a deep hatred for Ḥabīb Allāh Khān and so allied with Amān Allāh Khān's army. As a result, an order was issued to punish General ʿUmrā Khān by means of the "four nails" punishment [putting four stakes in the ground and tieing the victim's hands and feet to them] and to dismiss his father from his position as head of the Central Customs Office. His companions were all placed in neck-irons.

Also on this day, they brought eight wounded men to Kabul from the Wardak fighting.

The Events of Wednesday, 5 Z̲īḥijjah, Corresponding to 25 S̲awr and 15 May

During these recorded events, as a consequence of rumors and propaganda that Ghulām Nabī Khān [Charkhī], had attacked and captured Mazār-i Sharīf with a contingent of Russian Qazāqs disguised as Turkmāns, Ḥabīb Allāh Khān, with two of his closest confidants, went to the Russian Legation. He wanted to obtain reliable information about that government's intentions since it officially had not yet recognized his emirate as well as about the situation in Afghan Turkistān and Afghanistan. He was acting in accordance with the bidding of England as transmitted through Humphrys,[163] who had departed for India. The Russian minister repudiated the story of Russian interference in Turkistān and [Ḥabīb Allāh Khān] was reassured.

91 Also on this day, the Northerners spread rumors | that at the time of the attack and capture of Mazār-i Sharīf by Ghulām Nabī Khān, the brigadier

---

[163] Sir Francis Henry Humphrys (1879–1971) was appointed British minister to Afghanistan in 1922. See the online *Oxford Dictionary of National Biography*.

general of the army of Ḥabīb Allāh Khān, ʿAbd al-Raḥīm Khān, reportedly fled with sixty riders, arrived in Harāt, and captured it. The Russian and Iranian embassies officially congratulated Ḥabīb Allāh Khān on the victory. As a result of these false rumors, supporters of Amān Allāh Khān despair and the revolutionaries are elated.[164]

Also on this day, because Muḥammad Nādir Khān's army had crossed the Tīrah Pass, giving notice of their arrival [in Lahūgard] with a forty-one gun salute, the people of Lahūgard who were tired of the oppression and tyranny of Ḥabīb Allāh Khān's soldiers, who killed, stole, assaulted five-year old girls, /198/ chopped off the heads of five-year-old and seven-year-old boys, forced every family to pay a land tax of 120 rupees or be punished, and sent every man without exception off to fight, having learned of the arrival of Muḥammad Nādir Khān's army in Lahūgard, turned their faces from Ḥabīb Allāh Khān and joined forces with Muḥammad Nādir Khān. Because of the spread of this news and [news of] other problems and dangers [to Ḥabīb Allāh Khān] coming from Ghūrband, Panjshayr, and Wardak where, according to reports, his forces had suffered defeat in the Ghaznīn region and withdrawn to Qalʿah-yi Durrānī and the army of Amān Allāh Khān had occupied Ghaznīn and Shaykhābād and also because the population of Panjshayr and Tagāb had drawn the head through the collar of opposition, Ḥabīb Allāh Khān called a conference at 10 A.M. in the Arg in an upper room of the Gulkhānah Palace to find some solution. The discussions lasted until 5:30 P.M. but no one knows what, if any, decisions came out of it.

Later, it was disclosed that at the written request of Ghulām Nabī Khān, the Russians reportedly subjected Mazār-i Sharīf to aerial bombardment in the wake of which a vast army arrived and occupied the city. Ḥabīb Allāh Khān asked [his advisors] what was the best thing to do. They said that as long as there was fighting inside the country what could one say to the Russians and what steps could one take? They advised that it was best just to wait on developments and could offer no other opinion or decision.

Also on the eve of this day a large contingent of defeated and routed soldiers of the army of Ḥabīb Allāh Khān arrived in Chahārdihī after being defeated in Ghaznīn and Wardak. As they were hungry, they broke into

---

[164] On ʿAbd al-Raḥīm Ṣāfī's capture of Harāt and his "Harāt Republic," an episode in Afghan history that has drawn little scholarly attention, see V. S. Boyko, *Vlast' i oppozitsiia v Afganistane: osobennosti politicheskoi bor'byi v 1919–1953 gg.*, Moscow and Barnaul: Rossiskaia akademiia nauk, 2010, pp. 164–83. For more on ʿAbd al-Raḥīm Ṣāfī's career see Adamec, *Who's Who*, p. 102.

shops in Ūnchī Bāghbānhā, Dih Būrī, and Dih Mazang, and made off with everything edible including mulberries, peas, and raisins. In the dark of night, they then headed off to Kūh Dāman on the road through Shāh Mardān Pass and ʿAlīābād. As they had notified [the government] by telephone from Qalʿah-i Durrānī **/199/** about the defeat, Ḥabīb Allāh Khān, fearful that Amān Allāh Khān's army would enter the city in pursuit of the vanquished, in a state of anxiety raised several units and sent them to the heights of Kūḥ-i Āsmāʾī and Shayr Darwāzah. They awaited the enemy
92 attack there until morning, frightened and sleepless. |

The Events of Thursday, 6 Ẕīḥijjah, Corresponding to 26 Ṣawr and 16 May

The fighting which began on Wednesday in Lahūgard is still raging today. On the eve of this day, a detachment under the command of Captain ʿAbd Allāh Khān Panjshayrī and also Hazārahs of Bāmyān, Yakah Awlang, Turkmān, Shaykh ʿAlī and other regions, having barricaded the road to the Khāwāk Pass, prevented Sayyid Ḥusayn Khān from passing through on his way to Qaṭaghan and Mazār-i Sharīf. [Sayyid Ḥusayn Khān] and his detachment of cavalry who had made camp in Gul Bahār intending to cross the Hindū Kush then returned to Chārīkār from where he telephoned Ḥabīb Allāh Khān asking for reinforcements. At four in the morning Ḥabīb Allāh Khān ordered a mixed bag of 1,000 men from Chahārdihī sent to Sayyid Ḥusayn in Chārīkār. These men had been rounded up from the populace of Chahārdihī and were held in Shahrārā, the palace which earlier had been the Ḥabībīyah School.

Today at sunrise a large group of defeated soldiers returned to Kabul. They had been sent by Ḥabīb Allāh Khān to Lahūgard and the Southern Province and there had suffered defeat at the hands of Muḥammad Nādir Khān whose army pursued them as far as Kulangār, Kattī Khayl, and Muḥammad Āghah.

Also on this day, secret informers notified Ḥabīb Allāh Khān that Amān Allāh Khān had sent seven planes to bomb Kabul. These were the same ones that the day before had bombed the detachment in Gul Bahār, Sayyid Ḥusayn Khān's force, which was heading for Afghan Turkistān. On hearing this news, Ḥabīb Allāh Khān lost his head **/200/** and at the advice of a German advisor and convert to Islam he ordered that five of the twelve anti-aircraft guns that he had in Kabul be taken to the summit of Kūh-i Āsmāʾī. Guns were also set up on other peaks around Kabul. Until noon, he personally manned the guns on Āsmāʾī. Then, after firing off three rounds, he came back down from the mountain.

At 1:00 P.M. he received four letters by rider from Sayyid Ḥusayn Khān and one from the commander of the unit in Butkhāk from which he learned that 6,000 men of Muḥammad Nādir Khān's army had reached Khāk-i Jabbār by way of Ḥiṣārak.[xcvi] Straightaway, Ḥabīb Allāh Khān set off by motor vehicle for Butkhāk in order to organize its defenses. However, rumors spread from close confidants of his that Ḥabīb Allāh Khān broke down and cried after reading the letter from Sayyid Ḥusayn Khān and had gone not to Butkhāk but to Chārīkār. The populace of the city, having prayed to God day and night to deliver them from Sayyid Ḥusayn Khān, believed the rumors that he had been fatally wounded in the battle at Burj-i Guljān and Ḥabīb Allāh Khān had gone there to see him for the
93 last time. |

The Events of Friday, 7 Ẕīḥijjah, Corresponding to 27 Ṣawr and 17 May

During the calamitous times that have been described, on the advice of the Indian muhājir Mawlawī ʿAbd al-Laṭīf, who, when it came to deception, cunning and conspiracy, was a schemer second to none and whom the whole population considers a servant and spy for the English and an evil man, Ḥabīb Allāh Khān decided to write a letter to Muḥammad Nādir Khān and his brothers, Shāh Walī Khān and Shāh Maḥmūd Khān, proposing a truce. These [latter two] men were then in the Southern Province, having made preparations to snuff out the flames of revolution in the country, to provide tranquility and comfort to the nation, put an end to the bloodshed and re-establish security. /**201**/ After their relatives were arrested and their wives taken away to the Arg where they were subjected to humiliation and assault, on Saturday, the first of Ẕīḥijjah, Ḥabīb Allāh Khān wrote a letter in which he promised to send Muḥammad Nādir Khān money and invited him to become involved in the administration of the state. He also wrote,

> despite the fact that you did not come to Kabul, but opposed the new government and began a war, the road to peace is still open. But in order for this to happen, you must end the bloodshed and killing of Muslims and, in conformity with my original suggestion, come to Kabul. If not, all the blood which is shed, and all the property and wealth which is stolen will be on your conscience. If something happens to your families, you will also be to blame for that and not I. You may assure yourself of the sincerity of this offer through Mawlawī ʿAbd al-Laṭīf, who is my fully empowered representative, with whom you may conclude any agreement or understanding and on whom you may rely.

The mawlawī, who had orchestrated this affair at English bidding, with credentials signed by the minister of court, Shayr Jān, and bearing Ḥabīb Allāh Khān's seal, set off to see Muḥammad Nādir Khān and his brothers. God willing, his returning empty-handed, will be recounted below.

Also at this time, due to rumors circulating that seven airplanes were coming to bomb Kabul and, according to his spies who said they would be taking off from Mazār-i Sharīf, Ḥabīb Allāh Khān, because of misunderstanding, considered the Russian government responsible and sent an official protest to the Russian Legation in Kabul which said "if these planes actually bomb Kabul, they will be ones connected to [your] legation. This will then occasion objections to be lodged by representatives of other countries for this and for interference in the internal revolution of our country." But the acting Russian chargé d'affaires in Afghanistan replied,

> My government has never interfered and is not now interfering in the affairs of Afghanistan and [Afghan] Turkistān either at the time of the revolution
> **94** or at any other time. | But once the revolution settles down and an official emirate is established and its independence is secured, if [my government] should have some plan, it will see that it is carried out. For the time being, it will not interfere in any way.

The Events of Saturday, 8 Ẕīḥijjah, Corresponding to 28 Ṣawr and 18 May

Meanwhile, after Mawlawī 'Abd al-Laṭīf reached Muḥammad Nādir Khān and delivered Ḥabīb Allāh Khān's letter, Muḥammad Nādir Khān called a halt to hostilities until the ceremonies of 'Īd-i Qurbān (Day of the Sacrifice or 'Īd al-Aẓḥā) were over.

On this day it was learned that Ḥażrat Shayr Āqā had arrived in Zurmat and Katawāz from India supposedly at the request of the Muslims of India and was staying with the Sulaymān Khayl and Andar tribes in order to aid in putting out the flames of the revolution that the Afghans had raised against Amān Allāh Khān. In fact he was carrying out the instructions of the English who had not wanted Amān Allāh Khān as amir. So, this ḥażrat, after meeting with the Sulaymān Khayl and Andar elders and turning them against Amān Allāh Khān, set off to meet with the tribes of the Southern Province who had concluded an agreement with Muḥammad Nādir Khān. **/203/** They had resolved that after the capture of Kabul and getting rid of Ḥabīb Allāh Khān, then, after consultation with representatives and notables of all the people, they would put on the throne a man worthy of the honor of governing the country. He would be a representative from either the Durrānī, Ghilzā'ī, Hazārah, Tajik, or Ūzbak tribes and they would raise him to authority and obey his commands and prohibitions so the government would not be destroyed and its citizens would not be brought to the brink of disturbance but would be consorts of ease and comfort and could occupy themselves with farming, crafts, and earning a living. It was also agreed that the Afghan tribes of the Southern Province, who did not want Amān Allāh Khān to be amir because of the treachery and corruption of his ministers, would back Muḥammad Nādir Khān in the event that he agreed to be amir of Afghanistan. But he, being a judicious and pious man, considered this a provocation to the English who could cause great harm to the Afghan government and nation.

By getting the Afghans of the Southern Province to agree to such a resolution, Shayr Āqā first united them and then called on them to rise up and overthrow Ḥabīb Allāh Khān. In conformity with the plans of the English, he came to Muḥammad Nādir Khān and, using great cunning and deception, persuaded him to become amīr and so raised the flag of the sultanate in his name.

Meantime, as has already been mentioned, Mawlawī 'Abd al-Laṭīf had come to Muḥammad Nādir Khān and a truce had ensued until the end of the Festival of the Sacrifice. It is possible that as a result of this shortsighted policy, all-out war will commence and the revolution in Afghanistan will continue since Amān Allāh Khān has many supporters, like Russia and Turkey, the Muslims of India,[xcvii] the Durrānī Afghan tribes,
95 the Hazārahs and others. | **/204/**

Ḥabīb Allāh Khān's Preparations According to the Program and Instructions of the English Government

On the aforementioned Saturday [18 May], it was disclosed that secretly at night, Ḥabīb Allāh Khān's confidants, high-ranking figures in government business, and advisors, had all gathered at the Arg, among whom were elders of the tribes of the northern regions; the wakil, Muḥammad Walī Khān; Deputy Field Marshal Maḥmūd Sāmī; Deputy Field Marshal Muḥammad Na'īm Khān; Sardār Muḥammad 'Usmān Khān; the former minister of finance, Mīrzā Maḥmūd Khān; Muḥammad Maḥfūẓ Khān, son of Aḥmad Jān Khān; 'Aẓīm Allāh Khān; and Nūr Allāh Khān, the brother of Aḥmad 'Alī Khān who, during Amān Allāh Khān's reign, served as mayor [of Kabul]. Two or three spies for the English who occupy high positions and enjoy great trust and respect were present at this gathering and discussed things with them. At their bidding, rumors are circulating that Russian troops jointly with Ghulām Nabī Khān have bombed Mazār-i Sharīf and then attacked that city and Qaṭaghan. As was already mentioned, Ḥabīb Allāh Khān had protested this to the Russian mission in Kabul. It was decided to print up a circular with the following contents: "In connection with the Russian attack on Mazār-i Sharīf and Qaṭaghan and the marching of their troops into those regions, all residents of Afghanistan must put an end to the civil war and rise up to defend against Russian attack." But this proclamation, which, without question, is a provocation of the English, has yet to be published. One specimen of it, signed by the government, fell into the hands of the English. Probably on that pretext, they will bring troops into Afghanistan so that the revolution will go on and a general war in the center of Asia will eventually wind up being to England's advantage. **/205/**

The Events of Sunday, 9 Ẕīḥijjah, Corresponding to 29 S̱awr and 19 May

Despite the fact that the new moon for this month has not yet made an appearance, on Friday evening Ḥabīb Allāh Khān, though he has no special knowledge of astronomy but like a bear who is the mightiest on the mountain considers himself an Abū ʿAlī Ibn Sīnā[165] amongst ignoramuses, on the basis of the calendar which he had devised, the *Taqwīm-i Ḥabīb Allāh*, declared today to be the holiday (ʿĪd al-Ażḥā, the Day of the Sacrifice). Since on Friday, the crescent moon was not visible in the sky, still, if it appears on Saturday evening, then according to jurisprudence (*fiqh*) on the day of ʿArafat (the ninth of Ẕīḥijjah), the ceremonies and the holiday prayers and the sacrifice are forbidden. It is possible that someone sighted the crescent moon on Friday and therefore the *qāżī* declared the holiday. But if there is any doubt, then, according to Sharīʿah, the tenth of Ẕīḥijjah should correspond to the same day of the week as the first day of Ramażān and this year that day is a Monday. Therefore the holiday should be celebrated on the tenth of Ẕīḥijjah but today, Sunday, is the ninth and the festivities (of the sacrifice) and the holiday prayers are not permitted.

Also on this day news circulated that Sayyid Ḥusayn who had been wounded in the buttocks in fighting at Burj-i Guljān had died. This news brought joy to the hearts of the people of Kabul and other [regions of the country] who had been subjected to the oppression, tyranny, killing,

---

165 Ibn Sīnā (d. 1037 A.D.), physician, philosopher, and scientist, known in medieval Europe as Avicenna, was the author of many works perhaps the most famous being an enormous medical treatise, the *Qānūn*.

plundering, sinning, and fornicating of Sayyid Ḥusayn Khān and who had begged God for his death.

[Also] news spread of the victory of the supporters and partisans of Amān Allāh Khān, their reaching Chārīkār and their surrounding Ḥabīb
96 Allāh Khān's army | to the delight of the disgusted people of Kabul and others who were under tremendous pressure.

Also news circulated about raising the banner of Muḥammad Nādir Khān's emirate and about fixing the time for the assault on Kabul by his troops and those of Amān Allāh Khān to occur three days after the holiday. Other things that came out after the spread of this news were the rumors and propaganda of the Northerners that partisans of Ḥabīb Allāh Khān had surrounded Amān Allāh Khān in the fortress of Qalāt which is situated five stages from Qandahar. /**206**/ (It is rumored that) the fortress is just about to fall and Amān Allāh Khān about to be captured or killed. Ḥabīb Allāh Khān sent five iron cages by truck so that in the event they capture Amān Allāh Khān they would put him and his close associates in the cages bring them to Kabul and set them out for viewing as a lesson to others. Although this news had no basis or any truth to it, nevertheless lies and propaganda when widely disseminated are still considered to be "events" and so I recorded them so that in the future people would learn what was true and false and use these stories as examples.

On this day, in the ʿĪdgāh Mosque, having learned that Muḥammad Nādir Khān had been proclaimed amīr and that the tribes of the Eastern and Southern Provinces had sworn allegiance to him and also aware that he himself does not have the power to govern and defend the country, Ḥabīb Allāh Khān had sent, as already mentioned, that lackey of the English, Indian by origin, Mawlawī ʿAbd al-Laṭīf, with a letter in which he invited [Muḥammad Nādir Khān] to return to Kabul. This was something the residents of the city did not know. Ḥabīb Allāh Khān himself now ascended the pulpit of the ʿĪdgāh Congregational Mosque and delivered a speech in which he declared,

> I was a poor man, hiding out from the government up in the mountains and in fear of being punished for my banditry. When Amān Allāh Khān decided to undermine the foundations of religion and to turn the nation of believers into atheists, I opposed him and was victorious. He fled. As for me, having decided that I am not worthy of ruling the country, I sent a large sum of money to Muḥammad Nādir Khān in France and invited him to take charge of the most important matters of government and to put things in order in the country and in its sultanate. He refused. Having come instead to the Southern Province he has busied himself inciting the people to provocative acts. Today he is causing bloodshed and he wants to destroy the government

> and the nation and to intimidate /207/ and annihilate the people. But if he returns now, it is still not too late to avert the killing of Muslims and to put an end to the revolution.

In answer to this speech, those who were present cursed Ḥabīb Allāh Khān through clenched teeth for the fact that he had destroyed the government, plundered government reserves, and demolished the tranquility of the nation with murder and violence.

The Events of Monday, 10 Ẕīḥijjah, Corresponding to 30 S̱awr and 20 May

97 | Yesterday Ḥabīb Allāh Khān ordered that holiday celebrations be concluded. To mark the occasion, the amir held a reception and distributed gifts to his guests.

In response to the rumor that Amān Allāh Khān was besieged in the Qalāt fortress, Ḥabīb Allāh Khān ordered enough "little oranges and hand bombs" [types of hand grenades] sent there to destroy the fortress.

On this day, due to word of the acceptance of Ḥabīb Allāh Khān's proposal that he had sent to Muḥammad Nādir Khān by the hand of Mawlawī ʿAbd al-Laṭīf Khān, as mentioned above, and (word) that his charm had done its work on Muḥammad Nādir Khān to end the bloodshed and killing of Muslims, he (Muḥammad Nādir Khān) dismissed [the mawlawī] who had successfully completed his mission. Either from Barakī Barak or Muḥammad Āghah he informed Ḥabīb Allāh Khān by telephone of the effective outcome of his deceit and duplicity. The amir then ordered the freeing of all Muḥammad Nādir Khān's family members from prison and the restitution of their confiscated property, including their homes. He then let a rumor float that Muḥammad Nādir Khān had sent a letter of allegiance with an oath of obedience including acceptance of [Ḥabīb Allāh's] amirate.

On the dissemination of this news, the people of Kabul, who had been brought to the brink of despair by the oppression, humiliation, and violence perpetrated /208/ by Ḥabīb Allāh Khān, his officials, and the debauched fornicators from the North, and who found no refuge except in death, began to condemn Muḥammad Nādir Khān, whom they had considered a person unparalleled in their time, devoted to the religion, a man in whom were combined the best qualities of a son of the Afghan people. To themselves they said that if he had in fact sent such an oath to Ḥabīb Allāh Khān then he had neither pride, nor faith, nor honor, nor feelings of shame, nor does he recognize his own indecency because Ḥabīb Allāh Khān had taken his wife and the wives of his brothers at night to the Arg, women who were daughters of [the late] Amīr Ḥabīb Allāh Khān, held them there for some time with a total lack of respect, and dealt with them cruelly. [They said to themselves that] Muḥammad Nādir Khān knew all about this but because of a lack of pride he had overlooked it and so had demeaned Afghan honor and his own reputation which up until now had been famous and esteemed. The residents of the city finally reassured each other by saying this rumor is a lie and Muḥammad Nādir Khān's capacity for courage is limitless, for on the holiday [of the Sacrifice] more than 20,000 men, who had raised him to the amirate, yesterday read the *khuṭbah* and performed the prayers in his name. If thoughtlessly and precipitously he is complicit in fulfilling the desires of Ḥabīb Allāh Khān, then the mere recording of this case would pollute [the pages of] history.

The Events of Tuesday, 11 Ẕīḥijjah, Corresponding to 31 Ṣawr and 21 May

On this day, problems in Kūhistān due to the progress made by supporters of Amān Allāh Khān and their getting close (to Kūhistān) by way of [both] the Khāwāk Pass and Ghūrband and because of the plans of a Ṣāfī group to cause trouble in Tagāb, [all these] caused Ḥabīb Allāh Khān considerable anxiety and as a defensive move he ordered part of the army stationed in Kabul to be dispatched to Chārīkār and Rīzah-i Kūhistān in
98 eighteen "fire" vehicles and lorries (*mūtar-i ātishī wa lārī*). | He himself with his brother, Muʿīn al-Salṭanah Ḥamīd Allāh Khān, the high governor Malik Muḥsin, and a number of riflemen, **/209/** headed for Ghaznīn at five in the morning in nine Dodge motorcars (*mūtar-i dāj*) to get information about Amān Allāh Khān's situation.

Marginalia: Recently, it was learned that Sayyid Ḥusayn, having been wounded and then brought by a secret route to the Arg for treatment, had died from his wounds and they took his body [in a convoy of] eighteen vehicles filled with property and soldiers[xcviii] to Chārīkār. Ḥabīb Allāh Khān, pretending that he was going to Ghaznīn, now turned around at Dih Būrī and headed instead for Chārīkār for the burial of Sayyid Ḥusayn Khān. He passed by the *gardanah*[166] of Bāgh-i Bālā and the village of Afshār. In the late afternoon he made a secret return to Kabul by the

[166] According to Muḥammad Muʿīn, *Farhang-i Fārsī*, 6 vols., Tehran: Mu'assasah-i intishārāt-i Amīr-i Kabīr, 1371/1992, s.v. and Ḥasan ʿAmīd, *Farhang-i Fārsi-yi ʿAmīd*, Tehran: Mu'assasah-i intishārāt-i Amīr-i Kabīr, 1357/1978, s.v., a *gardanah* is a difficult road full of twists and turns leading to the top of an elevation. Bāgh-i Bālā, a palace built by Amīr ʿAbd al-Raḥmān Khān, was on an elevation. Thus here, the reference is probably to the road that led up to the Bāgh-i Bālā.

same road. They also say that he went to Ghaznīn in the clothing of a Jājī tribesman. The automobile in which he was riding and five other automobiles carrying his supporters drove straight into the hands of supporters of Amān Allāh Khān. By some trickery, he managed to get into another car and without encountering anyone arrived back in Kabul in the afternoon. So it happened that of the nine vehicles that had left three were seen at the Harten Bridge and those were headed for the Arg. There were no more vehicles than that. This latter rumor is probably closer to the truth. [End of the marginal note.]

[Ḥabīb Allāh Khān] also circulated rumors that Muḥammad Nādir Khān had sent an oath of loyalty and was going to come to Kabul. Meanwhile Muḥammad Ṣiddīq Khān, who was a major general under Amān Allāh Khān, having forgotten the kindness shown him and being untrue to his salt, came out against Muḥammad Nādir Khān and, having received the post of high commissioner of the Southern Province from Ḥabīb Allāh Khān, left Kabul for Lahūgard. Muḥammad Nādir Khān's force was large and when [Muḥammad Ṣiddīq Khān] realized that he did not have the wherewithal to confront him, he sent a letter to Kabul by secret courier (*sawār-i chār*) in which he requested adequate reinforcements from Ḥabīb Allāh Khān saying,

> Due to the deficient numbers of fighting men I have to be excused from engaging Muḥammad Nādir Khān. It simply isn't possible. Instead I would be throwing myself into a sea of fire and would be burned to ashes. If reinforcements don't arrive, it's impossible to set foot on the field of battle and advance along the road to victory.

However, aside from **/210/** some thieves whom Ḥabīb Allāh Khān called the "Arg Battalion," that is his personal bodyguards, there were no forces left in Kabul who could be sent to Lahūgard. So Ḥabīb Allāh Khān began to promote, even more vigorously, the rumor that Muḥammad Nādir Khān had sent his oath and was going to come to Kabul.[xcix]

Today, there is more and more talk about the death of Sayyid Ḥusayn Khān. These stories began two or three days ago. People so look forward to his death that they literally dream that he has died. It is possible that it is true that he has.

The Events of Wednesday, 12 Ẕīḥijjah, Corresponding to 1 Jawzā and 22 May 1929

On this day, when the military and civilian leaders in Ghaznīn had gathered to perform the prayers in the ʿĪdgāh Congregational Mosque which is situated a mile west of the city, false rumors were spread that Tarakī and Sulaymān Khayl tribesmen, expressing their devotion to tribal unity and Afghan honor, had come out in support of Amān Allāh Khān and had occupied Ghaznīn without firing a shot, not allowing Ḥabīb Allāh Khān's forces to return [from performing the holiday prayers]. Thus they drove them out [of Ghaznīn] and dispersed them [according to rumor].

After that, further fighting has spread as far as Shaykhābād, Wardak three stages from Ghaznīn. Primarily for this reason, Ḥabīb Allāh Khān left for Ghaznīn and spent a whole day there overseeing the strengthening of positions as was mentioned earlier. Then during the evening of the day before this day he returned to Kabul.

Also during this time, [the supporters of Ḥabīb Allāh Khān] derived great satisfaction from the arrival of the letter from Muḥammad [Nādir] Khān which, as was already mentioned, he sent by the hand of Mawlawī
99 ʿAbd al-Laṭīf and in which he wrote about his own coming to Kabul. | At the very beginning of the letter he expressed his views about coming to Kabul saying,

> In inviting me to Kabul, you wrote that the Russian government has bombarded the region of Mazār-i Sharīf and that therefore we ought /**211**/ to end the internal fighting; further, when I return to Kabul you expect me to occupy myself with getting government affairs back into order and you will begin to fight the Russians and cleanse our land of their encroachments. Very good. Having read your wishes, I will come to Kabul.

But having read the end of the letter, where Muḥammad Nādir Khān said, "I will arrive in Kabul with 60,000 soldiers and therefore an adequate quantity of fodder and provisions should be readied" the partisans of Ḥabīb Allāh Khān became distraught and regretted that they had spread the rumor that Muḥammad Nādir Khān had allegedly given an oath of allegiance and had recognized Ḥabīb Allāh Khān as amir. They realized that it would have been better to be truthful because with the aid of such lies it was impossible to govern the country and bring peace and prosperity to the nation.

On this day as retribution for the Northerners' shedding blood, fornicating, and doing prohibited things, a swarm of locusts swooped down along the Lahūgard road as far as Chār Āsyā in Kabul.

Also news arrived that in the district of Shinīz in Wardak 5,000 households of nomadic Afghan tribes had gathered in one place, intending to make their migration into the Hazārahjāt to summer pastures. Soldiers from the army of Ḥabīb Allāh Khān en route to Ghaznīn, due to the excessive lust and prurience that causes them to commit lecherous acts and fornication, violated the honor of a girl from a family of the nomads. These then attacked the soldiers who had perpetrated this outrage and put them to the sword. News of this reached the ears of other "servants of the religion" including the high governor, Malik Muḥsin, who was thrown into turmoil. He set off for the district by car and placated the nomads using language that he knew [would work]. With cunning, he patched up the business and covered this filth, whose smell was spread throughout the country, with the dirt of craftiness and trickery. **/212/**

The Events of Thursday, 13 Ẕīḥijjah, Corresponding to 2 Jawzā and 23 May

On this day, Ḥabīb Allāh Khān, out of expedience, ordered released some 200 Wardak tribesmen who had been taken captive and held in prison in Kabul. He ordered the rest kept as hostages so that the Wardaks would provide him with 2,000 soldiers. He felt that the people of Kabul and its environs supported him, a brigand, only because they were unhappy with the former corrupt government of Amān Allāh Khān, his ministers and high-ranking officials. But once he became *pādshāh*, straight from being an outlaw and roaming the mountains and wastelands, and his army began to commit such oppression and plundering and causing rape, fornication, and the arrest of [innocent] travelers, the people turned the face of supplication to the Eternal Lord and fervently wished for him to be exterminated.

100 | The elders and representatives of the Tajiks of Ghaznīn, who had risen up against Amān Allāh Khān and become partisans and well-wishers of Ḥabīb Allāh Khān, had, before the arrival of Amān Allāh's army, provided the governor, Muḥammad Karīm Khān, and the troops of Ḥabīb Allāh Khān with accommodations and food in the city, in their villages, and in their own homes and they expelled Amān Allāh Khān's governor, Jānbāz Khān, from Ghaznīn. But despite their assistance and their allegiance, they were robbed by Ḥabīb Allāh Khān's army and his governor and so they came to Kabul and sought justice. Each was given ten rupees and promised eventual compensation for their losses. At the time when they were present at the court and hearing [the amir's] pleasing promises, right in the midst of his talking to the Tajik representatives from Ghaznīn, a mounted courier arrived with a letter which said that Ghulām Nabī Khān had subjected the Qaṭaghan regions of Khānābād, Andarāb, Tāluqān, and

Ḥażrat Imām to aerial bombing. /213/ This drew Ḥabīb Allāh Khān's ire and, as in the case of the bombing of Mazār-i Sharīf, he attributed this to the Russians. He filed a protest with the Russian Legation and ordered the chargé d'affaires of the legation be brought to the killing ground and put before a firing squad. Due to this thoughtless, bandit-type order, the Ḥażrat of Shūr Bāzār intervened to solicit forgiveness and generosity of spirit and prevented the precipitous implementation of this unworthy order. He suggested that [Ḥabīb Allāh Khān] consult with dignitaries of the court and then be satisfied with their views. Each of them should decide whether to execute or pardon the chargé d'affaires and then he should carry out whatever is agreed to. However, such extreme actions [that is, ordering the chargé d'affaires to be shot] will not deceive the people—it has long been clear to everyone that Ḥabīb Allāh does not know anything and cannot utter a single word let alone such extreme barbaric talk and all of his public announcements are wholly designed to obtain support from England. His reckless actions are devoid of all sense. Muḥammad Nādir Khān, who had proclaimed himself amir, also has done that because of English help and provocation. Also, Ḥażrat Shayr Āqā [Mujaddidī's] arriving in Katawāz and Zurmat and coming to claim the amirate is due to English policy.

Also on this day, rumors circulated that a meeting took place in Lahūgard between Muḥammad Nādir Khān and Ḥabīb Allāh Khān mediated by Mawlawī ʿAbd al-Laṭīf Hindī. People are saying that they were reconciled and that they have mutually agreed that Ḥabīb Allāh Khān would become ruler of the North and Muḥammad Nādir Khān would sit[c] on the throne as amir but would not harass and oppress the Northerners. In connection with this, they freed from prison Muḥammad Nādir Khān's cousin, ʿAlī Shāh, and sent him to him accompanied by several mullahs. Besides that, eighteen machine guns with iron gun shields and a force of 300 men were sent to Lahūgard. People wrongly imagine that due to the deployment of the detachment and the weaponry /214/ Ḥabīb Allāh Khān will be plotting malice towards Muḥammad Nādir Khān since he sends an army detachment while the reconciliation talks are going on
101 | to deal Muḥammad Nādir Khān a crushing blow and put his own mind at peace.

On this day, when they were freeing the captured Wardaks, Ḥabīb Allāh Khān did not release the Hazārahs but instead ordered them sent to the prison in Shayrpūr. He said, "I will have a talk with you later." This was because Hazārahs had chosen to side with Amān Allāh Khān.

The Events of Friday, 14 Ẕīḥijjah, Corresponding to 3 Jawzā and 24 May

At 11 P.M. on the eve of this day. the high governor, Malik Muḥsin, went to the house of the [former] high governor, Mīr Zamān al-Dīn, son of Prince Ḥasan Badakhshī. Four years before, Mīr Zamān al-Dīn had been appointed governor of Harāt and there his soul suddenly departed his body. (Now) while his wife and two sons slept, Malik Muḥsin stole all their valuables. Without their having committed any misdeed, treachery, misdemeanor,[ci] or crime, he made off with all the valuable and precious things that they had, put locks on all the rooms of the house and said, "Tomorrow I will return and make an inventory of all moveable property and will also check several other homes." Due to this wicked behavior on the part of the high governor, which has been going on in Kabul for five months now all the residents of the city ask the Creator of Jinn and Men to help them get out of the city but have found no opportunity.

Meantime, during the events already recorded, Muḥammad Nādir Khān through Mawlawī ʿAbd al-Laṭīf had opened the gates of a truce with Ḥabīb Allāh Khān and now wrote and sent a message of his own that he would come to Kabul to see him on condition that, as evidence of good faith on Ḥabīb Allāh Khān's part, he would send his brother, the Muʿīn al-Salṭanah Ḥamīd Allāh Khān, as a hostage to Muḥammad Nādir Khān. He in his turn would then send his brother, Shāh Maḥmūd, with 6,000 men to Kabul /215/ for them to take control of the Arg, the artillery, and government weapons. Ḥabīb Allāh Khān will himself then depart for the Northern Province and be satisfied with it. After this, Muḥammad Nādir Khān will himself enter Kabul with the 40,000 regulars and tribals that he has with him. Ḥabīb Allāh Khān, who had spread the rumor of the Russians' aggression in bombing the region of Mazār and Chihil Dar, the governor's seat at Khānābād, accepted Muḥammad Nādir Khān's written proposal at the behest and instruction of the English.

On this day, he sent his brother, Ḥamīd Allāh off to Muḥammad Nādir Khān by motor car along with Mawlawī ʿAbd al-Laṭīf, so that Shāh Maḥmūd would arrive in Kabul according to Muḥammad Nādir Khān's terms. Ḥabīb Allāh Khān himself, in accordance with his own declarations which the English had also put him up to, would then begin jihad against the Russians. However, due to the fact that from the outset Muḥammad Nādir Khān had rejected Ḥabīb Allāh Khān's respectful request that he come to Kabul, some discord had arisen between them, the outcome of which was that his family and wives were disgraced and dishonored. Also since Ḥażrat Shayr Āqā had arrived among the savage border tribes and

Muḥammad Nādir Khān had raised the banner of (his) amirate, it became clear that the English had introduced this jiggery-pokery and had laid the
102 foundations for an international war in the middle of Asia. | We will see what time brings. As for now, the good name of Muḥammad Nādir Khān has been transformed into a bad one.

The Events of Saturday, 15 Ẕīḥijjah, Corresponding to 4 Jawzā and 25 May 1929

During these events, some of the people of Kabul who were worn out from the violence and oppression of those semi-human Northerners devised a plan to assassinate Ḥabīb Allāh Khān. With this aim in mind, to kill him twenty-five hand grenades were buried in the ground beneath a pavilion which had been set up for Ḥabīb Allāh Khān on the Chaman-i Ḥużūrī for a review of the army. Having learned about the plot from a secret informant, Ḥabīb Allāh Khān invited to the Chaman-i Ḥużūrī the combat units which were stationed in and around Kabul, like those manning **/216/** the mountain summits surrounding the city, Chahārdihī, Arghandah, and Butkhāk, to watch the review on this day with the aim to radicalize them, turn them against the people of Kabul, and plant hatred in their breasts for all Kābulīs. To incite his soldiers against the Kābulīs, Ḥabīb Allāh Khān gave a speech to 4,000–5,000 troops complaining about the people of Kabul. The story about the harm which Amān Allāh Khān had caused worked the soldiers up to a fever pitch. Then they were ordered to retrieve the buried hand grenades. At sight of them, the soldiers became enraged at the Kābulīs and began to attack the spectators who had gathered around the enclosure where the military review took place and who were themselves looking at the explosives with great interest and just observing. The soldiers beat them with rifle butts while calling them "Lātī," meaning "Lātīnī" and drove them back into the city. After dismissal from the review, the soldiers, following Ḥabīb Allāh Khān's automobile back to the Arg, cursed and vilified the people of Kabul and then dispersed and returned to their posts.

To the wise and educated of Kabul this speech of Ḥabīb Allāh Khān and the malicious behavior of his troops are merely pretexts for looting and plundering the city. Among themselves, people blame and complain of the treachery of the corrupt ministers of Amān Allāh Khān, the pseudo-mullahs, Sardār Muḥammad ʿUs̱mān, and the ḥażrats of Shūr Bāzār who, in supporting the thieves, looters and rapists have brought about the plundering, the bloodshed, the taking of usury, and have let

the revolution establish itself in the country. They have made the country subject to enormous losses and the government to lose respect, and they have been the ruination of the country so that Ḥabīb Allāh Khān, who is by habit and custom a looter, will seek any pretext, through deceit and perfidy, to accuse the residents of Kabul of rebelling and so subject them to being pillaged and annihilated. If this is not and should not be the case, then why did the high governor of Kabul at night secretly enter the house and steal the valuable cloaks, precious jewelry, and magnificent clothing of the family of Mīr Zamān al-Dīn, the former high governor [of Harāt] /217/ and then quickly convey to Ḥabīb Allāh Khān what had been taken, part of which [the latter] kept for himself, and part he gave back to the high governor? Furthermore, that same night he ordered the Qizilbāsh to obtain an oath of loyalty from the Hazārahs in order to have a pretext to
103 plunder them [in case they refused to give it]. |

On the night of the looting of the house of Mīr Zamān al-Dīn Khān, Muḥammad Maḥfūẓ, the Muʿīn al-Salṭanah Ḥamīd Allāh Khān's deputy, staged a provocation in connection with the Qizilbāsh which he had his subordinates execute. By telephone, Muḥammad Maḥfūẓ received an order from the Muʿīn al-Salṭanah to assemble several Qizilbāsh at the Ministry of War and send them to the Hazārahs to obtain an oath of allegiance. Having received this order, at 11 P.M. he summoned to the ministry Nūr al-Dīn Khān Jawānshayr; Ḥājjī Muḥammad Yaʿqūb Khān, son of Mīrzā Muḥammad Yūsuf Khān who had held the post of army paymaster during the reign of Amīr ʿAbd al-Raḥmān Khān; Mullā Mīr Āqā, son of Sayyid Ḥusayn, a wool weaver nicknamed "Āqā Bulbul *rawżah-khwān*;"[167] the Iranian subject Shaykh Muḥammad Riżā-yi Khurāsānī; Khalīfah Ghulām Ḥasan; ʿAbd al-Wāḥid, son of Mullā Malik; and some others. Having uttered words to frighten, to give hope, to instill fear, to warn, and to bring trouble to the Hazārahs he then ordered those he had assembled to go to the Hazārahjāt and bring back a written oath of allegiance from the Hazārahs. It was agreed that they would consult among themselves and decide to do one of three things: one was to select a governor and a high governor from among the Qizilbāsh; another was to send a commission and choose the spokesman [for it]; and another, by means of a letter from [the Qizilbāsh] people stressing their being united by religion with the Hazārahs, to perhaps persuade [the Hazārahs] to swear an oath and

[167] A *rawżah-khwān*, or reciter of the passion of Imām Ḥusayn, performed the rites at Shiʿi funerals and recited the *rawżah* during the first ten days of Muḥarram, the first month of the Muslim calendar.

accept obedience to Amīr Ḥabīb Allāh. On the day following the evening, the Qizilbāsh held a meeting and proposed a reasoned but apologetic response. In late afternoon they went to see Muḥammad Maḥfūẓ who had demanded a reply and said to him,

> /**218**/ At the time of the Hazārah wars, which dragged on for nearly three years, Amīr ʿAbd al-Raḥmān Khān did not oblige the Qizilbāsh to go to the Hazārahs, although many of them held important positions in the government and enjoyed the respect of His Majesty. If you have given us this responsibility because of having a common religion, then it would follow logically to send representatives of the same tribes and co-religionists from the Eastern and Southern Province who were in Kabul and others who held high positions and enjoyed respect to obtain written oaths of allegiance [from the tribes of those provinces]. Moreover, at the time of Ḥabīb Allāh Khān's conquest of Kabul, the Qizilbāsh not only failed to shelter the 1,800 Hazārahs who were in the city but even disarmed 800[cii] of them in Murād Khānī in the presence of the great sardār, Muʿīn al-Salṭanah (Ḥamīd Allāh Khān) and turned their weapons over to his men. Not one Qizilbāsh allowed a single Hazārah into his house for a single night [for safety]. Consequently, in the serais, Ḥabīb Allāh Khān's soldiers robbed and stripped the Hazārahs. In past attempts to persuade the Hazārahs to swear an oath of allegiance, already two such attempts, one time a governor from the Qizilbāsh, Mīrzā Muḥammad Muḥsin, and a peace delegation were sent, and another time a sayyid and a mullah from the Shiʿis and the Sunnis had been sent to them
> 104 and all have returned empty-handed. | Now, when the brother [Prince Amīn Allāh Khān] and the army of Amān Allāh Khān have made their headquarters among the Hazārahs, and [the Hazārahs] have offered them their allegiance and support, no Qizilbāsh can fulfill such an impossible task given the way we have mistreated them. In addition to this, Qizilbāsh have been treated as outcasts by the government and the nation already for forty years now. Vis-à-vis the Hazārahs, there has never been shown either respect or goodwill and therefore (we) not only cannot expect kindness from the Hazārahs following the principle "Is there any other reward for good than good?"[168] but, on the contrary, we expect ourselves to be the objects of retribution on the principle of "repay evil with evil" /**219**/ so how can we expect to get a letter of allegiance from those people?

Having offered this excuse, [the Qizilbāsh] were relieved of the obligation [to obtain a letter of allegiance from the Hazārahs].

Sunday, 16 Ẕīḥijjah, Corresponding to 5 Jawzā and 26 May

On this day a special announcement was broadcast on the radio concerning a telegram about the flight of Amān Allāh Khān from Qandahar with

168 Qurʾān 55:60.

his family and the dependents who had traveled with him from Kabul and about his arrival in Bombay by special train. This had a depressing effect on the residents of Kabul and on his supporters.

Also on this day, 1,000 soldiers were ordered to go from Kabul to Qaṭaghan and they set off. Also today rumors circulated that Sayyid Ḥusayn, who had been thought dead from his wounds, arrived in Khānābād and began to gather conscripts there to oppose Ghulām Nabī Khān and this caused anguish to those who wanted peace and tranquility now and for the future.

All around the city, word spread that Amān Allāh Khān's partisans had laid two bombs in the ʿĪdgāh Mosque on the eve of the ʿĪd al-Aẓḥā holiday under the bricks at the very spot where Amīr Ḥabīb Allāh Khān would perform his prayers. But by the will of the Inimitable Lord, the bombs did not explode either when he knelt down or when he stood up. A day or two ago, while sweeping, a janitor stepped on the spot and the bomb exploded. The janitor and one other man were killed. This incident increased even more the indignation and malice that Ḥabīb Allāh Khān felt towards the people of Kabul. But who knows the will of God?

Also news is now circulating ever more feverishly about the imminent arrival of Muḥammad Nādir Khān in Kabul and his intention of assuming the emirate, and about a jihad against the Russians planned by Ḥabīb Allāh Khān.

Also in the afternoon of this day, residents of Kabul were strolling as was their habit /**220**/ along Dār al-Amān Avenue and the river in groups of twos and threes. Some others were wandering about in the area of newly planted trees and others were just casually strolling. Along this road, the brother of Ḥabīb Allāh Khān, Muʿīn al-Salṭanah Ḥamīd Allāh Khān, was taking a pleasure drive. On the banks of the river he saw men sitting[ciii]
105 and enjoying | the fresh air to clear their heads. They were discussing their hopeless situation and the extraordinary tyranny and perfidy of the semi-human Northerners and speculating on how they were to be subjected to the various ways in which [the Northerners] were pillaging, murdering, and arresting people. [On hearing this conversation], Ḥamīd Allāh Khān pounced on them, beat them with the butt of his rifle and, cursing their wives, fathers and children, scattered them. While he was beating them he kept saying, "If you ever sit again beside [these] grassy fields, flowerbeds, or rivers, and [are found] ever again strolling about [here] you will be jailed and shackled and forever deprived of seeing the flowers, breathing the fresh air, and enjoying yourselves." Other people, witnessing this brutality and savage punishment, group by group quickly fled any way they

could, hurried to their own homes, and resolved not to leave their homes again, nor think about relaxing but have to put up with restlessness and turn the face of supplication toward the threshold of the Almighty. They prayed for salvation from the whirlpool and desert of adversity. Perhaps they would find freedom, an escape, and a place to go and be liberated from the clutches of the wild beasts and ghouls.

The Events of Monday, 17 Ẕīḥijjah, Corresponding to 6 Jawzā and 27 May

At the time of the disaster-entailing events that have been recorded above, intending to flee this country which had in fact become the lair of creation-harming devils, the homeland and headquarters of man-eating wolves, and a gathering place for semi-humans heedless of God and the Prophet and /**221**/ victims of their own selfish desires, I had gathered together a thousand rupees in preparation and, relying on the mercy of God and good luck, I resolved to flee with my son from this country and find salvation from the malignant and destructive jungle and from the teeth of these vicious beasts. This sum I would spend on food and travel expenses. But, at that time, I wanted to contract the marriage of my son[169] to his fiancée so that I might then set off with an easy mind. Thus, on the evening of this day, the aforementioned sum of money was spent on the wedding feast of my son's "henna night"[170] and so I [even] had to borrow money and was thankful for the favors of the Lord and grateful for His goodness. In complete firmness of belief, I relied on the most insignificant gifts of my Creator just as I have relied in the past so that this business [of the marriage] auspiciously begun and successfully concluded has been completed with divine help and it is hoped that God's favor will render easy the matter of [obtaining] the means for me to escape.

On this day, the high governor of Kabul, Malik Muḥsin had gone as far as Jalrīz and Takānah with the intention of obtaining an oath of allegiance from the Hazārahs. They had fortified Ūnay Pass with brave men, set up breastworks there, prepared to fight, and resolved to attack Kabul.

---

[169] Fayż Muḥammad had four sons by this time; his eldest was ʿAbd al-Ṣamad, who helped him with the writing of the third volume of *Sirāj al-tawārīkh*. The others were ʿAlī Muḥammad, Walī Muḥammad, and Muḥammad Mahdī. Which son was getting married at this point is unknown.

[170] Henna night is celebrated the night before the wedding and, in this case at least, was an obligation of the groom's family. It was clearly a major expense.

Malik Muḥsin sent someone to the Hazārahs inviting them to render obedience and swear an oath of allegiance. They proposed that he come to Sar Chashmah and negotiate together with them there about their offering an oath of obedience. But he was afraid to go to Sar Chashmah and
106 instead returned to Kabul. He went a second time to Jalrīz | and sent to the Hazārahs a group of elders from Maydān, Jalrīz, Takānah, Sanglākh, and Sar Chashmah with a threatening message warning them that if they turned their heads from obedience and refused to express their obedience and swear an oath [of allegiance], then the nomadic tribes which migrate into the Hazārahjāt for summer pastures and are now in Kabul awaiting permission to set off will occupy the Hazārahjāt along with regular army units, bring destruction down on the Hazārahs, killing, looting, and imprisoning them and so take control of the Hazārahjāt. Words having reached this point, up to now no answer, either yes or no, has been forthcoming from the Hazārahs who rose up in support **/222/** of Amān Allāh Khān and the Afghan emirate and are readying for a fight. It is possible that being aware of Amān Allāh Khān's flight, the Hazārahs will now set foot on the road of obedience and won't be drawn into bloodshed.

Meantime, during Ḥabīb Allāh Khān's ongoing negotiations, in the vicinity of Butkhāk and on the slopes of Kūh-i Quruq, he forcibly prevented 12,000 households of Afghan nomads from Peshawar and Jalālābād from moving towards the Hazārahjāt, collected the zakāt tax on their livestock before it was due, confiscated their camels which transported their household goods, their necessities of life, and the goods they traded in order to transport military supplies to Qaṭaghan, Badakhshān, Mazār-i Sharīf and its region, the Hazārahjāt, Qandahar, and the Southern Province and so caused the nomads to protest loudly. Also at the same time, he invited their elders to meet him in secret. With a fatwa from his pseudo-mullahs in hand, he incited them to kill, rob, and kidnap Hazārahs in the name of jihad and holy war and he urged them to usurp the Hazārahs' lands, estates, farms, and irrigation systems. But he fails to realize that having deprived the Afghans of the source of their power, he has made an enemy of them. And now, through intrigue, he wants to push them into war with the Hazārahs who rose to the support of the Afghans. Having brought the reins of the country's and the government's affairs into his own ignorant hands when he knows nothing about how to administer the country, he has then given power over the affairs of the army and the country to a handful of totally destitute thieves with no grasp of God or religion, and they do whatever they want.

The Events of Tuesday, 7 Jawzā, Corresponding to 18 Ẕīḥijjah and (28) May

People who claim to be thoughtful, have perceptive opinions, and consider themselves to be persons of feeling and sentiment, as well as politically savvy, these people maintain /**223**/ that Amān Allāh Khān fled because the Afghan tribes did not accept him as *pādshāh* and acted contrary to their promises.[171] Because of that they said that Amān Allāh Khān has reached an agreement with Muḥammad Nādir Khān, whom the Afghan had chosen as amir, that he would carry on military activities independently and when he takes the capital and cleanses it of the gang of robbers, then Amān Allāh Khān will return with his daughters and sons whom he has sent to Europe and will again sit on the throne
107 of the amirate.[172] |

Others harp on the story that Amān Allāh Khān took with him the English Colonel Lawrence[173] captured in the region of Farāh and Chakhānsūr who was disguised as a member of the Islamic ulema and had books of

[171] Fayż Muḥammad's use of the term *pādshāh* here refers to Amān Allāh's assumption in June 1926 of the title "shāh" signifying absolute monarch, reverting to the more imperial usage of his Saduzā'ī predecessors and breaking with the century-old use of "amir" as the sovereign title.

[172] Shkirando provides a note here that is worth repeating. It appears on page 267 of Faiz Mukhammad, *Kniga upominanii*, as footnote 151. "Upon his return from France, Mohammad Nadir Khān announced that he had come to end the civil war and restore peace to Afghanistan. On meeting with a delegation of the Afghan tribes from the frontier region with India, he emphasized that he would exert every effort to drive out Habiballah Khan and return the throne to Amanallah Khan. (See Sayyid Bahadur Shah Zafar Kākā Khayl, *Pakhtanah da tārīkh pa rana kih*, Peshawar, n.d., p. 1101.) Even the prominent Afghan leader, ʿAbdul Ghaffar Khān corroborates this. 'At the time of our private meeting,' he writes, 'talk turned to the future of Afghanistan. Nadir Khān said, "All that I do, I do for the sake of Amanallah Khan."'" (See ʿAbd al-Ghaffar, *Ema zhwand aw jidd wa jahd*, Kabul, 1983, p. 347] Using this propaganda, Mohammad Nadir Khān was able to garner the support of the Afghans of Afghanistan as well as the Muslims of India. Meanwhile he also had a plan to seize power himself. Subsequently, having put forward the idea of 'monarchical democratism,' the basis of which was the principle that 'electing the king is the right of the people,' he dissociated himself from Amanullah Khan and other claimants of the throne. English support played a large role in his struggle for power. It was not by chance therefore that the newspaper *Ḥabl al-matīn* on 29 January 1929 wrote, "The English government, convinced that Ḥabīb Allāh is not in a position to maintain himself as supreme ruler in Afghanistan, and is unsuitable, in any event, sent Nadir Khan from Paris to Afghanistan." [*Biulleten' pressy Srednego Vostoka*, Tashkent, 1929–30, special issue nos. 4–5 (12–13), p. 18].

[173] T. E. Lawrence was a private in the Royal Air Force at the time working as a mechanic. His presence at the airbase in Mīrānshāh, Wazīristān, led to all sorts of speculation, mostly sensationalist and unfounded, about his "real" role. When his presence became an embarrassment to the RAF he was transferred rather precipitously to England. See David Garnett, ed., *The Letters T. E. Lawrence*, New York: Doubleday Doran & Co., 1939, pp. 631–38, for Garnett's persuasive reconstruction of Lawrence's activities at Mīrānshāh and his becoming "a victim of his own legend."

Islamic legal principles and their practical applications on his person. Because (they believe that) he was the fomenter of the revolution in Afghanistan, although the English deny this, Amān Allāh Khān took him to Europe to seek justice by showing him to the great civilized governments of Europe [as proof of] the malign purpose of Europe (i.e. England) with whose backing a thief [could come to power]. Perhaps [Amān Allāh Khān] has advanced matters doing something like this. But most likely, these tales are without foundation and will prove to be merely propaganda from Amān Allāh Khān's partisans and will be of no use at all.

Meanwhile on this day, Ḥabīb Allāh Khān followed up on the obligation of the Qizilbāsh to get from the Hazārahs a written oath of allegiance (*bay'at-nāmah*) through a mediary, Muḥammad A'ẓam Khān, son of Jalandar Khān of Tutamdarrah.

Also, having launched the rumor of the amirate of Muḥammad Nādir Khān and his own [i.e. Ḥabīb Allāh's] oath of allegiance to him, he [Ḥabīb Allāh] now made deceitful propaganda so that by tricks and stratagems he can put off Muḥammad Nādir Khān who has neither a treasury nor supplies. Thus the peace negotiations which are in progress are purely deceptive and are to allow him to build up his own strength to destroy (Muḥammad Nādir Khān). If this is not the case, then why is he in such a rush to get an oath of allegiance from the Hazārahs? If this is not simply a conspiracy, then the Hazārahs would know what was going on and why then would it be to Muḥammad Nādir Khān's advantage to give Ḥabīb Allāh Khān an oath of allegiance? It will certainly be /224/ for the same reason that was recorded above.[174]

The Events of Wednesday, 19 Z̲īḥijjah, Corresponding to 8 Jawzā and 29 May

During the previously recorded events, Muḥammad Maḥfūẓ Khān, son of Aḥmad Jān Khān,[175] a Peshawarī physician, made a duplicitous and fraudulent proposal [regarding getting an oath of allegiance from the Hazārahs]. (See above, pp. 195–96) He and his father had been loyal servants of the government and from the earliest days of the reign of Amīr

[174] This is a vague sentence and it is not entirely clear what the reason is that he had "previously recorded" unless it is the immediately preceding one of gaining time to build up his forces.

[175] Aḥmad Jān Khān was a prominent official during the reign of Amīr 'Abd al-Raḥmān Khān. See the indexes to Fayż Muḥammad, *The History*, vol. 3 ("Aḥmad Jān Khān, Doctor, physician and Honorary Colonel") and vol. 4 ("Aḥmad Jān K., physician (ṭabīb) and honorary colonel"). We have no other information about his son.

ʿAbd al-Raḥmān Khān up to now had always enjoyed rank and status. But due to humble birth and lack of nobility and good family breeding, they had shut their eyes to the favors granted by Amīr ʿAbd al-Raḥmān Khān, the late slain Ḥabīb Allāh Khān, and Amān Allāh Khān. Along with his father, [Muḥammad Maḥfūẓ] had taken the path of opposition to Amān Allāh Khān while his father had attended Ḥabīb Allāh Khān, the usurper amir, as a clandestine friend while Muḥammad Maḥfūẓ himself became an assistant to Muʿīn al-Salṭanah Ḥamīd Allāh Khān. Having proposed a pretext for the extermination and annihilation of the Qizilbāsh of Kabul, as was already mentioned, he now noted, apropos of the subject of the *bayʿat-nāmah* and obtaining the allegiance of the Hazārah tribes, that officials of Amān Allāh Khān like ʿAbd al-Karīm Khān, the high governor of Qandahar, and two of the sons of [the late] Amīr Ḥabīb Allāh Khān because of their being trusted by that people (the Hazārahs) were in the Hazārahjāt and busy with preparing the means to get rid of Ḥabīb Allāh Khān, readying the instruments of war, and establishing fortifications.

Regarding the Qizilbāsh, he had made a proposal to Ḥabīb Allāh Khān and obtained a sanctioning order. [As mentioned above], late at night, he summoned seven men to the Ministry of War and charged them with the task of obtaining a *bayʿat-nāmah* from the Hazārah tribes. He imagined that they would not be able to get one and could then be accused of inciting the Hazārahs not to give an oath of allegiance, and would flee to the mountains in opposition instead, which would then make them susceptible to being plundered. This suited [Ḥabīb Allāh Khān's] inner malevolent inclinations. Subsequently, the Qizilbāsh provided credible reasons [why they should not do it] and were excused from this obligation. /225/ Because of the [ignoble] sentiments that he harbored, Muḥammad Maḥfūẓ presented their response to Ḥabīb Allāh Khān in such a way that [the amir] asked him to continue to pursue this as a responsibility [of the Qizilbāsh] so he then ordered Muḥammad Aʿẓam Khān, son of Jalandar Khān, to carry it out.

[Muḥammad Aʿẓam Khān, the president of the Islamic Regulatory Commission] then summoned them a second time to oblige them to send a delegation to the Hazārahjāt and obtain a *bayʿat-nāmah*. Since [the Qizilbāsh] considered themselves now to be facing death and destruction, they had no choice but to accept on condition that Muḥammad Aʿẓam Khān himself headed the delegation so he could observe whether the delegation behaved with integrity or not and be a witness to the success or lack thereof of the delegation and clear the Qizilbāsh of any suspicion [of false dealing]. He agreed [to the condition] and related it to Ḥabīb Allāh

Khān who approved. He [the amir] then ordered several Qizilbāsh to come to court. At 2:00 P.M. on this day about fifty Qizilbāsh leaders [actually fifty-three] were officially invited to come to see him and at 4:00 P.M. they presented themselves. This will be noted in due course, God willing.

Also on this day, because an Hazārah tribal force had marched right up to Kūhistān along the road through Ghūrband and had begun combat activity that caused much anxiety among the Kūhistānīs, at the plea for reinforcements from the leader of the Kūhistān army, five infantry regiments numbering 2,300 men were sent to the north from Kabul.

Also on this day, the high governor of Kabul, Malik Muḥsin, because of the cropping up of a number of problems related to the fact that he had opened negotiations with the Hazārahs, and had gone to Lahūgard to make some arrangements to resolve those problems, now returned to Kabul.

The Events of Thursday, 9 Jawzā, Corresponding to 20 Z̲īḥijjah and 30 May

At 4:00 P.M. the day before [as described above] the president of the Islamic Regulatory Commission, Muḥammad Aʿẓam Khān, assembled fifty-three representatives of the Qizilbāsh who had been charged with going to the Hazārahjāt to obtain an oath of allegiance from the Hazārahs [but had initially begged off]. **/226/** Qāżī Quṭb al-Dīn Jawānshayr, Nūr al-Dīn, and two other Qizilbāsh had gone to see [Muḥammad Aʿẓam Khān] and made the arrangements [for the fifty-three to meet him]. The group went to the Arg and waited until 6:00 P.M. for Ḥabīb Allāh Khān to come out of his office. After he emerged, because of a personal agenda and selfish desire, Nūr al-Dīn manipulated things in a calculated way. Originally he had stirred Muḥammad Maḥfūẓ up with provocative and misleading information [about the Qizilbāsh] but had been thwarted when they had given credible reasons [for their inability to obtain the desired *bayʿat-nāmah*]. He then began to manipulate Muḥammad Aʿẓam Khān and include him in his scheming. When Ḥabīb Allāh Khān came out of his office, Nūr al-Dīn had Muḥammad Aʿẓam Khān say that he should
109 give an oral order | according to which the Qizilbāsh had to leave for the Hazārahjāt to obtain the *bayʿat-nāmah* and were to give no excuses. For deviating from carrying out the order they might then be punished. [Nūr al-Dīn] was also successful in scheming to get himself named to head the delegation and it was agreed that he would select the seven people to be its members. At the request of the Qizilbāsh present Muḥammad Zamān Khān, son of Sarwar Khān Parwānī, was also included in the delegation.

He was to bear witness to any treachery or double-dealing by members of the delegation or by its leader.

On Thursday at 7:00 P.M. the Qizilbāsh were dismissed. Frightened by the machinations of Nūr al-Dīn Khān and Ḥājjī Muḥammad Yaʿqūb Khān who had asked the amir for the position of delegation head [for Nūr al-Dīn], they parted company for their own homes in a gloomy frame of mind. Due to the scandalous behavior of their ignorant fellow tribesmen, who out of self-interest and greed are prepared to destroy everything of this world, they prayed for the help of God who, perhaps, would defend them from evil, ignorance, and greed and save them from being murdered and robbed.

Because the times have become so dangerous and the government is utterly incompetent but exceedingly vicious, how is it possible for the Hazārahs to give an oath of allegiance and accept obedience /227/ when the high governor of Dāy Zangī, Dāy Kundī, and Bihsūd, Muḥammad Ḥusayn Khān, a supporter of Amān Allāh Khān, is still in the Hazārahjāt? Similarly, his brothers and the high governor of Qandahar, ʿAbd al-Karīm Khān,[176] is fervently preparing his army and artillery for the defeat of Ḥabīb Allāh Khān. Therefore, if Nūr al-Dīn possessed any sense or conscience at all he would not undertake such villainous intriguing. For in such circumstances, when the Hazārahjāt is in the hands of the partisans and confederates of Amān Allāh Khān and the northern Tajiks are engaged in fighting the Afghans, sooner or later, today or tomorrow, the Afghans will drive Ḥabīb Allāh Khān from the throne and Nūr al-Dīn will be driven to confusion and despair. Even if the Hazārahs, unbeknownst to their governor, to the brothers of Amān Allāh Khān, and to his partisans and military units in the Hazārahjāt, give an oath of allegiance in order to save their lives, belongings, and honor, then Ḥabīb Allāh Khān will want them to fight against the Afghans. But this they will not agree to do and then the Qizilbāsh will be forced to bear the malice of Ḥabīb Allāh Khān and the horror of being subjected to being killed and robbed.

In view of these [preceding] sentences, on this day it was ordered that preparations be made for the departure of the chosen members of the delegation. The author, who had no monetary means and was seriously

[176] ʿAbd al-Karīm Khān Bārakzāʾī was a son of Qāżī Saʿd al-Dīn Khān, governor of Harāt from 1886 to 1904 and then chief judge (*qāżī al-qużāt*) in Kabul, and the brother of Qāżī ʿAbd al-Shakūr. Their sister Shāh Sulṭān "Nawwāb Jān" was married to and then divorced by Amīr Ḥabīb Allāh Khān. For other aspects of ʿAbd al-Karīm's life and career see Adamec, *Who's Who*, p. 98 ("Abdul Karim Barakzai").

ill from a swelling that had appeared on his neck, was enrolled in the delegation against his will.

The Events of Friday, 10 Jawzā, Corresponding to 21 Ẕīḥijjah and 31 May

110 | This evening, the Muʿīn al-Salṭanah, Ḥamīd Allāh Khān, having resolved to marry the daughter of a butcher named Jān Muḥammad, made arrangements for the wedding to take place at the Zayn al-ʿImārah palace of the late Nāʾib al-Salṭanah, Sardār Naṣr Allāh Khān **/228/** which the meaning of this verse captures:

The royal palaces are in ruins / All have become abodes of ravens and owls.

However, the palace was decorated and the night passed in revelry, with music and drinking.

After sunrise, baseless and false rumors that Amān Allāh Khān had returned to Qandahar from Bombay were spread as propaganda by his supporters.

Also, [people were saying that] Ḥabīb Allāh Khān's army which had advanced as far as Bāmyān and was heading towards Mazār-i Sharīf, as a result of a clash with Hazārah tribal forces, had been routed and had turned its back to the fight and its face towards flight until it reached Jabal al-Sirāj. Also the army under the command of Sayyid Ḥusayn Khān, which numbered more than 10,000 men and was marching towards Mazār-i Sharīf intending to conquer it, had come under bombardment at Dasht-i Chīchak. A large part of the force was killed or wounded. The rest had fled back to Kūhistān and Kabul in disarray. This news angered Ḥabīb Allāh Khān so that at 9:00 A.M. he telephoned his brother, Ḥamīd Allāh Khān, and ordered him to immediately dispatch a vehicle for Khwājah Mīr ʿAlam, appointed [high] governor of [Afghānī] Turkistān, and for the six officers who fled from Bāmyān to Jabal al-Sirāj, stopped there, and were terrorizing the residents of the Northern regions. They were to be arrested, delivered to Kabul, and imprisoned in the Arg.

Marginalia: Also on this day, Ḥamīd Allāh Khān, at his own "little royal court" and at the order of his brother, Ḥabīb Allāh Khān, collected 200,000 rupees from the high governor [of Kabul], the chief of police, the minister of court, and other thieves who had attained high rank. It was called an official "fine" for this continuous soirée of savagery so they would not see it as expropriation of the property they had looted and homes they had plundered and thus would not take offense. [End of marginal note.] **/229/**

Also on this day, Nūr al-Dīn, head of the delegation to the Hazārahjāt, enrolled as members of it some men from Chandāwul, Murād Khānī, Qalʿah-i Ḥaydar Khān, Afshār, and Wazīrābād [all sections of Kabul], men of sound judgement and insight. He asked the government to assign ten riding horses for the delegation, ten pack horses, ten rifles with a sufficient supply of ammunition, and 15,000 rupees for travel expenses. This request was fulfilled only on Saturday while the rumors of fighting and of the return [from Bombay] of Amān Allāh Khān abounded.

Also on this day, Ḥabīb Allāh, in light of his populist and ignorant creed, with all pompous royal dignity and [to fulfill] a vow, ordered a phaeton for Shaykh Muḥammad Rizā Khurāsānī to go to the shrine of Khwājah Musāfir located near [the village of] Chihil Tan and to read [and transcribe] the lines inscribed and embossed on the tombstones at the shrine, which were in Kufic script.[177]

The residents of Kabul and all oppressed people rejoiced when they learned of the defeat of Ḥabīb Allāh Khān's armies in Qaṭaghan and Bāmyān and prayed to God to defend them from the Northern plunderers, beasts in the form of humans, because of whom they find themselves now in a miserable situation.

The Events of Saturday, 11 Jawzā, Corresponding to 22 Ẕīḥijjah and 1 June

[This is an account of] the cowardice and treachery of Aḥmad ʿAlī Khān, son of ʿAbd al-Wāḥid Khān, son of Muḥammad Rafīq Khān of the Lūdī tribe, who possesses neither foresightedness nor common sense. After Amān Allāh Khān's departure for France via Bombay, based on stories
111 [that I heard] | which somewhat approximated reality, [Amān Allāh Khān] gave up any expectation of support from the wild Afghan tribes who were neither true to their alliances nor to their oaths nor to the faith, and so he abandoned Afghanistan and went /**230**/ abroad with his family and his circle of courtiers. Aḥmad ʿAlī Khān, whose grandfather earlier had sown discord between Amīr Shayr ʿAlī Khān and Sardār Muḥammad Amīn Khān and by whose hand Sardār Muḥammad ʿAlī Khān, son of the abovementioned amir, and [the amir's] brother had both perished on

---

[177] This was the same scholar whom the martyred Amīr Ḥabīb Allāh Khān had commissioned to transcribe the tombstones of "the saints and the greats of ancient times" buried in the cemeteries of Ghaznīn. See Fayż Muḥammad, *The History*, vol. 4, pp. 1296–97. His work was published by the Historical Society of Afghanistan in 1967 as *Riyāż al-alwāh: mushtamil bar katībah-hā-yi qubūr wa abniyah-i Ghaznah*, Kabul: Anjuman-i Tārīkh-i Afghānistān, 1346/1967.

the same day, ended up in perdition for this evildoing, similarly, as the grandson of that miserable wretch, despite the fact that he had come from poverty and risen to the post of minister plenipotentiary and other high positions, in the final analysis, instead of showing gratitude, betrayed his salt.[178] As mentioned above, he gave weapons and money to Ḥabīb Allāh Khān and Sayyid Ḥusayn in Jabal al-Sirāj by which he helped them when they attacked Kabul. But as if this was not enough, like the devil, he approached Prince ʿInāyat Allāh, the three-day amir, in Qandahar, and expressed his allegiance to him, casting wide the net of his impudence. When Amān Allāh Khān departed [Qandahar for Bombay], this devilish one hoisted the flag of duplicity and summoned to the city from every corner of the region the elders of the five branches of the Durrānī tribe[179] on this day and said to them, "Now we must raise a person worthy of the amirate, someone like Aḥmad Shāh whom the Durrānī tribe elected as pādshāh after the assassination of Nādir Shāh." Having spoken these hypocritical words to the tribal leaders, with the dissemination of this misleading news, regiments which had set out for Kabul and had passed, one after another, all the halting places up to Qarā Bāgh, Ghaznīn, fortified them, and were awaiting the order to launch the attack, now abandoned all the strategic and fortified places and dispersed. In secret, Aḥmad ʿAlī Khān sent someone to Ḥabīb Allāh Khān's field marshal, Purdil Khān, with this message, "I performed this service for you and have brought matters to this point. The rest is up to you. Get yourself to Qandahar as quickly as possible and occupy the city." Purdil Khān [then] quickly captured Qalāt and without resistance left there [for Qandahar] drawing near the city at the time when the Durrānī tribes had assembled in [Qandahar] and were deeply preoccupied with the election of a *pādshāh*. The people of the city, seeing themselves on the brink of disaster, /**231**/, closed the city gates. They used the Qurʾān as intercessor and sought a seven-day truce at the end of which they would submit, swear an oath of allegiance, and obtain safety. Purdil Khān accepted their proposal, and settled at Manzil Bāgh.[180]

---

178 For his biography see Adamec, *Who's Who*, pp. 109–10 ("Aḥmad Ali, Ludin"). His title of minister plenipotentiary (*wazīr-i mukhtār*) came from his appointment as envoy to Germany in 1925.

179 In his *Nizhādnāmah-i Afghān*, p. 55, although it is somewhat uncertain, Fayż Muḥammad seems to name the five branches of the Durrānī as: Pūpalzāʾī, Bārakzāʾī, ʿAlīkūzāʾī, Sadūzāʾī, and Nūrzāʾī.

180 A garden estate just east of Qandahar on the road to Kabul, Manzil Bagh was first developed by Aḥmad Shāh Durrānī (r. 1747–1772) and re-developed by Amīr ʿAbd al-Raḥmān Khān and his son, Amīr Ḥabīb Allāh Khān.

He notified Ḥabīb Allāh Khān [of developments] and about the treachery of Aḥmad ʿAlī Khān which gave the amir great satisfaction.

Also on this day, fighting flared up anew in Burj-i Guljān and Gul Bahār
112 and created fear and anxiety amongst the Northerners. | Also on this day, an airplane took off for Qandahar in order to retrieve the plane on which the pilot Muḥammad ʿUmar had flown from Kabul to bomb the army of Amān Allāh Khān and which he had landed in Qandahar. The second airplane landed at night and was delayed there.

Also on this day, Ḥabīb Allāh Khān and his brother, Ḥamīd Allāh Khān, took custody of an arrested colonel named Dur Muḥammad, a recent convert to Islam from the Kāfirī people, drove him to Jabal al-Sirāj, and ordered him shot in front of the troops that had retreated and the regiment stationed in [Jabal al-Sirāj] as a lesson to the rest not to abandon the battlefield again but to fight to the death. *Marginalia*: In the end it turned out he was not killed. [End of marginal note.] This colonel, with the governor of [Afghan] Turkistān, Khwājah Mīr ʿAlam, and other officers had been defeated and retreated to Chārīkār. They were summoned to Kabul and imprisoned, but the colonel who had arrived in Chārīkār before the others, was detained by the local governor, Chighil Khān, and sent to Kabul. In the late afternoon Ḥabīb Allāh Khān returned to the Arg.

The Events of Sunday, 12 Jawzā, Corresponding to 23 Ẕīḥijjah and 2 June

On this day, the son of Quṭb al-Dīn Jawānshayr, Nūr al-Dīn, who from a lack of knowledge wanting to be a leader and seeking rank, without his own people knowing, sought to obtain a *bayʿat-nāmah* from the Hazārahs. As already mentioned, by tricks and stratagems, he assembled the leaders of the Qizilbāsh saying that Ḥabīb Allāh Khān had again asked for them and bringing them before [the amir], then selected seven of them and, forcibly put them in a situation of dubious outcome. By treachery and perfidy he made himself head of the peace delegation and officially invited to his house the seven men who were selected at his discretion as members of the delegation and also a number of other highly respected Qizilbāsh. Having attained his ends and having frightened his fellow tribesmen, he wanted, under the guise of consulting with them, in reality to make himself pleasing in their eyes through cunning. The chosen members of the delegation, referring to their miserable livelihoods and physically not up to such a trip, begged and supplicated this ambitious man and instigator of illicit acts. But he did not listen to their pleas and threatened them with the government's wrath. So they were forced to choose silence and to wrap the foot in the skirt of forbearance.

Also on this day, the aircraft which yesterday took off for Qandahar returned to Kabul at 10:00 A.M. It carried the oaths of allegiance which had been received from the cowardly and sly people of Qandahar, who lacked all pride, and also information about Field Marshal Purdil Khān's elevating ʿAlī Aḥmad Khān (*sic*—Aḥmad ʿAlī Khān)[181] to the post of mayor. The town crier [of Kabul] spread this regrettable news around the city. At the time of the evening prayer, a 101-gun salute was fired to celebrate the victory.

Also on this day, an order was issued to pay the monthly salary directly to those units first sent to Qandahar who, to defend against the attack of
113 Ghulām Nabī Khān on Kūhistān and Kūh Dāman, | were then ordered to be sent directly to Kūhistān and Kūh Dāman to the homeland of those savages and ghouls before Ghulām Nabī received reinforcements and captured these regions.

Also during these events, as was already described, due to the thievery of the high governor Malik Muḥsin /233/ and his entering the house of Mīr Zamān al-Dīn at night and stealing 25,000 rupees, several carpets, women's jewelry, and two of his own personal rifles, his poor wife appealed to the "servant of the religion of the Prophet," Ḥabīb Allāh Khān. He, in his turn, assigned the thieving high governor himself to investigate. By threatening murder, the high governor obtained from the plaintiff and her sons a letter stating their satisfaction [with his version of the episode]. It said, "aside from two carpets, nothing else was taken from the house." And although on that same night the high governor had brought Ḥabīb Allāh Khān some women's jewelry, half of which he took for himself, he considered this a thorough investigation. Indeed, from this government of thieves you could hardly expect better. All these acts are due to the evil pseudo-mullahs and ḥażrats.

The Events of Monday, 13 Jawzā, Corresponding to 24 Ẕīḥijjah and 3 June

On this day, at the time of the capture of the city of Aḥmad Shāh [Qandahar] by Ḥabīb Allāh Khān's forces, in the home of an Hazārah they

[181] Although both the manuscript and the print edition have ʿAlī Aḥmad Khān, in light of what has preceded, (the machinations of Aḥmad ʿAlī Khān to assist Ḥabīb Allāh Khān's forces in taking Qandahar) and what shortly follows (the arrest of ʿAlī Aḥmad Khān) Fayż Muḥammad clearly meant Aḥmad ʿAlī Khān here.

captured ʿAlī Aḥmad Khān [Lūynāb] who had declared himself amir in Jalālābād and, as already related, had been defeated and then gone with Ghulām Aḥmad and his son, Nūr Aḥmad, to Amān Allāh Khān in Qandahar.

Marginalia: Field Marshal Purdil Khān for whom ʿAlī Aḥmad Khān had done some favors in the past, killed Nūr Aḥmad in Ghaznīn. [End of marginal note.]

[Ḥabīb Allāh Khān's men] sent ʿAlī Aḥmad Khān along with the chief *qāżī*, Qāżī ʿAbd al-Shakūr Khān,[civ] son of (Qāżī) Saʿd al-Dīn Khān; ʿAbd al-Wāsiʿ; and one other mufti[cv] to Kabul and at eleven o'clock they arrived in the city. Barefoot and bareheaded, they were paraded around the streets and bazaars. For (ʿAlī Aḥmad Khān) this was just recompense for his betrayal of Amān Allāh Khān who had named him to the post of high commissioner of the Eastern and Southern Provinces and sent him to Jalālābād to completely extinguish the flames of rebellion raised by the semi-human and savage Shinwārīs and other tribes. But, dreaming of the amirid throne, he decided to deceive Amān Allāh Khān. He wrote him a letter telling him that 23,000 Shinwārī and other tribesmen were en route to Kabul. When his letter reached Amān Allāh Khān it terrified him. Also, by intuition **/234/** he realized that his cowardly and perfidious ministers would support Ḥabīb Allāh Khān and would arrest him and deliver him to him and so, having no other recourse, he abdicated the throne and fled. One might say that Amān Allāh Khān abdicated mostly because of this letter from ʿAlī Aḥmad Khān. Well, now ʿAlī Aḥmad Khān himself is forced to sit in shackles and endure punishment for his misdeeds. In Qandahar they also arrested Aḥmad ʿAlī Khān [Lūdī] who helped Ḥabīb Allāh Khān at the very outset and also later, at the taking of Qandahar, thus betraying the government and the people. But he has yet to suffer punishment for his indecent acts. ʿAlī Aḥmad, along with the chief *qāżī*,
114 ʿAbd al-Shakūr, and Mullā ʿAbd al-Wāsiʿ | were presented to His Highness Ḥabīb Allāh Khān. He asked (ʿAlī Aḥmad), "Why didn't you come to me from Jagdalak? If you had come I would have welcomed you with honors. ʿAlī Aḥmad replied, "There's no questioning fate." Mullā ʿAbd al-Wāsiʿ, in reply to the amir's question "Why do you accuse me of godlessness?" said, "I do not call and have never called any Muslim a kafir. This means that if I called you a kafir then that is what you are." Afterwards, Ḥabīb Allāh Khān ordered all four imprisoned.

All the residents of Kabul and also all the Hazārahs and Afghans—excluding the semi-human Shinwārī, Khūgyānī, Sulaymān Khayl, Andar, and Tarakī tribes—who had nurtured hope of salvation from the oppression and tyranny of the Northern plunderers and had supposed that a happy day would dawn for them, but having learned of these four men being brought to Kabul, of the capture of Qandahar, and the flight of Amān Allāh Khān, now fell into despair. They were especially affected by the arrest of ʿAlī Aḥmad Khān.

The Events of Tuesday, 14 Jawzā, Corresponding to 25 Ẕīḥijjah and 4 June

On this day, Aḥmad ʿAlī Khān [Lūdī],[cvi] who, as already related, had been shackled and chained and paraded in disgrace around the bazaars and then held in isolation at home, was released and for his services to the Kūhistānī and Kūh Dāmanī brigands his house in Murād Khānī was restored to him. As high governor he had frequently spared and released from prison those who had committed crimes, from the perspective of the government of Amān Allāh Khān, /235/ men who today hold the ranks of field marshal or minister of court or commandant. All those for whom he had interceded now came to his defense and asked that he be pardoned and released from jail. Field Marshal Purdil Khān sent a letter from Qandahar in which he requested a pardon for ʿAlī Aḥmad Khān (*sic*—Aḥmad ʿAlī Khān) and Commandant Sayyid Āqā Khān begged Amīr Ḥabīb Allāh Khān on his knees to spare him. Some ḥażrats who were the ringleaders of the brigands and thieves and who had destroyed the government and the religion and sowed dissension among the people also spoke up in his defense.

Also on this day, the high governor Malik Muḥsin and Nāʾib al-Salṭanah Ḥamīd Allāh Khān left for Qandahar by car to restore order to the city whose population had only just surrendered and sworn an oath of loyalty.

Also on this day, the force sent to Pamqān to barricade the road against Hazārah attack was ordered to occupy positions on the heights and be ready to defend the area. After a rumor circulated that the Hazārahs, on learning of the flight of Amān Allāh Khān, had decided to swear an oath of allegiance, part of the army was sent to Sar Chashmah. It was ordered not to fire on anyone who vows allegiance but only if unarmed since they cannot cause any harm then. They were to open fire only on armed individuals and not to let them pass lest, on the pretext of giving an oath of loyalty, they cause harm to the troops entrenched there.

Also on this day, ʿAlī Shāh Khān, son of Muḥammad Sulaymān Khān, who at Ḥabīb Allāh Khān's order had gone to Muḥammad Nādir Khān to negotiate a truce, returned to Kabul with an answer which not only did

115 not satisfy Ḥabīb Allāh Khān | but greatly distressed him because he had supposed that Muḥammad Nādir Khān would recognize him as amir and, forgetting about honor and nobility, would accept a high position and come to Kabul. Instead, he had sent a message saying that he should put an end to the bloodshed and abandon Kabul **/236/** forthwith for as long as one Afghan remained alive he would not be allowed to remain on the amirate throne. Otherwise he should prepare for all-out war. Muḥammad Nādir Khān sent this message, confident at the time of the alliance of the tribes of the Southern Province, who ultimately proved faithless. He had no idea that the Afghans were unbelievers and committed neither to an agreement nor an alliance, especially when that henchman of the English, Ḥażrat Shayr Āqā, settled amongst them. He is misleading them and inciting them to commit murder and robbery. It was primarily for this reason that the English sent him from India to these regions. He (Shayr Āqā) sent half of the Sulaymān Khayl, Andar, Taraki and ʿAlī Khayl towards Qandahar against Amān Allāh Khān and half towards Khūst against Muḥammad Nādir Khān. He achieved his aim as far as Qandahar is concerned for Amān Allāh Khān fled and Qandahar passed into the control of Ḥabīb Allāh Khān's forces.

The Events of Wednesday, 26 Ẕīḥijjah, Corresponding to 15 Jawzā and 5 June

Out of 15,000 rupees envisaged as the travel expenses necessary for the members of the peace delegation which was supposed to go to the Hazārahjāt and obtain a *bayʿat-nāmah* from the Hazārahs, Ḥabīb Allāh Khān approved only 10,000 and disbursed them to Nūr al-Dīn. He said that since the government had no money and the army had to be paid, the fellow tribesmen of the members of the delegation, which Nūr al-Dīn had volunteered to lead, should help with the provisioning. Since the Qizilbāsh were all living hand-to-mouth in extreme poverty and in need of daily sustenance, the members of the delegation whom the ambitious and opportunistic Nūr al-Dīn had forcibly enrolled and who received a meager wage, each agreed to receive 200 rupees, approved by Ḥabīb Allāh Khān. Each decided to buy himself 10–20 seers of flour. One seer of flour today costs 4–4.5 rupees; one seer of oil, 35–40 rupees, one seer of meat, 12 rupees, six *fals*; firewood by weight is one rupee for one and one-quarter seers; **/237/** one *pāw* of yogurt is ten *paysah*; one *khūrd* of cheese, 6 *paysah*; twelve eggs, one rupee. Each of them could also acquire cloth to be sewn into clothes and supply his family with money for 5–10 days and then set off. [Without this money] they could not have afforded these prices. The sum of 200 rupees was also sufficient to acquire a saddle and harness and the clothes necessary for the trip. Thus it was because of the ignoramus and opportunist, Nūr al-Dīn, that on this day they took the money and began their preparations [for departure].

During this time, leaders of the Sulaymān Khayl, who coveted the lands and property of the Hazārahs, arrived in Kabul thanks to the instigation of Shayr Āqā, and voluntarily offered to attack and plunder the Hazārahs.
116 Ḥabīb Allāh Khān | approved their offer but held back on giving them a definitive answer until the issue of the Hazārahs offering their allegiance was clarified. But he does not know that[cvii] today the influence of the policies of England and Russia in Afghanistan is very great. He is unaware that the Russian government is inciting Ghulām Nabī Khān in Afghan Turkistān to attack Hindūstān (British India) and is giving him support to make the territory as far as the Hindū Kush part of their colonial possessions while England, with the help of Muḥammad Nādir Khān, is trying to transform the lands stretching up to the Hindū Kush into a colony of its own and is inciting the misguided fornicating Afghans to attack the Russians. Despite the intrigues of the two governments, Ḥabīb Allāh Khān, in order to stay on the amirate throne, sets the poor benighted people against each other and encourages bloodshed and robbery. God willing, he won't remain much longer. /238/

The Events of Thursday, 27 Ẕīḥijjah, Corresponding to 16 Jawzā and 6 June 1929

At the time of these tragic events, which are brought about by the unbelief and treachery of the Afghans, of whom a section of the Sulaymān Khayl, at the instructions of Shayr Āqā, disavowed Amān Allāh Khān and supported Ḥabīb Allāh Khān in Qandahar, and also because of the beginning of fighting in the Southern Province against Muḥammad Nādir Khān, after Ḥabīb Allāh Khān had sent the latter a message, Muḥammad Nādir Khān sent him a message in Kabul which read,

> Send me in exchange for my homes and property, which you have confiscated, ten lakhs (one million) of rupees and also my family and relatives so that I may leave for abroad and abandon these wild Afghan tribes. Then the throne will be yours.

From another quarter, the Sulaymān Khayl, Andar, and Kharūtī tribes, having violated the agreements they had with each other, were now spilling each other's blood. Before long all those who have been acting according to Ḥażrat Shayr Āqā's instructions will be punished and annihilated for their misdeeds.

As instructed by the abovementioned ḥażrat, a group of Sulaymān Khayl elders arrived in Kabul and voluntarily expressed their willingness to attack the Hazārahs and seize their lands. Ḥabīb Allāh Khān agreed and, as a reward, distributed one lakh [or], twenty thousand tumans[182] to them and also issued a decree according to which the property of the Hazārahs was transferred to their ownership. Notwithstanding, on Friday, the 28th of Ẕīḥijjah, he dispatched the Qizilbāsh delegation to the Hazārahjāt. When they learned of his intentions, the Hazārahs sent him a reasonable reply which corresponded to the will of God and the Prophet but it was not accepted. /**239**/

117 *The Events of Friday, 28 Ẕīḥijjah, Corresponding to 17 Jawzā and 7 June* |

On this day, despite the fact that Amān Allāh Khān had fervently wished for the progress and civilization of the country and the nation and had longed for the prosperity of its people and the development of the country, he had turned his back on Afghanistan and its ignorant people in disappointment and left for Europe via Bombay. In Kūh Dāman and Kūhistān, rumors circulated about his declaration that Ḥabīb Allāh Khān was an unbeliever based on actual deeds of his and on verses from the Qurʾān. Some people refused to accept the pronouncement while others considered it valid.

At the time of these events, another son of Chief Qāżī Saʿd al-Dīn Khān, ʿAbd al-Karīm Khān, high governor of Qandahar, had already been in the Hazārahjāt for quite some time at Amān Allāh Khān's orders to raise the Hazārahs against Ḥabīb Allāh Khān. The Hazārahs had agreed to fight and, after erecting defensive works in many spots, were fully prepared and anxious for an attack on Kabul. ʿAbd al-Karīm Khān [now] decided to commit treason. Although Ḥabīb Allāh Khān confiscated and looted his property and home in Kabul, he secretly sent a message to him in which he expressed his allegiance and asked for a safe conduct guarantee. He also wrote, "If my safety is guaranteed, then I will deliver Muḥammad Amīn Khān, the brother of Amān Allāh Khān, in shackles to Kabul. He is now in the Hazārahjāt with me. I will also bring an oath of allegiance from the

[182] A tūmān was five rupees.

Hazārahs." Having discovered the duplicity [of ʿAbd al-Karīm Khān], the Hazārahs decided to seize and imprison him. But since he was just one person and could not do much, they treated him as if he were a refugee and guest of their tribes according to the saying, "Respect the guest even if he is an unbeliever"[183] and abandoned the idea of arresting him.

Also on this day it was rumored that three airplanes, which had taken off from Mazār-i Sharīf, landed on a specially prepared air strip at Bād-i Āsyā, in Bihsūd. The pilots informed the Hazārahs that several planes were going to bomb **/240/** Kūh Dāman, Kūhistān, and the Arg in Kabul. They then returned to Mazār-i Sharīf. Despite the fact that Ḥabīb Allāh Khān had already dispatched to the Hazārahjāt the empowered peace delegation for negotiations on a truce, he also ordered five military units numbering 6,500 men sent to that region. He also sent to Gardayz and Khūst a large quantity of hand grenades to Deputy Field Marshal Muḥammad Ṣiddīq Khān.

On this day rumors circulated once again [in Kabul] that tribal forces from the Eastern Province were about to come.

The Events of Saturday, 29 Ẕīḥijjah, Corresponding to 18 Jawzā and 8 June

On this day, Ḥabīb Allāh Khān did not allow a plane with Russian mail to land despite a long-standing bilateral treaty between Russia and Afghanistan. This was because he and his high-ranking officials are completely ignorant and have absolutely no say in important political questions but
118 act only on instructions from the English ambassador. Only yesterday, | after some deliberation, was permission given for Russian planes to land which were delivering the mail of the Turkish, Iranian, and German governments and today they took off with the mail of these governments. This was painful to the English authorities who, for the sake of strengthening their own interests, were keeping these countries in ignorance of the state of affairs in Afghanistan. Perhaps in the future, these governments, once they learn about the unsettled situation that prevails in Afghanistan today because of English plots, will give long deliberation to their own activities in order to avert the outbreak of a large-scale war in the center of Asia, the causes of which are already evident. Maybe then, peace will be granted to all people. **/241/**

On this day Nūr al-Dīn, an overweeningly ambitious and greedy fellow, having volunteered to obtain an oath of allegiance from the Hazārahs and

[183] The maxim is given here in Arabic.

having been named head of the delegation, left Kabul with the delegation heading for the Hazārahjāt. They spent the night in Afshār as guests at the home of Muḥammad Mahdī Khān, the grandson of Sulṭān Khān.

Various rumors are circulating: one is of the imminent approach of Ghulām Nabī Khān from [Afghan] Turkistān, although as yet they had no news that he had actually left. Another is of the creation of huge tribal formations in the Eastern Province under the leadership of Muḥammad Hāshim Khān and of the start of combat by the Afghan tribes under the leadership of Muḥammad Nādir Khān. And also the army of Son of the Water Carrier was sent via the road through Ghaznīn towards Gardayz. Once the parts of it reached Wardak, Qalʿah-i Durrānī, and Arghandah, they [then] planned to march as quickly as possible [towards Gardayz].

In spite of all this, at daybreak on Sunday, the 30th of Ẕīḥijjah, Nūr al-Dīn and the delegation, of which this writer was a member, departed Afshār and headed for the Hazārahjāt.

The Events of Sunday, 1 Muḥarram 1348, Corresponding to 19 Jawzā and 9 June

On this day when Nūr al-Dīn had arrived in Kūt-i ʿAshrū and taken lodgings in the caravanserai (*ribāṭ*) there, with ominous noises and fearful omens, rumors of bloodshed and grief inspired by the revolution due to the insecurity of the roads, which have taken on the aspect of cemeteries and the byways which are like perdition, are heard coming from every direction. Residents of Takānah, Jalrīz, and Kuhnah Khumār, who are Tajiks subject to the governor of Maydān, are delighted with the Saqqawī government, serve Son of the Water Carrier with great enthusiasm and fervor, and send to Kabul to the intelligence department and to the truth-ignoring ears of the thief Ḥabīb Allāh both false and accurate reports about the people of Sar Chashmah, Ūnay, and [the Hazārahjāt], many of whom are arrested, plundered, and murdered [on the basis of this information]. **/242/**

Seeing with their own eyes and grasping their parlous situation, the members of the delegation were gripped by the fear that if, God forbid, the Hazārahs did not tender their submission and refused to acknowledge the infidel and thief as amir, then they themselves might be accused, punished, and thrown into the arena of destruction and annihilation. This hapless tribe has no homeland called "Qizilbāsh," and will be cast to the winds of murder, plunder, and captivity.

In light of this, the writer, having been sent to the Hazārahjāt against
119 his will, | happening to find himself at a shop where a group of people

had gathered to drink tea, spoke cautiously, aiming to defend the delegation against accusations by these people who could be equated with the devils resident in Kuhnah Khumār, Jalrīz, and Takānah, people who are distinguished by their savage fanaticism and congenital hatred for Shiʿis, especially Hazārahs. In light of the fact that the Hazārahs had refused to submit to the government and had not given a *bayʿat-nāmah* to Son of the Water Carrier, with whom the Hazārahs were waging a courageous struggle and up to now had made no compromises or concessions, I thought that the members of the delegation and the oppressed tribe of the Qizilbāsh, who had no rights and whose representatives had involuntarily been enrolled in the delegation, might well be subject to being robbed and killed. Given this context, I said,

> I don't understand why the Hazārah people do not tender an oath of allegiance and do not express obedience to the Tajik government with whom they share the same language and who has always treated them well. Instead, they have risen up against them. Ever since the time of the reign of ʿAbd al-Raḥmān Khān through the reigns of Ḥabīb Allāh Khān and Amān Allāh Khān, Hazārahs have been oppressed, killed, plundered, and taken captive. Thousands of [their] people have been killed, enslaved, forced to leave their homeland and their ancestral places, and their residences, farms, and irrigation systems have been given to Afghan. Furthermore, before the reign of ʿAbd al-Raḥmān Khān, permission was never given to Afghan nomad tribes to bring their livestock into the Hazārahjāt for summer pasturing. But from his time onwards, access to the Hazārahjāt was opened to the nomads with full government backing and the aid and assistance of governors, *qāżīs*, and other government officials and they began to kill Hazārahs, rob them of their wealth and lives, kidnap their families and children, and destroy their farms. The government never held (the Afghan tribes) accountable nor provided justice nor does it do so now. Thus this ill-starred people in despair took their wives and children by the hand and set out for foreign lands /**243**/ and still do. So how is it that they don't want to offer allegiance to the Tajik amirate and be subject to its government when they share the same language? Instead they have risen up against it and show every intention of fighting it. God willing, when we arrive in the Hazārahjāt, they will recall their tragic fate and the misfortunes done to them by the [Afghan] government and the Afghan people and will express their allegiance and put an end to fighting [the Tajik government].

This speech was overheard by Muḥammad Zamān Khān Parwānī, who was concealed by a wall and whom we had asked to go with us to witness what we did. When I took myself off to my room in the caravanserai, he thanked me for my words and the sincerity which I showed for the Saqqawī government. I was reassured because—God willing—any accusations against us will be ineffective because this person, who is a witness accompanying us, will testify to [the nature of] my remarks, if it becomes necessary.

Monday, 2 Muḥarram 1348, Corresponding to 20 Jawzā and 10 June[184]

On this day, when everyone was spreading propaganda of an attack on Kabul by the tribes of the Southern Province under Muḥammad Nādir Khān and the Afghan tribes of the Eastern Province under Muḥammad
120 Hāshim Khān, | we left Kūt-i ʿAshrū and set off for Sar Chashmah. Nūr al-Dīn, due to stupidity and vanity, left the route with six members of the delegation, his son and son-in-law, and seven armed riders, sixteen people in all including himself, and headed for the homes of the elders of Takānah and Jalrīz. At each of the homes he bragged of his power, smoked a water pipe, and drank water and *dūgh* (a yogurt drink). He then paid a visit to the home of the head of the Aḥmadzāʾī tribe, Ḥażrat Muḥammad Khān, a good man with a good head on his shoulders. There, he had lunch, boasted about himself, and stayed until nearly **/244/** evening. This writer, who despite illness had been forced to join the delegation, reached Sar Chashmah along with the baggage train of eleven pack animals. He and the baggage stopped alongside a small pool (*ḥawż*) next to the Pusht-i Mazār fort—the last fort along the road from Sar Chashmah to Ūnay Pass and the nearest fort to the pass. Exhausted and downcast, I sat next to the pool and lay down on the dirt. Ḥasan Riżā, son of the late Zuwwār ʿAbd al-Ghiyas̱,[185] and the proprietor of the fort, Ḥājjī Sulṭān Muḥammad, who had 100 households subject to him, prepared food and tea.

As [the latter] had known me for a long time, was a fellow tribesman, and held me in high regard, he therefore in a sincere and friendly way asked me, "Regarding your dinner, should I slaughter a lamb or several chickens?" Angry with Nūr al-Dīn for having brought me to the Hazārahjāt against my will, I told Ḥājjī Sulṭān Muḥammad, "Nūr al-Dīn received 10,000 rupees from the government for travel expenses. Therefore don't trouble yourself. When he comes, whatever he tells you, that's what you should prepare."

At sundown, the powerless and useless Nūr al-Dīn arrived and, in a show of disrespect, arrogantly ordered the residents of the fort to prepare

[184] Here with the exception of 4 Muḥarram and 5 Muḥarram, Fayż Muḥammad stops introducing the date with the word *waqāʾiʿ-i* (the events of).

[185] The title *zuwwār* is given to someone who has made pilgrimage to shrines other than to Mecca, especially to those holy to Shiʿis—Mashhad, Qum, Karbalā, Najaf, Kāẓimayn.

dinner according to the current fixed official prices. In response to my reproach about his nawkar who had behaved inappropriately towards me and had ignored the fact that I was ill, Nūr al-Dīn reacted by admonishing me, using language that was unsuitable for a man in his position. I replied,

> You have not achieved the kind of rank and position that permits you to insult me. If the Hazārahs hear about what you have said, they will never show you any respect. They will refuse to recognize you as leader of the delegation and will not give you an oath of allegiance and submission on behalf of the one to whom you willingly agreed to go to the Hazārahjāt and so put the Qizilbāsh under the threat of death. You will thus not succeed in getting anything done.

Some minutes later, he regretted what he had said and came to see me in my tent to apologize. He brought with him members of the delegation to intercede for him and stand behind him. But according to the Qurʾānic verse, "... and if they pass by foolish talk, they pass by with dignity,"[186] before his intercessors could open their mouths to apologize, **/245/** I kissed his face and said, "For the sake of Islam and so as not to cause harm to our mission, I harbor no feelings of enmity nor of hatred. So do not worry." With that he was reassured and relieved of his anxiety.

Tuesday, 3 Muḥarram 1348, Corresponding to 21 Jawzā and 11 June 1929

121 | On this day, Nūr al-Dīn, because of the haste with which he wanted to take money from the Hazārahs and demanded they deliver it to him as quickly as possible and so fill the purse of his greed and ambition with the money of poor weak Hazārahs and also in his crude imagination that once he got an oath of allegiance and submission for Son of the Water Carrier from the Hazārahs he would spend his days as a high governor and in elevated service to Son of the Water Carrier, therefore, on this day without consulting other members of the delegation's leadership, he gave Colonel Ghulām Nabī, at his own request, permission to go to the forts and homes of his own tribe and they agreed that he would return within four days bringing back an agreement. Colonel Ghulām Nabī, son of Ghulām Riżā and grandson of Arbāb Yūsuf Hazārah, held the rank of colonel thanks to his mother who had been wet nurse to Sulṭān Jān Nūr al-Sirāj, the full sister of His Highness Amān Allāh Khān. After Son of the Water Carrier conquered Kabul, he found himself sitting at home out of work and I brought him into the delegation. Ghulām Nabī received instructions from

[186] Qurʾān 25:72.

Nūr al-Dīn to exert every effort to make the Hazārahs end their opposition and to get his tribe and the rest of the tribal elders to agree to be obedient and to give an oath of loyalty. He was also ordered to send back a report before he returned.

At the same time, I took him aside and advised him that this was an opportunity to raise the Hazārahs against Son of the Water Carrier and that he should not let them give an oath of allegiance. On the other hand, he should tell Nūr al-Dīn just the opposite to reassure him. Under no circumstances should he himself come back.

Also, to Walī Muḥammad, son of Muḥammad ʿAẓīm Beg, who was living in the village of Sih Pāy in Dāy Zangī and whose father had been killed by Amīr ʿAbd al-Raḥmān Khān, Nūr al-Dīn entrusted several farmans from Son of the Water Carrier which contained promises of promotion for Hazārahs in the army up to the rank /**246**/ of deputy field marshal and [in the civil service] up to governor, a reduction of the agricultural tax, and [promises] that the nomadic Afghan tribes would not appear again in the Hazārahjāt or in other places where even one Hazārah is found to be living. He was supposed to deliver these farmans to the leaders of the Dāy Zangī, Dāy Kundī, and Bihsūd Hazārahs. As a reward he was given 200 rupees.

[Nūr al-Dīn] handed over several other farmans addressed to the elders of the Jāghūrī and Mālistān Hazārahs to nine schoolboys who, fearful of being sodomized by the Northerners who were forcibly taking young boys to their lodgings and raping them, had gone into hiding in Kabul but were now heading home with the delegation. He also gave each one ten rupees for travel expenses. He also sent the people of Dāy Zangī and Dāy Kundī a personal letter borrowed from Prophetic hadiths and verses from the Qurʾān. At the time of their departure for the Hazārahjāt, this writer secretly enjoined [the schoolboys] to take all these documents to Fatḥ Muḥammad, the high commissioner of the Hazārah forces at the Ūnay Pass, where they had raised breastworks. These farmans ought to stay in the hands of Prince Muḥammad Amīn[187] who will not let the instructions of Son of the Water Carrier be published in the Hazārahjāt for they may mislead the Hazārahs and raise doubts in their minds about Muḥammad Nādir Khān. They did what I urged them to do.

---

[187] Prince Muḥammad Amīn (1911–1981) was the tenth son of Amīr Ḥabīb Allāh Khān.

The Events of Wednesday, 4 Muḥarram Corresponding to 22 Jawzā and 12 June

122 | In the late afternoon of this day, Ghulām Ḥabīb Khān, son of Ghulām Ḥasan Qizilbāsh and a resident of Qalʿah-yi Safīd, located at the mouth of its valley, came to the Pusht-i Mazār fort in Sar Chashmah with a letter from Colonel Ghulām Nabī. Ghulām Ḥabīb Khān was hostile to the Hazārahs of the Ūnay Pass due to their lands being adjacent to his and their sharing water and pastures. He was acting as an intermediary on behalf of Nūr al-Dīn. In his letter Ghulām Nabī had written,

> I met some arbābs who are inclined to proffer an oath of allegiance /247/ to end the hostilities and to express their submission to Son of the Water Carrier, the amir. All this gives me great pleasure and confidence that we will achieve our goals. From the [Ūnay] Pass, I am setting off for [my] tribe to meet with my friends. I will persuade them all to submit to Amīr Ḥabīb Allāh.

Nūr al-Dīn was pleased with the letter and believed that he had achieved his goals.

This writer, after convincing myself of the trustworthiness of two men—Aḥmad ʿAlī of Sar Chashmah and Ghulām Ḥusayn from Yakah Awlang who along with Mīr Faqīr Bihsūdī and Shāh Mīrzā Ḥusayn had led the fight in Bāmyān against the army of Son of the Water Carrier—through them informed Fatḥ Muḥammad, Miḥrāb ʿAlī, and other [Hazārah leaders] in Ūnay about Colonel Ghulām Nabī's letter. In [my] message, I called on them to resist Son of the Water Carrier and to refuse to give any oath of allegiance. I also promised to make inquiries about the situation in Kabul, about Muḥammad Nādir Khān and the tribes of the Southern Provinces who will oppose Son of the Water Carrier's forces in Gardayz and elsewhere, (*marginalia*: about Muḥammad Hāshim Khān in Jalālābād, and about the unity of purpose of the people of the East to attack Kabul [end of marginal note]) and to pass on any information I collect via these two men who, with the permission of the Saqqawīst, Colonel Niẓām al-Dīn, travel back and forth to the Ūnay Pass under the guise of purchasing wheat, oil, and mutton. In the letter I wrote, "Once you get the information, begin preparing your forces and if possible move against Kabul. According to some of their elders with whom I've met, if they're not lying, the residents of the city,[cviii] Chahārdihī, Pamqān, Bīktūt, and Maydān are all on the side of the Hazārahs."

The Events of Thursday, 5 Muḥarram, Corresponding to 23 Jawzā and 13 June 1929

On this day Ghulām Ḥabīb appeared and gave Nūr al-Dīn good news saying,

> Last night I went to the [Ūnay] Pass and met with Fatḥ Muḥammad, the leader of the Hazārah tribal forces /**248**/ who was stationed at a sangar there. I negotiated an agreement with him that on Friday Nūr al-Dīn and the members of the delegation would come to his fort as his guests. Fatḥ Muḥammad will be there with three or four tribal elders. Together they will negotiate and exchange ideas on the subjects of peace and an end to hostilities, the Hazārah tribes proffering an oath of allegiance, and their acceptance of obedience. Whatever the two sides agree is the best thing to do to end the carnage, that will suffice [for such a meeting].

It was not entirely clear from this whether Ghulām Ḥabīb was telling the truth. Ghulām Ḥabīb wanted to establish himself as the conduit for negotiations and, by cunning, make the Hazārahs pleased with him in order to achieve a good outcome for himself, and persuade them to submit to Son of the Water Carrier. He was doing all this so that afterwards he and his brother, ʿAlī Aḥmad, would receive high rank and status from Son of the Water Carrier. Prior to this, as was already mentioned, at the order of the high governor, Malik Muḥsin, he and his brother and representatives of Maydān, Takānah, Jalrīz, and Sar Chashmah had taken on the responsi-
123 bility | to obtain an oath of allegiance from the Hazārahs in ten days and return to Kabul. As a reward, each had been given a piece of turban cloth and Sayyid Zayn al-ʿĀbidīn of Takānah received the rank of "civil and military brigadier general." But they failed to give much thought to the fact that sooner or later consequences and punishment await them for every act. And as will be seen later, both brothers are killed and experience the results of their machinations.

Meanwhile during this time, Muḥammad Nādir Khān and his brother, Muḥammad Hāshim Khān, were doing their utmost to unite the Afghan tribes of the Southern and Eastern Provinces and encourage them to attack Kabul. However, because of the treachery of Ḥażrat-i Chārbāghī, Malik Muḥammad ʿAlam Shinwārī, ʿAbd al-Raḥmān, Malik Qays Khūgyānī, Ghawṣ al-Dīn, son of Jāndād Aḥmadzāʾī, and other tribal leaders, who had agreed to an alliance with the two brothers but hearing Son of the Water Carrier's proclamations with promises of rewards and the provocation of the misguided pseudo-mullahs had violated the agreement and decided either to seize or murder Muḥammad Nādir Khān, Shāh Walī Khān, /**249**/

Shāh Maḥmūd Khān, and Muḥammad Hāshim Khān, Muḥammad Nādir Khān and his brothers were unable to launch the campaign against Kabul and were again frustrated. As a precaution to avoid capture and death, they moved to a secluded place where they spent their days and nights in misery and hardship.

Because of the contradictory and unreliable announcements of an alliance of the Afghans of both provinces, the people would first rejoice then despair, continuing to live in bitter fear of the Saqqawī infidels, who were far beyond the pale of religion and faith. Women and men, children and adults, weeping and wailing and believing themselves to be on the brink of destruction, prayed to the Omnipotent to save them from murder and annihilation at the hands of the Northerners.

In brief, Ghulām Ḥabīb went home after delivering the invitation for Nūr al-Dīn and the members of the delegation to meet Fatḥ Muḥammad on Friday.

Friday, 6 Muḥarram, Corresponding to 24 Jawzā and 14 June 1929

On this day in response to the invitation, Nūr al-Dīn and the members of his delegation set off to join Ghulām Ḥabīb at his home at Qalʿah-i Safīd. There they had an elaborate lunch while awaiting the arrival of the three or four Hazārah leaders whom Ghulām Ḥabīb had hoped for. When they did not appear, Ghulām Ḥabīb sent one of his own horsemen to the Hazārahs. In response, they sent back the following message: "The arbābs left for their homes to mourn the son of the 'Ḥaydar-i Karrār'[188] and the beloved of the Prophet. Without their consent we cannot take part in negotiations, otherwise conflicts might arise amongst fellow tribesmen."

124 Before the arbābs had left Ūnay Pass for their own homes, they vowed | that each of them /250/ would choose one man of every four from among the valiant and courageous men under each one's authority and, on the 14th of the month, when the mourning period for the Lord of Martyrs (Imām Ḥusayn) and the partaking of votive offerings was over, they would straightaway dispatch them to the Ūnay Pass. Once they had mobilized, 2,000 men would take up strategic elevated positions in the Ūnay Pass, another 2,000 in Sar Chashmah, and a further 2,000 would occupy the heights commanding Jalrīz and Kūt-i ʿAshrū. After preparing their

[188] The "Ḥaydar-i Karrār" (Impetuous Lion) is a nickname for Imām ʿAlī, son of Abū Ṭālib. His son referred to here is Imām Ḥusayn.

breastworks they would await the sound of battle. They wanted to keep this group in battle readiness in the rear so that if the forces that will carry out the assault on Kabul suffer losses, then the first unit of 2,000 will go to attack Kabul while the second 2,000-man unit will move into the position of the first and the third force of 2,000 men will immediately move into the position of the second with the speed of the wind and scudding clouds. Four thousand men by way of Sanglākh and Qalʿah-i Kūh-i Pamqān while another 4,000 men by way of Kūtal-i Safīd Khāk, Maydān, Kūtal-i Takht, Qarghah, Chihil Tan, Qalʿah-i Qāżī, and Dār al-Amān will march forward in the dark of night for an attack on Kabul, ascending to the summits of Kūh-i Āsmāʾī, Shayr Darwāzah and Dukhtar-i Kāfir. After the night prayer, under cover of darkness, they will begin the assault on the capital by way of Kūtal-i Khayr Khānah, Qarghah, Chihil Tan, Qalʿah-i Ghāzī, and Dār al-Amān and will ascend the mountains of Āsmāʾī, Shayr Darwāzah, and Dukhtar-i Kāfir. If they conduct the attack by day between the forts of Chahārdihī and the open land located between Khayr Khānah Pass and Chīmtalah and the plain between Qarghah and Afshār they would suffer severe losses from the heavy artillery fire and will be unable to ascend and gain control of the mountains. At night, however, artillery fire goes into the air and is ineffective and the heights will be easily taken. After this, they can target the Arg and the Saqqawīs with artillery, rifles, and machine guns.[189] The hope is that they will be victorious and cleanse the city of the filth and pollution of the Northerners.

So in light of this plan they decided not to attend the meeting at the appointed place [Qalʿah-i Safīd]. In fact, the arbābs agreed that they ought to find a way to seize and kill Nūr al-Dīn and Muḥammad Zamān and arrest the members of the delegation. /251/

Saturday, 7 Muḥarram, Corresponding to 25 Jawzā and 15 June 1929

On this day Ghulām Ḥabīb who had gone to the [Ūnay] Pass to meet the Hazārah leaders relayed to them in a friendly way the complaint of Nūr al-Dīn and the members of the delegation that they had not shown up for the promised meeting. The Hazārahs responded,

> We Hazārahs are always accustomed to conduct our mourning ceremonies until the 12th of Muḥarram, i.e. the third day of the murder of the Lord

---

[189] Fayż Muḥammad uses here the French word for machine gun, mitrailleuse (*matrālyūz*), although in his previous references he has used the English (*māshīn gun*). Perhaps he's referring to a weapon here of French manufacture introduced by one of Amān Allāh Khān's Turkish military advisors.

of Martyrs, and are engaged in mourning, grieving, and lamenting, and although we are in our sangars, nonetheless we cannot ignore the sufferings of the son of the holy sayyid [Imām Ḥusayn] and go about other business. We regret that Nūr al-Dīn, who despite his claims to Islamism and making his own house in Kabul an official *ḥusaynīyah* at the disposal of the *pādshāh*, ministers, and his colleagues, now puts us in a vise and demands either that we express our obedience to Son of the Water Carrier and swear an oath or he will summon an army from Kabul to destroy us. His claim of Islamism is an out-and-out lie and his reciting the passion [of Imām Ḥusayn] and his mourning [for Ḥusayn] from beginning to end is a fraud and hypocrisy, a lamp without light. He does not seem to know that the Muslims of the whole world, including those of India, and even Hindūs there, put aside all their other business and stop making money for the ten days of Muḥarram and mourn the poor Imām, spending huge sums to do so while Nūr al-Dīn is quick to line his own pockets and threaten us. However, until the 12th of Muḥarram, we will undertake no other business nor are we afraid that the army of Son of the Water Carrier will attack us.

Ghulām Ḥabīb reached Nūr al-Dīn in Sar Chashmah and delivered the Hazārahs' response. Beside himself with anger, Nūr al-Dīn cursed them in the foulest terms and ordered Ghulām Ḥabīb once again to take them a message. In it he accused them of breaking their promise to attend the meeting. The Hazārahs, at the instructions of this writer which he had sent to them by way of Ghulām Ḥusayn, in response to Nūr al-Dīn through Ghulām Ḥabib, said that they were withholding an oath of allegiance to Son of the Water Carrier pending clarification of the situations of Muḥammad Nādir Khān in the South and Ghulām Nabī in Mazār[-i Sharīf]. /252/ Nūr al-Dīn wrote out a report of what had been conveyed orally and sent it by rider to Water Carrier's Boy[190] (*pisar-i sag qaw*) in Kabul. /253/

Sunday, 8 Muḥarram, Corresponding to 26 Jawzā 1308 and 16 June 1929

On this day, rumors circulated of a victorious assault by Muḥammad Nādir Khān on Gardayz and Lahūgard; the rout of Son of the Water Carrier; the treachery of Ghaws̱ al-Dīn Aḥmadzāʾī; the attack on his forces by the Sulaymān Khayl; and his retreat. Supporters of the Nādirid force, realizing that the incitement of the so-called mullahs and the announcements by Son of the Water Carrier concerning rewards have been effec-

190 Fayż Muḥammad deliberately writes *"pisar-i sag qaw"* for the usual *"pisar-i saqqā."* When uttered in a Kābulī pronunciation the two would sound virtually identical. Although *sag* (dog) is obviously derogatory it is unclear what meaning *qaw* is intended to convey other than emphasizing the intended denigration by the use of "dog."

tive among dishonorable Afghans in undermining agreements and negotiations, in despair clasp their hands in prayer and ask the All-High to assist Muḥammad Nādir Khān to victory, rout the Saqqawīs, and save the country and nation from the misdeeds of this infidel and also of his confederates—thieving murderers and blackguards all—each one of whom has a high position and rank and does whatever he feels like doing.

Also today Son of the Water Carrier received a letter informing him of the departure [from Afghanistan] of Ghulām Nabī, minister plenipotentiary, who had captured Mazār-i Sharīf and its environs with a force of 700 Hazārahs from Khurāsān, Transoxania, and those displaced to Afghan
126 Turkistān [from the Hazārahjāt]. | He had pushed [the supporters of Ḥabīb Allāh Kalakānī] back to Ay [Aybak?] and had intended to attack Kūhistān, Kabul, and Kūh Dāman. On the eve of Wednesday, 20 Ẕīḥijjah, having taken as much money as he could carry, he returned to Transoxania and Moscow.[191] With the arrival of a plane in Kabul, it was learned that the military and civil officials of His Majesty Amān Allāh Khān who were able to flee abandoned Mazār-i Sharīf in the dark of that same night for Tashkent experienced considerable hardship. Among their number were: the director of customs, Mīrzā Muḥammad Naʿīm Khān; the director of taxation (*mudīr-i māliyāh*) for Maymanah, Mīrzā Muḥammad ʿAzīz Khān; the governor of Darrah-i Ṣūf, Mīrzā Muḥammad Yusuf Khān; and his brother, Mīrzā Muḥammad Kāẓim, all of whose belongings were looted by followers of the "Khalīfah" of Qizil Ayāq-i[192] Turkmān and Mīrzā Qāsim Ūzbak.

Son of a Dog himself drove a car around /254/ the bazaars of Kabul (on this day) under the impression that the people of the city, who harbored in their hearts hope of an attack by Muḥammad Nādir Khān and prayed to God for his victory, would be in a state of confusion and distress [because

---

[191] According to Shkirando (Faiz Mukhammad, *Kniga upominanii*, p. 267, note 166) "Ghulām Nabī Khān made the decision to abandon Mazār-i Sharīf after receiving a telegram from the minister of foreign affairs under Aman Allah Khān who was in Kandahar, Ghulam Siddiq Khān. In it he was advised to leave the country since Aman Allāh Khān had already left. Even though, as Muḥyī al-Dīn Anīs tells it, the majority of the participants at a council of war were in favor of continuing the fighting, [nonetheless] 'on the night of 10 Jawza Ghulam Nabi Khān headed for the Amu Darya via the Tepe-i Kashir road taking with him eight lakhs of rupees, goods and carpets, as much as he could carry, and accompanied by his close associates. On Friday, they crossed into Russia." (See Muḥyī al-Dīn Anīs, *Buḥrān wa najāt*, Kabul: Anīs, n.d., p. 211.).

[192] The name of the "khalīfah of Qizil Ayāq" is unknown. The village of Qizil Ayāq appears on the Ayazi map as "Qezel Ayaq-e Khurd (Lesser Qizl Ayaq). Adamec, *Historical Gazetteer* vol. 4 tells us there were two villages, "Lesser" and "Greater" (*kalān*) Qizil Ayaq (s.v. "Kizil Aiak"). The villages were inhabited at the time the gazetteer was compiled (late 19th century) by Arsari (Erserī) Turkmens and their spiritual leader was the "Khalīfah."

of the news from Mazār]. He informed people and assured them of the success of his army and also the defeat and withdrawal of Muḥammad Nādir Khān's forces and sent off to Lahūgard the miscellaneous tribals whom he had rounded up and forcibly conscripted to defend it from attack by the tribes of the Southern Province. By promising a reward he also lured some deluded pseudo-mullahs and leaders of the donkey-stealing Sulaymān Khayl and some other miserable tribes who, besmirching Afghan honor, had come to Kabul, some with greedy hopes of getting money and some just out of ignorance, to go and exhort the Aḥmadzāʾī, Ṣabarī, Muqbil, Matūn, Jājī, Jadrān and other tribes and incite them to oppose Muḥammad Nādir Khān and the tribes supporting him. They were to persuade them all to turn against him and befoul the eye of pride, courage, and honor of all Afghans with the filth of infamy in the same way they were already contaminated with the dirt of disgrace.

Monday, 9 Muḥarram, Corresponding to 27 Jawzā and 17 June 1929

On this day, the son of Mullā Malik, Shaykh ʿAbd al-ʿAlī, who settled with his family in Ūnay and is living off the food handed out after the fasting [of early Muḥarram] and on *zakāt* from the Hazārahs, came to Sar Chashmah to meet with one of the members of the delegation, Mīr Āqā,[cix] a Shiʿi specialist in Imāmī law, and well-respected among the Shiʿis. After reaching Sar Chashmah, he began to boast that he had a great deal of influence and authority among the Hazārahs. Mīr Āqā confirmed what Shaykh ʿAbd al-ʿAlī said to Nūr al-Dīn, and told him that he was a secret emissary of the head of Hazārah tribal forces, Fatḥ Muḥammad. Nūr al-Dīn, after listening to his boasting and having heard Mīr Āqā's confirmation of his authority, believed him and sent him to Fatḥ Muḥammad with a message which suggested that he name a day, time, and place for a meeting and /255/ negotiations and, through ʿAbd al-ʿAlī, provide
127 guarantees of | safety for the leadership and members of the delegation. Nūr al-Dīn was still hoping that if Son of the Water Carrier's terms were accepted, he would succeed in realizing his own ambitions. ʿAbd al-ʿAlī departed with the letter as well as greetings for Fatḥ Muḥammad from Mīr Āqā whom Nūr al-Dīn also believed was very influential among the Hazārahs because they kept bringing him different sorts of fried sweet flatbread (*khajūr wa rawghan jūsh*[193]). He promised to return the next

[193] The *Dari-English Dictionary* (1993) equates *khajūr* and *rawghan jūshī* and defines them (s.v. *rawghan jūshī*) as "a flat round piece of sweetened dough folded from both

day and report the outcome. On the advice of the high commissioner of the Hazārahjāt, Prince Muḥammad Amīn Khān, and his deputy, Khwājah Hidāyat Allāh, as well as Ghulām Ḥusayn, Fatḥ Muḥammad designated the meeting place in a small village called Qūl-i Ghulām Ḥusayn, one of Ūnay's forts, near the pass and the Hazārah positions. There they planned to capture and murder Nūr al-Dīn and Muḥammad Zamān Parwānī.

Nūr al-Dīn was now in a hopeful frame of mind. The message [sent to the Hazārahs], the boasting of ʿAbd al-ʿAlī and Mīr Āqā's description of his own influence among the Hazārahs, corresponded nicely with [Nūr al-Dīn's] plans. Dropping off to sleep, he was at peace, confident that the morrow would bring him good fortune. Nūr al-Dīn had such a miserly nature that he was also pleased by the fact that those fried cakes which the Hazārahs had given to Mīr Āqā, he had added to his own travel trunk (*yakhdān*) and that from the first of Muḥarram the funds allocated for travel expenses still fattened his own purse since the delegation was living off food provided by the people of Sar Chashmah and their votive offerings. The daily expenses, of which in fact there were none, he recorded in his account book as expenditures. **/256/**

Tuesday, 10 Muḥarram, Corresponding to 28 Jawzā and the Eighteenth of the English June

On this day, despite the fact that it was ʿĀshūrā, the most important day commemorating the sufferings of Muslims, from sunrise, Nūr al-Dīn waited expectantly for the return of Shaykh ʿAbd al-ʿAlī who should have been bringing back information about the time and place of the meeting with Fatḥ Muḥammad. But hour after hour went by and the shaykh did not appear. Finally, along with some of the members of the delegation—Mīr Āqā, Mullā Ghulām Hasan, Mīrzā Qāsim, and Muḥammad Mahdī Afshār—[Nūr al-Dīn] left for the *ḥusaynīyah* to hear the re-telling of the story of the tragedy of Imām Ḥusayn, the Lord of Martyrs.

This writer was sitting alone in his tent when Shaykh ʿAbd al-ʿAlī, dressed in a great robe (*chūkhā-yi buland*) with long sleeves, came riding up on his horse. Although he had no desire to come near this humble one, still he called out to me and reluctantly I invited him to my tent and said, "Sit here for a bit. Nūr al-Dīn and Mīr Āqā will return after the *rawzah-khwān*'s narration is over." I asked him about Fatḥ Muḥammad. But he

sides into the middle [and] deep-fried in cooking oil." *An Afghān Recipe Book*, ed., Doris McKellar (1967), p. 28 calls them "khajoor or busrauq (Fried Cakes)" and provides a recipe.

was keeping everything secret and wouldn't tell me anything. He sat for a while, waiting for Nūr al-Dīn and Mīr Āqā. As soon as they appeared in the distance he jumped up and headed for their tent (*utāq*) which stood on an elevated place on the heights of the mountain. He met up with them on the way and they entered the tent together. Muḥammad Zamān Khān was also included in the group. Without this writer's being present, they heard from Shaykh ʿAbd al-ʿAlī the message of Fatḥ Muḥammad that the members of the delegation and Muḥammad Zamān Khān Parwānī should come to the *ḥusaynīyah* at Qūl-i Ghulām Ḥusayn to hear the recitation of the tragedy of Imām Ḥusayn and partake of the votive offerings for the
128 day of ʿĀshūrā of that Lord and meet and negotiate a truce. |

Nūr al-Dīn[cx] selected Mīr Āqā and this writer to go. He summoned me and explained the matter. /257/ Since I was in the dark regarding the actual situation, I refused to go, using the excuse that it was ʿĀshūrā. In reply I was told that Fatḥ Muḥammad had invited the leader and members of the delegation to celebrate ʿĀshūrā by listening to the narration of the tragedy and partaking of votive offerings. Therefore the writer had to go. Then I turned to Shaykh ʿAbd al-ʿAlī and said, "In this robe with the long sleeves will you be able to provide the delegation with security and guarantees against seizure and detention by Fatḥ Muḥammad and the others and will you be able to deliver us back [safely]?" He did not answer. Mīr Āqā who was his accomplice and was always "collecting *khums* for the *mujtahid*,"[194] acting as surrogate [for Shaykh ʿAbd al-ʿAlī] answered for him, "Yes, I guarantee it." Because of these casual and foolish words of his, the writer was forced to agree to go. Muḥammad Zamān Khān (Parwānī) [on the other hand] was not advised to go.

After ordering the horses saddled, Nūr al-Dīn happily mounted and then Mīr Āqā, the writer, and two armed Wazīrābādī horsemen of the regular army each mounted. The order to go was also issued to Khalīfah Ghulām Ḥasan, one of the members of the delegation, who, not having been [originally] selected was standing on the path about to redo his ritual ablutions [having voided his original ablutions, probably by a call of nature] when he was forcibly ordered to mount up. We all departed then accompanied by Shaykh ʿAbd al-ʿAlī who secretly was in full accord with Fatḥ Muḥammad and at his instructions performed the role of

194 The phrase "collector of *khums* [a 20% religious tax] on behalf of the *mujtahid*" has the sense of someone doing their job as a surrogate, here protecting Shaykh ʿAbd al-ʿAlī [and providing deniability] by answering for him.

intermediary, and without being forced to, was exposing the head of the delegation and his three companions to mortal danger.

In short, the group arrived at Qūl-i Ghulām Ḥusayn at the fort of the Hazārahs. After embracing and shaking hands with Colonel Hāshim; Mīrzā Zamān Shāh, the customs official of Bihsūd; and other people who were present, we took our places in the hall (*imāmbārah*) which they had started to build above[cxi] the mosque but hadn't yet finished. Fatḥ Muḥammad showed up with an armed force of 300 men after a few minutes, his absence explained by the fact that he was listening to the retelling of the tragedy [of Imām Ḥusayn]. Nūr al-Dīn greeted him and then showed Fatḥ Muḥammad a farman from Son of the Water Carrier authorizing him to act on the amir's behalf. He had issued it to him in order to deceive the Hazārahs. Then [Nūr al-Dīn] began to boast of his own rank and status among the Saqqawīs.

After we sat for a meal /258/ of lamb stew as a votive to the oppressed Imām (Ḥusayn) and an entire narration of the tragedy was performed, this writer and Khalīfah Ghulām Ḥasan began the daily prayer. Fatḥ Muḥammad, on the pretext of consulting and negotiating with Nūr al-Dīn, led him outside and instructed him to write Muḥammad Zamān Khān Parwānī and the other members of the delegation to "come to the (Ūnay) Pass from Sar Chashmah and be our guests." Nūr al-Dīn, unable to comprehend the situation he was really in and still believing himself respected and influential amongst both Qizilbāsh and Hazārahs, feared that they would arrest and murder Muḥammad Zamān Kūhistānī [i.e. Parwānī] refused to ask them [to come]. Aware that Nūr al-Dīn had willingly volunteered to obtain an oath of allegiance from the Hazārahs, Fatḥ Muḥammad was angered and signaled for a bugle to be sounded. He disrespectfully forced Nūr al-Dīn off his horse, disarmed him, put him on a different horse, and drove him before him to the Ūnay Pass. To three other members of the delegation he said, "Get on your horses and go home."

The writer, who was on good terms with Fatḥ Muḥammad, had given him a full and accurate account of the state of affairs, advised him regarding the strengthening of defensive positions and the readiness of his units, and convinced him not to tender an oath of allegiance but rather to fight Son of the Water Carrier, [now] approached him and whispered, "If we
129 go back, we'll be killed at the hands of Son of the Water Carrier. | All the poor Qizilbāsh, who due to the stupidity and opportunism of Nūr al-Dīn were forced to send this tribal delegation, expect to die. Take this and other things into consideration and consult with the arbābs. [It is best] to carry us off as if we are also under arrest." Fatḥ Muḥammad agreed with

the writer's whispered remarks and ordered that they all mount up and go off as if under arrest.

Colonel Gul Muḥammad, commanding 100 regular army Harātī infantrymen equipped with two artillery pieces, had joined forces with the Hazārah tribal contingent and was at Ūnay Pass in accordance with the orders of Prince Muḥammad Amīn. Having learned from Colonel Ghulām Nabī the whole story of Nūr al-Dīn's having freely volunteered to obtain an oath of allegiance from the Hazārahs and having deceitfully threatened the members of the delegation that Son of the Water Carrier would arrest them if they refused to go [to the Hazārahjāt], [Colonel Gul Muḥammad] was outraged and slapped Nūr al-Dīn so hard on the face and mouth that he drew blood. /259/ One of the Hazārahs then took Nūr al-Dīn's watch. Colonel Gul Muḥammad unleashed a barrage of curses at Nūr al-Dīn,

> You wretch! Did the martyred Amīr [Ḥabīb Allāh Khān] and His Highness Amān Allāh Khān show you so little kindness that you decided to serve Son of the Water Carrier and for his sake are willing to sacrifice yourself in order to undermine the strength of the community of Hazārahs who, being valiant and faithful to God, rose to support the Afghan government and to uproot the government of the Saqqawīs? And you volunteered to obtain an oath of allegiance from this warlike and courageous tribe in order to disgrace the feeble tribe of the Qizilbāsh and to place them in the arena of death, destruction, and plundering?

Nūr al-Dīn, ashamed of his behavior could only repeatedly mutter, "Son of the Water Carrier forced me to accept this mission." Nothing else was he able to say. Then, with the three other delegation members, they took him to Fatḥ Muḥammad's tent. Tea was drunk, then at sunset, Muḥammad Isḥāq, son of Khalīfah Ghulām Rasūl Kābulī, the tax collector and currently governor of Hazārah Bihsūd, [arrived]. He brought an order from Sardār [Prince] Muḥammad Amīn addressed to Fatḥ Muḥammad to send Nūr al-Dīn and his companions to the prince in Rāh Qūl. He also brought a forged farman of His Majesty Amān Allāh Khān's which reported his arrival in Gū-yi Qarābāgh in Ghaznīn. This farman had been concocted by the prince's aide, Khwājah Hidāyat Allāh, in order to bolster the spirits and strengthen the resolve of the Hazārahs in their opposition to Son of the Water Carrier. After reading this farman those who were present were heartened and delighted and congratulated each other on the arrival of His Majesty. At this moment, Colonel Gul Muḥammad turned to Nūr al-Dīn and said, "If you are telling the truth, that Son of the Water Carrier forced you to try and get an oath of allegiance from the Hazārahs, and that you are actually a sincere and loyal servant of the Afghan government, then what present did you bring for the prince?" Nūr al-Dīn replied, "A pistol and a watch which I had but you took away. Anyway we were invited here and so did not bring gifts."

Colonel Gul Muḥammad then said, "Your gift **/260/** was Muḥammad Zamān [Parwānī] Kūhistānī, whom you should have brought with you. Since you didn't bring him with you the first time, write him now in your own hand and with your signature so that he and the other members of the delegation will leave Sar Chashmah and come to the pass." But Nūr al-Dīn [again] refused and this writer warned [Fatḥ Muḥammad], "If this order is carried out and you kill Muḥammad Zamān Khān like they
130 killed ʿAbd al-Raḥmān, son of Dād Muḥammad | Kūhistānī, then all the Qizilbāsh in the delegation will be put to death and their property confiscated [by Son of the Water Carrier]." However, the words of this writer had no effect. In order to force Nūr al-Dīn to write the letter with his own hand, they grabbed him so hard around the throat that his spine cracked and his breathing was cut off. Licking his dry lips, he began to beg for mercy. But Colonel Gul Muḥammad was adamant and made up his mind to punish Nūr al-Dīn. Then Mīr Āqā took his turban off and began to plead for mercy for [Nūr al-Dīn]. The Hazārahs also interceded on his behalf and prevented the colonel from doing Nūr al-Dīn any real harm. In the evening, Nūr al-Dīn, Mīr Āqā, Ghulām Ḥasan and this writer were sent off on horseback to Prince Muḥammad Amīn in Rāh Qūl. The two armed Wazīrābādī horsemen, their heads now bare, were also sent with arms bound. All were guarded by Colonel Hāshim, Mīrzā Zamān Shāh, and seven armed Hazārahs. When [we] stopped for the night near Qalʿah-i Yūrt, a Qizilbāsh court usher (*ʿarż-bīgī*) arrived. At the request of Mīr Āqā and me, they put us up in a mosque which was swarming with fleas and reminded us all of a jail. The grandson of the usher, Aḥmad ʿAlī, who was a nice boy, brought us bread and soft-boiled eggs after the [night] prayer. [We] put our heads down to sleep but it was impossible because of the plague of fleas, which bit painfully. I sat on the bed my body feverish, my spirit downcast, and my mind afflicted due to the severity of the pain. My temperature rose and my body ached all over. I sat and scratched away at the flea bites with both hands.

Colonel **/261/** Hāshim Hazārah, who had assigned guards to the door and roof of the mosque was himself spending the night in the mosque. [I spoke to him] and the colonel replied, "I'm not asleep." So I asked him, "Now that you've decided to take the leader of the delegation prisoner, do you have any news about Muḥammad Nādir Khān in the Southern Province and the displaced Hazārahs [active in the Ghūrband area]? Do you have any contact with them and are your reserves of war materiel sufficient to defend yourself against attack from Son of the Water Carrier? If you don't have the reserves, and you're not going to have them, then it was rash to so hastily arrest the members of the delegation. If Son of the Water Carrier finds out about this he'll mobilize an army, make the situation very difficult for you and will destroy the Hazārahs, who don't have sufficient arms and strength." In reply he said, "no" and his answer made me feel regret. Then I said to him, "You should not have done that [arrested the delegation members] but should have made Son of the Water Carrier wait another month or two using delaying tactics so that the real situation of Muḥammad Nādir Khān and Muḥammad Hāshim Khān in the Southern and Eastern Provinces would be clarified and then you could act in conformity with the regulations of the holy lawgiver." Hāshim did not reply.

Wednesday, 11 Muḥarram, Corresponding to 29 Jawzā and 19 June

On this day when a decision was made to take the prisoners to the prince [Muḥammad Amīn] after morning prayers and tea brought by the luckless Aḥmad ʿAlī, who was eventually subsequently killed by Hazārahs who had
131 a dispute with him over land, those arrested were sent off. | At approximately 11 A.M. they stopped for lunch at the fort of the Qizilbāsh Mīrzā Ghulām Nabī, who at the order of the prince, had been appointed tax collector for Bihsūd. Nūr al-Dīn, although he knew that he had been condemned, nevertheless still hoped for mercy or that someone would intercede for him. Mīrzā Ghulām Nabī began /262/ to prepare food. When we were seated in the guest house, Mīrzā Zamān Shāh arrived. He had overtaken us along the way and said "I have a job for some sepoys from the Harāt regular army garrison stationed at Ribāṭ Jawqūl." He had brought with him a captain and three or four sepoys. By what he implied, he was threatening the prisoners. Ghulām Nabī brought bread, *dūgh*, butter, and soft-boiled eggs. They ate as if the food were poisoned, distressed by the fact that they had not been able to send anyone to Shāh Muḥammad Ḥusayn, the intermediary with the Hazārahs of Bihsūd, to intercede for Nūr al-Dīn and to try and save him. In utter despair, the prisoners set off again and at 3 P.M. drew near a fort situated near Ribāṭ-i Bād Āsyā. They knocked at the gate, intending to make a stop to smoke a water pipe, and drink some water. An elderly grey-haired woman brought water and asked Mīr Āqā, who was squatting by the road, "Which one of you is Mīr Āqā?" "I am," he replied. The woman then burst into tears and began to kiss Mīr

Āqā 's hands and feet. "When we learned of your arrest on ʿĀshūrā, the people blocked all the roads to Rāh Qūl so that they would not be able to deliver the prisoners to the sardār [Prince Muḥammad Amīn Khān] and Nūr al-Dīn would not be killed." Then [other] women of the fort heard the news and ran to the gate of the fort with their children. They kissed the hands and hem of Mīr Āqā, swore oaths on the heads of their children, asked him to pray for the long lives of their children, and wished him a long life. The first woman then informed the prisoners that a cavalry sergeant, Āqā Sayyid Jaʿfar, had sent someone to warn the prisoners not to go right away to Rāh Qūl but to stop at his fort in Khāk-i Āghah. Having heard Sayyid Jaʿfar's message and injunction and having set off again, near the caravanserai (Ribāṭ-i Bād Āsyā) they saw several sepoys with two cannons who had come here after their defeat in Bāmyān at the hands of Son of the Water Carrier. [At Bāmyān] /**263**/ Mīr Faqīr, a Dawlat Pāy Hazārah of Bihsūd, with 1,000 of his fellow tribesmen along with Sayyid Shāh Mīrzā Ḥusayn of Yakah Awlang with people from there and the Hazārahs of Bāmyān had surrounded the army of Son of the Water Carrier. But Mīr Faqīr went home to observe the ten days of ʿĀshūrā and Shāh Mīrzā Ḥusayn took [a bribe of] 12,000 rupees from an officer of the surrounded force and, having given an oath of allegiance to Son of the Water Carrier, returned to Yakah Awlang. This was the cause of their defeat. But they brought the cannons with them.

So on this same day it was seen with one's own eyes how in the place of Mīrzā Ghulām Nabī some members of the Dawlat Pāy tribal force cursed and vilified Shāh Mīrzā Ḥusayn and departed quickly for Bāmyān so as to fight the Saqqawīs and stop them from making any progress.

In short, not far from Khāk-i Āghah, a horseman came into view trotting along the road ahead. When he approached it became clear it was
132 the cavalry sergeant Sayyid Jaʿfar and he was searching for the prisoners |. He jumped down from his horse and warmly greeted them, shaking hands and embracing them. After having a look at Mīr Āqā and the writer, he began berating the guard, Colonel Hāshim, in the strongest language and very rudely ordered him to get off his horse and then said,

> Hey, you're just like that accursed Ibn Saʿd,[195] a treasonous and duplicitous enemy of the faith. You're guarding a sayyid and a mullah whom Son of the

---

[195] In October 680, Ibn Saʿd led a force sent against the man who came to be seen as the third Shiʿi imām, Ḥusayn, son of ʿAlī, at Karbalā, a city in Iraq some 100 kilometers southwest of Baghdad. Imām Ḥusayn's death in the battle that followed became a major moment of commemoration for the partisans of his also assassinated father, ʿAlī son of

> Water Carrier forcibly sent to get an oath of allegiance from the Hazārahs. These are like the prisoners of Karbalā taken into custody by that "Shimr,"[196] Fatḥ Muḥammad, on ʿĀshūrā, and sent under a treasonous guard like you to Sardār Muḥammad Amīn. But from a similar story told him by Colonel Ghulām Nabī, he is already well informed about them and knows that they are opponents of Son of the Water Carrier and do not serve that oppressive scoundrel. So why are you driving them under guard like prisoners, along with Nūr al-Dīn?

Colonel Hāshim and Zamān Shāh, seeing the large number of armed men standing in front of Sayyid Jaʿfar's fort, were afraid that they would be killed. They began to cringe and in voices shaking with fear babbled, "We brought them here with honor and treated them politely /**264**/ and did not harm them in any way."

Meanwhile, the prisoners, having experienced a situation quite opposite to the one in which they faced being killed, although they had endured all kinds of hardship, decided to end the strife and save Hāshim and (Shāh) Zamān from death. They turned to Sayyid Jaʿfar and said, "They treated us in an appropriate manner, with proper concern and respect." When he heard this, Sayyid Jaʿfar stopped abusing Hāshim and Shāh Zamān. Then everyone mounted up and together rode off to Sayyid Jaʿfar's fort and home. Near the fort, they were met by 500 Hazārahs who had gathered to prevent the prisoners being taken to Rāh Qūl to Prince Muḥammad Amīn. At the sight of Colonel Hāshim and Zamān Shāh, whom they knew were the prisoners' guards, they surged forward and shouts went up; some, loading their weapons, seemed intent on killing the two men. But Mīr Āqā, Khalīfah Ghulām Ḥasan, and I took our turbans off, rose to the defense of those two, and prevented them being killed.

After shaking hands and embracing all around, we sat down in Sayyid Jaʿfar's salon (*ṣālūn*) which was his guest house and a place furnished with carpets in which 200 people could be accommodated. Worried that they might kill Colonel Hāshim, Zamān, and the seven sepoys under their command, we put them in one of the rooms in the inner sanctum of Sayyid Jaʿfar's house and locked the doors behind them. The Hazārahs hung around until sunset at which time they rode off to spend the night in nearby villages.

Abū Ṭālib. Those supporters were called the "party of ʿAlī" (*shīʿat-i ʿAlī*) hence the name Shiʿi or Shīʿah.

[196] Shimr was the man who actually killed Ḥusayn. In the Iranian Shiʿi tradition, his name stands for cruelty and inhumanity.

Although I was ill and had eaten nothing, nonetheless, after performing my prayers I passed this night in complete rest and in gratitude for the piety, unshakable loyalty, and Islamic integrity of the Hazārahs.

Thursday, 12 Muḥarram, Corresponding to 30 Jawzā and 20 June

On this day after tea, the Hazārahs who had spent the night at other forts returned in groups. All told, about one thousand men gathered. Sayyid /265/ Jaʿfar, Shāh Ḥaydar, Shāh Muḥammad Ḥusayn and other ulema sent a messenger of theirs to Sardār Muḥammad Amīn Khān. In the letter which
133 the messenger was to deliver to the prince, | they said that they would not allow the prisoners to be sent to Rāh Qūl until all arbābs had been assembled and those arrested were given guarantees of personal safety. When [the messenger left], the Hazārahs began to prepare the midday meal. However, they were worried lest, God forbid, the prince send the Harātī regulars with cannons, take Nūr al-Dīn by force, and carry him off to Rāh Qūl to the trouble that awaited him there. In addition, they had [received] a message from the revenue collector Riżā Bakhsh in which he demanded that they not leave the prisoners with Sayyid Jaʿfar but send them to him under guard lest, God forbid, some misunderstanding should arise. So it was that, without giving the prisoners time to eat, they delivered them to [Riżā Bakhsh] in the district of Kajāb at 3 P.M. escorted by a guard of 500 armed infantry and horse. There they dismounted onto a large raised platform, twenty by ten *gaz* in area, covered with large multicolored kilims, and surrounded on four sides by a row of plane trees, their tops reaching to the sky. At the four corners pillows (*naʿlīnchahs*[197]) were set out. Bread, tea, halvah, meat, soft-boiled eggs, and bowls of *dūgh* were served and the prisoners and those 500 people ate and drank until they were full. Then the horsemen were dismissed, having been given advance notice that on the morrow they would attend as a group in order to provide protection if the prince should harbor some malice for Nūr al-Dīn. The infantrymen who had been appointed to guard him stayed behind, a small number of them scattering to nearby forts.

By Riżā Bakhsh's mien, one sensed that he was a Saqqawī. Sayyid Jaʿfar warned the writer about this saying, "Look, I hope he did not deceive

[197] A. I. Shkirando, the Russian editor and translator of this text, understood this word to mean a *ṣandalī*, a wooden frame over a charcoal brazier covered with a quilt which people put their legs under for warmth. But the word used here, *naʿlīnchah*, actually refers to the cushions placed around the sandali on which one rested one's legs under the quilt cover. We are grateful to Dr. Amin Tarzi for this information.

you or force you into getting an oath of allegiance from the people." [I] replied, "God willing, his intrigues will have no effect."

On the pretext of protecting Nūr al-Dīn, Rižā Bakhsh took him to spend the night /266/ in a special tower in the inner part of the fort, the same place he had hid the son of Maḥmūd Tāymanī, Naẓar Muḥammad. Naẓar Muḥammad had squandered 6,000 rupees on the road[198] to Dakkah for which he was sentenced and spent time in prison for his treachery. Son of the Water Carrier released him and appointed him governor of Hazārah Bihsūd. However, Rižā Bakhsh was worried that Prince Muḥammad Amīn might take [Naẓar Muḥammad] and put him in a house and then by means of him send Son of the Water Carrier an oath of loyalty, in order to prevent a rising of the people against him [Amīr Ḥabib Allāh Kalakānī].

The three of them [i.e. Naẓar Muḥammad, Rižā Bakhsh, and Nūr al-Dīn] discussed matters amongst themselves. By intuition I came to the conclusion that they are trying to get me to persuade people, by means of selections from the Qur'ān, to submit to Son of the Water Carrier. But they fail to consider my own feelings and conscience when it comes to what they want [me to do].

Friday, 13 Muḥarram, Corresponding to 31 Jawzā and 21 June

On this day after tea and the morning meal some Hazārahs arrived, one by one, some on horseback and some on foot. They reported that a number of arbābs had gone to Sardār Muḥammad Amīn Khān in Rāh Qūl and he had spoken to each of them in secret on the subject of the prisoners. No
134 one knows what they agreed to. | On hearing this news, but without knowing what it meant, Nūr al-Dīn became distraught, afraid that the arbābs had decided to hand him over to the sardār who would hang him. Out of fear he began to babble senselessly. Rižā Bakhsh turned in his direction and said, "Khān-ṣāḥib! Your demeanor, posture, and face appear fine. Just put something under your shoes and your bottom so that seated you'll be a little taller than others but keep your mouth closed and don't say anything that might spoil things. Let the writer [Fayż Muḥammad] do the talking." After these words of Rižā Bakhsh, I realized that either Nūr al-Dīn had disobeyed the instructions given to him at night in the tower, or [Rižā

198 Fayż Muḥammad introduces a Franco-Persian linguistic neologism here, *rāh shawsah-i* (*chaussée*) *Dakkah* by which he simply seems to mean the Dakka road, the main route from Kabul through Jalālābād to the border with British India.

Bakhsh] wants to provoke me, on whom people look favorably, to speak out. /267/ But I said nothing.

At this time the prince's deputy, Khwājah Hidāyat Allāh, came in, accompanied by two or three sayyids and arbābs. After asking, on behalf of the prince, how we all were, he conveyed [the prince's] pleasure and satisfaction [at the activities] of Mīr Āqā, Khalīfah Ghulām Ḥasan, and me. He particularly thanked and complimented me for not agreeing to accept a salary from Son of the Water Carrier, for having recited some Qur'ānic verses on declaring him and his army infidels in a public assembly before Son of the Water Carrier himself, for having to be forcibly assigned to [the delegation to] the Hazārahjāt, and for privately calling him "Son of the Water Carrier." [Hidāyat Allāh] said,

> The sardār is very pleased with you. You never forgot the regard shown you by his father, the martyred amir, and his brother, His Majesty Amān Allāh Khān. You refused to serve Son of the Water Carrier and you encouraged the Afghans in Kabul when you addressed them saying, 'What happened to your devotion to the religion, your valor, your Afghan honor about which so much used to be said in bygone times? You have expressed submission and have submitted to a dishonorable thief, a drinker of blood, a lecher, and an apostate. You are cutting off the very limb on which you sit and you have cast your own country, nation, and government to the wind of annihilation, violating your covenants, undermining faith, abandoning unity and concord, and involving yourselves in murdering, plundering, and enslaving each other.'

These were the words at the end of a letter from Sardār Muḥammad Amīn Khān personally addressed to me. In this letter the prince also expressed thanks to Mīr Āqā, Khalīfah Ghulām Ḥasan, and me for our frankness and sincerity. [Hidāyat Allāh] wanted to present us with this letter which in the future might serve as a confirmation of our successful efforts. But Mīr Āqā and I demurred saying, "Son of the Water Carrier will find out about this letter, one way or another, and will kill us."

Thereupon Hidāyat Allāh read out another letter signed by the prince and addressed to the sayyids, arbābs, and the tribal forces which had protected Nūr al-Dīn, prevented him from being taken to Rāh Qūl and thus saved him from death. [In it he said],

> Displaying sincerity, steadfastness and [also] honor and valor /268/ in support of the Afghan government, you not only refused to express obedience to Son of the Water Carrier but you encouraged confidence among the Afghans and [helped] unify several of their tribes. [What you have done is
> 135 so admirable that] | in addition to Nūr al-Dīn if you were to ask for Son of the Water Carrier to be forgiven, we would forgive him. So clearly his supporters and servants like Nūr al-Dīn would be forgiven. But this man ought

> to leave here and should not stay one [more] day with your tribe, or there might be trouble.

He handed the sardār's letter to the Hazārahs then grasped the hands of the writer and Sayyid Muḥammad Akbar, a sayyid of the Hazārahs of Bihsūd, who is a good person and can distinguish the true from the apocryphal, and said, "I want a word with you in private." We moved far away from the gathering and sat on the bank of a canal in the shade of a tree. Khwājah Hidāyat Allāh tried to guess the intention of Riżā Bakhsh who, unbeknownst to Sardār Muḥammad Amīn, had sent an oath of allegiance to Son of the Water Carrier and in spite of the wishes of all the tribes expressed his submission to him, thus deceiving his own tribesmen, and secretly instructing his friends to provide *bay'at-nāmahs*. Opening the conversation, [Khwājah Hidāyat Allāh] said, "Since you did not obtain an oath of allegiance, when you return to Sar Chashmah you will have to endure a great deal at the hands of Son of the Water Carrier." He said that because he wanted to know if Riżā Bakhsh had said something to me [trying to convince me to get the oath of allegiance] so that he could be sure about his claim regarding Riżā Bakhsh. When he did not hear anything about this from me, he said, "We must think this through so that your actions do not cause you any harm." So Hidāyat Allāh, Sayyid Muḥammad Akbar, and the writer began thinking about the problem but (Khwājah Hidāyat Allāh and Sayyid Muḥammad Akbar) could not think of a way to provide security to Nūr al-Dīn and the members of the delegation and said, "We don't know what can be devised."

I then asked for some paper and wrote a message as if from the Hazārah elders addressed to the leader and members of the delegation. It said,

> The leaders and members of the delegation have brought and shown us the government decrees and the messages full of good advice /269/ entrusted to them. Since the arbābs and elders of the Hazārahs have scattered to their homes because of 'Āshūrā, the tenth of Muḥarram, and because the land of Bihsūd is quite vast, it will be a few days before they return. On their return, they will set forth their conditions and will send them with the delegation which should deliver them to Kabul for the amir's approval. This same delegation should send the accepted conditions back to us. Naturally, if our best interests are taken into account, we will provide an oath of allegiance.

I then copied this message out in another hand and tore up the draft and said to Hidāyat Allāh,

> If the arbābs, sayyids and ulema sign this statement and send it to Son of the Water Carrier, it would be advantageous on two counts. First, the

correspondence will drag on for two months, there will be a cease-fire, and the situations of Muḥammad Nādir Khān in the Southern Province, Muḥammad Hāshim Khān in the Eastern and the displaced Hazārahs in Mazār-i Sharīf will become clearer. Then the right steps will be taken and Son of the Water Carrier will be annihilated. Secondly, once he receives this message, Son of the Water Carrier will have some hope that the Hazārahs will give an oath of allegiance and so will not punish the members of the delegation.

136 Khwājah Hidāyat Allāh | and Sayyid Muḥammad Akbar considered this [solution] acceptable. They agreed that after sending it for signing, they will hand the letter over to me. At that, I summoned Mīr Āqā from the majlis so that no one would accuse me of talking with these other two alone and would not report to Son of the Water Carrier that I had. Then, under my breath, I told Sayyid Muḥammad Akbar that I would draft [a document with] the conditions on which the Hazārahs would give an oath of allegiance. Then all four returned to the majlis[cxii] and Khwājah Hidāyat Allāh left to rejoin Prince Muḥammad Amīn.

From Sar Chashmah, Nūr al-Dīn had written Mullā Muḥammad Zamān, whom he thought influential among the Hazārahs, as he did Mīr Āqā, [and told him] to persuade the Hazārahs to give an oath of allegiance. /270/ To carry this out, he [Muḥammad Zamān] came from [the fort] of Qalʿah-i Nakhshī (Naqshī), about a day's ride away on horseback. Under the direction of Riżā Bakhsh and Mīr Āqā, [Muḥammad Zamān] began to threaten the Hazārahs that if they did not give the oath of allegiance then they would be killed, their belongings confiscated, or they would be arrested. They also called on the Hazārahs to stop fighting for it exposed them to destruction and annihilation.

The Hazārahs, hearing what these two mullahs had to say, were distraught and frightened. On the pretext of needing to relieve myself, I got up and advised those Hazārahs who had also gone outside not to give an oath of allegiance nor to stop fighting Son of the Water Carrier. I encouraged them to follow the Sharīʿah and so bolstered their resolve. Afterwards I secretly added the following conditions [which] Son of the Water Carrier would have to meet for the Hazārahs to offer their oath of allegiance:

First,[199] because an oath of allegiance is an expression of free will according to the Sharīʿah, therefore it is impossible to get such an oath from the Hazārahs by war or by force.

---

199 The author gives both the cardinal number and the ordinal written out. Since this seems unnecessarily repetitious, we have not bothered to include the cardinal numbers from the manuscript.

Second, because the throne was taken away from the Afghans and they are engaged in a war, so the Hazārahs will not give the oath of allegiance until all the Afghans have submitted. Only then will they swear an oath of allegiance.

Third, the taxes for this year are not to be levied again since they were [already] collected and spent by [Prince] Muḥammad Amīn, who was appointed by Amān Allāh Khān.

Fourth, since the nomadic Afghans constantly kill and rob Hazārahs, they must not confiscate the weapons of the latter which they have purchased for the defense and preservation of property, crops, families, and children.

Fifth, after their terms are acknowledged and an oath of allegiance given, the Hazārahs ought not to be drawn /271/ into fighting with Afghans. Should war with their brother-Muslim Afghans break out, then the blood of the dead will be on the conscience of the government. Furthermore, not only have God Most High and the Prophet forbidden the shedding of blood, they have damned those who murder Muslims and promised to send them to Hell for eternity.

Sixth, to avoid offending the honor of the Hazārahs, the government should not station any forces in the Hazārahjāt, either temporarily or permanently.

Seventh, security should be guaranteed to Muḥammad Amīn, his deputy, and his retainers. If he accepts the terms and comes to Kabul, then the government is obligated to pay him a salary equivalent to what is suitable for a prince.

137 *Eighth,* if he does not accept the terms | and does not return to Kabul, then we, with our forces, will escort him across the borders of Afghanistan either to Russia or Iran. The government should take upon itself the obligation of providing a guarantee that the governors and police will not interfere when he crosses [through their territory] nor attack him so that future generations of Hazārahs will not be consumed by the shame that their forebears denied him assistance.

Ninth, all Hazārah tribes who have taken steps to defend themselves and have hesitated to swear allegiance[cxiii] should be considered pardoned and not punished for their refusal to offer obedience.

The author handed these conditions over to Sayyid Muḥammad Akbar, tore his draft up into little pieces, and threw them in the canal there and thus set his own mind at ease about [the consequences of] the stipulations that he had devised himself.

Saturday, 14 Muḥarram, Corresponding to 32 Jawzā [sic] and 22 June

On the eve of this day, the tax collector, Rizā Bakhsh, whose heart was with Son of the Water Carrier, once again escorted Nūr al-Dīn to the tower where his sleeping accommodations were. There the two of them plotted with Naẓar Muḥammad. After the sun rose, /272/ the three of them had tea outside the walls of the fort in the guest house. During breakfast, Riżā Bakhsh, who was sitting beside the author, whispered to me, as if it were a secret, "As soon as Son of the Water Carrier's army comes to Sar Chashmah, let me know immediately, so that a general oath of allegiance could be sent." When I heard this, I thought that he, Nūr al-Dīn, and Naẓar Muḥammad had agreed that after the arrival [of the delegation] in Sar Chashmah, they will not wait for the Hazārahs to send the terms which are set forth in my letter; instead, they will summon military units from Kabul to Sar Chashmah which would frighten the Hazārahs and cause them to send a *bayʿat-nāmah* to Kabul expressing their obedience. After breakfast I discussed the supposition which had taken root in my mind with Sayyid Muḥammad Akbar and insisted to him that the Hazārahs should not give an oath of loyalty nor submit to any tricks of Riżā Bakhsh which could disgrace them.

Later, some 300 men arrived, both mounted and on foot, whom the day before Riżā Bakhsh had assigned to escort Nūr al-Dīn and his companions. At …[200] o'clock, they left Collector Riżā Bakhsh's house, mounted up, and headed for Sar Chashmah. They stopped for a midday meal at the mosque of the Garmāb sayyids. Its imām and caretaker was an Hazārah, Ghulām Rasūl. Lunch began after Mīr Āqā and Khalīfah Ghulām Ḥasan, who had also been invited, performed a recitation of the passion of Imām Ḥusayn. During the meal, I reminded Sayyid Muḥammad Akbar, who was sitting next to me, of my earlier instructions. After the meal, we continued on our way and reached the village of Tīzak in Dāy Mīrdād in the afternoon. There we stopped at the public *imāmbārah*.[201]

Sunday, 15 Muḥarram, Corresponding to 1 Saraṭān and 23 June

We spent the night as guests of the people of Tīzak. I and other members of the delegation were overjoyed at news we heard from two Wardak horsemen of Muḥammad Nādir Khān's successes in the Southern Prov-
138 ince and who were on their way to see | /273/ Prince Muḥammad Amīn. But Nūr al-Dīn, Riżā Bakhsh, and Naẓar Muḥammad, who were traveling with us, immediately began to disparage this information, declaring that the Wardaks were spreading false rumors and propaganda in order to pro-

200 The time is not indicated.

201 *Imāmbārah* is another name for a *ḥusaynīyah*, a congregational hall used for the recitation of the passion of Imām Ḥusayn and for other Shiʿi religious festivals and ceremonies.

voke the Hazārahs into a war with Son of the Water Carrier which would only expose their lives to danger and their property to being plundered.

Yesterday a courier came from Malik Ḥażrat Muḥammad Aḥmadzā'ī, who is a nomad and a landowner in Takānah. I personally heard from him (the courier) enough evidence about what Muḥammad Nādir Khān was doing to refute what those three men were saying. The messenger also mentioned [to me] that the rest of the members of the delegation had moved from Sar Chashmah to Takānah and also that Nūr al-Dīn had given him twenty rupees and a piece of turban cloth as a gift and a "robe of honor" (*khilʿat*). Nūr al-Dīn then sent him back to the other members of the delegation with a letter that he was leaving Kajāb for Sar Chashmah.

On this day after drinking tea we set off for Sar Chashmah. People whom we passed on the road warned us that the Hazārahs had occupied the (Ūnay) Pass and were bent on killing Nūr al-Dīn, Naẓar Muḥammad, and Riżā Bakhsh because they were allies of Son of the Water Carrier. Nūr al-Dīn and Naẓar Muḥammad were upset and frightened by this news and ordered that [the party] turn off the road at the Khirs Khān (*sic*—Khirs Khānah) Pass, ride along the road to Qalʿah-i Nakhshī, in two days cross the pass at Narkh, arrive in Maydān, and from there continue on to Sar Chashmah. Unhappy with their shameful decision, I galloped off with the Hazārahs who were accompanying the delegation. On my heels came other [members of the delegation] who had been trying to give Riżā Bakhsh some encouragement. At the summit of the Khirs Khān (*sic*—Khirs Khānah) Pass, we dismounted and said our farewells to Riżā Bakhsh and the three hundred-man escort. Nūr al-Dīn, afraid of being detained, pleaded with the Hazārahs to take him as far as the positions occupied /274/ by Son of the Water Carrier's forces which[cxiv] included people from Maydān, Kuhnah Khumār, Jalrīz, Takānah, and Sar Chashmah. But I objected, saying, "God forbid. This will surely lead to rebellion. The Hazārahs should not ride down from the pass with us." Then I turned to Riżā Bakhsh and said, "You should behave as Sayyid Muḥammad Akbar was ordered to do. God forbid that you should act in any other way."

Parting company, we set off and reached Sar Chashmah without incident. Nūr al-Dīn wanted to head straight for Takānah after those members of the delegation who had stayed behind and then gone there, fearing an Hazārah attack. I did not agree. "I'll never go there, otherwise we would be disgracing the honor of the people of Sar Chashmah. Word will get out that the people of Sar Chashmah are partisans of the Hazārahs and that is why the leader and members of the delegation did not stay there but went to Takānah."

[139]

At this time, the author's son[202] and another rider arrived from
139 Takānah. | The rider was the one who had brought the message to the members of the delegation that they should return to Sar Chashmah. He now brought a letter from Muḥammad Zamān Parwānī whom the people of Takānah and Jalrīz had browbeaten and wanted to take from Sar Chashmah to Takānah. In this way they could accuse the people of Sar Chashmah of supporting the Hazārahs, thereby dooming them to death and plundering by Son of the Water Carrier. They said to him, "Tonight, the people of Sar Chashmah will bind you hand and foot, hand you over to the Hazārahs and then, in the confusion, will shoot you and say that the Hazārahs attacked and kidnapped you. They will carry you away and kill you as they did 'Abd al-Raḥmān Kūh Dāmanī." Muḥammad Zamān's reply [to them] was, "I will never come. The rest may decide for themselves whether to go or not." Because of my saying that /275/ I would not go to Takānah because the people of that region and also of Jalrīz, due to ignorant religious fanaticism, will plunder Sar Chashmah, for this reason, my son returned [to Takānah]. Muḥammad Zamān did not come while the remaining [members of the delegation] came at night and told me why they had gone to Takānah. [Here is their story]:

> When we received the letter from the Hazārahs who wrote that Nūr al-Dīn along with the members of the delegation had gone as guests to Farākh Ūlūm and had asked them to notify us so that we would leave Sar Chashmah, we understood that they had arrested you. So if we were to remain here then they might attack us at night and arrest us, therefore we decided to go to Takānah. But the people of Sar Chashmah pleaded with us not to leave, assuring us that each of us was perfectly safe and no one would cause us the slightest harm. We believed them and refused to go to Takānah. However, the people of Takānah, having intimidated Muḥammad Zamān, began to abuse the people of Sar Chashmah and so we were unable to stay and were forced to go to them. He himself [Muḥammad Zamān] will come tomorrow and then we will again leave.

Monday, 16 Muḥarram, Corresponding to 2 Saraṭān and 24 June

On this day, at the time of the evening prayer, I gave to Nūr al-Dīn the letter of the Hazārahs in which their terms for an oath of allegiance were laid out. In a separate letter to Son of the Water Carrier Nūr al-Dīn described in detail his detention, accusing Fatḥ Muḥammad of being responsible for it. But I did not let him sign it and admonished him saying,

---

[202] This was probably his eldest son 'Abd al-Ṣamad. See Fayż Muḥammad, *The History*, vol. 1, p. xlviii.

> Look, the Hazārahs wrote in their letter that a regular army colonel and his sepoys had arrested the leader and members of his delegation. If that should be blamed on Fatḥ Muḥammad, then Son of the Water Carrier will try to take revenge on him. The Hazārahs, feeling oppressed, will begin to revolt.

So having said this, together we altered the text of Nūr al-Dīn's letter and sent it to Kabul to the godless one, the commander of the thieves. /276/ Muḥammad Zamān [Parwānī] also came from Takānah. He was relieved when he heard what the people of Sar Chashmah and I had to say and obliged me to tell Nūr al-Dīn that his legs were bothering him and that
140 he wanted permission to go to Kabul. I promised to help him, | passed his request on to Nūr al-Dīn, and got permission for him to return to the city.

At this time Malik Ḥażrat Muḥammad, Sayyid Abū'l-Qāsim, and Sayyid Zayn al-ʿĀbidīn arrived, on [the latter of] whom the high governor Malik Muḥsin had bestowed the title "military and civil brigadier" for having promised, as mentioned earlier, to get the Hazārahs to give an oath of allegiance. They had come to find out about the situation of Nūr al-Dīn, what happened to him in the Hazārah[jāt], and to ascertain whether the Hazārahs were going to give an oath of allegiance or not.

Having learned what had transpired with Nūr al-Dīn and that the Hazārahs are promising to give an oath of allegiance only if their terms are accepted, these men were delighted. Taking me aside, Malik Ḥażrat Muḥammad said,

> God grant that the negotiations and correspondence drag on for a long time until the situation with Muḥammad Nādir Khān and Muḥammad Hāshim Khān, the question of the alliance of the Afghan tribes of the Eastern and Southern Provinces, the activities of the displaced Hazārahs of Turkistān and Darrah-i Ṣūf and also the outcome of the struggle in Bāmyān between Mīr Faqīr and the forces of Son of the Water Carrier under the command of Brigadier General ʿAbd al-Rashīd are all clarified. By that time, with the help of the Almighty, Son of the Water Carrier will have been defeated, Muḥammad Nādir Khān with his brothers and the valiant Afghans will have taken Kabul, and it will not be necessary for Hazārahs to give an oath of allegiance.

Malik Ḥażrat Muḥammad took me aside and questioned me about the fighting in Bāmyān and about the siege there of the forces of Son of the Water Carrier. From me he heard that at the request of Nūr al-Dīn "Saqqawī," the Hazārahs sent a letter to Mīr Faqīr, who having suffered defeat, had again gone to Bāmyān with his tribal forces and engaged in renewed fighting. The message they sent was that he should stop fighting and hold his position until it became clear whether the terms of the Hazārahs were going to be accepted or not.

After this, Malik Ḥażrat Muḥammad gave an Afghan twenty-five rupees /277/ and sent him to the Southern Province to get information. (Malik Ḥażrat Muḥammad] promised me, "I will pass on any accurate information that I receive from the man I'm sending and you should keep me informed about the Hazārahs so that they don't tender their allegiance because they are in the dark about the lies and propaganda of Nūr al-Dīn." Also, as a result of the events that took place, the Hazārahs abandoned the plans they had made on the 14th of Muḥarram to attack. As already recounted, Nūr al-Dīn himself was soon handed over to the Hazārahs.

Tuesday, 17 Muḥarram, Corresponding to 3 Saraṭān and 25 June 1929

On this day, Muḥammad Zamān and Naẓar Muḥammad, worried that the Hazārahs would attack them, spent the night together with Nūr al-Dīn inside the fort at Pusht-i Mazār in Sar Chashmah. They resolved to tell Son of the Water Carrier that only a menacing presence of combat-ready forces would compel the Hazārahs to obedience. Otherwise, hoping that Muḥammad Nādir Khān would arrive in Kabul, they will just keep dragging their feet on the issue of the *bayʿat-nāmah* with various tricks and stratagems and offering "maybes" and "perhapses." Therefore, it was essential to send a powerful force from Kabul to Sar Chashmah which would terrify the Hazārahs and force them with all due speed to give an oath of allegiance and express their obedience, otherwise the matter will drag on for a long time and the government will get no satisfaction. Apparently
141 Riżā Bakhsh, who had earlier given an oath of allegiance in secret, | urged [Muḥammad Zamān and Naẓar Muḥammad] that night in the fort to do this provocative thing [to make sure that a force was dispatched from Kabul]. Probably Riżā Bakhsh had this in mind when he had said to me, "As soon as the army comes from Kabul to Sar Chashmah, tell me, so that I can send an oath of allegiance right away, not waiting for the acceptance of the [Hazārahs'] terms."

Muḥammad Zamān and Naẓar Muḥammad having set off for Kabul spent that night in Jalrīz and heard inflammatory statements from the Tajiks there and from Muḥammad Aman, a baker (*nānwā*),[cxv] a Tajik from Kuhnah Khumār who had received the post of district chief and also from local Tajiks /278/ who were the cause of all trouble, bloodshed, and looting in Maydān and Sar Chashmah.

Also on this day, Malik Ḥażrat Muḥammad, having received information about the situation in the Southern Province through the agent he sent there, told me of the treasonous activities of Mullā Shāh Naẓar and other pseudo-mullahs. Employing unsavory propaganda, these mullahs are causing the Sulaymān Khayl, Aḥmadzā'ī, Matūn, Ṣabarī, Muqbil, Jājī, Jadrān, Mangal and other tribes to forget Afghan honor and valor and are preventing the tribes from joining forces with Muḥammad Nādir Khān. Muḥammad Nādir Khān is without funds, in need, and isolated while Son of the Water Carrier, through proclamations and spies, has promised vast monetary rewards to the pseudo-mullahs and tribal elders. He has already given them a portion of the money and makes them greedy for more. Having shaken up all the Afghan tribes, he is turning Afghan unity and concord away from Muḥammad Nādir Khān and winning them to his side. Major General Ghulām Ṣiddīq, son of Khwājah Jān, having exerted every effort to gain the upper hand for the Saqqawīs, is working hard to obstruct Muḥammad Nādir Khān's plans. No one knows what all this will lead to.

I was quite upset after receiving this information from Malik Ḥażrat Muḥammad. Now I can only put my hope in the assistance and will of the Creator of Mankind.

Wednesday, 18 Muḥarram, Corresponding to 4 Saraṭān and 26 June

On this day, Muḥammad Zamān [Parwānī] and Naẓar Muḥammad, having left Jalrīz like the emissaries of Satan, arrived in Kabul. I had asked Muḥammad Zamān to deliver to my family some money which I had received from a person who owed me money and he brought the money himself to my house. He still believed that I was sincere in my service to Son of the Water Carrier because I had gotten a letter from the Hazārahs in which they promised to provide an oath of allegiance /279/ and express their obedience. He was ignorant of the fact that a deep pit had now been dug in the road of Son of the Water Carrier's plans and that the Hazārahs were not going to give an oath of allegiance.

On this day, with flags flying, drums beating, and shouting "Four Friends!" some 200 Wardak men marched towards Prince Muḥammad Amīn along the road to Rāh Qūl through Tizak and Kajāb in aid of the Hazārahs. This was distressing to the Saqqawīs and heartened the Hazārahs and the people of true religion and faith.

This evening an Afghan from the village of Zāy Manī in Maydān arrived, as did a rider sent by the sayyids of Takānah who had been calling for an alliance of Afghans and Hazārahs against Son of the Water Carrier.
142 | These two men, who had been keeping the Hazārahs informed of the course of military activities, arrived at the Ūnay Pass in the guise of buying wheat and brought two letters from Muḥammad Nādir Khān. Despite the

fact that Nūr al-Dīn, Mīr Āqā, Khalīfah Ghulām Hasan, Mīrzā Muḥammad Qāsim, and Muḥammad Mahdī Afshār were there, I asked [the two men] to conceal the letters from the others. I thanked them and asked them to deliver [the message] to the Hazārahs that they stand firm and not give an oath of allegiance.

Thursday, 19 Muḥarram, Corresponding to 5 Saraṭān and 27 June

On this day, Fatḥ Muḥammad, the high commissioner of the Ūnay Pass, sent Zaw, a sheep-seller from the Hazārah clan of Chulī, to Nūr al-Dīn, ostensibly to negotiate a truce but in fact to ascertain his and Son of the Water Carrier's plans regarding the Hazārahs. (Fatḥ Muḥammad) had sent a message, couched in polite terms, about a truce. Nūr al-Dīn gave the messenger a piece of *sundī*[203] turban cloth as a *khilʿat* and 70 rupees for oil as well as a message to Fatḥ Muḥammad which said that /**280**/ without waiting for approval of the conditions [submitted by the Hazārahs], he should send a tribal and general oath of allegiance in order that he subject neither himself nor the Hazārahs to being killed and plundered. In addition, he should also return what he had confiscated from Nūr al-Dīn—the farman which authorized his mission, the amirid decrees concerning his promises, and his watch, pistol, and knife. If he did, then everything would be satisfactorily resolved, the need to summon an army would not arise, nor the need to exterminate the Hazārahs. Zaw, having deduced the real plans of Nūr al-Dīn, decided to depart for the Hazārah positions at the [Ūnay] Pass. But I called him aside and told him that the residents of Kabul, Chahārdihī, Pamqān, Maymanah, Arghandah, Maydān, Lahūgard, and Wardak were united with the Hazārahs and were just waiting for the Hazārahs to attack Kabul and for Muḥammad Nādir Khān to attack Lahūgard. Having thus been given new hope, Zaw carried a message to Fatḥ Muḥammad which told him not to be hasty in giving an oath of allegiance for, with the help of various ruses, they could drag things out until Muḥammad Nādir Khān's situation could be ascertained.

At this time Ghulām Ḥabīb Qizilbāsh approached Nūr al-Dīn, the two of them having strong ties, carrying a small earthenware pot of yoghurt and several pieces of fried sweetened flatbread. He owned a fort in Ūnay and had a dispute going with the local Hazārahs, in particular the Hazārahs of the fort of Qalʿah-i Karīm, over water and pasture. Nūr al-Dīn asked him,

---

[203] The ms. (p. 142, line 9) adds the vowel "u" so there is no confusing the word *sundī* with "Sindi" or "sanadī." So far we have been unable to determine the kind of lungi cloth this was.

"Why haven't the Hazārahs up to now presented terms?" He answered, "If the residents of Ūnay would allow it, then the Hazārahs would give an oath of allegiance and right away conduct you across my land. But instead the people of Ūnay say all sorts of lies to them about Muḥammad Nādir Khān and keep them from giving an oath of allegiance and expressing their obedience." I was indignant and said,

> How is it possible for you, who consider yourself an adherent of Islam and a follower of the Infallible Imams, to heap dirt on the peasants who pay
> 143 one-quarter of their earnings in taxes | and who, from the very beginning right up to now, along with the residents of Sar Chashmah, day in and day out supply the 100 sepoys of Son of the Water Carrier with baked bread. In addition they have [already] provided the Saqqawī soldiers in Qalʿah-i Durrānī with fifty kharwārs of wheat, flour, barley, mutton, firewood, and cooking oil. /281/ You slander them because you have some issues with them about land and water. By means of such slander, you want all of them to be attacked, plundered, and destroyed.

I then encouraged him to "do good and eschew evil" and finally he repented his inappropriate words and affirmed his devotion to Islam and his willingness to protect other Muslims.

Also on this day, Son of the Water Carrier received the letter from the Hazārahs which contained the terms [under which they would give an oath of allegiance]. Muḥammad Zamān and Naẓar Muḥammad also delivered to his oppressive and unjust presence the message from Nūr al-Dīn. Son of the Water Carrier was furious when he learned from Colonel Niẓām al-Dīn and the district chief of Kuhnah Khumār, the baker Muḥammad Amān, that the Hazārahs had advanced one kurūh from the Ūnay Pass towards Sar Chashmah, had pitched their tents and thrown up breastworks. He ordered his brother, the Muʿīn al-Salṭanah Ḥamīd Allāh Khān, to go to Sar Chashmah the next day with 50 incorrigible bloodthirsty cutthroats and find out what was going on. If the Hazārahs [in fact] had advanced one kurūh, then he should bombard them with cannon and rifle fire and drive them off.

Friday, 20 Muḥarram, Corresponding to 6 Saraṭān and 28 June

On this day at 8 A.M. I was in my room, whose door was separated from the entryway door by a vestibule (*dihlīz*) off which was also the door to the room of Nūr al-Dīn. I was writhing from side to side in pain when I heard the sound of an automobile horn and people shouting. A few moments later, the younger son of the water carrier, Ḥamīd Allāh Khān, walked

into the room. He was on his way from the capital to Sar Chashmah with the group of fifty of his associates, a bunch of hardened thugs. They had left their cars on the highway since there was no road up the mountain towards the house where Nūr al-Dīn was staying. A number of soldiers were with him, some of whom were holding the handles, others the barrels of machine guns. Overcome by terror, Nūr al-Dīn called for me. /282/ To Mīrzā Muḥammad Qāsim he said, "Send a message to the Hazārahs who are in their positions at the Ūnay Pass and ask them why we don't yet have their terms for an oath of allegiance?" When I heard this order coming from the seriously frightened Nūr al-Dīn, I thought that if fighting broke out, they would accuse the members of the delegation of inciting the Hazārahs, persuading them not to send terms, warning them of the arrival of Ḥamīd Allāh, and provoking them to take action. Therefore, I quickly asked Mīrzā Muḥammad Qāsim for the register of documents, opened it, and showed it to Ḥamīd Allāh who had come in and failed to utter a greeting nor let slip even a single word. I said, "There's no need to write the Hazārahs. Here, look at the register. It is [clear] from it that the
144 contemplated plans | are nearing resolution. It's not worth being hasty or overanxious." However, that man, who was a stupid opinionated person of low origins and who earlier earned his living as a dancer at weddings, then participated in the raids and robberies of his brother, became used to a debauched life, and now, as a result of the shameful behavior of dishonorable pseudo-mullahs, who have absolutely nothing in common with the religion, is honored with the title "Muʿīn al-Salṭanah" and is puffed up with conceit and self-satisfaction like a fiery red balloon, paid no attention to the register or the notes in it and headed for the summit of the mountain on foot. Nūr al-Dīn and a son of Fatḥ Muḥammad, Muḥammad ʿAlī, a descendant of Khān Shīrīn Khān Jawānshayr, a Qizilbāsh, who hoped to become governor of Bihsūd for which reason he had volunteered to be on the delegation, accompanied Ḥamīd Allāh and the other brigands up the mountain which overlooked the forts of the Ūnay Pass.

From the heights they descended to Qalʿah-i Safīd, where Ghulām Ḥabīb [Qizilbāsh] lived. They asked him about the peasants of Qalʿah-i Karīm, well-to-do oilsellers: "And these people, are they with /283/ us or against us?" That infidel, lacking any conscience and at odds with them over land, pasture and water, said that they were the enemy and were partisans of the Hazārahs.

Ḥamīd Allāh, who was an ignorant libertine and would do anything that he took it into his head to do, now, showing consummate arrogance, ordered his men to open fire on Qalʿah-i Karīm with rifles and cannons.

One man was killed and an eight or nine year old girl was wounded. The men of the fort fled into the mountains. That heartless infidel, Ḥamīd Allāh, ordered his gangsters to set fire to the fort and to carry off the property and valuables of its inhabitants. The residents of Takānah, Jalrīz, Kuhnah Khumār and Qalʿah-i Majīd, wild fanatics all, had long been awaiting that day. At Ḥamīd Allāh Khān's order, they, who had saluted him when he passed their forts on the way to Sar Chashmah, poured down on Qalʿah-i Karīm with hundreds of men on foot under the command of the infidel Colonel Niẓām al-Dīn who had been guarding Sar Chashmah from Hazārah attack, beating drums, banners flying, and shouting "O Four Friends!" and consigned it and other forts of Ūnay to fire and sword. They burned practically all the forts in the region up to Ūnay, drove off the livestock, and looted anything that could be carried away. As for Ḥamīd Allāh, he set up a machine gun on the top of the mountain and began to fire down on the tents of the Hazārahs who had come down from the pass and set up their tents there. Taking down their tents, the Hazārahs headed back to their sangars at the top of the pass.

Into the night, rifle and machinegun fire rang out and the forts continued to burn. That night, when the residents of Ūnay Pass, having lost all their possessions had gone into hiding in the mountains, Ḥamīd Allāh took prisoner forty women and girls along with their children and brought them to Qalʿah-i Safīd where he handed them over to Ghulām Ḥabīb. After fortifying strategic places there with some brave souls, he went back to the city. /284/ During the evening, from the battlefield, he ordered Nūr al-Dīn to prepare one kharwār and 40 seers by the Kabul weight standard
145 | of baked bread. He told Ḥamīd Allāh that the residents of Ūnay are subject to the thieving Saqqawī government [and therefore would provide the food]. [Ḥamīd Allāh] ordered Ghulām Ḥabīb to keep the women at Qalʿah-i Safīd. Until midnight, Nūr al-Dīn busied himself delivering the one and a half kharwārs of baked bread to the regular and tribal forces of Son of the Water Carrier [Ḥamīd Allāh] on the shoulders of the peoples of Sar Chashmah who had baked the bread themselves. He himself spent the night in utter terror.

Saturday, 21 Muḥarram, Corresponding to 7 Saraṭān and 29 June

On this day in Bāmyān, after the Hazārahs agreed to send the list of terms they expected to have approved in return for their oath of allegiance, they left the passes and the fighting with Son of the Water Carrier's forces there subsided.

This evening Nūr al-Dīn wrote Ḥamīd Allāh a letter in which he asked for instructions as to what he and the members of the delegation should do now that fighting had started. He wrote that the one whom God has forsaken (Ḥamīd Allāh Khān) had returned from the battlefield to Sar Chashmah, where he will spend the night and the next day begin fighting the Hazārahs [again]. However, Ḥamīd Allāh left for the city and so Nūr al-Dīn received no reply. He imagined that Ḥamīd Allāh would return the next day and he would give him his letter and receive an order in return. While he was sitting and waiting for him, Ḥamīd Allāh with a large band of thieves, marched through the Ūnay Pass without coming to Sar Chashmah, headed for the Hazārah positions and paid no attention to Nūr al-Dīn's letter.

After Ḥamīd Allāh left the battlefield, a member of the delegation, Muḥammad Mahdī Afshārī, said that he had decided to return to Kabul. "Whether they permit me or not, I am going to leave anyway because now that war has started my responsibility [as a member of the delegation] is no longer relevant," he said. Mīr Āqā also supported him and they both decided to leave. I warned the two of them /285/ that before they left they should consult with Nūr al-Dīn as the leader of the delegation. They should be sure to act in such a way that he (Nūr al-Dīn) would not be able to tell Son of the Water Carrier that they had returned at their own behest and he would not avenge himself by persecuting the feeble tribe of the Qizilbāsh, whose members they are, even though they were chosen for the mission against their will. As I had advised, half an hour later they approached Nūr al-Dīn and it was decided that the entire delegation would return to Kabul together.

So, we rode out of Sar Chashmah on horseback. On the pretext that we were supposedly going to Takānah, we managed to get ourselves to the main road via secret paths, and then headed to Kabul. En route, I turned to Nūr al-Dīn and Mīr Āqā and said,

> Words may or may not have an effect but if I remain silent they certainly won't. Whether you listen to me or not, I must speak out. I advise that we go to the governor of Maydān and inform Ḥabīb Allāh by telephone of our situation and ask for instructions as to how to proceed while fighting is going on. This, so that we are not persecuted for willfully leaving the scene without instructions.

They agreed to my suggestion and so we headed for the governor in
146 Maydān. | At a shop near the caravanserai in Kūt-i ʿAshrū, we stopped for tea. My temperature was rising and I rode in last. Approaching an

automobile which was parked near the shops and in which four armed men were sitting, I tried to pass unnoticed. But a hearty bearded fellow sitting in the car, called out, "Whose convoy is this and whose riders are these?" I answered, "This is the Hazārahjāt delegation empowered to achieve peace. Since the Muʿīn al-Salṭanah has started fighting, we're returning to the city." Another sepoy sitting in the car whose beard was shaved off and whose appearance as a result seemed to be that of a bloodthirsty thief, rudely said, "This is the high governor [Malik Muḥsin], so get off your horse." /286/ I replied, "I didn't recognize him." I said, "Salaam ʿalaykum" and stood there for a few minutes [still mounted] and then apologized that I could not dismount and explained, "I'm very sick. If I dismount I won't be able to mount again." I then rode on and got down from my horse near the other riders.

At that moment they summoned Nūr al-Dīn since he had freely volunteered to obtain an oath of allegiance from the Hazārahs and, as has already been mentioned, headed a delegation made up of representatives from Maydān, Zāy Manī, Kūt-i ʿAshrū, Māmakī, Jalrīz, Takānah, Sar Chashmah, and Ūnay. The Hazārahs had asked that they be given a certain grace period. Eight days still remained until the deadline by which time the Hazārahs were supposed to swear an oath of allegiance. Since Nūr al-Dīn had volunteered to speed matters up and personally promised to obtain the oath of allegiance but had been unable to do so, the high governor, Malik Muḥsin, now whipped him with more than 100 lashes despite the fact that he was only wearing light summer clothing. He abused him verbally as well, cursing his religion and his family, and asked him, "What did you do with the ten thousand rupees?" and swore that he would get it back.

Having beaten Nūr al-Dīn black and blue, he set off by car towards Sar Chashmah to find out how the fighting was progressing. Ḥamīd Allāh, having arrived at [Ūnay] Pass before him, dispersed the Hazārahs, of whom fewer than 100 were still in position, the rest having scattered and gone home. He killed a number of men including the Hazārah leader, Colonel Khayr Muḥammad Niẓāmī, who had fought bravely, cut his head off, and sent it to the city where it was hung on the Chawk. With his forces, whose weapons included machine guns, he advanced to Yūrt, seized the pass and established his forces in the Hazārah positions. He then brought to the city a satchel which had fallen into his hands and which contained the correspondence of the slain colonel.

Nūr al-Dīn and the other members of the delegation changed their minds about going to Maydān and from there asking permission from Son of the Water Carrier and instead headed directly for Kabul. Fearing the high governor [Malik Muḥsin], who might arrest them on his return from the battlefield, they avoided the main road and made for the capital by way of Qalʿah-yi Ghulām Ḥaydar Khān and Chihil Tan. On the way, Nūr al-Dīn secretly sent the pack animals and most of the members of the delegation to Afshār[204] with the idea that he himself would go to the city to Muḥammad Aʿẓam, president of the Islamic Regulatory and Reform Commission[205] and his mentor and ally, in order to tell him what had hap-
147 pened and | that he had left the delegation in Maydān while he himself had come to the city to get permission. With this naive idea in mind, he arrived in the capital in the evening accompanied by his son, son-in-law, Muḥammad ʿAlī, and me, and went to his own home. That same evening he wanted to meet with Muḥammad Aʿẓam but out of fear of the high governor, (Muḥammad Aʿẓam) refused to see him.

Sunday, 22 Muḥarram, Corresponding to 8 Saraṭān and 30 June

On this day, the high governor, Malik Muḥsin, ordered the arrest of Nūr al-Dīn and the confiscation of the goods in his baggage train. Nūr al-Dīn placated him by sending some of his 10,000 rupees by the hand of the Qizilbāsh Ḥasan ʿAlī. Ḥasan ʿAlī was the former clerk of the aide-de-camp, Maḥmūd Khān (Yāwar). He was now on assignment to [Malik Muḥsin], and was deeply involved in extorting money and confiscating property for the high governor who was [therefore] quite pleased with him. Consequently, the high governor rescinded the order for Nūr al-Dīn's arrest.

Also on this day Ḥamīd Allāh again set off for [Qalʿah-i] Yūrt. When he had gotten as far as the caravanserai of Jawqūl without encountering any resistance he arrogantly thought that he would be able to capture all of the

204 Afshār, now a Kabul neighborhood, was established in the 18th century by the Iranian warlord and conqueror, Nādir Shāh Afshār, as a military camp. It had since been inhabited by Qizilbāsh claiming descent from the troops garrisoned there. In 1898, the amir, ʿAbd al-Raḥmān Khān, forcibly purchased the lands and forts of the Qizilbāsh there and made them leave. At the time it was a walled village with about 100 houses contained within high (15–20 foot) walls. (See Fayż Muḥammad, *The History*, vol. 4, pp. 361–62 and Adamec, *Gazetteer* 6, pp. 15–16.).

205 This is the same as the Islamic Regulatory Commission mentioned earlier now with the words "and Reform (*wa iṣlāḥīyah*)" added.

Hazārahjāt. He ordered his forces to occupy the mountaintops which the courageous [Hazārah] troops had left. Along the road from [Qalʿah-i] Yūrt to this place [Jawqūl] he had burned down all the forts and the men of his command had made off with livestock and belongings. A small group of Hazārahs, whose homes had been burned, kept up a resistance in the mountains until evening. /288/ Ḥamīd Allāh, in a happy frame of mind, came galloping into Sar Chashmah and from there returned by automobile to the city. At night he opened the satchel of the slain colonel, Khayr Muḥammad, whose head they had hung [at the Chawk], and found a number of unsigned letters from residents of Chahārdihī, Pamqān, Arghandah, Lahūgard, and Maydān addressed to the Hazārahs. These expressed support for the Hazārahs' struggle against Son of the Water Carrier and promised to give them help whenever they decided to attack Kabul. Among the letters, he found one from the residents of Sar Chashmah signed on the first of Ṣawr and addressed to the high commissioner of the Hazārahjāt. They expressed the hope that the Hazārahs would release and treat with respect ʿAbd al-Raḥmān, son of Dād Muḥammad Kūhistānī, a good and kind fellow, and an advocate of peace and good order. But the Hazārahs did not fulfill this request. They put ʿAbd al-Raḥmān to death after Son of the Water Carrier hanged their general representative or ombudsman (*wakīl-i ʿumūmī*), Mīrākhūr Aḥmad ʿAlī.

Although this letter was addressed to the high commissioner, [Ḥamīd Allāh], a wicked man deprived of all common sense, had no idea when it was written and even who the high commissioner was, although it was, in fact, Prince Muḥammad Amīn, and put all the blame on Nūr al-Dīn and also the members of the delegation, who represented the Qizilbāsh. In order to get authorization to investigate, he took the letter to his older brother, king of the thieves, who had awarded himself the title of "servant of the religion of the Prophet of God," although in fact all he did was destroy the religion of the Prophet of God.

Monday, 23 Muḥarram, Corresponding to 9 Saraṭān and 1 July

148 | On this day Ḥamīd Allāh went to Sar Chashmah, having postponed to a later date the investigation of the non-existent faults of Nūr al-Dīn, the members of his delegation, and the tribes of the Qizilbāsh. Because of the letter which should have proved to Ḥamīd Allāh that the people of Sar Chashmah are obedient and honest [because they asked the Hazārahs to release a Kūhistānī], /289/ Ḥamīd Allāh instead ordered the looting and burning of their homes and forts, notwithstanding the fact that the

[148]

majority of the residents of Sar Chashmah had the titles "hajji," "Karbalāʾī," and "Zuwwār," paid the *zakāt* and the *khums*, were devout adherents of the religion, worked, for the most part, as oilsellers, and were well-off. He ordered Ḥājjī Sulṭān Muḥammad, whose only way was God's way, put before a firing squad at the cemetery of Pusht-i Mazār and executed him.

[At Ḥamīd Allāh's order] they also looted the people of Takānah, Jalrīz and Kuhnah Khumār. These were people who were members of the disruptive and troublemaking Tajik tribe and enthusiastic supporters of Son of the Water Carrier. They plundered not only their trade goods—oil, carpets, dishes, livestock—but even the mosques and *imāmbārahs*. The looting even went as far as removing doors from homes. Over several days, [Ḥamīd Allāh's men] carted away the stolen goods to their own homes. It is said that they looted property worth fifteen lakhs of rupees.

Ḥamīd Allāh brought thirty-four male prisoners and forty women to Kabul. He resolved to sell the women and so lodged them in separate houses. The men he kept imprisoned with nothing to eat or drink. Although (Ḥabīb Allāh Khān Kalakānī) gave himself the title "servant of the faith of the Prophet of God" yet he had forbidden food and water be given the prisoners. Consequently, the Qizilbāsh, with the help of a kindly and sympathetic municipal official (*maʾmūr-i baladīyah*), Muḥammad Ibrāhīm, collected money and secretly passed it to some bakers. Ostensibly receiving the money from the residents of Sar Chashmah themselves, the bakers brought food to the prisoners and this lasted until the bakers themselves were repressed.

Tuesday, 24 Muḥarram, Corresponding to 10 Saraṭān and 2 July

Ḥamīd Allāh, formerly a dancer at wedding venues, who now had reached the rank of Muʿīn al-Salṭanah thanks to the godlessness of the ḥażrats and pseudo-mullahs who, in reality, are nothing but devils in disguise and, like animals, have no consciences, yesterday was defeated in a fight with Hazārah devotees of Islam in the region /290/ of Jawqūl. He lost many soldiers, machine guns, six-pound guns, rifles, and ammunition. On the road back, in a wild rage, he considered the inhabitants of Sar Chashmah to be Hazārahs, although they were submissive subjects, looted their property, took them prisoner, and burned their forts.

Taking these prisoners to Kabul, he decided to kill the men and, as already mentioned, sell their women. On the basis of a letter found in the satchel of the slain Colonel Khayr Muḥammad and the message of Nūr al-Dīn, sent through Naẓar Muḥammad and Muḥammad Zamān, in which he asked that an army be sent from Kabul to Sar Chashmah to frighten the Hazārahs, Ḥamīd Allāh accused Nūr al-Dīn and the members of his delegation of conspiracy, as a consequence of which the Hazārahs had started a war and he himself had suffered defeat. At night he appeared before his older brother, commander of the thieves, who from poverty, indigence, and wandering through mountain and desert, had now achieved the position of amir. He received permission from that stony-hearted and irrational thief to exterminate the Qizilbāsh, to sell the women and children into slavery, and to confiscate their property.

149 | At one o'clock in the afternoon, taking 800 pig-resembling blood-drinking mankind-oppressing bandits, Ḥamīd Allāh headed for [the Kabul quarter of] Chandāwul via Sar-i Chawk and Bāghbān Kūchah. Stopping at Sih Dukkān bazaar, which was adjacent to the gates of Chandāwul, he ordered his armed bandits to stand guard at every door in Chandāwul so that no man, woman, nursing infant, or old man could leave their homes. Then they either could be killed or taken captive and no one could escape one or the other fate. Having issued this order, he tried to enter Chandāwul and begin the killing and looting.

Marginalia: At this time, the residents of Kabul, having realized that while today this misfortune might happen to the Qizilbāsh, tomorrow it could happen to them, armed themselves, hiding small lances, pistols, axes, and other things under their coats or robes and headed for Chandāwul just /**291**/ as if they were a sociable group having an outing. They resolved, in the event of the slaying of the Qizilbāsh, to slaughter the bandit-infidels and let fate and divine will decide the winners and losers. [End of marginal note.]

The mayor, Khwājah Tāj al-Dīn, who in comparison with other Kūh Dāmanīs and Kūhistānīs was a very good-natured person and had consistently defended the residents of Kabul and other [regions] from the assaults, killings, muggings, and insults of the diabolical Northerners, now, on seeing this scene unfold like the Day of Judgement, was overcome by feelings of alarm. Using every means he knew and every trick at his disposal, he tried to prevent Ḥamīd Allāh from entering Chandāwul. First, he led him to his own headquarters located next to Qalʿah-i Bāqir Khān connected to Chandāwul and asked him why he was so upset and what had spoiled his usually happy frame of mind. Ḥamīd Allāh showed Khwājah Tāj al-Dīn the unsigned letter with the oaths of allegiance of many anonymous people. Therefore he did not know which village, region, or tribe these people were from. He also said,

> Nūr al-Dīn persuaded the Hazārahs not to give an oath of allegiance nor submit; he encouraged them to fight, and treacherously called for a force to be sent. Because of his scheming, we have failed and the Hazārahs have won. As a result, permission was received from the amir and so the Qizilbāsh must be punished for their treason.

When Khwājah Tāj al-Dīn saw the letter, he realized it was dated in the first days of Ṣawr while he had information that Nūr al-Dīn's departure was in the last days of Jawzā [i.e. almost two months later]. He then quietly explained to the ignoramus Ḥamīd Allāh,

> The residents of Sar Chashmah, out of goodwill, sincerity, integrity, and as a service to you, wrote this letter in Ṣawr (April–May) to Prince Muḥammad Amīn, who was named by Amīr Amān Allāh Khān to the post of high commissioner of the Hazārahjāt, only in order to intercede for ʿAbd al-Raḥmān Khān (Kūh Dāmanī). It is dated to Ṣawr and Nūr al-Dīn's was sent /**292**/ at the end of Jawzā (May–June) and there's a difference here of almost two months.

Ḥamīd Allāh [having heard what Tāj al-Dīn had said] now ashamed of himself wanted to leave but his nephew (sister's son), Iskandar, and others under [Ḥamīd Allāh's] command, having occupied themselves bringing the members of the delegation to an outbuilding of Nūr al-Dīn's along with all the Qizilbāsh officials from the reign of His Majesty Amān Allāh Khān
150 | to make short shrift of them, while the Qizilbāsh, far from their original homeland [Iran], awaited the Day of Resurrection. Now the *kalāntar*, Sulṭān ʿAlī, and Naṣr al-Dīn, son of Nūr al-Dīn, with extraordinary cruelty and fury dragged the author and several middle-aged Qizilbāsh civil servants from their houses to city hall under guard. Most of them, expecting to be robbed and killed, had hidden in their homes in fear behind locked doors, while I was sick and had kept to my bed, At the moment when Mīr Āqā and some other Qizilbāsh, who feared me, appeared before Ḥamīd Allāh, Nūr al-Dīn showed up. Standing above the crowd, Ḥamīd Allāh addressed the Qizilbāsh who had been rounded up and were standing below under the scorching rays of the sun, expecting the order of death to be passed on them. He said in an admonishing tone,

> As long as I live I will serve the faith and nation of Islam. Yesterday, had the Hazārahs killed me in the fight which took place because of the treachery of Nūr al-Dīn, how would I, being dead, be able to serve the government and the nation? Since this delegation represents the tribe [of the Qizilbāsh], therefore I ask of you, greybeards and elders of the tribe, how should I deal with them?

The voice of Sayyid Ṭahmāsp was heard, "Shoot them!" Mullā Ḥusayn ʿAlī, who ought to have said, "Since they represent the tribe, hand them over to their tribe and name a reliable person from your side. If it emerges that they have committed an offense, /293/ then the tribe will kill them," said only, "Pardon them!" Ḥamīd Allāh shouted at him, "Shut your mouth! (Literally, eat your beard!) How can I pardon them for such offenses when I almost died?" Then he ordered them to be caned and beaten black and blue. Afterwards if they were still alive, they should be shot and their corpses nailed to the [city] gates.

So they took Nūr al-Dīn, Mīr Āqā, and me from the large room on the upper floor [of city hall] where we had been waiting. Twenty-four bloodthirsty Afghans from the Hūd Khayl tribe along with Kūh Dāmanī and Kūhistānī bandits stood in a circle. Behind their backs they held bundles of cherry and almond sticks at the ready. First, they knocked Nūr al-Dīn and then Mīr Āqā to the ground and beat them almost to death. Nūr al-Dīn was only able to utter, "For God's sake ... for God's sake ..." While they were beating him, Mīr Āqā managed to utter a couple of times, "We were only doing our duty ..." As for me, one stick caught me in the forehead and blood drenched my face and beard. I whispered one of the prayers of Abū Ḥamzah al-Thumalī, the Ḥażrat Sayyid al-Sājidīn:[206] "Oh, God! Guard me with Your guarding and preserve me by Your preserving." I made no other cry and did not ask for justice.

We three were supposed to die from the beating. But because there were so many cane-wielding bandits taking part in the execution, [only] three or four of the canes actually hit us, the rest of the time the executioners managed only to strike each other's sticks and so we survived. After the beating, Mullā Muḥammad Yūnus, a diabolical person known
151 as Mawlawī Jang, demanded of Ḥamīd Allāh that he | throw us in prison and confiscate our homes. But Ḥamīd Allāh, who had had us caned without our having committed any crime or treachery, let us go home. [Then] Muḥammad Yūnus Jang said, "A number of times you have vowed that if you caught any Shiʿis, you would crush them into little bits with pliers. Now that God has delivered the opportunity to you, you should carry out your promise towards the people of the faith and earn the title *ghāzī*." But Ḥamīd Allāh did not respond.

---

[206] Thābit b. Ṣafiyah known as Abū Ḥamzah al-Thumalī, a contemporary of the early Shiʿi imams, Zayn al-ʿĀbidīn, Muḥammad Bāqir, and Jaʿfar al-Ṣādiq, was renowned for the efficacy of his prayer (*duʿā*) of supplication. See "Abu Hamza al-Thumali," *Wikipedia*.

[151]

The Qizilbāsh and the relatives of Nūr al-Dīn and Mīr Āqā collected them. /294/ One they took to his own home and the other to his sister's home. A member of the delegation, Muḥammad ʿAlī, a grandson of Khān Shīrīn Khān Jawānshayr, who had also been sentenced to a caning but then pardoned because he had accompanied Ḥamīd Allāh to the mountains at the Ūnay Pass, supported me under the arms and led me from Qalʿah-i Bāqir Khān to a nearby canal. I not only did not have the strength to move about, I couldn't even move my feet. So he left me there alone and set off about his own business. When they heard what happened, a tea seller named Sayyid Abū'l-Qāsim and his uncle Sulṭān ʿAlī became alarmed and hurried to the canal. [Sayyid Abū'l-Qāsim] lifted me onto his shoulders, took me to his shop and sat me down at the entrance. Then they brought a charpoy [a rope bed] and laid me on it. In a soft voice I uttered,

> Glory be to God![cxvi] They arrested [me] on the 10th of Muḥarram and on the 24th of the month my beard, face and whole body is covered with blood. Maybe they should consider me one of the friends of the Lord of Martyrs (Imām Ḥusayn).

When they heard my words, people who were standing there and those who lifted the charpoy onto their shoulders began to weep. With tears in their eyes, they carried me home. At home, my wife and children, along with other women and men who had gathered there, burst out sobbing. At this time, an infusion of iodine was brought from the Iranian Legation and rubbed on my back and sides. The Iranian military attaché, Sarhang ʿAlī Khān, had received instructions by telephone from the *shāhanshāh* of Iran [Riżā Shāh Pahlavī] to undertake everything possible to aid and comfort the Shiʿis of Afghanistan, without interfering in the internal affairs of the country in a way that might invite an attack on Iran. He did so and at a meeting with ʿAṭā al-Ḥaqq, the Saqqawī foreign minister, he demanded that the oppression of Shiʿis by Son of the Water Carrier stop. To some extent, he succeeded in reducing the attacks.

In the evening, Keeper of the Privy Purse Mīrzā Muḥammad Ayyūb Khān, and Mīrzā Muḥammad Mahdī /295/ returned from interrogation. Mīrzā Muḥammad Ayyūb asked the author, "Shouldn't the letter, which you wrote on behalf of the Hazārahs, have gotten to Son of the Water Carrier?" I answered,

> Fulfilling our duty, we sent the letter of the Hazārahs, in which they promised to give an oath of allegiance. We didn't write anything more than that to anyone. So you may tell the ignorant government, without any reservations,

> that your delegation sincerely fulfilled its duty. Nothing has been done that would cause harm to your tribe or to the members of the delegation.

152 [Mīrzā Muḥammad Ayyūb] was reassured and | left after about an hour. It was clear to him that this misfortune had befallen the tribe because of the idiotic ambitions of Nūr al-Dīn.

Wednesday, 25 Muḥarram, Corresponding to 11 Saraṭān and 3 July

On this day, Ḥamīd Allāh, a son of the water carrier, who is distinguished neither by intelligence nor reason, has cast religion and faith to the winds of pride and fantasy, is completely ignorant and misguided, and has trod the path of boasting, fantasy, vulgarity and debauchery, was bent on renewing combat operations against the brave Hazārahs. Having embarked on the road of impetuosity and folly, he arrived [again] at Jawqūl where a day ago he had arrived without meeting any opposition but had then been defeated at the hands of a small contingent of battle-hardened Hazārahs. Nurturing revenge in his heart, he resolved [on this day] to deal as harshly with the Hazārahs as he had dealt with the residents of Wardak, Lahūgard, Tagāb, and Qandahar before this.

When he arrived there with a mighty force of bloodthirsty thieves, he attacked the contingent of Hazārahs who had homes and domiciles in the region. He had just started to plunder their belongings, steal their livestock, and set fire to their homes and forts when suddenly a number of Hazārahs /296/ who had learned about his attack on the previous day and had come to fight, unexpectedly surrounded [Ḥamīd Allāh] and his force and opened fire. Their attack was such a surprise that [Ḥamīd Allāh] not only gave up the fight but also lost the route by which he might have been able to retreat. Out of eighty-four bandits, including those who yesterday had caned Nūr al-Dīn, Mīr Āqā and me, all but four were killed. Their "repeating guns" (machine guns), the six-pound field pieces which they had dragged along, and their ammunition stores all fell into Hazārah hands. He gave up in losses a great deal of money as well as the lives of his soldiers. He lost his own horse and his footman and groom were taken captive. As for that dog, Ḥamīd Allāh, he crept away on all fours from the battlefield in the evening, like a sly fox. His arms up to his elbows and his legs up to the knee from creeping along were full of thorns, lacerated, bleeding, and swollen. Aʿẓam, a thief from Maydān, lifted him onto his shoulders, and brought him to his car in Sar Chashmah by way of Darbūghā. From there he quickly fled back to the city and told the commander of thieves and chief of the atheists, who had awarded himself the title "servant of the faith of the Prophet of God" but in fact was its destroyer, what had happened. Already badly frightened by the activities of Muḥammad Nādir Khān and the Afghan tribes of the Southern Province and also Muḥammad Hāshim Khān and the Afghan tribes of the Eastern Province, his fear was compounded [by this news] and he said,

> I am generally not too worried about the Afghans because I can make them obey, like donkeys, by giving the leaders of each tribe a few rupees. But the Hazārahs fought for three years against the army of ʿAbd al-Raḥmān which numbered 120,000 soldiers and had 100 pieces of artillery and still were not defeated. The amir only managed to gain victory after the Hazārahs were decimated by cholera. You can't defeat them by force and drag them into the wadi of obedience and subjection.

After thinking about this for a moment, he scolded his brother /297/ saying,

153 The Qizilbāsh peace delegation | prevented the Hazārahs from fighting and attacking Kabul. Moreover, it obtained from them a letter in which they promised to give an oath of allegiance so that even if they didn't promptly offer allegiance, they also didn't fight. Now that you yourself have ignited the flames of war, you've stirred up a hornet's nest and on top of the problem of Muḥammad Nādir Khān and Muḥammad Hāshim Khān in the South and the East you've opened a front in the West.

After saying this to his brother, he pondered how to rectify the situation so that the Hazārahs would stop fighting and he then might enjoy the leisure to concentrate his forces on the struggle with Muḥammad Nādir Khān and Muḥammad Hāshim Khān and take the opportunity to reach [temporary] agreement with the Hazārahs concerning their promise of allegiance and obedience contingent on the terms they had written and then by strategic delay buy time so that he could achieve his [immediate] goal [of defeating Muḥammad Nādir Khān and Muḥammad Hāshim Khān].

Thursday, 26 Muḥarram, Corresponding to 12 Saraṭān and 4 July

On this day, the Qizilbāsh were in confusion after hearing about the defeat of Ḥamīd Allāh and the victory of the Hazārahs and became prey to dark thoughts. In particular, some of the more farsighted and conscientious Qizilbāsh thought that they who have been living in deprivation and oppression because of the fatwa of the ignorant pseudo-mullahs which barred them from their long-time work for the government and doomed them to death and destruction will [now] be in even more danger of being killed and plundered. They believe that frustration and disappointment confront them on all sides and they are extremely disturbed to think that because they are of the same sect as the Hazārahs they are despised by the government and the nation and are repugnant to Sunnis. Thus, they have been prevented from serving the government, they have no access [to regaining that service], and are on the brink of perishing with no other protector or helper but God. Humble and debased, they struggle to live; they do not have the wherewithal to travel and thus are deprived of the possibility of leaving the country. They will be trapped in this arena where they will be killed, plundered, /298/ or arrested.

Instead of expecting a reward from Son of the Water Carrier for the work the delegation had accomplished in the Hazārahjāt and instead of complaining about the insults, contempt, oppression, cruelty, and unwarranted caning meted out to their representatives, the Qizilbāsh decided to use flattery. In a message which they submitted in writing to Shayr Jān, the minister of court, counting on him to intercede for them, they expressed gratitude to Ḥamīd Allāh for punishing their fellow tribesmen and interpreted his censure as instruction and guidance, hoping that in this way they would be able to save their own lives, wealth, families, children, and belongings from death, looting, and arrest. When mentioning the Hazārahs' battle with Ḥamīd Allāh Khān, when the Hazārahs came down from the Ūnay Pass and pursued the remnants of Son of the Water Carrier's forces as far as Sar Chashmah, Mīrzā[cxvii] Sulṭān Ḥusayn Qizilbāsh asked the minister of court, "When the truce negotiations were going on, did the Hazārahs come down from the Ūnay Pass of their own accord or did you force them to come down and start fighting?" With these words he gave the minister to understand that the blame was on Ḥamīd Allāh,
154 for having instigated the fighting. The minister of court | answered, "We ourselves made the Hazārahs come down and fight." Then the minister of court delivered their message to Ḥabīb Allāh, chief of thieves, who had received the title *pādshāhs* and "servant of the faith of the Prophet of God" from the pseudo-mullahs and *ḥażrats*.

Thinking how best to extricate himself from this, [Ḥabīb Allāh Khān] said, "We will publish an announcement and send it to the Hazārahs accompanied by some Qizilbāsh chosen by you." The minister of court, having brought matters to this point, promised to present to him the delegation he selected on the morrow. /299/

Friday, 27 Muḥarram, Corresponding to 13 Saraṭān and 5 July

On this day, a group of conscientious Qizilbāsh elders, because of the evil intentions of the Saqqawīs, indeed because of the ill-will towards them of the general population of ignoramuses living in Afghanistan and also because of the battles between the Hazārahs and the Northern bandits, realizing they were in a bad situation and that their property and lives were in grave danger, fearful and anxious, began to prepare what was necessary to defend themselves, their property and their honor, and having made a promise to Son of the Water Carrier and the minister of court the day before, met at the home of Mīrzā Muḥammad Mahdī to select members for a peace delegation that would be sent to the Hazārahjāt. During the discussion and selection of the delegation's members, the sorrowful news spread that I had died as a result of the caning by that offspring of the water carrier (Ḥamīd Allāh), who, out of ignorance and misguidedness, had cast religion to the wind of his whims and selfish desires. They then began the necessary preparations for [my] ritual ablutions, enshrouding, and burial. The municipal official (*ma'mūr-i maḥallī*), Muḥammad Ibrāhīm,[207] an honest fellow and a sincere Muslim, sent some men to Afshār, Wazīrābād, and other areas on rented bicycles to spread the news to come and follow the bier [to the cemetery], perform the prayer for the dead, and, despite illwishers, lay me to rest among my own people. However, it soon became clear that the stories about my death following the caning were not true and I was still alive. So they stopped the funeral preparations and again turned to choosing the members of the intended delegation. They formed two groups—one of four men and the other of eleven and decided to tell the minister of court that if the purpose of sending a delegation was the same as the first one, their people had already gone and worthily fulfilled the mission but had nonetheless been subject to injury and insult. If [the purpose now] was only to deliver the announcement to the Hazārahs, then they had chosen four men who would see to the distribution of it. But if the purpose was a renewal [of the aims of the first mission], then eleven men had been chosen to be empowered by the government. **/300/**

With this in mind, they went to the Arg and handed their resolution to the minister of court and suggested that he himself take the responsibility of heading their delegation. But he declined, excusing himself on the grounds of the opposition of the high governor [Malik Muḥsin] and Ḥamīd Allāh to his heading it. But he promised to present them to Son of the Water Carrier the next day at Dār al-Amān.

207 This is the same Muḥammad Ibrāhīm, called a *ma'mūr-i baladīyah* above, p. 256.

Saturday, 28 Muḥarram, Corresponding to 14 Saraṭān and 6 July

155 | On this day, when rumors of fighting between the tribes of the Southern Province and Saqqawī forces and the bravery and steadfastness of Muḥammad Nādir Khān and Shāh Walī Khān were on everyone's lips, Son of the Water Carrier, despite the fact that his mind was uneasy and disturbed and did not know whether the proclamations to entice the Afghan tribes of Sulaymān Khayl, Aḥmadzā'ī, Andar, Tarakī, ʿAlī Khayl, Jadrān, Jājī and others to secure a pact appealing to their shared religion and faith [would be effective], knowing that the promise of money would turn them away from any pact or covenant with Muḥammad Nādir Khān, and by airplane and through the pseudo-mullahs had disseminated appeals which said that anyone who killed or captured Muḥammad Nādir Khān and his brothers could hope for a sum of money from the government, despite all this, he, his relatives, and followers set off for Dār al-Amān, which he had renamed Dār al-Ḥabīb, to enjoy themselves and relax.

According to the promise made to them by Shayr Jān, the Qizilbāsh drove out to Dār al-Amān by car. The minister of court presented them to Son of the Water Carrier and put their resolution before him. Because of his fight with the Hazārahs and because they were Shiʿis, Son of the Water Carrier bore ill-will towards the Qizilbāsh and because of the instigation of the pseudo-mullahs, he sought a pretext for destroying them. But now, hypocritically, he praised their outstanding and devoted service /**301**/ on behalf of the government and state of Afghanistan over the course of 200 years and said that during this long period, they had not grown rich, for they did not unjustly appropriate the wealth of the government and nation through corruption and instead lived on their fixed salaries. Thereupon Son of the Water Carrier began to denounce the ministers of His Majesty, Amān Allāh Khān, who, [despite] being Sunnis, had, in a short time, ransacked the nation and the country and its glorious buildings, wonderful serais, and spacious fields and gardens and had betrayed Amān Allāh Khān in the process. He referred to each one by name, calling them swindlers and rogues. Then Ḥabīb Allāh confirmed the four[cxviii] delegates who were supposed to distribute the announcements in the Hazārahjāt and postponed to the future any need for the delegation [of eleven] to go. At this moment, Mīrzā Ḥasan ʿAlī Qizilbāsh, a reliable employee, secretary, and right-hand man of the high governor Malik Muḥsin in the confiscation of money, and his helpful assistant [in corruption], volunteered to go the Hazārahjāt, saying "as a service to the government, I will deliver the announcements to the Hazārahjāt." The high governor,[cxix] who trusted him, praised him to Son of the Water Carrier and so he included him in the delegation. Ḥabīb Allāh also confirmed Ḥājjī Rustam ʿAlī from Wazīrābād, Mullā ʿAbd al-ʿAlī from Murād Khānī and Mullā ʿIważ from Afshār whom the Qizilbāsh themselves had selected. He ordered them to go to Sar Chashmah by car, thence to the Hazārahjāt to distribute the appeal and then to return to the capital. The Qizilbāsh went home in a good frame of mind, hopeful that their lives would improve after fulfillment of this mission. /**302**/

Sunday, 29 Muḥarram, Corresponding to 15 Saraṭān and 7 July

On this day, Mīrzā Ḥasan ʿAlī, having undertaken preparations for his companions' departure, and having received 1,000 rupees from the government for the four men's travel expenses, a motor car, and 400 copies of the announcement, which was prepared and printed on the 26th of Muḥarram, was now ready to leave. Here is the exact text of the announcement which Muḥammad Ḥasan Salīmī drafted and printed:

156 Let it be manifest to my ignorant subjects, the Hazārah tribes! | As a result of the agendas and incitements of enemies, you turned from the path of obedience. Although I have had to put up with a great deal I came to you with good advice and even dispatched a delegation to you made up of your fellow-tribesmen and staunch supporters like Nūr al-Dīn Khān, Mullā Fayż Muḥammad, and others so that they would encourage you to find a way out of the wilderness of error. It had all the effect of a drop of rain on solid rock. Moreover, you became even more insolent and misguided so that I resolved to send a small part of my triumphant army to punish you. You fled and they brought disaster to your property and lives. Consequently in fear of them you now obstinately flee. Notwithstanding this adequate force, I have prepared a mighty army which I am going to send to your region. Loyal tribes of Afghans also beg me every day to send them to annihilate you. But the characteristic quality of a *pādshāh* is mercy and that of leaders is compassion towards the creatures of God. The relationship of the *pādshāh* to his subjects is like that of a father to his children. Therefore (out of the goodness of my heart) I cannot subject you to such unbearable troubles and impositions. By this means I put you on notice that if, starting today and for the next ten days, your representatives come to the royal court with *bayʿat-nāmah*s and you tender your obedience, the pen of forgiveness will record your [previous] actions in the account book of politics /**303**/ and I will consider you subjects like all my other subjects. But if, at the expiration of this period, neither you, with pledges, nor your representatives, have arrived, then I will send a force against you and call up the Afghan tribes to destroy your world. When the troops and the [Afghan] tribal contingents are dispatched your prayers for forgiveness will be of no avail and by your

> own hand you will "lose both this world and the Hereafter."[208] Although I have had to put up with a good deal from you ignorant people and more than once [have tried] to guide you [in the right direction]; still my actions have not produced the desired results. Now I deem it necessary to bring this to your attention [again]. So you should choose now whether you know the value of your well-being and will not make yourselves a morsel for cannons and rifles. The end. 26 Muḥarram 1348 Hijrī.

The Qizilbāsh delegation, having reached Takānah and finding the road had been closed for several days, opened negotiations with the Hazārahs, their co-religionists, declaring that they were their supporters and had been forced to come to the Hazārahjāt under pain of death. So the Hazārahs escorted them, under guard, through the Ūnay Pass and brought them to Sardār Muḥammad Amīn Khān in Rāh Qūl. They were deemed to be friends of the Hazārahs and enemies of Son of the Water Carrier. In any event, they were given a certificate of affirmation (*taṣdīq-nāmah*) [that they were indeed friends of the Hazārahs and enemies of Son of the Water Carrier] signed by the prince and the Hazārah arbābs for a rainy day. In this way, the Qizilbāsh protected themselves against destruction.

Monday, 30 Muḥarram, Corresponding to 16 Saraṭān and 8 July

157 | The Hazārahs had now been fighting Son of the Water Carrier's troops for eleven days and driving them back each day. On this day, following another successive victory, they returned to their breastworks and positions in (Ūnay) Pass. Then, in anticipation of the next battle, they remained in their sangars /304/ on the hill tops. [Then] they set out to battle the Saqqawī army, which had come to number 5,000 bellicose men with bloodthirsty officers, each of whom was a thief, totally ignorant of the Almighty, and [each of whom] had volunteered. And they had numerous pieces of artillery and machine guns. Proudly, [the Hazārahs] turned the face of combat to the mountainous region in which [the Saqqawīs] were stationed and shouting "O, ʿAlī" their hands on their rifle stocks, loading and ejecting cartridges, they advanced. They pushed the Saqqawīs back as far as Jalrīz, capturing several pieces of artillery and a number of machine guns. They killed, wounded, and captured some and seized as booty the weapons of the dead and wounded and the prisoners as well as a large quantity of ammunition. They put so much pressure on the Saqqawī army that when they were fleeing they threw most of their rifles and bandoliers

208 Qurʾān 22:11.

into the river and tilled fields. In revenge for Ḥamīd Allāh's burning forts at Sar Chashmah, the Hazārahs set fire to the Qalʿah-i Majīd and several hamlets in Takānah and Jalrīz, and plundered them for whatever could be carried off.

The majority of Son of the Water Carrier's troops, who were from Chahārdihī, Maydān, and the environs of Kabul and were forced to fight, fled home and hid, because Son of the Water Carrier had issued an order to shoot deserters. Already, everyone was continually talking about the repeated victories of the Hazārahs. The residents of Kabul, Chahārdihī, Lahūgard, Maydān, and Wardak, delighted by this Hazārah victory, put their hands together in prayer at the threshold of God, and prayed for victory and [for the Hazārahs] to come and enter Kabul.

However, in accordance with a fatwa from one of their own religious scholars addressed to everyone and offering the following guidance,

> Because His Majesty Amān Allāh abdicated the amirate, the order to fight issued by Prince Muḥammad Amīn, who is his appointee as high commissioner, is invalid and the Hazārahs must consider it an obligation to defend their own lives and belongings and in the event of an attack by Son of the Water Carrier must defend their lives and property and their homes and homeland against him but must not leave their own soil to attack other Muslims, /**305**/ since in both cases, the slayer and the slain, will have to answer to God and the Prophet,

the Hazārahs abandoned an attack on Kabul. But until the end, they were steadfast in [defending] the religion and in refusing to give an oath of loyalty or to obey Son of the Water Carrier.

Tuesday, 1 Ṣafar, Corresponding to 17 Saraṭān and 9 July

Son of the Water Carrier, alarmed by the situation in the Southern and Eastern Provinces and the judicious Islam-supporting activities of Muḥammad Nādir Khān and his brothers, was even more disturbed by the Hazārah victory. With an eye to calling on the following tribes—Mullā Khayl, Sulaymān Khayl, Kākar, Tarakī, Andar, ʿAlī Khayl, Daftānī, Kharūtī, and the semi-nomadic Aḥmadzāʾī, all of whom had bound themselves to
158 the extinction | of the Afghānī sultanate and government and to assisting and supporting the Saqqawī [sultanate] of the Tajik tribe, which had no lineage and was of ignoble descent and had brought the nation to its knees, asked via numerous requests for them to volunteer to kill, plunder, and enslave the Hazārahs and take their homes and homeland.

On this day identical farmans were issued addressed to these tribes and their leaders. Affixing his signature and the seal of his depraved amirate, [Ḥabīb Allāh] called upon all of these tribes to attack the Hazārahs.

Here is a verbatim copy of the farman addressed to Raḥīm Khān of the Kākar tribe which came into my hands and which I included in my journal of the revolution:

> May it be manifest to Your Excellency, Raḥīm Khān Kākar! Your piety and praiseworthy service to your Muslim government has been reported to His Highness by Brigadier Khatak Khān. For your service to my government, I, servant of the religion of the Prophet, express satisfaction and gratitude and by this /**306**/ farman, having expressed to you my great pleasure, I want in future for you to serve the clear religion of Islam and thereby gain the satisfaction of the All High, His Prophet and me as the servant of the religion. You and your tribe should attack the Hazārahs who have not expressed their obedience to the *pādshāh* of Islam. Any village that you capture will be deemed yours and its belongings and lands will be given to you and your tribe from His Highness, as compensation both in this world and the next. After the jihad comes to an end and the Hazārah issue is resolved, every tribal leader will get a title and a gift, depending on his contribution to the victory. 1 Ṣafar 1348 Hijrī. (28 June 1929)

Because of the publication of this dissension-sowing hypocritical decree, the foolish Afghans became the consorts of vanity and arrogance. They had not a drop of human honor and conscience let alone religious and Islamic understanding and they had not the slightest inkling that they were cutting off the branch on which they were sitting. It never occurred to them that the result of this would be the humiliation of the nation, the impoverishment of the government, and the destruction of the country. They would cast to the wind and ravage the monetary and material resources and the arsenals of the country which had been built up over 100 years by the blood, flesh, and skin of the miserable subjects for the defense of the frontiers, the independence of the country, the protection of the people and their honor, for building up the country, improving the lot of its people, and for repelling the attacks of foreign enemies. But they are only interested in acquiring high ranks and positions in a world of misery, futility, ignorance, and savagery.

As for this Raḥīm Khān, as well as his fellow tribesmen, they were people who had already taken ownership, by decree of the government, of lands and forts in Pul-i Jangalī, Gazak, and Arghandāb which belonged to the Maskah Hazārahs of Jāghūrī, by which [the Kākars] demonstrated their zeal for the Afghan government. Son of the Water Carrier legitimized all of this usurpation and destruction, and declared them worthy of reward as if what they had done was a service to the government and the nation. /307/

Wednesday, 2 Ṣafar, Corresponding to 18 Saraṭān and 10 July

159 | On this day, [General] ʿUmrā Khān, son of Malik Zayn al-ʿĀbidīn Dāʾudzāʾī, an infamous brigand and libertine, announced to the commander of the fornicators, Ḥabīb Allāh, Son of the Water Carrier, that he would voluntarily take upon himself the duty of intimidating the Hazārahs, either to force their submission or to crush them. He said,

> Field Marshal Purdil Khān has performed the services of taking Ghaznīn and conquering Qandahar; Major General Muḥammad Ṣiddīq and ʿAbd al-Qayyūm Ibrāhīm Khayl Pamqānī are advancing in the direction of the Southern Province; and General Muḥammad ʿUmar has achieved what he desired[209] against his opponents in numerous battles. Having made it my responsibility to smash and crush the Hazārahs, I don't want to be lagging behind my peers and equals. I would bring the matter to a close and place the halter of obedience around the neck of the Hazārahs.

His arrogant request was welcomed and he set off for Jalrīz with one regiment of experienced fighters from the Kūh Dāmanī and Kūhistānī army as well as some artillery pieces (literally, fire-emitting and raining-down guns). He linked up with the soldiers who had earlier marched against the Hazārahs, were skirmishing with them daily, and finding it difficult to stop the lion-like Hazārahs. He encountered a small force of Hazārahs who had reached Sar Chashmah and were conducting combat operations as far as Takānah. The Hazārahs, planting the foot of valor, killed or wounded 500 soldiers of the regular and tribal forces and nineteen of the Saqqawī officers. ʿUmrā Khān himself was gravely wounded in the leg. He thus never had the chance to achieve his goal (literally: "they crippled the leg of his promise and kept him from gamboling in the field of his wishes") and [the Hazārahs] seized the artillery, rifles, and ammunition of his force as booty. Consequently, late in the afternoon, wounded, embarrassed, and apprehensive, /308/ he reached the city by motor car. The victorious Hazārahs returned to Ūnay Pass and re-occupied their sangars in a contented frame of mind. From the battlefield, they carried off the heads of the slain, mounted them on poles like scarecrows, and planted those

---

[209] Fayż Muḥammad uses an expression "*sūr-i satranj-i* [sic] *ārzū-yi khūd ... az ḥarīf burdah*" that appears to be a metaphor from chess (*shatranj*).

poles at the summit of the pass so they could "see" the bazaar in Kabul. The (dead) would bemoan the fact that they would never again get to eat mulberries and from beneath the ground they would curse the impudent bloodshedding Son of the Water Carrier.

The Events of Thursday, 3 Ṣafar Corresponding to 19 Saraṭān and 10 (sic 11) July[210]

As was noted earlier, ʿAlī Aḥmad Khān, son of Khūshdil Khān "Lūy Nāb," was arrested in Qandahar at the premises of an Hazārah from Ḥajaristān named Ṣamad ʿAlī, who was known for having fucked[211] his sister and his aunt. ʿAlī Aḥmad Khān's mother was the daughter of Amīr Dūst Muḥammad Khān and his wife was a full sister of His Majesty Amān Allāh Khān, whom he had twice betrayed by declaring himself amir, in Jalālābād and then in Qandahar. The Saqqawīs brought him back to Kabul along with two other arrested men, Qāżī ʿAbd al-Shakūr, and Mullā ʿAbd al-Wāsiʿ, as has already been mentioned. On this day, they paraded him around the bazaars barefoot and bareheaded. He was suffering from thirst and appealed to the Kūhistānīs as Muslims—since they gave themselves the name "servants of the religion"—to give him water. But these non-
160 Muslims, bereft of religion and faith, | instead of a cup of water gave him a taste of their rifle butts, hitting him on the back, and giving religion and the [Hanafi] maẕhab a bad name. Having strapped him and Mawlawī ʿAbd al-Wāsiʿ to the muzzles of cannons, they blew them both to bits. When Son of the Water Carrier issued the order to tie him to the cannon, Amān Allāh Khān's sister, her head bare, prostrated herself before that tyrant and threw her small child at his feet. She begged for permission to see her husband for the last time but he did not give it. Also, (ʿAlī Aḥmad's) people were forbidden to go to the place where the cannon stood but the woman who served as his sons' nurse endured insults and **/309/** sustained blows from rifle butts, but, due to her great loyalty for the favors she had received from the family and from [ʿAlī Aḥmad Khān] himself, managed to make her way to the killing ground and bring his head back to his wife. This was the cause of weeping, lamentations, and great distress on her

[210] By an error, the author repeats the Gregorian date, July 10. From here on the Gregorian calendar dates are off by one day in the Persian original as well as in the Russian translation. We have corrected the Gregorian dates.

[211] Fayż Muḥammad uses the verb "gāʾīdan" here, for which "fuck" seems the most appropriate translation.

part. After some time, with the permission of the *pādshāh*[212] his wife left Afghanistan in the company of Prince Amīn Allāh Khān, her uncle, and her brother, Muḥammad Kabīr, to join her [other] brother [Amān Allāh] and mother.[cxx]

Friday, 4 Ṣafar, Corresponding to 20 Saraṭān and 12 July

On this day, due to the Hazārah victory, Son of the Water Carrier, worried lest braves from this tribe would come down from Kūh-i Pamqān along the road through Qattān attack Pamqān and Kabul and win the day, set out from Kabul, ostensibly for pleasure and relaxation for he did not want the populace to see his anxiety and fear. He went to Pamqān and there spent the day supervising his men building breastworks and digging trenches at strategic spots.

At this same time, Ḥabīb Allāh telephoned to the police station [in Kabul] and ordered the arrest of Mīr [Muḥammad] Hāshim, the former minister of finance in His Highness Amān Allāh Khān's administration, and Mīr Hāshim's brother. At this same time, Mīr Hāshim received a letter from Muḥammad Nādir Khān in which he learned that the latter would arrive in Kabul in the near future. The letter encouraged him to begin a campaign to incite the population of Kabul and its environs who already hated the leader of the thieves and to fan the flames of that hatred.

Out of fear of what might befall him, Son of the Water Carrier also ordered the arrest and imprisonment of Prince ʿAbd al-Majīd,[213] Mīrzā Sulṭān Ḥusayn Qizilbāsh, and the sons of Mullā Malik, who were accused of secretly sending weapons and ammunition to the Hazārahs. Due to the issuing of this order, (Son of the Water Carrier) directed that all the sons of the assassinated amir, Ḥabīb Allāh Khān, be brought to the gates of the Arg. But there was nothing to be gotten from them—some of whom were still quite young and their mothers had already paid out bribes of 200, 300 and 400 rupees [for their safety]. So they were allowed to go home.

[212] This word comes at the end of the line (ms. p. 160, line 6) and is very difficult to read. The print edition (p. 309, line 4) transcribed it as "shāh" which would raise questions since Fayż Muḥammad has never used the word "shāh" for Son of the Water Carrier. A. I. Shkirando, the Russian translator elides the problem by leaving "with the permission of" out of the translation entirely (Faiz Mukhammad, *Kniga upominanii* 1988, p. 203, second paragraph). Under considerable magnification, *pādshāh* seems the most likely reading.

[213] On Prince ʿAbd al-Majīd see Fayż Muḥammad, *The History*, vol. 4, index ("ʿAbd al-Majīd Khān Muḥammadzāʾī") and Adamec, *Who's Who*, pp. 98–99 ("Abdul Majid, Sardar, Muḥammadzai").

/**310**/ They have so far escaped imprisonment and punishment from the Saqqawīs and are not being bothered.

Of the detainees from Qandahar, Qāżī ʿAbd al-Shakūr and the mufti of Qalāt (at the time of His Majesty Amān Allāh Khān's stay in Qandahar) had issued a decree anathematizing Son of the Water Carrier and the Northerners as infidels. The day before, along with ʿAlī Aḥmad Khān and Mullā ʿAbd al-Wāsiʿ [they were to be executed.] But Qāżī ʿAbd al-Shakūr escaped death because his brother, ʿAbd al-Karīm, betrayed His Highness Amān Allāh Khān in the region of Darāz Qūl which lies next to the lands of the Hazārahs of Bihsūd [and switched loyalties]. He had compelled the Dāy Zangī and Dāy Kundī Hazārah contingents (numbering 900 men),
161 who had been conducting operations | in Bāmyān and Ūnay Pass, to stop fighting against Son of the Water Carrier's army. Unbeknownst to Prince Muḥammad Amīn Khān [the high commissioner of Hazārah Bihsūd], he and the governor of Dāy Zangī, Mīr Muḥammad Ḥusayn, had sent a letter pledging loyalty to the chief[cxxi] of the Saqqawīs. The letter said that he personally would follow up with a general oath of allegiance from all the Hazārahs under his own high commissionership [of Hazārah Dāy Zangī and Dāy Kundī]. [ʿAbd al-Karīm] chose the path of betrayal [of Amān Allāh] to save his house and belongings in Kabul from confiscation by Son of the Water Carrier and also to receive title and rank from the sardār of thieves. Because of his treachery, consigning to oblivion the honor, dignity, and respect which his fathers and forefathers, who had lived well and held high positions, had enjoyed for 150 years from the time of Shāh Maḥmūd Saduzāʾī until now [his older brother escaped death and] the pages of this work are contaminated by mentioning his base character and conduct.

Saturday, 5 Ṣafar, Corresponding to 21 Saraṭān and 13 July

On this day, the minister of finance, Mīr Hāshim, and his brother, Sayyid Ḥabīb, who, as already mentioned, had been in communication with Muḥammad Nādir Khān; Mīrzā Sulṭān Ḥusayn Qizilbāsh and a son of Mullā Malik, who were accused of delivering rifles and ammunition to the Hazārahs, purchasing /**311**/ the arms through a number of bakers, were arrested and imprisoned. The bakers, to whom the Qizilbāsh [also] secretly transferred funds to take food to the imprisoned Hazārah men and women from Sar Chashmah, [were also arrested]. Because the elder brother of the accused son of Mullā Malik, ʿAbd al-Wāḥid,[cxxii] was a member of the delegation sent to the Hazārahjāt to distribute copies of the appeal referred to above, he was released. Mīrzā Sulṭān Ḥusayn, after paying a bribe of

3,000 rupees to the warden [of the Arg], ʿAbd al-Ghanī, also was released after a few days. The bakers also bought their way out, escaping prison and saving themselves from humiliation and persecution at the hands of Saqqawīst officials who, by denouncing people, could extort money from them. It cost the bakers from 500 to 1,000 rupees each. Outwardly, [the bakers] appeared calm but inwardly they lived in constant fear of being arrested again. The Saqqawīs did not release the minister of finance and, as will be seen, they soon put Prince ʿAbd al-Majīd to death.

Also on this day a decree was broadcast which anathematized the Hazārahs as infidels. It was signed by the pseudo-mullahs at the order of the ringleader of the debauchers, Son of the Water Carrier. When they learned of the proclamation, the Hazārahs stepped up their struggle against the Saqqawīst gang and intensified their propaganda about this "servant of the religion of the Prophet of God" who was, in fact, its nemesis, as the verse has it: "they call a black person (*zangī*) camphor (*kāfūr*)."[214] They declared that an oath of allegiance which is actually a pact and covenant and a contract with "offer" and "acceptance" is given voluntarily. Since the Hazārahs up to now have not given an oath of allegiance, how
162 | is it possible to call them rebels and rabble-rousers and to consider the theft of their property and the shedding of their blood legal? From this it follows that the Hazārahs must defend themselves from destruction, not turn away from killing and being killed in order to obtain a good outcome. Since the Hazārahs are devoted to their faith and religion, have refused to express obedience to an amir-libertine, a thief, and a murderer, therefore this decree they treated **/312/** as a call to arms, to devote themselves to killing and wounding and they courageously took the path of striving [to defend themselves].

Sunday, 6 Ṣafar, Corresponding to 22 Saraṭān and 14 July

At the order of the leader of the oppressors and profligates, Ḥabīb Allāh, Son of the Water Carrier, three members of the royal family—the Muḥammadzāʾī Prince Ḥayāt Allāh Khān, ʿAżud al-Dawlah, and Prince ʿAbd al-Majīd, sons of the murdered amir, Ḥabīb Allāh Khān, and Sardār Muḥammad ʿUs̠mān, son of the late Sardār Muḥammad ʿUmar, son of Sardār Sulṭān Khān, the latter of whom (Sardār Sulṭān Khān) had obtained the post of governor of Harāt from Nasir al-Dīn [Shāh] Qajar as well as the

[214] A euphemism, racist in this case, which conveys a meaning contrary to the reality. Camphor in its raw state is white.

nickname "Sarkār," along with Ḥabīb Allāh, the deputy minister of war under His Majesty Amān Allāh Khān, were all condemned to death by hanging. They were executed and buried in a ditch.

All of this was kept secret and the guard standing watch at the gates of the prison ate the men's breakfasts and dinners for a period of time so that their relatives would not find out about this tragic event and hatch any plots. This, despite the fact that the murdered men had committed no crime nor even a misdemeanor. Although Son of the Water Carrier anticipated the possible consequences, nonetheless in a situation where general terror reigned no one believed that there was anyone who would sacrifice himself in the name of saving an unhappy nation from the yoke of thieves and, at night when Son of the Water Carrier went out for a drive in his car towards Dār al-Amān, would shoot him so that the people would live in peace and an end would come to the bloodletting, thievery, and debauchery.

At 10 o'clock in the morning of this day, the courageous forces of Muḥammad Nādir Khān entered **/313/** Lahūgard. At Pādkhwāb-i Rawghanī they clashed with the Saqqawī forces, shed much blood of the highway robbers, [enemies] of the religion and faith, and advanced to Surkhāb. They surrounded the infidel Muḥammad Ṣiddīq and his force at Kārīz-i Darwīsh and he sent a courier to Kabul with a request for reinforcements.

Also on this day, a contingent of the Karū Khayl tribe, intending to attack the force stationed in Butkhāk, reached Chakarī and Khūrd Kābul. However, they were unable to prevail over the [Saqqawī] force there. The fighting with the Saqqawīs lasted until night with much killing and wounding, and [the Karū Khayl] withdrew in frustration.

Monday, 7 Ṣafar, Corresponding to 23 Saraṭān and 15 July

On this day, the army that took Qandahar and had only just arrived back
163 in Kabul was dispatched to Lahūgard to help Ṣiddīq Khān | who yesterday had asked for reinforcements. Also on this day 200 Saqqawī soldiers were lost. They say that at the height of the fighting, they turned the face of flight towards the mountains. A large group was taken captive in Gardayz or Kārīz-i Darwīsh, General Muḥammad ʿUmar, known as "Sūr,"[cxxiii] was encircled and Muḥammad Nādir Khān's tribal army earned a victory which evoked joy among the Kābulīs and among all those who were facing the oppression and tyranny of the Saqqawīs and had come to the end of their ropes due to [the Saqqawīs] hateful and vile deeds. So they were praying to God for some small sign of security and had not yet found a way either to flee or the means to fight.

Muḥammad Nādir Khān at first showed benevolence to the prisoners, considering them Muslims. He distributed one English gold pound **/314/** to each of them, took away their rifles and cartridges, and advised them to go home and stop fighting their Islamic brethren. But as the poem says,

Even if you give royal blood to a bad seed / Only evil comes from evil

these people would forgot the kindness, forsake religion, (again) get rifles and cartridges, and return to the battlefield. So Muḥammad Nādir Khān (soon) handed over [the prisoners] in tens and twenties to the maliks of the Southern Province tribes, ordering them to provide food, make them work in the fields and gather firewood, and always keep them under guard so that they could not escape and return to fight again. In this way, he divided up the prisoners among the maliks. But at the height of the victories and success of the southern braves, out of [innate] rivalry and competition amongst the tribes and because Muḥammad Nādir Khān's money and provisions had now run out, tribes began to envy others who had received booty and, no longer paying heed to their agreements, pacts, and oaths to God on the Qur'ān, began to go home.

At this point, in the atmosphere of mutual envy, Ghaws̱ al-Dīn, son of Jahāndād Aḥmadzā'ī, turned traitor, on the promise of money from the water carrier's son, and formed a villainous plan [to kill] Muḥammad Nādir Khān. Meanwhile, southern fighters turned back from Surkhāb and Pādkhwāb, thus bolstering the spirits of the Saqqawīs and causing sorrow and disappointment among those who hated them.

Tuesday, 8 Ṣafar Corresponding to 24 Saraṭān and 16 July

On this day, a "Kānkarīs"[215] plane, a single-propeller Russian aircraft, which had delivered mail from Tirmiẕ, took off at 5:30 A.M. and headed back with the return mail.

The army detachment force that had been sent to help Brigadier General Muḥammad Ṣiddīq resist Muḥammad Nādir Khān, since it had not heard about the retreat of the battle-eager southern braves, fearing attack [by the Southerners], was unable to move forward and at the village of Muḥammad Āqā-yi[216] Lahūgard it built breastworks and stood

[215] Fayż Muḥammad may possibly have been referring to the Kalinin-1 or Kalinin-2, two Russian aircraft of the period.

[216] Fayż Muḥammad clearly means Muḥammad Āghah not Muḥammad Āqā, the former both a district and a town on the main road through Lahūgard (Logar).

ready /315/ to block the passage of the Southerners and prevent their attacking Kabul.

Also on this day General of Artillery ʿAbd al-Qayyūm of the Ibrāhīm Khayl of Pamqān, a skilled artillerist, was sent to fortified positions in Kārīz-i Darwīsh to use artillery to defend against the Southerners.

Rumors having spread around the city about the preparations to attack Kabul being made by the Hazārahs and the tribes of the Eastern and Southern Provinces, Son of the Water Carrier, who had inadequate forces
164 in Kabul, | was perturbed but in order to conceal his distress from the people, and also to prevent trouble, on this day ordered the publication of an announcement of the flight of Muḥammad Nādir Khān and Shāh Walī Khān, his brother, the absence of any news or sign of the two, and the opposition [to them] of the Afghan tribes who had no conscience or feeling about adhering to their pacts, covenants, their [duties as] Muslims, and Afghan honor and could be called "donkey-thieves" and "animals." He ordered the publication of this announcement so that those who hated his ignorant and misguided government would be disappointed [of any] expectation of a victory by the two brothers. In light of their lack of any religious feeling, the Sulaymān Khayl tribe, especially the donkey thieves of the Sulṭān Khayl clan of this ignorant, misguided, and deviant tribe; the Manzāʾī clan of the ʿAlī Khayl; the Ṣāliḥ Khayl, Māmūzāʾī; Khwāzak; Landīzāʾī; the Mīlan ʿAlāyi clan of the Par Khayl; the Ibrāhīm Khayl, the Zālū-yi clan of the ʿAlī Khayl tribe; the Andar; the Sahhāk; the ʿĀshūzāʾī clan of the Durrah; the Jadrān; the Darī Khayl; the Fakhrī tribe; the Kharūtīs; and the Tajiks living in Katawāz, Zurmat, Gardayz, and other regions, had all come out against Muḥammad Nādir Khān and in support of the leader of the scoundrels, Son of the Water Carrier. But that genius of the age and the best of Afghans, [despite] having no money, being sick and hungry and sleeping at night on the ground, on rocks, and on dry grass, by day, through exhortations, pleasing flattery, and persuasion was able to rally and unite [some of] the savage Afghan tribes and manage to achieve some success. But those [Afghan tribes] at the slightest disagreement, would again scatter. In such a situation, the water carrier's son /316/ was right to issue such announcements.

Wednesday, 9 Ṣafar, Corresponding to 25 Saraṭān and 17 July

At four o'clock in the afternoon of this day, courageous Hazārahs (literally: the hair of pride standing erect on the body of courage), due to reading the water carrier's son's declaration calling on the Afghan tribes and his threatening [the Hazārahs] with attack by willing Afghans, grasped their weapons and shouting "O ʿAlī, help us" attacked the Saqqawī forces that were stationed in the Ūnay Pass and Qalʿah-i Safīd. They crushed and routed them, pursuing them to Takānah and Jalrīz. After killing, wounding, and capturing many of them, they returned to the Ūnay Pass in triumph.

Also on this day, braves of the Southern tribes, who had joined forces with Muḥammad Nādir Khān to uphold Afghan honor, and, as already noted, successfully advanced as far as Surkhāb but then turned around, now carried out a surprise attack and took prisoner a large part of the water carrier's son's defenders. Some of them willingly surrendered with their weapons while the rest scattered and fled back to their homes. After this, the high governor, Malik Muḥsin, forcibly conscripted 1,500 men from Chahārdihī and the environs of Kabul in the name of ethnic duty and quickly sent them, some with and some without weapons, towards Lahūgard, hoping that the southern tribes, when they saw the silhouette of this force, would halt any further advance. But after these conscripted troops had been forced to go to [Lahūgard], they deserted and fled back
165 to their homes. /317/ |

Thursday, 10 Ṣafar, Corresponding to 26 Saraṭān and 18 July

On this day, 2,000 battle-eager braves from Chaprahār and the Khūgyānī tribe, who were followers of Malik Muḥammad Jān, an ally of Muḥammad Hāshim Khān and an enemy of the Saqqawīs and Malik Qays, in accordance with the agreement about the attack on Kabul by the tribes of the Southern Province, entered Chakarī and Khūrd Kabul and attacked the Saqqawī force which was impeding the advance of the tribes of the Eastern Province, having cut the road to Butkhāk. The battle lasted until late afternoon but after sustaining many losses without achieving their objective, [the Easterners] withdrew.

As a result of this attack by the tribes of the Eastern Province, Son of the Water Carrier decided that the campaign involving all the tribes of the Eastern Province, which Muḥammad Hāshim Khān had been preparing over the course of several months, had begun. While this battle was still in progress, the frightened [Ḥabīb Allāh] would climb up to the top of the Arg gate every minute and hourly would go out by car to Maranjān Hill. Having seen the red flag of the Easterners through a telescope and how hot the battle was becoming and trembling so much with fear it was as if he had fleas in his trousers, sand in his shoes, and lice in his turban, he locked the gates of the Arg. His brother, Ḥamīd Allāh, went out to the battlefield and managed to drive off the enemy. During the battle, the leader of the misguided wretches ordered all the soldiers in the Arg and in Kabul to climb into motor cars and hired (horse-drawn) phaetons, and go to the battlefield. He ordered all those who were concealing their motor cars or buggies (*gadīs*) to be immediately shot in front of their garages. As a result of this appalling order and the reckless driving of the cars and buggies, these rag-tag thieves rendered completely useless 400 government vehicles and private carriages.

In late afternoon, Ḥamīd Allāh reported his victory and defeat of the Easterners by telephone, thus relieving the anxiety and confusion of Ḥabīb Allāh, the wrecker of the religion of the Prophet of God. /**318**/ On horseback Ḥamīd Allāh pursued the defeated troops as far as Khāk-i Jabbār, Tīzīn, and Barīkāb. The ringleader of the bandits ordered Ḥamīd Allāh to pursue them and detached a force from the rear to help him. Having won the battle, he ordered cannons taken to the summit of Samāwī [*sic*—Kūh-i Āsmāʾī] and Kūh-i Shayr Darwāzah and to the ramparts and towers of the Arg. He gave orders to the units sent to those heights to remain constantly on the alert since, judging by talk that was circulating, the tribes of the Eastern and Southern Provinces were going to attack Kabul from two sides and the populace is expecting this attack.

Friday, 11 Ṣafar Corresponding to 27 Saraṭān and 19 July

Despite the anxiety and fear which had not left the water carrier's son for a single minute, he spent this night in peace. On Friday, during the day, he ordered the hands and feet of an Afghan of the Khūgyānī tribe,
166 the owner of a buggy who had been taken prisoner, severed. | They cut an ear off fourteen other prisoners from this same tribe. For the rest, they smeared filth on their faces and paraded them around the bazaar. They always paraded Muslims in this manner while the town crier shouted, "This fate awaits anyone who thinks about rebelling and about ceasing to obey and be subject to the *pādshāh*, the *ghāzī* of Islam and the servant of the religion of the Prophet of God." /**319**/

Saturday, 12 Ṣafar, Corresponding to 28 Saraṭān and 19 and 20 July

On this day an article was published in *Ḥabīb al-Islām* about a banquet held by the Hindūs of Kabul on the twenty-ninth of Muḥarram at the

Chihil Sutūn Palace located next to the village of Hindakī.[217] The water carrier's son, his ministers, the high governor Malik Muḥsin, the aide-de-camp Muḥammad Saʿīd and other notables of the court were invited to a midday meal. The Hindūs message to the water carrier's oppressive son was read out by Mangal Singh. It said,

> May we be a sacrifice on behalf of the luminous and blessed Amīr-ṣāḥib Ghāzī! We Hindūs, residents of the province of Kabul, express our gratitude because the fortunate and valorous Amīr-ṣāḥib Ghāzī, disseminator of justice, casts an eye of kindness on the multitude of his dear children of the land and, as a beloved parent, shows paternal concern and affection more and more for our situation and well-being, we who pray for the God-given government. In view of these blandishments and the benevolence for [his] slaves, we will always pray to the Almighty with the wish that He not lessen or shorten the Phoenix-like shadow of the Amīr-ṣāḥib Ghāzī cast over the heads of the weak and heartbroken. Today our brothers in faith live in total tranquility and boundless prosperity and we, a humble and weak tribe to whom a strong wind has brought good news from Qandahar, heeding the consolation of the Almighty in addressing the unfortunate on the part of His Most Excellent Majesty, Sardār of Greatest Eminence [Ḥamīd Allāh], and their excellencies, holders of high positions, the respected high governor-ṣāḥib, and the aide-de-camp to His Majesty, cannot find the appropriate words to express our gratitude for their valuable concern. For the paternal kindness and benevolence of our kingly father, we hardly know how to act in order to warmly show our appreciation of the beloved pādshāh. Therefore, first of all, we raise our hands to the Almighty in prayer that he will assist you **/320/** in realizing all your dreams and desires in this world. Each time we bow in prayer, we pray to the Almighty to give you happiness in this world and the next. Amīr-ṣāḥib Ghāzī! (verse)
>
> Every morning when we bow before God / first we pray for your long life and good fortune. // We want to express our love for you, / We worship you and want to sacrifice ourselves for you.
>
> O great *pādshāh*! May the All-High aid and assist you. Our wish is that you make short work of your enemies; may they be like tent pegs—their heads beneath a stone, their bodies in the ground, and a rope around their necks. Therefore, rest assured that this humble tribe will always be praying for you. 30 Muḥarram 1348 Hijrī (27 June 1929).

---

[217] On this palace, first built by Amīr ʿAbd al-Raḥmān Khān for his son, Ḥabīb Allāh, then completely rebuilt by Ḥabīb Allāh, see Schinasi, *Kabul: A History*, pp. 71–72, 100, 206, 207.

This adulatory message, which hardly corresponded with reality, was signed by Dīwān Mangal Singh,[cxxiv] Naranjan Dās,[218] Kūsingh Arjan Dās, Dīwān Mūhan Laʿl, Dīwān Ḥukm Chand,[219] Mīr Singh Lachman Dās, Kishn Singh, Mishr Bāl Makan, Shūḥī Bartarz, Bhakwān Dās,[220] Mīr Singh, Amīr Chand the broker (*dallāl*), Nānak Chand, Lachman Dās, Tūlah Rām, Lakmī Chand, Kaniyah Laʿl, a Kūh Dāmanī clerk (*daftarī*), and several others.

Son of the Water Carrier replied to this obsequious petition of the
167 Hindūs in the Kūh Dāmanī dialect of Persian |[cxxv] in which he knew only such words as chicken, eggs, wood, selling grapes and other such village-talk nonsense. His minister of court, Shayr Jān, also the supervisor of the press, published it in the paper under the headline "The Gracious Response of the Amir." It went as follows:

> Mangal Singh and other Hindūs! Truly, we, following the guidance of our great leader [Prophet Muḥammad] who 1,348 years ago kindled the rays of our religion in the glittering sublime palace and by that light has spread justice to Muslim and non-Muslim alike, and has taken them under his shield and protection. As concerns you, o Hindūs, we have given you our support to the extent we have been able. It is also necessary to recognize that we have allowed you civil and political freedoms equal to those of Muslims, Jews, and other subjects. We have not allowed anyone to have special tribal advantages and privileges. What we have said is confirmed by proofs we see in everyday life. In my actions, I have maintained the principles of the sacred religion. Today, events are taking place before my eyes which took place at the beginning of this millennium between Iran and Rūm. From the perspective of religion, we protect you just like we protect others. As it has been, so is it now and will be in future. I assure you in all sincerity that no force will bring any harm to your religious freedom if civil calm and tranquility is maintained. You can live peacefully, maintaining the principles of the holy Sharīʿah, and your prosperity is hoped for.

Namely because of such obsequious declarations and speeches, the unfortunate peoples of the East are always vulnerable to destruction and cannot find the right path. Thus in this case the water carrier's son, his high-ranking officials, and even the editors of newspapers write and disseminate mendacious articles (on the one hand) and on the other they accuse the Shiʿis and the Hazārahs of unbelief, who up to now have not

---

[218] On this prominent bureaucrat, see Fayż Muḥammad, *The History*, vol. 3 index ("Dīwān Naranjan Dās"). and vol. 4 ("Dīwān Naranjan Dās") and Adamec, *Who's Who*, p. 207.

[219] See Fayż Muḥammad, *The History*, vol. 4, p. 449.

[220] Ibid., vol. 4, p. 256.

given an oath of allegiance and have not expressed obedience, and call them rebels.

Sunday, 13 Ṣafar, Corresponding to 29 Saraṭān and 21 July

In the afternoon of this day, approximately 100 men of the Karū Khayl tribe and other braves, who earn their living by theft and only think about pillaging, attacked the airstrip and artillery emplacements in the Khwājah Rawāsh plain with plunder in mind. They continued the fight until night but to no avail and eventually they retreated to Tangī Ghārū.

Also on this day, tribal contingents under Muḥammad Nādir Khān, after much effort and encouragement, and recalling the past valor and honor of the Afghans, united in a strong alliance and captured Gardayz and the Tīrah Pass. Driving out Son of the Water Carrier's soldiers, they marched triumphantly through the villages of Khūshī and Tangī Āghūjān and on to Shikār Qalʿah and Surkhābād, fighting all the way.

The residents of Kabul, Chahārdihī, Pamqān, Bīktūt, Arghandah, and
168 Maydān, beset by the tyranny and oppression | of the Saqqawīs, secretly prepared to offer their support as soon as the southern battle-eager braves reached the vicinity of Hindakī and Chahārdihī. They thought that with the assistance of God perhaps they would succeed in driving out Son of the Water Carrier and his Saqqawī followers and, when Muḥammad Nādir Khān entered Kabul, **/321/** their lives would become easy and peaceful.

But for the time being (literally "today and tomorrow") the Southerners strive manfully and have pushed the Saqqawīs to the brink of despair and in the city Son of the Water Carrier is in great distress. The Hazārahs have attacked the Saqqawī forces in the region of Ūnay Pass and Sar Chashmah. They have driven his soldiers from several strategic places where they had erected sangars and have pursued them as far as Jalrīz and Kūt-i ʿAshrū, killing and wounding many soldiers, capturing their rifles, ammunition, and machine guns. [The Hazārahs] delayed their advance to Takānah and Jalrīz for one night. But since the Saqqawī soldiers hid in caves like jackals the Hazārahs returned triumphantly to Ūnay Pass and there stood ready for a fight. Son of the Water Carrier, distraught and anxious and fearful of a two-pronged attack by the Hazārahs and the Southerners, began to ready his army.

Monday, 14 Ṣafar, Corresponding to 30 Saraṭān and 22 July

On this day, Malik Muḥsin, the high governor, than whom no Northerner was more evil, tyrannical, and licentious, because of the fighting in Lahūgard and the advance of the army of the Southern tribes, which Muḥammad Nādir Khān had united using every possible means and sent into battle by appealing to their sense of Afghan honor and Islamic sentiments, forcibly conscripted unarmed residents of Chahār Āsyā (Chār Āsyā) and sent them against the Southerners to stop their advance towards Kabul. He thought that perhaps from a distance the appearance of such a multitude would stop [the Southerners].

Also today, the brave Hazārahs, whose valorous struggle diluted the poison of Son of the Water Carrier, kept up the fight. A detachment of reinforcements with sangar- and fort-smashing artillery was sent from Kabul to Jalrīz so that if the Hazārahs, as they were accustomed to do, should pursue the defeated troops as far as Jalrīz and then turn back, that would be the best thing. **/322/** But should they not turn back but instead take up positions in the forts of Jalrīz preparatory to advancing on Kabul, [the Saqqawī troops] should level the forts which they've occupied with the artillery so that perhaps [the Hazārahs] would be unable to fight from those forts and would then withdraw.

[Elsewhere] for six months Muḥammad Hāshim Khān had advised, counseled, flattered, and welcomed the residents of the Eastern Province, since there are no Afghans more evil or savage than they, guiding them away from abandoning religion and leading them to the high road of Islamism and Afghan honor and pride. On this day, rumors circulated that thanks to his persistence, they had assembled a mighty 24,000-man force which included Muhmands, Ṣāfīs, Chaprahārīs, Surkh Rūdīs, Lamqānīs and others. They were divided into two groups and they resolved jointly to attack Kūhistān, Kūh Dāman, Butkhāk and Kabul, half the men moving
169 via | Sūlāng, Tagāb and Nijrāb and the other half of the force by way of the Lataband Pass, Tangī Ghārū, Tangī Khūrd Kabul, and Manār-i Chakarī. By this they would restore their reputation for Islamism and Afghānī honor which they had cast into the dirt of degradation and the barrens of ignorance.

Rumors of this possible attack from three directions—the south, the east, and from the Hazārahs—pleased the residents of Kabul and frightened the allies of Son of the Water Carrier. In the west the Hazārahs and in the south Muḥammad Nādir Khān would ignite the flames of battle. And perhaps the Easterners would repent their betrayal of Islam and of Afghan honor and, following the wide road of Islamism, would attack Kabul [from the east] in order to put an end to the oppression, humiliations, and debauchery of the godless Saqqawīs.

In the midst of these hopeful thoughts, talk turned to the Ḥażrat of Chārbāgh; the Khūgyānī and Shinwārī tribes; ʿAbd al-Raḥmān, son of ʿIṣmat Allāh Khān; Malik Qays; ʿAbd al-Raḥmān [Shinwārī] and Malik Muḥammad ʿAlam who, incited by foreigners and being irreligious, continually strove to incite and **/323/** ruin the country, to plunge the nation into a sanguinary conflict, to avoid the path of tribal and Islamic unity, and to smash holes in Muḥammad Hāshim Khān's attempts to organize appropriate measures. In talking with each other, people could not conceal their worry that even if the Hazārahs joined forces with the Afghans to crush Son of the Water Carrier, the savage Easterners, guilty of destroying the government and plundering the nation, as a result of outside instigation and the incitements of the abovementioned persons, especially the Ḥażrat-i Chārbāghī, would never stay on the path of unity, faith, and Afghan honor. Because of such discussions amongst themselves, they regretfully agreed that it was necessary [first of all] to rely on the Hazārahs and the Southerners and not on the Easterners.

Tuesday, 15 Ṣafar, Corresponding to 31 Saraṭān and 23 July

On this day, Son of the Water Carrier was in despair: the gallant Hazārah attack and defeat of his army plunged him into despondency. Moreover, after sending 450 soldiers with siege weapons yesterday to Jalrīz to reinforce his army there, not a single soldier remained in Kabul, since prior to this forces had been sent to Lahūgard, Sar Chashmah, Butkhāk, Khāk-i Jabbār, and Tangī Ghārū. Even those 150 soldiers who guarded the airport and the Arg, he had already dispatched in vehicles to Sar Chashmah to defend it against Hazārah attack. Not only were there no tribal contingents in the capital, there weren't even any policemen left. The chief of the misguided and the deviant himself departed for Sar Chashmah and the high governor Malik Muḥsin for Lahūgard. En route, the high governor had four Saqqawī soldiers shot for deserting the battlefield. When the fighters who had fought at Lahūgard and been defeated learned about the execution by firing squad of these four, they were infuriated and **/324/** decided that if [Malik Muḥsin] came to the army they would send him to Hell. But, in the nick of time, he came to his senses and fled back to Kabul.

170 Also, at Kūt-i ʿAshrū, Son of the Water Carrier | disarmed and shot sixteen soldiers who had been defeated in fighting with the Hazārahs and fled towards Kabul. Among those slain were four Shiʿi residents of Wazīrābād, who had been forced to go to the battlefield. Their execution increased the anger and indignation of the residents of Wazīrābād and also that of all Shiʿis, opponents of the water carrier's son. He took other deserters forcibly picked up on the road to Jalrīz where fighting was going on with the Hazārahs. There, having climbed to the summit of a hill opposite the Hazārahs from where he had a good view over the forts of Takānah, he opened fire with machine guns and rifles targeting the brave Hazārahs.

During this, the Shiʿi Sayyid Abū'l-Qāsim, who had a house and plot of land in Takānah, baked thin loaves of leavened bread from one and a half Kābulī seers of flour, and prepared a skinful of fresh *dūgh*, some butter, and the roasted lamb of a sheep he had slaughtered at midday. He set off with the food in the direction of the oppressor and infidel, the water carrier's son and his bandits, who were faint with hunger and thirst. When the sayyid approached the leader of the thieves, that infidel, he was asked who he was and where he came from. A Tajik from Jalrīz, a Sunni, blinded by a savage, fanatical hatred for all Shiʿis, introduced him as a sayyid as well as a Shiʿi who the night before had given shelter in his fort to a Hazārah, the son of Shāh Nūrā. When he heard this, Son of the Water Carrier was enraged. The fact was that Hazārah contingents had captured forts in Takānah, lodged there that night and during the day had climbed the mountain heights and continued the fight. Without thinking, he made that sayyid, who had brought to him in his time of need bread, meat, oil, and *dūgh* for which he should /325/ have been pleased and thanked him, the target of his own pistol and brought him down with seven shots. He also ordered his home burned to the ground and his belongings confiscated. He handed his two wives and his betrothed daughter over to the Kūh Dāmanīs. The younger brother of that wretch, Ḥamīd Allāh, who was present at the battlefield, came by to participate in torching the fort, ransacking the sayyid's belongings, and taking prisoner his wives and children. Tearing an eight-month-old son of that sayyid from its mother, he grabbed the baby by the feet, swung him around his head a few times, and then smashed him on the ground with all his might, killing him. The Tajiks of Takānah and Jalrīz plundered everything in the sayyid's house. Since he had been a person of considerable means, each one carried off a [substantial] share. In the afternoon, the Hazārahs realized that the water carrier's son was there and attacked him from four sides in order to capture and send him to Muḥammad Nādir Khān. But he fled the battlefield and escaped in his car back to Kabul.

On this day 125 men of the Saqqawī army were wounded in Lahūgard, 500 were taken prisoner and many were killed. In fighting with the

Hazārahs, twelve were wounded and several killed and the Hazārahs took possession [of the countryside] as far as Jalrīz.

Wednesday, 16 Ṣafar, Corresponding to 1 Asad and 24 July

171 | Ḥamīd Allāh, the younger son of the water carrier, audaciously running to and fro to fight on all fronts, set off for Jalrīz by car to engage the Hazārahs. Two days before [detachments] had been sent to Jalrīz as reinforcements but, afraid of fighting the Hazārahs, who were known for their ferocity, unable to advance, they stopped at Arghandah and Maydān in fear of their lives. On this day, he forced them to move towards Jalrīz. He himself, /**326**/ fearing for his own life, would not take a single step forward and turned around and went back to the city.

Also due to rumors mentioned above of the Easterners being formed in two groups to attack Kabul, Kūhistān, and Kūh Dāman via two different routes and their sending a letter to the people of Tagāb in which they set the day for their arrival there and calling on the Tagābīs to take up arms on that day against the Northerners, (due to) this message and the Tagābīs taking up arms against the Saqqawīs, Son of the Water Carrier was trapped with no way out.[221] Because there were no soldiers remaining in Kabul, he ordered that unarmed tribal people be recruited from the Kabul suburbs and the northern provinces. Armed with sticks, axes, sickles, swords, and ancient sabres, if they had them, they were supposed to appear to the enemy as if they were an army.

With regards to the bill for [paying] the tribal army, from Shaʿbān to the present, that is for about seven months while fighting has been going on continually on all sides, they were paying each sepoy of the 50,000-man tribal army 140 rupees a month for living expenses. As a result, the residents of Kabul and the villages and forts belonging to it have shouldered the burden of paying out some 12 million rupees.[222] The ongoing, intolerable monetary extortions, the murders, looting, torchings of homes and forts, the ransacking of the treasury and the arsenals, the disabling of automobiles, and the misappropriation of valuables, carpets, and

221 *dar shashdar-i ḥayrat furūmāndah* ("helpless at the 'six doors' of perplexity"). The "six doors" refers to a position in backgammon where the player's piece is immobilized by his opponent's having six consecutive points ("doors") on the board secured with two or more of his pieces.

222 These figures give results of 700,000 rupees a month and 49,000,000 for seven months. Perhaps 12,000,000 represents the difference between what the treasury could pay and the actual cost.

household dishes have brought the government, the nation and the country to the brink of destruction. All this is a consequence of the activities of the ḥażrats and mullahs. One hundred fifty thousand people have perished. If there were no further fighting in the country it would take 100 years to reinstate the original conditions and even with that it is doubtful that the wickedness and ignorance of the people of this nation would allow for such conditions to be reestablished. /327/

Thursday, 17 Ṣafar, Corresponding to 2 Asad and 25 July

On this day, the Hazārahs, having learned about the murder of Sayyid Abū'l-Qāsim, the torching of his home, the looting of his property, the seizing of his wives and daughter, and the murder of the eight-month old infant, all of which has been recorded above, decided to avenge this and attacked the Saqqawī force which was in Jalrīz, killing and wounding many. Fifty wounded bandits, the backbone of the Saqqawī contingents, infamous thieves and (the amir's) favorite individuals, were loaded in vehicles and driven to the hospital in Kabul. The rest, bleeding and
172 smeared with dirt, | became the prey of dogs and foxes. Taking revenge for the sayyid, the Hazārahs burned several houses in Takānah and shot three or four men who had participated in his murder.

Due to the rumor that the Hazārahs, having taken Jalrīz, intend to come over the mountains through Sanglākh and attack Pamqān and Kabul, Sayyid Ḥaydar Shāh Sanglākhī vowed to stop the Hazārahs and not let them pass through Sanglākh and so received 150 English muzzle-loading rifles from Son of the Water Carrier and went to Sanglākh. But since he was in accord with the Hazārahs, he advised them not to be too hasty in attacking Kabul through Sanglākh and Pamqān, at least until it was clearly ascertained when the people of the south would attack Kabul and those of the east would attack the northern regions because although the people of Maydān, Arghandah, Bīktūt, Pamqān and Chahārdihī hate Son of the Water Carrier and await the attack of the Hazārahs on Kabul with impatience and pray to God that having joined forces, together they will wipe him out, nonetheless, the things (the Easterners and Southerners) say cannot be relied on. Therefore, it is not worth the risk of the harm that would befall them for the Hazārahs [to prematurely attack Kabul]. On the basis of this message from Sayyid Ḥaydar, the Hazārahs curtailed the offensive /328/ against Kabul until Muḥammad Nādir Khān's victorious approach and so, with peace of mind, they returned to their sangars in the Ūnay Pass in triumph.

Friday, 18 Ṣafar/3 Asad/26 July

Field Marshal Purdil, *khalīfah* and skilled pillager of the bloodthirsty thieves, the previous day entered Maydān with the force which had taken Qandahar and with a new regiment drafted from the people of the region. He halted there to rest from the incessant skirmishes with the Hazārahs. From there he dispatched his army to Sar Chashmah and the Hazārahjāt while he himself came to Kabul. On this day he set off with a contingent of 200 men towards Lahūgard to reinforce Major General Muḥammad Ṣiddīq. At Kārīz-i Darwīsh, units from the Southern Province had Muḥammad Ṣiddīq surrounded and he requested reinforcements from Son of the Water Carrier by telephone. The high governor [Malik] Muḥsin, who, as already reported, had shot four deserters, thereby enraging the soldiers, did not dare to go to Lahūgard. Instead he headed for Jalrīz where fighting was continuing with the Hazārahs. As soon as he arrived, fighting broke out and lasted until 4:00 P.M. A number of his soldiers were killed. He sent the wounded—60 men—by car to Kabul and he himself retreated there.

Also today, the home of the prime minister, ʿAbd al-Quddūs Khān, was confiscated by order of the water carrier's son. Many carpets and other
173 valuables, which had been hidden in a secret room | constructed behind a false wall, fell into the hands of the plunderers and their leader.

Also on this day, a pseudo-mullah from the Andar tribe whom Son of the Water Carrier /**329**/ had summoned during the night to a private meeting, was instructed that when people crowded into the Pul-i Khishtī congregational mosque for the Friday prayer he was to deliver the *khuṭbah* and read a decree declaring Shiʿis to be infidels making it licit to steal their property, shed their blood, and enslave their families and children. By inciting the people to holy war against the Hazārahs and feeding the flames of religious fanaticism, Son of the Water Carrier hoped to annihilate the Hazārahs. So the pseudo-mullah ascended the pulpit, recited some verses [from the Qurʾān] and some hadiths [of the Prophet], texts completely inappropriate to the present situation, and then declaimed it permissible, nay obligatory, to kill, plunder, and enslave Shiʿis. Those in attendance, who were fed up with the water carrier's son, and the irreligion, lechery, and licentiousness of the Northerners and heartily wished for an Hazārah victory, despised and denigrated the ignorant and evil mullah, his utterances having the opposite effect from what Son of the Water Carrier had thought. The mayor, Khwājah Tāj al-Dīn, seeing that the exposition had had quite an opposite effect to what the commander of the degenerate had imagined, straightaway went to Son of the Water Carrier and received permission from him to imprison [the mullah].

At the same time, some of the leading Qizilbāsh came to the office of the mayor, who had led this pseudo-mullah off to the prison in the Arg, and, expressing apologies, addressed the following complaint to him:

> If accusing the Shiʿis of unbelief and heresy is solely based on the fact that up to now the Hazārahs have not been obedient to the government and so have been labeled kafirs and rebels, then since they have not up to now sent an oath of allegiance, this is another question and should be resolved by the Illumined Law. But if what is claimed means that all Shiʿis are kafirs then this will lead to nothing good and will only be the cause of great carnage which no one will be able to stop. Only the weak Qizilbāsh will suffer, they will be killed, robbed, enslaved, and their homes will be confiscated. This will only bring loss in this world and the next. And if the Qizilbāsh of Kabul perish, this does not in any case mean that all Shiʿis will be annihilated. And if there is carnage, the other side will also suffer great losses.

Khwājah Tāj al-Dīn, after listening to this troublesome speech of the Qizilbāsh, reassured them and said, "the amir, for the sake of the Qizilbāsh **/330/** people, ordered the arrest of the libertine mullah and has given permission for him to be made a public example. Tomorrow some Qizilbāsh should come and verify this with their own eyes, as well as see the discretionary punishment that will be meted out."

On another front, officials of the Iranian Legation accused Son of the Water Carrier of ignorance and made him aware of his deviant behavior.

Saturday, 19 Ṣafar, Corresponding to 4 Asad and 27 July

As was already reported, Purdil Khān, the number one commander of the forces of Son of the Water Carrier, had gone to Lahūgard in support of Major General Muḥammad Ṣiddīq and to counter the tribal army under Muḥammad Nādir Khān. On this day he won a victory over the Southerners who turned out to be two-faced and faithless to their covenant. They
174 fled in defeat, abandoning six machine guns and two six-pound guns. | Purdil reported his victory to Son of the Water Carrier by telephone and warned him not to send any unarmed conscripts[223] to Lahūgard to deter the Southerners because there would be no food for them. The retreat of the southern tribal force, which Purdil Khān reported to Son of the

[223] The term used for these conscripts was *siyāhī nishān dādan* (showing a silhouette) because they were a kind of "shadow army" only useful to give an impression from a distance of a mass of soldiers.

Water Carrier as a victory, was instigated by the fact that Muḥammad Nādir Khān, after observing the distrust and defiance among the tribes, declared a three-day truce, ostensibly for negotiations with Major General Muḥammad Ṣiddīq, who was in Kārīz-i Darwīsh.

Also on this day, the Hazārahs resumed combat operations in the Sar Chashmah area and entered Jalrīz in triumph. The 1,300-man regiment of Son of the Water Carrier which was stationed there was unable to withstand their onslaught. His soldiers, passing through Bīktūt and Pamqān, scattered to their homes in Kūh Dāman. They were afraid to return to Kabul /331/ since the water carrier's son and the high governor, Malik Muḥsin, usually shot deserters.

Already, the soldiers had not been paid [but see above] for seven months. They survived only by stealing from the subjects. This was another reason for them to return home (to protect their families and belongings). Both military and civilian officials nursed extreme hatred and loathing for the Saqqawī regime of infidels and libertines, who after Son of the Water Carrier's entry into the Arg, had begun looting the government treasury, hauling money away in trucks to their homes. After a while, they realized that without money it was difficult, indeed impossible, to administer the country and advance [government] business. So they stopped taking away the money, held tightly to what was left, and put it under guard. Out of this sum, they paid bribes to the avaricious, mercenary, and unscrupulous Afghans, thus provoking them to destroy the government and to kill and ravage each other. They reckoned that this was sufficiently effective to neutralize the Afghans. But they failed to pay their own soldiers their monthly wages.

Also on this day, employees of a number of the international legations applied to the Foreign Ministry to visit Jabal al-Sirāj and the hydroelectric power station there that supplies Kabul with electricity. Today, they received permission and, after preparing everything necessary for the trip—rugs, utensils, tables, chairs and food, they set off. They spent the day inspecting the surrounding area and the power station and then returned to the city in the evening.[224]

---

[224] On the hydroelectric plant at Jabal al-Sirāj see especially Marjorie Jewett Bell, *An American Engineer in Afghanistan*, Minneapolis, University of Minnesota Press, 1949 for the letters of the American who constructed the plant. Also Schinasi, *Kabul: A History*, index under "Jabal al-Serâj." Shkirando, in a note, cites a Russian source that describes this visit to the power station, Iu. Irkin in "Istoriia Afganistana," *Aziia i Afrika Segodnia* 1983, no. 3. p. 127. (Cited in Faiz Mukhammad, *Kniga upominanii*, p. 268, note 183.).

Also during these events, Deputy Field Marshal Malik Qays Khūgyānī, Deputy Field Marshal Muḥammad ʿAlam Shinwārī and ʿAbd al-Raḥmān Shinwārī, despite the fact that Muḥammad Hāshim Khān was in Jalālābād, trying to rally the tribes into a single coalition, came out in opposition to him and set about creating their own force. Malik Muḥammad ʿAlam and ʿAbd al-Raḥmān gathered a force of 1,800 men and Malik Qays, a force of 800.

Also /332/ ʿAbd al-Raḥmān,[225] son of ʿIṣmat Allāh Khān, who was allied with them and had come out opposed to Afghan honor and the faith, was
175 named to the post of high commissioner | of the Eastern Province. Pleased, he set out from Kabul for the Eastern Province, intending to widen even more the divisions and discord that existed there.

Sunday, 20 Ṣafar, Corresponding to 5 Asad and 28 July

On this day some of the Easterners, who had remained true to the principles of Afghan honor and whose hearts were with Muḥammad Hāshim Khān, entered Khāk-i Jabbār and clashed with contingents of Son of the Water Carrier that had been sent there.

As was already mentioned, the Easterners were divided into two groups, one of them assigned to head for Kabul and the other for Kūhistān. They had written to the men of Tagāb and had a pact with them that they would fight the Saqqawīs [when it was time] and now they wrote them and told them the time had come for the Tagābīs to take up arms against the Saqqawīs. The Ṣāfī tribe, which lived in Tagāb, immediately took up arms, fought valiantly, and gave the Saqqawīs cause to fear.

Also on this day, in accordance with the promise that had been made to subject the Andarī mullah in the presence of Qizilbāsh to discretionary punishment and make a public example of him because of his anathematization of the Shiʿis as infidels, the mayor (Khwājah) Tāj al-Dīn sent a written invitation to the elders of this tribe [the Qizilbāsh] through Āqā Jān, son of Nawrūz ʿAlī Khān, to come to city hall. But in the message he indicated that it would be wise of them to forgive this mullah. Some of the Qizilbāsh, who felt that if they were asked anything regarding issues of religion they would not be able to answer, came to me for advice. Ever since the beatings by Son of the Water Carrier my back and sides had been in great pain and I had been confined to bed. They reported that a decree had been prepared for some days now accusing the Shiʿis of unbelief and

[225] ʿAbd al-Raḥmān Khān was a Jabbār Khayl Ghilzāʾī. See Adamec, *Who's Who*, p. 103.

yesterday 120 mullahs had signed it, by which they were inciting all Sunnis to holy war (*ghazā*) and jihad against Hazārahs in order to kill /333/ and enslave them. The Qizilbāsh, who feared they too might be punished and humiliated at city hall, asked me how they should behave. I gave them Abū Ḥanīfah's precept:

> 'It is wrong to consider a person an infidel if he is a "person of the *qiblah*".' Concerning the unity of all Muslims, Abū Ḥanīfah also says, 'Everyone who utters the words "There is no god but God, and Muḥammad is the Prophet of God" is Muslim by consensus.' In the chapter 'Kitāb al-Shahādah' of the *Hidāyah*,[226] according to a fatwa from Nuʿmān b. Thābit, Shiʿis are considered Muslims because they profess the Muslim faith. Moreover, the law written down in the Sharīʿah reads as follows: 'The profession of faith given [even] by people who have erred or by the Khaṭṭābīyah[227] is acceptable.'[228] and by 'people who have erred' they mean Shiʿis and others. So how can someone whose profession of faith is acceptable be considered an infidel?

However, the Qizilbāsh, out of fear, said that they themselves will not be able to respond like this and cite the *Hidāyah* at the municipality. They proposed to carry me on a litter (dhooli) so that I could do it. But I, who was not even able to move, said reproachfully, "Oh wicked, cowardly tribe! Can't you even cite a book written by the Sunnis themselves? Why then have you stayed here, worked for this government, and [yet] force me, a sick man, to respond and cite this book for you?" Then I asked them to
176 send to me Shaykh Muḥammad Riżā [Khurāsānī], | who was an unusually eloquent public speaker so that he could quote the book at city hall and say that Shiʿis should be treated just like the adherents of Abū Ḥanīfah in conformity with his fatwas and that they should stop accusing the Shiʿis of unbelief. Otherwise, [the Qizilbāsh] will be excluded from their own religion. So they left and sent [the shaykh] to me along with the chief of the quarter (*kalāntar*), Sulṭān ʿAlī. They came at the moment when a merchant from Tabrīz, named Asad Allāh, and an employee of the Iranian Legation, Ṣafdar,[cxxvi] had come to visit me. However much I tried to persuade Shaykh Muḥammad Riżā, he did not have the courage to quote the book at city hall, /334/ and so, with harsh words, I admonished him. Finally, in the presence of the *kalāntar* and him, I sent the book to the Iranian Legation by the hand of Ṣafdar. The military attaché and his secretary

---

[226] The twelfth-century *al-Hidāyah fī sharḥ al-Bidāyah* by Burhān al-Dīn ʿAlī al-Marghīnānī (d.1197) remains a standard work of Hanafi jurisprudence.

[227] On the "extremist Shiʿi sect," the Khaṭṭābīyah, see W. Madelung, s.v., *The Encyclopedia of Islam*, New Edition, volume 4, pp. 1132a–1133a.

[228] The quotations are in Arabic.

[then] went to see Son of the Water Carrier and used official [diplomatic] language to resolve this religious conflict. By the following day announcements were posted in mosques and in other frequented places forbidding the denunciation of Shiʿis as infidels. Son of the Water Carrier was thus unable to publish the proclamation which the pseudo-mullahs had endorsed. This afternoon, a number of representatives of the Qizilbāsh went to city hall to intercede for that infidel mullah. Son of the Water Carrier kissed him and released him. In this manner, thanks to the actions of officials of the Iranian Legation, the problem of the anathematization of the Shiʿis was resolved and the Qizilbāsh were reassured.

Monday, 21 Ṣafar, Corresponding to 6 Asad and 29 July

On this day, twenty-six of the wounded from the battle at Tangī Āghūjān between the Southerners and the troops of the water carrier's son were taken by car to the hospital. Many of his soldiers were killed. At this battle, the hypocritical Southerners, unfaithful to their pledges, withdrew their support for Muḥammad Nādir Khān and Shāh Walī Khān.

Also on this day, the Hazārahs who had defeated the Saqqawī force at the Ūnay Pass began to pursue the fleeing soldiers to Jalrīz. Fighting continued right up to this same evening in Jalrīz. However the Saqqawī forces, who had fortified their positions in Jalrīz, continued to fight. In the dark of night, when both sides were resting from the fatigue of fighting, two Hazārahs, one of whom was a sayyid from Sanglākh, fell into the hands of the Saqqawī troops. The Hazārahs had been returning home from the Hazārahjāt where they had gone to get a bullock and grain. Both were brought to Kabul as prisoners. The sayyid, who was a Saqqawī subject and had not taken part in the fighting, was released. Son of the Water Carrier summoned [the other] Hazārah /335/ for questioning to learn the Hazārahs' situation, their preparedness for war, and their intentions with regards to fighting. He threatened him saying, "If you don't tell me the truth, I'll kill you, because I already have accurate facts obtained from Afghan nomads." [The Hazārah] replied,

> I don't care whether you have the facts or not, I would not lie in any case because lying is the worst sin of all and is the source of all corruption. I'm not afraid of being killed. I joined the struggle, knowing in advance that I
> 177 would certainly perish. | However, if I were to obey anyone except God and his Prophet, I would then consider myself to be the follower of an accursed devil. Therefore if I die while defending my property, family, the honor of my tribe, the legal Islamic government and my homeland, birthplace, and home, I will count it a great honor.

Son of the Water Carrier then said, "Why then do you oppose me and refuse to obey me, I who am the *pādshāh* of Islam and hold the reins of government in my capable hands." [The Hazārah] replied,

> The *pādshāh* of Islam is His Majesty Amān Allāh Khān, whom ignorant mullahs accused of unbelief but none of the things he has been accused of that would make him an infidel are the causes of unbelief, according to the Sharīʿah of the Prophet. He was forced to abdicate, but forced abdication is not accepted in Islam. The Hazārahs fight so that, once they take Kabul, they can invite him back by telegram and declare him amir although he has shown them nothing but oppression and tyranny for which no one is held accountable.

"And where are you going to get the rifles and ammunition to fight the government?" the water carrier's son asked. "We are going to get them to fight just as we've gotten the artillery, rifles, and cartridges in the past, by capturing them from your army." Son of the Water Carrier said, "You know, all the Hazārahs are going to perish and how is a dead man going to fight?" He replied, "There are 2,100,000 Hazārahs and before they perish they will kill double this number and only then **/336/** will they perish." Son of the Water Carrier said, "Then according to you, the Hazārahs, who had promised to give an oath of allegiance, will not now give it?" He said, "Never! They promised to give an oath of allegiance in order to end the war and secure themselves from destruction. In fact, they are waiting for the time when Muḥammad Nādir Khān approaches Kabul to resume the struggle."

Since the Hazārah had told the truth, Son of the Water Carrier ordered him imprisoned and abstained from killing him.

Also on this day rumors spread that Sayyid Aḥmad, son of Muḥammad Mīr, son of Shāh Nūr, had ascended the heights of Kūh-i Surkh with a group of braves intending to launch an attack on Kabul and Pamqān. This was troublesome news to the water carrier's son.

Tuesday, 22 Ṣafar, Corresponding to 7 Asad and 30 July

On this day when people were talking about the ongoing fighting in Lahūgard and Tagāb, an article with the deflating headline "Defeat for Muḥammad Nādir Khān" was published in issue No. 20 of *Ḥabīb al-Islām* written by its editor and chief bootlicker. It said,

> Muḥammad Nādir Khān has wanted to ignite rebellion and sedition in the Southern Province. To some degree he has succeeded in raising part of the

> tribes against the central government. But lately he has seen the regrettable and bitter result of his illegal and illegitimate activities. As you know from issue No. 19 of *Ḥabīb al-Islām* and also as reliable facts at our disposal attest, Muḥammad Nādir Khān has now gone missing. His brother, Shāh Walī Khān, left Afghanistan for Pārah Chinār [in British India]. The general situation of the tribes and the intentions of their leaders inspire confidence
> 178 | that soon all the tribes will express their submission to the lawful central government and will never again yield to the provocations of the enemies of Islam and the opponents of Afghan honor and valor. Besides, we are convinced that the English government, which is our neighbor, /**337**/ upholding the principles of good-neighborliness and of international agreements, will prevent the return to Afghan territory of persons who are the sources of trouble and corruption and would bring harm to the security and general tranquility of the country.

This report made its way to the Hazārahs. The Saqqawī deputy field marshal Muḥammad Ṣiddīq, who was known by the nickname "Bī-bīnī" ("No Nose"), his nose having been cut off during a raid, sent [to the Hazārahs] this issue of the paper. (The Hazārahs) had pinned their hopes on Muḥammad Nādir Khān but were now disappointed and returned to the Ūnay Pass from Jalrīz.

The report about the pullback of the Hazārahs, which had been recorded in my journal of the rebellion, greatly distressed me because I had persuaded them to be steadfast in fighting the Saqqawīs. I cursed the editor of the newspaper, that ignoramus. I knew that Kabul and its environs have been encircled since the first day of Son of the Water Carrier's regime and there is not a single safe road. The whole country is engulfed in the flames of rebellion, The Saqqawī gang is busy killing and looting, and people are killing each other. Despite this, he (the editor) calls the government with Son of the Water Carrier at its head the legitimate one—these brigands from the North, unbelievers, destroyers of the country, pseudo-mullahs, in whom not a single ounce of humanity remains, while the people, devout defenders of Muslim honor, who spend day and night in misery and deprivation, exerting every effort to drive out the gang of unbelievers and libertines, so as to reassure the nation, end the rebellion, and restore the destroyed government and country, are called by the editor, enemies of Islam and the foes of Afghan /**338**/ honor. He calls the gang of bandits and despoilers of the country the legal government! May this report be cursed and this Satan-like behavior be cursed. Anyway, with the help of a secret agent he conveyed it to the Hazārahs and detoured them from the path of what is right.

So, all these things—the abovementioned [newspaper] report; a Qur'ān sent by Son of the Water Carrier; the propaganda of Mīrzā Ḥasan ʿAlī, a scribe in the employ of the high governor, Malik Muḥsin, who had arrived in the Hazārahjāt and introduced himself to the backers of Muḥammad Amīn Khān who had received in advance a document about him which confirmed his loyalty; the activities of Nādir ʿAlī, the son of Sulṭān ʿAlī, who was one of the Hazārahs of Jāghūrī and who had obtained an oath of allegiance from the tribes of Fūlādah, Mīr Ādīnah, Pūsht, Shayr Dāgh and Jāghūrī, and had frightened [other] Hazārahs—all this resulted in my admonitions and instructions going for nought.

Wednesday, 23 Ṣafar, Corresponding /8 Asad/31 July

179 | Akram, a thief from the Shiʿi sweepers (*farrāshān*) of Pamqān, whose brother, Ḥasan, the insolent high governor, Malik Muḥsin, had killed and then confiscated two or three houses belonging to the poor people of Afshār, accusing its residents of having sheltered and fed [Akram], now gathered some 300–400 men and launched raids against Son of the Water Carrier. During this day's night, he led a foray against Qarghah and skirmished with the local population. But after several such raids, he went into hiding on the heights of Kūh-i Pamqān and then fled.

On this day, Son of the Water Carrier, fearing that the Hazārahs, having reinforced their sangars on Kūh-i Surkh, might begin an offensive against Kabul, ordered a unit with artillery to go to Pamqān and take up positions there.

Nādir [ʿAlī], son of Sulṭān ʿAlī, son of Sardār Shayr ʿAlī, /339/ was one of the Hazārahs of Jāghūrī. During the reign of His Majesty Amān Allāh Khān, he had been hostile to the governor for which he, the governor, and also the tribal *arbāb* (elder), Jumʿah by name, had been summoned to Kabul. [There] he was investigated and ultimately acquitted. Mīrzā Muḥammad Yaʿqūb, son of Muḥammad Ayyūb, who was the elder brother of Mīrak Shāh Kābulī, vice-president of the National Council, helped him in the process, and became his benefactor. [Nādir ʿAlī] became a member of the National Council, a post which he occupied for a year. In the first days of the revolution, when Son of the Water Carrier captured Kabul, [Nādir ʿAlī] received appointment as governor of Jāghūrī and Mālistān but was unable to take up his post. He got only as far as Lahūgard, before he had to return to Kabul. Fearing that the high governor, Malik Muḥsin, would persecute him because he had not gone to Jāghūrī, he went into hiding at the home of the mother of ʿAbd al-Karīm, a concubine of [the late] Amīr Ḥabīb Allāh Khān.[229] At the time [Nādir ʿAlī] was a member of the National Council, he had tricked her into marrying him.

So [Nādir ʿAlī] bided his time and, at the first opportunity, he walked to Bihsūd by night through Pamqān and from there made his way to Jāghūrī. When rumors spread that His Majesty Amān Allāh Khān was intending to attack Kabul, he concealed the farman [of appointment] issued by the Saqqawī government, went to see [Amān Allāh Khān] and received money and arms. And after the latter's defeat, he allied himself with an Afghan, Muḥammad Khān, who was deputy field marshal for Son of the Water Carrier. He went with Muḥammad Khān's units to Muqur and Qalāt, leading raids and forays along the way and trying with all his power to prove his devotion to Son of the Water Carrier.

At this time, [Nādir ʿAlī] obtained an oath of allegiance from his clan (*khānwādah*). Like a dog ready to serve whoever throws him a scrap of bread, after arriving in Ghaznīn, he called the high governor, Malik Muḥsin, on the telephone and reported the services he had performed including [his claim] that he had received [the oath of allegiance] from 40,000 men of his tribe and from the Mālistān, Jāghūrī, Mīr Ādīnah, Pashahʾī and Shayr Dāgh Hazārahs. [Nādir] hoped that his tricks and stratagems would be effective and they would honorably invite him to Kabul and indeed he was asked to go to Kabul by car. As soon as he arrived, Son of the Water Carrier ordered him to set off for Bihsūd to obtain an oath of allegiance from the Hazārahs of Bihsūd, Dāy Zangī, and Dāy Kundī **/340/** in the same way that he had gotten the oath from the Hazārahs living in the vicinity of Ghaznīn. But Nādir ʿAlī sidestepped the commission. Relying on the fact that he was the grandson of Sardār Shayr ʿAlī,[230] he also dreamed up other fraudulent ways and means in order to obtain high rank and title. He enjoyed no respect from his fellow tribesmen. He proposed to Son of the Water Carrier that he summon the elders of the Muḥammad Khwājah, Jīghatū, and Chahār Dastah tribes of Ghaznīn so that through them and by using tribal connections he would obtain an oath of allegiance from the Hazārahs of Bihsūd.

---

229 ʿAbd al-Karīm's mother was an Hazārah concubine named Ḥakīmah. Her title was ʿIzzat al-Haram (Glory of the Harem). (Adamec, *Who's Who*, Table 66 and May Schinasi, *Généalogie Mohammadzay*, Table 11.1.1.2, unpublished ms.).

230 Shayr ʿAlī Khān Jāghūrī was a strong supporter of Amīr Shayr ʿAlī Khān (r. 1863–66, 1868–79) and may have been given the life-title "sardār" usually reserved for Bārakzāʾī and Muḥammadzāʾī by him. As far as is known, he was the only Hazārah to have held the title, certainly the only one Fayż Muḥammad ever records.

180 | Son of the Water Carrier himself understood nothing of this and, like a dog, would scamper in any direction, yipping and yapping, as soon as he heard someone call. Nādir ʿAlī, fearing for his life and afraid that these tribes which, according to him, had given the oath of allegiance although [in fact] they had not, would unite with the Muḥammad Khwājah, Jīghatū, and Chahār Dastah of Ghaznīn, begin to fight the Saqqawī troops and take himself captive, convinced Son of the Water Carrier to summon the elders of these three tribes to Kabul. [His argument was that] it might be possible to get an oath of allegiance from the obstinate Hazārahs and, once the representatives of these three groups arrived in Kabul, the Hazārahs of Bihsūd would lose hope and break their alliance with other Hazārahs and would have to swear allegiance.

By telephone Son of the Water Carrier ordered the governor of Ghaznīn to send the leaders of these three tribes to Kabul. Since they were in Ghaznīn to pay their taxes, the governor sent them by car to Kabul under escort.

Thursday, 24 Ṣafar, Corresponding to 9 Asad and 1 November (sic—August)[231]

On this day, two elderly and greedy leaders of the Mangal tribe, donkey thieves whose avarice knew no bounds—they were ready to kill for as little as an onion—wanting to enrich themselves, brought Son of the Water Carrier eight captives from his army who during fighting had been taken prisoner by Muḥammad Nādir Khān. The latter, being a charitable man and a sincere Muslim, had not killed the prisoners but had handed them over to leaders of the Southern tribes and had ordered them to give them food and drink in return for their labor. These two men, getting themselves to Kabul by an unknown route and having handed over the prisoners /341/ who had been entrusted to them, told him of the service they had done him. But Son of the Water Carrier gave them nothing and dismissed them.

Also on this day, in response to rumors of the arrival of Easterners in Nimlah and Gandamak under the leadership of Muḥammad Hāshim Khān, the water carrier's son dispatched reinforcements from Kabul to Butkhāk.

---

[231] From here on the author mistakenly calls August, November. To avoid confusion, we have used the correct name of the month.

The fact that Son of the Water Carrier had sent a Qur'ān to the residents of Sar Chashmah was regarded by the Hazārahs as a sign of weakness and they attacked Deputy Field Marshal Muḥammad Ṣiddīq "No Nose" whose units were garrisoned at Qalʿah-i Majīd near Siyāh Baghal and Qalʿah-i Safīd, the fort of Ghulām Ḥasan Qizilbāsh in the Ūnay Pass. [The Hazārahs] chased his forces as far as Jalrīz.

As a result of the Hazārah attacks, Ḥamīd Allāh, the youngest son of Amīr [Hidāyat] Allāh, the water carrier, hitched up horses to several field pieces and sent them to Jalrīz at 2:00 P.M. He himself, with a gang of battle-ready thieves also set off for that region.

Also on this day, twenty-four Easterners, who earlier had formed an alliance with Muḥammad Hāshim Khān, but then, having turned their backs on him, had broken the pact, ascended the mountains which towered over Khāk-i Jabbār and Butkhāk. One of them appeared on the heights directly in front of the Saqqawī forces in Butkhāk. The soldiers opened fire with artillery and rifles. The man on the heights waved a piece of cloth which they took as a sign of surrender. They sent someone for him, brought him and his comrades down from the mountain, and took them to Butkhāk from where they sent them under guard to Son of the Water Carrier in Kabul who commended them for their action.

Also on this day, they severed the hands of an Hazārah who resided in Qalʿahchah and confiscated his belongings after Saqqawī soldiers found two rifles in his house. A friend of his had informed on him. /342/

Also on this day, the high governor Malik Muḥsin captured a woman
181 | from Chahārdihī, whom one of the Saqqawī debauchers had raped and impregnated. The rapist himself was also caught. Malik Muḥsin ordered the woman imprisoned until she gave birth and afterwards for her and her infant to be killed. The *qāżī* objected to killing the infant, declaring that this contravened the laws of the Sharīʿah. The high governor attacked him saying, "Whether my order conforms with the Sharīʿah or not, it must be carried out. So do not argue!"

Friday, 25 Ṣafar, Corresponding to 10 Asad and 2 August

On the eve of this day a number of the Karū Khayl, the tribe of the wife of Muḥammad ʿAlī Khān, brother of Her Majesty [ʿUlyā Ḥażrat], and [the tribe of] the mother of His Majesty Amān Allāh Khān, decided to advance along the road to Tangī Ghārū and attack Dih-i Sabz and Khwājah Rawāsh. They began the attack at 2:00 A.M. Son of the Water Carrier's soldiers, who were occupying positions there, opened fire with artillery and rifles.

The fight continued for half an hour /343/ and the Karū Khayl withdrew without having achieved their objective, but without losing any dead or wounded either.

Today wounded were brought to Kabul Hospital from Lahūgard where fighting has already lasted several days.

Also on this day, leaders of the Jāghūrī, Mālistān, Mīr Ādīnah, Pashah'ī, Shayr Dāgh, Muḥammad Khwājah, and Chahār Dastah Hazārahs who due to the scheming of Nādir ʿAlī, the grandson of Sardār Shayr ʿAlī Khān Jāghūrī, some of whom were with him and some having been deceived by him, proffered their oath of allegiance now were summoned to Kabul. There, on behalf of Son of the Water Carrier, they were commissioned and compelled to go to Bihsūd and bring back an oath of allegiance from the militant Hazārahs. When the Hazārah leaders, with the exception of Nādir ʿAlī, as already mentioned, had come to see me to ask how I was doing after the beating by Son of the Water Carrier, I had advised them to stand firm. They, who had been snared by the tribal betrayal of the treacherous and duplicitous Nādir ʿAlī, in view of the enormous consequences for all Hazārahs of swearing allegiance to Son of the Water Carrier, now with apologies [to Son of the Water Carrier] said,

> We have no tribal ties to the Bihsūd, Dāy Zangī, Dāy Kundī, Surkh wa Pārsā, Turkmān, Bāmyān, Shaykh ʿAlī, and Balkhāb Hazārahs and our only relationship to them is that we are all Hazārahs. These tribes will not follow our advice and admonitions and will pay no heed to our guidance and instructions.

Prior to this, Son of the Water Carrier had sent the Hazārahs a Qur'ān, and, separately, Deputy Field Marshal Muḥammad Ṣiddīq had sent a Qur'ān and two sheep along with a message appealing nicely to the Hazārahs to submit and put an end to the bloodshed and promising to fulfill any of their demands. Son of the Water Carrier did not take the Hazārahs of Ghaznīn to task for their refusal to go and simply said, "If you don't want to go yourselves, then just draft a letter to them on your own behalf which you will send along with some admonitions and warnings. The minister of court, Shayr Jān, will compose it." Nādir ʿAlī promised to draft this letter and have it in final form the next day and they were granted permission to leave the presence of Son of the Water Carrier and go to their own lodgings. /344/

Saturday, 26 Ṣafar/11 Asad/3 August

182 | Today rumors circulated that the Saqqawī forces had been routed at /228/ Jalrīz at the hands of Hazārahs and at Lahūgard by the Aḥmadzā'ī

who, due to the two-faced, hypocritical, disloyal actions of Ghawṣ al-Dīn, son of Jahāndād [Aḥmadzā'ī], were cursed by the southern tribes allied with Muḥammad Nādir Khān. They also attacked [the Saqqawīs] in order to remove the accusation [of being traitors] and were victorious. Rumors also circulated about fighting by the people of Tagāb, who, in hopes of the arrival of the Eastern Province tribes, had begun engaging contingents of the army of Son of the Water Carrier. From all three directions, the defeated turned the face of flight from the battlefield towards their homes and concealment. In the face of this situation, Son of the Water Carrier became desperate and ordered a decree printed and posted in all the places where people gather including the city mosques and in [surrounding] villages saying,

> *kalāntar*s of the city and *kadkhudā*s of the villages should not conceal deserters fleeing the battlefield but must hand them over to government officials who will return them to the place from which they had fled and where they had turned their backs on the enemy and shoot them so that no one would ever again flee from the battlefield. Should the *kalāntar*s or *kadkhudā*s harbor anyone and they are discovered, then they will be subject to a fine of twelve rupees cash and the deserter will be shot. The same things holds for each deserter up to a total fine of 5,000 rupees for any individual *kalāntar* or *kadkhudā* who hides more than one deserter.

After the issuing of this decree, all deserters sought refuge in the mountains where they could not be found.

Also on this day, braves from the Karū Khayl and Hūd Khayl tribes attacked the Saqqawī detachment which was dug in at Butkhāk and took 100 soldiers prisoner with their weapons. After disarming them, they let them go. /345/

Also on the evening of this day, battle-eager Hazārah braves carried out a foray against the Saqqawī force in Jalrīz and killed 800 soldiers.

During this time, Nādir ʿAlī, as cunning as a fox and as villainous as a jackal, appeared at the house of Sayyid Jaʿfar and appealed to him for advice on the letter he had promised to write to the Hazārahs. I was there and chastised him for getting an oath of allegiance from the Hazārahs of Jāghūrī.

> You managed to do this without Son of the Water Carrier being forced to send an army and you broke the unity of the Hazārahs and set them against each other, introduced the breach of hypocrisy, and have done a very wicked thing. And you've done it purely out of avarice hoping that Son of the Water Carrier will give you something. Because of this vile deed, you've caused the Hazārahs to be cursed by the whole world.

That one, who had no justification for what he had done, showed me a farman from Son of the Water Carrier that was addressed to Raḥīm Khān Kākarī.[232] It said, "All the lands of the Hazārahs, their belongings, wealth, and families that you seize will be yours." [Then] [Nādir ʿAlī] said, "We were forced to obtain the oath of allegiance because of fear that the Afghans, who believe this farman to have the force of law, would attack us." But since the dreams of Son of the Water Carrier have not been realized, the Afghan could not unleash a religious war that would stretch from the [frontiers of] Afghanistan to Khurāsān. [Nādir ʿAlī] promised to bring the draft copy of the letter for correction in order to then take it to the
183 minister of court. |

After the departure of Nādir ʿAlī, Sayyid Jaʿfar told me as a friend, "What you did was not wise. This man is very greedy and envious. God forbid that he should report you to Son of the Water Carrier." This frightened me but there were no consequences. **/346/**

Sunday, 27 Ṣafar/12 Asad/4 August

On this day Nādir ʿAlī came [again] to Sayyid Jaʿfar, with whom I was staying. Nādir ʿAlī, as already reported, had promised to bring the draft copy of the letter but he did not bring it. He had already written the letter to the Hazārahs on the advice of Son of the Water Carrier and the minister of court and gotten the leaders of the Muḥammad Khwājah, Jīghatū, and Chahār Dastah of Ghaznīn, whom Nādir ʿAlī had dragged into the snares of Son of the Water Carrier and been forced to come to Kabul, to sign it. Already yesterday he had sent the letter accompanied by Mustawfī Sayyid Qāsim Sarābī, who, of the highest Saqqawīst officials, had received the rank of "civilian general" (*janrāl-i*[cxxvii] *kishwarī*); Shaykh Sulṭān ʿAlī Jāghūrī; Walī Muḥammad, son of Bāz ʿAlī Mālistānī; and Muḥammad Nāṣir, who came from the Aḥmadī clan which lived in Jāghūrī. Glibly, Nādir ʿAlī said, "Son of the Water Carrier and the minister of court forced me to write the letter and the Hazārah elders to sign it in their presence. Then he immediately entrusted it to [those] four men and sent it by motor car to Sar Chashmah for them to pass on to the Hazārahs."

Although this Nādir ʿAlī, who, for a crust of bread, is ready to run anywhere and for a half-rupee is ready to chase after a hundred horsemen, it was clear that he himself had devised all these subterfuges in order to gain his own ends. He has made and is making the Hazārahs, like the Afghans,

232 This would appear to be from the same farman quoted in full above.

to be known for lacking religion and pride and for abandoning honor and reputation. And, by these duplicitous statements he is trying to make sure that there won't be any evidence to indict him.

I asked Nādir ʿAlī, "Did you have a copy of this letter?" In reply, he pulled out his original draft. After it was seen and read and falsely praised, he was pleased and said, "I first wanted to bring this draft to you and then take it to Son of the Water Carrier but the latter, not giving me the time, straightaway forced me to write it and then quickly sent it off. /347/ But I brought you the original draft." In this letter [Nādir ʿAlī] tried to inspire fear in the Hazārahs by asserting the power of his tribe and of the elders who had signed the letter. He also warned them about what Son of the Water Carrier might do and also gave promises on his behalf. This is a summary of the text of the message:

> Hazārah brothers of Bihsūd and others! Being your fellow tribesmen and co-religionists, we want what is best for you and would like to offer our advice. Why have you let yourselves be led about by villains and mercenary-minded people, opposed the *pādshāh* of Islam, and gone astray and become rebels? You never had any high posts and ranks. When the Afghans were in power, you were subject to humiliation and abuse. Now that you and we have been
> **184** freed from the cruel regime of the Afghans, | and power has passed into the hands of a *pādshāh*, a sincere Muslim, who speaks the same language we speak, God willing, we will be masters of our own lands, wealth, honor, and rights of which we have been deprived for so many years. We will also become holders of high posts and ranks. For this it is necessary that as soon as you read this letter, you immediately put the cord of obedience around your necks and end the bloodshed and war. If you don't do that, the government will not have to send forces to fight you; we ourselves, the Hazārahs, will attack and destroy you. The end.

This letter of Nādir ʿAlī [in a play on his name] became known as "*nardallah-ī*"[233] and people cursed him for it.

Rumors spread that the residents of Tagāb, after receiving the message from the tribes of the Eastern Province in which they promised to attack Kūhistān with Muḥammad Hāshim at their head, had taken up arms and joined the struggle. Son of the Water Carrier was frightened and confused and ordered four treasonous khans of Kūhistān and Kūh Dāman, namely Muḥammad Aʿẓam /348/ Tutamdarraʾī, Muḥammad Zamān Jabal al-Sirājī, Khwājah Bābū, and a son of Mīr Akbar who was known as Mīr Bachchah, all of whom had major responsibilities and held high posts in Kabul to

233 *Nardallah-ī* is the adjective from *nardallah* "faggot."

go to Kūhistān to defend their own families, belongings and wealth from any attack by the Tagābīs and to prepare the people there to repel them.

Farmans intended to bolster spirits and encourage support were sent to all the people of the North to remind them that the sovereign and the government were of their own people, to ask them to join forces and spare no effort to aid and protect the authority of the government from the Afghans, and to realize that if they abandoned unity and defense [of the government] they would be annihilated by the killing and plundering which the Afghan nation and others would make them subject to.

Also on this day, due to the fact that Sarhang ʿAlī Khān, the military attaché (*ātāshah-i militar*) of the Iranian Legation, visited Prince Amīn Allāh Khān, Ḥamīd Allāh, the youngest son of the water carrier, verbally attacked him and said that he would cane him and that his older brother (Ḥabīb Allāh) would [also] punish him. However, at the request of the minister of court, Shayr Jān, they pardoned him from the caning and ordered a complete severing of contacts with foreigners. The guard at the Iranian Legation was replaced and the people of Kabul were prohibited from visiting it. For eight years, I had visited the legation twice a week. But after receiving word from the secretary at the legation I stopped going there for some time. This affair was the cause of [Prince] Amīn Allāh's emigrating from Afghanistan.

Monday, 28 Ṣafar, Corresponding to 13 Asad and 5 August

Because people are more and more frequently saying that the Tagābīs are intent on taking up arms, Son of the Water Carrier, who yesterday dispatched an appeal to the people of the North, remains the consort of anxiety and confusion. On this day, he again resolved to send [the Northerners] leaflets and farmans in which he ordered /349/ that they prepare 6,500 men to fight the Tagābīs with whatever weapons they had and prevent them from entering Kūhistān. He ordered these farmans speedily distributed to the people of the Northern regions through the aforementioned Kūhistānīs and Kūh Dāmanīs who held high posts in Kabul.

185 The populace, | already inclined against the amir, now expresses even more support for the valorous Hazārahs and Afghans. In order to win the people over to his side and to reassure them that the government is confident and not involved in fighting on several fronts, Son of the Water Carrier ordered a Victory Arch built and flower beds planted all along the road from the Shāh Dū Shamshīrah Mosque, situated near the bridge, up to the Monument of Knowledge and Ignorance, which was erected

by His Majesty Amān Allāh, and the road to Dār al-Amān decorated in honor of Independence Day. He assigned the responsibility of preparing everything necessary for the celebrations, including assembling singers, to the minister of education, Fayż Muḥammad; Ghulām Muḥyī al-Dīn Khān, the director of the Kabul Museum; and others, sycophants who in fear for their lives have continually curried the favor of Son of the Water Carrier. He warned them that if they did not make better preparations than had been made for the holiday in preceding years, he would have them shot. And although Son of the Water Carrier, being an ignorant unbeliever and more used to roaming through mountains and deserts, had no conception of what constituted beauty, nevertheless, these people, afraid of slanderers, zealously applied themselves to the holiday preparations. **/350/**

Tuesday, 29 Ṣafar, Corresponding to 14 Asad and 6 August

Today in Chamargand, announcements from Muḥammad Nādir Khān printed at the Chamargand Press situated in the homeland of the Muhmand tribe in the free frontier zone were sent out as a final warning to the North and to Kabul, Chahārdihī, Lahūgard, Pamqān, Arghandah, and Maydān. Based on incontrovertible proofs, the announcements called on people to stop supporting Son of the Water Carrier and, if they were able, to capture or kill him. If unable, the valorous Afghans would attack from four sides and annihilate him. The residents of these regions should be aware that if they do not take up arms against him, but rather deem themselves the consorts of ease and comfort and oppose what is written in this proclamation, which has only been issued because of incontrovertible proofs, then by their degrading actions they would be bringing death and destruction down on themselves. This decree, like a fire, scorched the heart of the oppressor, Son of the Water Carrier, and pushed him to the brink of desperation and terror.

On this day, on the Tagāb front, the forces of Son of the Water Carrier that had been sent there to suppress the local population, set up their thunderbolt-loaded artillery on Kūh-i Ṣāfī, targeted the Tagābīs with fire from those guns and their rifles, smashed a breach in the fortress of Tagābī solidarity, and took two or three prisoners.

On the Hazārah front, the bearers of the tribal letter that, by intrigue, Nādir ʿAlī had written on behalf of the tribes, reached the Hazārahs. After listening to the fear-inspiring words of the bearers of the letter, they stopped fighting and began negotiations with Deputy Field Marshal Muḥammad Ṣiddīq "No-Nose" who had sent them a Qurʾān and some

186 sheep. | The message that they sent him suggested meeting in a mutually satisfactory place to negotiate. After reaching an agreement [on a satisfactory place for the negotiations], every matter which is agreed to by the two sides and sworn to by oath, Hazārah obedience to the government according to their conditions /351/ will be fulfilled and the cord of discord will be severed. Since the Hazārah stance in opposition[cxxviii] to Son of the Water Carrier had come to this point through the cunning of Nādir ʿAlī, their firmly planted feet were now dislodged, and they had no choice but to make peace. As will come below, they met and negotiated with Deputy Field Marshal "No-Nose" and broke the chain of conflict.

Also, Mīrzā Ḥasan ʿAlī, secretary to the high governor Malik Muḥsin, having voluntarily gone to Bihsūd to obtain an oath of allegiance, as was mentioned above, had been detained along with his personal assistant (nawkar). But having obtained a letter from Prince Muḥammad [Amin] and the leaders of the Hazārahs of Bihsūd, attesting to his loyalty to the prince and to the Hazārahs, at night, his nawkar secretly got over the walls of the fort and escaped and went to Kabul to deliver reliable information to the high governor, Malik Muḥsin. On this day, they asked this messenger, who had just arrived, "What are the losses that both sides have sustained since the outbreak of fighting between the Hazārahs and the Saqqawīs?" [The nawkar], who had been locked up with Mīrzā Ḥasan ʿAlī for a time and had obtained reliable information, explained that among the Hazārahs there have been two men killed and wounded and one taken prisoner while more than 2,000 Saqqawīs have been killed, wounded, or captured. He then said,

> About 30 pieces of artillery have also fallen into Hazārah hands along with a large quantity of rifles and ammunition. At the moment, the Hazārahs have ample artillery, rifles and ammunition for conducting combat operations. They have fought bravely and well. But because of the arrival of the letter and the Hazārah delegation from Jāghūrī and other places, they have undone the belt of their resolve.

Wednesday, 1 Rabīʿ al-Awwal, Corresponding to 15 Asad and 7 August

Muḥammad Nādir Khān sent to Son of the Water Carrier a number of the ulema and leaders from the southern tribes and the Aḥmadzāʾī who had caused him grief by breaking their covenants with him, along with Adam Khān, son of Malik Pīr Dūst /352/. Through them he asked Son of the Water Carrier to release his and his brother's families who were languishing in prison and send them to him. When that happened, he would give up the ill-starred alliance of Afghan tribes and leave the country. The delegation arrived in Kabul in three automobiles. They were accorded a very warm reception, but, as will become clear, they returned empty-handed.

During the night of this day, the youngest son of the water carrier, Ḥamīd Allāh, learned that a beardless youth from the North had been brought to the village of Bībī Māhrū for a wedding festival to entertain the guests with dancing and to satisfy their lust. Ḥamīd Allāh suddenly broke into the house with a gang of bandits and arrested more than 100 people who were enjoying themselves. Ḥamīd Allāh himself was an incorrigible dancer and, more than that, a great libertine but, in order to appear in the eyes of the people as an advocate of Islam, he shackled those he arrested,
187 took them to the city | and threw them in jail. During the day, they paraded them around the bazaars as an example and caned the young dancer to death. The rest were fined 20,000 rupees, each person having to pay a fine ranging from 100 to 600 rupees. He also ordered the homes of the parents of the bride and the bridegroom confiscated. Despite the fact that during the time of his brother's brigandage, [Ḥamīd Allāh] himself worked as a dancer, and at the time his brother came to power he would have his way with young girls and young boys at night while by day he would torture people, nevertheless he took these steps to try and make himself appear to be a true Muslim and an upholder of the Sharīʿah in people's eyes. /353/

Thursday, 2 Rabīʿ al-Awwal, Corresponding to 16 Asad and 8 August

A rumor circulated on this day that the son of Jahāndād Aḥmadzā'ī, Ghaws̱ al-Dīn, an infamous rebel who had always followed the way of "partnering with the caravan and befriending the thief" attacked the Saqqawī detachment stationed in Butkhāk with 8,000 fighters. Had he been victorious he planned to attack the city and sack it. But the rumor turned out to be unfounded and no one knows where Ghaws̱ al-Dīn actually is. Since everyone heard the rumor was false, this night passed quietly for the people of Kabul and Butkhāk.

At this time Prince Muḥammad Amīn and his deputy, Khwājah Hidāyat Allāh, were in a state of despair because of the arrival of the delegation of Hazārahs from Ghaznīn,[cxxix] their letter, and the threats of Nādir ʿAlī who was warning that if the Hazārahs of Bihsūd refused to submit, then he would attack at the head of a force from his own tribe and crush and subjugate them. Hazārah leaders reassured both of them, reminding them of those same terms which I had urged on them and for which I had drafted a memorandum listing them. They said, "As long as there is one Hazārah still alive, then no harm will come to you or your deputy." The prince was reassured. He knew that the Hazārahs were champions of the religion and faithful to their covenants and he had never heard them tell lies.

Also on this day, by order of the water carrier's son, the managing editor of *Ḥabīb al-Islām* published an article about Nādir ʿAlī's obtaining an oath of allegiance under the headline "Praise to the Hazārahs of Jāghūrī and Mālistān." This was meant to break the Hazārah coalition against the Saqqawī government. It read:

> As has become known, thanks to the grace of God and to the wisdom of the sublime and auspicious *pādshāh*, who is true to the religion, a large part of the Hazārah tribes with pure hearts presented to His Highness an oath of allegiance and created the propitious opportunity for other Hazārah tribes to express their obedience. During these days, /354/ the grandson of Sardār Shayr ʿAlī Khān Hazārah, Nādir ʿAlī; Shaykh Sulṭān ʿAlī, and Walī Muḥammad
> **188** Khān, staunch leaders of Jāghūrī, Mālistān, | Mīr Ādīnah, Pashah'ī, and Shayr Dāgh, have been honored by being received by His Highness and have presented an oath of allegiance from themselves personally and on behalf of their co-tribesmen. Moreover, they have declared, 'The Hazārahs of Bihsūd are our fellow tribesmen and co-religionists and they live the same kind of life that we do. Therefore, we beg His Highness to permit us, in the course of talks, and also as an object lesson, to direct them to the path of truth and eliminate the misunderstandings which exist. We hope that they will perceive us as fellow tribesmen and will take our advice and stop the internecine bloodshed. If they do not put an end to rebellion, then permit us by ourselves, making use of tribal alliances, to force them to stand on the true path and to submit to your Islamic government.'

After hearing such avowals, His Highness expressed his satisfaction and pleasure and having accorded to each of them royal favor and blessing, he sent them off with all honors in motor cars to fulfill the noble task.

Thus, on the basis of this newspaper article, the readers of *Kitāb-i* [*taẕakkur-i*] *inqilāb* will form for themselves some idea of people like Nādir ʿAlī Jāghūrī; Riżā Bakhsh, the Bihsūdī collector; Ghaws̱ al-Dīn, son of Jahāndād Aḥmadzā'ī; Muḥammad Hasan, son of ʿAtīq Allāh Wardak; and others. /355/ In the grip of insatiable greed and avarice, they continue to threaten destruction, ruin, and ransacking both to the entire government and to their fellow tribesmen in this world and the next. As a result of the intrigue and conspiracies of Nādir ʿAlī, which the newspaper article confirmed, the coalition of Hazārahs was destroyed. I pray to the Almighty to direct Nādir ʿAlī to the path of truth.

Friday, 3 Rabīʿ al-Awwal, Corresponding to 17 Asad and 9 August

In three places in Lahūgard—Khūshi, Dūbandī, and Shāh Mazār—and in Kūhistān—up to Bagrāmī and Khwājah Chāsht where some strong adherents of the religion and faith and upholders of their covenants and pacts from the tribes of the Southern Province along with the proud residents of Tagāb, had attacked the Saqqawī forces, on this day well-armed units under the command of Major General Muḥammad Ṣiddīq, the high commissioner of the Southern Province; the aide-de-camp Saʿīd Muḥammad; and Muḥammad ʿUmar, /356/ better known as "General Sūr," were dispatched to those places. However all three were beset by confusion. Fed up with the oppression and licentiousness of the Saqqawīs, people were hopeful that the Southern tribes and the Tagābīs would win this battle and impatiently awaited their assault on Kabul. However, the Southerners, as is their unfailing custom,[cxxx] carry out attacks only with the object
189 of booty and loot, | and so went home despite their success in battle.

Another of the sons of the slain Jahāndād[234] as well as the deluded Ghawṡ al-Dīn entered the wadi of broken promises, false oaths, and loss of influence [and decamped]. The substantial Saqqawī force commanded by Saʿīd Muḥammad, the aide-de-camp, was heartened and resumed its advance towards Gardayz, Machalghū, and Darrah-i Mangal; another sizeable force led by Field Marshal Purdil Khān marched in the direction of the Southern Province and Jājī by way of Dūbandī and Qāsim Khayl in Lahūgard; and Muḥammad Ṣiddīq and Muḥammad ʿUmar /356/ "Sur" occupied positions in Kārīz-i Darwīsh. They were relieved of any concern because the bellicose southern tribes had gone home.

Also on this day, as a result of the courage and manly resolution of the Tagābīs, the Saqqawī force was bested in battle and fled. A number of them reached Kabul. Son of the Water Carrier had one of the deserters shot and imprisoned the rest so that no one else would desert the battlefield. However, since he had no forces now, having sent them all to the Eastern and Southern (Provinces), the Hazārahjāt, and Tagāb, and there was no one left in the city, he released (the deserters) and sent them towards Tagāb.

Also during the events that have been recorded, thanks to Nādir ʿAlī's letter; the Ghaznīn Hazārah delegation; the secret activities of Mīrzā

---

[234] Jahāndād, a very troublesome Aḥmadzāʾī Ghilzāʾī to Amīr Ḥabīb Allāh Khān's government, was eventually put to death (blown from a gun) in 1912. (Fayż Muḥammad, *The History*, vol. 4, pp. 1029–30.).

Ḥasan ʿAlī, secretary to the high governor Malik Muḥsin; and Riżā Bakhsh, some Hazārah braves had turned their hearts towards Son of the Water Carrier. But some other brave Hazārahs still remained resolute in the struggle and were not influenced by Nādir ʿAlī's threats. They regarded the Qurʾāns sent by Son of the Water Carrier and Deputy Field Marshal "No-Nose" and the proposal of a truce as mere deception. Thus, in the dark of night, descending from Ūnay Pass, Hazārahs attacked the Saqqawī force that was in Sar Chashmah and believed that a truce had gone into effect. The Hazārahs took 700 prisoners, their rifles, ammunition, and six-[pound] field pieces and returned in triumph. At the water carrier's son's order, four soldiers who had fled to Kabul from the battlefield were shot by firing squad as a lesson to others not to turn their backs on a battle and run away.

Saturday, 4 Rabīʿ al-Awwal, Corresponding to 18 Asad and 10 August

On this day, rumors circulated in Kabul that rupees and half-rupees had appeared minted with the name of ʿInāyat Allāh Khān, whom His Highness Amān Allāh Khān had left on the amirid throne after his abdication /357/ and departure for Qandahar. Disloyal ministers, the Ḥażrat of Shūr Bāzār, and Sardār Muḥammad ʿUs̱mān Khān, having expressed their obedience to Son of the Water Carrier, warned ʿInāyat Allāh Khān what might happen to him and forced him to go into exile. He left for Tehran and settled there permanently. But a few days ago, a rumor made the rounds that he had entered Jalālābād. The rupees and half-rupees minted in his name came into people's hands thanks to opponents of Son of the Water
190 Carrier. | The people of Kabul were excited by this rumor and it heartened them. They told each other,

> Although it may be untrue, where there's smoke, there's fire (literally: where there's light there's a lamp). ʿInāyat Allāh Khān is in Tehran, no longer amir, and the Indo-British authorities whose protégé is Son of the Water Carrier, do not wish and will not allow ʿInāyat Allāh Khān to enter Afghanistan from Tehran by passing through their territory in order to drive out Son of the Water Carrier. From this it follows that the coins with ʿInāyat Allāh's name on them were apparently minted by counterfeiters in Tīrāh, who are always producing counterfeit money. They probably acted on instructions from Muḥammad Nādir Khān in order to unite, by the use of [ʿInāyat Allāh's] name, the Afghans who have forgotten their pride and the need to defend their honor and homeland and instead have engaged in discord and dissension. In the final analysis, they have set for themselves the goal of eliminating Son of the Water Carrier.

Such stories were heard for several days but gradually they died down and nothing more was heard of them. It is not known who was behind this but it brought no advantage either to Muḥammad Nādir Khān or Muḥammad Hāshim Khān for all the Afghans by their very nature are untrue to their alliances and agreements and are [more] accustomed to thievery. They deserve no commendation. Through error, they gained high positions, but during this revolution they lost the esteem they had in the eyes of the people, fell into the dirt of bad reputation, /358/ and were condemned by all.

Sunday, 5 Rabīʿ al-Awwal, Corresponding to 19 Asad and 11 August

For a long time, the brother of Muḥammad Nādir Khān, Muḥammad Hāshim Khān, had been operating in Jalālābād and its environs. But all his attempts to create a coalition of the tribes of the Eastern Province had come to nought since those people usually did not honor their oaths and ended up turning their faces away from religion and towards Satan and could never be true to an alliance even with the backing of their leaders. Even if they had concluded an agreement and were on their way to the battlefield, even then, as a result of the activities of foreigners, local pseudo-mullahs, bootlicking leaders, and Ḥażrat-i Chārbāghī, the foundations of any coalition could always be undermined. Each time rumors were heard about their getting together, it would evoke feelings of optimism among people who were sick and tired of the tyranny of Son of the Water Carrier and feelings of despair among his supporters. But as of yet no breeze was blowing from that direction. However, on this day, rumors spread that a huge force of Easterners had arrived in Jagdalak and Barīkāb. Son of the Water Carrier ordered a proclamation printed advising the Easterners to obey [his government]. On this day at 5:00 A.M. he
191 sent the proclamation by plane to Jalālābād. He stressed to the pilots | that they obtain information [about where to drop the proclamations] and then drop them on the camps of the Eastern tribal forces.

Meanwhile, Mīrzā Ḥasan ʿAlī, the secretary of the high governor Malik Muḥsin, on the twenty-seventh of Muḥarram, as previously noted, had voluntarily gone with four Qizilbāsh to the Hazārahs to get an oath of allegiance and had been detained. /359/ But Mīrzā Ḥasan ʿAlī continued his clandestine activities, persuading the Hazārahs to give an oath of allegiance. Also, the Ghaznīn and Jāghūrī Hazārah delegation arrived with the letter which contained threats that were confirmed by Mīrzā Ḥasan ʿAlī. The Hazārah leaders of Bihsūd, expecting the arrival of Muḥammad Nādir Khān in the environs of Kabul, dragged their feet on offering the oath of allegiance using any pretext they could think of, and continued to oppose Son of the Water Carrier and to fight against his forces. Eventually, they lost hope in Muḥammad Nādir Khān and the Southerners and on this day they promised the Hazārah delegation from Ghaznīn, Mīrzā Ḥasan ʿAlī, and Deputy Field Marshal Muḥammad Ṣiddīq "No-Nose," who more than once had suggested they either give an oath of allegiance or let the war continue, that they would come to Sar Chashmah for negotiations about tendering the oath of allegiance under the terms that they wanted. The delegation and Mīrzā Ḥasan ʿAlī reported the Hazārahs' promise to Deputy Field Marshal "No-Nose" and he in turn reported to the governor of Maydān who, in his turn, let the high governor, Malik Muḥsin, know about it by telephone in order to prepare everything necessary to receive the Hazārahs who had promised to come to Sar Chashmah. After a successful conclusion of negotiations there, they would then go on to the city to present their oath of allegiance. These stories had a very depressing effect on the opponents of Son of the Water Carrier's regime, who had linked their hopes to salvation at the hands of the Hazārahs. Some of them shared their disappointment with me. But I reassured them,

> The Hazārahs are acting according to the advice given them. As far as I know, Son of the Water Carrier will never manage to obtain an oath of allegiance from them. They will not recognize his government as long as the situation of Muḥammad Nādir Khān and the Afghans remains unclear. If they come to Kabul then it will only be for the sake of gathering intelligence about Son of the Water Carrier's army and the number of troops stationed /**360**/ in the capital.

These words reassured them.

Monday, 6 Rabīʿ al-Awwal/ 20 Asad/12 August

On this day, Ḥājjī Muḥammad Ṣāliḥ, the son of Mīrzā Muḥammad Ṭāhir Qizilbāsh, who had paid a bribe of 4,000 rupees to Son of the Water Carrier's minister of court, Shayr Jān, hoping thereby to leave Kabul, go to Iran, and escape the tyranny of the Saqqawīs, received the post of director of the customs office at Harāt and left for Harāt. As soon as he arrived in Ghaznīn, a resident of Kabul by the name of Aḥmad ʿAlī, a functionary with responsibilities in the Ministry of Trade | to whom [Ḥājjī
192 Muḥammad Ṣāliḥ] had promised a bribe but had not paid it before he left, complained to the minister of trade that [Ḥājjī Muḥammad Ṣāliḥ] had not done his job properly and was escaping to Harāt via Qandahar. As a result of these aspersions, the minister telephoned the governor of

Ghaznīn and ordered him to send Ḥājjī Muḥammad Ṣāliḥ back to Kabul. At the governor's order they somehow summoned him from the caravanserai to the Bālā Ḥiṣār [in Ghaznīn]. They did it in such a way that an onlooker would have thought they had arrested someone who had just committed murder or was guilty of something indecent like fornication or drunkenness. They held him that night under guard and sent him the next day to Kabul. The 500 rupees which he had paid to get himself and his servants to Qandahar were for nought. When he arrived in Kabul, he was straightaway sent to the high governor, Malik Muḥsin. Ḥājjī Muḥammad Ṣāliḥ even offered him a bribe, for he was trembling with fear because the savage Saqqawī had summoned him back. He recounted in detail what had happened to him, and showed the farman of Son of the Water Carrier and the instructions of the minister of trade. The high governor escorted him to Son of the Water Carrier along with his farman and reported that he was not guilty of anything. Ḥājjī Muḥammad Ṣāliḥ was relieved and asked Son of the Water Carrier now not to appoint him to the post. After this, he swore before his relatives and friends that he would never again serve this government because /361/ he knew that every Kūhistānī and Kūh Dāmanī, whether a purveyor of eggs, vinegar, grapes, firewood, grape syrup, and dates, or a thief, having now taken up arms and strapped on a bandolier, strove to become a minister, a warden of a fortress, an aide-de-camp, a high commissioner, a high governor, a field marshal, a deputy field marshal, a brigadier, a colonel or a governor. Every thief and unbeliever, devoid of any sign of intelligence; every vagrant and stranger to religion and reason spending his life in the hills and desert and living in caves; every brigand; and every murderer and robber of true believers sees himself as the *pādshāh*. It is clear that in such a government there is nothing for a rational person to do. Despite this, as will come, [Ḥājjī Muḥammad Ṣāliḥ] having obtained a position in Harāt and having set out to take it up, failed to achieve his goal, having in the meantime spent around 30,000 rupees in vain. After this, he emigrated to Mashhad, travelling by way of Quetta and Duzdāb (?).

Also on this day, a large arsenal of war matériel was shipped from Kabul to Sar Chashmah, Lahūgard, and Kūhistān because of the fear of attacks by Hazārahs, Muḥammad Nādir Khān, and the Tagābīs. A farman was sent to the people of the North with an order to arm themselves with saws, hatchets, and axes and cut down any fruit or other tree that they could find in the region of Tagāb. This kind of order from Son of the Water Carrier violated the precepts of Ḥażrat-i Rasūl (Prophet Muḥammad), when at the time of the [Islamic] conquests, he had prohibited the army of Islam and his Companions from cutting down trees, destroying crops, or killing the elderly, middle-aged women, or children of the unbeliever. Because of this order, the frightened Tagābīs set out, Qurʾāns in hand, to ask for mercy and to express their obedience. However, the Northerners paid no heed to the Qurʾān and cut down the trees. This was due to the false messages of the Easterners who incited the Tagābīs to fight and promised to come [and assist them] but did not do so and as a result the Tagābīs bore the brunt of the damage. /**362**/

Tuesday, 7 Rabīʿ al-Awwal, Corresponding to 21 Asad and 13 August

193 | As was already reported, a group of ulema and leaders from the Aḥmadzāʾī and other tribes had come to Kabul to seek the release of the immediate and extended families of Muḥammad Nādir Khān and his brothers, who were languishing in prison. On this day they presented a petition to the ringleader of the oppressors to release them and send them to Muḥammad Nādir Khān so that the latter, disappointed in his hopes of a coalition of the Southern tribes and having accomplished nothing for seven months, would take the path of extending his own life and leave for foreign lands with his family and retainers. Then perhaps the flaming fire of this grief-causing revolution would subside and the carnage would end. However, Son of the Water Carrier, who could not tell good from bad due to ignorance and could have cared less for the contempt of the time, refused the request. After giving each member of the delegation a piece of *sūndī* turban cloth, he permitted them to leave. This whole affair and the barely veiled insults that this ignoble person cast on the family of Muḥammad Nādir Khān left a very negative impression on them and evoked wrath in their hearts due to their pride and feelings of protectiveness, so they cursed him and returned home.

Also on this day Kāzik, the nephew of Babrak of the Jadrān tribe, along with a group of his fellow tribesmen, came to Son of the Water Carrier in Kabul to express obedience and offer an oath of allegiance. Son of the Water Carrier met them with great courtesy. But rumors circulated in Kabul that those who had come to Kabul to save the family of Muḥammad Nādir Khān had, in concert with Kāzik, promised to assassinate Muḥammad Nādir Khān for a lakh of rupees. The agreement was that Son of the Water Carrier would pay half the sum immediately and the rest on completion of the job.

Also on this day, the Tagābīs justified their excuse for accepting obedience to Son of the Water Carrier by blaming the promise and [as it turned out] the false message from the Easterners that the men of Tagāb should prepare for fighting /363/ and they [the Easterners] would be there without delay. But they had not come and brought the Tagābīs to the brink of death and destruction. In their message, the Tagābīs wrote, "You violated the agreement and from the very outset of the rebellion up to now you have been to blame for all the destruction and loss this has brought to us."

Nādir ʿAlī, who had obtained the farman from Son of the Water Carrier giving him the title "sardār," had promised to summon the Hazārahs to obedience and had sent a letter and a delegation to the Hazārahs of Bihsūd, as was already reported. Having broken the unity and undermined the steadfastness of the Hazārahs but without attaining his goals [completely], on this day he wrote a second letter to the displaced Hazārah settlers and residents of Darrah-i Ṣūf who were fighting against Nā'ib al-Salṭanah Sayyid Ḥusayn and the Turkmān supporters of Son of the Water Carrier. This letter was printed up and here is an exact copy of it:

> Let it be known to our brothers in religion and to the honorable Hazārah settlers living in Mazār-i Sharīf: At this time when the present esteemed government has firmly established its influence in most of the territory of
> 194 Afghanistan and all the Afghan tribes, who are like brothers to us, | have, with pure hearts, expressed their obedience, many tribes of the Hazārahjāt have also chosen us to act on their behalf and have sent an oath of allegiance to the capital, Kabul. And now some two weeks have already passed since we arrived in the city and had the honor to be received by His Highness to whom we submitted the oath of allegiance. His Highness was sincerely grateful to all of us and expressed the hope that in future we would live in peace and tranquility. It is also evident to us that you, our brothers and fellow tribesmen, who are living in that province, up to now have not been aware of how sincere the (amir's) feelings are and so have not given an oath of allegiance to His Felicitous and Noble Excellency, the Āqā Nā'ib al-Salṭanah Sayyid Ḥusayn. Whether from a powerful fear or from unfounded rumors spread by self-interested people, you have withheld [your obedience]. Since we and you both have the same tribal affiliation, /364/ we feel exactly whatever evil or good, whatever benefit or loss befalls you and do not want to see you subject to any distress and anxiety. In particular, from the standpoint of tribal solidarity and rights we tell you that for the past seven months, we, the residents of the Hazārahjāt, were not in accord with the current government. You all know that we had no wish for precedence nor did we lose such glory and rank in this revolution as to cause us sadness and grief. Nor did any personal or tribal enmity between us and the present powers cause us to resist. There was only one reason for us to be steadfast

[in opposition]. Our only motive was the former oath of allegiance which we had given to the person of Amān Allāh Khān. Until that time when he was still in Afghan territory, he had a claim on our assistance, which we would render him. When he relinquished everything and fled abroad, the conditions that pertained to us and had been set out in the former oath of allegiance lapsed and there is no cause for us to feel ashamed or be obliged any longer to anyone. However, from now on it would be unreasonable, contrary to what is good, and the very essence of ill fortune to again raise the flag of opposition and to throw to the winds one's own means by one's own doing. If you think things through carefully [then it will be clear] that it was because of this lucky happenstance that from the beginning of this revolution up to now, day by day [success] appears on the cheeks of the actions of His Highness, "Servant of the Religion of the Prophet of God," that is, Amīr Ḥabīb Allāh Khān. Again and again, about these mind-dazzling successes which spontaneously appear from every direction, every sound and perceptive mind realizes that in all these activities of his there is divine assistance and support and that His will is at work. Thus any person who in this regard expresses /365/ anything to the contrary will receive nothing else but the endurance of eternal suffering. Therefore, we promptly advise all of
195 you, [our] brothers, with pure hearts and as quickly as possible | to bow the head of submission to the present esteemed government, to ask His Excellency, the most esteemed ḥażrat, the Nā'ib al-Salṭanah-ṣāḥib Sayyid Ḥusayn who, God be praised, possesses all nobility, both acquired and by birth, to forgive your past actions and in future to cinch tightly the belt of commitment to serving the government. God willing, your sincere protestations will evoke the concern and esteem of the blessed shah as well as His Excellency Āqā Nā'ib al-Salṭanah-ṣāḥib. All of us, representatives of the tribes of the Hazārahjāt, [like you] also absent from that very place, wish and hope that the Nā'ib al-Salṭanah-ṣāḥib will overlook your past actions and will deal with you with kindness and beneficence, as befits his sublime sayyidly nature for in forgiveness there is an enjoyment not to be found in revenge. It is hoped that our loving words in their entirety will affect the pure hearts of our friends. Moreover, [it is hoped] that the false rumors of self-interested people will not perplex and confuse you nor will you make the revered leaders of the present government unhappy with you and us, bring affliction to [our] people, and discomfiture to you yourselves. The End. Dated 7 Rabīʿ al-Awwal 1348 A.H.Q. (13 August 1929 A.D.)

Nādir ʿAlī, having written this disgraceful letter in his capacity as a "sardār" at the court and in a private court session of Son of the Water Carrier, signed it himself with fifteen of the Hazārah leaders of the Muḥammad Khwājah, Jīghatu, Chahār Dastah, Bayāt, Fūlādah, Jāghūrī, Shaykh ʿAlī, Turkmān, and Surkh wa Pārsā namely: Shaykh Sulṭān ʿAlī, Walī Muḥammad, Mustawfī Sayyid Qāsim, Niyāz Muḥammad, Ḥaydar ʿAlī, Muḥammad Nāṣir, Muḥammad Bāqir, Żabṭū,[cxxxi] Ḥasan Rižā, Muḥammad Ḥusayn, ʿAlī Rižā, /366/ Fayż Muḥammad *tūpchī* (artillerist), Khudā Raḥm,

Shāh Ḥusayn, and Khayr Allāh, all of whom had been lured by deception into Son of the Water Carrier's snare and summoned to Kabul where they were kept under surveillance as if they were prisoners. By order of the leader of the people of divisiveness, this letter was printed many times over and sent by plane to Mazār-i Sharīf where it was scattered from the air on the God-fearing and religious Hazārah settlers and the Day Mīrdād [Hazārahs] residing in Darrah-i Ṣūf.

But a few days before this, Ghulām Nabī Khān, son of Gulak *mangbāshī*, had come to Bihsūd with 100 horsemen with the aim of finding out what was going on and saw that [the residents of Bihsūd] were continuing the struggle against Son of the Water Carrier and heard from them the advice I had given to the Hazārahs in Bihsūd as well as the Qur'ānic verses that I had recited to them: "And (as for) the male thief and female thief cut off the (right) hand as a recompense for that which they have committed, as punishment from God."[235] "And whoever deliberately kills a Believer, his recompense is Hell, to dwell therein; and the wrath and curse of God are upon him and a great punishment is prepared for him."[236] As a result, when he left, [the Hazārahs of Mazār-i Sharīf and Darrah-i Ṣūf] were even more encouraged and, disregarding the letter, cursed Nādir ʿAlī and those who had signed it. Taking the ordinances of the Sharīʿah and their own consciences as their guide, they refused to bow the head of obedience to the murdering thief, the one who has earned the wrath and curse of God. Their courageous actions and their refusal to offer their obedience
196 frustrated Sayyid Ḥusayn.[cxxxii] |

Wednesday, 8 Rabīʿ al-Awwal, Corresponding to 22 Asad and 14 August

On this day, the high governor Malik Muḥsin, having gone to Ghaznīn to gather information [about the situation there] brought back to Kabul the notorious thief, Aḥmad Shāh, son of Bāz [Muḥammad] Andarī, and presented him to Son of the Water Carrier. In giving his support to Son of the Water Carrier, he had caused much harm to His Highness Amān Allāh Khān. Allied with the Andar, Sulaymān Khayl, Tarakī and ʿAlī Khayl tribes, he had defeated Amān Allāh Khān, his regular troops, and Durrānī and Hazārah tribal contingents. After His Majesty's departure /367/ abroad, he was guilty of many murders and depredations. The high governor disarmed Aḥmad Shāh and other brigands from his band who had supported

235 Qur'ān: 5:38.
236 Qur'ān: 4:93.

and continued to support Son of the Water Carrier and imprisoned him, producing evidence of his guilt for looting, murders, and raids in the region of Ghaznīn, for which the high governor had received an order to arrest him.

During this time when the country stood on the brink of destruction, people were being plundered, tortured, and killed, road junctions appeared to be cemeteries and highways killing fields, when people could not travel from one fortress home to another, and Son of the Water Carrier and the residents of Kabul and its environs were so encircled that it was as if the entire government facing extinction and nonexistence, spent its days and nights in utter terror of being killed and plundered and had lost all hope of salvation from this misery and misfortune, (it was at this time that) Son of the Water Carrier naively made attempts to get foreign governments to recognize him officially as amir of Afghanistan and to resume official ties. However, he did not seem to be aware that most of the people of Afghanistan still called him a thief and did not recognize his amirate. For example, the Hazārahs have not submitted to the government and the eastern and southern Afghan tribes spend their days and nights in ambivalence. Nevertheless, with the approval of the Northern thieves, the State Council, telegraphed a request to the Russian and English governments to send a minister plenipotentiary with a delegation in order to re-establish relations and conclude agreements. But those two governments, which did not recognize him and instead hoped that Muḥammad Nādir Khān or someone else would come to power to whom the nation was not averse and who could consolidate power in the country and defend its borders and subjects, did not telegraph a response. To counter the rumor that no answer had been received, /368/ [the amir] circulated the false rumor that [minister plenipotentiaries] would be sent after Independence Day celebrations.

Thursday, 9 Rabīʿ al-Awwal, Corresponding to 23 Asad and 15 August

Rumors spread on this day of the approach of the army of Muḥammad Nādir Khān about whom nothing had been heard in recent days. Due to the hypocrisy and treachery of some of the Southern tribes he had given up fighting and was in Dūbandī trying to restore the reputation and the
197 honor of those people. | As a result of the rumor, hope again manifested itself among the residents of Kabul and those suffering the oppression and tyranny of the Saqqawīs.

Also during this time, Khūgyānī brigands raided the Jabbār Khayl, whose leader was ʿAbd al-Raḥmān, son of ʿIṣmat Allāh Khān. ʿAbd al-Raḥmān had stolen three lakhs of gold English pounds sterling (gold sovereigns?) from ʿAlī Aḥmad Khān [Lūynāb], who, as previously noted, had declared his own amirate and, intending to attack Kabul and drive out Son of the Water Carrier, had gotten as far as Jagdalak. ʿAbd al-Raḥmān had placed the money in his treacherous purse in his own home. [The Khūgyānī] plundered all the belongings and money of the Jabbār Khayl, who lived in Ḥiṣārak, and then burned down their homes and took some of their women captive.

In Turkistān, Hazārah settlers, armed with government rifles, artillery, and ammunition, occupied positions in Darrah-i Ṣūf, Kūh-i Shādyān, and Mārmal and were fighting with the Turkmāns, who due to a letter from the dethroned amir of Bukhārā who was in Kabul and, at the provocation of Khalīfah-i Qizil Ayāq, their leader, and Mīrzā Qāsim Ūzbak, had chosen to side with Son of the Water Carrier and had attacked the Hazārahs who opposed the Saqqawīs. Due to the circulation of Nādir ʿAlī's letter, [the Hazārahs] were even more offended and fought even harder. Led by Ghulām Nabī, son of Gulak *mangbāshī* from Darrah-i Ṣūf; Nūr Muḥammad, son of Ghulām Ḥusayn Khān, a grandson of Khān Shīrīn Khān Jawānshayr, who held the post of /369/ high commissioner; and Major General Muḥammad Iklīl, son of Muḥammad Afżal Darwāzī, they heroically assaulted the Turkmāns and killed and wounded a number of them and besieged the army under Sayyid Ḥusayn in the well-built fortress at Dih Dādī. The surviving Turkmāns fled to their felt tents in the steppe. This is the result in Mazār-i Sharīf to which Nādir ʿAlī's letter led, that and the actions of the Hazārahs of Ghaznīn, who had been ensnared by Son of the Water Carrier. We will see to what extent Nādir ʿAlī succeeded in normalizing the situation among the Hazārahs of Bihsūd and in making Son of the Water Carrier content.

Friday, 10 Rabīʿ al-Awwal, Corresponding to 24 Asad and 16 August

A while ago, the high governor, Malik Muḥsin, went to Tagāb, placated its people, returned to Kabul, and then planning to go again to Tagāb, went to Chārīkār by motor car. There he listened to [the complaints of] the people about the wicked deeds and lewd activities of the Saqqawī forces who everywhere were besetting and afflicting the subjects of the prurient, misguided government. They were taking women, young girls, and beardless youths to their hideaways and raping and sodomizing them. [He discovered that] they were ready to sacrifice themselves and were prepared for hard times and to light the fires of tumult and turmoil. On this day, Malik Muḥsin dropped his plan to go to Tagāb and straightaway returned to Kabul and told Son of the Water Carrier about the explosive situation [around Chārīkār].

On this day too, the rumor spread that Saqqawī soldiers in Qandahar had abducted a young boy at night, taken him to a party they had organized, and forced him to dance to the tune of the *nāy* (flute) and their own
198 singing. They then took him to a private room and sodomized him. | Due to this unspeakable act by the Kūh Dāmanī and Kūhistānī brigands—miscreants and infidels all—people of perception and conscience in Qandahar denounced them as kafirs. In their gatherings, the Qandahārīs talked about the "divine commands and prohibitions" /**370**/ of the holy law of the Prophet and decided that death and destruction were preferable to the effects of the actions of the Saqqawīs, which every second and every hour were penetrating their hearts, souls, and bodies like a conflagration. They wished that someone able to lift his head through the collar of pride would appear and cinch the belt of commitment to expunge and exterminate those errant people. They would give him any assistance they could to cleanse their way of life and the land of Qandahar from the filth of the existence of the gang of murderers. They discussed this in private amongst themselves but dared not start anything without the involvement of the tribes outside the city. The accursed Northerners, having learned about the intentions of the residents of the city, began to exert every effort to try and prevent news of their obscene escapades reaching the populace outside the city and leading to an uprising and the lighting of the fire of revolution. They therefore began to post misleading announcements to persuade the residents of the city of their piety and religious devotion.

As was already noted, thirty ulema and leaders of the Aḥmadzāʾī tribe and [leaders] from the Andar tribe as well had come to see Son of the Water Carrier with a request that he release the relatives of Muḥammad Nādir Khān and the household of Shayr Āqā but to no avail and so they had returned home. But due to [their] firm belief in the Mujaddidī ḥażrats which they have always had, they now turned against Son of the Water Carrier whom up to now they had supported. Thus, the chiefs of the Andarīs, who have an unwavering belief in Shayr Āqā [Mujaddidī], prepared to express their opposition to Son of the Water Carrier. In the vicinity of Ghaznīn, a clamor arose and opposition appeared on every side.

Through propaganda, [the Andarī chiefs] began to spread rumors, both true and false, which perhaps would light a fire and achieve their desired ends. /371/

Saturday, Rabīʿ al-Awwal, Corresponding to 25 Asad and 17 August

As was reported earlier, agreement was finally reached on a truce. The arbābs of the Hazārahs were supposed to arrive in Sar Chashmah to negotiate a time limit for the acceptance of their terms and for safe passage to Kabul with Deputy Field Marshal Muḥammad Ṣiddīq "No-Nose" who had sent a Qurʾān and sheep to the Hazārahs and persuaded them to accept the truce. On this day a number of Hazārah arbābs arrived in Sar Chashmah accompanied by an armed contingent of 300 brave men. They met with the deputy field marshal, that Satan, the worst evil-doer of all. After a midday meal and fruit and tea that Son of the Water Carrier and the high governor, Malik Muḥsin, had sent two or three days earlier
199 for hosting the Hazārahs, | the deputy field marshal signaled his sepoys who had surrounded the gathering. By prearrangement they were supposed to blow a bugle as soon as he winked his eye and seize the Hazārahs who had come to the majlis. But before the signal could be passed to the sepoy-bugler, who stood some distance away from the majlis, one of the Hazārahs, excusing himself to answer a call of nature, left the gathering, quickly climbed a nearby hill and fired three rifle shots in rapid succession. Meanwhile, the Saqqawī sepoys began disarming the Hazārahs who were calmly sitting in the majlis. But then 3,000 brave Hazārahs, lying in wait behind the hills, and on the alert to act if Son of the Water Carrier's soldiers tried anything to harm the arbābs, heard the three shots which was their signal to attack. They sprang from ambush and, with cries of "O ʿAlī, help!" they fell upon the sepoys. They disarmed, captured, and led away the 400 soldiers who had been guarding the majlis but the unbeliever, Deputy Field Marshal Muḥammad Ṣiddīq, /372/ managed to make his escape by car back to Kabul.

Also on this day, a number of Hazārah horsemen, who had promised Prince Muḥammad Amīn, his deputy Khwājah Hidāyat Allāh, and his retainers to escort them safely through their territory, came to the prince who was worried about the negotiations going on between the Hazārahs and Son of the Water Carrier and felt himself in danger being among the Hazārahs. He therefore decided to leave. But they assured him that as long as one Hazārah remained alive, neither he nor any of his associates would be subject to any harm from Son of the Water Carrier.

The events which took place in Sar Chashmah, Deputy Field Marshal Muḥammad Ṣiddīq's return to Kabul, and the willingness of the Hazārahs to conduct Prince Muḥammad Amīn safely across their territory to Wardak if he wished it, all these things disturbed Son of the Water Carrier. Consequently, from evening until 2:00 in the morning he dispatched to Sar Chashmah in vehicles those tribal conscripts who had been assembled in Kabul. They were ordered to stop any Hazārah offensive.

Sunday, 12 Rabīʿ al-Awwal, Corresponding to 26 Asad and 18 August

From the day before, the shopkeepers of Kabul have been forced to set up a market on the fairgrounds on the southern edge of Dih Mazang which Son of the Water Carrier has designated as the site for the Independence Day celebrations. Originally, he had planned to hold the celebration at Dār al-Amān but worried about attacks from Muḥammad Nādir Khān and the Hazārahs he changed his mind and ordered the shopkeepers to set up their stalls in Dih Mazang. Ghulām Muḥyī al-Dīn, the director of the museum, and his staff, busy with preparations for the celebration, were assigned to decorate the streets and other spots planned as gathering
200 places for | the festival. They began to hang colored banners and strings of electric lights. Minister of Education Fayż Muḥammad, /373/ was assigned to gather singers who had been trained in the schools. He selected a group of singers and then continued quickly [to complete] the preparations for the holiday so that the chief of those who have gone astray, Son of the Water Carrier, would not punish him.

Elsewhere during the events that have been recorded, a frustrated Muḥammad Nādir Khān abandoned his old headquarters and chose to live among the ʿAlī Khayl and Jājī tribes who assured him of their genuine loyalty. Over the preceding seven months he and his brothers, Shāh Walī Khān and Shāh Maḥmūd Khān, had exerted every effort to forge an alliance between tribes utterly lacking in any sense of Afghan loyalty, honor, conscience, and mutual aid. He spent his days and nights hungry and cold, sleeping on bare earth, stones, and camel thorn for the sake of uniting the promise-breaking Afghans who live in the mountains of the Southern Province. But some of them, completely devoid of any sense of honor or belief and possessed by an avarice that knows no bounds, offered themselves to Son of the Water Carrier and, in reward, he paid each of them from three, five, and eight [thousand] up to fifteen thousand rupees. Others promised to murder Muḥammad Nādir Khān and his brothers for a reward of one lakh of rupees. Son of the Water Carrier, supposing that

Muḥammad Nādir Khān's efforts had now failed, felt himself to be the wholly legitimate amir of Afghanistan. But he was unaware that although God had brought him to punish His ignorant and ungrateful people, He will also save them for the sake of the children and the weak and will rid them of [Ḥabīb Allāh's] viciousness. We hope that He will save the people of this country from the oppression and mischief caused by the Saqqawīs and will provide tranquility. /374/

Also during these recorded times, Sayyid Nādir Shāh Kayānī, of the Ismāʿīlī sect of Shiʿism, joined forces with the Shaykh ʿAlī Hazārahs and became a cause of the anguish and exhaustion of Son of the Water Carrier. (Kayānī) made life very difficult for the Saqqawī forces stationed in Bāmyān, Ghūrī and Baghlān. In the fighting, he drove the Saqqawī forces back to Ghūrband and blocked their route to Turkistān. The Hazārah settlers and the Dāy Mīrdād tribe living in Darrah-i Ṣūf, having learned that the Kabul mullahs had signed a proclamation anathematizing Shiʿis as infidels, left their homes and forts and marched to Darrah-i Ṣūf and Kūh-i Shādyān armed with government-issue rifles and artillery captured when Ghulām Nabī Khān, son of the late Ghulām Ḥaydar Khān [Charkhī], established his control in those areas and attacked Mazār-i Sharīf. They began operations in Turkistān, besieging Sayyid Ḥusayn in Mazār-i Sharīf and preventing him from establishing his administration there.

A group of the chiefs and leaders of Tagāb, who had put themselves on the brink of death and destruction because of the promise and message
201 of support from the eastern Afghans | and had begun to fight Son of the Water Carrier, due to the fact that the message was a lie and the Easterners violated their promise and did not come to assist, [the Tagābīs] suffered defeat at the hands of the Saqqawīs and [these leaders] were taken prisoner. Also on this day, that group of captured leaders was transported to Kabul and imprisoned. The once good name of the Easterners was recorded in the register of salutary examples of disgraceful behavior and [their reputation for] religiosity and courage disappeared into the whirlpool of non-existence.

Monday, 13 Rabīʿ al-Awwal, Corresponding to 27 Asad and 19 August

During the reign of His Majesty Amān Allāh Khān, the celebration of independence was called Independence Day (*ʿīd-i istiqlāl*). Eight days were set aside for it and it was held annually in the summer resort of Pamqān. /375/ Money which had been collected in the form of rental fees for motor cars, carriages, and phaetons, and from the sale of tickets to the celebration—in all some 60,000 rupees—and one lakh of rupees from theater and cinema tickets—would be distributed to master craftsman, wrestlers, and others as prizes. But today it was announced that the holiday would be planned for only five days on a field on the banks of the Kabul River near the southern edge of Dih Mazang. Around eight in the morning, when they heard the call of the town crier, all citizens—the common folk and the well-off, the weak and the strong—were supposed to line both sides of the street from the Victory Arch which stands beside the Shāh Dū Shamshīrah Mosque to the place where the celebration is to be held and await the arrival of Son of the Water Carrier's car. Although everyone was loath to look at Son of the Water Carrier, still, fearing punishment if they did not, residents stood until 10 A.M. under the scorching heat of the sun. When the car with the leader of the thieves passed them, the people, overcoming their true feelings, raised their hands to their foreheads in greeting.

Son of the Water Carrier drove up to the festival grounds, climbed up on a wooden stand before a huge crowd and, in imitation of His Majesty Amān Allāh Khān's royal speeches and stately appearance, opened the festival with a royal speech. However his address, which had been written by the minister of court, Shayr Jān, who had also coached him, most of all sounded like the peroration of a thief. I did not include his speech in this book about the revolution because it would have ruined it.[237]

The message of the Hazārahs to Muḥammad Ṣiddīq "No-Nose" in which they promised that their leaders would come to Sar Chashmah to negotiate and asked for safe passage had reassured Son of the Water Carrier. Convinced that there would not be an Hazārah offensive, he therefore on this day ordered nine regiments (*ghunds*) numbering 12,000 men armed with artillery to prepare to march from Butkhāk towards /376/ Jalālābād to suppress the insurgents there. En route, they were to fortify each stopping place and prepare a vanguard which would attack and crush the Easterners whom Muḥammad Hāshim Khān, by guile and cunning, had
202 united and set against the government of Son of the Water Carrier. |

Tuesday, 14 Rabīʿ al-Awwal, Corresponding to 28 Asad and 20 August

On this day, the army having left Kabul for Jalālābād, due to a letter from Deputy Field Marshal Muḥammad Ṣiddīq to Son of the Water Carrier, the rumor that the Hazārahs had offered their obedience reached people's

---

[237] See M. G. M. Ghubar, *Afghānistān dar masīr-i tārīkh*, Kabul, 1346/1967, p. 827 for the speech.

ears. In the letter, he wrote that the innocent men and women of Sar Chashmah, who had been taken captive, had set the following conditions: release them and pay them fifteen lakhs of rupees as compensation for their plundered property and for the burning of their forts because they had been obedient subjects of the government; had faithfully paid their "one-quarter" taxes; in winter and through the snow had sent fifty Kābulī kharwārs of provisions to the forces fighting with the Wardakīs; and, hoping to get compensation from the government, for seven months had fed the 100 sepoys stationed in Sar Chashmah to defend against Hazārah attack. Moreover, they wanted released the relatives of one or two men who had come to Kabul in winter to sell 100 kharwārs of oil but whom the Muʿīn al-Salṭanah Ḥamīd Allāh had had shot and then burned their homes. These relatives had themselves been forced to go to Kabul as prisoners. They also had to be compensated for the damage caused to their forts. Then the Hazārahs would be convinced that the government has not deceived and swindled them.

Also, he wrote that after the release /377/ of the captives, the Hazārahs had promised to come to Sar Chashmah and begin to negotiate on the question of an oath of allegiance based on the conditions they had set out. If their terms were accepted, they would come to Kabul and swear their allegiance. The government must therefore undertake to make the necessary arrangements.

Son of the Water Carrier was overjoyed by Deputy Field Marshal Muḥammad Ṣiddīq's letter because he was always saying,

> If the Hazārahs bow their heads in obedience and unite with the people of the North, then I could care less about all the Afghans because if I reward their leaders with a rifle and a few rupees, they will make their entire tribe obedient and content. But the business of the Hazārahs is difficult because they can neither be placated with gifts nor can they be driven from their fortifications by force and compelled to give up the fight.

For the expenses of hosting the Hazārah leaders, Son of the Water Carrier ordered a sum of 12,000 rupees be taken from the treasury and transported to Sar Chashmah. He also released the men and women of Sar Chashmah and ordered that they be driven to Sar Chashmah in a dignified fashion in twenty hired phaetons. In conjunction with their release and respectful conveyance to Sar Chashmah, the residents of Kabul would say to each other,

> It must be the case [that the Hazārahs are powerful] for this blinds the tyrannical eye of Son of the Water Carrier. If this is not the case, then why

> doesn't he send Afghan prisoners home, wherever they come from, with comparable honors? He behaves in this fashion with their prisoners because the Hazārahs are powerful and are always steadfast. This is what it means to be strong!

Also on this day, a rumor circulated concerning the unity, common purpose, and willingness to sacrifice themselves expressed by the Jājī tribe
203 in support of Muḥammad Nādir Khān, who, | having lost hope in all the southern Afghan tribes, had now set up his headquarters among the ʿAlī Khayl of the Jājī tribe. In harmony, the tribe cinched the belt of support for him and resolved to fight and get rid of the Saqqawīs. Also, in Kabul, Chahārdihī, and Lahūgard, and among the Hazārahs, the residents of Wardak and in other /378/ regions, Muḥammad Nādir Khān's proclamations of admonition and warning were distributed and evoked fear and anxiety in Son of the Water Carrier but hope in the hearts of the people who cursed his misguided, licentious, and tyrannical government.

Wednesday, 15 Rabīʿ al-Awwal, Corresponding to 29 Asad and 21 August

During these events, Sayyid Nādir Shāh Kayānī, a sayyid from the Shaykh ʿAlī Hazārah tribe, refused to express obedience to Son of the Water Carrier, and with the support of a kindred spirit, Mīrzā Ṣafdar ʿAlī Qizilbāsh, tax collector for Ghūrī and Baghlān, aroused the Hazārahs and Tajiks who were under the latter's [tax] jurisdiction to oppose the Saqqawīs. Willingly accepting the "commands and prohibitions" of Sayyid Nādir Shāh [as their leader], they engaged the Saqqawīst contingents, together with Hazārah and Tajik volunteers from Qaṭaghan, and made life difficult for them. They fought them up to Khānābād, Andarāb, and Ghūrband and were everywhere victorious. Having done much killing and plundering and having closed the Kabul–Mazār-i Sharīf road to caravans, Son of the Water Carrier could do nothing but issue threatening proclamations. On this day, he ordered copies of a proclamation of admonition and threat printed up and dropped by plane over those areas where the fire of revolution was in full flame. The proclamation called for an end to opposition and for the people to choose obedience. Otherwise, they should consider themselves targeted for annihilation. Sayyid Nādir Shāh paid not the slightest attention to it and just as he had been doing he continued to fight. Due to the outbreak of revolution everywhere, the encirclement of Kabul, and the fact that in the course of the eight months of the government of Son of the Water Carrier roads and byways were blockaded to traffic and killing had become universal, people of sound opinion and right mind were saying to each other that because of the ignorance, lack of religious feeling, and sheer stupidity of Son of the Water Carrier and the immorality and licentiousness of his appointees and high officials, killing and plundering show no signs of stopping and as long as he sits on the throne, /379/ the country and the people will not be safe and secure from being consumed by fire and utterly destroyed. The truth is that these perceptions and enlightened thoughts were absolutely correct, accurate, apparent, and obvious so that day after day unfortunate things kept happening and with every day that passed people faced ever greater hardships.

Thursday, 16 Rabīʿ al-Awwal, Corresponding to 30 Asad and 22 August

Meanwhile, Muḥammad Nādir Khān, having decided to make his headquarters among the ʿAlī Khayl of the Jājī tribe to try and revive the reputation and honor of the Afghans, encouraged by the promises, pact, alliance,
204 and agreement | of that tribe, the sincerity with which they had offered to help him, and their promise to conquer Kabul and drive out Son of the Water Carrier, now addressed a proclamation to the people which he sent out by secret couriers on clandestine routes. During the night of this dark day [in accordance with his instructions] leaflets with the proclamation under the heading[cxxxiii] "Rectification of the Southern Province" were posted in popular gathering places. The text read,

> Despite extremely difficult circumstances and bloodshed among Muslims, we have been calling for a ceasefire and a truce and we have avoided raiding and attacking, so that, perhaps, the destroyer of religion, Son of the Water Carrier, who calls himself "servant of the religion" would come to his senses and put an end to subjecting the country and nation to death, plundering, and destruction and return to his former way of life where he was happy to herd two or three goats and sheep in the open air and be content with the life which his father had led. However, the fact is that this ignorant unbeliever, who used to wander through mountain and desert, earning his living by killing and robbing Muslims, /380/ and sometimes even going hungry, having seized the amirid throne and having experienced a comfortable way of life, is not going to just give it up. He has not stopped boasting, 'Even if one hundred thousand people were to perish and one thousand homes, the country, and the nation were to be destroyed, having taken the throne by sword and the help of God, I will never abandon it so long as I live.' So having effected his criminal plans, Son of the Water Carrier has plundered all the resources of the government and the nation and brought the country to the brink of disaster by his sedition. The southern tribes proudly joined forces and resolved to attack Kabul and cleanse it of Son of the Water Carrier and the larcenists who support him. This is the plan of attack: a force of 10,000

> militiamen will march on Kabul via Chahār Āsyā; 10,000 via Butkhāk and 12,000 through Sar Chashmah and Maydān. In view of this agreement and the resolution of the valorous Afghans of the south, it is incumbent upon the residents of the northern region and elsewhere to either arrest this villain or drive him out of the capital. Otherwise, they should understand that their having to face all the kinds of trouble, injury, and loss that will follow will be the consequence of their own actions.

One of these proclamations reached Son of the Water Carrier and alarmed and frightened him.

Also on this day the secretary to Sayyid Ḥusayn, Ghulām Qādir, who flew in the day before from Mazār-i Sharīf with secret dispatches, arrived on the fairgrounds of Dih Mazang and greeted Son of the Water Carrier. In the evening he spoke with him behind closed doors about the situation of the irreconcilable uprising in [Afghan] Turkistān, the disobedience and active resistance of the Hazārah settlers there, the activities of the Turkmāns who had received a letter from the Bukhāran amir who was in Kabul attempting to gain their support for Son of the Water Carrier, and about the secret supporting directives of the Russian government. He asked Son of the Water Carrier for instructions to take back to Sayyid Ḥusayn. Son of the Water Carrier promised to give him instructions and to send him back when the holiday was over. **/381/**

205 | Also today fighting took place in Gardayz and Kārīz-i Darwīsh between the southern [Afghan] braves and the Saqqawīs. It is not known which side was victorious.

Sayyid Nādir Shāh [Kayānī] with a force of Shaykh ʿAlī Hazārahs entered Ghūrband in victory having been resolute in heavy fighting.

Also during the days of the holiday as well as on this day when the southern Afghans who were supporters of Son of the Water Carrier would dance to drums at festivals for money as they did during the reign of His Majesty Amān Allāh Khān, the Kūhistānīs and Kūh Dāmanīs were much amused and made fun of them. "Look how splendidly the Tajiks make you southern Afghans dance!" And the Afghans, feeling totally ashamed, accepted these insults in silence so that Son of the Water Carrier would not take back the two or three rupees he paid them for dancing and they would not return home empty-handed.

Friday, 17 Rabīʿ al-Awwal, Corresponding to 31 Asad and 23 August

On this day some 150 soldiers were brought in nine lorries to Kabul, men wounded in the fighting in Gardayz and Kārīz-i Darwīsh, and left at the hospital. Also twenty men who had deserted came back to Kabul and two of them were shot, as a warning to others not to turn their backs to the battlefield and flee.

In the afternoon of this day, Malik Muḥsin's nawkar returned to Kabul. At the end of Muḥarram, accompanied by Mīrzā Ḥasan ʿAlī, Ḥājjī Rustam ʿAlī, Mullā ʿIważ ʿAlī, Mullā ʿAbd al-Wāhid and ʿAlī Jān, son of Āqā Khān, he had delivered a proclamation containing threats to the Hazārahjāt from Son of the Water Carrier. The whole group had been detained there. He [Malik Muḥsin' nawkar] spread the rumor that the Hazārahs had come to Sar Chashmah to express submission to Son of the Water Carrier. /382/ This news made the father and relatives of Mīrzā Ḥasan ʿAlī happy since they had decided that Son of the Water Carrier would give Mīrzā Ḥasan and them high ranks for this service and thus they would acquire status. Several people, disposed against Son of the Water Carrier, dismissed this news. But they did not know that the [tax] collector, Riżā Bakhsh, had already sent Son of the Water Carrier his oath of allegiance and assured him that, no matter what happened, the united front of the Hazārahs would be destroyed.[cxxxiv]

Because of another deception of Riżā Bakhsh, [the Hazārahs] did not yet know that Deputy Field Marshal Muḥammad Ṣiddīq, after receiving those 12,000 rupees, which, as was already mentioned, Son of the Water Carrier had sent to Sar Chashmah for the expenses of hosting the Hazārahs, had placed them in a basket used for picking grapes just heavy enough that they could be carried by a donkey. He covered the money with bunches of grapes so that it would appear that the donkey was only carrying grapes. Several donkeys were fitted out in this way, money inside and grapes on the outside, and sent to Riżā Bakhsh to use to sow discord among the Hazārahs. [Riżā Bakhsh], a Saqqawī who always maintained good communications with Son of the Water Carrier, made sure that the path for Hazārahs to go to Kabul and offer their pledge [of obedience] to Son of the Water Carrier would always remain open. Along with the fifteen
206 Hazārah leaders and their retainers, twenty-five men in all, | he [now] set off for Kabul and on this day reached Sar Chashmah. Mīrzā Ḥasan ʿAlī, who had been of great service to Son of the Water Carrier and, with Riżā Bakhsh, had engaged in duplicity and deception, now embarked on a new ruse. He came as far as Sar Chashmah with the arbābs. From there [he left them] and went to Takānah where he spent the night in the home of the people of Sayyid Shāhanshāh and the next day set off for Kabul in order to report his accomplishments to Son of the Water Carrier as quickly as he could. The arbābs, for whose reception and entertainment 12,000 rupees had been sent but all of which had been diverted to Riżā Bakhsh, dined

and spent the night, thanks to the hospitality of Deputy Field Marshal Muḥammad Ṣiddīq "No-Nose."

Also on this day 100 horsemen from Khānābād and Andarāb, perplexed and confused by the attacks of Sayyid Nādir Shāh Kayānī, having set off for Kabul to get help, /383/ arrived there. Son of the Water Carrier promised them reinforcements.

Also news [arrived] of fighting between the Hazārah settlers and the Turkmāns who, incited by the letter from the amir of Bukhārā who is in Kabul, and egged on by Khalīfah Qizil Ayāq and by the Uzbek, Mīrzā Muḥammad Qāsim, violated their agreement and killed three Hazārahs. Sayyid Ḥusayn, the *nā'ib al-salṭanah* (vice-regent) of Son of the Water Carrier, himself refused to exact legal vengeance for the killing of the Hazārahs and so [the Hazārahs] decided to retaliate and attacked the Turkmāns and made life difficult for them. [This news] brought pleasure to the minds of those who cursed the misguided and immoral government of Son of the Water Carrier, someone beyond the pale of religion.

Saturday, 18 Rabīʿ al-Awwal, Corresponding to 1 Sunbul and 24 August

On this day at 1:00 P.M. Mīrzā Ḥasan ʿAlī arrived in Kabul and reported to the high governor, Malik Muḥsin, the impending arrival of the Hazārah leaders. [Malik Muḥsin] offered his congratulations to Son of the Water Carrier. [The amir] commissioned a military band to lead the cars which would be carrying the Hazārah arbābs from the Harten Bridge and beyond it in a parade with musical accompaniment and shouts of "Four Friends" around every part of the city and through the bazaars until after dark. Therefore, a group of military bandsmen went to the end of the Harten Bridge and waited for the arrival of the cars with the Hazārahs. They arrived at about sunset. The bandsmen marched off ahead of the cars, playing and shouting "O Four Friends." Until late evening they paraded the Hazārahs through every nook and cranny of the city and the bazaars. While they were parading through the bazaar and the Saqqawīs were shouting "O Four Friends," the notorious Hazārah thief, Sayyid Aḥmad, son of Muḥammad Mīr, son of Shāh Nūr, began to curse their sisters and mothers, "When you used to fight or run away, at that time you forget "O Four Friends" and shout "O ʿAlī, help!" So why don't you shout "O ʿAlī, help!" now that the Hazārahs are not attacking you?" But since the Saqqawīs considered the Hazārahs guests, /384/ they did not respond. They led their guests into the Hotel Cafe Walī and gave them something
207 to eat and drink. As for the horses which their servants | were riding,

because the time was late and the shops where straw and barley were sold were closed, the bakers, water carriers, and bearers [of Kabul] most of whom were Hazārahs from Bihsūd, took [the horses] to their own homes, and gave them hay and barley.

On this day, due to a rumor of heavy fighting in Lahūgard which the Southerners have started with the Saqqawīs, as was his invariable custom at such difficult moments, Son of the Water Carrier forced the military units stationed in Kabul to march around the city to band music and shouting "O Four [Friends]" so that the Kābulīs would not accuse him of cowardice and weakness, and not incite tumult and turmoil and through propaganda introduce any fissure into the solidarity of the army. Also on this day due to the innate hatred that the people of Kabul and its environs manifested every day for the Saqqawīs and which Son of the Water Carrier was well aware of, he began to organize demonstrations of strength in the city and in the bazaars by the army so that the people would not unfurl the banner of disobedience.

Also, because of the parading of the Hazārah representatives from Bihsūd around the city, the Hazārah arbābs and all the Hazārahs living in Kabul condemned and cursed Riżā Bakhsh, the collector, who introduced dissension in Hazārah ranks and caused the representatives of the Hazārahs of Bihsūd to be brought to Kabul. They also cursed and vilified Nādir ʿAlī.

Sunday, 19 Rabīʿ al-Awwal, Corresponding to 2 Sunbul and 25 August

On this day, the high governor, Malik Muḥsin, presented to the ringleader of the evildoers twenty-five Bihsūd Hazārah arbābs, who, as was already reported, arrived the previous day, and eleven Hazārah leaders from Muḥammad Khwājah, the Chahār Dastah, Jīghatū, Jāghūrī, and Surkh wa Pārsā [Hazārahs] who had been drawn into Son of the Water Carrier's snares by Nādir ʿAlī, grandson of Sardār Shayr ʿAlī Jāghūrī. He now got them to sign a letter which he dispatched to the Hazārahs of Bihsūd, Dāy Zangī, Dāy Kundī, the displaced Hazārah settlers in Turkistān, and the Dāy Mīrdād in Darrah-i Ṣūf with the request that they affirm their obedience to the government of Son /385/ of the Water Carrier for which the title "sardār" would be bestowed on them.

Despite the fact that the Hazārahs fought him so tenaciously, Son of the Water Carrier received the delegation with pronounced deference because he understood that their submission and alliance with the residents of the northern territories would be a guarantee of his personal security. But he also reproached them for their taking up arms against him. The collector, Riżā Bakhsh, who earlier had sent an oath of allegiance and felt secure about his own life said, in answer to this admonition,

> We sent a letter with a promise to give an oath of allegiance. Your brother loosed the hounds of war and attacked Sar Chashmah and Ūnay Pass where loyal subjects of your government live. As a result of his attack, we thought that if we gave an oath of allegiance and expressed obedience then we would be attacked and plundered like the people of Sar Chashmah and Ūnay Pass and so we entrusted our fate to the Almighty and, in accordance with the holy Sharīʿah, undertook to defend ourselves and our families. Now that we have come [to you] we are not afraid of death, imprisonment or punishment for insubordination because we are by no means all the Hazārahs. As
> **208** is known, although Amīr ʿAbd al-Raḥmān | killed, pillaged, and drove into exile 600,000 Hazārahs and illegally, contrary to the norms of the Sharīʿah, seized their cultivable lands and pastures, nevertheless he was unable to exterminate them. And now thousands of Hazārahs are to be found in this country and abroad and all of them are devout Muslims and proponents of Islam. Therefore if something should happen to a few people who have come to Kabul, this will have no effect on the wider community of Hazārahs.

As for the war, Son of the Water Carrier knew that his brother had started it and therefore it was not worth dwelling on the past. In future, the Hazārahs, who had been under the yoke of an Afghan government and deprived of their legal rights for a very long time, ought to join forces with the Tajiks in the name of a greater interest so that they would not again become slaves of the Afghans who continually oppressed and tyrannized them. Later he addressed a request to the arbābs to help him with money and 3,000 fighters for the struggle with the Afghans. Despite the fatwa of the ḥażrats and pseudo-mullahs which only emphasized the continuation of hostility between Afghans and Hazārahs, and despite the fact that this writer had strongly advised them not to accept (the Saqqawī demand for) an Hazārah force to fight Afghans, as long as Son of the Water Carrier had not managed to bring all Afghans under his control, and [advised them] that [the Afghans and Hazārahs] are Muslim brothers and their blood should not be shed, [the Hazārahs] did not bring up this stipulation and accepted [the amir's] suggestion.

After the audience with Son of the Water Carrier, the Hazārahs dispersed and went to the lodgings assigned to them. For a day and a night each of them had to subsist on two rupees. For two or three days they were entertained as guests of the *pādshāh*. But these ignoramuses did not appreciate the respect that was rendered to them and did not take advantage of the benefits of their position. They refused to eat alongside others in the guest room but dispersed to the homes of their fellow clansmen, some of whom were bakers. Thus instead of pilau, they received two rupees.

Also on this day, 1,000 conscripts were sent to Lahūgard who had been conscripted in Kabul. Fighting continues in Gardayz and its environs. The partisans of Muḥammad Nādir Khān captured Dih-i Bālā and Son of the Water Carrier's troops are in difficult straits. /387/

Monday, 20 Rabīʿ al-Awwal, Corresponding to 3 Sunbul and 25 August

On this day, Sayyid Ḥusayn's secretary, Ghulām Qādir, who had come from Mazār-i Sharīf to obtain instructions relating to secret matters with the Russian government today received permission from Son of the Water Carrier to return. He wanted to fly out of Kabul but the weather did not cooperate so he postponed his departure until the next day.

Also on this day, news that Hazārah settlers had successfully taken Mazār-i Sharīf and defeated Sayyid Ḥusayn were circulating in Kabul.

Mīr Hāshim, the minister of finance during the reign of His Majesty Amān Allāh Khān, with his brother, Sayyid Habib, was imprisoned and his house was confiscated. This was because Muḥammad Nādir Khān had sent a letter to Mīr Hāshim and it had fallen into the hands of Son of the
209 Water Carrier.[238] |

Also, a number of the chiefs of the Sulaymān Khayl tribe, who up to this point had traveled the road of partisanship with Son of the Water Carrier, had risen against His Majesty Amān Allāh Khān along with the Andar, Tarakī, ʿAlī Khayl, and other tribes, and had participated in the destruction of the country, the government, and administration of the Afghans, now, having received instructions from Ḥażrat Shayr Āqā, ended their fighting with the backers of Muḥammad Nādir Khān and with the Afghans. This aroused the ire of Son of the Water Carrier. Consequently, those leaders who had come to Kabul fell from favor and ended up being arrested and humiliated.

On Tuesday, 21 Rabīʿ al-Awwal [corresponding to 4 Sunbul and 26 August] Muḥammad Nādir Khān sent letters of propaganda to tribal leaders via two couriers. He was writing so that they would change the minds of his opponents, force them to follow the teachings of the Prophet, and stir them up to rout Son of the Water Carrier as well as those who

[238] Mīr Hāshim had been arrested more than a month earlier. See above p. 273.

[209]

were the authors of sedition and had destroyed the country's government and the nation and in this fashion purge the country of this vermin.

Also on this day, Son of the Water Carrier made arrangements to send 5,200 forcibly conscripted men to Jalālābād, along with seven six-pound guns and five /388/ mountain guns. He ordered them to drive Muḥammad Hāshim Khān from the town so that, although the Easterners are not allied with [Muḥammad Hāshim] and have no plans for [an attack on] Kabul there won't be any basis for them to form a coalition which could undermine the new government.

Also on this day, Nādir ʿAlī, son of Sulṭān ʿAlī, son of Sardār Shayr ʿAlī Khān Jāghūrī, who had been given the nickname "Dog-for-warm bread" by his fellow tribesmen, was named to the post of high commissioner of the Hazārahjāt, helped by the minister of court, Shayr Jān. He was unable, however, to go there since the arbābs of Bihsūd did not believe he deserved this post.

On Wednesday, the 22nd of Rabīʿ al-Awwal ...[239]

Notes

i The printed Persian edition (p. 48, line 11) omits the words *ashrār jarī* (evil-doers [became so] audacious). Cf. ms. p. 2, line 15.

ii The Persian print edition (p. 49, line 8) has *Jamāl Pāshāh* and the ms. p. 3, line 2 *Jamāl Pādshā*.

iii The print edition (p. 49, line 15) misspells *lajājat* (quarrelsome) as *lajālat* (no sensible meaning). Cf. ms. p. 3, line 7.

iv The print edition (p. 50, line 5) omits a full line of text here after "local governors" up to "criminal judgments." Cf. ms. p. 3, lines 11–12.

v The print edition (p. 51, line 9) misreads *ḥasb al-marām* as *hasb-i ilzām*. Cf. ms. p. 3, line 23.

vi The print edition (p. 51, line 13) incorrectly read the number as "20." Cf. ms. p. 4, line 3.

vii The print edition (p. 51, line14) misread *rikhwat* (weakness, softness) as *riżwat* (no known meaning). Cf. ms. p. 4, line

viii "Italy" was first written and then crossed out.

ix The print edition (p. 57, line 20) added an extra ligature to produce Kīpak. Cf. ms. p. 8, line 8.

x The print edition (p. 58, line 4) misreads *bī-mānīʿī* (without hindrance) as *bih mānīʿī* (with hindrance). Cf. ms. p. 8, line 14.

xi The preceding two sentences are missing from the print edition (p. 58, line 9). Cf. ms. p. 8, lines 17–18.

xii The parentheses appear in the manuscript, p. 9, lines 1, 4.

239 The manuscript suddenly stops here.

xiii The print edition (p. 60, line 16) inserts the Hijrī lunar year date of 1347 in place of the ms. 1307 Hijrī solar date.

xiv The ms. (p. 10, line 7) mistakenly writes "1229" for 1929.

xv The print edition (p. 74, line 16 writes *martūsīn* (no meaning) for *mar'ūsīn* (followers). Cf. ms. p. 18, line 20.

xvi The print edition (p. 81, line 13) omits "Khān." Cf. ms. p. 23, line 5.

xvii The print edition (p. 92, line 10) misreads *az pā dar āwardan* as *az pā wa wārūn āwīkhtan*. Cf. ms. p. 30, line 2.

xviii This sentence is separated slightly from the text and appears to have been Fayż Muḥammad's note to himself.

xix Fayż Muḥammad first wrote "since he did not have definite information" and then crossed it out.

xx The words *wa Jamāl Āghah taṣarruf* were first written and then crossed out. See ms. p. 36, line 23.

xxi The print edition (p. 103, line 16) omits the title *mu'īn al-salṭanah*. Cf. ms. p. 37, line 4.

xxii Fayż Muḥammad first writes "Wednesday, then corrects it to "Tuesday." See ms. p. 37, line 10.

xxiii "The night of this day" (*shab-i īn rūz*) was first written and then crossed out. See ms. p. 37, line 18.

xxiv The print edition (p. 106, line 19) misreads *Sanjan* as *S-kh-n*. Cf. ms. p. 38, line 18.

xxv The print edition (p. 107, line 19) omits the negative particle *na* on *maḥbūs na-shudah*. Cf. ms. 39, line 10.

xxvi The print edition (p. 112, line 20) omits the negative particle *na* on *qabūl-i imārat-ash-rā na-namūdand*. Cf. ms. p. p. 42, line 14.

xxvii The print edition (p. 114, line 5) misreads Shawwāl as Shahrīvar (the name of the Iranian month). Cf. ms. p. 43, line 11.

xxviii The print edition (p. 114, line 7) mistakenly gives the date as 15 Shawwāl. Cf. ms. p. 43, line 12.

xxix The print edition omits the final letter of Arsalāḥ Khān's name. Cf. ms. p.45, line 7.

xxx A sign of momentary inattention on Fayż Muḥammad's part: After writing "the first of Sha'bān corresponding to," he then wrote "23 Sha'bān" which he then crossed out and wrote "23 Jady" instead.

xxxi Originally the author had written "No one knows what the outcome of this was" but then he crossed it out and replaced it with the sentence beginning "Eventually, the Hazārahs themselves were released ..." See ms. p. 49, line 10.

xxxii Fayż Muḥammad had originally written "the army of Turkistān, Ghulām Rasūl Khān Isḥāqzā'ī and the displaced Hazārahs" then crossed it out. See ms. p. 49, lines 17–18. On line 18 he also crossed out "*Amān Allāh Khān-rā kih ū*) and replaced it with *ū-rā*. On line 19 he crossed out "and established on the throne of his government." Pages 49 and 50 of the ms. have ten segments crossed out and replaced.

xxxiii The translation here is of the sentence written above the crossed out line. Originally the line read, "The *ra'īs-i tanẓīmīyah* of Ḥabīb Allāh Khān, Mīrzā

Muḥammad Qāsim, who for supporting Amān Allāh Khān …" See ms. p. 49, line 20.

xxxiv The print edition (p. 125, line 20) misspells *mismār* as *samār*. Cf. ms. p. 50, line 8.

xxxv The sentence "It is not known whether this rumor was just propaganda from Kābulīs fed up with the oppression of the Northerners or was true" was crossed out. See ms. p. 50, lines 4–6.

xxxvi Originally the author had written then crossed out the following: "They say that maybe he got as far as Ghaznīn and if along his way there was no obstacle then he would enter the city." See ms. p. 50, line 17.

xxxvii Originally the author wrote then crossed out: "He escaped through Sih Āb-i Wardak." See ms. p. 51, line 3.

xxxviii Above the line is written: "However, this talk turned out only to be propaganda." See ms. p. 51, line 6.

xxxix Immediately following this sentence "It is not known what the outcome of this was" is crossed out. See ms. p. 51, line 8.

xl Originally [Fayż Muḥammad] had written "Karīm Khān Wardak and the elder brother of Amān Allāh Khān, the prince Ḥayāt Allāh Khān "ʿAżud al-Dawlah" and then crossed it out. See ms. p. 52, line 1.

xli The print edition (p. 128, line 14) omitted "Allāh." Cf. ms. p. 52, line 2.

xlii Fayż Muḥammad here (ms. p. 52, line 3) misspells the Arabic *laṭmat* as *latmat*.

xliii The author crossed out "according to information I have heard." See ms. p. 52, line 5.

xliv In the manuscript, Fayż Muḥammad crossed out "Five aircraft bombed Ḥabīb Allāh Khān's army dispatched to Ghazni and the governor of Ghaznīn, Muḥammad Karīm Khān, fled to Kabul." See ms. p. 52, line 8.

xlv A note in the margin reads: "one ringleader of the thieves was killed and hacked to pieces." See ms. p. 53, second marginal note.

xlvi Fayż Muḥammad crossed out: "Ḥabīb Allāh Khān, who, as already mentioned, had driven to Wardak with Sayyid Ḥusayn, his brother, and minister of war, returned to the Arg at 5:30 in the evening. They say he left Wardak so soon because he heard that his father, Amīr Allāh Khān, had been taken prisoner. But he was unable to do a thing about it. Also one of his generals was killed and hacked to pieces." See ms. p. 54, lines 11–13.

xlvii Fayż Muḥammad crossed out: "He (Ḥabīb Allāh Khān) killed them using their own bomb." See ms. p. 54, line 20.

xlviii Fayż Muḥammad crossed out: "The father of Ḥabīb Allāh Khān—Amīr Allāh *saqqā*, the brother of the governor, Malik Muḥsin; the *qalʿahbegī* Sayyid Ḥusayn, who had the rank of *ghundmishr* (*birgid*); the minister of war and *sipāhsālār*, Purdil Khān …" See ms. p. 55, lines 9–10.

xlix Fayż Muḥammad crossed out "is still living." See ms. p. 55, line 13.

l Fayż Muḥammad crossed out "And now he cannot leave. I don't know how this will end and what this mutiny will bring." See ms. p. 56, lines 6–7.

li Fayż Muḥammad originally wrote "the first" (*gharrah*) and the word "Thursday" (*panjshanbah*). He then realized his mistake, crossed out Thursday and replaced it with "Friday" but neglected to change "the first" to "the second."

The print edition (p. 136, line 7) also failed to make the change. See ms. p. 56, line 10.

lii The print edition (p. 136, line 23) omits "Khān." Cf. ms. p. 56, line 19.

liii A crossed-out sentence reads: "They say that Ḥabīb Allāh Khān's father, Amīr Allāh Khān, was arrested by Shāh Pasand Khān, son of ʿAbbās Ghulām Riżā Khān, son of ʿAbbās Khān, from the clan of the ʿAlā al-Dīn Hazārahs of Ghaznīn. [Shāh Pasand Khān] laid a waterskin on Amīr Allāh's shoulders and, hobbling him [like a horse], ordered that, as previously, he should serve as a water carrier and deliver water to the troops. He assigned a soldier to him who was supposed to prod him with his rifle butt if he flagged at all." See ms. p. 57, lines 10–13.

liv A crossed-out sentence: "I don't know whether this is the truth or a lie." See ms. p. 57, line 19.

lv From here on this sentence is crossed out: "God willing, the story of their departure will come in due course." See ms. p. 58, line 4.

lvi The words "another male" was crossed out. See ms. p. 58, line 11.

lvii The following sentence has been crossed out: "We will see how this shedding the blood [of the people] by those who aspire to the status of spiritual leaders ends up." See ms. p. 58, line 16.

lviii First he wrote, "of Fatḥ Muḥammad Khān" and then crossed it out. Ms. p. 58, line 21.

lix He further wrote, then crossed out "the wife of Aḥmad Shāh Khān." See ms. p. 58, line 19.

lx This name is written in above: "the sister of ʿAlī Aḥmad Khān, son of Khūshdil Khān, son of the late *īshīk-āqāsī* Shayrdil Khān," which has been crossed out. Ms. p. 58, line 20.

lxi This sentence is crossed out: "They say the Hazārahs retreated to Band-i Sulṭān and that the greater part of them was killed. However, I don't know whether this is true or not." Ms. p. 61, lines 8–9.

lxii The following sentence has been crossed out: "[The Hazārahs] swore oaths of allegiance in order not to be annihilated." Ms. p. 61, line 19.

lxiii The following sentence is crossed out: "No one knows what the Almighty has in store for this unhappy benighted nation." Ms. p. 62, line 8.

lxiv The rest of the sentence is crossed out: "Evidently, next Monday fighting will commence in the Ūnay Pass because the Hazārahs, aware of the evil-minded Kūhistānīs and Kūh Dāmanīs and their treatment of the people of Kabul, give them no opportunity to invade their lands. Therefore war is inevitable." Ms. p. 62, lines 22–23.

lxv The following sentence is crossed out: "Along with him, Sayyid Ḥusayn departed for Ghaznīn. This trip of his is quite likely since in the northern regions …" Ms. p. 63, line 14.

lxvi The print edition (p. 151, line 14) has *p-n-ı p-k* while the ms. (p. 64, line 17) clearly has *pīnī bīk* (i.e. Pini Bīk/Beg).

lxvii The print edition (p. 153, line 11) has *būdand* (they were) instead of *birawand* (they should go). Cf. ms. p. 65, line 21.

lxviii Over the line is written: "However the Hazārahs continued to oppose Ḥabīb Allāh Khān and support Amān Allāh Khān." Ms. p. 67, line 12.

lxix Fayż Muḥammad crossed out [Muḥammad Nādir Khān] “with a very large army entered Tangī Āghūjān.” See ms. p. 67, line 17.

lxx The print edition (p. 158, line 50) misreads Shalgīr as Salīgar. Cf. ms. p. 68, line 11.

lxxi Originally the author wrote, then crossed out: “From these regions a detachment under the command of General Muḥammad Ghaws̱ Khān and an Hazārah tribal militia arrived in Wardak and cut the road in the rear of Ḥabīb Allāh Khān’s force.” See ms. p. 68, lines 14–15.

lxxii A crossed-out phrase: “who had seized the amirid throne.” See ms. p. 71, line 15.

lxxiii The following sentence is crossed out: “It is not known how all this business will end up.” Ms. p. 71, line 19.

lxxiv A crossed-out phrase: “of the Andar tribe from Shalghār.” See ms. p. 72, line 11.

lxxv A crossed-out phrase: “from twenty to twenty-five men.” See ms. p. 72, line 12.

lxxvi Written above the line: “In the end it turned out that these were all lies.” See ms. p. 72, line 19.

lxxvii The following sentence is crossed out: “I don’t know whether this is true or not.” See ms. p. 72, lines 20–21.

lxxviii Then comes another sentence which the author has crossed out: “Sayyid Ḥusayn, having departed for Chārīkār to repel the attack of the Hazārahs from Shaykh ʿAlī, Surkh-i Pārsā, Turkmān, Bāmyān, Yakah Awlang and Balkhāb and to conduct operations in Ghūrband, sent him to Kabul.” See ms. p. 73, lines 15–16.

lxxix The print edition (p. 168, line 15) transposes the numbers into “36.” Cf. ms. p. 74, line 2.

lxxx These words are written above the crossed-out “and also rumors spread.” See ms. p. 74, line 10.

lxxxi The following sentence is crossed out: “Besides this raid, they carried out no other military activity in Lahūgard.” See ms. p. 74, line 12.

lxxxii The following sentence is crossed out: “I don’t know how this concluded.” See ms. p. 75, line 12.

lxxxiii The following was deleted (after Lahūgard): “located close to Kabul which up to now the hand of aggression of the Kūh Dāmanīs and Kūhistānīs had not yet been curtailed from bringing harm and news of Muḥammad Nādir Khān and the affairs of [the Southern Province] had not yet been brought.” See ms. p. 75, lines 15–16.

lxxxiv The print edition (p. 171, line 23) omits the next several words up to “he returned to the city.” Cf. ms. p. 75, line 21.

lxxxv “… defeated and routed” is written above the line. See ms. p. 75, line 23.

lxxxvi Crossed out is: “The Mangal tribe had carried out an attack on Charkh.” See ms. p. 76, lines 10–11.

lxxxvii Crossed out is: “they plundered them” before “were burned.” See ms. p. 76, line 11.

lxxxviii Crossed out: “No one knows what he will next undertake.” See ms. p. 77, line 17.

lxxxix The print edition (p. 176, line 13) omits the word *amr* in the phrase *bi-amr-i* (at the order of). Cf. ms. p. 78, line 5.

xc The following sentence is crossed out: "About whether Ḥabīb Allāh Khān's conditions are acceptable or not will be recorded after [Amān Allāh's] reply arrives. However, it is likely that his conditions are acceptable because [Amān Allāh Khān] awarded the pilot a shawl and a robe (*chūkhā*)." See ms. p. 78, lines 21–23.

xci The following sentence is crossed out: "But now, when a truce is achieved, it is possible to put an end to war and bloodshed, however …" See ms. p. 80, line 9.

xcii The print edition (p. 180, line 4) inserts an extraneous conjunction *wa* (and) between *ghundmishr* and "Ḥabīb Allāh Khān." Cf. ms. p. 80 first marginal note line 2.

xciii Crossed out is: "After being [released from] detention, under the pretext that he was heading for Ghaznīn, he left for Qalʿah-i Durrānī." See ms. p. 80, line 9.

xciv The print edition (p. 181, line 2) has Patī for Bīnī. Cf. ms. p. 80, line 16.

xcv Originally he had written the words "military" and "civilian." See ms. p. 84, line 15.

xcvi The print edition (p. 200, line 7) mistakenly writes Ḥiṣār. Cf. ms. p. 92, line 17.

xcvii The print edition (p. 203, line 22) has "Sind" rather than "Hind." Cf. ms. p. 94, line 22.

xcviii The print edition (p. 209, line 4) renders what appears to be *sipāhī* as *aspānī*. Cf. ms. p. 98, marginal note line 2. The third letter (whether *nūn* or *hā-i dū chashm*) is not clear but it is clear that there is no initial *alif*).

xcix In transcribing the text, the print edition (p. 210, line 3) inadvertently skipped a line in the text. Cf. ms. p. 98, line 12.

c The print edition (p. 213, line 20) substitutes the Persian *jānishīn* for the Arabic *jālis*. Cf. ms. p. 100, line 20.

ci The print edition (p. 214, line14) misspells *junḥah* (misdemeanor) as *ḥ-n-j-h* (no meaning). Cf. ms. p. 101, line 8.

cii The print edition (p. 218, line 10) erroneously has "600" instead of "800." Cf. ms. p. 103, line 5.

ciii The print edition (p. 220, line 5) mistakenly wrote *tashnah* (thirsty) instead of *nishastah* (sitting). Cf. ms. p. 104, line 23.

civ Originally, "with Muḥammad ʿAlīm Khān son of ʿAbd al-Karīm Khān" was written then crossed out.

cv Originally he had written, "two mullahs" and then crossed it out. See ms. p. 113, line 12.

cvi The author here mistakenly wrote ʿAlī Aḥmad Khān when he meant Aḥmad ʿAlī Khān. See ms. p. 114, line 9.

cvii Above the line is written "As people say". See ms. p. 116, line 1.

cviii The print edition (p. 247, line 17) omits the conjunction *wa* between *ahālī-yi shahr* (people of the city) and Chahārdihī making it read *ahālī-yi shahr-i Chārdihī* "the people of the city of Chārdihī." Cf. ms. p. 122, line 13.

cix The print edition (p. 254, line 20) has inserted an extraneous *radd* (rejection, refusal) which changes the meaning and is not in the manuscript.

cx The print version (p. 256, line 19) inserts an extraneous conjunction *wa* (and) here changing the meaning. Cf. ms. p. 128, line 1.

cxi The print version (p. 257, line 19) misreads *zibar* (upper part) as *zīr* (lower part). Cf. ms. p. 128, line 13.

cxii The print edition (p. 269, line 19) mistakenly reads *majlis* (gathering, meeting, session) as *maḥbas* (prison!). Cf. ms. p. 136, line 4.

cxiii The print edition omits about half a line of text (p. 271, line 17, middle) which renders the sentence incomprehensible. Cf. ms. p. 137, line 5.

cxiv The print edition (p. 273, last line) has omitted one line in the manuscript represented here by the words between the words "which" and "objected." Cf. ms. p. 138, line 17.

cxv The print edition (p. 277, line 22) misread *nānwā* (baker) as *nām wa* (name and) which changes the meaning of the sentence.

cxvi The print edition (p. 294, line 10) has omitted the next sentence (from "They arrested ..." to "... with blood.") Cf. ms. p. 151, lines 11–12.

cxvii The print edition (p. 298, line 10) inserts the errant preposition "bih" between the word "Mīrzā" and "Sulṭān." Cf. ms. p. 153, line 21.

cxviii The print edition (p. 301, line 9) erroneously writes "fourteen." Cf. ms. p. 155, line 13.

cxix The print edition (p. 301, line 14) erroneously writes *wa dāʾī* (and the uncle) for *wālī* (high governor). Cf. ms. p. 155, line 16.

cxx The print edition (p. 309, line 5) writes *barādar-i shawhar-ash* (the brother of her husband) while the manuscript (p. 160, line 7) has *barādar wa mādar-ash* (her brother and [her] mother).

cxxi The print edition (p. 310, line 10) misspells *sālār* (chief). Cf. ms. p. 161, line 3.

cxxii The print edition (p. 311, line 4) misspells ʿAbd al-Wāḥid's name as ʿAbd al-Waḥd. Cf. ms. p. 161, line 13.

cxxiii The print edition (p. 313, line 16) misspells Sūr as *sawār*. Cf. ms. p. 163, line 3.

cxxiv The print edition (p. 320, lines 13–17) makes several mistakes transcribing the Hindū names, adding an extra 'h' at the ends of the names with 'Singh'—Dīwān Mangal Singhah for example, and misreading Kūsingh Arjan Dās as Kūsinghah Darjan Dās; Mishr Bāl Makan as Shar Bāl Makan; and Lachmī Dās as Lachmanī Dās. Cf. ms. p. 166, lines 21–23.

cxxv The print edition at this point (p. 320, line 18) omits an entire page of the manuscript (p. 167).

cxxvi The print edition (p. 333, line 21) omits a letter and reads the name "Ṣadr." Cf. ms. p. 176, line 4.)

cxxvii The print edition (p. 346, line 9) misreads *janrāl-i* (general) as *jazāʾī* (reward, punishment). Cf. ms. p. 183, line 8.

cxxviii The print edition (p. 351, line 2) misspells *mukhālafat* as *mukhālat*. Cf. ms. p. 186, line 3.

cxxix The print edition (p. 353, line 10) skipped an entire line here. Cf. ms. p. 187, the middle of line 12 to the middle of line 13.

cxxx The print edition (p. 355, line 16) transposes the letters in *ʿādat* (custom, habit) into *duʿāt* (prayers). Cf. ms. p. 188, line 22.

cxxxi The print edition (p. 365, line 24) misspells Żabṭū as Ẕabṭū. Cf. ms. p. 195, line 13.

cxxxii The print edition (p. 366, line 16) dropped the name "Ḥusayn." Cf. ms. p. 195, line 23.

cxxxiii The print edition (p. 379, line 12) omits the word *ʿunwān* (title). Cf. ms. p. 204, line 3.

cxxxiv The print edition (p. 382, line 3) starting with the words *bar ʿAlīyah* omits a line of the original. Cf. ms. p. 205 middle of the line 16 to middle of line 17.

NIZHĀDNĀMAH-I AFGHĀN

NIZHĀDNĀMAH-I AFGHĀN

The Book of the Afghan Lineage

In the name of God, the Merciful, the Compassionate

With the help of the Creator of the Upper and Lower Worlds, the One who brought humanity into existence beginning with Adam and Eve, I undertook to establish the origin of the race of the Afghans and have organized and written a modest account including an introduction, seven chapters, and a conclusion. Should any omission or inadvertent failure to mention any ethnic groups (*firaq*) or clans (*qabā'il*) of this people (*qawm*) occur, (the author) should deem himself negligent and hope for the generosity of fault-finders but "because man is subject to forgetfulness and oversight" [an Arabic saying], I hope for those people's forgiveness. And it is my wish that they correct errors as they appear and so make the writer the consort of success.

Introduction

The author of *Nāsikh al-tawārīkh* wrote that the migration of this people (the Afghans) and their settling in the Kūh-i Sulaymān in northwestern Hindūstān took place 3,820 years after Adam's fall (peace be upon him), 1,765 years before the birth of Christ (Ḥażrat-i Masīḥ—peace be upon him), and after the exodus of Moses and the Israelites from Egypt and the drowning of [the pharaoh] Walīd ibn Musʿab in the Red Sea. It is thought that they [the Afghans] are of the Coptic people.

/46/ The author of *Tārīkh-i Firishtah* has recorded that during the time of the Islamic sultans (the Afghans) sought to settle in the city of Patnah, in the land of India.

Hāshim Shāyiq Bukhārī, deputy director of the Text Book Office of the Ministry of Education of Afghanistan, has noted in a general history intended as a classroom textbook that the "Pukht, Pukhtū, Pushtū, and Pushtūn/Pashtūn" are documented as being of the Aryan race and that their homeland was in eastern Persia, by which is meant Afghanistan.[1]

[1] Bukhārī was Fayż Muḥammad's supervisor in the Textbook Office (*dār al-ta'līf*). The title of this history textbook is unknown to us.

 | DOI:10.1163/9789004392441_004

[2]

The author of *Makhzan-i Afghānī*[2] noted, without any documentation, that this tribe was of the progeny of Afghanah, the name of a son of Ārmiyā, commander-in-chief of the army of Solomon (Ḥażrat-i Sulaymān—peace be upon him) and that it established its homeland in the Ghūr mountains, Fīrūzkūh, and the mountains of Khurāsān after Nebuchadnezzar's conquest of Jerusalem and the diaspora of the Israelites. He notes that [the Afghans] are the progeny of Qays ibn ʿAyṣ who was one of (the Israelites).

How the Afghans Were Named Patān

The most compelling reason (for the name) is their having chosen to settle in the land of Patnah, which is mentioned in *Tārīkh-i Firishtah*, which was the cause of their being known as Patān. Up to today, the majority of the people of India refer to them metonymously (as Patāns). /47/

2 The author of *Makhzan*, in contrast, writes that due to some service | that Qays, the forebear of this people, had rendered in bringing Islam to them, the Prophet, gave him the name ʿAbd al-Rashīd and the nickname "Patān" meaning the mast of a sailing ship. At this time (the word with) the Persian 'b' and the Hindi (Urdu) 't'[3] is no longer used in Arabic.

How This People Came To Be Called Pashtū or Pashtān and Pukhtū/Pakhtū or Pakhtān/Pukhtān

According to a persuasive note by Hāshim Shāyiq, "In olden times, (the Afghans) had this name when they lived in northern Iran. In his history, Ḥayāt Khān[4] attributes this name to a place called 'Pusht/Pasht' located in Ghūr-i Harāt which is the first place they lived. He also wrote that Pashtūn/Pushtūn is derived from *pushtah* meaning 'mountain' since they first took refuge in the mountains of Ghūr and the Kūh-i Sulaymān. Thus, by a slight phonetic alteration, it gave them the name 'Pushtū.' Their language spread and became known as Pushtū. Coincidentally, the word mountain and Pushtūn both derived from *pushtah*. The two correlate to each other and produce the meaning, 'mountain Pushtūn' or 'Pushtūn of the mountain region.'" That is the end of (Hāshim Shāyiq's) note.

---

[2] Khwājah Niʿmat Allāh b. Ḥabīb Allāh Harawī, *Tārīkh-i Khān Jahānī wa Makhzan-i Afghānī*, edited by S. M. Imāmuddin, 2 vols., Dacca: Asiatic Society of Pakistan, 1960–62.

[3] Fayż Muḥammad is referring to his orthography in which the Arabic 't' (*tā'*) is written with the small Arabic velarized 't' (*ṭā'*) added above it (called the *ṭe* in Urdu) to indicate the retroflexive consonant.

[4] Deputy Muḥammad Ḥayāt Khān, *Ḥayāt-i Afghānī*, Lahore: Kūh-i Nūr, 1867. In Urdu.

Pukhtūn is how the Afghans pronounced the word by changing the letter *shīn* [the "sh" in Pushtū] to the letter *khā'*. They call themselves Pushtū/Pashtū and Pushtūn/Pashtūn as well as Pukhtū/Pakhtū and Pukhtūn/Pakhtūn while Indians call them Patāns and Persians call them Afghans. /48/

How This People Came to Be Known as Afghans

The author of *Makhzan-i Afghānī* imagined that they were the progeny of the mythical Afghanah ibn Armiya and thought that this was the origin of their name. In the *Shāhnāmah*, Kak Kūh Zād Afghan bore this name before the birth of Jesus (peace be upon him). In any case, the origin of this word and name was the result of usage by Persian speakers. Thus, the Afghans call themselves Pashtūn and Pakhtūn and their language Pashtū and never call themselves "Afghan."

With the pen of clarity, the author of *Tārīkh-i Firishtah* has recorded how they were named. He writes that in the year 143 A.H. this people raided the environs of Peshawar. The rajah of Lahore sent an army to repel them, several battles were fought, and the rajah's army was defeated. At that point people from Kabul, Ghūr, and the Khalaj, who had come out of religious solidarity to assist (the Pashtūns), returned home.

Some who were asked about /49/ the situation of Muslims of the mountain region of the frontier would say in response, "Because of the great amount of conflict, hardship, great turmoil, quarrelsomeness, and complaining (*faghān*) (in that region), the word "mountain region" should not be uttered, instead you should say "Afghanistan"" (i.e. "Faghānistān," ["land of complainers"]). Thus, they became known as Afghans and their abode (*saqnāq*) was eastern Iran. In ancient books of the Hindūs it extended to Balkh Bālīk Dīs [i.e. Bakhdi, the Avestan name?] and during the era of the Iranians [Achaemenids, i.e.] [it included] Harāt, Kābulistān, and Zābulistān. At the time of the conquests of Alexander of Macedon and
3 the Greeks, (the region) was named Bactria | and then became known as Afghanistan. In addition, during the time of the Mughal sultans it was called the *ṣūbah* of Kabul and [the *ṣūbah*] of Qandahar.

The Origin of the Pashto Language

Deputy Ḥayāt Khān, who was an Afghan and a resident of Ḥasan Abdāl, a district of Rawalpindi, quoted from *Makhzan-i Afghānī* in his own history saying that the Pashto language is taken from demons with whom the Afghans collaborated in the work of building *Bayt al-Muqaddas* [or *Maqdis*—Jerusalem]. The Afghan themselves allege and claim that there were a number of Afghans at the court of King Solomon (peace be upon him). They were his close companions and confidants and the king [in particular situations] would speak to them in Pashto [so others would not understand]. This claim by Afghans is also recorded in the *Makhzan-i Afghānī*. However, it is well-known from the speech and pronunciation of Afghans and their sentences and conversation[i] that the words and inflections [are] new Persian, Pahlavi, and ancient Zand and it is well-understood that the majority of Persian words are found [in Pashto] with only slight or no changes at all. For example, the honorable English [author] in his book writes that two hundred /50/ and eighteen Afghānī words correlate to words in Persian, Zand, Pahlavi, Sanskrit, Hindi, Arabic, Armenian, Georgian, Hebrew, and Babylonian.[5] Only ten percent of the words do not correspond to words in other languages. The majority of the remaining ninety per cent are Persian with some (correlating to) Pahlavi, some to Zand, and some actual Zand and Pahlavi words and then a very few Sanskrit words and five or[ii] six Hindi words. As for Hebrew, which was the principal language of the Banī Isrāʾīl, there's not a single word in Pashto. Similarly, another person compared the meaning of one hundred words or so of the Afghānī dialect to Panjābī words but no more than six correspond.

Thus this evidence proves that the Afghans are Aryans and not from the Banī Isrāʾīl [nor] are they Arab or Copt, for they [also] say they are descended from Khālid ibn Walīd, a well-known leader of the Quraysh and an Arab. The dialect that they speak is a potpourri of old Aryan words from Persian, Pahlavi, and Zand mixed with those [few] words [from other sources] and so a separate language came into being.

The fact that the Afghans consider themselves Banī Isrāʾīl may be because during the fighting and battling of Tiglath Pileser[6] and his son [*sic*] Shalmanāṣir, the Banī Isrāʾīl conquered Jerusalem. After a short time, Nebuchadnezzar, King of /51/ Chaldea and Babel, extirpated the Banī Isrāʾīl and carried a large number off as prisoners, along with Prophet Daniel (on him be peace). Of the twelve tribes of the Banī Isrāʾīl, he returned
4 two, the Banyamīn and Yahūd, to Jerusalem and Syria. | The others fled towards the east and became foreigners in the land. One of them Qays, the forebear and first ancestor of the Afghans converted to Islam, as indi-

[5] Fayż Muḥammad might have been referring to Henry George Raverty, *A Dictionary of the Puk'hto, Pus'hto, or the Language of the Afghans: With Remarks on the Originality of the Language, and Its Affinity to the Semitic and Other Oriental Tongues*, London, 1860.

[6] Tiglath-Pileser II r. ca. 967–935 B.C. Shalmenasir II reigned 1039–1013 B.C.

cated above, and was given the name ʿAbd al-Rashīd. Because of their mixing with Arabs and a variety of other peoples and tribes they entirely lost Hebrew. Other than this, there is no evidence of their being from the Banī Isrā'īl.

Similarly, there is no source for their being related to Khālid ibn al-Walīd other than their having intermarried with Arabs after the sending of the Ḥażrat, the Seal (of the Prophets) with the revelations, the appearance of the religion of Islam, and the Arab conquests of Iran and Afghanistan and their occupation of the mountain regions, the Kūh-i Sulaymān, and [its] valleys and farmlands. The Afghans, who have not a word of Arabic in their dialect, nonetheless say they are related to the Arabs. On the pattern of those who came to speak Tājīk and Fārsī, the Afghans adopted this language that they speak. They have no documentation to distance themselves from the Aryans or the Copts and instead concoct a fictitious Banī Isrā'īl or Arab lineage.

Pashtūn or Afghan Peoples and Tribes

Scholars and historians from this great people and contentious nation, which now numbers in the hundreds of thousands of individuals and thousands of distinct tribes, clans and lineages (*khayl*s), date the beginning of their family tree and their ancestry /52/ to a time after the appearance of Islam and to Qays ʿAbd al-Rashīd and Shāh Ḥusayn Ghūrī. Their ancestry is based on seven original lineages: Sarbanī, Ghurghushtī, Bītanī, Matī/Matay, Sarwānī, Garrānī (Karrānī),[7] and Usturānī. By way of clarification, each lineage will be depicted in a separate chapter along with its subsidiary clans and the different tribes speaking Afghānī so that everyone, whether noble or commoner will know everything about them.

---

[7] The spelling of this name and its transliteration vary between texts and modern scholarly studies. Fayż Muḥammad spells the name with a 'g' (Garrān), what is known as the "Persian k.' Since in texts the 'g' is simply a small mark over the 'k,' it is often written as 'k,' the mark omitted and the reader expected to know that it is 'g' and not 'k.' Modern scholarship has largely accepted the pronunciation of the name with a 'k' (see e.g. Willem Vogelsang, "The ethnogenesis of the Pashtuns," in *Cairo to Kabul: Afghan and Islamic Studies*, edited by Warwick Ball and Leonard Harrow, London: Melisende, 2002, pp. 228–35, p. 232.) Typically in Arabic orthography, the doubled consonant *rā'* ('r') would be written only once and would have the doubling symbol (*shaddah, tashdīd*) either written or understood to be above it. However, Fayż Muḥammad writes the *rā'* twice, suggesting at first that the name is to be pronounced "Garrarān" or "Karrarān" as some scholars have rendered it (e.g. Robert Nichols, *Colonial Reports on Pakistān's Tribal Areas*, Karachi: Oxford University Press, 2005, p. 52). We have chosen to adhere to Fayż Muḥammad's spelling of the first letter but assume that his writing the *rā'*-s separately was to tell the reader the consonant was doubled, hence "Garrān" and not "Garrarān."

/55/ CHAPTER ONE

The Sarbanī Tribes[8]

The peoples and tribes of the (1) Tarīn, (2) Shayrānī, (3) Barīch, (4) Ūrmur, and (5) Miyānah are of the lineage of Sharaf al-Dīn, better known as Sharkhbūn, son of Sarban, son of Qays named ʿAbd al-Rashīd. Several ethnic groups and clans were formed from each of the abovementioned. For example, the Tūr Tarīn, Aspīn Tarīn, Abdāli—now known as Durrānī—Zīrak, and the Panj Pāy which includes (1) Pūpalzāʾī, (2) Bārakzāʾī, (3) ʿAlīkūzāʾī, (4) Sadūzāʾī, and (5) Nūrzāʾī, which in turn includes Adūzāʾī, Isḥāqzāʾī, and Khūkyānī[9] and Mākū, in all 105 clans (*khayl*s) are (all) the descendants of Tarīn of which (only) the largest tribes have been recorded
5 (here). |

Sadūzāʾī

This clan together with the Pūpalzāʾī (comprises some) 15,250 households, most of whom are connected to Shahr-i Ṣafā[10] located six farsangs northeast of the city of Qandahar. A few households are in Peshawar. A certain number have mixed with others of the Tarīn lineage and live in Multān, Dīrahjat, and other places. Aḥmad Shāh was from this clan and, having been enrolled as one of Nādir Shāh Afshār's *yasāwul*s, he attained royal rank, wrested Afghanistan from Iran /56/ and created an independent sovereign kingdom. Four of his progeny [sons and grandsons] were Tīmūr Shāh, Shāh Zamān, Shāh Shujāʿ, and Shāh Maḥmūd. The first two enjoyed sovereignty, as did Aḥmad Shāh himself, over Lahore, Kashmīr, Sind, and the Panjāb; the other two, thanks to the conquests of Ranjīt

---

[8] It should be noted at the outset that Fayż Muḥammad uses several terms often interchangeably to indicate "tribe, people, or clan." These include (with their plural forms): *qawm/aqwām, qabīlah/qabāʾil, īl or ayl /īlāt or aylāt, ahl/ahālī, firqah/firaq, ṭāʾifah/ṭawāʾif, khayl/akhyāl, dastah/dastahjāt, rishtah,* and *shaʿbah/shuʿāb.* The best that can be said is that *qawm, firqah, ṭāʾifah, ahl, īl* appear when speaking of large groups and *shaʿbah, khayl* and *dastah* for smaller units or subdivisions of tribes. However, he consistently introduces each new tribal group with the word *firqah*, irrespective of its size or relationship to any other group. We have omitted it in the translation.

[9] The commonly accepted pronunciation is "Khūgyānī" but we adhere to Fayż Muḥammad's spelling.

[10] Because of the large number of toponyms, we will only identify the location of each place in Afghanistan in the index if it appears in Adamec, *Gazetteer*, especially volumes 5 ("Kandahar and South-Central Afghanistan") and 6 ("Kabul and Southeastern Afghanistan") and/or on the 1:1,500,000 scale map, "Afghanistan," Ayazi Publishing, 2001. For the locations that fall in Pakistan today, the sources are listed at the beginning of the index.

Singh, surrendered control over the regions of the Panjāb, Lahore, and Kashmīr and (only) governed Sind and Afghanistan. Three other royals, namely the princes Kāmrān, Qayṣar, and Fatḥ Jang spent time governing Harāt, Qandahar, and Kabul but without enjoying [full] sovereignty. The offspring of Shāh Shujāʿ still live in Lūdyānah (Ludhiana) on the east bank of the Satlaj [Sutlej], one of the rivers of the Panjāb. This clan [the Sadūzāʾī]—known today as Durrānī—held sway over the entire Abdālī tribe. They had a document, a farman, from one of the Safavid shahs concerning their chieftainship that said that the Saduzāʾī clan serves as *khān*, *raʾīs* and *sardār* of the entire Abdālī tribe and holds jurisdiction over them as their governor.

Pūpalzāʾī

This clan, which, in terms of numbers, is equal to the Sadūzāʾī, the Sadūzāʾī being a branch of it, are mostly located in the northern mountains of Qandahar, adjacent to the Hazārahjāt. A certain number are found in Khākrīz, some in several places east of Qandahar, some in Ẕākard, Bālā Qarż, Shūr Andām, and other places south (of Qandahar); some (in) the district of Zarasht which is one of the districts of Girishk located on the west bank of the Hīrmand (Helmand) River; in two locales in Garmsīr, in three places west of the lower Arghandāb (River); a few households in Hazārah Uruzgān where they settled when the government gave it to them. All Pūpalzāʾī are farmers and are the most noble of Afghans. /57/

Bārakzāʾī

This clan group comprises 43,750 households. They are found in Arghastān south of Qandahar and along the Hīrmand River and reside in Khushk Maydān. Due to the fine conditions of the soil, almost all spend their days as farmers. Some (on the other hand) eke out a mere subsistence on barren ground gathering what they need [only] through much toil and hardship. Most also work as herders and drive their flocks to summer pas-
6 tures. Amīr Dūst Muḥammad Khān | emerged from this clan and seven of his [direct] descendants have ruled down to Amīr Amān Allāh Khān, namely: (1) Amīr Shayr ʿAlī Khān, (2) Amīr Muḥammad Afżal Khān, (3) Amīr Muḥammad Aʿẓam Khān, (4) Amīr Muḥammad Yaʿqūb Khān, (5) Amīr ʿAbd al-Raḥmān Khān, (6) Amīr Ḥabīb Allāh, and (7) Amīr Amān Allāh Khān. Because of the revolution (*inqilāb*) launched by the thief,

Ḥabīb Allāh, son of Amīr Allāh[11] *saqqā* (water carrier), the reins of the emirate passed to Muḥammad Nādir Khān, a descendant of Sardār Sulṭān Muḥammad Khān, the brother of Amīr Dūst Muḥammad Khān, and he is presently the *pādshāh*.

Achakzāʾī

This tribal group of 7,500 households resides in and around Kūh-i Kūzhak. Most are subjects of the English but some occupy the district of Hazārah Chūrah which the [Afghan] government gave them. The majority have flocks and pasture their sheep on Kūh-i Khwājah ʿImrān and Kūh-i Tūbah. They pasture their camels in the steppe northeast /58/ of Shūrābak. A few of the Achakzāʾī work as farmers. The majority of them spend time in thievery and highway robbery. They are an extremely wicked, rebellious, dishonest, vicious, lying, and deceitful people.

ʿAlīkūzāʾī

This clan comprises 17,750 households. They live in the district of Jaldak in eastern Qandahar; northwest and west of Khāṣṣ-i Arghandāb; in Panjwāʾī; in other places west and north of Khākrīz district and Kuhistān (the mountain area north Qandahar); north and northwest of Maymand; and (in) Chakah district and Sarban Qalʿah along the eastern banks of the Hīrmand River; several places south of the city of Qandahar; in Baghnī and Bāghrān northwest of Zamīn Dāwar; Nawzād and Kanjak of Zamīn Dāwar proper. Some are found living here and there [away from their clan] in Harāt, Ghaznīn, and Kabul. Most pursue farming as an occupation while a small number are herders and roam the wastelands. They also earn livings through crafts and commerce. The lands they possess are generally rich and fertile ones. Āqā-yi Asadī,[12] the current trustee for all

[11] On the question of the name of Ḥabīb Allāh Khān Kalakānī's father see note 19 in the *Taẕakkur al-inqilāb* section of this book.

[12] According to Ḥājj Kāẓim Yazdānī, "During the time of the first Pahlavī [Reza Shah], Āqā-yi Asadī was deputy trustee of the Riżawī shrine [in Mashhad]. The insurgency at the Gawhar Shād Mosque shrine occurred in 1314/1935 under his leadership and about 4,000 people of Mashhad and its environs, the greater number of whom were Khāwaris, were martyred. The details of how this Asadī came to perpetrate such a terrible crime are still unknown. But given what Mullā Fayż Muḥammad brings to light here about his origins and roots, it is not far-fetched to think that such an outrage was concocted by a mind governed by tribal fanaticism and sectarianism. In any event he was then put to death by the Riżā Khānī government. To know more about this one should read the book *Qiyām-i Gawhar Shād* by Wāḥid Sīnā [Sina 1982]. (Fayż Muḥammad Hazārah, *Nizhādnāmah-i Afghān*, Qum: Muʾassasah-i Maṭbūʿāt-i Ismāʿīliyān, 1372/1993, note, p. 58.).

of Khurāsān [for the Riżawī shrine at Mashhad], is from this ethnic group and one of the offspring of Wazīr Yār Muḥammad Khān. Two clans **/59/** of this ethnic group, the Nasūzā'ī and the Sarkānī live in the Hazārah District, Rawalpindi. A number of the Sarkānī live in Kunar, Jalālābād and in Dūābah district of Peshawar. A few households reside in Balūchistān and the Deccan in India. Zarghūnah, the mother of Aḥmad Shāh, was from the ʿAlīkūzā'ī clan.

Nūrzā'ī

This clan, also like the Barakzā'ī, is made up of 43,750 households. Most live in Garmsīr, the district of Dihrāwut [Dihrāwud]; the mountain region north of Qandahar adjacent to the Hazārahjāt; Farāh; and Isfizār as far as Harāt; in the sand desert (*rīk/rīg*) south of Qandahar; Spīrawān west (of Qandahar); and on the eastern banks of the Helmand River. They spend
7 their days farming, moving flocks to summer pastures (*yaylāmīshī*), | and roaming barren areas (grazing their herds). They raid, plunder, and murder the people of the frontier, those subject to Iran. They deem it legal and morally permissible to take their blood and property because they are Shiʿi and therefore heretics. They have always perpetrated this kind of thing and continue to do so. The majority of Afghans and Sunnis of Afghanistan adhere to this same creed. In short, the members of this clan who own herds travel in spring and summer to Siyah Band, which belongs to the Tāymanī people and is situated adjacent to the Hazārahjāt. There they pasture their animals for the summer and in winter return to their headquarters and homelands, while pursuing the path of ignorant and wicked behavior. **/60/**

ʿAlīzā'ī

This tribe is made up of 20,000 households. Its homeland is opposite that of the ʿAlīkūzā'ī tribe. The dividing line between the two groups is the Hīrmand River. The farmlands of the ʿAlīkūzā'ī are mostly river bottomland while those of the ʿAlīzā'ī are irrigated by underground aqueducts. There are a few sub-clans of the ʿAlīzā'ī in Panjāb and in nineteen locales in the Chahchah district of Rawalpindi.

Adūzā'ī/Adawzā'ī

This clan includes 6,250 households. They live in Maʿrūf District, in two places in the Dihrāwut district, and in three locales in Garmsīr.

[7]

In their lifestyle and in terms of good and evil behavior, each of these groups conforms to that of their neighbors. They are farmers and cultivators.

Isḥāqzā'ī

This tribe comprises 12,750 households. It lives in the following places: west of Qandahar at the edge of the sand desert, along the banks of the Arghandāb River as far as Qalʿah-i Bust, in a few places below Chakah District along the eastern bank of the Hīrmand River, in Garmsīr District, in Farāh, in Isfizār, in Lāsh wa Juwayn, southeast of Harāt and north of Sīstān, and a few households in Harāt itself. One thousand families of their herders pasture their flocks summer and winter in the vicinity of Balkh. The majority of the people of this group are herders and the minority are farmers. In terms of their morals, they are hardly human and are the consorts of bestiality and utter ignorance. **/61/**

Mākū and *Khūkyānī*

These two clan groups comprise 1,000 households. Deprived of having a separate territory [of their own], some live in Qandahar; some amongst the Nūrzā'ī, and a small number in fortress homes (*qilāʿ*) west of Ghaznīn and connected to the Qiyāq and Gulbūrī Valleys belonging to the Bayāt tribe. The Khūkyānī clan inhabits two separate places around Qandahar called Greater Khūkyānī and Lesser Khūkyānī. Their people living in Ghaznīn are known as Mākūwān. Some Durrānīs call them "godson" (*pisar-khwāndah*) of their [own] ancestors and so do not count them as sharing their lineage. Because of their small numbers, among the rest of the Afghans they hold a subordinate status.

Aspīn Tarīn

This clan is made up of 4,000 households and inhabits the three valleys of (1) Zhūr, (2) Tal, and (3)[13] Chityālī, adjacent to Kākar territory. Despite the line separating them from the Tūr Tarīn, these three pieces of land are similar to the lands of the Tūr Tarīn. All three valleys are connected and the farmland of Tal and Chityālī is equal to the land of Sīwī in terms of development and productivity. Despite the fact that Sīwī is known as "the

[13] The numbering is Fayż Muḥammad's.

inferno of the world," its climate is better [than people think] and /62/ good-quality indigo is produced there in commercial quantities.

Tūr Tarīn

This tribe comprises 7,500 households and lives in Fūshanj District between Quetta and the Chaman mountain range. Fūshanj is flat and lies south of the territory of the Durrānī people and in the colonial hands of the English. It falls within the Kūzhak Mountains. On the west side it is bordered by Shūrābak district, homeland of the Barīch people, and on the south is bordered by Quetta. The Kūh-i Takah Tū [also] borders it and is located between it and Kākar territory. [Its territory] is eighty miles long and forty miles wide. Over and above the Tūr Tarīn, 5,000 households of sayyids and clients (*hamsāyahs*)[14] of the Kākar people amount to 12,500 households in all in that homeland. There are wealthy merchants among the sayyids living there. The ordinary people of the Tūr Tarīn earn their living as farmers driving plows drawn by cattle and camels.

Shayrānī

This branch consists of approximately 20,000 households. They make their center and place of residence between Wazīrī territory, the Gūmal Valley, Zhūb district, the Kākar homeland, and the lower skirts of the Sulaymān mountain range. There are also people from this group living in other places which will be listed below. In the mountains where they live there are various types of trees suitable for construction use and for their fruits, such as pomegranate, piñon pine, walnut, and olive and all in commercial quantities. /63/ As a result, the majority of Shayrānīs transport long pole lumber and milled planks to Kulāchī and Dīrah Ismā'īl Khān to sell. Winter and summer, in Dāman and Afghanistan, nomadic Afghans would travel back and forth through the territories of this clan group. They themselves are subjects of the English.

[14] Akbar S. Ahmed, *Pukhtun Economy and Society: Traditional structure and economic development in a tribal society*, London: Routledge & Kegan Paul, 1980 (Reprint 2011), p. 366 defines *hamsāyah* among Afghan tribes as "literally 'one who shares shade'. It is used for client or low status groups" and he gives examples on pp. 64, 133, 140, and 173. *Hamsāyagī* is the abstract noun "clientage."

The Bābar Clan of the Shayrānī Branch

This clan numbers 5,750 households. It resides south of the homeland of
9 the Miyān Khayl. The western section of the territory | they inhabit is very rugged mountainous terrain. A road called Ghawāy Lārī[15] (Gūmal Road) leads towards Afghanistan. This entire tribe, except for the Usturānī branch, resides in Dāmān and the district of Chawdwān on land under English colonial rule. They are traders and a number of them reside in Qandahar. A few households live in Sūznāy, one of the environs of Qandahar adjacent to Arghandāb; in the suburbs of Kabul; in Lahūgard; in Surkh Rūd of Jalālābād; and in the Kunar Valley. These miscellaneous groups in total do not number more than 800 households. Generally speaking, they are more righteous than other Afghans.

Harīpāl Clan of the Shayrānī Branch

This small clan lives in the southern mountains of the Gūmal Valley opposite Wānah District. In terms of their customs and ways, they correspond with other Shayrānīs and in terms of moral behavior they do no harm. /**64**/ They occupy themselves with farming.

Jalwānī Clan of the Shayrānī Branch

This clan is small and lives in places in the mountain areas where the rest of the Shayrānis live as well as in a few places in Hindūstān. Due to their low numbers they are not counted among the major Afghan tribes.

Barīch

This clan comprises 3,750 households. It inhabits Shūrābak district which is bordered to the north by the territory of the Durrānī people, to the south by a mountain range under the control of the Brāhūy-i Balūch people, to the east by Kūh-i Khwājah ʿImrān, and to the west by sand desert. Its area is about seven miles square. The southwest portion of it is under the control of the Balūch. The Lūrah River which flows from north to south towards the Fūshanj plain irrigates this district.[iii] The clan group is made up of four subsections (*dastah*). Each subsection has its own individual chief (*sar kardah*). Because of a shortage of horses, they're used to riding

[15] Fayż Muḥammad (marginal note): "In Afghānī| (Pashto) *ghawāy* is cow (*gāw*) and *lār* is road (*rāh*). They call a person *mal* who is heading for a destination (*jānibdār*). So Gūmal (Gawmal) supposedly is used for heading towards a cow."

camels. Some of them [the Barīch] live in the district of Rūdbār-i Palālak located beside the Hīrmand River adjacent to Sīstān. A few households live in Qalʿah-i Bust in Chakhānsūr. The ruins of Qalʿah-i Bust, which was the winter headquarters of Sulṭān[iv] Maḥmūd-i Sabuktagīn [d. 1030 C.E.] are situated on the east bank of the Hīrmand River. When it rains, pieces of Kufic inscription and ruby and turquoise gems may be found [there].

Ūrmur(ī)

The provenance and homeland of this clan is an area in the Kūh-i Sulaymān which is /65/ now in the possession of the Masʿūd-i Wazīrī people. The
10 town | of Kānī Gūram, built by the Ūrmurī clan in the Badr District, is now inhabited by Masʿūds. Presently, it is the longstanding home of five tribes of the Ūrmurī clan—(1) Khīkanī with seventy-five households, (2) Khurram Jānī with fifty households, (3) Mullā Tātī with seventy-five households, (4) Bīkanī with 250 households, and (5) Jarānī with twenty-five[v] households, in all 475 households. The rest [of the Ūrmurī] have abandoned their homeland and emigrated, forcibly driven out by the Wazīrīs. Dispersed and separated, some have settled in Barakī Barak in Lahūgard, a few in Peshawar, and a number in Hindūstān. Wherever they happen to be, that is where the number of their households and individual souls is recorded in the census. Through agriculture they earn what they need to live on. They survive in a very abject state. Those of the tribe who live in Kānī Gūram spend their lives persecuted by the Wazīrī. Those who reside in Kānī Gūram and Lahūgard speak a strange mixture of Afghānī, Hindī, Persian, Panjābī, and Kashmīrī amongst themselves.[16] If some time should pass, it is possible that on the pattern of other Afghans who relate their language by its symbols and ciphers to the secret language of King Solomon—peace be upon him—as was mentioned above, these people too would claim relationship to (his) prophethood. Even more astonishing, they say their dialect derives from the code of King Solomon—peace be upon him—and they trace their own lineage to the coming of Islam. They have written made-up books /66/ about their unknown lineage. They are a people of unknown genealogy and of concocted heritage.

[16] According to Yazdānī, "The Ūrmurī dialect current among the Ūrmur tribes living in Lūgar (Logar, i.e. Lahūgard) is so distinct from Pashto that it is actually considered an independent language." (Fayż Muḥammad, *Nizhādnāmah*, p. 65, note.) Louis Dupree, *Afghanistan*, Princeton: Princeton University Press, 1980, p. 72 places speakers of an "Ormuri" dialect in Nuristan.

Miyānah Clan of the Sarban Lineage

This clan group has from ten to fifteen or twenty [thousand] households with homes scattered all over. The Tūgh tribe of this ethnic group dwells in the environs of the homeland of the Bangash people who are Shiʿi and inhabit the Kūhāt district, which is in the grasp of the English. The rest are around Qandahar. The *kihtarān* (junior) tribe of this clan group lives in the district of Girang. Shaykh Chishtī, whose resting place is a shrine for both high- and low-born alike and is located in the large village of Tūsah, a dependency of Dīrah Ghāzī Khān, was one of these people. In addition they say that the ethnic group of Gharshīn is related to the offspring of Miyānah. Gharshīn was a righteous man. Through his prayers, a barren mountain became verdant, they say. Since in Afghānī they say *ghar* for mountain and *shīn* for green, he and his offspring became known as Gharshīn. Most of them [the Gharshīn] have established themselves in the mountain region of Qandahar as managers of a shrine. A few households [of the Gharshīn] live in the village of Gharshīn situated in Burhān district, one of the dependent districts of Rawalpindi.

The Second [Group of] Sarbanī Afghans

The clan groups that have been recorded to this point and conclude with the Miyānah clan are from the lineage of Sharkhbūn, named Sharaf al-Dīn, [the first] son of Sarban. From this point onwards, the discussion will deal with the Sarbanī Afghan clans who were the offspring of
11 Kharshbūn, given the name Khayr al-Din, the second son of Sarban. | Fifteen clans are descended from Kharshbūn and from each clan group there are several thousand households. /67/

Kamālzāʾī

This clan group is divided into two sections: Mashrān ('big') zāʾī and Kashrān ('small') zāʾī. They reside in the locale of Ṭūrū wa Hūtī Mardān, a dependent district of Peshawar. Since the census of households and individual persons was not available [these figures] have therefore not been recorded. Initially, the lands and farms of each of those sections were equivalent. Now, the number of the people of the smaller zāʾī (i.e. Kashrānzāʾī) has increased and it also owns and occupies more than half the farms and irrigation works.

Amāzā'ī

This clan lives on the banks of the Sadhūm River, one of the dependencies of Peshawar. There are [also] nearly 2,000 households of them residing in the locale of Charūray wa Nukray, one of the districts of Mahāban belonging to Kūhāt. They work as farmers and cultivators and are subject to the English.

Utmānzā'ī

This clan is in the eastern part of the territory of the Yūsufzā'ī people along the edge of the Abāsīn River; on the southern slopes of Kūh-i Mahāban; and in the locales of Tūpī, Mīnī, and Kūtah in Gurmārī district; Kahbal on the western bank of the Abāsīn River; and Tūr Bīlah. Some [of the Utmānzā'ī] dwell in the district of Gundgahar and Harū. A number inhabit Kalābat in the Hazārah District,[17] under the jurisdiction of Rawalpindi. They are numerous in the census [but] are recorded with the people of /68/ each district and place where they live and are not counted separately.

Kanāzā'ī

This clan inhabits those places where the Utmānzā'ī live. In the census of households and individuals they are combined. In a similar way, the 'Alīzā'ī clan is numerous but mixed with the Utmānzā'ī and counted together with them.

Sadūzā'ī and *'Umar Khayl*

These two groups include the Zalūzā'ī clan and the Darizā'ī clan and (they reside) in the locales of Zuhdah, Hind, Ṣawābī, and Manīrī. These last two places are where high-quality snuff in commercial quantities is produced. They are sedentary and their homeland is in Tahand, Kār-i Manārah, Kalābat, Panjtār, and Chagla'ī. The census of their households and individual persons along with the rest of those resident in the aforementioned places has been recorded together with other ethnic groups who reside in

[17] According to Yazdānī, Hazārah District is a vast region stretching north of Lahore as far as Chitral. It is where the Chach Hazārah tribe live. They share the same origin as the Hazārahs of Afghanistan but the Chach Hazārahs speak Urdu and Pashto. They are [also] Sunnis and intermarry with the Pashtūns and other neighboring tribes. (Fayż Muḥammad *Nizhādnāmah*, p. 67, note.).

the aforementioned places. They are all subject to the English government and are not a part of the Afghan nation.

Razar or *Rasar*[18]

12 | This tribe includes the clans of Khiżrzā'ī and Maḥmūdzā'ī and all three groups, together with the Utmānzā'ī, Kanāzā'ī, and the Sadūzā'ī, form a four-part entity known as the Mandir or Mandhan people. They live in Sadhūm on the banks of the river, in Yūsufzā'ī district, Chamlah district, Kūh-i Mashriq of Sadhūm, the northern part of Mahāban,[vi] Panjtār, Chagla'i, and [among] the eastern part of the Yūsufzā'ī people. The census of persons and number of households **/69/** of those mentioned above is calculated in the total of the Mandir people. They are subjects of the environs and dependencies of Peshawar. They do not identify with, aid, or lend support to Afghanism (*Afghānīyat*) but are obedient to the English.

Yūsufzā'ī

This tribe includes the Akūzā'ī and Rānīzā'ī clans. All three live together in the long mountain range of the Hindū Kush north of Peshawar in which Swāt and Bunīr are the large populated districts. They also make a homeland in Panjkūrah. Together with all the descendants of Mandir they number 1,250,000 households and are subjects of the English.

Kakyānī

This tribal group numbers 6,250 households. The majority lives in the locale of Dūābah which is situated between the Kabul River and the Swāt River. It is a dependency of Peshawar and subject to the English. They are outside Afghan social structures.

Tarkalānī

This clan is quadripartite and numbers 15,000 households. It resides in Chār Ming, Barāwul, Nāwagī, Jandūl, and Miyākulī of the Bājāwur district. After the delimitation of the border separating the English and Afghanistan by the treaty with ʿAbd al-Raḥmān Khān,[19] the district of Bājāwur

[18] Fayż Muḥammad: '*Razhar*' with the letter *ḥa'* with three dots over it is the Afghānī (Pashto) *s̱ā'* and is pronounced '*ras̱ar*'.

[19] This is the agreement negotiated by the Indian foreign secretary, Mortimer Durand, with the Afghan amir in November 1893.

was annexed to the colonized territory of the English. It is a flat place twenty-five miles long and twelve miles wide and its area is three hundred (square) miles. Wheat is planted and the yield is good. Besides /70/ the Tarkalānī clan living there, north of [Bājāwur] the Siyāh Pūsh Kāfirs newly converted to Islam (*jadīd al-Islām*), live in the depths of the mountains. (Also) 5,000 of the Ṣāfī people, 37,500 Tājīks, and 5,000 Shinwār, in all 47,500 people, are well-established on both sides of the Bājāwur River. They are English subjects and spend their days engaged in inter-tribal fighting.

Ṣāfī

This tribe is in six segments: (1) Qandahārī, (2) Maswūd, (3) Gurbuz, (4) Dahīr, (5) Kākīzā'ī, and (6) Khawīzā'ī. They number 15,000 households. They consider themselves Sarbanī Afghans. Some people deem them to be the brother or the offspring of Ghilzā'ī and others (consider them) affili-
13 ates (*ilhāqī*) [of Ghilzā'ī]. | They live in Sūr Kamar of Bājāwur between the homeland of the Tarkalānī clan, the Muhmand, and the Utmān Khayl; in Lamqān and Tagāb located northeast of Kabul; and in Kunar, Jalālābād. One or two households live in the villages of Swāt. During the revolution of Son of the Water Carrier (Pisar-i Saqqā), at the instigation of Pīr Muḥammad Khān and Ghulām Muḥammad Khān, the son and grandson respectively of Mu'āẕ Allāh Khān Ṣāfī, these people came out against [Son of the Water Carrier] and refused to tender their obedience, instead supporting Prince 'Ināyat Allāh Khān, whose mother was from the family of Mu'āẕ Allāh Khān, the chief of the Ṣāfī tribe of Tagāb. In the hopes of having the backing of the people of Jalālābād, who sent them a message offering assistance and telling them of their [imminent] arrival with reinforcements, [the Ṣāfīs] fought two or three engagements with an army of Son of the Water Carrier but when the Jalālābādīs did not come to help them they were both times routed. In the end, they were overwhelmed and wiped out. 'Abd al-Ghafūr, the son of Muḥammad Shāh, from the family of Mu'āẕ Allāh, who /71/ ('Abd al-Ghafūr) had chosen to cast off his paternal uncle, Ghulām Muḥammad's, supervision and taken up the cause of Son of the Water Carrier in opposition to Amān Allāh Khān, eventually turned his back on the revolutionaries because of the evil deeds of the Saqqāwīs. At night in secret, he was killed by the Saqqāwīs, put in a coffin, and surreptitiously buried. He thus earned the reward of his treachery to the government whose favor and benevolence he had enjoyed for years.

Ghūryā Khayl

This clan group is made up of seven tribes: (1) Muhmand, (2) Dāʾūdzāʾī, (3) Khalīl, (4) Chamkanī, (5) Zīrānī,[vii] (6) Kūkū, and (7) Mūsāzāʾī. It resides in the mountains, valleys, hills, and dales of Peshawar and Bājāwur and in the midst of the region between Peshawar and the Jalālābād border. God willing, each one of these will be recorded in turn along with its household census.

Muhmand

This tribe is divided into two parts, the Bar (Upper) Muhmand and the Kūz (Lower) Muhmand. The Kūz Muhmand reside in Maydān-i Pīshāwar, numbers 15,000 households, is subject to the English, and, in terms of its customs and traditions, completely differs from the Bar Muhmand. The Bar Muhmand are established in the valleys of the mountain range west of the range which is the homeland of the Utmān Khayl as far as the Kabul River, in the Khaybar Valley, along the Kāshghar River which is [made up of] the Kunar, Kāmah, and Gushtah Rivers, and in the locale of Pandyālī. They comprise 12,500 households and can muster 37,500 armed men. They are known as the "free Afghans of the frontier" for whom ʿAbd al-Raḥmān Khān made it a condition of his agreeing to the delimitation of the border and the demarcation of the frontier with the English that the peoples and tribes living in the mountains of the frontier be free /72/ and it was agreed that the governments of Afghanistan and the English would not interfere with them. The chief of this tribe [the Bar Muhmand], Saʿādat Khān, lives
14 in Laʿlpūrah. The majority of its people | are farmers. Some engage in highway banditry and some sell reeds, fans made of reed, and slippers made of grass which are called *mazar*. From these things, they earn enough for the basic necessities of life. They do not obey the English and are constantly engaged in skirmishes and raids against that government. Two of their clans specialize in herding. In the spring and summer they pasture their animals in the Hazārahjāt and in winter they return to their homeland where they earn a living by hiring out animals for transport. Currently, Muḥammad Nādir Khān, due to a lack of funds and seeing himself incapable of preparing the means and tools of governance, has ignored the [treaty] stipulation about the liberty of the frontier tribes, and has surrendered that region to the interference and control of the English. He has received 16,000,000 rupees cash from that government as well 7,000 rifles and an adequate quantity of ammunition. On this subject, both he and

the English government have misread the situation and by not providing internal security and also because of the ferment of rebellious tribes, they have made Afghanistan a battlefield for war between the Russians and the English. The hope is that in the event of war, Iran will get to keep what rightfully belongs to it.

Dāʾudzāʾī

This clan (of the Ghūryā Khayl) numbers 12,500 households and 15,000 fighting men. It resides (mostly) in Maydān-i Pīshāwar, but a few households live in Qandahar while some live with the Muhmand in Bardarānī under the chieftainship of a family of the Shinwārī people. /73/ A few live in Kūh Dāman, Kabul and Chārīkār where they live as farmers and traders. During the uprising of Son of the Water Carrier they were instigators of evildoing [by supporting the uprising] and so they were attacked and plundered by the warriors of the Wazīrī and Jājī (Zāzī) people and were seized in the talons of hate. Some households then took refuge in Tīrāh.

Khalīl

This clan (of the Ghūryā Khayl) numbers 7,500 households and 15,000 brave fighting men. For the most part, it has its lair and dwelling place in Maydān-i Pīshāwar. A few households along with some Muhmand have lived and still live honorably in Qandahar City.

Chamkanī

This clan has 12,500 people and resides in Kūh-i Safīd north of Kurram District and also has a large estate in Peshawar. The lands they own are rain-watered and produce wheat, barley, and maize. Honey and yellow oil are [also] produced in quantity, which they transport to Kurram and Kūhāt to sell. They harbor a deep antagonism towards the Mangal people.

Zīrānī

This clan is quite small and it is mixed with and dispersed among Tājiks
15 in and around Jalālābād. They are not included in the count of Afghans. |

Mullā Gūrī

This clan,[20] numbering 750 households, is established in the locale of Tātarah and is all mixed in with the Muhmands. The Mullā Gūrī make their living by theft and farming and pass days of wickedness and nights of ignorance practicing evil and so go astray by day and by night. /74/

Zamand or *Jamand*

This clan group traces its lineage to Zamand, the second son of Kharshbūn, son of Sarban. It is made up of five subdivisions: (1) Khwīshagī, (2) Katānī, (3) Bangīzā'ī, (4) Muḥammad(zā'ī) or Mamanzā'ī, and (5) Tūkhī. They live in a variety of locales like Multān, Hind, Ghūrband-i Kabul, Zamīn Dāwar, Qandahar, and the town of Quṣūr east of Lahore. The Bargalī, one of [the Zamand's] subdivisions, is on the west side of Lahore and the Lurgalī, a branch of another of their subdivisions (resides) east of Quṣūr, in Qaṣabah-i Jūrjā, Qaṣabah-i Tāndah, the Fūshanj district, Qandahar, and in a variety of other places. They have a large estate in Hashtnagar, Peshawar. Several households reside north of the Kabul River adjacent to the Muhmand people residing in the mountains and in the Khaybar Valley. The Muḥammadzā'ī [or Mamanzā'ī] subdivision resides in Chār Ṣadah, Tangī, Nawshahrah, and Parāng, all villages of Hashtnagar. The number of their households and individuals is recorded in the count for each of the places where they reside.

Kānsī

Of this clan are the seven Shinwārī tribes: (1) Shaykh Mal Khayl, (2) Khūgā Khayl, (3) Mīrdād Khayl, (4) Pīrū Khayl, (5) Sangū Khayl, (6) Sarakī Khayl, and (7) Salmān Khayl. Along with the (other) Shinwārīs, they inhabit Bājāwur, the Shīgal Valley, and Kunar and number 12,500 households. Besides the residents of those places, the rest (of the Kānsī) live in Kūh-i Safīd south of Jalālābād, and in the environs of the Khaybar along with Afrīdī and Arūkzā'ī clans. Consequently, they are also called Khaybaris. They are extremely wicked and are without equal for their thievery, killing, and pillaging. From this particular /75/ clan (the Kānsī) other than these seven khayls of Shinwār evildoers there is no other (Kānsī) person in Afghanistan.

[20] It would appear that Fayż Muḥammad has ended his description of the "seven" subdivisions of the Ghūryā Khayl omitting the Kūkū and Mūsāzā'ī (see *supra*).

In [the late] solar year 1307/1928, at the instigation and provocation of the Englishman [T. E.] Lawrence, in disguise and with a fake identity, he infiltrated [the Khaybaris] and urged them to fulfill the religious 'commands and prohibitions,' and so the first flames of insurrection were ignited. The city of Jalālābād was set ablaze and lofty government buildings were burned down. [These buildings were] patterned after European buildings by which the government provided a symbol both of what was indigenous and what was foreign and gave a glimpse of the great progress of the government, the beauty of the kingdom, and the civilization of the country. [The Khaybarīs also] plundered and destroyed the belongings and furnishings of the people of the city and the government's equip-
16 ment and arsenal. | At the very height of the conflagration, the fighting, and destruction by this rapacious group, people from Kūh Dāman and Kūhistān north of Kabul [rose up] urged on by Ambassador [Sir Francis] Humphrys and Shaykh Maḥbūb ʿAlī, a member of the British Legation who once or twice a week would pass through Istālif, Farzah, Shakar Darrah, Qalʿah-i Murād Beg, Sarāy Khwājah, Chārīkār, and other places, on the pretext of traveling for rest and recreation, and arouse and incite local leaders to rebel.

In addition, treacherous ministers and treasonous and disloyal officials took the path of opposition to Amān Allāh Khān. Secretly, (these traitors) set the nation against him and continued to do so. They confounded (true) religion with the catalyst of their own reprehensible ambitions. They proclaimed the chief fomenter of the conflict, Son of the Water Carrier, to be the emir, drove Amān Allāh Khān from the country, and cast government, kingdom, and nation to the wind. The recently independent government [of Amān Allāh Khān], which existed in (the view) of other regions and in the sight of the [Afghan] public, /76/ was so disrupted that even if the deep yet quickly changeable politics of its eastern [English] and northern [Russian] neighbors were to give up their own particular ambitions and let Afghanistan return to its (former) condition, even if fifty years pass it will not achieve the state it once was in. Now that those two neighbors are not remaining quiet they will not [let Afghanistan] rest for a moment in order to gain what they want.

In short, 700 Kānsī households have residences in the southwest corner of Quetta, Balūchistān in a large fort as big as a village (*qaṣabah*), adjacent to the city. In light of this close connection, the residential quarters near where the fort touches the city are known as Kānsī Rūd. Also, some households live lives scattered in the Indian Deccan.

CHAPTER TWO

Tribes of the Ghurghushtī People

This people, one of the seven original Afghan (peoples), constitutes seven clans: (1) Dānī, (2) Bābī, (3) Mandū, (4) Kākar, (5) Nāghar, (6) Panī, and (7) Dāwī. In what follows they will be mentioned, recorded, and briefly sketched with their homelands and a census of their households and their individual members. Dānī, son of Ghurghusht, son of Qays ʿAbd al-Rashīd, is the first (ultimate) progenitor of four ethnic groups: (1) Kākar, (2) Nāghar, (3) Panī and (4) Dāwī. [Ghurghusht's] two other sons, (1) Bābī and (2) Mandū formed a separate people; and the offspring of each one of them is known by its own name, as will be recorded.

Kākar

This tribal group, according to some, [numbers] one *milyān*, one *kurūr* (crore),[21] and three hundred thousand [people, i.e. 1,800,000] [while according to others] one crore, four hundred thousand (i.e. 900,000). The most correct is 750,000 equivalent to one crore and 200,000 (*sic*—250,000) people. They inhabit an extensive mountain area some one hundred miles
17 square lying between the territory of the Ghilzāʾī people, Balūchistān, | and the Durrānī homeland, Afghans of the Sarbanī people. Part of their territory coincides with Kūh-i Sulaymān. To the north, they dwell as far as the southern border of the Ghilzāʾī; on the northwest as far as the district of Arghastān of the Durrānī people, a dependency of Qandahar. On the south they live adjacent to Balūchistān and on the east to a spur of the Kūh-i Sulaymān bordered by an annexed part of the area colonized by the English. The larger locales inhabited by this ethnic group are the Barshūr (Barshwar) Valley and Hunnah situated northeast of Quetta, Balūchistān. The water of the Mahnā-yi Ghawārāy /80/ flows past several newly constructed grist mills. The water is then piped to the city, the bazaar, and to homes. [The places which receive this water are] Kanjūghī and Būrī and smaller locales like are Targharī, Sanītah, Zhūr, Kūsah, Ṣaḥrā, Kūtah, and Tūdah.

---

21 In most South Asian contexts one crore is ten million. Here clearly the *kurūr* (crore) is five hundred thousand.

Nāghar

This clan is small and in the census of households and individuals is combined with the Kākar and counted with them. It has no separate homeland.

Panī

This clan numbers nearly 100,000 persons and has its homeland in Sīwī, a territory colonized by the English and attached to the Kākar clan. Most of the Panī have flocks and pasture them in the district[s] of Chakhan and Kandar. They also come to Afghanistan and go to the Hazārahjāt for summer grazing and then return home in the autumn. A number of them have taken possession of the districts of Gazag and Arghandāb in Hazārah Jāghūrī by [Afghan] government decree.

Dāwī

This clan is also known by the name Khūndī. It is small and affiliated with the Kākar tribe and is censused along with them. In the *Makhzan* and other history books and genealogies of the Afghans, it is written with regard to the clan name "Khūndī" that [an individual named] Dāwī had gone to Khujand to trade and brought along a beautiful girl, no longer a virgin, as well as her young son named Sayyid Ḥasan. He made her his consort for sex and sent Sayyid Ḥasan out to thieve and prostitute himself but ultimately he repented, asked the girl to marry him, /81/ and produced four sons. Their offspring were known as "Khujandī" and little by little because of Afghānī pronunciation it changed into "Khūndī." ʿAbd al-Hādī, the son of ʿAbd al-Wāḥid, one of the fakirs of this clan, reached the rank of minister in the era of Amān Allāh Khān.[22]

Bābī, Second Son of Ghurghūsht[23]

This clan of 3,700 individuals travels on business to Qandahar and Qalāt-i Nāṣir, Balūchistān. They are well-off.

---

[22] ʿAbd al-Hādī Dāwī, whose pen name was Parīshān, was born in 1895 and attended the Ḥabībīyah School or Lycée. He worked as a journalist, editor, translator (from Ottoman Turkish to Persian), diplomat, minister (of commerce), secretary (to the king), and poet. He became president of the Afghan Senate (Meshrano Jirgah) in 1970. He died in Kabul in 1982 and a high school in Kabul was named after him. See Adamec, *Who's Who*, p. 287; May Schinasi, *Afghanistan at the Beginning of the Twentieth Century: Nationalism and journalism in Afghanistan: A Study of* Serāj ul-akhbār *(1911–1918)*, Naples: Istituto Universitario Orientale, 1979, pp. 66, 79, and 98; and Wikipedia, "Abdul Hadi Dawi."

[23] Fayż Muḥammad changes the spelling here from Ghurghusht to Ghurghūsht.

[17]

Mandū Khayl, Descendants of the Third Son of Ghurghūsht

This clan resides on both sides of the valley of Zhūb District, which extends from the beginning of the Hindū Bāgh mountain range and the northeastern part of the mountain range to a point touching Sar Maghah in Gūmal. [The Mandū Khayl] is a very large group of people and is subject to the English. This district, whose agriculture benefits from the small river of Zhūb, is bounded on the north by the southern limits of Kūh-i Siyūnādāgh and on the south the mountain range and valley of Gūmal which is situated between Zhūb, Būrī District, and Kūh-i Sulaymān. In the southeast corner of this defined region are the farms of the Harīpāl and Bābar clans of the Shayrānī Sarbanī. The entire area is annexed to the territory colonized by the English. The Mandū Khayl clan does not cause much trouble, is engaged in agriculture, and is counted in the census with the Kākar. In comparison with other Afghans they are credulous people, easy-going, patient, and straight-talking.

Tāymanī[24]

This ethnic group is quite small and is considered one of the four clans of the Ūymāq [the Chahār Ūymāq]. They speak Persian but are fanatical Sunnis and their homeland is in the environs of Siyāh Band in Ghār, a part of Harāt. They are divided into two sub-groups, the Qipchāq and the Darzā'ī. They consider themselves Afghans of Kākar lineage. They earn their living through agriculture and maintain ties of friendship with the Hazārahs.

Gadūn

This tribe is divided in two sections: 1) Salār and 2) Manṣūr. They reside to the west of the Abāsīn River, in the southern part of Kūh-i Mahāban, in the villages of Gundāb, Bābanī, and in the hamlets of /83/ Pādah, Shanī, Kūlāgar, Pūlā Achpulī, Bīsak, and Malikā Gadāy, territories under the

---

24 Ḥājj Kāẓim Yazdānī's note is interesting and worth quoting. "The Tāymanīs have no lineal connections to the Pashtūns. Instead, they are of Turkish origin and of the same race (*tabār*) as the Hazārahs. The word Tāymanī is formed of *tāy* and *manī*, the first part of which is the same as *dāy* which is attached to the names of some Hazārah peoples. The word *dāy* is found in three distinctive forms: *dāy*, *tāy*, and *zāy* in the form Dāy Zangi, Dāy Kundī, Dāy Mīrdād, etc.; in the form *tāy* in Tāymanī, Tāy Bughā, and Tāy Tīmūr; and as *zāy* in the names Zāy Badal, Zāy ʿAṭā, Zāy Wulāt, Zāy Naṣīr, Zāy Lughānī, etc., all of which are names of Hazārah tribes. In my research, I found nearly 30 tribal names which begin with the prefix *zāy*." (Fayż Muḥammad, *Nizhādnāmah*, p. 82, note.).

colonial administration of the English. They engage in herding and agriculture. The sell yellow oil (ghee) and lumber for construction, which is plentiful in the mountains adjacent to them. They buy whatever cloth is necessary for clothing as well as salt for consumption. They count 15,000 men at arms.

[There are] Ghūrghushtī [*sic*] Afghans, besides those that have been recorded above, [living] in the Hazārah district of Chahchah, one of the dependencies of Rawalpindi, and a Kākar clan group. This clan numbers 3,750 individuals in the small town of Kūhānah, a dependency of Ruhtak, Hindūstān; and 1,250 living in the Deccan. They are intimates with Indians and except for the fact that they think of themselves as Pathans, they do not know their original homeland. Besides these people, there is not a place in Hindūstān that doesn't have some Afghans and they are more civilized than the Afghans of Afghanistan.

[19]

CHAPTER THREE

Bītanī Afghans

This clan group, one of the seven original Afghan [peoples] is comprised
of two sub-groups: 1) Warsabūn and 2) Kajīn. They reside in the frontier
area north of Kūh-i Kapar, south of the Sarāghar Valley which goes as
far as Tāk Valley, east of Kūh-i Masʿūd-i Wazīrī, and west of the Marwat
19 people. | There are 3,750 of them that are armed and the rest are with-
out weapons. Among the Bītanī Afghans, the Kūtī, Awlād-i Tattā, Dannā,
Kattā, and Ratanzā'ī are affiliated and are not Afghans. In terms of language, customs, traditions, ethics, and habits they are called Afghans and
among ordinary people they are called Pashtū[n].

/91/ CHAPTER FOUR

Mītī Afghans

This people comprises the following tribes: Lūdī, Sarwānī, Hūtak, Tūkhī, Sulaymān Khayl, ʿAlī Khayl, Ākā Khayl, Mūsā [Khayl], Tarakī, and Andar. They occupy the lands south of the Hindū Kush and north of the Safīd Kūh range. Because of the varied locales in which they reside—uplands, lowlands, hills, and dales—the temperature is very different in different places. From the north looking south and west [this region is] approximately 180 miles long and from west to east it is 50 miles wide and forms a long irregular rectangle. Originally they were from the line of Shāh Ḥusayn Ghūrī, one of the offspring of Żaḥḥāk-i Tāzī. They are called Ghilzāʾī because during the caliphate of Walīd, the son of ʿAbd al-Malik (r. 705–715 A.D.) Ḥajjāj, the son of Yūsuf-i Ṣaqafī, was ordered to conquer Ghūr, did so, and because of the Arab conquest the peoples of Ghūr were dispersed and scattered. One of them, the prince Shāh Ḥusayn Ghūrī, in exile took refuge with Shaykh Bīt, the original bequeather (*mūriṡ-i aʿlā*) of the Afghan Bītanī people, fell in love with the shaykh's daughter Matū, had sexual intercourse with her until, after repeated sex, Matū became pregnant and her father then contracted her in marriage to Shāh Ḥusayn. When she gave birth her son became known as Ghilzāʾī. They called him that from the Afghānī word '*ghil*' meaning thief and '*zāʾī*' from the word *zāʾīdah* (born). Thus he became known as Ghilzāʾī, "born to a thief." /92/ Although his offspring were not Afghans, in the mouths of ordinary folk they became known as Afghans.

Lūdī

This people is comprised of three [major] clans: Siyānī, Niyāzī, and Daftānī and includes the tribes of Sūr, Lūḥānī, Marwat, Parangī, Dawlat Khayl, Maʾī Khayl, Bakhtiyār, Tatūr, Hūd, Tīj, Khaysūr, and Balch all of whom will be recorded below.

Sūr

Shayr Shāh [Sūrī] was from this group in India and attained the position of shah. Of his sons, Salīm Shāh and Muḥammad Shāh known as 'the Just' (*ʿadlī*) also came to power. Their rule collapsed, their family and tribe

broke up, and their power came to an end.[25] Consequently in Hindūstān, Dāmān, and Afghanistan they all went their separate ways. Thirty-eight
20 households still exist in Chahchah district, a dependency of Rawalpindi. | The rest are in Afghanistan and nearly extinct. As a result, none of them remembers or recalls their [own] name.

Lūḥānī

This clan has more than 4,000 households. All are nomadic traders. They go to Dāmān in winter, come to Afghanistan in the summer, and camp at Shāh Jūy, Muqur, Jahān Murād, Qarābāgh[viii], and Shalgīr, [all] of Ghaznīn. They sell their goods in Kabul, Qandahar, and Ghaznīn and to the ordinary people from those areas as well as /93/ to the people of Harāt, Balkh, Mazār, Maymanah, Bukhārā, and Mashhad. They have either bought or leased most of the forts and farms located near their camping sites. They pay a little or a lot in the form of customs duty on their trade goods to the government. But they also engage in smuggling and bring most of their goods to market that way. They never give any thought to their social responsibility to aid and assist the Afghan nation in time of need.

Marwat

This clan includes four tribes: Mūsā Khayl, Patī, Nūnā Khayl, and Salār. They in turn include the clan groups of Sandar, Bahrām, Khadū Khayl, and others, 17,500 households in all. They reside in Banūn, Dāmān, on both the north and south sides of the Kurram River, and [make up] all of Tal, one of the dependencies of Dīrah Ismāʿīl Khān. The locales of their homeland are divided in three parts: in the western part the clans of Bītī, Mūsā Khayl, and Nūnā Khayl; in the middle part Bahrām; and in the eastern section, Darī Palārah. They are subject to English colonial rule.

Parangī

There is no one in Afghanistan bearing the name of this clan but in Hindūstān there is a smattering by the name Lūdī. The cities of Rūpar and Ludyānah (Ludhiana) were founded by this clan. A few households live in the Deccan and are known by the name Parangī.

25 The Sūrī dynasty briefly displaced the Mughal dynasty and ruled northern India from 1540–55. Before them, the Lūdī clan from which the Sūrīs came, had held Delhi and Agra in the last half of the 15th century and was the dynasty that lost northern India to the Tīmūrids from Kabul, Ẓahīr al-Dīn Bābur in 1526.

Dawlat Khayl

This clan numbers 10,000 households and resides in Tāk district, an area in the clutches of English colonialism. A small number dwell in Kārandah and Zimmah in Kūh Dāman-i Kabul /94/ and in Kāfir Qalʿah which belongs to Maydān and there live in abject conditions.

Ma’ī Khayl

This clan of 3,750 households lives in Darāban, land seized by the English. Some are traders and have become wealthy. They are known and highly regarded from Calcutta to Bukhārā. As traders they travel back and forth to far-off lands. Nearly all of them live independently [i.e., not with other members of their clan]. A number of them are nomadic. They spend time in Darāban and Chawdwān with the people of their tribe who till
21 the land. In summer, | they come to the vicinity of Ghaznīn to trade and spend the summer [pasturing their animals]. They do not participate in any tribal, national, or clan organization. Some of the Bakhtiyār and a few households of the Daftānī[ix] and the Matī are included [in the Ma’ī Khayl]. Except when it is in their own personal interests and according to their own personal desires, no one ever takes an interest in protecting, aiding, or abetting what is in the best interest of the tribe as a whole.

Bakhtiyār

This tribal group was originally from the Bakhtiyārī people living southwest of Iṣfahān, Iran. Some think they are sayyids. A number of them live in Bukhārā. A thousand households are in Darāban mixed with the Ma’ī Khayl. Seven hundred and fifty households live in Marghah[26] and almost 500 households reside in Peshawar in a separate quarter known as Marwī-hā. Some of those living in Peshawar maintain their Iranianness and adhere to Shiʿism. They include reliable men whom the English consider respectable and who conduct themselves properly and so they assign them important tasks which they carry out with integrity. But those of their group who mix with Afghans are fanatical Sunnis and have abjured and forsworn the sect of their forefathers. /95/

---

[26] 32 See Adamec, *Historical and Political Gazetteer*, vol. 5, pp. 330–31.

Tatūr

This clan [numbers] 375 households. They have their lair west of Tāk. In terms of morals and habits they correspond to the Dawlat Khayl. Most make their living through agriculture; some extend their lives by doing various kinds of things for the English.

Hūd and *Tīj*

These clans, except for what the two names would suggest, do not have particular areas belonging to them. They [live] mixed with the Lūḥānīs and there is no distinction [between them]. People don't remember their original name; it is as if they were rendered non-existent and exterminated.

Khaysūr

This clan believes that it is of Lūdī lineage but the Lūdīs reject their [claim of] co-tribalism. According to what the rejecters say, there is no mention of their name in any genealogy of Lūdī offspring. Whatever the case, they reside on the west side of the Indus River, north of ʿĪsā Khayl District and east of Kūh-i Kūchak and below Panyālah or Palyānah. They number 375 households. They are wealthy and live an easy life owning commercial palm and date groves.

Balch

This group sometimes calls itself Niyāzī and sometimes Dawlat Khayl.
22 Although it is understood that they are of Lūdī lineage | they have no source that provides certain proof for their genealogy. They are few in number and reside in Patyālah, south of Kūh-i Ghund Shaykh Badīn, belonging to Dīrah Ismāʿīl Khān and in Pīlān in Miyān Wālī District. **/96/** They are subject to the English government.

Niyāzī

Regarding this ethnic group, the ʿĪsā Khayl, Mūshānī, and Sarhang all live under English colonial rule. Separate villages and social groups related to them do not exist in Afghanistan. Except for a few households scattered in Qandahar, Ghaznīn, Kūh-i Gar, and in the environs and village of Shīwakī in Kabul and [in] Hindūstān where they live an abject life. Among them are the Marhal, Kandī, and Matī tribes who are nomadic herders and traders. A number go to Bukhārā to trade. In the spring they spend some time in summer pasturage in the Hazārahjāt and in the winter they live in Qandahar and other places. In relation to other Afghans they don't cause much trouble, are quiescent, [even] incapable [of causing trouble] and they avoid evildoing.

Daftānī

They [number] 250 households. Some are nomads and traders and some reside in Wānah District. At government order some forcibly occupied and took possession of the Hazārah farms of Zartak. Some of those who are traders, with the backing and support of the [Afghan] government, became the owners of the principal Hazārah forts and farms of Qarābāgh[x], Ghaznīn for one-half, one-quarter, one-third, or even one-fifth of their value. The Hazārahs were driven out of their homeland and faced hardship and suffering both abroad and within the country.

ʿĪsā Khayl

A large contingent of this clan makes its home along the banks of the Indus River at a place called Tarnah. There because of the flooding of the river, since this prevented the water from flowing to their fields, they provided a way to convey it [to their fields] by means of a large [wooden] water trough, and thus gave a name to the place [Tarnah = *tarnāw*, a wooden chute or trough]. The lands /97/ and farms are divided amongst them into four [*sic*—five] parts. The Mamūn Khayl, Badīnzāʾī, Zakū Khayl, the Apū Khayl, and Bambīrah each own and possess a share. They pass their days farming and in other occupations and are subject to the English.

Mūshānī

This group [numbers] approximately 4,000 households. They live in a place called Dāwud Khayl and Tatī in Miyān Wālī District along the western bank of the Indus River. They wear the ring of slavery in their ears and the saddle cloth of obedience to the English on their backs. They are cultivators and tillers of their own farms and fields.

Sulṭān Khayl

This clan is the offspring of Sarhang and [numbers] 4,954 households. They make their homeland near the mountain which is home to the
23 [word missing] people. |

[23]

Sarhang

This tribe includes the clan of Bharat and Sunbul and [numbers] 2,943 households. It resides in Miyān Wālī District.

Hūtak

This group [numbers] 10,000 households, It resides in Marghah and on both sides of Bārī Ghar, Sūr Ghar, Girdī Jangal, Ghābūlān, Khaznāy, Sūrī, and Atā Ghar. Their homeland is four stages northeast of Qandahar and a distance of one stage southeast of Kalāt-i Tūkhī. Mīr Ways, Maḥmūd, and Ashraf were from this group. They conquered Iṣfahān and parts of southeast Iran, and did not fail to subject all males, young and old, of the Ṣafavid royal family to the edge of the blade of fanaticism /98/ and the peoples of Iran to plunder, murder, and rape. They were the cause of much destruction until Nādir Shāh Afshār slaughtered them with the sword of vengeance, took possession of Afghanistan as far as the Indus River, and banished 1,500 of the rebels and seditionists from their homeland, sending them to Turkistān, Iran, and Hindūstān. He ordered them to stay in Bukhārā, Balkh, Māzandarān, and Ardabīl and until this day they remain in those places and are content. Because they are free of anxiety [and life is easy], they don't [think about] their original homeland.

Tūkhī

This clan [numbers] 15,000 households and lives around Qalāt, and along the Tarnak River from Pul-i Sangī to Shībār District. They [also] went and took possession of locales along the Arghandāb (River) adjacent to Hazārah Dāy Chūpān which by government order was given over to usurping Afghans. [These locales were] the middle and southern part of the Nāwah Valley as well as the lower part of that valley, Khākhāk, Sarāsp, Jangīr,[xi] Shāh-i Mardān, Nāwah itself, Shībār, Baltāgh, and Mandān. Several households reside in Dih Afghan[an] in Kabul. Ghulām Qādir, whose father was a baker, is from this clan and is currently the mayor of the city.[27]

Sulaymān Khayl

This clan [numbers] 37,500 households and is divided into two sections, the northern and the southern. The southern section [includes] the Qayṣar Khayl, Samalzā'ī, Adīn Khayl, Nasū Khayl, Qalandar Khayl,

[27] See Adamec *Who's Who*, p. 151 for a short biography of Ghulām Qādir Tūkhī.

Shakī Khayl, Shāh Tūrī, Jalālzā'ī, Kalā Khayl, /99/ Maḥmūd Khayl, and Mish Khayl. Their homeland is Katawāz District, half of Zurmat District,
24 Wāzkhwāh and Nālī Ghund and they occupy adjoining places as well. | In the northern section, the Sulṭān Khayl, Aḥmadzā'ī, Jabbār Khayl, and Bābakr Khayl are established in, and are the owners of, Taytīmūr,[28] Darrah-i La'l Andar, Maydān District, Tīzīn, Jagdalak, Gandamak, Surkh Rūd of Jalālābād, Darrah-i 'Alīshang in Lamqān and [locales] in the eastern part of Lahūgard, such as Altīmūr, Aspīkah, and Surkh Āb. This clan [the Sulaymān Khayl] with its various branches together with the clan of the nomadic Mullā Khayl, who, at the order of the government, took possession of Dāyah and Fūlādah in Hazārah Ḥajaristān,[29] are the most wicked of all Ghilzā'ī clans, [indeed] of all Afghans. They constantly travel the path of robbing, murdering, and pillaging the inhabitants of the country, both Hazārah and Afghan. They are all disciples and followers of Shayr Āqā, known as "Ḥażrat-i Shūr Bāzār."[30] They keep their eyes open for any signal from him and their ears attuned to any command of his. At his clandestine sign they [immediately] plunge the affairs of the government into disorder and attack ordinary people, especially Hazārahs, who are Shi'ah.

'Alī Khayl

This clan and the Sulaymān Khayl were the offspring of two brothers and are equal to each other in terms of wicked and vicious character. They number 10,000 households. Half of them inhabit Zurmat, which in Afghānī, is pronounced "Zurmal." The rest reside in Muqur and Rasanah, which is separated by a mountain range from Hazārah Zīrak and Nīrān-i Jāghūrī, while a few households, thanks to a farman of permission from the government, took possession of some Hazārah Qalandar forts in Ūlūm Lālā. The Nabīdā Khayl and /100/ another khayl known as Kūtī number 500 households. ([These latter] live in Khūst, which is also where the governor of the Southern Province resides. They are perennial accomplices of the Sulaymān Khayl on the path of robbery.

---

[28] According to Yazdānī, "Taytīmūr was once the name of an Hazārah tribe. Altīmūr was also the name of an Hazārah tribe, which lived in Lūgar." (Fayż Muḥammad, *Nizhadnāmah*, p. 99, note.).

[29] See Fayż Muḥammad, *The History*, vol. 4, pp. 671–72.

[30] See Adamec *Who's Who*, "Fazl Umar," p. 141 for a short biography of Shir Agha (Shayr Āqā). Also see Senzil Nawid, *Religious Response to Social Change in Afghanistan: King Aman-Allah and the Afghan Ulama, 1919–29*, Costa Mesa: Mazda Publishers, 1999 index entry "Fazl Umar Mujaddidi."

Ākā Khayl[31]

This clan [comprises] 1,250 households. They are independent, without fixed abodes and an estate of their own. Some are found in Muqur and work as sack- and kilim-weavers; the rest nomadize. In the eyes of Afghans, they are contemptible because they weave sacks and kilims, an occupation Afghans consider degrading.

Andar

This group [numbers] 22,500 households. Most reside in Shalgīr in the southern part of the city of Ghaznīn; some in Jahān Murād, in Hazārah Qarābāgh; and a certain number in Zurmat. [Some] live on a large estate in Shībār, territory of the Tūkhīs; and some live in the village of Gazag in Hazārah Jāghūrī which they took by force with the help of a government order. There isn't a single place in Afghanistan where at least one or two households of this ethnic group have not settled down as neighbors [or clients of the indigenous group]. One section of them, the Mūsā Khayl, is in Wāghaz west of Shalgīr and Haft Āsyā adjacent to Kakrak District of Hazārah Jīghatū. Some live in Gīrū south of Shalgīr. In general, they are farmers and /**101**/ in winter they go to Peshawar, Bannū, Dāmān, and
25 Panjāb to find jobs as paid casual laborers. |

Tarakī

This ethnic group [comprises] 18,750 households. More than two-thirds have fixed abodes of their own and nearly one-third are nomadic herders and move to summer pastures. Because of the occupation by the ʿAlī Khayl and the Khadūzāʾī of territory originally the homeland of the Tarakī in Muqur, the lands there no longer were sufficient to support the Tarakīs' needs and one-third of them were forced into nomadism. Winters they lived in the desert and in the environs of Qandahar and summers they spent in Muqur until, during the era of Amīr ʿAbd al-Raḥmān Khān, the Hazārah people were reduced to submission and exterminated. At that time, the Tarakī were given fertile farmlands in the Hazārahjāt. Having

[31] According to Yazdānī, "The Ākā Khayl ethnic group had Hazārah roots originally and was from the Hazārah Āqā tribe which was accepted as a Pashtūn tribe once it changed its religion. It intermarried with the Pashtūns and spoke Pashto. If a researcher should go among them he would notice that there are still traces of Hazāragī culture amongst them. The fact that their profession is weaving sacks and kilims is one such trace. The name Ākā Khayl was originally Ākā Khayl." (Fayż Muḥammad, *Nizhādnāmah*, p. 100, note.).

thus gained access, they completely abandoned the arid plain of Muqur and invaded Hazārah territory by way of Tamazān. There they destroyed the Hazārahs' farms and fields and made the lands forage for their livestock. They plundered and murdered the Hazārahs and then would return to their winter quarters around Qandahar. The government, which was bent on wiping out the Hazārahs, did not hold [the Tarakīs] to account and would force the Hazārahs, whether they had the means or not, to pay the property taxes and other assessments [on the land seized by the Tarakīs]. The Hazārahs had not the wherewithal to stay **/102/** and fled for refuge to Khurāsān, to territory in the grasp of the English, and to Russia and still continue to emigrate today. As for the refugees who went to Khurāsān, hardly had they found respite there then, thinking that the Iranian people would be friendly and kind to strangers because of their sharing the same religion and so out of ignorance and obstinacy [the Hazārah refugees] began harassing [the Iranians] because of their generosity to strangers, and still do. Because of all the killings, plunderings, oppression, and tyranny carried out by Afghans and their government, they were unable to live in their original territory and homeland and so fled abroad, especially to Khurāsān and Iran, where they make themselves despised. It is as if, except for adhering to the firm creed of Shiʿism, they [the Hazārahs], have no humane feelings or natures.

Isḥāq, known as Sahhāk

This clan [comprises] 8,850 households. The Yūsuf Khayl [clan] is larger than any other clan of theirs and it resides in Kharwār District. Some live in Zurmat and the rest in Pamqān [Paghmān], Bīktūt, and Tagāb. A few are scattered in Lamqān and in other valleys south of the Hindū Kush mountains. They live by farming and other professions.

Nāṣir

This clan is known by three names: Surkh (Red) Nāṣir, Safīd (White) Nāṣir,
26 and Siyāh (Black) Nāṣir. [It numbers] 18,750 | households. They live in the villages of Kāh Darrah, Shakar Darrah, and Ḥājjī Kak [Ḥājīgak] in Kūh Dāman-i Kabul. Most are nomad herders. Some people think they are sayyids, some believe they are Balūch, and because [they speak] the Afghānī language some link them to the Afghans. In summer they go to the Hazārahjāt to pasture their animals **/103/** and make their winter quarters in Dāmān, a dependency of Dīrah Ismāʿīl Khān. Most engage in trade. Muḥammad ʿUmar Khān, the son of Ghulām Nabī Khān and known as the

"Red General," during the revolution of Son of the Water Carrier fought hard against Amān [Allāh] Khān and caused a great deal of trouble and a considerable amount of damage to property.[32]

Kharūtī

This group [numbers] 7,500 households and its homeland is in Katawāz east of the Kūh-i Sulaymān. [Its members] reside as far as the locales of Parmal, Urgūn, and Sar-i Rawżah. Most practice agriculture and some live by tending herds and by trade. Their traders live in Qarābāgh. Through purchase they have come to own some Hazārah forts. In summer their herders pasture their animals in Hazārah Nāhwur and Mālistān and they harass the Hazārahs and bring a great deal of trouble.

Their [true] genealogy and lineage remains unknown because [of the story that] Sahhāk and Īzab, the names of two Ghilzāʾīs, one day came across a donkey carrying barley bread and a young boy. They divided it amongst themselves and gave the young boy the name Kharūtī [combining] the Hindī word for bread (*rūtī*) [and donkey, *khar* in Persian]. Consequently, his offspring were known as Kharūtī and were associated with the Ghilzāʾī Afghans. [The Kharūtī] have a bitter animosity and an innate hostility for the Sulaymān Khayl. They continually pillage and kill each other and are never at a loss for blood or money (by killing and looting each other).

Khadūzāʾī

This clan group is small and comprises the Qawm-i ʿAlī in Muqur and 250 [households] living in Dih-i Khwājah adjacent to the Kabul Gate of Qandahar. They believe themselves to be sayyids. **/104/** Some pass their lives as farmers and some are traders. Sometime they call themselves Pūpalzāʾī, a branch of the Durrānī, and sometimes Ghilzāʾī. In all of Afghanistan there are 2,500 households of them. They are extremely fanatical and hate Shiʿis. Consequently, they try to bring harm to the wealth and health of the Shiʿah by any means possible.

---

[32] For some of General Muḥammad ʿUmar Khān's exploits refer to the index in this volume.

Zhamaryānī

This clan is the "threshold of the Tūkhī people" (*āstānah-i qawm-i Tūkhī*). Most of this clan lives amongst the Tūkhīs. From Kabul to Qandahar there are one or two households living in most places. They spend their lives working in agriculture, trade, and in service [professions] Throughout all
27 of Afghanistan they number 250 households. | **/105/**

CHAPTER FIVE

The Sarwānī Afghans

Sarwānī, the half-brother (by the same father) of Ghilzāʾī, emerged from the womb of Mahī the daughter of Kakh Dūr, wife of Shāh Ḥusayn Ghūrī. His offspring were known as Sarwānī and, through their upbringing, became known in the tribe of Matū, the mother of Ghilzāʾī, as Afghans of the Matī tribe. They lived in the city of Darāban. Shaykh Malīḥ Qitāl emerged from this murderous (*qattāl*) tribe. He became the one to whom men and women turned with their desires and hopes until during the reign of Humāyūn[33] a bloody war broke out between the Sūrīs and the Sarwānīs over a woman. Because of the great number of fatalities on both sides they were [both] greatly weakened and lost power. The Miyā Khayl Lūḥānī joined forces with the Bakhtiyār clan to take possession of [the Sarwānī and Sūr] lands and estates. They seized control of the Darāban District and only a small number of Sarwānīs remained; the rest were driven from their homeland and fled. Some took refuge with the chief of Malīr Kūtalah District; some took the path of vagabondage and vanished from among the Afghan tribes, their name forgotten. A few households permanently settled in Chahchah District, part of Rawalpindi District.

Shaykh Ṣadr-i Jahān, the son of Shaykh Aḥmad Z[h]andah Pīl [Shaykh Aḥmad of Jām][34] to whom people were devoted and turned [for religious guidance], came to India from Jām where his father, Shaykh Aḥmad, had chosen to live and there [in India] he was the object of admiration and reverence. His progeny up until today have ridden the horse of their desires and hopes. They found worldly prosperity in Malīr Kūtalah and have received the respect and honor of the English. Other descendants of Shaykh Aḥmad Z[h]andah Pīl reside in the village of Turbat-i Shaykh Jām, the fields and irrigation works of which are an endowment for the shrine and burial place of His Holiness. They live easy and prosperous lives by taking, holding, and spending the income of those endowments. Also they engage in a vast amount of smuggling of cash, weapons, destitute women, and opium. And they plunder and murder pilgrims to the

[33] The reference is to Humāyūn, the son of Ẓahīr al-Dīn Bābur, founder of the Mughal dynasty in India. Humāyūn reigned from 1530–40 and 1555–56.

[34] On Aḥmad-i Jām (d. 1141 A.D.) whose shrine at Turbat-i Jām is an object of great veneration in Khurāsān, see H. Moayyad, "Aḥmad-e Jām," *Encyclopaedia Iranica*, New York & London: Routledge & Kegan Paul, 1987, vol. 1, pp. 648–49 and Shivan Mahendrarajah, "The Ṣūfi Shaykhs of Jām: A History, From the Īl-Ḵhāns to the Tīmūrids," Ph.D. dissertation, Downing College, University of Cambridge, 2014.

shrine of the Eighth Imām [in Mashhad, Iran] by being "friend of the thief and partner in the caravan." Due to religious fanaticism and as coreligionists [of Afghans], they are enemies of the Iranians and supporters of the Afghans. On occasion, on the pretext of seeking justice from oppression, they come to Harāt and then go on to Kabul. There, in secret, they collect a stipend for living expenses from the government and then go back to Turbat. With Shujāʿ al-Mulk,[35] the Bākharzī Tīmūrids, and the [people of] the "Sunni-house" of Qā'in[36] all of whose hearts incline towards Afghanistan, much detriment and criminal activity was secretly directed at Shiʿis and is still being directed at them. They consider it permissible to cause trouble for Shiʿis and they deem spilling their blood to be without moral consequence, and deserving of reward.

[35] Shujāʿ al-Mulk was a title awarded by the Qājār government to Sartīp Muḥammad Riżā son of Yūsuf Khān Hazārah. He served as governor of Bākharz and was assigned to guard the eastern frontier of Iran with his Hazārah followers. (See Fayż Muḥammad *The History*, vol. 4, pp. 577 and 920.) According to Ḥājj Kāẓim Yazdānī, during the era of Riżā Shāh Pahlavī, Shujāʿ al-Mulk's son, Ṣawlat al-Salṭanah, rebelled against the Pahlavī government and was able to take possession of areas of eastern Khurāsān and advanced as far as Sang Bast-i Mashhad before he was defeated. (Fayż Muḥammad, *Nizhādnāmah*, p. 108, note.)

[36] Qā'in was famous as a center of Sunnism in Shiʿi Iran.

/111/ CHAPTER SIX

The Garrānī[37] *Afghans*

There is considerable difference of opinion about the lineage and genealogy of Garrān. Today there are many tribes, descendants of his, who are called Afghans. Some would say he is the seed of Sayyid Qāf while some old men of the Shītak people say that he was born of some imaginary
28 prince while the Khūkyānī tribe says he is the son of | ʿAbd Allāh Ūrmurī of the Sarbanī Afghans. Some Garrānīs say with conviction that either a newborn infant was found under an iron frying pan, which Afghans call *karāʾī* and in which they cook bread, meat, and fish, at the camping place of an army which had camped during the night and then during the day had set off on its march, or, alternately, that ʿAbd Allāh Ūrmurī had taken the infant in exchange for a frying pan and had named it Garrānī.

In an old Pashto book it is recorded that Garrān was found in a winter pasture area as a newborn. His descendants, who make up a very large group, introduce themselves and have come to be known as Afghans with a fabricated genealogy as follows. It is here recorded and laid before [my] gentle readers that Garrān was made up of the original tribes of Kūdī, Kakī, Dilāzāk, Arūkzāʾī, Mūsāzāʾī, Mangal, Tūrī, Hunī, and Wardak. Each tribe in turn is made up of several distinct groups, thousands of households and hundreds of thousands of individuals.

Kūdī and *Dilāzāk*

Most members of these two groups live with their families in the Deccan, Hindūstān. Some reside in Hazārah District, one of the dependencies of Rawalpindi, in Taktak Khānah in Chahchah District, and in Peshawar. They are not found in Afghanistan. /**112**/

Arūkzāʾī

This tribe has 20,000 fighters. It inhabits the mountain region west of Kūh-i Safīd and north of Tīrāh District. A few [households] reside in Kūhāt District, the territory of the Bangash people. Of those people, the Muḥammad Khayl clan is Shiʿi along with most of the Bangash. The rest [of the Arūkzāʾī] are generally Sunni, bigoted, and hostile to Shiʿis. They

[37] See p. 349, note 7 regarding the orthography of this name. Fayż Muḥammad took pains to make it clear that the first letter was a 'G' and his spelling is consistently "Garrān" rather than the more commonly used "Karrān."

continually raid and pillage areas under English jurisdiction. The family of Sayyid Maḥmūd resides in Tīrāh. The "Pir-i Khānah" and the center of the Shiʿis is there and the Arūkzāʾī there are Shiʿi.

Mangal

This group comprises 15,000 battle-hardened warriors. They reside in Khūst District, the seat of the governor [located] south of Kabul in a mountainous area and west of Kurram District, the territory of the Shiʿi Tūrīs. To the north they have the Jadrān as their neighbor. [The Mangal] are brave. They cut wood and sell it as beams [for construction].

Muqbil

This group lives in rugged mountains difficult of access, north of the Mangal and south of the Jājī. Some live in Khūst District in the locale of Lakan as clients (*hamsāyahs*) and in small numbers. In relation to other Afghans, they are a simple folk and cause little trouble.

Kakī

29 | This clan group includes the Afrīdī, Khatak, Jadrān, Utmān Khayl, Khūkyānī, Sulaymān [Khayl], and Shītak. The Afrīdīs have 23,750 armed and bellicose fighters. They live deep in a mountain range **/113/** [bordered] on the east by the homeland of the Khatak tribe, adjacent to the shrine of Kākā Ṣāḥib.[38] This mountain range where they have made their homeland lies west and south of Peshawar. To the south of it is the homeland of the Arūkzāʾī clan and the Bangash, the Kūh-i Safīd, and Chamkanī. To the west is the Sangū Khayl Shinwār clan and to the north [their land] is bordered by the mountains where the Muhmand people live and by Peshawar.

The people of this clan [the Afrīdī] are thieves and highwaymen and are utterly corrupt. Except for the plain around Tīrāh they have little land suitable for agriculture. They live by selling charcoal, salt, and straw; by stealing; by serving in the English army and by other sorts of policing-type service for the English. Shaykh Maḥbūb ʿAlī, a member of this clan, by treachery and trickery and working in concert with the English envoy Humphrys, both of whom were in Kabul, created discontent among the

[38] The Kākā Ṣāḥib shrine is today in Nawshahrah (Noshera) District in Pakistan. The internet has no shortage of information about it.

people of the North (the Shamāl) and caused the revolution of Pisar-i Saqqā (Son of the Water Carrier) and thereby [the shaykh] gained a higher rank and status and a larger stipend [from the English].[39]

Khatak

This clan group is made up of the Anū Khayl, Tarakī, and Būlāq and [numbers] 62,500 individuals. They occupy [the region] from the Yūsufzā'ī district around Peshawar and Landī north of the Kabul River to Kālah Bāgh, [up to] the territories of the ʿĪsā Khayl, the Marwat, and the Wazīrīs in /**114**/ Banūn District. These lands and locales have been made the homeland of the Khatak people on the west side of the Indus River. [This territory] has an irregular shape nearly 100 miles in length from north to south and 40 miles in width from east to west. It is enclosed by the Kabul River to the north and Kūh-i Maʿdan-i Namak [Salt Mine Mountain] to the south. Most of the eastern part [of Khatak territory] is enclosed by the Indus River. A branch of the Khatak, the Sāghirī Makhad, is located in Rawalpindi district. The region to the south as far as Mārī, located on the east bank of the Indus River, is also occupied by this tribe. In the west what they have made their homeland is bounded by [the lands of] the Afrīdīs, the Bangash, and others. South of them are the tribes settled in Banūn District. All [the Khatak] are followers and subjects of the English. They keep themselves aloof from any feelings of Afghan tribal solidarity and do not identify with their own people and heritage.

Jadrān[40]

This tribal subdivision has made its homeland in the mountains west of Khūst and east of Zurmat. It has 18,700 armed men. Although they have
30 plenty of water and a good ecology (lushness, verdancy, and trees) | they have little cultivable land. So [in order to increase their cultivable lands] they use stones to build a wall-like structure and then they pour dirt behind it and make small terraces where they could plant one *pāw*, one *chārak*, or half a seer of seeds. They also carry dirt using the skirt of their (loin) cloth or baskets and pour it on top of large boulders and then cultivate there. They endure pain and hardship far above the norm in order to obtain the

[39] For more on the shaykh and Humphrys see the *Taẕakkur al-inqilāb* in this volume, p. 365.
[40] In Pashto the name is pronounced Zadrān.

food and clothing necessary for survival. They continually migrate inside and outside the country /115/ working as bearers, rock breakers, and mudders to provide for their food and clothing, whether a little or a lot. In their mountains they have some trees which provide nutritious fruits [and nuts] such as apples, pomegranates, walnuts, almonds, and pine nuts in such abundance that they can trade them in Khūmah. But since they don't have a head for business, they remain impoverished. The people who make their homes on the four sides [of the Khatak] live lives of ease and plenty [in contrast to the Khatak] whose lives are full of hardship.

Utmān Khayl

This clan [numbers] 15,000 households and lives in Arang Barang District. The mountains where they reside are in the southern part of the mountains between Bājāwur and Sawāt (Swāt); the western head of [those mountains] extends to Bājāwur and its eastern side to the southern part of Swāt. Their largest villages are located in Maydān-i Yūsufzā'ī. The northern part of the mountain chain where they reside is flourishing. On the uneven heights of that [mountain chain] they build three-to-four-foot high walls of stone, throw soil behind them, and cultivate it. Two thousand five hundred households of them reside in the locale of Sih Ṣadah and engage in raiding and robbing the people of ʿAlī and Rāghib. They take Hindūs as captives, demand ransom for them, and then free them. A few of them reside in Kūh Dāman-i Kabul where they sell fruit. They spend the spring there and live in Jalālābād in winter.

Khūkyānī

This Khūkyānī is not the same as the Sarbanī Khūkyānī. They [number] 6,925 /116/ households. The Shayrzād, Khiżr Khayl, Bārak, and Būbū tribes [of the Khūkyānī] live west of Jalālābād on the northwestern slopes of the Kūh-i Safīd along with other Garrānī tribes like the Ṣabarī, Malī, Landar, Akībī, Qadam, Hārūn Khayl, Lakan, Rakī Khayl, Nukat Khayl, Shādīzā'ī, Ayyūb Khayl, Ṣādiq, ʿAlīshayr Khayl, Bakr Khayl, and Nūn Khayl. All are subject to Khūst and live in subdistricts of Khūst. Altogether these number 7,500 households. In the mountainous areas where they reside, especially in their homeland along the skirts of Safīd Kūh, they produce many
31 grapes, mulberries, and figs. | Malik Qays from this group, along with a number of fellow tribesmen, took the path of evildoing in the revolution of Son of the Water Carrier and caused a great deal of harm.

[31]

Tūrīs

This tribe is [made up of] 15,000 bellicose and brave fighting men. It inhabits Kurram District north of Khūst and south of Kūh-i Safīd. The territory it occupies lies on both sides of the [Kurram] River. It constantly wages a sectarian war with tribes of the Sunni sect and it always prevails. It is known by the names of five of its clans: Ḥamzah Khayl, Mastū Khayl, Pīrzāʾī, ʿAlīzāʾī, and Ghundī Khayl.

Of the Ḥamzah Khayl, 250 households are nomadic. In the cold season they spend the winter in Tal-i Buland Khayl and when it is warm they pasture their livestock in Kūh-i Safīd. Two hundred and fifty households of the Malah Khayl engage in raiding and pillaging the herds and the goods and furnishings of Sunnis. But the English have forbidden them from fighting with Sunnis and from raiding and plundering their wealth and livestock. /117/ Whenever the Afghans came to blows with the English, they would urge the peoples of Kurram to rise up in defense. [But] this is how (the English) defend themselves [by using other Afghans]. Indeed they always make Muslims fight each other and then pretend to be the peace-loving intermediary.

A number of families of the [Tūrī] people of Kurram have established themselves in Mashhad and make life easy for Tūrī pilgrims by acting as agents and surrogates on their behalf, finding them hotel rooms, and accompanying them in performing the pilgrimage rites. This is in contrast to the Barbarīs [Hazārahs living in Iran] for the Barbarīs will not help their own [i.e. Hazārah] newly arrived pilgrims and will not give them good directions. Through deceit and trickery, they will empty their purses of money for provisions and so force them to immediately return home.

The Tūrī people asked for a scholar from Lucknow well-versed in the principles of the Jaʿfarī school of law [the legal school of Shiʿis] and their practical application to come to Kurram and serve as *qāżī* of the "commands and prohibitions" of the sect and to adjudicate the litigation, appeals, and disputes they had over their dealings with each other. From the English they obtained a monthly salary for him of 200 English rupees and they revived and restored the settling of all claims of rights relating to justice between themselves, according to the Jaʿfarī legal school.

Six hundred Tūrīs serve in the English military. As long as their sons and daughters have not performed pilgrimage to Mashhad they do not marry. They are united heart and soul with Hazārahs despite the fact that they live far apart.

Jājī[41]

This clan shares with the Tūrīs a common paternal lineage as brothers of the same father. But they differ in terms of sect and **/118/** are deeply antag-
32 onistic (literally, seek each others' blood). | They live apart from the Tūrīs, west and a little bit north of Tūrī territory and are separated by Kūh-i Paywār. They are well-established in the locales of Aryūb and Maydān. They [number] 6,250 households and are always eager to support and give aid to tribes of their own sect [Sunnism], raiding and plundering the Tūrīs but they tend to be defeated and unsuccessful. The Tūrīs, due to the English telling them not to, do not fight unless defending themselves; they never attack the homes and places of the Jājīs.

Parbah, a Branch of the Khūkyānī

This branch of the Khūkyānī, which [lives] separate from it, numbers 1,250 households and includes ten subdivisions: (1) Mardī Khayl, (2) Miyā Khayl, (3) Basī Khayl, (4) Sardār Khayl, (5) Maḥmūd Khayl, (6) Narīzā'ī, (7) Malīzā'ī, (8) 'Āshizā'ī, (9) Dadah Khayl, and (10) Pūchī Khayl. [The Parbah tribe] lives in Khūst and engages in agriculture. Some engage in commerce at which they are diligent and for which they are well-suited.

Darmān/Durmān or *'Abd al-Raḥmān*

This clan comprised three major tribes—Ḥājjī Khān Khayl, Sūdī Khayl, and Aḥmad Khayl—and three affiliate tribes—(1) Mūdī Khayl, (2) Kūndī, and (3) Mangas. In total [the Darmān] number 1,250 households and are known as Mamūrī. In terms of their residence, by metonymy they are called Matūn because the name of the place where they live is Matūn. This is a locale in Khūst where those [three] affiliates work at agriculture. **/119/**

Wazīr

This clan group includes the Ibrāhīm Khayl, Walī Khayl, Aḥmadzā'ī—but not the Ghilzā'ī Aḥmadzā'ī—Kālū Khayl, Mas'ūd, Bahlūlzā'ī, Lālī, Madah Khayl, and others. [The Wazīrs number] 48,320 armed fighters and warriors. [Their territory is] 140 miles in length measured from the

---

[41] In Pashto, the name, though spelled Jājī, is pronounced Zāzī and it is in this form that it is most commonly rendered in Western sources today.

border of Kūhāt District to Darrah-i Sāmanī Wāl in Dīrah Ismāʿīl Khān District.[42] They occupy the land [in this region] and own a number of subdistricts—Shawāl, Shakī, Parmal, Razmak, Sham, Darrah-i Khaysūr, Shahr Nuh, Sharakī, Shayr Talah, Wānah, Badr, Shahr-i Makīn, Khasūrah, Maydān, Duwatūy, Darrah-i Tāk, Kūh-i Bābar, Zangarah, Shahīr, Shaktū, and Girishtū. Less than one-third [of the Wazīrs] are subject to Afghanistan. The rest all live on soil in the grasp of the English. One thousand of them along with another 1,000 from the Jājī clan who for seven months did not cinch the belt of resistance to Son of the Water Carrier, only after much effort on the part of Muḥammad Nādir Khān, and thanks to the firm stand taken by the Hazārahs who, at the propagandizing and incitement of this writer,[43] fought Pisar-i Saqqā (Son of the Water Carrier) and did not submit to him, finally **/121/** [the Wazīr and Jājīs] moved by a sense of
33 honor, attacked Kabul, and were victorious. | They looted the treasury, the arsenal, and the government property and armaments [depots] which remained from the pillaging and looting by the Saqqawīs, and had even been collected by the thieving emirate and barbaric government of the son of the water carrier. [The Wazīr and Jājīs] also stole money, furnishings, and belongings of the people of the North and the goods that [those people] had plundered from nation and government. They thus brought the government and nation to the brink of impoverishment. You could say that this was no help, assistance, or defense against chaos and **/122/** corruption, nor did it work to guard and protect sovereignty and country or the money and lives of [people of] the nation. What they did in the way of creating misery and misfortune is illustrated by this verse:

> The love of an idiot is just like the love of that bear/
> His hate is like love and his love is like hate.[44]

---

[42] Note that no measurement of the width of their territory is given in the published text. It seems unusual that Fayż Muḥammad would have omitted it.

[43] See *Taẕakkur al-inqilāb* (Memoir of the Revolution) accompanying this text, especially pp. 220–54.

[44] The poetry refers to the story of a man who had a bear and the bear loved him so much that once, when the man was asleep and a fly landed on his forehead, the bear, wanting to get rid of the fly, picked up a rock and smashed the fly (and the man's head) with it. The line is from Rumi's *Maṡnavī*.

Gurbaz, a Branch of the Wazīrī

This clan [numbers] 1,250 households. They live in the northwest corner of the territory of the Wazīrīs, in the southeastern part of Khūst, and the northwest part of Dūr District. The mountain areas they inhabit are under snow for two months. They build their humble homes of reed and are extremely poor. Beyond this mountain area, they also call home a small part of Maydān-i Khūst. In physical form and identity they resemble the Wazīrī but are quite their opposites when it comes to doing good or evil.

Laylī, a Branch of the Wazīrī

This clan has 6,250 fighting men and it inhabits the northwest slopes of the Kūh-i Safīd in such places as Āgām, Pachīr, and Chaprahār, adjacent to and neighboring the Shinwār and the Khūkyānī people. They [the Laylī] are known as Wazīrī but are far removed from the Wazīrī [in terms of behavior].

Shītak

This clan includes the following tribes: Dūr, Tanī, and Surānī, known as Banūchī /**123**/ or Bānūzā'ī. Its [Banūchī] subdivisions, the Malakh, ʿAbdak, Darpah Khayl, and Imrūnī or Imkhānī live deep in the mountains on both sides of the Tūchī River. Aside from the Banūchi subdivisions, they number 27,000 individuals. They are known in terms of their place of residence; they live in Dūr District and are known as the Dūr people. They seek a life of ease and play. They are unreliable and have vicious natures. They fornicate with the women (wives) of outsiders and sodomize beardless youths. Several people may have intimate relations with a single boy. The door of this kind of sexual intercourse is open throughout all of Afghanistan and among all Afghans. It is widespread and is the occasion of pride and boasting.

Tanī

This clan dwells in the mountains in the southwest corner of Khūst. Some of them live in Darakī on the skirts of the mountains and in the villages
34 of Ḥiṣārak, | Kūkhah, Narkhī, and Utmān. Of those residing in the mountains of Khūst, on the plain and on the mountain slope (in Khūst)], and Darakī there are 750 armed men. The remaining segments of the group have 12,000 men under arms. The western mountains where they reside

are verdant with lots of hunting falcons and large shade trees. In the main they are brave warriors who like to think about fighting and about armies.

Banūchī or Bānūzā'ī

The tribes of this clan are from the offspring and lineage of Sūrānī and are known as Bānūzā'ī after the name of their great grandmother. They corrupt the name and, using the Afghānī articulation, pronounce it Banūchī. This clan includes the tribes of Pak, Gharażżā'ī, Mandā Khayl, and Hasībak. It [numbers] 295,372 individuals including the clans of Marwat, ʿĪsā Khayl, Tājīk, and Wazīrī. They are subject to and obey the farman of **/124/** the English. They live along both sides of the Tūchī River whose source in the mountains is owned by the Kharūtī people in the Urgūn District and in Kūh-i Parmal. Their homeland, where Hindūs are also settled as well as the remnants of the army of Alexander of Macedonia, later became known as Dand. Then, due to the settlement there of this clan it became known as Banūn. It is 3,611 [square] miles in area. Besides the Tūchī River, there is the Kurram River which rises in the Kūh-i Safīd. From Aryūb it passes a place adjacent to Paywār. It thoroughly waters Kurram District and the territory of the Bangash, enters Banūn, irrigates it, and supports its lushness.

Nine Groups Affiliated with the Afghans but Not Themselves Afghans

These nine are: (1) Bakhtiyār, (2) Usturānī, affiliated with the Shayrānī people, (3) Mushwānī affiliated with the Kākar people, (4) Hunī, (5) the Wardak mixed with the Garrān, (6) Khūndī mixed with the Dāwī, (7) Sipandzā'ī affiliated to Tarīn, (8) Gharshīn affiliated with the Miyānah, and (9) the Kūtī, tied to the Bītanī. This latter group considers its members sayyids but they don't publicly declare themselves to be sayyids. Given this lack of acknowledgement, their people say about being sayyids, "we separated from the sayyids and chose to be affiliated and related to the Afghans. We came to speak their language, merged with them in terms of behavior and customs, became united with them in their customs and manners, and correspond to them in terms of habits, character, and nature. In this regard announcing that we are sayyids would be a violation of good manners and disgraceful. One of our leaders said to us, 'Whoever declares he is a sayyid is not one of us.'" **/127/**

CHAPTER SEVEN

The Tribal Groups Affiliated With the Afghans

Suturyānī or *Ūsturānī* [*sic*]

This group comprises the Shaykhī, Gandah Pūr, Humar, Yaʿqūbzā'ī,
35 ʿImrānzā'ī, Khūbīzā'ī, and Darī Palārah tribes | and [numbers] 37,500 individuals. They live in Chatākūt Ẓafar Rūrī, the rail transfer node for Karachi, Lahore, Bombay, and Quetta, and in Kulāchī, Takwārah, and the eastern skirts of Kūh-i Sulaymān along the banks of the Lūnī River. These places are all dependencies of Dīrah Ismāʿīl Khān. [Their territory] goes as far south as the territory of the Miyān Khayl people and northwards to the homelands of the Dawlat Khayl. On the west [their border is] the skirts of Kūh-i Takht-i Sulaymān and to the east Dīrah Ismāʿīl Khān District. They are within the territory colonized by the English. The people of this clan gain their livelihoods in agriculture and commerce.

Mushwānī

This clan is not to be confused with the Mūshānī mentioned earlier. It [numbers] 525 households. Some are engaged in farming and commerce in Kūh Dāman-i Kabul. A few households live in Qandahar, and a number of others in the northern part of the Kūh-i Gandagar in the locale of Sīrī Kūt in Hazārah District, a dependency of Rawalpindi. Some live dispersed among the Tūkhī people. Aḥmad ʿAlī Khān, son of ʿAbd al-Wāḥid Khān, son of Muḥammad Rafīq Khān, son of Mullā[xii] Bīd, son of Mullā Nasī is a member of this group. He is a brave person and competent but he is not farsighted and cannot think properly and thus went astray and erred. Thus, because Son of the Water Carrier /128/ and Sayyid Ḥusayn gave him money, a rifle, and the rank of colonel, he gained power and capability and became trusted and acquired influence among the evildoers. In the fighting of the coup, he himself was [often] successful. Later, in the amirate of Nādir Khān he was named high commissioner for Qaṭaghan and Badakhshān. Hardly had he arrived there when, without carefully weighing the consequences and because he had a quick temper and a foul mouth, he created trouble, launched a coup and tried to take control of the government. But he was defeated and consequently made Ibrāhīm Beg Lukhāy victorious over the army of the government.[45] /129/

[45] Ibrāhīm Luqāy was a commander of the Muslim mujāhidīn (more familiarly known as basmachi) fighting the Soviets in Russian Turkistān. During the reign of Amīr Amān

Hunī

This clan has some 10,250 armed and warlike men. A number of [the members of this clan] live in the western mountains of the Mangal people's homeland. Their Dū Musht clan resides among the Bangash, Arūkzā'ī, and Tūrī people in Kurram to the southeast of Kūh-i Safīd. They engage in farming and the sale of commodities. Some others live by mining and selling salt from the Bahādur Khayl mine. This provides them with a life of considerable ease.

Wardak

[The members of] this clan believe themselves to be sayyids. The clan
36 comprises ten tribes having 12,500 households | and occupying the fertile valley of the Shinīz [River] which is more than two manzils long from north to south [stretching] from Shaykhābād to Kārīz-i Bahā'ī and Nāwagī and from the mountain range of the Sajāwand Pass separating Lahūgard and Kharwār. This valley from east to west is two to two and one-half miles wide. It is continuous from the valley of Khawāt, Sih Āb, Kūdah, and Dāy Mīrdād to Hazārah-i Dāy Mīrdād, and Gīrū-yi Rashīd connected to Hazārah-i Jīghatū. This is their homeland. These places are all occupied by Wardaks, the whole area being bounded on the west side by the mountain range of Hazārah-i Bihsūd, on the north by the villages of Zaranay and Tūp, on the south by the territory of Khayr and villages on the northwest by the city of Ghaznīn, the forts of the Bayāt people, and the Hazārahs of Jīghatū. The lands are fertile[xiii] and the farms produce grain.

Most Wardaks are hardworking, deliberate, and patient, and earn their living as farmers. /**130**/ One of them, Karīm Khān, in hopes of Amān Allāh's arriving in Kabul from Qandahar, valiantly fought the son of the water carrier with a force but was ultimately captured and killed. Due to his zeal and bravery, the entire Wardak people in the eyes of the public came to be seen as heroic. They gained a good name, and became honored, respected, and recipients of office and rank from the government.

Also, one of them, ʿAbd al-Aḥad Khān,[46] the son of Qāẓī Ghulām, who fled with Amān Allāh from Qandahar and went to Iran, is currently

---

Allāh Khān, he took refuge in Afghanistan and would launch attacks on Russian forces across the Amū (Oxus) River. In 1929, he threw in his lot with Amīr Ḥabīb Allāh Kalakānī. When Nādir Khān came to power. Ibrāhīm Beg was forced to give up his sanctuary in Afghanistan, crossed back over the border, and was captured and killed.

[46] Adamec, *Who's Who*, p. 93 identifies him as an Ismāʿīl Khayl Ghilzā'ī but says he was known as Wardakī because of long residence there.

president of the (National) Council and is a kind and modest individual. However, it is regrettable that during this time of the overthrow and extermination of Islam [by the son of the water carrier and Muḥammad Nādir Khān] he has not exerted much effort to unify and harness the social power of Islam but instead has introduced division and aversion into the nature of Islam. In gatherings he has slandered and denigrated Iran and the Iranians and boastfully declared, "We've taken their 'sun-worship' to the toilet and used it to purify [our bottoms]."

Humar

This clan comprises the Amānzā'ī and Gugalzā'ī and it [numbers] 3,750 households. Some of them live in Maydān south of the Bābar people, some live in the mountains. South of where they live are the Kasrānī Balūch people. To [the Humar's] west is the mountain region of the Amrzā'ī people. [The Humar] people themselves subsist as herders and farmers, and by hiring out their livestock [for transport].

Bangash

This clan believes itself to be Quraysh and descended from Khālid [ibn al-Walīd][47]. It comprises the tribe(s) of Garī and Samilzā'ī and numbers 22,500 households. Most of them live in Kūhāt District and the rest in the western part of Kurram District and in the locale of Shalūzān. Their homeland from east to west **/131/** is long and flat and enclosed by mountains. To
37 its southeast are the mountains of the Khatak, to the north | the Arūkzā'ī people, to the southwest the Wazīrī people, and to the west the district of Kurram, the homeland of the Tūrī. The Bangash living in Kurram and Paywār are dominated by the Tūrī. The Shalūzān are the most capable [of the Bangash] and the ones who make the decisions. Most Bangash are Shi'i of the firm Imāmī Twelver creed. Some are Sunni and downtrodden. In sectarian disputes, the Tūrīs unite with and support the Bangash. All are ready to fight and are as brave as lions and they always prevail over the Sunnis. In fighting they always overcome, win, and are victorious.

The English, for their own political objectives, sometimes prevent any fighting and sometimes provoke it and decide whether to support one side or the other in order to achieve their own ends. Having made both sides capable and strong, it then weakens them and renders them impotent.

---

[47] Known as the "Sword of Islam" Khālid ibn al-Walīd was a leading Arab commander in the earliest Muslim conquests. He died in 642 A.D.

[37]

The Bangash mostly make a living through agriculture, although some pursue commerce and some sell salt. A few households of them live in Māzandarān and Khurāsān, Iran, as well as in some districts of Hindūstān, In Farrukhābād there are quite a few and there they are zamindars [wealthy landowners]. Among their peers they are esteemed and respected, behave with dignity and good manners, and are well-spoken.

/135/ EPILOGUE

The Non-Afghans of Afghanistan

Of Afghans living in Afghanistan, having beat the drum of self-interest in the name of Afghanism and an independent Afghanistan and having made themselves visible to the eyes of the world and so are [now] well-known to the far horizons, it has been established and recorded that there are not more than 300,000 households [of Afghans] that are settled and reside in this country. The rest of the people are Tājīk, Uzbek, Hazārah, Jadīd al-Islām [formerly known as Kāfirs, now Nūristānīs], and a variety of other peoples. Whatever Afghans there are beyond these 300,000 [households] live on the territory under the colonial rule of the English and follow English laws and directives. No one knows anything more [than what has been presented here] about any other situation, homeland, dwelling place, or clan [of Afghans] or where any such might be.

In what follows, by way of informing the readers of this *Nizhādnāmah*, we only provide a brief record of the various [other] peoples that are counted as subject to the Afghan government and number approximately 5,400,000. As the [Arabic] proverb says, "It's only people's kindness that makes their excuses acceptable" ("*al-ʿudhru ʿinda kirām al-nās maqbūlun*") [and so the author] asks to be forgiven [for his failure to give] a detailed account [of the non-Afghans] due to physical frailty and the difficult straits [he is in] caused by a lack of the food, drink, and clothing necessary for survival. He hopes that fair-minded people will forgive him.

Sayyids

There is not a single place in Afghanistan, be it city, town, or village, where there are not one, two, or several households of Ḥasanī, Ḥusaynī, ʿAlawī, Mūsawī, or Riżawī sayyids living there. All the people of Afghanistan honor and revere [these descendants of the Prophet Muḥammad],
38 each tribe identifying them in its own terminology | as "sayyid, amir, āqā or shah." /136/

The Hazārah people, especially, show the greatest respect to sayyids and do not seek to marry women from sayyid families. At seven years of age (Hazārahs) give their male children a [circumcision] feast and have a sayyid tie a [ceremonial] waistband or belt [on the child]. This tying of the waistband means that their waistband-bound progeny will be bound to the commands of the religion, submit to the law of the Lord of Messengers, and carry out the 'commands and prohibitions' of the Lord of the Two Worlds in accordance with the commands of the [Twelve] Pure Imāms (peace be upon them). The sayyids of Dīrah Ismaʿīl Khān, the Hazārahjāt, Kurram, the Bangash, and Tīrah are Shiʿi. Other [sayyids] who associate with Sunnis are Sunni. Some of the Sunni [sayyids] are fanatics while some [sayyids] are neither Sunni nor Shiʿi because they know nothing about religious matters.

Among sayyids, those of Fūshanj are fanatical Sunnis. Most are wealthy merchants and are arrogant and conceited. In the districts of Zurmat, Urgūn, and Banūn there is a large number of the descendants of Shāh Muḥammad Rūḥānī and an esteemed family living on the edge of Jalālābād [whose males] are called "shah." In Kūh Dāman [and] Kūhistān-i Kabul, sayyids are numerous. All are esteemed, serve as the chiefs of tribes, and are referred to as "khwājahs."

Most revolutions and general turmoil have been due to their incitement, for example, the revolution of Son of Water Carrier and the second assault [on Kabul] by the miserable felons from the people of the North.

Hazārah sayyids live off the income and yield from lands and estates which [other] Hazārahs set aside as votive offerings. **/137/** The sayyids' share from the *khums* [20% religious tax] and votive offerings lets them live a life of ease. Some of them, in imitation of the pseudo-mullahs of Iran,[48] choose to be spongers and like the sayyids of the Barbarīs of Mashhad, lead the common folk into troublemaking and evildoing. The Sunnis view them with the eye of fanaticism and hatred and attribute to them illicit and obscene acts.

Quraysh

This group claims the same lineage as the sayyids. A few families of them are found in every district. Most work as mosque muezzins, madrasah teachers, and prayer leaders (imāms). They live off donations of charitable gifts made at the end of the month of the fast, Ramażān (*zakāt-i fiṭrah*), other charitable gifts, and alms. Some earn the necessities of life working as farmers. In the census, they are counted with the people of the village in which they live.

[48] It is not clear whom Fayż Muḥammad means by the "pseudo-mullahs" (*mullā-namāyān*) when applied to Iranian mullahs. It is a term he uses here and elsewhere for the Afghan Sunni mullahs who backed Ḥabīb Allāh Kalakānī. Perhaps he only means the sayyids of the Barbarīs, those Iranian Hazārahs whom he has already condemned for their treatment of Hazārah pilgrims from Afghanistan.

Non-Quraysh 'Arabs

This ethnic group numbers more than the sayyids and Quraysh [combined]. Nearly 5,000 households bear the name 'Arab. They have no tribe per se but live scattered in Bihsūd and near the city of Jalālābād. In summer, they work as reapers in Bīktūt and in the environs of Kabul and sell chickens and fresh paneer [cheese]. In winter they return to Jalālābād. Some of them were the 'Arabs of Bālā Ḥiṣār, Kabul who were Shi'is and served as soldiers and as craftsmen in the bazaar. Because of the destruc-
39 tion of the Bālā Ḥiṣār by the English they disappeared.[49] | /138/ The household of Barāt 'Alī Khān, one of their leaders, spent a very difficult time in Tehran as did [other] Afghans.

A group of 'Arabs live in Afghan Turkistān, Qaṭaghan, and Badakhshān as tent-dwelling pastoralist nomads. They sell thousands of sheep in Russia, thereby exacerbating the scarcity of meat in the daily life of Islam while providing the Russians a sense of ease and fulfilling their needs. This is due to the unconcern of the government which has not concluded a commercial agreement with the Russians to close the path for smuggling.

Tājiks (a Contraction of Tājīk)

This group's lineage goes back to the 'Arabs. When Islam first appeared and ['Arabs] conquered and occupied Europe, Africa, and Asia, they took up residence and mixed with the [local] peoples in those places. Then gradually, with the addition of the letter 'k,' which creates a diminutive, to the word Tāzī, the Persian name for 'Arabs,[50] [the name] became Tāzīk. Then with the change of the 'z' to a 'j' and the dropping of the long 'i' in most usage, the word became Tājik.

In Darwāz, Badakhshān, the head of the community and the high governor [is Tājīk]. [Another is] Muḥammad Walī Khān, one of their offspring, [who] obtained the rank and office of *wakīl* (representative, attorney) of Amān Allāh /139/ Khān. During Son of the Water Carrier's revolution, he was accused of treason and with the [confirmatory] signatures of the

[49] The destruction charged to the British was the result of two accidental explosions in the ammunition stores within the precincts of the Bālā Ḥiṣār. There seems to have been no deliberate attempt by the British to blow up the Bālā Ḥiṣār. See Brigadier C. W. Woodburn, "The Bala Hissar of Kabul: Revealing a fortress-palace in Afghanistan," The Institution of Royal Engineers, Professional Paper 2009, No. 1.

[50] The name was based on the name of the 'Arab tribe, the Ṭayyi' or Ṭayy, prominent in the seventh-century A.D. Muslim conquest of Iran. The adjective from its name is Ṭā'ī from which the Persian "Tāzī" was derived.

leaders of the nation, and the ulama and chiefs on the government council, he was sentenced to ten years in prison.[51]

Forty-five thousand households of Tājiks reside in the Shamāl (the North), that is Kūh Dāman and Kūhistān-i Kabul, Panjshayr, Sanjan, Durnāmah, Nijrāb, Ghūrband, Takānah, Jalrīz, and Kuhnah Khumār. Twelve thousand five hundred households make their homes in Khinjān and the same number in the villages close to the city of Ghaznīn as well as inside it; in the large villages of Arzū, Shālīj, Ribāṭ, Rāmak, Tāsan; in villages around Harāt; in most villages of Badakhshān; in all of Darwāz; in Jalālābād, Gardīz, Kulālgū, Lamqān, Sardah, Urgūn, Parmal, etc. Except for the Tājiks of Bāmyān, Gīzāb, and Chūrah who were Shiʿis and whose properties, forts, and farms the government gave to Afghans, the Tājiks are all bigoted Sunnis and bitter enemies of Shiʿis.

The entire number of Tājiks residing in Afghanistan amounts to eighteen lakhs seventy-five thousand (1,875,000) persons, nearly one-third of all inhabitants of Afghanistan. Of the Tājiks, those living in the Shamāl lit the fires of an uprising [by Son of the Water Carrier] and brought so much adversity and disaster to government authority, the country, and the nation, that it will not recover in fifty years.

Hazārah Clans and Tribes

These people are one of the subdivisions of Mongols and Tātārs who settled and made their homes in Afghanistan. Currently, whether in
40 their own homeland | or living in the cities and provinces [outside it] or amongst other tribes and clans of Afghans, Tajiks, and Uzbeks, due to the oppression and tyranny of the government and terrorizing and pillaging by nomad Afghans and the even greater oppression and mercilessness of their own tribal elders, headmen, and leaders, they are abandoning house and home /**140**/ and enduring days of adversity and victimization and living in a state of subservience and clientage (*bi-hamsāyagī*).[52]

[The Hazārahs as a whole] number 650,000 households and 2,250,000 persons. All are Twelver Imāmi Shiʿis except for a small number of Shaykh ʿAlī Hazārahs and the Hazārahs of Bihsūd[53] who are Ismāʿīlī and disciples

---

[51] See Adamec's *Who's Who*, p. 262, for a short biography. There the name is reversed to "Walī Muḥammad."

[52] On clientage, *hamsāyagī*, see note 14 above.

[53] According to Yazdānī, "A very small number of Isma'īlīs, not exceeding thirty households, is scattered in the Siyāh Sang Valley, Bihsūd, and on the slopes of Kūh-i Bābā. The rest of the people of Bihsūd, whose number at the present time has reached 500,000,

and followers of Āqā Khān Maḥallātī who lives in Bombay. They are known as "extremists" (*ghulāt*, pl. of *ghālī*).

Other [Hazārahs] in general are firm in their religion, devoted friends of the Pure Imāms (peace be upon them), brave, warlike, hospitable, and generous. Due to illiteracy and ignorance they are [also] obstinate, litigious, bad-tempered, foul-mouthed, and quarrelsome. Due to the harshness of government repression and the affliction caused by the dislike of the Afghan nation, the Hazārahs have turned the face of flight in the direction of Iran. Group after group they have gone to Khurāsān and are still going. The part of the country of Afghanistan that they have owned is 250 miles square. It includes warm areas and cold ones (*garmsīr wa sardsīr*, i.e., subtropical and temperate) and verdant mountains that are the sources of the rivers of Balkh, Kabul, Panjshayr, Lahūgard, the Arghandāb (River) of Qandahar, the Hīrmand (Helmand) and the Harāt River (Harī Rūd). **/131/** [Their land] has waterfalls, meadows, and numerous hunting grounds. It is fertile and grain-producing and was the cause of abundant blessings and general prosperity for all the people of Afghanistan for its ability to provide meats and fats, [other] comestibles, and floor coverings [in the form of kilims].

[Their land] is situated in the very heart of Afghanistan. On the west it is bounded by Dawlatyār and Ghūr of Harāt; on the east by Kabul, Ghaznīn, and the Andar, Tarakī, ʿAlī Khayl, Tūkhī, and Hūtak Ghilzāʾī tribes; to the north by Balkh and its environs and by some locales of Qaṭaghan; and on the south by Qandahar and some of its dependencies that touch on dependencies of Harāt. It is bounded on four sides by Sunnis all of whom are out for [Hazārah] blood.

There are twelve large tribal divisions [among the Hazārahs]: Dāy Zangī, Dāy Kundī, Dāy Mīrdād, Dāy Mīrakshāh, and Dāy Mīrak—these five known as Sādah Suwaykah—Dāy Chūpān, Dāy Khitāy, Dāy Nūrī, Dāy Mīrī, and Dāyah—these five known as Sādah Qabr—Bihsūd, and Jāghūrī. Each of these comprises several subdivisions. Now, only a small number from Dāy Zangī, Dāy Kundī, Dāy Mīrdād, Bihsūd, and Jāghūrī, and from [other] subdivisions of the Sādah Suwaykah remain. They face adversity and persecution and are turning their faces toward Iran. The rest, whose farms, fields, forts, homes, and residences the Afghan government handed over to Afghans, have all gone abroad and live in exhausted hardship.

---

are all Twelver Shiʿis and are pure in their belief." Fayż Muḥammad, *Nizhādnāmah*, p. 140, note 2.

This great people pursued the occupations of farming and raising sheep and cattle. Their hardworking, resigned, and patient men and women pro-
41 duced *barak* [wool cloth], felt, and kilims. They processed yellow oil | in commercial quantities and nomad Afghan retailers transported hundreds of /142/ kharwars of it to the Panjāb, India, and Sind, to sell. Also, all the cities of Afghanistan with their environs and dependencies lived contentedly and at ease [because of these products]. Now that they have taken an ax to their [own] roots and out of ignorant fanaticism have been exterminating the Hazārahs, the lives of all the people of Afghanistan have been adversely affected by the reduction of meats, fats, and other foodstuffs and by a weakening of the vigor of society. Despite of all that, the Hazārahs are supporters and backers of the present government [of Muḥammad Nādir Khān].

Ūymāq

Ūymāq is a Tātār term meaning a people, a section, or a group from the same origin. In Afghanistan, four subdivisions [of the Ūymāq] exist: 1) the Tāymanī; 2) the Hazārah, but not the Hazārahs mentioned above; 3) the Taymūrī [Tīmūrī]; and 4) the Zūrī. These are known as the "Four Ūymāqs" (*chār ūymāq*). The Tāymanī includes two subdivisions: Qibchāq and Darzī. The Hazārah also comprises two sections: Jamshīdī and Fīrūz Kūhī. The Jamshīdī has several branches including Khūk Rū, Gālkandī, Qāqchī, Zayn Gar, Zulfī, Amfalīdī, Juwālī, Khayr Qirk, and Dāy Zabarī. The Chār Ūymāq live in the valleys and heart of the mountain range to the west and south of the territory of the Hazārahs. The Jamshīdīs live in the northwestern section of the lands which make up the homeland of the Chār Ūymāq along the banks of the Murghāb River, including locales in Mārūchāq, Kūshk, Tannūr-i Sangī, and other places. The Tāymanī live in Ghūr and Kūh-i Siyāh Band. All are subject to [the government of] Harāt. The dwellings of the Zūrī are in the southern section of Ghūr, where Isfizār or Sabzawār and their environs are. Most of this section (southern Ghūr) is occupied by the Nūrzā'ī, ʿAlīzā'ī, and Isḥāqzā'ī tribes, all Sarbanī Afghans. /143/

Evildoers from the midst [of the Nūrzā'ī, ʿAlīzā'ī, and Isḥāqzā'ī] due to ignorant fanaticism, the fatwas of mullahs, and the orders of [Afghan] government functionaries responsible for the border, all of whom consider [taking] the wealth and the blood of Shiʿis to be permissible, morally without consequence, and even commendable and deserving of reward, continually plunder and kill the subjects of Iran living along the border.

The Karā'ī branch of the Fīrūz Kūhī Chār Ūymāq resides south of Mashhad. Two large communities of Hazārahs and Taymurīs live in and around Bākharz, west of Harāt, and they are all subjects of Iran.

During the time of Shāh Maḥmūd Saduzā'ī,[54] these Hazārahs rebelled and took refuge on Iranian soil. The Iranian government, which always actively works to protect Islam, gave them farms, residences, and places to live. Up to now, they are content, peaceful, and powerful. One of their number, Mullā Yūsuf, attained the rank and office of tribal chief. His sons, Muḥammad Rizā Khān and Muḥammad Afżal Khān, in turn, have held the title "Shujāʿ al-Mulk."[55] Notwithstanding this boon from the govern-
42 ment of Iran, those two groups, the Taymūrī and Hazārah, | along with the "Sunni house" of Qā'in, and the descendants of Shaykh Aḥmad Zhandah Pīl living in Turbat-i Shaykh Jām, by way of sectarian unity embarked on the path of clandestine collusion with the Afghan government and nation and at the secret instigation and incitement of Shujāʿ al-Mulk caused much harm in the form of thievery, murder, pillaging, money-and weapons-smuggling, and trafficking helpless women for prostitution. They constantly advise, support, and aid Afghan outlaws and highway robbers.

Qizilbāsh

Nādir Shāh Afshār transported from Iran 20,000 warlike and combat-ready men from the Shāh Sawand, Jawānshayr, Bakhtiyārī, Kurd, Bayāt, and Rīkā tribes with their families and armaments, as well as people **/144/** from Shīrāz and Khwāf to guard the country [Afghanistan] and punish and intimidate any Afghan insurgents. He ordered them to settle in Harāt, Qandahar, Ghaznīn, and Kabul and to guard the borders and the hinterland.

Also, Aḥmad Shāh, a Saduzā'ī Afghan and one of Nādir Shāh's personal bodyguards who attained the position of ruler, separated Afghanistan from Iran and formed a distinct state.[56] He invited to Afghanistan, in an honorable way, a number of noble people of the *dīwān* from Sabzawār, Iṣfahān, Khurāsān, Shīrāz and other places with whom he was acquainted

---

[54] Shāh Maḥmūd or Maḥmūd Shāh, as he is more usually named, had fitful control of Harāt between 1817 and his death in 1828–29. The Hazārah "rebellion" cited here by Fayż Muḥammad involved a frontier warlord named Bunyād Khān Hazārah, about whom Fayż Muḥammad has much to say in Fayż Muḥammad *The History*, see index to volume 1 for Bunyād Khān.

[55] See above p. 383.

[56] Aḥmad Shāh Durrānī, the widely recognized founder of the state of Afghanistan (r. 1747–1772).

and on occasion had become close to because of his service to Nādir Shāh and entrusted to them the reins of administration of the country, management of affairs of the nation, and putting the affairs of government in order, something which Afghans and other people of Afghanistan did not know how to do.

Serving with sincerity and integrity from about the year 1160/1747 until 1337/1919 they gave 177 [lunar Hijrī] years of good service to the king, the nation, the government, the army, and the subjects. Until the beginning of the reign of Amīr ʿAbd al-Raḥmān Khān, they were the ones carrying out all important matters, seeing that orders were fulfilled in the best possible way from beginning to end, and enjoying a life of ease and comfort. But during the era of that emir, when, to make a long story short, Afghans and Sunnis became the drafters of documents and learned how to conduct the business of the diwan, little by little they removed the hand of the Qizilbāsh from this work and today except for Mīrzā Muḥammad Ayyūb, the minister of finance,[57] who **/145/** on his own cannot do the work and, in the view of his own people, is completely devoid of high-mindedness, ambition, courage, generosity, manliness, or concern for supporting others of his tribe, except for him no one else has obtained any position of responsibility and for the most part (all) are faced with impoverishment. In truth, due to the envy, avarice, and personal agendas which they [the Qizilbāsh] have, they deserve what they get and don't merit any sympathy. Their forebears, who were truly men, were humane people and had good reputations. Their descendants today are worthless, in fact they are hardly men.

Kayānī

Some people of this ethnic group left Sīstān and chose to lead a somewhat oppressed existence in Harāt and its surroundings. Some of these

---

[57] In the words of Ḥājj Kāẓim Yazdānī, "This Muḥammad Ayyūb Khān Qizilbāsh, who was a literate man but very conservative, was appointed to the post of minister of finance in the first year of the government of Nādir but it was for less than a year, with the idea of gaining the approval of the Shiʿis, especially the Hazārahs who had resisted the Son of the Water Carrier. But as soon as the foundations of the government of Nādir Khān were firmly in place, he fired this one Shiʿi minister. His firing appears to have come a little after the death of Mullā Fayż Muḥammad Kātib." According to British records, after service as private secretary to Amīr Amān Allāh Khān and manager of the king's private properties, he was appointed by Nādir Shāh in November 1929 as minister of finance, then after a stint as special envoy or minister without portfolio to Qaṭaghan and Badakhshān, he was re-appointed in 1932 as minister of finance and then dismissed in September 1933, well after the death of Fayż Muḥammad. (See Adamec, *Who's Who*, p. 195.)

were known as Shīrwānī, believing themselves to be descended from Anūshīrwān.[58] They [number] 720 households. The Shīrwānīs are Shiʿi. Of the rest [of the Kayānī], some are Shiʿi and some Sunni. The offspring of Āzād Khān Khārānī are also Shīrwānī and Shiʿi. [There is] one [Kayānī] family in Kūhāt. Most of this group [the Kayānīs] has dignity and good morals and lives a modest existence with the Jat people who are their clients.

Jaghatāy Mongols

This group [numbers] 1,250 households. Their homes are scattered throughout the villages in Kūh-i Jamshīdī. They speak Mongolian. Some of this group live in the village of Kakrak, one of the western villages of Ghaznīn, known by the name Hazārah Jīghatū.[59] They are all Shiʿis and some, because of this tie, at the incitement of a certain Sayyid Muḥammad, a student from Karbalā, who had chosen the Akhbārī way,[60] became his followers and thus he [Sayyid Muḥammad] introduced evil thoughts among the people.[61]

---

[58] Anūshīrwān (or Khusraw I Anūshīrwān) a Sāsānian king (r. 531–579 A.D.) was one of the rare pre-Islamic figures to enjoy high regard in Islamic literature and to be held up as an exemplary ruler, as "Anushirwan the Just."

[59] ʿAbd al-Ḥayy Ḥabībī has raised the possibility that the name Jīghatū was derived from the name of a prince who governed in this area in the pre-Islamic period because there is a rock inscription in northern Ghazni where a word has been carved that some have read as "Jīghatū Shāh." (Cited by Yazdānī, Fayż Muḥammad, *Nizhādnāmah*, p. 146, note 1.)

[60] The Akhbārī-Uṣūlī dispute was a major controversy in Shiʿi jurisprudence over the issue of the proper sources of authority, coming to a head in the late 18th century. The Akhbārīs held that only the Twelve Imāms, as known through their teachings and rulings could serve as the basis of legal reasoning while the Uṣūlīs, who eventually prevailed, asserted that the *mujtahid*, the learned legal scholar, was capable of using rational judgment in legal matters and his rulings had to be followed. (See Hamid Algar. "Religious Forces in Eighteenth- and Nineteenth-Century Iran," Chapter 19 in *The Cambridge History of Iran*. Vol. 7 *From Nadir Shah to the Islamic Republic*, edited by Peter Avery, Gavin Hambly, and Charles Melville, Cambridge: Cambridge University Press, pp. 710–16.) Fayż Muḥammad was clearly an Uṣūlī and considered the Akhbārīs to be schismatics.

[61] Yazdānī is worth quoting here although he cites no source: "This Sayyid Muḥammad went to Sublime Karbala and Noble Najaf to learn from Akhbārī scholars and there embarked on the Akhbārī path. After his return, he settled in Jīghatū and won over two or three villages to this path. He built a fort for himself and collected funds from the people living there. Later, tension arose between Akhbārīs and Uṣūlīs until the late Āyat Allāh Shaykh ʿAzīz Allāh Ghaznawī, who was truly one of the great āyatullāhs and a learned professor, put an end to these disputes and reconciled the two groups. Little by little, there came to be more Uṣūlīs than Akhbārīs and today I don't believe that anyone in that region is a follower of the Akhbārī path." (Fayż Muḥammad, *Nizhādnāmah*, p. 146, note 2.).

The Uzbeks Displaced from Their Homeland

One hundred and twenty thousand households, having decided to emigrate from their homeland in [Russian] Turkistān, settled in a small place in the Muqur district which is home to the Tarakī and ʿAlī Khayl people, who speak Afghānī. They also settled in some other locales and pursued the occupation of farming. They speak Persian.

Dīgān

This ethnic group lives in Kunar and Bājāwur. Their language is mostly derived from Sanskrit with a little Persian and Afghānī (Pashto) mixed in and is of Indian provenance. Common folk consider Dīgāns and Tājīks to be the same. But the opposite is the case because Tajiks came to this land and settled after the coming of Islam. The Dīgān on the other hand came before the Tajiks at the time of Dharam and were Hindūs.

*Hindī*s

The group named Jat is found in most districts of the Panjāb. Also a large group lives in Sind among the Balūch, and in Dāmān, Banūn, and around Peshawar. They are farmers. In Balūchistān they are called Chakdāl. A large group called Jat lives in Sīstān and a group known as Āwān settled in Kālah Bagh and in eastern Afghanistan. The Āwān say that they are the offspring of [Imām] ʿAlī (peace be upon him). A people named Parāchi better known as Parānchah live in Kabul and work in the textile trade and in business. A large number of the Gūjars who believe themselves to be Rājpūt live among the Yūsufzāʾī and speak Hindī, Panjābī, and Afghānī. They are subordinate to the Afghans. All are Hindūs and live in the above-
44 mentioned places. |

*Hindū*s

Of the various Sūdar, Katrī, Bīsh, Brahman, Arūrah, and Sikh peoples, approximately 100 households live in and around Qandahar, Ghaznīn, Khūst, Urgūn, Kabul, and Jalālābād and in their dependent villages. **/148/** They earn their livelihoods as shopkeepers, textile dealers, and as clerks in government departments, provincial offices, and municipal dīwāns. Some engage in commerce and money-changing and some work as land owners, brokers in commercial transactions, and as goldsmiths. In contrast with the rest of the Hindūs they eat bread baked in a clay oven [rather than chapattis, fried bread]. In commercial transactions their way of doing business is the opposite of the way the Jews, who are deceitful, do business. [The Hindūs] are straightforward, humble, cool-headed, and well-behaved.

Numerous remains of ancient Hindū, Buddhist, and other structures and temples (*butkhānahs*) are easily dug up in Qandahar, Qalāt, Ghaznīn, the Hazārahjāt, Bāmyān, Kabul, Khūst, and Jalālābād, especially in the mountains and in [mountain] valleys, where idols and ancient utensils may [easily] be uncovered. In some locales like Haddah in Jalālābād and Khwājah Ṣafā in Kabul, which were [sites of] temples and with the passage of time became shrines for Muslims, at this time from those two places the discovery of idols establishes that these were idol temples. In Āqā Sarāy in Kūh Dāman there is a cave called Gazak Tīpū (Brahman temple) which Hindūs consider to be sacred. In Khūshī, Lahugard, there is a spring which the Hindūs imagine to be *tīrtah* [a Sanskrit word meaning any place, person, or text that is holy].

*Swātī*s

This group is of Indian descent and sometimes has the name Dīgān. A number of them live in the subdistrict of Pakalī in Hazārah District, one of the dependencies of Rawalpindi, and in the mountains of that area. Those found in and around Swāt include some Yūsufzā'ī. They [the Yūsufzā'ī of Swāt] live a downtrodden life and speak Afghānī. The Swātīs call them fakirs. /**149**/

*Shalmānī*s

This group took its name from its initial place of residence, Shalmān, along the bank of the Kurram River. They now live in Ilah Dand in Swāt District and are dominated by the Yūsufzā'ī people [there]. The Afghans call them Dīgān without any source or evidence.

*Tīrāhī*s

This group originally worshipped idols and wore the thread (*zunnār*). In the campaign of Sulṭān Shihāb al-Dīn Ghūrī[62] they were ennobled by the religion of Islam. Now a number of them live among the Shinwārī and
45 | speak a language different from Afghānī, a language which came from Sanskrit and includes many Pashtū words.

---

[62] This Ghūrid ruled in Ghaznīn from 1173–1203 A.D.

*Kashmīrī*s

Because of difficult living conditions, a group left Kashmīr, took refuge in northern Afghanistan, [came] to Kabul and even to Qandahar where they earned their livings as common laborers, husking rice (*shālī-kūbī*), baking, shawl-washing, tailoring, embroidering, mending [holes in clothing and cloth], weaving wool, in brokerage, working as porters, cart (dhooli) pullers, and draftsmen. They are established in Swāt, Bājāwur, and Lamqān and they speak Afghānī. Despite being aliens, they are extremely wicked and are troublemakers.

The Kashmīrīs living in Kabul are Shiʿi, weavers of *patū* [fine wool used as a wrap or blanket], narrators of the martyrdom of Imām Husayn (*rawżah-khwān*), and breast-beating mourners. Ḥasan Salīmī, the son of Mullā Āqā Bābā, whose relatives and (immediate) family were draftsmen, went [permanently] to Mashhad.

Kurds and *Rīkāʾ*[63]

The Mukrī and Rīkā, the name of [the latter of] whom was mentioned earlier among the Qizilbāsh, are **/150/** branches of the Kurds who elected to settle in Kabul with detachments of the Nādirid army [in the mid-18th century]. At the outset there were 3,000 households and now nearly 5,000 households live in the Chandāwul quarter under the name "Qart." Two hundred households called the "Rīkā" remain in Kabul's Kūchah-i Darwāzah-i Lāhawrī (Lahore Gate Street).[64] The Rīkāʾīs are Sunni and the Qarts are Shiʿi. The [Qarts] are miserable and are gradually going to Iran but because of greed, avarice, and arrogance, they find no place in Iran either and keep coming back.

Muḥammad Akbar Khān and Ghulām Ḥaydar Khān, son and grandson of ʿAlī ʿAskar Khān,[65] at the time of the uprising of Son of the Water

---

[63] The final *ḥamzah* (ʾ) on Rikaʾ is an unstable letter in Fayż Muḥammad's manuscript (e.g., p. 46, lines 8, 9, 11) and is given here as it appears there.

[64] Cf. Schinasi, *Kabul: A History*, p. 34. She says the residential quarter of the Rīkā was called Rīkākhānah and was north of the Bālā Ḥiṣār which corresponds with the location of Lahore Gate Street. See also her unpublished work, "De la ville historique à la vieille ville," p. 88.

[65] Muḥammad Akbar Khān appears in Fayż Muḥammad, *The History*, vol. 4, p. 663 as composer of a verse admonishing the late Amīr Ḥabib Allāh when he was still a prince and in a fit of sectarian bigotry was trying to convert a Shiʿi *ḥusaynīyah* into a Sunni mosque by hacking out a mihrab with a pickax.

"O shah! See how lofty is our heretical place / That when it is destroyed, it becomes the house of God."

Carrier, left Kabul with their families, went to Harāt and then went on to Mashhad. There they remain in limbo, unable to return.

The Rīkā'īs spend their lives farming their own land holdings, as shopkeepers, and working for others (as nawkars). Since they are comfortable, they do not think about Iran. Instead, they call the Iranians infidels and curse them roundly. This is in contrast to the Qizilbāsh who, out of ignorance, lack of ambition, and hypocrisy, have found no place to find ease or comfort either in Afghanistan or Iran and remain in an abased contemptible state.

Līzagī or *Lakzī*

At the order of Nādir Shāh [Afshār], nearly 500 households of this group settled in Farāh. There they had gardens, farms, estates, and were very well-off. Up until now they have lived a life of ease and honor serving in the irregular cavalry (*sawār-i kushādah*), and as clerks, farmers, and merchants, and they've earned respect. But now due to the tyranny and repression of the government and the murderous assaults by Afghans, they have not had the power to stay and in the solar year 1308/1929 they abandoned their lands, gardens, and houses and emigrated to /151/ Sīstān. The Iranian government welcomed them and by giving them crown lands
46 made them feel safe and secure [at first]. | But [when the immigrants] gained control of the crown lands, through the deceitful behavior of their own elders, they were deprived of the government grant, which caused them disappointment and perplexity.

Armenians[66]

It is a characteristic of Armenians that they go to any country where, with the eye of calculation and avarice, they see that there is a good opportunity to make money. They work hard to achieve their personal ambitions and desires, using every means at their disposal. In the beginning there (was) a (small) number of them in Afghanistan—two families in Peshawar, three in Kabul, and eight choosing to live in Harāt. [Later on], at the order of Amīr ʿAbd al-Raḥmān Khān, the one remaining family in Kabul was expelled to Peshawar. In Harāt, through natural increase, there are now

[66] On the Armenian community in Afghanistan see Jonathan Lee, "The Armenians of Kabul and Afghanistan," in Warwick Ball and Leonard Harrow, eds., *Cairo to Kabul: Afghan and Islamic Studies presented to Ralph Pinder-Wilson*, London: Melisende, 2002, pp. 157–62.

more than thirty families. They are Christians, they read the Old Testament and the Gospels in Greek, and they do not know Hebrew or English.

Qalmāq

Tīmūr Shāh, the son of Aḥmad Shāh Sadūzāʾī, brought a few members of this ethnic group from Balkh to Kabul.[67] The group is of Tātār lineage and was idol-worshipping in Tātāristān. [The shāh] lavished royal favors on its members and assigned them to the affairs of government. Up until now a few still exist but wherever they live it is in a state of anonymity. No one really knows anything about them except the people who live where they do. /152/

Ethiopians (Ḥabashī)

Individual members of this ethnic group were brought to the port of Muscat and were taken as slaves by upper-class people. Most are in Iran and some reached Afghanistan until the slave trade was curtailed and this practice was abandoned. During the era of the Sadūzāʾī sultans, Ethiopian slaves were relied on by the royal family and they were honest and faithful. Nearly 250 households of them existed in all of Afghanistan. Most were in Harāt, some in Kabul, and all were Muslims, the majority Shiʿi but some Sunnis. Every year in Saraṭān (June/July) they would organize a festival called "Qanbar" but in the time of Amān Allāh Khān, it was abolished.

Jews

This ethnic group is of the lineage of Ḥażrat Yaʿqūb (on him be peace) and are known as Banī Isrāʾīl. They are divided into twelve tribes (*asbāṭ*) and are spread throughout all five continents. Most are well-to-do traders and are extremely tricky, treacherous, and deceitful. There are fifty households in Afghanistan and all are in Harāt. They firmly adhere to the Hebrew religion and currently they travel back and forth from Bukhārā to Mazār [-i Sharīf] and Kabul on business. They conduct business throughout Hindūstān by way of Peshawar. They [also] do business in Mashhad and Europe.

[67] Tīmūr Shāh (r. 1773–93) is particularly noteworthy for having moved the Afghan capital from Qandahar to Kabul, trying to put distance between himself and the Durrānī tribes. He began to rely more and more on a non-Afghan military and it is reasonable to assume the Qalmāq played a role in this.

Balūch

47 | Much of their vast territory belongs to Iran while [another] /153/ large area including places like Khārān, Qalāt, Mastung, and Shāl (Quetta) with all their environs and individual dependencies [was] once included in Afghanistan but now is annexed to the territory colonized by the English. Thus these people are not worth mentioning in the total population of Afghanistan except for a small group of them. Of that small band, some are in Qandahar and some in Kabul. There are [also] 750 households in Kajrān who in summer come to the Hazārahjāt to pasture their flocks and then return to their winter quarters come winter. They are Shiʿi and persecuted by the Afghans. There are no other [Shiʿi Balūch] to be found. Also there are a few Balūch in Chakhānsūr and in the region of Kūh-i Malik Siyāh and in Shūrābak and one or two households in various other locales. One of the Balūch of Qandahar, Muḥammad Anwar Khān, son of Aslam Khān, has the rank of general and ʿAlī Akbar Khān, his brother, the rank of brigadier general. Each of their other three brothers also hold [army] ranks. They follow the path of Twelver Shiʿism.

Various Other Individual [Groups]

In every city there are one, two, or several households of people from Sīstān, Qā'in, Birjand, Kirmān, Mashhad, Hamadān, Kāshghar, Chitrār, and Bukhārā. Also there are a number in Harāt who have come from the "Sunni house" of Qā'in. They are a problem for Iran because they advise thieves, highwaymen, and smugglers about the best routes and the [various] halting places. They cause a great deal of harm to Shiʿis. /154/

Dawlatshāhī

Two hundred fifty households of this group are resident in Afghanistan. During the era of the Sadūzā'ī sultans [1747–1826], they were shown much respect and most had a [judicial] position as *qāżī* or mufti. One of Kabul's quarters is known as Kūchah-i Qāżī (Qāżī Street) It is said that they used to be captives and slaves but Aḥmad Shāh released the fetters of slavery from their feet and gave them the title "Dawlatshāhī" (Royal Fortune). However, they consider themselves to be Quraysh.

The Qāżī Khayl of Peshawar is not part of this ethnic group but is from the Amāzā'ī people and of the lineage of the Afghan Mandir. They (the Qāżī Khayl) are well-off, influential, and respected by the English. They have a good natural disposition, are humble, self-effacing, and forbearing.

Jadīd al-Islām

This ethnic group [numbers] approximately 500,000 individuals. They live deep in the heart of the Hindū Kush mountains from Panjshayr and Kutal-i Munjān, Badakhshān to Lamqān, Chitrār, Kāshghar, and the valleys of Arīt, Shamās, Kulmān, Asmār and other places. Included among them are the inhabitants of the Nūr Valley and the valleys of Lamqān, Asmār and other places. Long ago some of them accepted the religion of Islam. As for the rest, in the lunar year 1313/1895–96, Amīr ʿAbd al-Raḥmān[xiv] Khān ordered an army mobilized and they were conquered, made obedient, and accepted the religion of the Best of Men.

48 There is a difference of opinion about their lineage and stock. | Some aver that they are the offspring of Żaḥḥāk-i Tāzī, some that they are Quraysh, and some others that they are Greek and the remnants of /155/ the army of Alexander of Macedon. When one considers their height, facial appearance, and physique, the latter view would seem to be more correct. Their language is an Indian dialect with Sanskrit, Greek, Sogdian, Bhāshah [Pasha'ī?] and other words [mixed in]. They comprise four tribes namely: (1) Kāmūz, (2) Halār, (3) Salār, and (4) Kāmūj and several subsections, their names [based on] where they live: Sūkūy, Tarī, Gūmā, Kambīr, Katār, Bīrah Galī, Chanīsh, Damdū, Dūwaylī Wāy, Kāmah, Gūshtah, Dīnag, Wāy, Kāmūz, and Kāntūz. [Also they are] in the following locales: Kāmdīsh, Waygal, Kambīr, Chīmī, Amīsh, Dīsh, Jāmij, Kīgal, Nasī Girām, Katār, Kalā-yi Gal, Rājgal, Sūnindīsh, Dīwgal, Pandīsh, Dīrī, Gāwāchī, Jamāmīsh, Manj Gal, and Walī Gal. Also, there are other groups named Āmshī, Sanū, Nashī, Jamakah, Ashkāmak, Parūnī, Tuyūnī, Pūnūz, Dīmash, Khullum, Ayrat, Haran Siyah, Wāmā, Chūniyā, Anīshwar, Pashākarī, Kastūz, Pīm, Awrang Siyah, Minchīyāshī, Mandīgal, etc. By the clothing which they produce from goat hair and homespun cotton, they have been and still are known as "Black-clothed Kāfirs" (*kāfir-i siyāh pūsh*) and "Red-clothed Kāfirs" (*kāfir-i surkh pūsh*). Women do the farming. Their raising of animals [is based on] goats. The mountains they inhabit have such fruit- and nut-bearing trees [and vines] as walnut, grape, pomegranate, apple, almond, apricot, jujube, and others, both wild and orchard-grown. They themselves are uncivilized and behave like jungle animals.

Uzbeks (*Ūzbak*) and *Turkmans*

These two ethnic groups make their homes in Afghānī Turkistān, Qaṭaghan, and Badakhshān and are mixed in with Tajiks, Afghans, Hazārahs, and

ʿArabs. They live in and around the cities of Maymanah and Mazār-i Sharīf, /156/ and the towns of Sar-i Pul, Tāshqurghān, Andkhūd, Shibarghān, Ay Bīk, Khānābād, Andarāb, Qunduz, Tāluqān, Ḥażrat-i Imām, and in the dependencies [of those places]. They farm and raise livestock.

The Turkmāns are nomads and felt-tent dwellers and keep busy herding their animals between winter and summer pastures. They [number] approximately 1,500,000 souls.

Except for the Hazārahs and the people of Shighnān and Wākhān, everyone is a bigoted, uneducated, and uncivilized Sunni. And due to tribal differences they are hostile to each other.

All the peoples and tribes which have been recorded here number between 5,700,000 and 6,000,000 subjects of the government of Afghanistan. The rest [of the Afghans] are under the sway of English imperialism. Currently, [Muḥammad] Nādir Khān's surrendering the border tribes to the English and foreswearing any interference in their affairs, has caused great harm. These were the border tribes which ʿAbd al-Raḥmān Khān had prevented the governments of Afghanistan and England from interfering with and he created a solid foundation. For thirty-seven years, from 1310/1892–93 up to now [i.e. 1347/1928–29], the tribes have been continuously fighting the English and killing and plundering them, under the banner of freedom. But now [because of what Nādir Khān has done] the English are free to fortify the border and to make the tribes there obedient. The Russians also have started to make trouble in Turkistān. One wonders where all these things will lead.

Notes

i The print edition (p. 49, line 16) misspells *muḥāwarah* as *maḥārah*. Cf. ms. p. 3, line 8.

ii The print edition inserts an extraneous conjunction (*wa*) here (p. 50, line 5; cf. ms. 3, line 13).

iii The print edition (p. 64, line 13) writes *mīkunand* instead of *mīkunad*. Cf. ms. p. 10 line 17.

iv The print edition (p. 64, line 17) and the manuscript (p. 9, line 20) both have Sulṭān Sulṭān Maḥmūd, an apparent mistake on Fayż Muḥammad's part.

v The print edition (p. 65, line 5) omits the conjunction *wa* in the number twenty-five (*bīst wa panj*). Cf. ms. p. 10, line 3.

vi The print edition (p. 68, line 17) omits the conjunction *wa* between Mahābān and Panjtār. Cf. ms. p. 12, line 3.

vii The print edition (p. 71, line 9) mistakenly gives the spelling as Zirātī. Cf. ms. p. 13, line 13.

viii The print edition (p. 92, line 16) has *qarah bāgh*. Cf. ms. p. 20, line 4. This mistake recurs through the printed text.

ix The print edition inserts an extraneous conjunction (*wa*) before "Daftānī". Cf. ms. p. 21, line 2.

x The print edition (p. 96, line 16) has *qarah bāgh*. Cf. ms. p. 22, line 12.

xi The print edition (p. 98, line 13) misreads Jangīr as Jangīrad. Cf. ms. p. 23, line 17.

xii The print edition (p. 127, line 19) twice misreads "Mullā" as "Mawlā." Cf. ms. p. 35, line 10.

xiii The print edition (p. 129, line 20) misreads *zarkhīz* (fertile) as *zarkhaz*. Cf. ms. p. 36, line 7.

xiv The print edition (p. 154, line 15) misspells "Raḥmān as "Raḥmāniyān." Cf. ms. p. 47, line 23.

APPENDICES

APPENDIX 1

MĪRZĀ ʿABD AL-MUḤAMMAD MUʾADDIB AL-SULṬĀN IṢFAHĀNĪ ĪRĀNĪ, *AMĀN AL-TAWĀRĪKH*, VOLUME 5, PP. 7–130/134

7 An Account of the Tribes and Clans of Afghanistan[1]

In 1340 Hijrī [in this case January–May 1922] when I journeyed to Afghanistan my only purpose for this long trip was first to pay my respects to the sublime and shining threshold of the Afghan revitalizer and the man who gave Afghanistan its independence, the wise, just, and glorious sovereign of the world of Islam and the Muslims, His Majesty Amīr Amān Allāh Khān Ghāzī, king and refuge of the Afghans, through whose kindness we succeeded in paying homage at the threshold of that embellisher of crown and throne. Secondly, my goal was to collect some historical information including an explanation of the condition of the tribes, peoples, and clans of Afghanistan, and the origin of each tribe. Praise God, all that was made easy and provided. The virtuous and highly educated gentleman, Mullā Fayż Muḥammad Kātib, who is a font of sublime perfections and /8/ valuable information, made this writer indebted to the writings of his artistic pen.

Since the origin and complete organization of the tribes of Afghanistan was divided into three original branches whose names are "Sarbanī" (with the velarized marker over the rāʾ [r]), "Ghurghushtī," and "Bītanī" [with the velarized marker over the tāʾ (ṭ)] and this (basic) tripartite division is further subdivided into many branches, therefore in setting out what follows the various lineages of each branch will be written down name by name and tribe by tribe with the name of its locale and homeland and the number of its members.

---

1 As noted earlier, there are two versions of this part of volume five, one is the manuscript held by Fales Library, the rare books department of New York University Libraries, and the other, a reduced-size facsimile edition of the work (Kabul: Riyāsat-i Intishārāt-i Kutub-i Bayhaqī, 2013) produced from the seven-volume Fales Library manuscript. The manuscript of volume five was not originally paginated and when page numbers were added, two page numbers were inadvertently omitted in the pagination, page numbers 28 and 48, although the pages themselves are not missing. The facsimile edition, rather than follow the pagination of the manuscript, re-paginated its version eliminating the two omissions. Readers of this section should know that at page 28 we write 28/29 to indicate the two different page numbers for the same page and at page 48 we write 48/50 and from that point on all the page numbers are given in that format with the print edition page number first. To further complicate matters, the print edition itself omits two full pages of the original, pages 121 and 122. Thus page 118 of the print edition is page 120 in the manuscript but 119 of the print edition is actually 123 of the manuscript. We have thought it prudent to give both page numbers in the text of the translation.

In addition, either because the manuscript was poorly photographed or the photographs were poorly reproduced, diacritics are often very difficult, if not impossible, to distinguish. Therefore the editors have relied entirely on the manuscript.

 | DOI:10.1163/9789004392441_005

The First Sarbanī Tribes and Clans

Sarban (retroflexive *ṭ* over *rā'*), the son of 'Abd al-Rashīd, had two sons: Sharkhbūn, named Sharaf al-Dīn, and Kharshbūn, named Khayr al-Dīn. The eldest son, Sharkhbūn, had five sons: the first was Tarīn; the second, Shayrānī; the third, Miyānah; the fourth, Barīch; and the fifth, Ūrmur. From these five together came the tribes and clans, each lineage of which will be recorded. The first, Tarīn, had three sons whose names were Abdāl, Aspīn, and Tūr. We begin with an introductory account of the Abdālī clan who were of the lineage and descent group from Abdāl.

How the Abdālīs Were Named and [The Name's] Transformation into the Name Durrānī

People who are of the Abdālī lineage say that [first] the name came from Dur. When Dur grew up, they brought him to see Khwājah Abū Aḥmad Abdāl Chishtī who was a great shaykh. Khwājah Abū Aḥmad called him "Abdāl" and that remained his name. Gradually his progeny came to be known as Abdālī. Or perhaps it was because he lived with Khwājah Abū Aḥmad Abdāl for a time as a servant that people called him "Abdāl." In fact, this tradition exists in most of the lands of the East: that a servant is called or named after his master and lord. Then in conversation among Afghans they gradually changed Abdāl to Awdāl until Aḥmad Shāh Sadūzā'ī who was the founder of (Afghan) sovereignty in Afghanistan. In this volume there will be an account of his coming to power, which occurred in 1161/1747. The eminent scholar Mullā Fayż Muḥammad Khān Kātib also writes in volume one of *Sirāj al-tawārīkh* about him in telling about Ṣābir Shāh, a dervish, who gives him the name Durrānī. The present-day Durrānī tribes are the Fūfalzā'ī, Alkūzā'ī, Bārakzā'ī, Mūsāzā'ī /9/ and Panj Pāy (the latter including), Nūrzā'ī, 'Alīzā'ī, Adūzā'ī, Isḥāqzā'ī, Khūkyānī and Mākū. The Sadūzā'ī, of which tribe Aḥmad Shāh Durrānī was a member, is of the line of the offspring of Fūfal. Most of the Fūfalzā'ī and Sadūzā'ī have their homelands in the northern villages of Qandahar, a small number in Khākrīz and Kūhistān and a few in regions to the south and east of that country (Qandahar) such as in Ẕākard, Bālā Qarż, Shūr Andām, and other places including some dependencies of Girishk west of the Hīrmand (River), in two locations in Garmsīr, and in three places to the west of the Arghandāb (River). Most of their developed lands are connected to Shahr-i Ṣafā and the Tarnak Valley and some are in the city of Qandahar. A few households live in Peshawar and Lahore in Hindūstān. Some of this tribe (the Sadūzā'ī) and other Durrānīs live in Multān. The royal family of the Sadūzā'ī resides in Lūdiyānah, India. They are also scattered in the Dīrajāt and other spots. They number some 15,000–17,000 households. Most of them are engaged in agriculture and pass their lives in farming.

The Bārakzā'ī tribe from Which His Majesty the Amīr Ghāzī (Amān Allāh Khān) Comes

The name Bārak (Sulaymān ibn 'Īsā ibn Abdāl) is mentioned [above]. This clan consists of 40,000 households and they live and reside in Arghastān District just south of Qandahar and along the Hīrmand (Helmand) River. They support themselves through agriculture and raising cattle and sheep.

The Chakzāʾī [sic-Achakzāʾī] Tribe a Branch of the Bārakzāʾī Lineage

This tribe has not more than 5,000–6,000 households. Most are audacious, wicked, and seditious. They live in the Kūh-i Kūzhak. It sometimes happens that they raid and plunder their neighbors in the night and they also don't leave travelers alone. Now, a number of them have taken possession of fertile lands belonging to Hazārahs at the order of high government officials. The pastures for their stolen flocks and cattle have been the locales of Khwājah ʿImrān, Tūbah, and Kuhsārān in the past but now they have made the Hazārahjāt their summer pastures and they raid in those lands. Pasture for their camels /**10**/ has been the wasteland to the north and east of Shūrābak but all of the Hazārahjāt is now their grazing area.

The Alkūzāʾī Tribe

The Alkūzāʾī tribe numbers 17,000 households. They make their homeland especially in Jaldak located in the eastern part of Qandahar, in Arghandāb, and in Panjwāʾī northwest especially west of that country (Qandahar). Similarly, they are found scattered in the northwestern locales (of Qandahar) like Khākrīz, the mountainous areas of north and northwestern Maywand or Maymand District, Chakah District and Sarbān Qalʿah on the east bank of the Hīrmand River, in several places south of the city of Qandahar, also in the mountain district named Nafl wa Bāghrān of Zamīn Dāwar located in the northwest, in the district of Nawzād and Kunjāk located in the western part of Zamīn Dāwar, and others in Harāt, Ghaznīn, and Kabul. They earn their living also as farmers, cattle owners, and in trade. The Nawzānī and Sarkānī branches of the lineage of this tribe reside in the Chahchah District of Rawalpindi and are affluent and wealthy. One branch of the Sarkānī tribe resides in Gaz, Jalālābād. A few households of this tribe are located in Duābah-i Panjāb, some in the environs of Peshawar, a few households in Balūchistān, and some households in the Deccan of Hindūstan. They spend their lives in utmost comfort and pleasure. The late Zarghūnah, the mother of Aḥmad Shāh Abdālī Sadūzāʾī, was from this tribe, which has produced such an illustrious and royal son.

The Mūsāzāʾī Durrānī Tribe

The Mūsāzāʾī Durrānī tribe is too small to count. It is counted along with the Nuṣratzāʾī people, a branch of the Bārakzāʾī. At the time of recording the Bārakzāʾī tribe, they will be mentioned, too.

The Nūrzāʾī Tribe of the Panj Pāy Durrānī

This tribe, like the Bārakzāʾī, numbers 40,000 households. Most are located in Garmsīr, the Dihrāwud District of Qandahar, and in the northern mountains of that land (Qandahar) which touches on the Hazārahjāt. They also make their homes in Farāh District, Isfizār as far as the territory of Harāt, in the sand desert south of Qandahar, in the village of Sapīrawān or Sapīd Rawān of Qandahar, which is located along the east bank of the Arghandāb River, and (in) the west part of the city of Qandahar. /11/ They own a great deal of farmland and pasture-land. They also have many cattle and sheep and in winter they take them to their winter quarters and in summer they take them to Kūh-i Siyāh Band of Ghūr for summer grazing. They are comprised of two groups (*dastah*), one *dastah* occupies itself with agriculture and the other *dastah* spends its days taking care of the herds of cattle and flocks of sheep.

The ʿAlīzāʾī Tribe of the Panj Pāy Durrānī

This tribe is counted as having 18,000 households. They live in Zamīn Dāwar, Qandahar. Their properties and lands are well-irrigated by open channels (*rūdbār*). The Hīrmand River is the border between them and the Alkūzāʾī tribe. The lands of the Alkūzāʾī which are located across (the river) from the lands of this tribe (are watered by) underground aqueducts. Some households of the ʿAlīzāʾī who had gone to Panjāb became wealthy. One very large household of this tribe lives in Islām Kadah of Ḥasan Abdāl, three miles west of that town and are the owners of several villages and hamlets.

The Adūzāʾī Tribe of the Panj Pāy Durrānīs

This tribe numbers approximately 6,000 households. They inhabit several villages of Maʿrūf District, two villages of Dihrāwud District, and three villages of Garmsīr District. They earn their livings like the rest of their neighbors [in agriculture and animal husbandry].

The Isḥāqzāʾī Tribe of the Panj Pāy Durrānīs

This tribe numbers 12,000–13,000 households. They inhabit the edge of the sand desert along the banks of the Arghandāb River west of Qandahar as far as Qalʿah-i Bust, and in a few other places in the lower part (*pāyān-hā-yi*) of Chakah District on the east bank of the Hīrmand River. A few of them are found in Garmsīr, Farāh, Isfizār, and Lāsh wa Juwayn District southeast of Harāt and north of Yalistān, which belongs to the government of Iran. Also, a small number of them are also zamindars. Now, all the owners of cattle and sheep once having gone to the environs of Balkh for summer pastures, gradually got places there and chose to reside there permanently.

The Khūgyānī and Mākū Tribe of the Panj Pāy Durrānīs

/12/ This is a very small tribe. They have no separate district or place of their own. Some are in Qandahar, a group of them is also included among the Nūrzāʾī tribe and pass their time there. This tribe is known by two names: "Big Khūgyānī (Khūgyānī-yi Kalān)" and "Little Khūgyānī (Khūgyānī-yi Kūchak)." The Khūgyānī of Qandahar are scattered about. The Khūgyānī of Ghaznīn have several forts of their own. The village of Mākū is adjacent to (the village of?) the Khūgyānī and thus is remembered by the name Khūgyānī.

All the aforementioned tribes of the Durrānī Afghans have several *zāʾī*-s (subclans) the mention of all of which would require a large book. To be brief, (all these different *zāʾī*-s) would total eight [hundred thousand] to one million people, i.e. ten lakhs. Up until now, there has been no census of these people registered in the Census Bureau (*daftar-i iḥṣāʾīyah*). They say that Nādir Shāh Afshār conducted a census of them and counted 60,000 households and all these 60,000 were Durrānīs. Many of the rest of the tribes who lived and were intermingled among (the Durrānīs) were not counted (by Nādir Shāh). Their number has certainly increased by now. The total that has been written here has been copied from *Kitāb-i Ḥayāt Khān Afghān* which was composed in 1281/1864–65.[2]

The Tūr, Son of Tarīn, Tribe Known as Tūr-i Tarīn

This tribe numbers 13,000 households. Their place of residence is Fūshanj District which today is subject to the Government of England. Its being separated off from Afghanistan is recounted by both *Sirāj al-tawārīkh* and *Amān al-tawārīkh* in relating the unfolding of events in 1295/1878 during the reign of Amīr Muḥammad Yaʿqūb Khān. In short, Fūshanj District is located on the southern side of Durrānī territory separated (from it) by the Kūh-i Kūzhak. West of (Fūshanj) is Shūrābak, the territory of the Barīch tribe, and to its south is the territory of Shāl separated from it by Kūh-i Taktū. Fūshanj District is 80 miles long from northeast to southeast. The occupation of this tribe is raising cows and camels and working at agriculture. They also engage in commerce. They carry their stock to Qandahar and Sind and exchange it or sell it. Many sayyids also live in this district and their occupation is mercantile trade. /13/

The Aspīn, Son of Tarīn, Tribe Known as Aspīn-i Tarīn

This tribe is smaller than the Tūr-i Tarīn and resides in Darrah-i Zhūrah, Tal, and Chityālī. Between their territory and the Tūr-i Tarins there is a small section of the territory of the Kārgar (*sic* Kākar) tribe. Consequently they share the traditions and customs of both the Tūr (Tarīn) and the Kākars. All three aforementioned districts where the Aspīn-i Tarīn live are contiguous. However, towards Darrah-i Zhūrah close to Kūh-i Chapar which is where (the valley) begins the (topography of the) mountain is tortuous with deep defiles and because of that there is no open wide place to traverse it. The plain of Būrī and Chityālī is open and the land of Chityālī is comparable to Sīwī in terms of revenue yield except the soil's "air" in Sīwī is much better.

The Tribe of Shayrānī, the Second Son of Sharkhbūn

The Shayrānī tribe, whose lineage is to Shayrān, descended as follows: Shayrānī had one son named Chār. Chār had three sons—Jalwānī, Wadam, and Harīpāl. From Jalwānī comes the Sālār Khayl, Marwat Khayl, Kūngarī, Yangī Khayl, Sapanzāʾī. and Mahār. From Wadam came Bāyir. From Bāyir came Ranjar, Sanjar,

[2] Muḥammad Ḥayāt Khān, *Ḥayāt-i Afghānī*, Lahore, 1867.

and Aḥmad. From Sanjar came the Mas'ūd Khayl, Ghuryā Khayl, Ibrāhīm Khayl, Ismā'īl Khayl, and Ya'qūb Khayl (clans). From Wadam came 'Umar and from 'Umar came Ḥamīm and from Ḥamīm came the Ūbah Khayl, Ḥusayn Khayl, Mūs(ā?) Khayl, and Dawlat Khayl whose names will be mentioned again.

The Tribe of Bāyir, Great-Grandson of Shayrānī

This tribe inhabits a region south of the homeland of the Miyān Khayl who will be mentioned in their proper place. Their occupation is trade. Nearly 5,000 households of them live in the wasteland (*ṣaḥrā*) of the Kūh-i Sulaymān. Several notable households reside in Qandahar and Tapah Sūzanā'ī which is in the environs of that country (Qandahar) and is adjacent to the territory of Arghandāb. In the environs of Kabul, Lahūgard, Jalīlābād [*sic*] and Gaz District (Jalālābād) they have several flourishing villages. They number 700 households and are scattered all over. /**14**/

The Tribe of Harīpāl, Wadam's Brother

The Kīpzā'ī tribe is from one of the sons of Harīpāl. They have their homes in the mountainous region adjacent to the territory of the Wadam tribe south of the Gūmal Valley. They are very peaceful and quiet people.

The Tribe of Jalwānī, Son of Chār, Son of Shayrānī

Their situations and stories are not known in any detail. However, a few households of them have gone to Hindūstān as muhājirs and there dispersed and live. Due to the fact that their numbers are quite small and they have scattered they have not been counted among the large Afghan tribes.

The Tribe of Miyānah, the Third Son of Sharkhbūn

This tribe is dispersed and doesn't live in one place. Because their numbers are so small there is also very little known about them. The Tūgh people of Bangash District and others, some in the environs of Qandahar and some like the offspring and progeny of Shakūn who are called "the junior tribe" (*qawm-i kihtarān*), are settled on territory in Gurāng District.

The Tribe of Gharshīn, Son of Miyānah

Several households of this tribe live in Burhān District, one of the dependencies of Rawalpindi, Hindūstān but most live in the western mountains of Afghanistan subject to Qandahar. They call this tribe Gharshīn for this reason: In the Afghānī language they call a mountain *ghar* and green is *shīn*. Since the [founding] father of this tribe had prayed to a barren mountain and because of his prayer the mountain turned green and bloomed, they (his tribe) then gradually became known by this name. Today his family is highly respected and ordinary people make pilgrimage to see them. The grave of La'l Shāh, a person from this tribe, is a place of pilgrimage for various tribes and he is counted as one of the great saints and shaykhs.

The Tribe of Barīch, the Sons and Grandsons of Barīch, the Fourth Son of Sharkhbūn

Most of this tribe lives in Shūrābak. North of Shūrābak is the territory of the Durrānī tribe. To the south are mountains held by /15/ the Ibrāhūy (or Brāhūy) Balūch tribe. To the east is Kūh-i Khwājah ʿImrān and to the west the Rīgistān sand desert. Shūrābak is located in the middle of these four boundaries. To each boundary it is six miles across [i.e. the land of Shūrābak is six miles square.] The lands of the Balūch lie in the southwest section of the district and are well-developed and flourishing. The Lūrah River, which flows from the Fūshanj Plain irrigates the farms of Shūrābak. The residents of Shūrābak number 3,000 households. This tribe is divided into four branches and practices agriculture using camels not oxen, and like the Arabs [who use oxen] of the environs of Chahrah, Sūq al-Shuyūkh, Markaz, Shaghāfiyah, Samā, Ūchahārah, they make their homes of grass (reeds). In their own dialect they call [those houses] *gazaki*. The tribes of Yalīzāʾī, Chūpānzāʾī, Shakarzāʾī, Basūkzāʾī, Badalzāʾī, Shaykh Nāʾit, Mardānzāʾī, Manhīnzāʾī, Bārakzāʾī (this Bārakzāʾī is a different Bārakzāʾī from the one already recorded), Basāzāʾī and Zakūzāʾī are related to Barīch.

The Tribe of Ūrmur, the Fifth Son of Sharkhbūn

The five divisions of the Ūrmur tribe namely Khīkanī, which is 100 households; Khurram Khānī which is 80 households; Mulātānī, which is 100 households; Bīkanī, which is 260 households; and Jarānī, which is 40 households thus the total number of households of this tribe is counted as 580. Their homeland is in Kān-i Kurram in the Masʿūd Wazīrī Tribal District. Nearly 1,000 households of this tribe 550 years ago because of famine and inflation left their homeland there and fled and went to Lahūgard District located south of Kabul in the town of Bar[akī] Barak and to Peshawar and a group also having gone to Hindūstān made its home there.

The Tribe Related to Khayr al-Dīn Known as Kharshbūn, the Second Son of Sarahban

Kharshbūn, the second son of Sarah Ban [*sic*—Sarban] produced three sons: the first, Gund;[3] the second, Jamand or Zamand; and the third, Kānsī. We will begin by writing about the sons and grandsons of Gund and then we will write about the tribes and progeny of these three brothers.

Gund had two sons, the first Shakhī or Khashī and the second Ghūryā. Khashī took two wives /16/ and from them produced three sons namely Mand, Makh Bāmak, and Tarak. We will record the lineage of each of them separately. Mand

3 The Iṣfahānī scribe who copied out volume five for ʿAbd al-Muḥammad "Muʾaddib al-Sulṭān" was inconsistent in distinguishing the letter 'k' (*kāf*) from the 'g' (the Persian *kāf*). In deciding whether to translate here as "Kand" or "Gund" we have consulted other sources, notably the translation of *Makhzān-i Afghān* and J. Wolfe Murray, *A Dictionary of the Pathan Tribes of the North-West Frontier of India*, Calcutta: Office of the Superintendent, Government Printing, India 1891 (2017 reprint).

had two sons, ʿUmar and Yūsuf. ʿUmar had one son, Mandir. Mandir also took two wives and produced three sons from them—ʿUs̱mān, Utmān, and Razar. ʿUs̱mān had two sons—Kamāl and Amā. Kamāl, the son of ʿUs̱mān from whom the Kamālzāʾī are descended, had three sons—ʿInāyat, Akā, and Yūsuf. ʿInāyat had two sons—Mashrān and Kas̱rān. From Mashrān came the Mīkhā Khayl, Mūsā Khayl, Abā Khayl, Būsī Khayl, Karā Khayl, Amā Khayl, ʿAmū Khayl, Ṣiddīq Khayl, Nīk Pay Khayl, and Zayd Khayl.

From his second son, who was Kas̱rān, came Maʿdūd Khayl, Qāsim Khayl, Rustam Khayl, Khumārī Khayl, Balar Khayl, Jānī Khayl, Alah Dād Khayl, Barah Khān Khayl, Nūr Mal Khayl, Dīkan Khayl, Muḥammad Khayl, Tatar Khayl, Yaḥyā Khayl, Saʿdī Khayl, Sikandar Khayl, Ḥamzah Khayl, Dalw Khayl, Bāmū Khayl, Bāy Khayl, Bahādur Khayl, Shakarī Khayl, Muḥammad Khān Khayl, Ismāʿīl Khayl, Bābū Khayl, Rajā Khayl, Būnah Khayl, Muḥtasham Kūr, Sulṭān Kūr, Sayr Khānī, Ḥaydar Khān Khayl, Shāhū Kūr, Shadar Khayl, Shādī Khān, Ḥājat Khayl, Muḥram (Muḥarram, Maḥram?) Kūr, Shahbāz Khān, Jalāl Khān, Haybat Khayl, Mushwānī Khayl, Buland Khayl, and Nazd Khayl. Later, they named all these Kas̱rānzāʾī.

The Amāzāʾī Tribe, the Progeny of Amā, the Second Son of ʿUs̱mān, Being Known as ʿUs̱mānzāʾī

The Amāzāʾī tribe came from Amā who had two sons—Dawlat, known as Dawlatzāʾī, son of Amā, and Ismāʿīl, known as Ismāʿīlzāʾī. The Ḥusaynī Khayl, ʿAmbārah Khayl, Ṣuḥbat Khayl, Matī Khayl, Rānī Khayl, Ismāʿīl Khayl, Khayr al-Dīn Khayl, ʿAlī Khān Khayl, Pāyandah Khayl, Ghāzī Khānī, Dalā Khān Kūr, Kabūr Khayl, Qābil Khayl, Malī Khayl, Maʿrūf Khayl, Sangar Khayl, Bahrām Khayl, Baliyā Khayl, Dar Khān Khayl, Saʿīd Kūr, Khānah Khayl, Khwājah Khiżr Khayl, Sulṭān Maḥmūd Kūr, Bāzīd Khayl, Saʿīd Khayl, Sulaymān Khayl, Jamāl Khayl, Jalāl Khayl, Nīk Nām Khayl, Mullā Mīrū, /17/ Mīrdād, Alahdād Khayl, Pīr Khayl, Payraw Khayl, Mīr Hawas Khayl, Nuqrah Dīn Khayl, ʿĪsā Khayl, and Jānī Khayl are all related to Dawlat and known as the Dawlatzāʾī, the son of Amā, known as Amāzāʾī, son of ʿUs̱mān known as ʿUs̱mānzāʾī.

The other line includes Būqah, Baqqāl Khayl, Jūnah Khayl, Sikandar Khayl, Yaʿqūb Khayl, Ṭāwūs Khayl, Palar Khayl, Wadar wa Bam Khayl, Ūryāzāʾī and Isḥāqzāʾī all descend from Ismāʿīl known as Ismāʿīlzāʾī, the son of Amā, the son of ʿUs̱mān.

Most of the aforementioned Amāzāʾī tribe resides in Yūsufzāʾī District along the river and in Sadhūm. They are subject to and obey the English government. Of them all, ʿAmbārah Khayl or Mubārak Khayl and, a bit of Pīr Khayl and Bām Khayl, and a few others make their homes in Charūrī and Nagarī located in Mahāban District. They have 4,000 battle-ready armed men.

The Utmān Tribe Known As Utmānzāʾī, the Son of Mandir, Son of ʿUmar, Son of Mand, Son of Shaykhī [sic—Shakhī] son of Gund, son of Khayr al-Dīn Known As Kharshbūn, Who Was Mentioned Above

Utmān had four sons—Ākāzāʾī, Kanāzāʾī, ʿAlīzāʾī, and Sadūzāʾī. These were of the Ākāzāʾī lineage: Chār Ṣadah, Ibrāhīmzāʾī, Shārah Khayl, ʿArabzāʾī, Bilkhayrzāʾī, Pīrakzāʾī, Shaykh Malī Khayl, Saʿid ʿAlī Khayl, Khiżr Khān Khayl, Nīkī Khān Khayl,

Khudādād Khayl (I)smā ʿīl Khayl, Pāyū Khayl, Pātū Khayl, Madad Khayl, Ūryā Khayl, Ṣāḥibī Khayl, Iskandar Khayl, Manṣūr Khayl, Pāyandah Khayl, Nīk Nām Khayl, Mazīd Khayl, Jahāngīr Khayl, Khānah Khayl, Ḥabīb Khayl, Jūnā Khayl, Kābul Khayl, Bahrām Khayl, Amarzāʾī Khayl, Awsahī Khayl, Shāh Dam Khayl, Saʿīd Khayl, Sham Khayl, Būsī Khayl, and Sikandar Khayl.

The Kanāzāʾī Tribe Which Was Descended from Kanā, the Second Son of Utmān

The Kanāzāʾī tribe which is known as the Kanāzāʾī [*sic*] and are the descendants of the second son of Utmān who is known as Utmānzāʾī. Originally Kanā had two sons named Sih Ṣadah and Bābakr. Bābakr is known as Bābakr Khayl. /18/ From Sih Ṣadah came Sanā Khayl, Bārah Khayl, Shamakī Khayl, Haymah Khayl, Āzī Khayl, and Chūr Khayl. From Bābakr Khayl came Ghulām Khayl, Muḥammad Khān Khayl, Mūsā Khayl, Rukyā Khayl, Mazīd Khayl, Khwājī Khayl, Ḥaydar Khān Khayl, Khān Khayl, Bārū Khayl, Khālah Khayl, Salīm Khān Khayl, Būchah Khayl, Rasū Khayl, Haybū Khayl, Bārah Khayl, Laʿlah Khayl, and Yaltā Khayl.

The ʿAlīzāʾī Tribe From the Lineage of ʿAlī, the Third Son of Utmān

The ʿAlīzāʾī tribe who are of the lineage of the third son of Utmān are as follows: ʿAlī known as ʿAlīzāʾī had four sons—Būbā, known as Būbā Khayl; Panj Pā; Samū, known as Samū Khayl; and Ismāʿīl, known as Ismāʿīl Khayl. From Būbā Khayl came Mīkī Khayl, Brahīm Khayl, Haybū Khayl, Mand Khānī, and Saʿīd. From Panj Pā came ʿUmar Khayl, Pāyandah Khayl, Kālā Khayl, Shāwis Khayl, and Bābā Khayl. From Samū Khayl came Sū Khayl, ʿAlī Khayl, Dawī Khayl, Khwājī Khayl, and Chārandah. From Ismāʿīl Khayl were born also Saʿīdū Khayl, Pāyandah Khayl, Bīrā Khayl, Zangī Khayl, Jūkī Khān, Adīn Khayl, and Ṭāhir Khayl. All (parts) of this tribe are the lineage of Utmān, son of Mandir, son of ʿUmar, son of Mand, son of Shakhī, son of Gund, son of Kharshbūn, are called Utmānzāʾī. Most of them reside in the eastern part of Yūsufzāʾī territory along the Abāsīn River and on the southern slopes of Kūh-i Mahāban and they spend time in the locales of Lūpī, ʿAynī, and Kūnah in Garhārī District. A few of them are also found on the skirts of Kūh-i Mahāban.[4]

Of them all, the Saʿīd Khwānī [*sic*] Khayl live in Kalābat in Hazārah-i Chach District. The rest of the ʿAlīzāʾī live in Tūr Bīlah and elsewhere in the hamlets connected to those places.

An Account of the Sadūzāʾī Tribe Who Were of the Lineage of Sadū, the Son of Utmān

The Saduzāʾī tribe being originally of the lineage of Sadū, son of Utmān, are divided as follows: Originally Sadū had two sons namely Zalū and Darī from whom came the Zalūzāʾī and Darīzāʾī (tribes). Zalū had two sons, /19/ Abāy, known as Bābā Khayl, and ʿUmar, known as ʿUmar Khayl. From Abā(y) came two offspring: one known as Nuṣrat Khayl and one known as Dawlat Khayl. (From them) came the

[4] The author (or copyist) may have inadvertently left something out here such as distinguishing these mountain slopes from the immediately preceding ones.

Ṣībū Khayl, Sīsī Khayl, Bahlar Khayl, Ṭā'ūs Khānī, Ābap Khayl, Panj Pāy, Tājū Khayl, Zakariyā Khayl, Ra'nā Khayl, Asū Khayl, Ghālī Khayl, Darī Talī, Manṣūr Khayl, Khiżrī Khayl, Bābū Khayl, Khūgā Khayl, Makā Khayl, and Ḥasan Khayl, all of whom are remembered as Nuṣrat Khayl and are related to Nuṣrat, son of Abā, son of Zalū, son of Sadū, son of Utman.

The Qāsim Khayl, Mūtī Khayl, and Brāhīm Khayl who are named after their mother, a lady called Marjānah, are called Marjānah Khayl. Dunyā Khayl, Sih Ṣadah, Hīm Khayl, Ḥasan Khayl, La'lū Khayl, Pandū Khayl, Shahdār Khayl, Ya'qūb Khayl, Ma'rūf Khayl, Barah Khān Khayl, Sharghah Khayl, Khachī Khayl, Rādū Khayl, Būdalah Khayl, 'Azīz Khayl, and Adīn Khayl are all descended from Dawlat known as Dawlatzā'ī, son of Amā son of Zalū, son of Sadū.

The 'Umar Khayl Tribe of the Lineage of 'Umar, the Second Son of Zalūy Known As Zalūzā'ī, son of Sadū

The tribe known as the Zalūzā'ī [*sic*—'Umar Khayl] are from the lineage of 'Umar known as 'Umar Khayl, the son of Zalūy who is known as Zalūzā'ī son of Sadūy known as Sadūzā'ī, son of Utmān, known as Utmānzā'ī. 'Umar had three sons—Mā'ī known as Ma'ī Khayl; Basūy, known as Basū Khayl; and Muḥammad, known as Muḥammad Khayl. Ṭāwūs Khānī, Shammah Khayl, Kurram Khayl, Shayrzād Khayl are descended from Ma'ī Khayl. Mazīd Khayl, Ma'ī [Matī?] Khayl, Sulṭān Muḥammad Khalīl, Rajū Khayl, and Qumī Khayl are descended from Basū Khayl. Nīk Nām Khayl, Būqān Khayl, Khamal Khayl, and Mīr Khayl are descended from Muḥammad Khayl. These three sons are known as 'Umar Khayl.

The Darīzā'ī Who Are the Lineage of Darī, the Second Son of Sadū, Who Has Been Written About

The Darīzā'ī are descended from Darī. Darī, the son of Sadū, has three sons—Mīr Aḥmad, known as Mīr Aḥmad Khayl; Bīzār, known as Bīzār Khayl; and Khadūy, known as Khadū Khayl. Thus Abū Khayl, Nawrang Khayl, /**20**/ Bārah Khayl, Chajū Khayl, Jalāl Khayl, Jānah Khayl, Barah Khān Khayl, Ṣiddīq Khayl, Darwīzah Khayl, Dūd Khayl, Ḥasan Bīk, Ādah Khayl, Tarkiyā Khayl, Dilāzāk wa Bārā Khayl, Khudādād Khayl, Balar Khayl, Alahdād Khayl, Aḥmad Khayl, Ḥabīb Khayl, Sikandar Khayl, Jalāl Khayl, Gadāy Khayl, Mālā Khayl, Muḥammadī Khayl, Sar Gund Khayl, Agā Khayl, Adī Khayl, Shabkhān Khayl, Māhā Khayl, Qamarāl wa Jānā Khayl, Salṭū Khayl, and Ūryā Khayl are all related to Mīr Aḥmad known as Mīr Aḥmad Khayl, the son of Darī.

Qarah Khayl, Kajū Khayl, Jalū Khayl, Ādam Khayl, Pāndū Khayl, Bakhshi Khayl, Mazīd Khayl, Būmī Khayl, Mīrdād Khayl, Walīdād Khayl, Guwār Khayl, and Banī Khayl are connected to Bīzād, known as Bīzād Khayl, son of Darī, and they are called Darīzā'ī.

'Uṣmān Khayl, Bīrī Khayl, Wadar 'Uṣmān, Raḥmat Khānī, Afżal Khānī, Bahādur Khānī, La'l Khayl, Bām Khayl, Madā Khayl, Sulaymān Khayl, Balū Khayl, Tarakī Khayl, Ja'far Khayl, Khālū Khayl, Ziyārat Khayl, Anīs Khayl, Bāzīd Khayl, 'Ayb Khayl, Jadū Khayl, Bangī Khayl, Būdilā Khayl, Bayān Khayl, Chūryā Khayl, Qāsim Khayl, Mūsā Khayl, Khwājah Hawas Khayl, Alahdād Khayl, and Sargīn Khayl, are connected to Khadūy known as Khadū Khayl, the third son of Darī, known as Darīzāʾī, and all were said to be Darīzāʾī.

The abovementioned tribes that are the sons and grandsons (progeny) of Sadū son of Utmān are all called Utmānzāʾī. Of the descendants of Sadū are a branch of the grandsons of Utmān. In the western part of their homeland are many estates and they live well. The already mentioned offspring of Zalū, the son of Sadū, in the branch of Abā Khayl, and the family of Raʿnā Khayl, live in Zuhrah Rāīs. The ʿUmar Khayl reside in Māyazī Ṣawāpī. The mentioned sons and grandsons of Darīzāʾī who have been recorded have their homeland with the offspring of Mīr Aḥmad Khayl in Kār [with the velarized 't' over the 'r') Manārah and Dand [with the velarized 't' over both 'd-s'] Salīm Khān, and Marghaẕ. Bīzād Khayl spends their time in Kalābat [velarized 't' over the 't'] while the Khadū Khayl are in Chaglaʾī and Panj Tār. The people of Bām Khayl have their homeland in Bājah.

The Tribe of Razar or Rajar, the Son of ʿUmar, Son of Mand(ir), Son of Shakhī, Son of Gund, Son of Kharshbūn

/**21**/ The tribe of Razar, son of Mandir is as follows: originally three sons came to Razar son of Mandir: Mānī, known as Mānīzāʾī; Malik, known as Malikzāʾī, and Akū, known as Akū Khayl. All three were from the same wife. Two other sons, namely Khiżr, known as Khiżrzāʾī, and Maḥmūd, known as Maḥmūdzāʾī, were from another wife. So there was a total of five sons. Mānī had three sons—Bāzīd, Bahlūl, and Aḥmad, known as Aḥmad Khayl.

Surghat, Aḥmad Khayl, Panj Pāy, Āzī Khayl, Ibrāhīm, Dāwud Khayl—known as Daʿwat Khayl, Hayb Khayl, Khiżr Khayl, Mūsā Khayl, and Sulaymān Khayl are through Bāzīd, son of Mānī.

Alahdād Khayl, Ṣiddīq Khayl, Zāngī Khayl, Sulṭān Khayl, Ḥamzah Khayl, Jūnā Khayl, Mubārak Khayl, ʿAlīkhān Khayl, Kālah Khayl, Jānib Khayl, ʿAẓamat Khayl, Bābī Khayl, Sindī Khayl, Janāb Khayl, Dawrān Khayl, Mardān Khayl, Burhān Khayl, Mīr Khayl, and Bāt Khayl are through Bahlūl son of Mānī, son of Razar, known as Mānīzāʾī.

Khwātūn Khayl, Aḥmad Khayl, Ismaʿīl Khayl, Alahdād Khayl, Karīmdād Khayl, Sardār Khayl, Muḥammad Khayl, Kamāl Khayl, Shamʾī Khayl, Sayyid Khayl, Bahlūl Khayl, Sulaymān Khwāh, Bābā Khayl, Bahrām Khayl, Zayyidah Khayl, Balar Khayl, Matah Khayl, Darwān Khayl, Bangī Khayl, Fātūn Khayl, Langar Khayl, Sih Sadah, Maʿrūf Khayl, Bādīn Khayl, Yūnus Khayl, Yaʿqūbī, and Nīkī Khayl are the offspring of Malik, son of Razar, and carry the name Malikzāʾī.

Khiżr known as Khiżrzāʾī, son of Razar, had four sons—ʿUmar known as ʿUmarzāʾī, Shamūrī known as Shamūrīzāʾī, Gadāy known as Gadāy Khayl, and ʿAyp known as ʿAyp Khayl. Aḥmad Khayl, Nijābat Khayl, Ṣāḥibī Khayl, Dāwud Khayl, Bahrah Khayl, Ghulām Khayl, Chūrah Khayl, Mughul Bīk Kūr wa Brāhīm Khayl, Rūgī wa Pāyandah Khayl, Būs Khayl, and Saʿīd Khayl are through Shamūrī all of whom are his and offspring and are remembered as Shamūrīzāʾī and Khiżrzāʾī.

Maḥmūd known as Mamūzāʾī, the fifth son of Razar, had three sons—Ākā known as Ākā Khayl, Būyāy, known as Būyāy Khayl, and Khānī, known as Khānī Khayl. Thus Walī Khayl, Nīk Khayl, Mīr Khayl, Kamal Khayl, Ṣāḥibī Khayl, Aʿẓam Khayl, Būstān Khayl, Zawāl Khayl, Agar Khayl, Muḥammad Khayl, Ghaznī Khayl, and Mīrdād who are the offspring of Ākā, through him are called Ākā Khayl and /22/ Mamūzāʾī.

Similarly Aḥmad Khayl, Dawlah Khayl, Pāyandah Khayl, ʿAlī Shayr Khayl, Sayf al-Dīn Khayl, Shāhī Khayl, Qarah Khayl, Muḥammadī Khayl, Shāndī Khayl, Sulṭān Kūr, Nikū Khayl, Yaḥyā Khayl, and Bahrām Khayl, who are the offspring of Būyā, son of Muḥammad, are called Būyā Khayl and Mamūzāʾī.

Also Khamārī Khayl, Shādīn Khayl, Khiżr Khayl, and Sargīn Khayl who are the offspring of Khānī are called Khānī Khayl and Mamūzāʾī.

The majority of this tribe lives in the Yūsufzāʾī District. The Khiżrzāʾī have their homes in Shīwah. The Mānīzāʾī are established in Tarlāndī and Dākī. The homeland of the Malikzāʾī is Yārḥīn. The Mamūzāʾī are established and settled in the territory of Naw Dahanah, Shaykh Khānah, and Astūrūz.

The Tribes of the Lineage of Yūsuf, Son of Mand, Son of Shakhī, Son of Gund, Son of Kharshbūn, and Known as the Yūsufzāʾī

The Yūsufzāʾī are as follows: Yūsuf, known as Yūsufzāʾī, son of Mand, had five sons—ʿĪsā, Mūsā, Mālī known as Mālīzāʾī, Akūy known as Akūzāʾī, and Ūryāy known as Yārī Khayl.

Thus Ḥasanzāʾī, Yaʿqūbzāʾī. Madā Khayl, and Akāzāʾī, through ʿĪsā, whose sons they were, are called Yūsufzāʾī.

Similarly, Ilyāszāʾī, Sālārzāʾī, Ayyūbzāʾī or Āyib Khayl, Burhān Khayl, ʿAli Shayr Khayl, Kambū Khayl, Milī Khayl, Jalāl Khayl, Ḥasan Khayl, Miṣrī Khayl, Bahrām Gur, Dād Khayl, Khān Gul Khayl, Hujūm Gūr, Māmūlī Gūr, Hūtī Khayl, Mazīd Khayl, Fatḥ Khayl, Wilāyat Khayl, Ṭāwusī Kūr, Brāhīm Kūr, Ṭāʾwus Khayl, Haymal Khayl, Sulṭān Khayl, Kamāl Khayl, and Mihtar Dād Khayl all of whom are the progeny of Sālār, son of Ilyās, son of Mūsā, son of Yūsuf. Sālārzāʾī, Ilyāszāʾī, and Yūsufzāʾī are referred to by the respective intermediate links (i.e. Sālār, Ilyās, and Yūsuf)

Panj Pā and Makhūzāʾī, through Māsū, a brother of Sālār are remembered as Ilyāszāʾī and Yūsufzāʾī.

Gadāyzāʾī, Ḥasan Khayl, Bahrām Khayl, ʿAlī Shayr Khayl, Sīn Khayl, ʿAʾishahzāʾī, Bā Khayl, Khadīn Khayl, Mūsārah Khayl, and Khākīzāʾī, who are all progeny of Tājī and Mamī, brothers of Sālār and sons of Ilyās, for that reason are also called Yūsufzāʾī.

Also Dawlatzāʾī, Mandīnzāʾī, Barkhīzāʾī, Ismāʿīlzāʾī /23/ Chighrzāʾī, Nurzāʾī, Abāzāʾī, and ʿĪsūzāʾī are the progeny of Mālī, known as Mālīzāʾī, son of Yūsuf, and are called Yūsufzāʾī.

The Tribes of the Lineage of Akūy Known as Akūzāʾī, the Son of Yūsuf Known as Yūsufzāʾī

The Yūsufzāʾī tribe that is of the lineage of Akū is segmented as follows: Akū was the fourth son of Yūsuf and he had four sons—Khwājū known as Khwājūzāʾī, Abā known as Abāzāʾī, Sharak, and Bāzīd known as Bāʾīzāʾī, all from one wife. Rānī, known as Rānīzāʾī, was from another wife. All had fine offspring.

Thus Adīnzāʾī, Shamūzāʾī, Nīk Pay Khayl, Abā Khayl, ʿĀyishī Khayl, Shamīzāʾī, Sabt, Jūnā, Yalīzāʾī, Sulṭān Khayl, Naṣr al-Dīn Khayl, and Pāyandah Khayl who were the sons of Khwājū and for that reason are called Khwājūzāʾī and Akūzāʾī.

Suhayl, Abā Khayl, ʿAzīz Khayl known as Bāzī Khayl, Khān Khayl, Sharghā Khayl, Bītā Khayl, Tarkhān Khayl, Miqdād Khayl, Mīr Aḥmad Khayl, Khānā Khayl, Pāchah Khayl, Bāzīd Khayl, ʿAlī Khayl, Kandā (Gundā?) Khayl, Nāguwāl, Shamālī Khayl, Ḥājī Khayl, Ismāʿīl Khayl, Basū Khayl, ʿAlī Khān Khayl, Shayr Khān Khayl, Bārah Khayl, Shāhū Khayl, ʿAyyār Khayl, Aḥmad Khayl, Khānagī Khayl, Bashīr Khayl, Ghālī Khayl, Mandir Khayl, Isḥāq Khayl, Jalāl Khayl, Ismaʿī l Khayl, Rustam Khayl, Dil Khah Khayl, Pīrū Khayl, Bankūrkah or Nabkūrkah Khayl, Qāsī Khayl, Malik Dīn Khayl, Pāʾī Khayl, and Dūr Khayl and it was through Suhayl, ʿAzīz, and Abā who were the sons of Suhayl—and he was the son of Bāzīd, the fourth son of Akū—that they were named Bāʾīzāʾī and Akūzāʾī.

Also the Matūrāzāʾī, Alā Khayl, Bahlūl Khayl, Mūsā Khayl, Khatūn Khayl, Darwān Khayl and Dawlat Khayl who were of the line of Sulaymān son of Bāzīd, the fourth son of Akū were known as Bāʾīzāʾī and Akūzāʾī.

The Abā Khayl, Bābī Khayl, Barat Khayl, Akā Khayl, Maʿrūf Khayl, Maghdūd Khayl, Pīr Khayl, Bāzīd Khayl, Mīrā Khayl, Dādī Khayl, Zānkah Khayl, Barchī Khayl, and Khuwaydād Khayl, who were of the line of Bābū, son of Bāzīd, son of Akū, are called Bābūzāʾī, Bāʾīzāʾī, and Akūzāʾī.

The Tribe From the Line of Rānī, Fifth Son of Akū, Son of Yūsuf and for This Reason are Called Rānīzāʾī, Akūzāʾī, and Yūsuf [*zāʾī*]

/**24**/ The Rānīzāʾī tribe is formed as follows: Rānī, known as Rānīzāʾī, the son of Akūy known as Akūzāʾī, had three sons—Jīlam, Utmān, and Makhah [*sic*—Makhad].

Thus ʿAlī Khayl, Bahrām Khayl, Khwāzā Khayl, Yalī Khayl, ʿAbdal Khayl, Shihābah Khayl, Mīr Khān Khayl, Ghaybī Khayl, Sulaymān Khayl, Mullā Khayl, and Machā Khayl who are the progeny of Jīlam, son of Rānī, carry the name Rānīzāʾī.

Similarly, Sīn Khayl, Madī Khayl, and Brāhīm Khayl the sons of Utmān son of Rānī are known (both) as Utmānzāʾī and Rānīzāʾī.

Also the Sulṭān Khayl, ʿAmbārah Khayl, Mardān Khayl, Kar Khayl, Ismāʿīl Khayl, ʿUs̱mānī Khayl, Landah Khayl, ʿAzīz Khayl, and Dūr ʿUs̱mān, the progeny of Makhad, third son of Rānī, are known as Makhad Khayl and Rānīzāʾī.

The Yūsufzāʾī tribes which regularly are named reside in a mountain area that is remote and vast.

The progeny of Mandir son of ʿUmar brother of Yūsuf—ʿUmar and Yūsuf as already recorded were the sons of Mand, the son of Shakhī, son of Kand, son of Kharshbūn. or, the progeny of Yūsuf, son of ʿUmar—are all called Yūsufzāʾī. Today the progeny of Mandir are separate tribes and live on both sides of the Kabul River and in Miyārān Samah located north of the Indus River. They call it Samah despite the fact that they have made it their homeland.

The Yūsufzāʾī tribes reside in the mountains of Sawād (Swat), in Bunīr, Panjkūrah, and Dīr in Panjkūrah. The inhabitants of these places, Yūsufzāʾī and others, number ten lakhs or one million persons. The Yūsufzā'ī themselves are 300,000 and the Mandir 200,000 for a total of 500,000. The other 500,000 are Afghans from a variety of tribes and clans like the Khatak, Muḥammadzā'ī, Utmān Khayl, and others. The Muḥammadzā'ī or Mumanzā'ī are the progeny of Zamand, the second son of Kharshbūn who has been mentioned above. They are attached to the Yūsufzā'ī and make their homes in Hasht Nagar. In aggregate they number 30,000 persons. The Utmān Khayl are the progeny of Burhān, the grandson of Kakī, second son of Karrān.[5] There is some difference of opinion as to whether Karrān is of the Sarah Bān [Sarban] lineage; some call this tribe sayyids and some say it's Afghan. They have written that it is in the genealogy of the Kakiyānī Kharshbūns through the lineage of Makh or Mak, son of Shakhī, son of Gund, son of Kharshbūn. In short, of all the Karrānī tribes which will be recorded from here on, one is the Utmān /25/ Khayl. Since their homeland is situated in the mountains along the Swat River in east Bājāwur among the Yūsufzā'ī, they are mentioned here. One should mention their place of residence and the numbers of those who live in the mesopotamian region between the Kabul River and the Swat River. They number 7,000 persons.

The Tarkalānī Tribe, Known as the Tarkānī

The Tarkānī tribe is the progeny of Tarkalānī, the son of Shakhī, son of Gund, son of Sharkhbūn, as was written above. The tribe of Tarkalānī, known as Tarkānī, was divided into four branches. The first is the Salārzā'ī, which resides on the land of Barāwul and Chār Ming and numbers 15,000 individuals. The second, Mamūnd or Māmūnd, which is divided into two sections, the Kakāzā'ī and the Dūr Mamūnd, numbers 14,000 individuals. The third is Sūzānī which numbers 10,000 individuals and the fourth is the Ismāʿīlzā'ī which also numbers 10,000 people. These (four) live in Bājāwur District on the west side of which are the Hindū Kush mountains, on the east the mountain homeland of the Utmān Khayl, on the north the Hindū Kush mountains on whose lands the people of Kāfiristān, now known as Nūristān reside, and on the south the Kūh-i Muhmand. The Bājāwur Valley is level, open and pristine. From the east slanting towards the north the valley is twenty-five miles long and in the south slanting towards the west it is twelve miles wide.

The Ṣāfī better known as Ṣābī

The Ṣābī tribe is made of six subdivisions whose names are: Qandahārī, Masʿūd, Gurbuzū, Dahīr, Kākī, and Narā'ī Ḥāwī Khayl. They all consider themselves Sarah Banī (Sarbanī) Afghans. Sometimes they consider themselves to be from the brother and son of Ghiljā'ī. However there is no doubt that the father of this tribe was one of the *waṣlī*[6] successors of Shakhī a grandson of Kharshbūn. In any

[5] The orthography of this name throughout this section of *Amān al-tawārīkh* is a little odd. Normally a doubled consonant is only written once and either the context or the diacritic signifying a doubling (the *tashdīd*) would alert the reader. But here Karrān is written uniformly with two 'ra'-s thus Kar-rān.

[6] *Waṣlī* is contrasted with *aṣlī*. The latter means a blood relative; the former means a relationship other than by blood—adoption, marriage, or clientage, for example.

case, most of them have their place on the land of Sūrkamar, one of the areas of Bājāwur located between the Tarkalānī tribe and the place of the Muhmand tribe and most villages of Swat have one or two households of them living there. A few live in Tagāb located east of Kabul and northwest of Lamqān and in Gaz, east of Jalālābād. /26/

The Tribe With a Lineage to Ghūryā, Known as Ghūryā Khayl, Second Son of Kand, Son of Kharshbūn

The Ghūryā Khayl tribe, which is the lineage of Ghūryā, son of Gund, son of Kharshbūn are as follows. It was indicated earlier that from Ghūryā, son of Gund, son of Kharshbūn there were four sons—Dawlatyār, Khalīl, Chamkanī, and Zīrānī—whose offspring will be listed. Dawlatyār, the eldest of Ghūryā's sons, had two sons—Muḥammad and Dāwud, known as Dāwudzāʾī.

Thus the Mūsā Khayl, Katah Khayl, Bāzīd Khayl, Dawlatzāʾī, Yaḥyāzāʾī, Nūrzāʾī, Bakhtiyār, Mūsāzāʾī, Bānīzāʾī, Khwājahzāʾī, Tājūzāʾī, ʿUmarzāʾī, Bāqīzāʾī, Ḥājjī Khayl, Sayyidū Khayl, Abūzāʾī, Ḥalīmzāʾī, Tārikzāʾī, Ismāʿīlzāʾī, Natāzāʾī (?), Sih Pāy, ʿUsmān Khayl, Burhān Khayl, ʿĪsā Khayl, Shāh Manṣūr Khayl, Mūriyah Khayl, Utmānzāʾī, Ākāzāʾī, Rāmī Khayl, Māmā Khayl, Naẓar Khayl, Bārah Khayl, Sulṭān Khayl, Atū Khayl, Daryā Khayl, Mūsā Khayl, and Khākā Khayl, who is recorded as Khūkā Khayl in *Tārīkh-i Ansāb*, Anmar Khayl, Matā Khayl, Būtū Khayl, Żarb ʿAlī Khayl, and Harū Khayl, the sons of Mūsā and Kūkū, who are the sons of Muhmand are called Dāwudzāʾī. This tribe is well-known in the dialect of the Kūz Muhmand and Bar Muhmand (the words *kūz* and *bar* mean "lower" and "higher"). The Kūz Muhmand number 15,000 households who live in the flat lands in the vicinity of Peshawar, Hindūstān. The Bar Muhmand tribe resides in the mountains that are bounded on the west by a mountain located in the western part of the territory of the Utmān Khayl up to the Kabul River and the Gaz River which flows from the west from Kūh-i Kāshghar and runs to the Kabul River. To the north, their land abuts the southern edge of the bed of that river (the Gaz River?). To the south, it is bounded by the Khaybar which is the route for caravans between Kabul and Peshawar; on the north side, by the Hindū Kush and Asmār; and to the east, the lands and mountains of the Yūsuf[zāʾī] tribe. They [the Bar Muhmand] are numbered at 15,000 to 20,000 households. After the demarcation of the frontier as has been written in *Amān al-tawārīkh* and *Sirāj al-tawārīkh*, most of [their land] became part of the land of the English. Of all (the Muhmand land) Laʿlpūrah, Kūshtah, and Kāmah with their mountains and valleys were attached to, and came under the control of, the government of Afghanistan. /27/

The Tribes and Clans of the Lineage of Dāwud Known as Dāwudzāʾī the Second Son of Dawlatyār ibn Ghūr[yā]

The Dāwudzāʾī tribe which is of the lineage of Dāwud, the second son of Dawlatyār the first son of Ghūryā is organized in this fashion: it is written that he had three sons—Mandakī, Māmūr, and Yūsuf. The Māmūzāʾī, Ḥusaynzāʾī, and Nīkūzāʾī are from the sons of Mand[akī] and so are related to the Dāwudzāʾī. Similarly the Mājū Khayl, Muḥammad Khayl, Saʿīd Khayl, Yūnus Khayl, Bāzīd Khayl, ʿAlīzāʾī, Bībīzāʾī, and Bāgilzāʾī who are of the sons of Māmūr, the second son of

Dāwud. Through him they are related to the Dāwudzā'ī. Also Mandir, Wafā Khayl, and Ṣafāzā'ī who are of the progeny of Yūsuf and through him are related to Dāwudzā'ī. On flat lands that are dependencies of Peshawar, south of the Kabul River, they have their homeland. They are numbered at 13,000 households.

The Tribes from the Line of Khalīl, the Second Son of Ghūryā, Known as Ghūryā Khayl, From Whom There are Several Clans

Sālārzā'ī, Afūzā'ī, Nūrzā'ī, Matīzā'ī, Akāzā'ī, Bārūzā'ī, Tarak, and Sāk, the sons of Khalīl, the son of Ghūryā, through him are related to the Ghūryā Khayl and in their dialect they are called Khalīl's tribe. They number 8,000 households and include 15,000 armed warriors. Their area of residence is also the flatlands of Peshawar. A few households of this tribe along with a few households of the Muhmand tribe and some others live in Maḥallah-i Bar Durrānī and are known as Bar Durrānīs.

Tribes from the Line of Chamkanī, the Third Son of Ghūryā, Known as Ghūryā Khayl

Chamkanī, whom they call Chūkanī in the Afghānī language, had three sons—Āzī, known as Āzī Khayl; Khānī, known as Khānī Khayl, and Khwājah, known as Khwājah Khayl. Consequently, Daryā Khān Khayl, Darī Palārah (who is called "Darī Palārah of three fathers" in Afghānī), Naṣr Khayl, Brāhīm Khayl, Tuwaykī Khayl, Khūnīzā'ī, Ḥusayn Khayl, Lashkarī Khayl, **/28/29/**[7] and Qamar Khayl, who were offspring of Āzī, are called Āzī Khayl and Chamkanī.

Mamūt Khayl, Badī Khayl, Gūrgah Khayl, Ambārak Khayl, Sulṭān Khayl, Balājuwā Khayl, Muṣṭafā Khayl, Tūlah Khayl, Jamāl Khayl, and Shayr Khān Khayl, who are the offspring of Khānī Khayl, the second son of Chamkanī, are known as Chamkanī.

Similarly, Darī Khayl, Shūlī Khayl, Ḥakīm Khayl, Walī Khayl, Fatḥ Khayl, Mīrzā Khayl, Gul Shayr Khayl, Jalāl Khayl, and Langar Khayl are said to be offspring of Khwājah Khayl, the third son of Chamkanī. The Chamkanī people are scattered. A group of this tribe have their homes in Peshawar District. [But] most make their homeland in Sapīd Kūh north of Kurram and southwest of Jalālābād. They can raise 9,000 armed men.

The Tribes and Clans of the Line of Zīrānī, Fourth Son of Ghūryā, Known as Ghūryā Khayl Son of Gund, Son of Kharshbūn

This tribe has no family tree. Their homes are somewhat scattered in Nangarhār and other places. They are attached to the Tājīk people and for this reason are known as Tājīks.

[7] As noted above, the manuscript pagination skips the number '28'.

The Mullāgūrī Tribe and How They Got Their Name

This tribe comprises four khayls: the first is Bahār Khayl, the second is Tār Khayl, the third is Aḥmad Khayl, and the fourth, Dawlat Khayl. On the tribal lineage (*nasab*) there are different accounts. This much is clear: they are said to be Muhmand by a non-blood relationship (*waṣlī*). There is another story that one day a few men of the tribe were to be punished for highway robbery. At the same time, a certain mullah and scholar by mistake was taken as one of the robbers. Regarding the punishment, one of the robbers in Afghānī said to another (robber), "Mullā Gūrī" i.e. "Do you see the mullah who was captured as one of us thieves?" After that mullah was freed from that [near-fatal] abyss, his offspring were called Mullāgūrī. They are mixed in with the Muhmand in the Kūh-i Muhmand and most of them live in Tātar Valley. They occasionally engage in highway robbery and bloodshed and [otherwise] pursue rain-fed agriculture. Their numbers are calculated at 700 individuals.

The Tribes and Clans of the Line of Zamand or Jamand, Second Son of Kharshbūn, Son of Sarban

Zamand, son of Khayr al-Dīn known as Kharshbūn, had five sons—Khwīshakī, Katānī, Bangī /29/30/ known as Bangīzāʾī, Maman or Muḥammad known as Mamanzāʾī or Muḥammadzāʾī, and Tūkhī. Thus Shūryānī, Khalafzāʾī, Tūzāʾī, Chanūzāʾī, Shihābanzāʾī, ʿĀrifzāʾī, Ibrāhīmzāʾī, Muḥammad, ʿĀshūzāʾī, Ḥīnzāʾī, Mahlīzāʾī, Bahdīnzāʾī, ʿĪsā, ʿAlīzāʾī, Utmān, Shak, Badā, Mūsā, Salmāk, Ismāʿīl al-Dīn, Amchūzāʾī, Kazlāni, Zīrzāʾī, ʿAzīzzāʾī, ʿUmarzāʾī, and Batakzāʾī, were the offspring of Khwīshakī, the first son of Zamand and through him, who was the second son of Kharshbūn, son of Sarban, they carry the name Sarbanī.

Similarly, the ʿUmarzāʾī, Ālāzāʾī, Mullāzāʾī, ʿĪsāzāʾī, Mūsāzāʾī, Khadr, and Sabīl, who are the offspring of Katānī, the second son of Zamand, are called Sarbanī.

Bangī, the third son of Zamand remained without sons.

The Ilyāszāʾī, who are called Chār Ṣadah, and the Bārakzāʾī, who are remembered as Parāng, Batūzāʾī, ʿUmarzāʾī, Utmānzāʾī, Tahdūzāʾī, Parchah Khayl, Ḥawāzāʾī, Shamūzāʾī, Faṭimahzāʾī, Tūrumzāʾī, Tangī, Razar, and Shayryād are Sarbanī through Maman whose offspring they are. He was the fourth son of Zamand.

Banīzāʾī, Amchīzāʾī, Pāchūzāʾī, Jamalzāʾī, and Manṣūrzāʾī are from a grandson of Tūkhī, the fifth son of Zamand son of Kharshbūn. Through him they are said to be Sarbanī.

In the beginning, all the abovementioned tribes and clans that are related to Zamand had their homelands in the environs of Qandahar like Arghiyān [Arghastān/]and other places. Later they came to Fūshanj District and occupied that place. From there the Tarīn tribe, whose name was previously recorded, drove them out by force so some of them went to Multān and the sons and grandsons of Khwīshakī, the first son of Zamand [first] went to Ghaznīn, [then] set off for the Ghūrband Valley north of Kabul and for Ghūrband District itself. Now they live in those locales. A few had no choice because of difficulties [in surviving] but to leave their homes [in Ghūrband] and settle in the city of Quṣūr east of Lahore. Due to assaults and attacks against them by the Balūch, the Batakzā'ī, Ḥīnzā'ī, 'Ārifzā'ī, Shābanzā'ī, Kazlāni, Salmāk, in order to forestall further attacks from the Balūch, attacked them and the Balūch chose to settle in Bargalī located to the west of Quṣūr and so they stood as an obstacle to the Balūch.

Similarly, the 'Azīzzā'ī, Chanūzā'ī, and Brāhīmzā'ī settled to the east of that place (Quṣūr) in the locale of Bargalī. Because of internecine fighting, a few of them were expelled from the tribe and settled in the town of Tāndah. Presently, not very many from this tribe are to be found in Afghanistan except a very few in Fūshanj and Qandahar District who live in downtrodden conditions. **/30/31/** A branch of the tribe of Khwīshakī have their homeland in the Ghūrband Valley. A few live in Hasht Nagar and several households in a locale adjacent to the Kūh-i Muhmand north of the Kabul River and the Khaybar Valley. Those who live in Quṣur, Lahore are called "Afghans of Quṣūr" and in the Quṣūrī dialect are called Patāns. The Muḥammadzā'ī clan of the offspring of Zamand live in Hasht Nagar, Chār Ṣadah, Tangī, Naw Shahrah, Parāng, and other places. The whole Zamand tribe is reckoned at 10,000 households.

The Tribes and Clans from the Line of Kānsī, the Third Son of Kharshbūn, and They Are Called Sarbanī

The offspring of Kānsī included the Alūzā'ī, Zhamryānī, Katīr, Kūhyār, Muḥammadzā'ī, Shinwārī, Sām, Siyān, Mūsalīgh, Salmat, Humar, Shaykh Mal Khayl, Khūkā Khayl, Mīrdād Khayl, Pīrū Khayl, Sangū Khayl, Sarakī Khayl, and Salmān Khayl. The Shinwārī tribe of those tribes related to Kānsī lives in Nangarhār. There is no information on the situation of any other Kānsī tribes except for a few households scattered about in various places. Some are also found in Hindūstān and the Deccan. The Shinwārī, who are known as a Kānsī tribe, because of their homeland being adjacent to the Khaybar Valley are called "Khaybarī."

The people of the Khaybar, other than the Bar Muhmand who have been recorded earlier, are the three tribes of the Afrīdī, Arūkzā'ī, and Shahnawārī. All of them are thieves, highway robbers, harass people, and are bloodthirsty. The Shahnawār tribe is numbered at 15,000 households. They live in Bājāwar District, the Ashīkal Khāk Gaz Valley, and other places. The known original homeland of the Shahnawār is Hazār Nāw.

Of the Shinwārī, the Sangū Khayl has 4,000 armed fighting men. They too are highwaymen and wicked people. They have their safe havens and residences in Sapīd Kūh of Jalālābād to the east of the homeland of the Khūgyānī people.

The Tribes and Clans of the Line of Ghurghusht, the Brother of Sarban, Second Son of Qays 'Abd al-Rashīd

Ghurghusht, the second son of Qays 'Abd al-Rashīd, known as Patān, had three sons—Dānī, Bābī, and Mandū. Dānī, the first son, **/31/32/** had four sons (Kākar, Nāghar, Bītī [Pītī], and Dāwī). The offspring of Kākar, son of Dānī, son of the aforementioned Ghurghusht, were Shām Khayl, Yūnus Khayl, Mūsāzā'ī, Tarah Gharī, Sargarī, Darbī Khayl, Damar, Jalāl Khayl, Khatan Khayl, Bakrān Khayl, Shādī Khayl, Bājū Khayl, Ayyūb Khayl, Mandūzā'ī, Tājūzā'ī, Mamā Khayl, Mastak, Mamī Khayl,

Zan Ghūzī, Tabarruk, Shīrād, Jah Rām, Abā Bakr, Ḥīn, Anchzāʾī, Charmī Khayl, Pindār, Karkarātū, Saptan, Sūrān, ʿĪsāzāʾī, Walīzāʾī, Yaʿqūb or Kībzāʾī, Tāran (Tāran is *waṣlī*), Sanzar or Sanjar-i Sūrān, Yūnus Khayl, Sālār Khayl, Sūdānzāʾī, Shādzāʾī, Angūzāʾī, Fāṭimahzāʾī, Anūzāʾī, Ādamzāʾī, ʿUmar, Husām, Sitām, ʿAlī Khayl, Barāt Khayl, Harmzāʾī, Utmān Khayl, Kīway, Khiżr Khayl, Arpī or ʿArgi Khayl, Awdal or ʿAbd Allahzāʾī, Sanītā, Yūsuf, ʿĪsā, Pītī, Marzāʾī, Ghūrī Nānī, Badāzāʾī, Shādūzāʾī, Ḥusayn Khayl, Yāsīn Khayl, Shams al-Dīn, Shamūnzāʾī, Atūzāʾī, Muḥammadzāʾī, Rajarzāʾī, Abā Bakr, Sūrī, Malīzāʾī, Pūkhīzāʾī, Amīzāʾī, Akāmzāʾī, Shāzali, Tarkūzāʾī, Shamʿūnzāʾī, Ibrāhīmzāʾī, Qabūl, Asmām, Sulaymān Khayl, Ayyūb, Adū Khayl, Shakūr Khayl, Dādar, Sabāk, Aḥmadzāʾī, Kamālzāʾī, Abū Saʿidzāʾī, Mardānzāʾī, Jalāl, Rawīzāʾī, ʿAyn al-Dīn, Abuʾl-Maʿālī or ʿAbd al-Mālī, Pīsh al-Dīn, and Shādī. All of these are called the Kākar tribe. This tribe, which is the seed of one of the four sons of the abovementioned Ghurghusht, has its homeland in an extensive mountain region. North of that is the land of the Ghiljāʾī tribe. Northwest of that mountain region is Arghasān District and a part of Tūbah, the residence of the Achakzāʾī tribe, a branch of the Durrānī tribe. Southwest of it is Balūchistān, a piece of Aspīn-i Tarīn District, and Kūh-i Sulaymān. The mountains in which they live have valleys with a flat area (*maydān*) and a total extent of 100 by 100 miles. The known homelands of the Kākar people have been Tūrah, Marghah, Barshūr, Narīn, Tūkī, Hunah, Kanchūʿī, and Būrī. The population of this tribe has been said to be as high as 18 lakhs (1,800,000) or [as low as] 5 lakhs. Now they say they number only 9,000 by virtue of the progress of the world (*taraqqī-yi kawnīyat*) The [actual] number of them therefore cannot be known because where are the hundred thousand and the million and where the 9,000?

The Tribes and Clans of the Line of Nāghar, the Second Son of Dānī, Son of Ghurghusht

/32/33/ Nāghar had two sons: Yunus and Mish. Barandū, Turk, Salāḥ, and ʿAbd al-Raḥmān were the sons of Yūnus and Chandar, Wasīlatī, Handar, Palkat, Banādū or Fād, and Tīrū were the sons of Mish. These are mixed with the Kākar tribe and have no territory or place of their own.

The Tribes and Clans of the Line of Panī, the Third Son of Dānī, Son of Ghurghusht

The offspring of Panī are: Sāhang, Khitānī, Marghānī, Sitan, Utmān Khayl, Shadī Khayl, Marghistan, Qāsim, Zamrī or Marzī, Dahyāl, Naṣrzāʾī, Pak Khayl, Anzar or Ashkhar Khayl, Mūlazāʾī, Ḥusaynzāʾī, Mūsā Khayl, Bulbul, Ḥamzah Khayl, Sīnzāʾī, Mafdūdzāʾī, Ḥasan Khayl, Kamālzāʾī, Jalālzāʾī, Bahrzāʾī, Ḥalālzāʾī, Mānīzāʾī, Bahdīnzāʾī, Khadūzāʾī, Aḥmadzāʾī, Shālimzāʾī, ʿUmarakzāʾī, Karmūzāʾī, Shādīzāʾī, Shīrūzāʾī, Karamzāʾī, Ṭūṭīzāʾī, Dārūzāʾī, Ādīnahzāʾī, Tawallazāʾī, Malīzāʾī, Khānūzāʾī, Kānūzāʾī, Khwājakzāʾī, Bābzāʾī, Marsīnzāʾī, Kabulzāʾī, ʿAlī Khayl, Bābarzāʾī, Larzāʾī, Aṣghar Khayl, Haybat Khayl, Darī Palārī, ʿUmar Khayl, Mamīzāʾī, Mardū Khayl, Bābakrzāʾī, Khūrak, Sāmī, Masʿūd Khayl, Gurbuz, Wadīr, Ayyūb, Shakūn, and Lahūn. Through Panī they are all called Ghurghushtī and this tribe (the Ghurghushtī) also includes the Kākars. They have their residences in Yahway and Dādar.

The Tribes and Clans of the Line of Dāwī, Fourth Son of Dānī, Son of Ghurghusht

Damar, Humar, Khūndī, Bulbul, Sikandar, Mūsā, and ʿAlī are the offspring of Dāwī. Of them Khūndī is *waṣlī*-related and the others are *aṣlī*. This tribe is also attached and connected to the Kākar. The Khūndī are by origin Khujandī [from Khujand] and sayyids.

The Tribes and Clans of Bāpī, Second Son of Ghurghusht

/33/34/ Mīrzāʾī, Sarū, ʿAzrāʾīl, Katūzāʾī, Shīlūyzāʾī, Najīzāʾī, Yāsīnzāʾī, Jandarzāʾī, Idrīszāʾī, and Ṣāyibzāʾī are the offspring of Bāpī son of Ghurghusht. They are not more than 4,000 individuals and have built their homes in Qandahar and Qalāt. Most of them make their living by retail trade and are well-off.

The Mandū Khayl, who are the offspring of Mandū, third son of Ghurghusht, does not have many clans. Whatever there are are called Mandū Khayl. This tribe has its homes on two sides of the Zhūb Valley from which Kūh-i Sirhind and Kūh-i Bāgh branch off. These mountains run on the east side (of the valley) towards the north and they stretch to Sar Maghah which touches the Gūmal [Valley].

The Gadūn Tribe Which Considers Itself of the Kākar Tribe and Was Not Mentioned Among the Kākar Tribes Who Have Already Been Described

As far as we understood, Sāhang, the first son of Panī, son of Dāni, son of Ghurghusht, also had two sons other than those already mentioned. And both those two fled because of internal conflicts. A few spent some time in Sapīd Kūh of Jalālābād and after that made a place for themselves in Hazārah Chach. Since they considered the Bītī tribe and the Kākar to be one tribe they call themselves Kākar. In any event, the Gadūn are known for having two lineages: Salār and Manṣūr. Thus, the Matkhūzāʾī, Atūzāʾī, Sulaymānzāʾī, ʿĪsā Khayl, ʿAbd al-Raḥīmzāʾī, Muḥammad Khayl, ʿAli Shayr Khayl, Qalandar Khayl, ʿAlī Khayl, Dawlat Khayl, and Dāwud Khayl have all been related to Salār.

ʿUmarzāʾī, Gawār Khayl, Qamar Khayl, Yaʿqūb Khayl, ʿĪsā Khayl, Karam Khayl, Bārah Khayl, Alāwzāʾī Khayl, Walī Khayl, Qāsim Khayl, Shāhī Khayl, Alahdād Khayl, Khwājah Rustam Kūr, Adīnzāʾī, Matīzāʾī, Dawlahzāʾī, Yaʿqūbzāʾī, Ḥasanzāʾī, Īdū Khayl, Tūrah Khayl, Zakariyā Khayl, ʿAbbās Khayl, Shāmānzāʾī, Bahlūlzāʾī, Khiżrzāʾī, Shāʾibzāʾī, Māmāzāʾī, Khalīlzāʾī, and Amrāzāʾī (Umrāzāʾī?) have all descended from Manṣūr.

The majority of the Gadūn tribe related to Salār have their homes in the mountain region located in Hazārah Chach District on both sides of the Dūrtā River connected to Ūrash. Those people of Gadūn who have their homes along the Abāsīn River located west of Kūh-i Mahāban are called Mahāban. In Sanskrit, *mahā* means big and *ban* means jungle. Since there was a big jungle there, they are called Mahāban. The Gadūn tribe comprises 1,000 households. Moreover, /34/35/ the Matkhūzāʾī clan of the offspring of Salār live in the locale of Bā Bīnī. Also, the Sulaymānzāʾī clan of the offspring of Salār have homes in the hamlets of Pādah, Shanī, Kūlākar, Pūlā Achap Lī located in Mahāban. The Aldūzāʾī and Dawlahzāʾī clans, offspring of Manṣūr, number 500 households and live in Bīk in

Maydān-i Ḥāmin Kūh. And 1,500 people of the Ghurghusht tribe are established in the Deccan, Hindūstān. Likewise, the ʿAlī Khayl, Abū Saʿīdzāʾī and others of the Kākar tribe who are Ghurghushtī and comprise 5,000 households are established in the districts of Hindūstan such as the town of Kūhand, one of the dependencies of Rohtak, and other places. These people between 96 and 132 households of the Kākar tribe live … mostly there are many more because 4,000 individuals have been counted from them.[8]

The Bītī, Known as Bītan, Tribes and Clans

Like the offspring of Sarban and Ghurghusht, the Bītī are the descendants of the well-known ʿAbd al-Rashīd. It is necessary to begin with mention of the offspring of Bītan, the third son of ʿAbd al-Rashīd. Shaykh Bīt, the son of ʿAbd al-Rashīd, who was known as Bītan, had three sons—Ismāʿīl, Raspūn (i.e Warsapūn, Warsabūn), and Kajīn—and one daughter—Bībī Matū, from whose belly and the loins of Shāh Ḥusayn Ghūrī came all the Ghilzāʾī tribes and clans.

Thus, Ibrāhīm, with his sons such as Rūtānī and Kūtī are related as *waṣlī* kin. And Biman Dādgarī (?), Yūsuf Khayl, Tunguz Lānī, Lashkarī, Abū'l-Faraḥ, Bāghī, Bālmīr, Shahmīr, Band, and Mazyānī with his own grandsons, Marūchākī, Hīran, Hamdānī, Niswānī, Bashūr, Khākī, Niyāzī, Mullā Khayl, Tājū Khayl, Chīnī, Shāh Malik, Bābī Khayl, Ram Dīv, Sīkrī, and Gaz Būnī, as well as his [more distant] seed like Jabalī Khayl, Mandī Khayl, Alif Dīn Khayl, Jānī Khayl, Ḥasan Khayl, Dalālī Khayl, Samarzāʾī, Darī Khayl, ʿUmar Khayl, Jangī Khayl, Galī Khayl, Sarmat Khayl, Shan Khayl, Mānī Khayl, Dūn Khayl, Matah Khayl, and Rikāzāʾī, along with his grandsons like Ādam Khayl, Rasūl Khayl, Maʿrūf Khayl, Khwājī Khayl, Char Gul Khayl, Raḥīm Dād Khayl, and Gharūn with the clans descended from him like Sītī, Arūkzāʾī, Darakī, Zarkanī, Bānī Khayl, Ghūrīzāʾī, Darī, and Shaykhi along with his clans like Darī Palārī, Fatḥ Khayl, Chalāk Khayl, Gharbūn, Ṣāḥib Khayl, Ismāʿīlak, Faryānah and all six sons with Rasbūn, the second son of Shaykh Bīt, and through that link they are called Bītanī.

Likewise Kajīn, the third son of /35/ Shaykh Bīt, who had six sons—Kīsū, Ādīzāʾī, Pashākanī, the last three sons with their clans and seed, which will be recorded below, are not the sons of Kajīn, rather they were *khānazād* (born into the household) and became mixed in with the offspring of Kajīn and so no one could distinguish who was *waṣlī* and who was *aṣlī*. Moreover, the offspring of Nā and Tahā are leaders of the Bītanī tribe because of their large number.[9]

Thus Bālah Khayl, Mandān, Khījī, Tūrān, Abā Khayl, Shān Khayl, ʿUmar Khayl, Rūzī Khayl, Salmī Khayl, Chankah Khayl, Mamī Khayl, ʿAmī Khayl, ʿĀlim Khayl, Bah Khayl, Saʿīdī Khayl, Niʿmat Khayl, Shāh Gul Khayl, Aṣgharī Khayl, Fīrūz Khayl, Kakā Khayl, Basī Khayl, Abā Khayl, Ḥasanī Khayl, Shakar Khayl,

[8] This last sentence makes no sense and we assume something has been omitted either by the copyist or the author. Moreover after the word *dū* [the 2 in 132] there is a word that appears to be *ḥadd* which only adds to the confusion.

[9] The sentence ends with a puzzling phrase *dānā wa katah girām bāz guzāsht* which the translators have been unable to decipher and we assume some thing has been omitted here by the copyist or the author.

Jāwul Khayl, Sīn Khayl, ʿĀshah Khayl, Shān Khayl, Qārī Khayl, Tāran, Dādī, Shabchah, Bābū Khayl, and Jalāl Khayl are all descendants of Tatā, the third son of Kajīn and through him are called Ghurghushtī.

Also Būbā, Bāgil Khayl, Tāj Bīk Khayl, Pā Khayl, Ram'ī Khayl, Māsūr Khayl, Rasūl Khayl, Hūd Khayl, Bīkī Khayl, Īsab Khayl, Bilā Khayl, Būbak, Shādī Khayl, Shamā'il Khayl, Ghāzī Khayl, Hānī Khān Khayl, Aṣghar Khayl, ʿAlī Khayl, Sarād Khayl, Bībī Khayl, Pīrah Khayl, Madī Khayl, ʿUmar Khān Khayl, ʿAbdū Khayl, Ḥusayn Khayl, Ratanzā'ī, Dardakī Khayl, Musāzā'ī, and Dadūrī who were offspring of Danā, the fifth son of Kajīn, through him were called Kajīn.

Kanazī, Parah Khayl, Tār Khayl, Khiżr Khayl, Azhgharī Khayl, Khānī Khayl, Nādir Khayl, Kā'in Khayl, Sīnzā'ī, Mānī Khayl, Siyāngī Khayl, Shaykh Milī Khayl, Ḥasan Khayl, Bāzūy Khayl, Darī Khān Khayl, Mīdād Khayl, Rāz Mīr Khayl, Qalandar Khayl, Malik Khayl, Kakā Khayl, and Abū Khayl are the descendants of Katah Girām, the sixth son of Kajīn, and through him, who was the third son of Shaykh Bīt, they were called Bītanī.

Some of the branches of the Bītanī tribe, due to the large number of people and the scarcity of land, put their homes on their backs and travel winter and summer. By means of their more powerful relatives, in winter they go to Hindūstān and in summer go up into the mountains for winter and summer pastures respectively and so go back and forth. Most of the Kajīn tribe and a small number of the progeny of Warsabūn, the second son of Shaykh Bīt, dwell in the eastern part of the Kūh-i Sulaymān. Because in relationship to the Sarbanī and Ghurghushtī tribes, the Bītanī are few in number and live dispersed throughout the districts of Hindūstān, a large number of them live established in the mountains, valleys, and plains of the eastern and southern frontier of Afghanistan and the northern frontier of Hindūstān, **/36/37/** and occupy the northern lands of Kūh-i Gabr whose range begins in the south in a mountain valley. Sarā Girāy (Kūh-i Surkh) and the slopes of it as far as Nāk Valley is their place of settlement. To the west of this homeland of theirs are the mountains belonging to the Masʿūd Wazīrīs. To the east is situated the plain inhabited by the Marwat tribe.

The number of persons of this tribe living in the frontier area is not more than 5,000.

The Kūtī Section Which is Recorded Among the Progeny of Warsapūn Son of Shaykh Bīt As Being Waṣlī

The most accurate and clearest (explanation) is that Kūtī was originally a sayyid. Ibrāhīm, one of the sons of Warsapūn, who was mentioned earlier, raised him (Kūtī) until he grew up. It (the section derived from Kūtī) is counted among the Bītanī. There is a group of sayyids living in Kūtī in Banūn District who are descendants of Ibrāhīm. Likewise Ratan better known as Ratanzā'ī who is a descendant of ʿAlī, known as ʿAlī Khayl, son of Būbak, son of Danā, the fifth son of Kajīn and waṣlī, originally was not Bītanī" because the aforementioned ʿAlī raised him as a child of unknown lineage. When he grew up, he entered the Bītanī tribe.

The Matī Clans and Tribes Which Came From the Womb of Bībī Matū, Daughter of Shaykh Bīt and the Loins of Shāh Ḥusayn Ghūrī. These Are the Ghiljāʾī, Lūdī, and Sarwānī All of Whom Are Said To Be of the Matī Tribe

These three tribes, as will be recorded below, are not of Afghan lineage but are outside the genealogy of the Sarbanī, Ghurghushtī, and Bītanī tribes because Shāh Ḥusayn Ghūrī left his (original) homeland and came to Shaykh Bīt who, out of compassion and mercy, allowed him to stay with him. He blandished and nurtured him and after Shāh Ḥusayn had spent some time in the shaykh's house he came to be at ease, like one of the shaykh's own sons, reliable, sharing in the work, and soon came to enjoy respect. Little by little he fell in love with Bībī, the daughter of Shaykh Bīt and the passion of love scorched the harvest of his life until gradually in secret he laid his hands on her and professed his love. The daughter was seduced by him, shared her bed with him, and /37/38/ became pregnant. When the mother of the girl and Shaykh Bīt, the father, became aware of their daughter's secret and her pregnancy, there was nothing for it but for them to marry her according to the (holy) law to Shāh Ḥusayn Ghūrī. When the term of her pregnancy arrived, she gave birth to a son and they called him Ghiljāʾī because in Afghānī they call a thief *ghil* and a son *zāʾī* meaning that through the 'theft' by Shāh Ḥusayn Ghūrī of having sex with the daughter that boy appeared. Afterwards, Shāh Ḥusayn Ghūrī also coupled with Mahī, the daughter of Kākh Dūr and from her he also produced a son whose name was Sarwānī. Later, Bībī Matū bore another son whose name was Ibrāhīm. Ibrāhīm, at the request of Shaykh Bīt, his maternal grandfather, became known as Lūdī because one day Shaykh Bīt ordered his wife to bake some bread and after she baked it, to bring it to be distributed in order to see which of these two grandsons' stars was in the ascendant. So Shaykh Bīt's wife baked some bread and Ibrāhīm the young son of Bībī Matū came first before his brother, Ghiljā, and quickly brought the bread to his grandfather. Shaykh Bīt, being hungry, was pleased with him and spoke to him in kind tones calling him Ibrāhīm Lūdī, *lūdī* in the Afghānī language meaning 'great.' Thenceforth he was known as Lūdī.

The Ghilzāʾī Tribes and Clans Who Are Bītī Afghans on the Mother's Side and of the Lineage of the Sultans of Ghūr on the Father's Side

Ghilzāʾī, the son of Shāh Ḥusayn, had three sons—Tūlar or Tūrān, Ibrāhīm, and Būlar or Burhān. Būlar had no sons. Tūlar or Tūrān had two sons—Bābū and Bārū. From Bārū there were two sons, Hūtak and Tūkhī. From Bābū three sons came—Yaḥyāzāʾī, Shāhū Khayl, and Ṭāhiri. The clans and progeny of each of these, God willing, will be recorded. Hūtak, the son of Bārū had four sons—Malikyār, Yūsuf, Dawlat, and ʿArab.

Thus Ḥusayn, Alḥaq, Quṭb, Jalāl al-Dīn, ʿUmar, Mand, Karam, Shah ʿĀlam Khayl, Ḥājjī Mīr Khān, Shāh Maḥmūd, the conqueror of Iṣfahān, the birthplace of the author of these lines, Shāh Ḥusayn, who was overpowered and defeated by Nādir Shāh Afshār, Shāh ʿAbd al-ʿAzīz, Shāh ʿAbd al-Qādir, Shāh Ashraf, Yaḥyā Khān, Muḥammad Khān, Nūr Allāh Khān, Ḥājjī ʿAbd al-Raḥmān, Shayr Shah, ʿAbd al-Raḥīm Khān, Shukr Allāh Khān, ʿUmar, ʿĪsakzāʾī, Katīzāʾī, Kadīnzāʾī, Kandalīzāʾī or Banādīzāʾī (?) **/38/39/** ʿUmarzāʾī, and Mandīn Khayl were all the lineage of Malikyār, the son of Hūtak and are said to be of the line of Hūtak.

Similarly, Malīzāʾī, Khūdīzāʾī, Tadazāk, Bidastzāʾī, Rāmīzāʾī, and ʿUmarzāʾī who were the offspring and descendants of Yūsuf, son of Hūtak are called Hūtak. Also Tūnzāʾī, Sāʾūtzāʾī, Ṭāhirī, Ayf Khayl, Absūzāʾī, Maʿrūfzāʾī, and Utmān Khayl, who are of the line of Dawlat, the third son of Hūtak, are also called Hūtak.

The Akāzāʾī, Bāqīzāʾī, Sitandzāʾī, ʿAlīzāʾī, and Pūlad are the offspring of ʿArab and are Hūtak. After the disappearance of their sultanate, the numbers of the Hūtak decreased and Nādir Shāh Afshār transferred 1,500 of their households to Turkistān, Hindūstān, and Iran and he dispersed them in those places. Thus they were scattered in Balkh, Bukhārā, Māzandarān, and Ardabīl and made their homes in those places. Now in Afghanistan there are between 14,000 and 15,000 Hūtak households, most of whom live in Marghah and near Bārī Ghar and Sūr Ghar (mountains). Of the lot, the ʿĪsakzāʾī live in Marghah and Atā Ghar, the Malīzāʾī in Ghābūlān and Girdī Zangal, the Baratzāʾī in Ghināy, the Ākāzāʾī in Khaznāy and Damandyār, the Tūnzāʾī in Sūrnay, the ʿUmarzāʾī in Mandāwar, and the Rāmīzāʾī in Atā Ghar. All these places are situated four manzils north of Qandahar and one manzil southeast of Qalāt-i Ghiljāʾī.

The Tribes and Clans of Tūkhī, the Second Son of Bārū, Son of Tūlar, Son of Ghiljāʾī

Tūkhī, the son of Bārū and of the line of Ghiljāʾī brought forth four sons—Rahmand, Ayyūbzāʾī, Ḥasanzāʾī, and Nūr Khayl. Of these four brothers, three had no sons. But Rahmand had offspring and a clan. Thus Maʿdūd Khayl, Bāsū Khayl, Akāzāʾī, Pūpal Khayl, Sabtū Khayl, Yūnus Khayl, Muḥammadzāʾī, Kālū Khayl, Faqīrzāʾī, Babrī, Mūsāzāʾī, Shāh Ḥasan Khayl, Sīgāk, Ādamzāʾī, Hūtakzāʾī, Aqrabīzāʾī, Babrak Khayl, ʿĪsāzāʾī, Burhān Khayl, Pātūzāʾī, Karmūn Khayl, Pīr Walī Khayl, Ḥasan Khayl, Khān Khayl, Bārakzāʾī, ʿUmar Khayl, Nashūzāʾī, Pīrūzāʾī, Saʿīd Khayl, ʿĀshūzāʾī, ʿIrāqī, Sūrīzāʾī, Mūsā Khayl, Barān Khayl, Khuwaydād Khayl, Shākī Khayl, Māmī Khayl, Naẓar Khayl, Shamalzāʾī, Bābakr Khayl, ʿAlī Shayrzāʾī, Ānīzāʾī, Matah Khān Khayl, Jalālzāʾī, **/39/40/** Fīrūz Khayl, Bahrām Khayl, Daʿwat Khayl, Bahlūl Khayl, Siyāhzāʾī, Tājū Khayl, Nājū Khayl, Mīzānzāʾī, Nūr al-Dīn, Akīzāʾī, Hawāzāʾī, Sīn Khayl, Khatīzāʾī, Mughulzāʾī, Rustam, and Bātā Khayl, all are sons and grandsons of Rahmand, the son of Tūkhī and they are all called "Tūkhī." The population of the Tūkhī tribe is counted as 17,000 households. They have their homes in Qalāt-i Tūkhī and its environs such as the locales of Tarnak and Pul-i Sangī as far as Shībār District and its dependencies and environs, in the Arghandāb Valley adjacent to Hazārah Dāy Chūpān, the properties and lands of which have now been transferred to Afghan muhājirs by the government. They also live in Mīzānah, Dādī Nāwah, and Khākāk. Of them all, the Bābakrzāʾī live in the locales of Nāwah, Shāh Mardān, Sarasp, and Jangīyah. The Shamalzāʾī reside in Mandān, Hiltāgh, Shībār, and elsewhere. There is a street of Tūkhīs in Kabul, adjacent to the Dih Afghānān quarter.

The Tribes, Clans, and Peoples Whose Lineage Went Back to Ibrāhīm, the Second Son of Ghiljāʾī, the Son of Shāh Ḥusayn Ghūrī

Ibrāhīm Ghiljāʾī had two sons—Īzab and Musā. Consequently, the Sulaymān Khayl, Aḥmadzāʾī, Bābakr Khayl, Maʿrūf Khayl, Mūsā Khayl, ʿĪsā Khayl, Yaḥyā Khayl, Karū Khayl, Taghrū Bārān Khayl, Allāh Dīn Khayl, Nūrī Kūtī, Ṣāliḥ Khayl, Sayyidū Khayl, Dawlatzāʾī, Ghanī Khayl, Guldād Khayl, Shamāʾilzāʾī, Darakī, Landīzāʾī, Khwājak or Khwāzak Khayl, Ismāʿīlzāʾī, Dāsū, Ibrāhīm, Sulṭan, Bachah, Qayṣar, Qalandar Khayl, Kalā Khayl, Shah Khayl, Sarwān Khayl, Babrī, ʿAmūzāʾī, Manshurī, Nasū Khayl, Khwājah Dād Khayl, Bāstānīzāʾī, Alūzāʾī, Quṭb known as Kūtī Khayl, Chūnzāʾī, Payārū Khayl, Ūtū Khayl, Utmān Khayl, Zuʾīzāʾī, Shayr Pāy, Mughul Khayl, Jābū Khayl, Bābakr Khayl, Amīr Khayl, Adrīm or ʿAbd al-Raḥīmzāʾī, Sarāz, Pāyandah Khayl, Jalālzāʾī, Shāh Tūrī, Dīnār Khayl, Sulṭān Khayl, Yazab Khayl, Dāwudzāʾī, Manzāʾī, ʿAlī Khayl, Mamūzāʾī, Sarmast Khayl, Āzār Khayl, Fatḥ Khayl, Daryā Khayl, Nīknām Khayl, Mīrzā Khayl, Gaydzāʾī, Qarār Khayl, Mish Khayl, Fīrī Khayl, Jabbārī, Ādam Khayl, Jānū Khayl, Ākhūnd Khayl, Yūsuf Khayl, Karīm Khayl, Mashtī Khayl, Nawrūz Khayl, Bārī Khayl, Mitā Khayl, ʿAjību Khayl, Fatḥ Khayl, Jānī Khayl, Yahyā Khayl, Ḥasan Khayl, Adīn Khayl, Maḥmūd Khayl, Shakī Khayl, Sar Parīgarī, Āzād Khayl, Karū Khayl, ʿAlī Bughān Khayl, Ghūrakī, Mīr Khān **/40/41/** Khayl, Āzād Khayl, Dūrī Khayl, Kamāl Khayl, Aʿẓam, ʿAlī Shayr Khayl, Muḥammad Khayl, Malikī Khayl, Shālī Khayl, Nīk Zan Khayl, Tājū Khayl, Shahbāz Khayl, Kattī Khayl, Haybat Khayl, Yārū Khayl, Sulānī, Ismāʿīlzāʾī, Pīrā Khayl, and Bārī Khayl all were progeny of Īzab, son of Ibrāhīm, son of Ghiljāʾī, and all are Ghiljāʾī.

The Tribes, Peoples, and Clans of the Mūsā-yi Ghiljāʾī

Mūsā, the second son of Ibrāhīm, the son of Ghiljāʾī, had three sons whom the Lord granted him—Sahhāk, Andar, and Tarakī.

Thus, the Ḥasan Khayl, Yaʿqūb Khayl, Yūsuf Khayl, Gadā Khayl, Ismāʿīl Khayl, Panj Pāy, Tūtā Khayl, Uryā Khayl, Alūzāʾī, Khadr Khayl, and Bakhtū were the offspring of Sahhāk, the first son of Mūsā, son of Ibrāhīm, son of Ghiljāʾī. They are called the Sahhāk tribe of the Ghiljāʾī.

Similarly, the Adū, Jalālzāʾī, Sulaymānzāʾī, Khīrū Khayl, Kābulī, Nūr Khān Khayl, Lūtab Wāl, Khānī Khayl, Kibrī, Bakhshī Khayl, Hārūnī, Gharī Khayl, Kandī Khayl, ʿAlī Shayr Khayl, Kūtī Khayl, Ḥabīb Khayl, Patān Khayl, Pūlād Khayl, Shamshī Khayl, Brāhīm Khayl, Bāzī Khayl, Mahān Khayl, ʿAlī Bīk Khayl, Bātā Khayl, Tangī Wālah, Sih Pāy, Chūri Khayl, Karīm Khayl, Sulaymān, Marjān Khayl, Bakhshī, Mushkī Wālah, Aʿẓam Khayl, Sayf al-Dīn Khayl, Dīsī Wālah, Mūsā, Lakin Khayl, Arān Khayl, Shāyib Khayl, ʿĪdū Khayl, Ḥaydar Khayl, Shālī Khayl, Būtī Khayl, Kārān Khayl, Nafrah Bārak Dīn Khayl, Aymal Khayl, Hit Khayl, Ghālī Khayl, Nasū Khayl, Naẕr Khayl, Rashīd Khayl, Wālī Khayl, Rīmah Khayl, Shīrī Khayl, Shābū Khayl, Ḥasan Khayl, Sarakī Khayl, Zāhib Khayl, Mūsā Khayl, Mamūzāʾī, Sardār Khayl, Ḥaydar Khayl, Shīngī Khayl, Rūzī Khayl, Sayyidū Khayl, ʿAli Khayl, ʿĀlim Khān Khayl, Iran Khayl, Lāghar, Girūy, Najī Khayl, Shamshīr Khayl, Changā Khayl, Khwājahgī, Khūrjah Khayl, Jabbār Khayl, Imām Khayl, Sayyid Aḥmad Khayl, ʿAlīkī

Khayl, Pāchakī, Islām Khayl, Daryā Khān Khayl, Saʿīd Khayl, Shāh Tūrī, Ghundī Khayl, Garmī, Dawlat Khayl, Miʾī, Pīr Khayl, Badwān, Alū Khayl, Shīṣ Khayl, Shākhūzhī, Bālā Wālah, Janatī, Faqīrī, Dalīl Khān, Brāhīmzāʾī, Lāsī Khayl, Qalandar Khayl, Yārū Khayl, Shamshī Khayl, Nūr Khān Khayl, Shāyr Khān Khayl, Liwān, Shātūrī, Rustam Khayl, Mumīrī (?) Katī, ʿAlī Khayl, Mīr Pawāl, Matī Khayl, Darī Palārī, Khānī Khayl, Garmū Khayl, Raʿnā Khayl, Mandī Khayl, Pāy Lūchī, Sagū Wāl, Lālā Khayl, Ẕākir Wāl, and Ghafūrī were all of the tribe and clan of Andar, the second son of Mūsā, son of Ibrāhīm, son of Ghiljāʾī. /**41**/**42**/

Rustam Khayl, Kharīwālah, Bātūrī, Shaṣt Wāl, Atal Khayl, Nūr Bīk Khayl, Shamshīr Khayl, Darāz Khayl, and Mikmāl Khayl are of the line of Mūsā, a Kākar, which are attached to the Andar tribe.

The tribe of Sahhāk, the brother of Andar, numbers 10,000 households. Of those, the Yūsuf Khayl has the most people.

The third section of this tribe lives in Kharwār District. Some also make their homes in Zurmat, and in Pamqan and Bīktūt of Kabul, and in Tagāb. A group lives in Lamqān and in the southern valleys of the Hindū Kush. These tribes and clans mostly have their homes in Shīgar District in the southern environs of Ghaznīn [Province]. A group has also chosen to live in Jamrār of Qarābāgh. A group of the Jalālzāʾī lives in Zurmat; another group has made a haven in Shībār, the territory of the Tūkhīs. This tribe (the Andar) numbers 23,000 households. The Mūsā Khayl of the Kākar tribe who have attached themselves to the Andar live on the territory of Wāghaz located in the western part of Shīgar adjacent to Hazārah Jighatū and some of them have their places in the villages of Gīrū located south of Shīgar.

The Tribes and Clans of Tarakī, the Third Son of Mūsā, Son of Ibrāhīm, Son of Ghiljāʾī

Tarakī, the son of Mūsā, son of Ibrāhīm, son of Ghiljāʾī had six sons—Bādīn Khayl, Nā Khayl, Sāk Khayl, Fīrūz Khayl, Taswīl Khayl, and Gurīz Khayl.

The Khīrū Khayl, Shahbāz Khayl, Tūrzāʾī, Malik Dīn Khayl, Mūsā Khayl, Gardan Khayl, Brāhīm Khayl, Qubād Khayl, Satīzāʾī, Zalū Khayl, Khān Khayl, Ṣāḥibdād Khayl, Firāq Khayl, Bangū Khayl, Shāh ʿAbdal Khayl, Kabīr Khayl, Sālī Khayl, Qattāl Khayl, Tarmī Khayl, Bastām Khayl, Lājmīr Khayl, Akbar Khayl, and Zarrīn Khayl were the offspring of Bādīn and through him were related to Tarakī.

Similarly, the Maʿarrī Khayl, Qudrat Khayl, Dawrān Khayl, Khajal Khayl, Ḥasan Khayl, Ẓālim Khayl, Shāyib Khayl, Ḥatim Khayl, Turāb Khayl, Salīm Khayl, Lālū Khayl, Nawrūz Khayl, Tājū Khayl, Anārī Khayl, and Ṣābir Khayl through Nā Khayl, the second son of Tarakī are called Tarakī.

Sāk, the third son of Tarakī, had no sons.

The Jamāl Khayl, Shāgul Khayl, Shaykh Nūr Khayl, Shīrīn Khayl, Nūr Khān Khayl, Sadū Khayl, Gūr Khayl, Ḥarīf Khayl, Ganjū Khayl, Mīrī Khayl, Galū Khayl, Kalān Khayl, Nāzik Khayl, Dildār Khayl, Shabakī, and Almarī were the progeny (sons and grandsons) of Fīrūz, the fourth son of Tarakī, and so are called Tarakī.

Taswīl, the fifth son of Tarakī also had no offspring so there was no foundation for a clan or tribe. Barak Khayl was of the offspring of Gurīz Khayl and Tarakī. /**42**/**43**/

These tribes which are all called Tarakī number 20,000 households. Two-thirds of them have their own independent places of residence and homeland and so live at ease in one place. One-third of them are nomads (*kūchī*) who do not engage in agriculture. The original homeland of this tribe was the territory of Muqur and Nāwah. Of them all, the ʿAlī Khayl and the Khadūzāʾī [still] reside in Muqur. The nomadic clans of this tribe go and stay for the winter in the vicinity of Qandahar. They return in the spring and settle around Muqur. Presently, they summer-pasture in the Hazārahjāt and are a great nuisance and cause the Hazārah tribes a good deal of trouble. It is likely that they will not cease their depredations and assaults and the government will not curtail their oppression and tyranny. Except perhaps now when the throne of authority and world-rule is adorned with the existence of a subject-blandishing, enemy-crushing, and justice-spreading pādshāh like His Majesty Amīr Amān Allāh Khān, the illuminating rays of subject-nurturing will warm the crowns of the heads of all subjects near and far and the tribes of the Hazārahjāt too will be soothed and the people of the Hazārahjāt will no longer be scattered.

The Tribe of the Ghiljāʾī Sulaymān Khayl Which in Terms of Numbers Is the Largest of the Ghiljāʾī Tribes

This tribe numbers 40,000 households. They comprise four well-known clan groups and possess and own vast lands in mountains, valleys, and barren areas. They divide their lands in two parts, the southern and the northern. The south is controlled by the Qayṣar Khayl and Shamalzāʾī or Ismāʿīlzāʾī, along with other tribes attached to them like the Adīn Khayl, Nasū Khayl, Qalandar Khayl, Shakī Khayl, Shāh Tūrī, Jalālzāʾī, Kalā Khayl, Maḥmūd Khayl, Mish Khayl, and others. They reside in Katahwāz. Similarly, half of Zurmat district is under the control of the Sulaymān Khayl tribe. Also, they have places in Nānī Ghund District dependent on Katahwāz, in Wāzkhwāh, and other scattered places.

In the northern division live the Sitānīzāʾī or Sulṭānzāʾī and the Aḥmadzāʾī, the latter in terms of numbers larger than the Astānīzāʾī [*sic*]. Of the branches of the Sulaymān Khayl, the Jabbār Khayl and the Bābakr Khayl are always preying upon and robbing people on the road between Kabul and Jalālābād, the Jabbār Khayl in the environs of Jalāl [ābād] and the Bābakr Khayl near Lamqān. The Payārū Khayl from this tribe (the Sulaymān Khayl) has its homelands on the territory of Taytimūr located west of the Laʿl Andar Valley of Kabul, in Maydān District, one manzil west of Kabul City, and in the locales of Tīzīn, /**43**/**44**/ Jagdalak, Surkh Rūd, and Gandamak. The Jabbār Khayl and Bābakr Khayl have their homes in the dependencies of Lamqān. The Jabbār Khayl particularly used to spend time in the village of ʿAlīshang. The Aḥmadzāʾī, one of the branches of the Sulaymān Khayl, [have their homelands] in the eastern part of Lahūgard District, Altimūr, Sapīkah, and Surkh Āb located on the western slopes of Kūh-i Sulṭān Aḥmad-i Kabīr.

The Tribe of ʿAlī Khayl, Brother of Sulaymān Khayl

This tribe numbers 10,000 households. Half of it resides on the territory of Zurmat which is known in the Afghānī language as "Zurmal." The other half resides in

Muqur District and elsewhere. The Mandūzā'ī clan of this tribe, a branch of the Ismā'īlzā'ī, numbers 500 households and resides in Khūst.

The Ghiljā'ī Akā Khayl Tribe

This tribe has very low numbers and has no agricultural land or territory of its own so that they could spend their springs and winters there. Most of them work as muleteers. A group of them work as weavers, weaving flat-weave rugs and sacks, and selling coal. Their craft skills were handed down father to son. They number approximately 1,200 households.

The rest of the Ghiljā'ī are households scattered throughout Afghanistan one by one and two by two. In Turkistān and Iran too there used to be a lot (of Ghiljā'īs) whom Nādir Shāh Afshār had banished and moved to those places. The Ghiljā'ī have settled on the banks of the river of Balkh and work as agriculturalists. There are many in Bukhārā who earn their livings as servants and soldiers. In Narmāshīr District, Kirmān, Ṭabas, and Iṣfahān, Iran, a few hundred households of Ghiljā'ī still are found but they adopt the Iranian way of life and have set aside the customs and ways of their forefathers. No one now would recognize that they were originally Afghānīs. There is also a group in Hindūstān and some are found in Dāghistān, the Caucasus, and in the Ottoman lands.

The Nāṣir Tribe Which Considers Itself Ghiljā'ī and Part of the Hūtak Tribe While the Hūtak Consider Them To Be Their Wards

There is some disagreement over the Nāṣir as to whether they are from the Ghiljā'ī or not. Some say they are Ghiljā'ī and from the Shāh Ḥusayn Ghūrī lineage and some don't know [whether they are or not]. One group thinks they are from the Balūch tribe. It is more likely that they were included in the Ghiljā'ī tribe by way of some sort of relationship other than blood (marriage, clientage, etc.)./44/45/ At one time, this tribe divided into three sections—the first group, the Tūr Nāṣir are called 'Umarzā'ī, the second the Sarah Nāṣir, and the third Aspīn Nāṣir—Tūr, Sarah, and Aspīn meaning black, red, and white. The Surkh (Red) Nāṣir are the Nasū Khayl; the Sapīd (White) Nāṣir are called Malīzā'ī. Altogether these tribes number 20,000 households. A small number of them live in the areas around Kabul such as Kuh Dāman, Kāh Darrah, Shakar Darrah, Ḥājjī Kak, and other places. Most are nomads. In the winter, they go to Dāmān and in spring they come to Afghanistan.

The Tribes and Clans of the Kharūtī Who Consider Themselves Ghiljā'ī

This tribe considers itself related to the Ghiljā'ī and included in the Tūkhī tribe. The Ghiljā'īs do not consider them to be of the same stock (*nasl*) and not sharers in their lineage. The Ghiljā'īs say that one day Īzab, the son of Ibrāhīm, son of Ghiljā'ī, had gone out together with his brother, Ishāk, the son of Mūsā. Suddenly they spied a loaded donkey without an owner. When they looked more closely they saw that on one side of the donkey was a load of barley flour and bread and on the other side a nursing infant. Therefore, because they say *rūtī* for bread in the Hindūstānī language and the donkey (*khar*) was carrying it, they named the child who was riding the donkey, "Khar-rūtī" and gradually that was shortened to "Kharūtī." When the infant grew up, took a wife, and had children, the Lord gave him three sons—Zakū Khayl, Bah Khayl, and Ādah Khayl.

Thus Amand, Shāyib Khayl, Bāyir Khayl, Tar Khayl, Bustān Khayl, Mūyak Khayl, Bandār Khayl, Parwatī, Pā Sīnī, ʿAnbar Khayl, ʿIṣmat Khayl, Shukr Dād Khayl, ʿAlī Dīn Khayl, Saʿīd Khayl, Mumand Khayl, Mūsā Khayl, Yāsīn Khayl, Lālī Khayl, Sanchah Khayl, Shāmū Khayl, Madad Khayl, Sandar Khayl, Shāh Tūrī, ʿAlīzāʾī, Khāwar Gārī, Ghūrī Khayl, ʿAlī Khayl, Darī Malārī, and Shāmūzāʾī, all of them were of the lineage of Zakū, the first son of Kharūtī, and they are called Zakū Khayl Kharūtī.

Similarly, Khiżr Khayl, Zāwulī, Jamālzāʾī, Tūrzāʾī, Mālī Khayl, Lalī Khayl, Kharmūzī, Zhūniyā Khayl, and Ḥufr Khayl are all of the lineage from the second son of Kharūtī (Bah Khayl) and they carry the name Bah Khayl Kharūtī.

Alū Khayl, Nūrā Dīn, Ḥarīf Khayl, Bājū Khayl, Bahrām Khayl, Basnās Khayl, Yaḥyāzāʾī, Sawt Khayl, Sawrān Khayl, Panchū Khayl, Karīm Khayl, Dawlat Khayl, Badīn, Kākulzāʾī, Shihāb al-Dīn, Kirāyah Din, Matū Khayl, Khuwaydād Khayl, Najabī Khayl, Marī Kat Khayl, ʿAbbās Khayl, Aṣghar Khayl, Bahādūr Khayl, Nawrūz Khayl, Shālī Khayl, Nādir Khayl, Shahbāz Khayl, Barkhān Khayl, Mālīk Khayl, **/45/46/** Dārū Khayl, Ashraf Khayl, Dārā Khayl, Pāpū Khayl, Shādī Khayl, Ṭāwus Khayl, Ghaybī Khayl, Naw[r]ūz Khayl, Lajmīr Khayl, Ṣāf Khayl, Mārzak Khayl, Kūndī, Lāyichī Khayl, Shādīzāʾī, Ḥaydarzāʾī, Sulṭān Khayl, Bahrām Khayl, Kūndah Khayl, and Bāndzāʾī, all are of the lineage of Adah Khayl, the third son of Kharūtī, and all are called Adah Khayl Kharūtīs. The total number of the Kharūtī tribe is 8,000. Most of them live in the mountains of Katahwāz west of the Sulaymān Mountains up to a point close to the Kūh-i Barmal. They occupy one section of Urgūn District, Parmūlī or Parmalī, who are Tājīks. One branch of the Kharūtī tribe also lives there. One thousand households of the Kharūtī tribe live in Sar-i Rawżah, 500 of whom are merchants. The rest are all nomads and property owners. Their bazaaris and traders have purchased all the property of Qarābāgh owned by the Chahār Dastah Hazārahs and have strong forts and well-fortified places (there).

The Khadūzāʾī Tribe Which Sometimes Says It Is Īdū, Sometimes of the Fūfalzāʾī Durrānī, and Sometimes Ghiljāʾī

This tribe numbers 3,000 households. Of that total, 300 households live in Dih-i Khwājah, adjacent to the eastern side of Qandahar. Most of the rest lives in Muqur attached to the ʿAlī Khayl tribe and they remain with them as one. All of them earn their living in agriculture.

A Tribe That Calls Itself Sayyid Most of Whom Live on the Territory of the Tūkhīs

This tribe numbers 1,500 households and is dispersed around the country, anywhere from one or two households found in Kabul, Qandahar, and other places. Their occupations vary. One group lives off agriculture and another from crafts and trade.

The Tribe and Clans Known as the Lūdī Tribe Named After Ibrāhīm, the Son of Ghiljā'ī Whose Name Was Previously Mentioned /46/47/

Lūdi, the second son of Ghiljā'ī, had three sons with these names—Sayānī, Niyāzī, and Dūbānī or Daftānī.

Parangī, Arand, Zaytūn Khayl, Didī, 'Umar Khayl, Alḥaq, Shāmū Khayl, Basīn Khayl, Aḥmad Khayl, Maḥmūd Khayl, Marchī Khayl, Bahrām Khayl, Malik Kālā, Sulṭān Bahlūl, Fīrūz, Muḥammad, Bārak Shāh, Mubārak Khān, 'Ālim Khān, Sulṭān Sikandar, Maḥmūd Khān, Ibrāhīm Khān, Jalāl Khān, Ḥusayn Khān, Ismā'īl Khān, A'ẓam Humāyūn, Jamāl khān, Ya'qūb, Fatḥ Khān, Mūsā Khān, Sulṭān Shāh, Fīrūz, Malik Muḥammad, Malik Khwājah, Yusuf Khayl, Anchī, Jīr, Mānī, Malik Aḥmad, Nasū Malik, Biyū, Bihdīn, Samū Khān, Mīr 'Alī, Nakar al-Dīn, Fīrūz Shāh, Dawlat Khayl, Rustam Khayl, Muḥammad Khānī, Tatār Khānī, Tāj al-Dīn, 'Alā al-Dīn, Ghūrī, Sūr, Isḥāqzā'ī, Shaykhzā'ī, Mūsāzā'ī, Abū Sa'īd Khayl, Sayyidū Khayl, Ḥasanzā'ī, Yūsuf Khayl, Payārū Khayl, 'Umarzā'ī, Tūr, Tūjī Khayl, Aḥmad Khayl, Sayyidī Khayl, Gadāy Khayl, Maḥmūdzā'ī, Zakariyā Khayl, Alif Khayl, Andar, Rāmdī, Turghundī, and Ismā'īl, mention of whose clans and lineage will be recorded after this, all of whom were the offspring of Sayānī, son of Lūdī and were known as the Ghiljā'ī Lūdī tribe. In volume two of this book, *Amān al-tawārīkh*, we wrote an account of the sultanate and world rule of the Lūdī kings who ruled over Hindūstān for some time. (There) we wrote "Lūdhī" following the style of the people of Hindūstān.

The Tribes and Clans of the Lineage of Ismā'īl, the Second Son of Sayānī, son of Lūdī

Ismā'īl, the son of Sayānī, had three sons—Sūr, Lūḥānī, and Mahpāl.

Thus, Shādū Khayl, Wālā Khayl, Yūnus Khayl, Tarakī, Maḥmūdzā'ī, Shayr Khayl, Utmān, Muḥammad, Bahā al-Dīn, Rukn al-Dīn, Ṣadr al-Dīn, Ibrāhīm, Ḥasan, Sulaymān, Yazīd given the nickname Shayr Shāh, Jalāl Khān, 'Ādil Khān, Niẓām, Mubāriz Khān, 'Alī, Yūsuf, Khwājah, Bāk, Nashū', Ghāzī Khān, Sulṭān Ibrāhīm, Sadū, Muḥammad Kālā Pahār, Sulṭān Sikandar, Maḥmūd, Shayr, Jahān Khān, Tandī Khayl, Dawlat Khayl, Shādī Khayl, Dāwud Khayl, Kūtī, Bahrām, Nūrā Khayl, Muḥammad, Zalī, and Bakī, all were the offspring of Sūr, the son of Ismā'īl. The Sūrī sultans who raised the banner of their rule in India and beat the drum of their pādshāhship were from this very genealogy. In volume two of this book an account of their sultanate has been written. /47/49/*

The Bībīzā'ī were of the lineage of Mahpāl, the third son of Ismā'īl.

The Tribes and Clans from the Lūḥānī Lineage, the Second Son of Ismā'īl, the Son of Sayānī, the Son of Lūdī

Lūḥānī had one son, named Marwat from one wife whose lineage and genealogy will be recorded in its proper place. He had five sons from another wife—Mamā

* The manuscript skips number 48 here, thus the page numbers now differ by two from the facsimile edition.

Khayl, Miyā Khayl or Maʾī Khayl, Tatūr, Hūd, and Patakh. The last two had no offspring. The three who had sons will be recorded before mentioning the promised account of the offspring of the first son of Lūḥānī, Marwat.

Thus Yasīn Khayl, Dawlat Khayl, ʿĪsā Khān, Luqmān, Jalāl Khān, Katī Khayl, Bihdīn, Khwājah Khiżr, Mūsā Khān, Dawlat Khān, Shahbāz Khān, Ghāzī Khān, Salīm Khān, Qattāl Khān, Masrūr Khān, Alahdād Khān, Nawwāb Shahnawāz Khān, Muḥammad Akbar Khān, Khudādād Khān, Ṣāḥibdād Khān, Akbar Khān, Haybat Khān, Hamrīz Khān, Ṣāḥib Khān, Ḥayāt Khān, Muḥammad Khān, Shayr Khān, Dalīl Khān, Bahādūr Khān, ʿIzzat Khān, Fīrūz Khān, Bar Mazīd Khān, Mūsā Khān, Yaḥyāzāʾī, Tājīzāʾī, Bandarzāʾī, Mūsāzāʾī, Mandūzāʾī, Palang, Ismāʿīl, Zakū, Ḥasan Khayl, Ḥaydar Khayl, and Yaʿqūb Khayl were all of the lineage of Mamā Khayl, the second son of Lūḥānī.

Sīn Khayl, Zakūrī, Wardakī, ʿUmarzāʾī, Abā Khayl, Mūsāzāʾī, Akā Khayl, Barzū Khayl, Pītī (this person was related as *waṣlī*), Sawt Khayl, Shādī Khayl, Saʿīd Khayl, Tārū Khayl, Ghulām Khayl, Shāhī Khayl, Jalīl Khayl, ʿAlī Khān Khayl, Qamar Khayl, and Mullā Khayl were all offspring of Miyā Khayl or Māʾī Khayl, the third son of Lūḥānī.

Asū Khayl and Mūsā Khayl were the offspring of Tatūr, the fourth son of Lūḥānī.

The Tribes and Clans of the Lineage of Niyāzī, the Second Son of Lūdī, As Promised Earlier

For Niyāzī, the second son of Lūdī, three sons came into the arena of existence—Bāhī, Jamāl, and Khākū. Bāhī had no sons.

Rukn, Ḥamīm, Tūrā, Zām or Jām, Khar, ʿUmar, ʿĪsā Khayl, whose lineage will be recorded below, ʿAlī Khayl, Shādū Khayl, Sunbul Khayl, Dawlat Khayl, Bandār, Sanjar, Yasīn Khayl, **/48/50/** Ismāʿīl Khayl, Nār Khayl, Sahl, Ākā Khayl, Ismāʿīlzāʾī, Bakā, Naṣr Khayl, Khān Khayl, Marhīl, Laylī, Marham, and Jakī were all the offspring of Jamāl, the second son of Niyāzī, son of Lūdī.

Ḥaydar, Miʿyār or Mihyār, Mūsyānī known as Mūshānī whose genealogy will be recorded after this, ʿĪsā, Ālā, Sūd, Jām, Machin Khayl, Nīkū, Sūr, Sarhang whose genealogy will also be written down after this, Kūndī, and Sipānī were all offspring of Khākū, the third son of Niyāzī, son of Lūdī.

The Lūdī tribe which is of the lineage of Sayāni, Niyāzī, and Dūtānī or Daftānī, his (Lūdī's) three sons, is according to what has been written down above.

In olden days, due to the large number of people possessing power, wealth, and ability most of whom went to Hindūstān, a few people, according to what is in the history of the Afghans, ascended the throne of power and rule in Hindūstan. But now that large number having decreased, in Afghanistan, except for the Lūḥānī tribe none of the offspring of Sayānī has sizeable numbers and power.

The Lūḥānī tribe is also nomadic so that in winter it goes to Dāmān, Sind, and Hindūstān and in summer stays in Qarābāgh and Shīgar, Ghaznīn. Most are wealthy merchants and traders.

Of the line of Lūdī, the Niyāzī tribe, except for the ʿĪsā Khayl and Sarhang [clans], has been dispersed over time and afflicted by misfortune. The Dūtānī tribe [too] has been very reduced in numbers.

The Tribe of Parangī, the First Son of Sayānī, Son of Lūdī, Who was Written About Above

At first, this tribe spent all its time in the mountains of western Afghanistan. It then migrated and then established itself in Dāmān District in the eastern part of the Kūh-i Sulaymān in the village of Tāk [Tank] wa Rūrī. After long years spent there, when they had come to possess power and wealth and led an easy life, the Dawlat Khayl, Miyā Khayl, Marwat, and other Lūḥānī tribes, during the reign of Bābur Shāh Gūrgānī, were forced to leave there and all the lands, properties, and estates were seized by force from those tribes. Scattered, they went to various places in Hindūstān. Today, in Afghanistan, not a single person from the Parangī tribe can be found bearing that name nor is there any trace of them. Only in Hindūstān is the name Lūdī Afghān remembered. /**49**/**51**/ They built up the cities of Rūpar and Lurhiyānah (Ludhiana?) and made them prosper and in the Deccan a few households of this tribe remain.

The Bakhtiyār Tribe Whom Some People Call Sayyids While They Themselves in (Their) Traditions and Faith Link Themselves to the Miyā Khayl Tribe

Originally, the Bakhtiyār tribe came from Iran. In Iran, particularly near Iṣfahān, the tribe is numerous. In recent years, because of the revolution and government changes which occurred in Iran, at the wish of the people of Iṣfahān, [the Bakhtiyārīs] came to Iṣfahān from their villages and set off on the road to Tehran. After deposing Muḥammad ʿAli Shāh and seating Sulṭān Aḥmad Shāh, they gradually found high office and even came to possess the Ministry of the Interior, the Prime Ministry, the governorships of large provinces, and positions as assembly deputies. They came to hold power and influence beyond measure. I, the author of these lines, swear by God that over the course of sixteen years of their (i.e. the Bakhtiyārīs) constitutionalism I did not see one *shāhī* from their being in power in the kingdom of Iran. I regret that I even have to introduce them into this reputable royal book and mention their good qualities in the luminous page of the history of this era because I can't find a single line to write capable of commending and praising them.

To sum up, the Bakhtiyār, who in Iran are known by the name Bakhtiyārī, and are some 800–900 households in Afghanistan, have their homeland in Marghah. Some work as artisans, some as farmers, and some are nomads. It is possible that Nādir Shāh Afshār, as he did with other tribes, removed them from Iṣfahān to Afghanistan. Those in Afghanistan then attached themselves to the genealogy and clans of the Miyā Khayl. But in that tribe there is no sign of their name. Perhaps with the passing [of time] they became genealogically absorbed but it still remains common knowledge that they come from the Bakhtiyārī tribe of Iran.

The Tribe of Tatūr, the Third Son of Lūḥānī, Son of Ismāʿīl, Son of Sayānī, Son of Lūdī Whose Name Was Mentioned Above

The tribe of Tatūr is very small and few in number, only about 500 households. Most of them live in the western part of the territory of Tāk (Tank) and are not mixed in with other tribes.

The Tribe of Niyāzī, Son of Lūdī, Whose Tribal Genealogy and Lineage Has Already Been Recorded /**50**/**52**/

Originally, this tribe dwelled in the environs of Ghaznīn. Now, several households still reside in the dependencies of Ghaznīn. From Ghaznīn, during the time of the reign of Bahlūl Shāh Lūdī they went to Hindūstān and during the rule of Shayr Shāh Sūrī great figures from this tribe emerged who rose to become, in the terminology of the time, *ṣāḥibān-i manāṣib-i ʿalīyah* (persons of high rank). One of those people, Haybat Khān Niyāzī, was honored with the title "high royal' (*aʿẓam-i humāyūn*) and was singled out to be the governor (*ṣūbahdār*) of Lahore. In volume two of this royal book, *Amān al-tawārīkh*, many of them are mentioned in various places. Today in Afghanistan, aside from the ʿĪsā Khayl, Mūshānī, and Sarhang, no other tribe known as Niyāzī is to be found. They live in the village of Tūgh on the territory of the Bangash and in other scattered spots [on Bagash territory], there are a few households in Qandahar, a few in Ghaznīn, some in the mountains around the village of Shabūgī, Kabul, and some in Hindūstān. The clans of Marmal [Marhal?], Kandī, and Matī of the Niyāzī tribe are nomads who come to Afghanistan in summer, especially to the territory of the Hazārahjāt, and in winter go to Qandahar and the territory of Dāmān.

The Tribe of Dūtānī [Daftānī?], Third Son of Lūdī, Whose Tribal Genealogy Has Been Given Already

The numbers of this tribe, too, are every small, reckoned at not more than 300 households. Some of them are nomads; some are artisans, and some are well-to-do and influential merchants. Those who are nomads transport their own goods by oxen to their winter and summer quarters. A segment of this tribe lives in Wānah where they work and earn their living in agriculture. They are not more than 80–100 households.

The Tribe of Khaysūr Which Considers Itself Related to Lūdī But Others Deny That It Is From Lūdī

There is no evidence to be found that places this tribe in the Lūdī genealogy but since they are Afghānī, and consider themselves Lūdī, therefore it behooves us to make some mention of them. The tribe of Khaysūr is quite small and lives on the west bank of the Indus River. To the north of their territory is the ʿĪsā Khayl District and to the west /**51**/**53**/ the low mountain of Patyālah or Patyānah. There too is the Marwat tribe, clients of theirs. Their household census is counted as no more than 160 households.

The Tribe of Palaḥ Which Sometimes Says It Is a Branch of the Dawlat Khayl of the Lūḥānī Lineage and Sometimes That It Is From the Lūdī Lineage

Although the Lūhānī are also from the lineage of the offspring of Lūdī and through his father, Ismāʿīl, son of Sayānī, son of Lūdī they (the tribe of Palaḥ) are called a Lūdī tribe, this tribe calls themselves offspring of Dawlat Khayl, offspring of Yasīn Khayl, offspring of Mamā Khayl, offspring of Lūḥānī. It seems that they separated themselves from Lūḥānī and falsely say they are (offspring of) Dawlat Khayl. Anyway, they are a very small tribe. Most live in locales of Patyālah at the terminus of Kūh-i Ghund Shaykh and thus belong to Dīrah Ismāʿīl Khān. One household of them lives in the village of Yīyilān of Miyān Wālī District and has its homeland in two places. (?)

The Tribe and Clan of Sarwāʾī, Son of Shāh Ḥusayn Ghūrī, Who Emerged from the Belly of Mahī, Daughter of Kākh, As Was Recorded Earlier

The Lord bestowed on Sarwāʾī, son of Shāh Ḥusayn Ghūrī, the son-in-law of Shaykh Bīt, three sons—Sarīpāl, Sīnī, and Balī. Thus Jaʿfarī, Kakūr, Rashīd, Pūpīzāʾī, Jawānmard, Sadū, Shaykh Sulaymān, Anā, Shaykh Maḥmūd, Shaykh Malīḥ Qattāl, Shaykh Bāzīd, Riyāʾī, Shaykh ʿAlī Shahbāz, Shaykh Aḥmad Zandah Pīr known as Zhandahpīl, Ṣadr al-Dīn Ṣadr-i Jahān, Shaykh Khwājah, Mālīzāʾī, ʿAlī Shayr, Shāh Sikandar, Shaykh Ḥasan-i Sarmast, Mamūzāʾī, Āghūk Khayl, Malānah, Alūt Khayl, Saknūt Khayl, Shahbāz, Malik Yār, Ayyūbzāʾī, Tundak, ʿAlī Khayl, Ẓahr Khayl, Dawī Khayl, Haybat Khayl, Shaykh Saʿīd, Ḥasan Khayl, Mulānā, Bandar, Darū Khayl, Talkhān, Surī, and Aḥmad were all the offspring of Sarīpāl, the first son of Sarwāʾī, son of Shāh Ḥusayn Ghūrī and they are known as Sarwāʾī.

Similarly, Ḥusayn Khayl, Baryā Khayl, Abu'l-Faraj, Sahyā, Khiżr Khayl, Tāhirzāʾī, Rustam, Amūt, Sanjar, Jinānzāʾī, Zakūzāʾī, Yūnus Khayl, Yūsuf Khayl, Ismāʿīl, Nūrzāʾī, Majāzāʾī, Shām, ʿAmā Khayl, Bahdīn Khayl, Amīk, Alīk, Aḥmad Khayl, Gadāy, Hūtīzāʾī, Hatūzāʾī, Harūzāʾī, Ajā Khayl, Matā Khayl, and Sarsīr were all the offspring of Sīnī, **/52/54/** the second son of Sarwāʾī. All are referred to by this name, Sarwāʾī.

There is no offspring or successor to Balī, the third son of Sarwāʾī.

The Tribe and Clan of Shaykh Ṣadr al-Dīn, son of Shaykh Aḥmad Zhandah Pīr [i.e. Pīl], and How Mālīr Kūtalah, Which Is Where They Were Settled, Got Its Name

Shaykh Ṣadr al-Dīn, known as Ṣadr-i Jahān who lived in Mālīr Kūtalah had one son whom he named Bāzīd [i.e. Bāyazīd] Khān. He had three sons named as follows—Fīrūz Khān, Ikhtiyār Khān, and Ḥusayn Khān.

Thus, Khwājah Khiżr Khān, Shayr Muḥammad Khān, ʿAẓīm Khān, Jamāl Khān, Bīgan Khān, Wazīr Khān, Amīr Khān, Maḥbūb ʿAlī Khān, Sikandar ʿAlī Khān, Fatḥ Khān, Bahādur Khān, ʿUmar Khān, Asad Allāh Khān, ʿAṭā Allāh Khān, Mīrzā Khān, and Ghulām Ḥusayn Khān, were the sons, grandsons, and great-grandsons of Fīrūz Khān, the son of Bāzīd Khān.

Nāhir Khān, Walī Muḥammad Khān, and Tustar Khān were the offspring of Ikhtiyār Khān, the second son of Bāyazīd.

Khwājah Muḥammad Khān was from the loins of Ḥusayn Khān, the third son of Bā[ya]zīd Khān.

Of the five sons of Shaykh Aḥmad Zandah Pīr, Shaykh Ṣadr al-Dīn, who was the father of this tribe and the founder of this genealogy chose the path of celibacy and moral purity and from the place that had been his native land and home he headed for Hindūstān. He then settled in Mālī on the banks of the Sutlej River, one of the five rivers of the Panjab and there he built for himself a wooden house (*karīj*) in the form of a qalandar's lodge (*takiyah-i qalandarān*). A woman of the people of Mālī became a devotee and tied the belt of service to him. Gradually his reputation for asceticism and piety spread everywhere. (Meantime) Bahlūl Shāh Lūdī advanced on Dihlī in quest of the crown of the sultanate and one day happened to come to meet Shaykh Ṣadr al-Dīn. In his heart it was his intention that "If I conquer Dihlī, and am successful in this campaign I will give my daughter to Shaykh Ṣadr al-Dīn." After his meeting and departure from Shaykh Ṣadr al-Dīn and his continuing on to capture Dihlī, as was explained in the second volume of this book, he easily occupied Dihlī without a fight and without bloodshed and then brought his daughter into a contract of marriage to Shaykh Ṣadr al-Dīn. The shaykh built a house at the place where he resided and affixed the letter 'r' which is the first letter in *rabb* (lord) as a blessing to the name Mālī so that it became Mālīr. After this /53/55/ he also contracted marriage with a woman from the Rājpūt people. In the Christian year 1515 he died and was buried in the middle of the courtyard of the Mālīr khānqāh. His offspring who emerged from the line of the daughter of Bahlūl Shāh, served as trustees of his tomb generation after generation. Their living came from the votive offerings of pilgrims and the alms of those who passed by the tomb. Those of the line of the Rājpūt daughter became property owners, chiefs, etc.

The Tribe and Clans from the Line of Karrān

The progenitors (ancestors) of Karrān have been described in a variety of ways. Thus his sons and grandsons who formed great tribes [sometimes] give an account of Karrānīs which is not reliable. Concerning the tribe of Dilāzāk, one of the descendants of Karrān, they say that the father of Karrān was a sayyid who through eight generations was descended from Ḥażrat Ḥusayn, the son of ʿAlī, peace be upon him. The tribe of Khatak indicate that the father of Karrān was in the family tree of the Sarbanī Afghans. The leaders of the Shītak tribe state that Karrān was the son of a certain prince. The Khūgyānī tribe says that he was the son of ʿAbd Allāh Ūrmurī. Despite these differences concerning tribal affiliation, the offspring of some of the tribes are in agreement that Karrān was a newborn child and nursing when he was abandoned at a certain place where a military unit arrived in the dark of night. In the morning, when they arose to leave, they most unwillingly sold that boy to ʿAbd Allāh Ūrmurī for an iron pot-like vessel (*karāhī*) and then left. Since in Afghānī, they call a *karāhī* a *karbarī* therefore ʿAbd Allāh named that infant Karrārān. When he reached the age of maturity and discretion he saw signs of bravery and goodness in him and so married his own daughter to him. Thus Karrān became related to ʿAbd Allāh as an adopted son. From the belly of the daughter of ʿAbd Allāh the Lord gave him two sons—Kūdī and Kakī.

Thus, Dilāzāk, Lūrī Khayl, Aḥmad Khayl, Watakzāʾī, ʿUmar Khayl, Yaḥyāzāʾī, Samarzāʾī, Ardakzāʾī, Yaʿqūb Khayl, Zakariyā Khayl, Yasīn Khayl, Mandīzāʾī, Mūtīzāʾī, Amāzāʾī, Ḥaydarzāʾī, Sakhizāʾī, Ḥasīzāʾī, ʿAlīzāʾī, Mastūrī, Dawlatzāʾī, Muḥammad Khayl, Sih Pāy, Sulṭān Khayl, Amīrah Khayl, Lashgarī or Lakhgarī Khayl, ʿAbd al-ʿAzīz or Abdalīz Khayl, Bīdā Khayl, Aṣghar or Azghar Khayl, Mānī Khayl, Ṣabūrah Khayl, Aḥmad Khayl, Sārūzāʾī, Mast ʿAlī Khayl, Salār Khayl, Ḥājjī Sar Khayl, Mīr Wāʿiẓ Khayl, Badā Khayl, Tāghah Khayl, /54/56/ Bar Aḥmad Khayl,

Khuwaydād Khayl, ʿAlī Khwājah Khayl, Saʿīd Khayl, Mīrāzī Khayl, Sattārī Khayl, Fīrūz Khayl, Bīrūnī, Ismāʿīlzāʾī, Rābiyā Khayl, Mamāzāʾī, Abā Khayl, Khūdīzāʾī, Lashkarzāʾī, ʿAlī Shayrzāʾī, Māmūzāʾī, and Pārī all were descended from Kūdī, the first son of Karrān and all these lineages and decent lines were born of the womb of (Kūdī's) first wife. The Musāzāʾī, Mangal, Mūsā Khayl, Mīral Khayl, Khūcharah, Haybī, Mūkī, Kamāl Khayl, Jānī, Tūzāʾī, Hunī, Wardānīdī Akhīrah and others originally of the descendants of Kūdī were from the womb of his second wife.

The tribes and clans from the line of Kakī, the second son of Karrān, will be recorded in their own place below.

The Tribes and Clans of Dilāzāk Who Were Descended from Kūdī, the son of Kararān [*sic*]

Originally this tribe was quite large and mighty. At the time when a group of Afghans took control of the Khaybar Valley, due to the weakness of the rajah of Lahore, they built a long wall out of stone from the summit of the mountain to the depths of that valley and erected an impregnable fortress the traces of which wall still remain today. Later, they attacked Peshawar, which was known as Bagrām. With swords and strong arms, (the Afghans) conquered until they had gained control of the lands east of the Indus River. During the reign of Sulṭān Maḥmud [r. 997–1030 A.D.], son of Sabuktigīn, a large contingent of this tribe under the leadership of Malik Yaḥyā fought alongside the army of Sulṭān Maḥmūd in the Sūmnat (Somnath) campaign. During that campaign, as was recounted in detail in the second volume of this royal book, Malik Yaḥyā acquired much booty and raised the tribe to a much higher level. Some of the old men from the Dilāzāk tribe said in this regard that in the beginning the Dilāzāk tribe entered the eastern part of Afghanistan and in the time before their incursion into that region they conquered a group of Surkh Pūsh Kāfirs from Peshawar and from the east and west banks of the Indus River. They called them Surkh Kāfirs (red infidels) thinking that perhaps they were from the tribe of the Greeks and Bactrians.

In short, the Dilāzāk tribe, little by little took control of Swat District of Peshawar, Rawalpindi as far as Jalālābād out of the hands of the "red infidels." In the era of the government of Mīrzā Ulugh Bīk they became extremely powerful and extended the hand of raiding and plundering in this direction and that direction until eventually Jahāngīr Pādshāh Gūrgānī [r. 1605–1627 A.D.] /55/57/ extended his rule and exterminated them. Consequently, the majority of them were forced with wives and children to decamp and go to the Deccan, Hindūstān and settle there. Now of that haughty and arrogant tribe a very small number are found in Hazārah District [India] and another small group is found in Chahchah. The rest have disappeared.

The Tribes, Clans, and People Who Were of the Lineage of Arūkzāʾī, the Second Son of Kūdī, son of Karrān

The Arūkzāʾī tribe and people are divided in five sections. Most reside in the mountains; some live in Kūhāt District and in locales in the eastern Kūh-i Safīd of Jalālābād and in the southern valleys of Tīrā territory. The Bangash people, who are of the Shiʿah sect, conquered the land of Kūhāt 470 years ago. Eventually, the Bangashes united and attacked the Arūkzāʾī, defeated them, and retrieved their own lands and fields.

The Arūkzāʾī tribe numbers 20,000 people. They live in the mountains and the Bangash have the flat lands with the farms and fields.

The Tribes of Mangal, One of the Offspring of Kūdī, Son of Karrān, Who Comprise Several Clans and Sub-Clans

Six hundred years ago [i.e. ca. 1326] this tribe was living together with the Sanī tribe on the territory of Banūn and then because of the Shītak tribe's victory over them—they abandoned that place and took up residence in the western mountains of Kurram District and Khūst. Several times during the reign of Amīr ʿAbd al-Raḥmān Khān [r. 1880–1901] and once during the time of Amīr Ḥabīb Allāh Khān [r. 1901–1919] they rose in rebellion and were massacred, beaten back, and routed. Today, their total number amounts to 15,000 individuals.

The Muqbil Tribe Resident in the Mountains Belonging to Khūst

This tribe is small and lives in a confined and impenetrable mountain area of the Khūst District in the direction of Kabul, west of the Jājī tribe and north of the Mangal tribe. A few households live in the village of Lakan, Khūst District, as clients [of an unnamed tribe]. **/56/58/**

The Clans of the Tribe of Kakī, the Second Son of Karrān

Kakī, the son of Karrān had four sons—Burhān, Khūgyānī, Sulaymān, and Shītak. The clans of the last three will be recorded after writing about the Afrīdī.

The Tribes and Clans of the Line of Burhān, the First Son of Kakī, Son of Karrān

To Burhān, son of Kakī, the Lord granted four sons whose names are as follows: 1) ʿUs̱mān, known as Afrīdī, an account of whom takes precedence over the others; 2) Luqmān, known as Khatak; 3) Jadrān, and 4) Utmān Khayl.

ʿUs̱mān, known as Afrīdī had two sons: Māpī and Chālnī.[10] The offspring of the second were very few and they lived amongst the Bangash tribe. Māpī, the first son of ʿUs̱mān, son of Burhān, son of Kakī had five sons—Mītā Khayl and Ādam Khayl from his (Māpī's) first wife; and Ūlā Khayl, Akā Khayl, and Mīrī from his second wife.

Mītā Khayl had no offspring.

The Ḥasan Khayl, Zūkī, Gulī, Sīnī Khayl, Naẓar Khayl, Shahbāz Khayl, Razm Khayl, Astū Khayl, Yāghī, Kalā Khayl, Muḥammadī, and ʿAlī Khayl were from these three full brothers (Ūlā Khayl, Akā Khayl, and Mīrī) and were known by their mother's name, ʿĀyishah Khayl.

---

[10] The copyist has created an unknown letter here (where we have chosen "Ch") by placing three dots inside the *ḥāʾ* as well as three dots over it. For other possible readings see p. 27, note 67 above.

Fīrūz Khayl, Mīr Aḥmad Khayl, Malik Dīn Khayl, ʿUmar Khān Khayl, Ramā Khayl, Shāhī Khayl, Kūdī Khayl, Gulāb Khayl, Bībī Khayl, Jand Khayl, Matah Khayl, Nuṣrat Khayl, Natū Khayl, Dawlat Khayl, Jaʿfar Khayl, ʿUmar Khayl, ʿAbdal Khayl, Ismāʿīl Khayl, Miyār Khayl, ʿAlim Khayl, Rashīd Khayl, Naẓar Khayl, Maḥmūd Khayl, Mīrzā Bīk Khayl, Tār Khayl, Khūbī Khayl, Qanbar Khayl, Darbī Khayl, Zūnah Khayl, Shaykh Mal Khayl, Khwājah ʿAlī Khayl, Mat Khānī, Yārān Khayl, Mīrān Khayl, Qāyim Khayl, Sulaymān Khayl, ʿAlī Khayl, Karminah or Karminā Khayl, Darwī Khayl, Mīrī Khayl, Yār Muḥammad Khayl, Bahrāmī Khayl, Alpī Khayl, Kalah Khayl, Aymal Khayl, Qamarī, Kūkī Khayl, Abdān Khayl, Bārī Khayl, Mādar or Padar Khayl, Bītā Khān, Iskandar Khayl, Zalūr Palārah (*zalūr* in Afghānī is 'four' and *palārah* is 'father'), Tūr Khayl, Qārūn Khayl, Madad Khayl, Wālī Khayl, Ḥasan Khayl, Mūyinah or Mūtanā Khayl, Kattī Khayl, Sih Pāy, Abā Bakr, Landī, Hurmuz, Shān Khayl, Būdī Khayl, Pakhī, Żiyā al-Dīn or Zād al-Dīn, Amānī, Naṣr al-Dīn, Pāyindī, and Khusrawkī of the Shān Khayl—up to this point the last eight clans are known by the name of the mother, Zakhah Khayl /57/59/ and the clans from Fīrūz Khayl to Hurmuz are altogether remembered as Ūlā Khayl. Akā Khayl, Basī Khayl, Madā Khayl, Kamāl Khayl, Sulṭān Khayl, Garīrī [Gurīzī?], Shayr Khayl, Lat, Sīrī Khayl, Sazl or Naḥl Khayl, ʾĪsāzāʾī, and Mīrī Khayl along with all the clans heretofore listed are named and known as the Afrīdī tribe.

This is how they say it came to be named Āfrīdī: One day a few people with no food and provisions entered the house of ʿUs̱mān as guests. He was the founder and progenitor of these numerous clans. Since it was the cold season and the weather was severe the guests were clinging to each other trying to stay warm with their natural body heat. Then ʿUs̱mān, the host, came in and the guests said to him, "Who are you?" In reply he said in Afghānī "*Da ham āfarīdah wa khudā dī*" meaning "This one, too, is but a creature (*āfārīdah*) of God." From that day onward they were called and became known as "Āfarīdahs." Through much usage, it became more commonly Āfrīdī and now the entire tribe of ʿUs̱mān and all the clans carry the name Afrīdī.

The Āfrīdīs are well-known to the English government for being punished because most of them are on the frontier of Hindūstān, are constantly harassing the frontier guards, and most of the time are victorious.

The majority of this tribe is known as Ūlā Khayl, Fīrūz Khayl, and Mīr Aḥmad Khayl, the offspring of Ūlā, Fīrūz and Mīr Aḥmad. They are extremely courageous, valiant, and already ready for a fight and they dwell in impenetrably mountainous territory. During the reign of Aḥmad Shāh Sadūzāʾī their numbers amounted to 19,000 [people] and today they are reckoned at 25,000 to 30,000. Their mountain lands are bounded on the east by those of the Khatak tribe and are adjacent to the shrine of Kākā Ṣāḥib. On the west they are bordered by Kūh-i Rājkul and Khaybar District up to Nangarhār. To the south and southwest the border is the mountain region belonging to Peshawar and to the north the Kabul River and Kūh-i Muhmand. To the south of the homeland of this tribe are the Arūkzāʾī, the Bangash, the Chamkanī people who live in the Safīd Kūh and to the west of that tribe (i.e. the Afrīdī) are the Sangū Khayl Shinwārī. To the north the Muhmands have their residences. Of all the clans, two descent groups of the Afrīdī, the Saml and Gārī, fight each other over being Shiʿah or Sunni and most of the time they fight on sectarian grounds.

The Tribes and Clans of the Line of Burhān, the First Son of Kakī, Son of Kararān [Karrān]

Except for those of this tribe making their homeland in the plain of Tīrāh District, all the others /58/60/ are forced to make their domiciles on the little bit of arable land found in both the low areas and on the heights of the stony mountain gorges and so in order to make a living they engage in theft and highway banditry. They also sell wood and salt and do unskilled labor in order to live. (The Āfrīdī) comprise two factions, one is called the Saml and the other the Gārī. Malik Dīn Khayl, Zakhah Khayl, Akā Khayl, Sih Pāy, and Qamarī are the auxiliaries of the Saml. The Qanbar Khayl and Kūkī Khayl side with the Gārī faction. From time to time, because of fighting amongst themselves, they withdraw from the factional fighting but after a while start up again.

Luqmān, known as the Khatak tribe, the second son of Burhān son of Kakī, second son of Karrān, had two sons—Tūrān and Būlāq.

The tribes and clans of the line of Būlāq will be recorded after those of the line of Tūrān. The clans of Tarī, Bar Kūpaṭah, Ismāʿīl Khayl, Gharī, Māshī, Khwājī, Sīrī Khayl, Yasīn Khayl, Bārak, Amanzāʾī, Kūdī Khayl, Hānī Khayl, Saraī Khayl, Kāmil Khayl, Allāh Khān Khayl, Kamī Khayl, Alif Khayl, Nafḥal Khayl, Bahrām Khayl, Jand Khayl, Khūshḥāl Khayl, Makhal Khayl, Mīrā Khān Khayl, Dalīl Khayl, Qajīr or Kajīr Khayl, Shaykh Ḥāṣil, Mīr Bāz Khayl, Mīnā Khayl, Pistī Khayl, Sardast Khayl, Gulzāʾī, Ismāʿīl, Māshī Khayl, Bānīd Khayl, Ḥaydar Khān Khayl, Khazīn Khayl, Kamī Khayl, Shūmī, Shakhāwat Khayl, ʿAzīz Khayl, Mishr, ʿArī, Tarakī, Bayān Khayl, Mandhan, Darshī, Mandūy, Madī, ʿĪsak, Matī, Akū, Babar, Idrīs Khayl, Khurram, Tar, and Ānū Khayl are all clans of the line of this last one (?) and will be mentioned later. These are all offspring of Tūrān, son of Khatak and they are called Khatak. Also Yūsuf Khayl and Īstūrī (*īstūrī* in Afghānī is *sitārah* (star) and the annexed *yāʾ* is the *yāʾ* of diminution so it means *sitārah-i kak* or *sitārah-i kūchak* [i.e. little star]). In the introduction of this very volume [volume five] there is a discussion concerning the sharing of words between nations and the word *istūr* which is from *stār* and *sitārah* is also in English as "star."

Amandī, Bahrām, Khwājah Khayl, Nuṣratī, Gandā Khayl, Būgar Khayl, Jalī Khayl, Bashar Khayl, Sandar Khayl, Darkhān Khayl, Kashīd Khayl, Mīr Gul Khayl, Alahdād Khayl, Ashraf Khayl, Dāwar Khayl, Sitan Khayl, Badīn Khayl, Guldīn Khayl, Charkī Khayl, ʿAlī Khān Khayl, ʿĀlam or Alam Khayl, Lashgar Khayl, ʿAbdalī or Awdalī Khayl, Lagārī, and Mapāl, which are the progeny of Tarakī son of Tūrmān [*sic*—Tūrān], whose name has not been mentioned before but here they are recorded with the clans of his lineage through whom the line of Tarī, the son of Tūrmān [*sic*], whose name has been mentioned, are given the name Khatak. /59/61/

The Tribes and Clans from the Line of Ānū, Which has been Mentioned and Whom We Promised to Record

Ānūy named Ānū Khayl of the Khatak tribe, had two sons—Baṭiʾ Khayl and Muhmandī.

Thus, the Hūtī, Fatḥ Khayl, Kīmal Khayl, Mushrī (Mashrī, Mishrī?), Shaykh ʿAlī, Ḥasan Khayl, Utmān Khayl, Darbī Khayl, Bārak Khayl, Mandū, Janjū, Akūr Khayl,

Yaḥyā Khān, Shahbāz Khān, Jamāl Khān, Khūshḥāl Bīk Khān, Muḥammad Ashraf Khān, Muḥammad Afżal Khān, Sa'd Allāh Khān, Shahnāz Khān, Nāṣir 'Alī Khān, Aṣlākhā Khān known as Arsalākh Khān, Khwājah Muḥammad Khān, Ja'far Khān, Sa'ādatmand Khān, Kaẓim Khān, Muḥammad 'Alī Khān, Ḥasan 'Alī Khān, 'Abd Allāh Khān, Nāmdār Khān, Bahrām Khān, 'Abd al-Qādir Khān, Mīrdād Khayl, Machūrī, Ghāzī Khān, Nāṣir, Shāhid, Malī Khayl, Aḥmad Khayl, Karīm Khayl, Chīnī Khayl, Alak Khayl, 'Amī Khayl, Yasīn Khayl, and Bakī Khayl were all the offspring (sons and grandsons) of Baṭī Khayl, the son of Ānū Khayl and through him are said to be Khatak.

Sūryā Khayl, and Mamā Khayl are the offspring of Muhmandī, the second son of Ānū, and are called Yāsinī and Kashīnī and they are named one of the branches of the Khatak.

The Tribes and Clans Who Emerged from the Lineage of Būlāq, the Second Son of Khatak and Whom We Promised to Report On

The Lord blessed Būlāq, son of Khatak, with three [*sic*—two? see below] sons from two wives—Shāghirī and Marwazī.

The Makūrī, Yangī Khāyl, Turkah, Bābar, Bāzdīd Khāyl, Mamarakī, Mashūn Khāyl, Dakat Khān Khāyl, Mal Khān Khāyl, Hujūm Khāyl, Riyā Khāyl, Mashwī Khāyl, Haybat Khāyl, Tarakī, Mihr Gul Khāyl, Kūrūb Khāyl, Murawwij Khāyl, Abī Khāyl, Jūtū Khāyl, Jamālī, Jaldīn Khāyl, Sūd Khāyl, Karīmdād Khāyl, Khārak, Mīrzā Khāyl, Chūrī Khāyl, Bītī, Mānakī Khāyl, Sagū Khāyl, Miryam Khāyl, 'Alam Shāh Khāyl, Dilāwar Khāyl, Sadū Khāyl, 'Aṭā, Tū, Dar Malik, Mandī, Mushk, Khurram, Tarah, Gulī, Rūzī, Shān, and Tandarak are the offspring of Sāghīrī (*sic*—Shāghirī), the first son of Būlāq, son of Khatak and therefore are called Khatak.

Similarly, the Mahmūtī, Achū Khāyl, Ghūr Khāyl, and Māmūn Khāyl, are the offspring of Marwazī, the second son of Būlāq, son of Khatak, and so carry the name Khatak.

The fact of the matter is that the Mughlakī, Sīnī, Ūryā Khāyl, and Chalūzā'ī clans which all carry the name Khatak, in truth **/60/62/** don't belong to the Khatak lineage because they came from a different place, entered the territory of the Khatak, and gradually, because of a great deal of intermixing, today they call themselves Khatak. They say, and it has been written, that the way they became connected [to the Khatak] was that there was a certain Mughulakī from the Mongol people who took a wife from the Khatak tribe and lived in the same place with them. Little by little he came to be known as Khatak.

As for the Sīnī, a person named Sīnī from the Dilāzāk Karrānī tribe which was written about with the clans of the line of Dilāzāk son of Kūdī, son of Karrān, took a wife from the Khatak tribe and established himself at a place called Sarāl. His children were known as Sīnī and it may be that the genealogy of these two men became connected to the line of the Būlāk (*sic*—Būlāq) Khatak through conjoining and intermixing.

Ūryā Khayl was the son of a widow. A person by the name of Hamandī of the Khatak tribe married her. Out of respect for the mother he (Hamandī) gave a share in his estate of both movables and immovables [to Ūryā Khayl]. This was one of the reasons that Ūryā attached himself to the Khatak. Ūryā took a wife from the Khatak and so attached his children to the Khatak.

As for the Chalūzāʾī there was a man named Rashīd, son of a certain Yaʿqūb who was of the Khalīl tribe. He took the daughter of ʿAlī Khān Khatak to wife and settled in the homeland of the Khataks. His descendants took the name Chalūzāʾī after his wife whose name was Chalū.

Similarly, the Dangarzāʾī were also related by *waṣlī* connection (rather than by blood) and these three *waṣlī* clans entered the Tarīn tribe and were named Ulūs-i Tarīn.

This is how Luqmān came to be called Khatak. One day, he went out hunting with ʿUs̱mān, better known as Afrīdī, Jadrān, and Utmān—all three being his brothers who earlier were written about at the end of the (description of the) tribes that were the offspring of Burhān, the son of Kakī, son of Karrān. They went to a barren area and as it happened they encountered four young women of lovely appearance and dressed in silk [but veiled.] On seeing the women they were smitten and when they began to speak to them, they fell in love. It soon became known that the four had no spouses and it was resolved that the four men would marry the four women. Luqmān, who was the oldest of the four brothers, said, "We should choose them by lot. But I have already settled on the woman who has the fine dress and chador and will have her but not by lot. You then will choose among the other three women by lot." To this the other three agreed. They drew lots and each one took a woman. When the women then revealed their faces, the woman whose clothing and adornments had smitten ʿUs̱mān turned out to be ugly, fat, revolting to look at, and in terms of her figure she had the worst shape, bar none! When those brothers saw her awfulness **/61/63** /they said to ʿUs̱mān or they spoke to each other in Afghānī and said "*ʿUs̱mān bakht lār*" that is "ʿUs̱mān ended up in mud and is stuck." This proverb is well-known among Afghans until today so that when anyone is helpless and unhappy in some affair they say to him *bakht lār* has happened. And thus Luqmān became known as Khatak and all his tribe and lineage from then on were known as Khatak.[11]

Originally, the Khatak tribe had their place in Kūh-i Shawāl. This mountain range extends to the west of Kūh-i Sulaymān. Now that mountain is occupied by the Wazīrī people. Approximately 670 years ago, the Khatak together with the Mangal tribe and the Hunī entered the territory of Banūn and took control of the lands and the Sad Rāwan River which at the time was the homeland of the Bīzhan Khayl and the Isparakī Wazīrs of the Aḥmadzāʾī. Later, the Shītak clans forcibly drove the Mangal and Sanī out of that place and scattered them. The Khataks were enemies of the Banūchī clans and not having the capability to defend it, they gave up the Sad Rāwan territory and made a place for themselves in a mountain region to the northeast of Banūn. Consequently, those mountains are presently known as Kūh-i Khatakān. They occupy that mountain and the locales of Kar Būghah, Tīrī, Chūtarah, Lāchī, and Shakardarrah as far as the Sīlāb River, that

[11] There would seem to be something missing from the text that would connect the *bakht lār* story to Luqmān becoming a Khatak.

is the Indus River. The mountain region at that time was undeveloped and no one bothered them until the time the Bangash people began to frequent Kūhāt by way of Kurram. At that time, Kūhāt was inhabited by the Ūrakzā'ī tribe. The Bangash fought with the Ūrakzā'ī and the Khatak tribe at first allied with the Bangash and assisted them and [together] they removed Kūhāt from the hands of the Ūrakzā'ī and then surrendered it to the Bangash. They themselves (the Khatak) occupied the locales of Rīsī, Payālah, and Zīrah as far as the territory of Chirah. They agreed that one mountain would separate and intervene between those two tribes, the Khatak and Bangash, with the Gadā Khayl and Lāchī in the midst of this borderland. Then the Khatak tribe, because of its large population, became predominant and independent and occupied all of that land. Consequently, the four borders of the lands of the Khatak became the Yūsufzā'ī District of Peshawar, the Kabul River north of Landī Kutal, Kālah Bāgh, 'Īsā Khayl, the homeland of the Marwat, the [homeland of the] Wazīr, and Banūn District to the western banks of the Indus River. The territory of this tribe which currently is in their possession happens to be quite irregular. Lengthwise, from north to south it is about 100 miles and from east to west its width is 40 miles. Most of **/62/64/** its eastern boundary is the Indus River.

One branch of the Sāghirī Khatak tribe occupies Shahr-i Makhad and Aqḥah in Rawalpindi District, to the south of which is the eastern side of the Indus River. The western boundary of the Khatak territory is the land of the Afrīdīs, the Bangash, and others. South of their territory is Banūn. The southern part of the possessions of the Khatak tribe are very high mountains.

The total number of households of the Khatak tribe, whether scattered about or assembled in one place, is reckoned at 20,000 and the number of its people at 60,000.

The Clans and Tribes of Jadrān, the Son of Burhān, the Son of Kakī, the Report about Which Was Promised Earlier

For Jadrān, or Zadrān, the third son of Burhān, son of Kakī, son of Karrān, three sons came into existence—Tūlā Khayl, Bīd Khayl, and Tīpah.

The Mazī, Aḥmad Khayl or Aḥmat Khayl, Brāhīm Khayl, Akhtar Khayl, Walī Khayl, Naẓar Khayl, Darī Palārah, Mūsā Khayl, Alīk, Tūgar Khayl, Khūjād Khayl, Madad Khayl, Ghanī Khayl, Pāw Khayl, 'Umar Khayl, Khar Khayl, Tūrah Khayl, Bāzīd Khayl, Sulṭān Khayl, Parangī, and Sūrī Khayl were all offspring (sons and grandsons) of Tūlā, the first son of Jadrān.

Also, Sar Khayl, Akhūn Khayl, Abū Khayl, Shayr Khayl, Bābar or Būbar Khayl, Dankī Khayl, Bāzakī, Walah Khayl, Tūrakī, Walīdī, Dīdī Khayl, Jūl Khayl, Jamakī, Dawī Khayl, Hawas Khayl, Khūy Khayl, Mawsim Khayl, Bībah Khayl, Khānī or Khūnī Khayl, Mīr Ḥusayn [or] Mīr Sīn Khayl, Kūbān or Kī Bun Khayl, Alū Khayl, Ni'mat Khayl, Yarmīst Khayl, Fīrūz Khayl, 'Alī Khān, Zanī Khayl, Būlā Khayl, Mumal Khayl, Zang Khayl, Sandal Khayl, Isparakī Khayl, Wāl Khayl, Khurmiz Khayl, Multān Khayl, Shahādat or Shawdat Khayl, Bishkah Khayl, Najī, Nabat Khayl, Matah Khānī, and Gurzā'ī, all were the offspring of Bīd, the second son of Jadrān and they were called Bīd Khayl of the Jadrān.

Tīpah, the third son passed away without producing offspring.

These tribes and clans of the Jadrān people have made their homeland in the verdant mountain range to the west of which is Khūst and to the east Zurmat District. These are a people enduring great hardship. Whenever there is war, [the Jadrān] will raise 20,000 armed men. In the mountain region where they live, everywhere there is running water they have many piñon pines. But they have very little cultivable land. Thus, with great difficulty **/63/65/** they have brought topsoil to places in the mountains that have been graded and to the base of the mountains and poured it on top of those places to carry out proper cultivation. Then they cultivate it. Their homeland to the east adjoins Khūst District, to the west the land of Gardīz, to the south the territory and homes of the Ghiljāʾī tribe and to the northeast to the Mangal. These are the details of [the Jadrān's] boundaries.

The Peoples and Clans of the Lineage of Utmān, Known as Utmān Khayl, Son of Burhān

The Lord favored Utmān Khayl, who was the fourth son of Burhān, son of Kakī, son of Karrān and for whom (Utmān Khayl) we promised earlier to provide an account, with six sons—ʿAzīz Khayl, Karāʾī, Bamrī, Hamrī, Dakhlah, and Māndal. Four of these six brought forth no sons but two, the second and third were particularly prolific.

Thus the blood relationship (*aṣīl*) stems from the loins of Karāʾī, the second son, and so back to Utmān Khayl.

Ismāʿīl Khayl, Pāyandah Khayl, Adan Kūr, Ḥamzah Kūr, Akhalī Khayl, Haybat Khayl, Dawlat Khayl, Shaykhā Khayl, Walī Khayl, ʿUmar Khayl, Yār ʿAlī Khayl, Rasūl Khayl, Tīrāwī, Shaykh ʿAlī Khān Khayl, Shaykh ʿAlī, Alḥaq Kūr, Barah Khān Kur, Khān Kūr, Zamandī Kūr, Mihtar Khayl, ʿAbbās Khayl, Pūkhān Khayl, Adrū Khayl, Fatḥ Khayl, Daʿwat Khayl, Bākī Khayl, Jān Bīk Khayl, Pūlād Khayl, Ḥayāt Khayl, Bātūzāʾī, Faqīr Khayl, Mulūk Khayl, ʿAmbārah Khayl, Miskīn Khayl, Kattī Khayl, Yābū Khayl, Khūshḥāl Khayl, Sulṭānī Khayl, Akūr Khayl, Achū Khayl, Ṣadr Khān Khayl, Wālī Khayl, Andān, Mīrūs Khayl, Alū Khayl, Muḥammad Khān Kūr, Zayn Khān Kūr, Barī Khayl, Dawlat Khayl, Ṭāwūsī, Dād Khayl, Jūkī Khayl, Akhtarī Khayl, Sar Badāl Khayl, Payandī Khayl, Bādū Khayl, Salīm Khān Kūr, Shamūzāʾi, Sih Ṣadah, Tūrzāʾī, ʿAjab Khayl, Ayā Khayl, Ṣālī Khayl, Shābī Khayl, Īzabzāʾī, Hārūn Khayl, Changā Khayl, Anīs Khayl, Ṭāwūs Khayl, Manṣūr Khayl, Dilāzak—this individual being related not by blood (i.e. *waṣlī* not *aṣlī*), Muʾmin Khayl, Sharīf Khayl, and Swātī—this one [also] being *waṣli* not *aṣlī*—all these clans both blood related and related by other than blood were the offspring of Bamrī and through him were called Utmān Khayl.

The tribes and clans inscribed above who were Utmān [Khayl] in 1004 A.D. headed for Peshawar by way of Kabul and Nangarhar, i.e. Jalālābād, from the locale of **/64/66/** Tāk (Tank) and the Kūh-i Gumāl included in [the territory of] the Yūsufzāʾī tribe. They went there and the Yūsufzāʾī, in consideration [of the fact that] they were accompanying them, made them their partners in Dūābah and Hasht Nagar. Later, the Dilāzāk tribe, the Yūsufzāʾī and others began to fight with each other in Mīr Langar Kūt or Karī Kapūrah. In this fight, the Utmān Khayls attacked and overcame the Dilāzākīs. For this great effort expended by the

Utmān Khayls in defeating the Dilāzāks, the Yūsufzā'īs showed no respect. Consequently they (the Utmān Khayl) were offended and moved from Hasht Nagar and Dūābah and settled in the southern part of the mountains of Bājāwur and Swat (Sawād) which is near the western end of Bājāwur and that mountain range and extending as far as the southern end of the territory of Sawād.

Of the Bamrī clans, the clans of Ismāʿīl Khayl, Daʿwat Khayl, and Sih Ṣadah made their homeland in the northeast corner of Miyāran belonging to the Bā'īzā'ī clan of the Yūsufzā'ī. The population of the Bamrī tribe there is counted as 3,000 armed men. The entire Utmān Khayl tribe is reckoned at 15,000 households. Of that total, a few have their homes in Kūh Dāman north of the city of Kabul. They are fruit sellers and make their living that way. There is also one clan from this tribe that is nomadic. In winter it goes to Jalālābād and in summer comes to Kabul. They also earn a living as reapers and cheese-(*panīr*) sellers, etc.

The Tribes and Clans Which Were the Lineage of Khūgyānī, the Second Son of Kakī, Son of Karrān

The Lord provided Khūgyānī, son of Kakī, son of Karrān, for whom we earlier promised to provide a full account, with six sons from one wife—Shayrzād, Parbah, Khadr Khayl, Bārak, Būbū Khayl, ʿAbd al-Raḥmān—and four other sons from another wife—Kharbūnī, Tūrī, Ḥājjī, and Mandūzā'ī—so in all he had ten sons. Three of them, who became the founders and heads of numerous tribes, peoples, and clans, will be inscribed below with the tribes that were their lineages. The seven other sons who had no separate clans will be mentioned now. Thus ʿAmrakī, Tarakī, and Kānkah Khayl were the sons of Khadr Khayl, the third son of Khūgyānī and so are called Khūgyānī.

Luqmān and Shādī Khayl were the grandsons of Bārak, the fourth son of Khūgyānī and because of this are called Khūgyānī.

Ḥamzah Khayl, **/65/67/** Mastū Khayl, Daparzā'ī, ʿAlīzā'ī, and Ghundī Khayl who were the sons of Tūrī, the eighth son of Khūgyānī, were thus called Khūgyānī. Now they are known as Tūrī. They are all of the Imāmī Twelver Shiʿah sect.

Of all these Khūgyānī clans, Shayrzād, Khiżr Khayl, Bārak, and Būbū Khayl, make their homes in Sapīd Kūh located in the western part of Nangarhar, i.e., Jalālābād, in the northwestern part of that mountain range. In the first year of the reign of the Mughal, Shihāb al-Dīn Shāh Jahān [r. 1628–1658] a minor dispute arose between the Shādī Khayl and Luqmān, offspring of Bārak which grew into a major conflict. The Khiżr Khayls supported and aided Luqmān against the Shādī Khayl. The Shādī Khayls were defeated in battle and fled, taking refuge among the Ghiljā'ī. With the help of the Ghiljā'ī, they attacked Saʿīd Khān, the governor (*ṣūbahdār*) of Kabul who took the side of their enemies, and 1,000 of the offspring of Bārak were killed. In the end, Shayrzād and Khiżr Khayl drew the collar of royal obedience around the neck of submission and the fires of *fitnah* were quelled. Now the Khūgyānī tribe are well-known and the mountain where they make their homes is very difficult (of access) and heavily wooded. Leaving the Tūrī and Jājī tribes aside, their numbers reach 7,500 households.

The Tūrī Tribe and People Descended from Tūr, the Eighth Son of Khūgyānī, Son of Kakī, Second Son of Karrān

This tribe has its homes on both banks of the river of the Kurram Valley south of the Sapīd Kūh and north of Khūst. Kurram District which has fertile land for growing grain at first was occupied by the Bangash tribe but due to exigencies of the time and constant factors which affected their situation, they abandoned their original homes and set out for different parts. Today, many of those from the Bangash tribe who are (still) there live difficult, hardscrabble lives. Of them one section, the Būʾl-Yamīn, confront extreme pressure (in their lives) at the far end of that district.

The Tūrī tribe, which has made its home there, comprises five khayls, namely, Ḥamzah Khayl, Satū Khayl, Parzāʾī, ʿAlīzāʾī, and Ghūndi Khayl. They have 16,000 armed and battle-ready men. They earn their livings from agriculture, trade, fruit sales, (government) service, and by other means. They are very brave and always ready for a fight. They are always fighting with the Afghans who are their neighbors and who are all of the Sunni sect. **/66/68/** They fight out of ignorant fanaticism and inherent hatred. They slaughter each other and in the midst of the river of fire they persist in protecting and preserving their own.

Concerning the lineage of the Tūrī and Jājī tribes Afghans have different opinions. Khūshḥāl Khān Khatak wrote in his book that they were of Karrān's line. He himself lived at the time of Shāh Jahān and included them among the tribal groupings of the Karrān. Some people from those very tribes (Tūrī and Jājī) confirmed this and considered themselves to be of the line of Kakī, son of Karrān. Some say that Tūr and Jāj were brothers and from the Awān tribe of the Mūnd branch and lineage. They became estranged from another brother of theirs, seized some lands west of the Indus River, went there and gradually grew strong. They then conquered the mountains and valleys that they presently inhabit. The descendants of Tūr came to be known as Tūrī and those of Jāj, Jājī. Although the tribe that makes its homeland and prospers in Jahlum (Jhelum) District, still what Khūshḥāl Khān says is not proof. Yet, what Khūshḥāl Khān Khatak said is reliable and most accurate because these two tribes have become all mixed up with other Afghans so no one is able to distinguish between them for it cannot be said that they are anything other than Afghans.

The Tribe of Parbah, Second Son of Khūgyānī, Son of Kakī, son of Karrān

Parbah originally was related to a branch of the Khūgyānī tribe except today they are separate and distinct and they think themselves so far removed [from the Khūgyānī] that they don't consider themselves as belonging to it. This tribe comprises ten clans and khayls—Mardī Khayl, Miyā Khayl, Basī Khayl, Sardār Khayl, Maḥmūd Khayl, Tarīzāʾī, Malīzāʾī, Āshīzāʾī, Dah Dah Khayl, and Būjī Khayl. Together they produce 1,250 sword-wielding men. They live in Khūst and are in the Aspīn Gundī faction.[12]

---

[12] As in other societies, the Pashtūns of the Khūst area divide into two factions, the Aspīn (or Spīn) Gundī and Tūr Gundī (the Whites and the Blacks).

It is recognized that the Khūgyānī clans of the Karrānī tribe and others in the beginning occupied all the district and territory of Khūst. During the reign of the Mughal, Jahāngīr, some clans of the Ghiljā'ī tribe living in Zurmat came out in revolt and seized the greater part of Khūst. During the time of Shāh Jahān, because of infighting, the numbers of the Khūgyānī tribe were reduced. Thus it is well-known that in former times the Purbah tribe had 3,000 fighting men and now /67/69/ they earn their living by farming and a few by trade.

The Tribe of ʿAbd al-Raḥmān, the Sixth Son of Khūgyānī, A Grandson of Karrān

This tribe was comprised of six clans—Ḥājjī Khān Khayl, Sūdī Khayl, Aḥmad Khayl and these three were related by blood (*aṣlī*). Madī Khayl, Kūndī, and Mankas were not related by blood [they were *waṣlī*]. All were also called Mamūrī and Matūn. Duzī Khayl also was incorporated in the Matūn tribe. The name Matūn is the name of a place in the district and territory of Khūst and so their name is by virtue of metonymy [the name derived from the name of the container]. The number of people in this six-segment tribe is as much as 1,200 to 1,300 people and all are farmers.

Another Six-Segment Tribe from the Karrānī Tribe and Residing in Zurmat

[The six]: Ṣabarī (4,000 [people]), Malī (800 people), Landar (200 people), Akībī (150 people), Qadam (150 people), and Hārūn Khayl (150 fighting men). All of them belong to the Aspahīn (Aspīn) Gūnd faction (the Whites). Their homes are in Little Khūst (Khūst-i Kūchak). Another four clans of the Lagan tribe—Rakī Khayl, Nukat Khayl, Shādīzā'ī, and Ayyūb Khayl—are reckoned to have 1,300 men. The Ṣādiq tribe is counted as having 300 men, ʿAlī Shayr 150, Bakar Khayl with 150, and Lūn Khayl with 100. All of these are in the Tūr Gūnd (the Black Faction) in Khūst. All these tribes which have been written about in the preceding as being from the Aspīn Gūnd or the Tūr Gūnd are in the Karrānī tribe. Two antagonistic tribes, namely the Ghiljā'ī and the Karrānī, have their homelands in Khūst territory and each has its own particular language, customs, and habits. All the clans of the Karrānī tribe belong to the Aspīn Gūnd faction while the Ghiljā'ī belong to the Tūr Gūnd. *Tūr* and *aspīn*, which in Persian mean *siyāh* and *sapīd* (black and white), have a visceral and endemic hatred for one another and never cease fighting with each other.

The Tribes and Clans of Sulaymān, the Third Son of Kakī, Son of Karrān

Sulaymān, son of Kakī, had one son named Wazīr. Wazīr had two sons—Khiżrī and Lākī.

Mūsāy known as Darwīsh, Aḥmadzā'ī, Maḥmūd, Masʿūd, Mubārak, Garbāz or Garīz, Utmānzā'ī, Maḥmūdzā'ī, Mumīt Khayl, /68/70/ Ḥasan Khayl, Khiżr Khayl, Sahbī Khayl, Īz Khayl, Ḥaydar Khayl, Muḥammad or Mamad Khayl, Mihtar Khayl, Khadr Khayl, Rajī Khayl, Tarkalī Khayl, Shayr Khayl, Darī Palārī, Balal Khayl, Tūr Khayl, Darī Nāmī, Bahār Khayl, Chalāk Khayl, Shayr Khayl—*sic*, Shādū Khayl or Shayūdī Khayl, Shaml Khayl, Dar Mal Khayl, Dūrī Khayl, Mandī Khayl, Gūgī Khayl, Bakhshī Khayl, Dardānī, Babar Sari, Haybat Khayl, Wazī Khayl, Ghalīb Khayl,

Pūchī Khayl, ʿĪsā Khayl, Lak Khayl, Mahrimān Khayl, Tūrakī Khayl, Dūsakī Khayl, Barkhānī, Sarmast Khayl, Muḥibb Khayl, Zargar Khayl, Shīrū Khayl, Jamāl Khayl, Mamarīz Khayl, Musakī, Būzī or Bāzī Khayl, Tar Khayl, Lālī or Lūlī Khayl, Shakhr Khayl, Darnī, Razānī or Razūnī, Darī Khayl, Asad Khayl, Mīr Khān Khayl, Mīrzā Khayl, Nānā Khayl, Armiyā Khayl, Tūlā Khayl, Zar Khayl, Darī Palārah, Sulaymānī, Bārak or Būrak Khayl, Lakī Khayl, Māt Khayl or Mad Khayl, Shaykhūdī, Ismāʿīl Khān Khayl, Mīr Khān Khayl, ʿAbdāl Khayl, Marchī Khayl, Khwājah Khayl, Kharmuz or Khūrmakh Khayl, Nazal Khayl, Sikandar Khayl, Rīshumīn Khayl, Pīnakzāʾī, Machī Khayl, Mamah Khayl, Sarmat Khayl, Ḥakīm Khayl, Jangī Khayl, Tūlī Khayl, Ibrāhīm Khayl, Walī Khayl, Aḥmadzāʾī, Maḥmūd, and Masʿūd—these were the clans of the line of those three individuals (i.e. Wazīr, and his sons Khiżrī and Lākī)—Mubārak and Gurbuz.

Similarly, the clans that are the progeny of Ibrāhīm, son of Utmān, who in the following text carries the name Darwīsh but is known by the name Mūsā, such as Manẓar Khayl, Khūnah Khayl, ʿAbbās or Abāz Khayl, ʿĀlam Khayl, Bajal Khayl, Qalandar Khayl, Shayr ʿAlī Khayl, Madī Khayl, Lājī or Lūchī Khayl, Shaykh Bidīn Khayl, Maḥal Khayl, Barīm Khayl, Dūdī Khayl, Lakhī Khayl, Tar Pashī, Iskandar Khayl, Tūlak Khayl, Khwājah Dīn Khayl, Dawlatān Khayl, Māsim or Mawsim Khayl, Sikandar Khayl, Ṣāḥibdād or Sūdād Khayl, Karī Khayl, Makhr Khayl, Walīdād Khayl, Madah Khayl, Būzī or Bāzī Khayl, Smāʿīl Khayl, Khūjī Khayl, Katī Khayl, Bahrām Khayl, Sarakī Khayl, ʿAlī Khān Khayl, Khiżr or Khiẕr Khayl, Naẓar Khayl, Khwājah Aḥmad Khayl, Jahān Bīk Khayl, Niʿmat Khayl, Ramī Khayl, Bahādur Khayl, Matī Khayl, Mīwā Khayl, Andas Khayl, Shāwat Khayl, Machkān Khayl, Tūrī Khayl, Khūshālī or Khūshāl Khayl, Shakhah Khayl, ʿAlī Khānī, Ratā Khayl, Jamālī, ʿUs̱mān Khayl, Mal Khayl, Haybatī, Ḥadī Khayl, Rasīl or Rasūl Khayl, Razbarī Khayl, Sūkī, Nūyinah Khayl, Tūr Khayl, Jangī Khayl, Būbalī, Yakhs Khayl, Salīmī Khayl, Pīlah Khayl, Sāmī Khayl, ʿAlī Khayl, Ūdī Khayl, Mīrālī or Mir ʿAlī Khayl, and Shāh Mīrī, the descendants of these [last] two, based on what was said, are called Darī Palārī and with all the recorded clans through /69/71/ Ibrāhīm, son of Utmān, who were offspring of Wazīr are called the Utmānzāʾī of the Wazīrī tribe.

Likewise, the offspring of Walī Khayl who bore the name [Ūtmānzāʾī]—and were mentioned above before the Aḥmadzāʾī—are now called Utmānzāʾī Wazīrīs. The clans of this lineage are as follows: Walī Khayl, Kabul Khayl, Sayfalī, Badā Khayl, Shayr Aḥmad Khayl, ʿĪsā Khayl, Miyāmī, Madā Khayl, Rīshumīn Khayl, Darī Khayl, Khawāṣṣ Khayl, Khūzī Khayl, Tatī Khayl, Palīpalī, Malū Khayl, Baṣwāl, Matī Khayl, Malik shāhī, Khūjah Khayl, Kharmish [or] Kharmīz Khayl, Sulṭān Khayl, Pāl or Pūl Khayl, Shūbar Khayl, Mītā Khayl, Shakhal Khayl, Gulī Khayl, Mandir Khayl, Kājī Khayl, Khāndar Khayl, Sharbat Khayl, Rīshumīn Khayl, Bakā or Bakī Khayl, Sardī Khayl, Lah Khayl, Shaykh Badīn Khayl, Mānak Khayl, ʿUmar Khān Khayl, Kakah or Kakā Khayl, Tūrak Khayl, Kakat Khayl, Ramkas Khayl, Bābā Khayl, Fatā Khayl, Shakhān Khayl, Daryā Khayl, Barīm Khayl, Abā Khayl, Jābī or Jūbī Khayl, Jabbār Khayl, Ḥasan Bīk Khayl, Kakah or Kakā Khayl (this one is different from the first one mentioned) Mīnkat Khayl, Khaybī Khayl, Pīrah Khayl, Mīrah Khayl, Takhtī Khayl, ʿUs̱mān Khayl, Jānī Maʿrūf or Yā Marīp Khayl, Kakī Khayl, Ḥasan Bīk Khayl, Khwājah Uways or Khwājah Hūs Khayl, Kakah or Kakā Khayl (also a different khayl with the same name),

Madī Khayl, Karam Bīk Khayl, Azūy Khayl, Miyāwar Khayl, Rūdī Khayl, Dīkān Khayl, Shahādat Khayl, Dilbat Khayl, Khalīf Khayl, Khān Khayl, Jalāl or Zalūl Khayl, Jāmīlī Khayl, ʿAlī Muḥammad Khayl, Laday Khayl, Shibar Khayl, Fażl Khayl, Kulayṣ Khayl, Tatar Khayl, Dādiyah or Dūdiyā Khayl, Khurram Khayl, Khūjah Khayl, Sanī Khayl, Khuwaydād Khayl, Pīr Dād Khayl, Pūlīd Khayl, Amzī Khayl, Ṣāḥib Khayl, Bīkam Khayl, Narmī Khayl, Mashwanī Mashūnī [?] Khayl, Gārī Khayl, Akbar Khayl, Jīkī Khayl, Andī Khayl, Shaykh ʿAlī, Sīnī Khayl, Shibr Khayl, Aral Khayl, Nūr Khayl, Yaḥyā Khayl, Mūsā Khayl, Jāmī Khayl, Tūr, Maḥmūd Khān or Mumīt Khān Khayl, Rīshumīn Khayl, Hindū or Hindī Khayl, Fatḥ Khayl, Kūtar Khayl, Bachahgī, Diram Khayl, Tarah Khayl, Būr or Sīr, Īdiyā Khayl, Yalī Khayl, ʿAlī Khayl, Shaykh ʿUṣmān Khayl, Malik Khayl, Khūjah Dar Khayl, and Rūgī or Wargī—these are all Utmānzāʾī with the name Wazīrī.

The Tribes and Clans of Aḥmadzāʾī of the Wazīrī People Who Have Had the Name in the Past

The Lord favored Aḥmadzāʾī, one of the sons of Khiżrī, the first son of Wazīr, the son of Sulayman with two sons—Sīn Khayl and Kālū Khayl. **/70/72/**

Thus the clans of Hātī Khayl, Aydal Khayl, Kamāl Khayl, Bakr Khayl, Abūlī Khayl, ʿĪsā Khayl, Kīmal Khayl, Amūsū Khayl, Tūrī Khayl, Brāhīm Khayl, Jān Bīk Khayl, ʿAlī Khayl, Barbād Khayl, Kandaʾi, Sanjar or Sanzar Khayl, Matīn Khayl, Ghalab Khayl, Miyā Gul Khayl, Ṭamūs Khayl, Marwat Khayl, Lalah Khayl, ʿAlī Khānī, Khiżr Khān Khayl, Barhamī Khayl, Madak Khayl, Dūdī Khayl, Patūl Khayl, Bāyik Khayl, Walīgī, Gulī Khayl, Babar Khayl, Zīrakī, Miyān Khayl, Madī, Sarakī Khayl, Tūlah Khayl, Būlah Khayl, Nānā Khayl, Alahdād Khayl, Ismāʿīl Khayl, Madīd Khayl, Walīdak, ʿUmarzāʾī Saʿīd Khayl, ʿIzzat Khayl, Apzap Khayl, Jangar Khayl, Landī Khayl, ʿAmal Khayl, Mīrzā Khayl, Tūrak Khayl, Marīz Khayl, Bāzah or Būzah Khayl, Barkhān Khayl, Barat Khayl, Shamī Khayl, Tīrah Khayl, Manẓar Khayl, Pānī Khayl, Gundī Khayl, Kararah Khayl, Salīmī Khayl, and Pīragah Khayl—all are of the offspring of Sīn Khayl, the first son of Aḥmadzāʾī and all of them are thus considered Aḥmadzāʾī and Wazīrī.

Similarly Naṣrī, Bāmī or Būmī Khayl, Tājī or Tūzī Khayl, Shamshī Khayl, Mastī Khayl, Mullā Khayl, Zalī Khayl, Utmān Khayl, Shaykh Bāzīd Khayl, Kakah Khayl, Gangī Khayl, ʿAlī Khānī, Shādī Khayl, Khūjah Khayl, Bābar or Būbar Khayl, Kharī Khayl, Kakah Khayl, Bābiyah Khayl, Pīr Muḥmmad Khayl, Zakariyā Khayl, Kandar Khayl, Sīnī Khayl, Shakhriyah Khayl, Agar Khayl, Kabīr Khayl, Bahādur Khayl, Bajal Khayl, Khāniyah Khayl, Badīn Khayl, Naẓar Bīk Khayl, Nakhī Khayl, ʿUṣmān Khayl, Bīzan Khayl, Īsū Khayl, Madī Khayl, Darwīsh Khayl, Akī Khayl, Darbah Khayl, Andas Khayl, Qulī or Gulī Khayl, Miyān Gul Khayl, Shaykh Mumīt Khayl, Dīrah Khayl, Barah Khān Khayl, Nafar Khayl, Nakrah Khayl, Darwīzah Khayl, Nūr Khayl, ʿĀshiq or Ashik Khayl, Banāt or Nabūt Khayl, Sangī, Mughul Khān Khayl, Balūch or Balīch Khayl, Siyāhī Khayl, Pīrakah Khayl, Payand or Pamdah Khayl, Lalah Khayl, Basī Khayl, Datak Khayl, Siparakī, Muḥammad Khayl, Zā or Zū Khayl, Naẓm Khayl, Miṣrī Khayl, Multān Khayl, Kakah Khayl, Zamānī Khayl, Mulūk or Malīk Khayl, Gūr Khayl, Karrānī Khayl, Gulāb Khayl, Khatak Khayl, Lāl or Lūl Khayl, Shakhr Khayl, Tabrīz or Tawrīz Khayl, Lālī or Lūlī Khayl, Andakī Khayl, Īsap Khayl, Yarzā Khayl, Mandak Khayl, Shakhr Khayl, Fāṭimah Khayl,

Matā Khayl, Qamar Khayl, Patī, Qāżī or Kūzī Khayl, Mughul Khayl, Khuwaydād Khayl, Kūdah Khayl, Bahādur Khayl, Katī Khayl, Ashpilāl Khayl, Sadī Khayl, ʿUmar Khayl, Sanjar Khayl or Sanzar Khayl, Shayrak Khayl, Suyūkī, Kūtwāl or Kītwāl, Galah Khayl, Sadan Khayl, Shayr Khayl, Bītan Khayl, Aḥmad Khayl, Bajal Khayl, /71/73/ Bagal Khayl, Bāghwān Khayl, Mīrā Khayl, Nānā Khayl, Lālah Khayl, ʿĀlam Khān Khayl, Bābā Khayl, Barat Khayl, Zargar Khayl, ʿAlī Khayl, ʿUmar Khayl, and Gulī Khayl—all these are offspring of Kālū Khayl, the second son of Aḥmadzāʾī because of which they are called Aḥmadzāʾī and Wazīrī.

The Clans and Tribes of Masʿūd Who Was Earlier Indicated Right After Maḥmūd

Masʿūd, the grandson of Khiżrī, the first son of Wazīr, son of Sulaymān, had two sons—ʿAlīzāʾī and Bahlūlzāʾī.

Thus Fatḥ or Pūtah Khayl, Shābī Khayl, Patānī Khayl, Astānī Khayl, Barhamī Khayl, Bangash Khayl, Tajil Khayl, Anā Khayl, Ḥaydar Khayl, ʿUmar Khayl, Dūdī Khayl, Bahramī, Mīrkhah Khayl, Khadī Khayl, Khān Khayl, Khūjakī, Sulṭānī, Aḥmad Khayl, Mīrzā Khayl, Marībī, Bībīzāʾī, Samanzāʾī, Kadāʾī Khayl, Langar Khayl, Kībī Khayl, Palī Khayl, Salīmī Khayl, Pachī Khayl, Mullā Khayl, Kūrar Khayl, Malik Dīnī, Shaman Khayl, Chapār Khayl, Pīlah Khayl, Naẓam Khayl, Zarīyah Khayl, Madah Khayl, Bajī Khayl, Qāsim Khayl, Tahrīm Khayl, Tatar Khayl, Gārī Khayl, Mullā Khayl, Shayr Khān Khayl, Sipānī Khayl, Ḥaydarī, ʿAlī Khayl, Salīmgī, Shakhah Khayl, Akā Khayl, ʿUlyā or Allāh Khayl, Landī Khayl, Kīmal Khayl, Badī Way, Dūtak Khayl, Bahādur Khayl, Shayr Gul Khayl, Bādīnzāʾī, ʿUṣmān Khayl, Absap Khayl, ʿAbdal Khayl, Ghalab Khayl, Darī Khayl, Katt Khayl, Jamūn Khayl, Kull Shay, Pīlī Khayl, Datī Khayl, Bah Bah Khayl, Kakah Khayl, Mankah Khayl, Bakhtī Khayl, Kīkhī Khayl, Balī Khayl, Matī Khayl, Tarakī Khayl, Mīrak Khayl, Bajī Khayl, Shabānī, Bīrī Khayl, Gulī Khayl, Ṭūṭīyah Khayl, and Sarak Khayl—all of these were of the line of ʿAlīzāʾī, the first son of Masʿūd, the grandson of Wazīr. All of them are called Wazīri and Masʿūd.

Likewise, Haml Khayl, ʿAbdalī or Awdalī Khayl, Khānī Khayl, Naṣrī Khayl, Shamak Khayl, Sarakī Khayl, Azūy Khayl, Ẓarīf Khayl, Kand Khayl, ʿAbbās Khayl, Lalah Khayl, Pāyū Khayl, Qatīl Khayl, Nūrnak Khayl, Qiyāmak or Kīmat Khayl, Ghūzakī, Salīm Akī, Malik Shī, Khuwāydādī, Langar Khayl, Katī Khayl, Sūmī Khayl, Bābul Khayl, Bāzīdī, Panjī Khayl, Bilāl Khayl, Naẓar Khayl, ʿAzīz Khayl, Fatḥ Khayl, Zargar Khayl, Khūrmakh Khayl, Ḥasan Khayl, Māmīyah Khayl, Bānd Khayl, Abkam Khayl, Ṭūṭīyah Khayl, Nānū Khayl, Haybat Khayl, ʿAbbās Khayl, Qādir Khayl, Rustam Khayl, Shayr Khayl, Jalāl Khayl, Shamī Khayl, Mīrat Khayl, Sandar Khayl, Shīrāz Khayl, Gulī Khayl, Tājī or Tūjī Khayl, Bābā or Babah Khayl, Darman Khayl, Pīrdād Khayl, Mīrdād Khayl, Karīmdād Khayl, Rūzī Khayl, Muʿīb or Muḥibb Khayl, Kamāl Khayl, Khūdī Khayl, Ṭālib Khayl, Kīkā Khayl, Sawdā Khayl, Sarmat Khayl, Ladī Khayl, /72/74/ and Batī Khayl—these are all of the line of those two and are named Nīk Zan Khayl. ʿUmar Khayl, Shīrīn Khayl, Bakhtī Khayl, ʿAlī Khānī, Darwīsh Khayl, Qarār Khayl, Mīr Khānī, Machī Khayl, Fatḥ Khayl, Gulmīr Khayl, Barham Khayl, Mand, Shinānī Khayl, Pīrā Khayl, Mīr Aḥmad Khayl—the clan of these [latter] three is called Kūkūkarī—Barnī, Mihr Khānī—these two are named Ūrmur Khayl—Shingī or Ashnakī, Muḥammadī, Jūkī, Milāy, Būbī, Būzyā Khayl, Dajī Khayl, Kharman Khayl, Māmiyah Khayl—this group which was just mentioned are the offspring of Bahlūlzā'ī, the second son of Mas'ūd, and because of that are called Bahlūlzā'ī of the Mas'ūd Wazīrī tribe.

Since the genealogy of the various clans of the Wazīrī tribe has been written down name by name, it behooves us to mention the situation and locales or the homelands, residences, and houses of this very large tribe and much needs to be said which my readers will find agreeable because they would surmise that the *wazīr* [meaning minister or even prime minister] is one of the ministers of the *pādshāhs*. But no! As has been written, he is Wazīr, the son of Sulaymān, and was one of the grandsons of Karrān. He had two sons—Khiżrī and Lālī. At that time, Wazīr was enrolled in the Shītak tribe and they occupied the land of Barmal, adjoining Kūh-i Shawāl and its environs. One of the members of the tribe, Mas'ūd-i Wazīrī resolved to acquire a farmstead and in a struggle they took control of the district of Badr and Shahīr. They seized the mine of Gūrūm and its environs which would be a jewel [in their (figurative) crown]. Hardly had any time passed when they went to war with the rest of the Ūrmur tribe and shed so much blood that the result was that they drove them out of the Tāk Valley which joined the mountains. Some of the clans from the line of Utmānzā'ī and Aḥmadzā'ī occupied the area to the north of the lands and mountains occupied by the Mas'ūdīs. Thus they managed to expand their territory significantly. They occupied from the edge of Kūhāt to the borders of Dīrah Ismā'īl Khān, a distance calculated at 140 miles and because of its importance, we will describe below the extent of the territory of this tribe.

The Territory, or in the Terminology of the People of Afghanistan, the Shawāl District, Which is the Residence and Homeland of the Wazīrī Tribe

This territory and district is in the form of a valley and is located within the links of the chain of mountains of the Kūh-i Sabz and (Kūh-i) Khurram. From east to west it is about twelve *kurūhs* (long) and from south to north six *kurūhs* wide. Its area is [thus] seventy-two square *kurūhs*. /73/75/ In the mountains there are many *nashtar* and *ṣanūbar* (piñon) pines. In winter, the snow lasts in those mountains for three months. Many of the locales and settlements of the Wazīrīs, except for Kūh-i Pīrghal and Kūh-i Shawāl, are cold. In this district, the Biryālī River arises at the top of the mountain and provides irrigation to a certain amount of land. The villages at the head of this parcel of [irrigated] land like the land of Dabarah, Miyāmī, and Malikshī are in the possession of the Kabul Khayl Wazīrī clan. Below the Kabul Khayl are the houses of the Bakā Khayl. Farther down from them the Jānī Khayl is established. Also in this district the Utmānzā'ī Wazīrī, namely the Purwālah, Kabul Khayl, and Malikshī, live.

The Land of Shakī Which is One of the Homelands of the Wazīrī

This district is also located within the chain of mountains and the valley and level place. From the northwest to the southeast it is eleven *kurūhs* in length and three *kurūhs* in width. It is surrounded by many *archah* pines. On this territory live the Malikshī, Miyāmī, and Utmānzā'ī Wazīrīs. Below them live the Shādīgī clan of the Khūyinā Khayl of the Badīn Khayl. In the section between the clans live the Bahlūlzā'ī and 'Alīzā'ī.

The Land and District of Barmal Which Is [Also] One of the Wazīrī Homelands

This land is located within the western mountains belonging to the Wazīrīs and is in the form of a valley. From east to west it is eighteen *kurūhs* long and four *kurūhs* wide. Most of the land of this valley is flat and a small amount of it is grassland (meadow). The clans of the Sīpalī and Pīpalī are branches of the Kabul Khayl and Saʿīdakī and have their homes here.

The Land of Zarmak (Zurmak?) Which Is (Also) One of the Places Where the Wazīrīs Live

This piece of land is small and is valley-like. Nature created it. It is some six *kurūhs* long and four *kurūhs* wide. The tribes living here are the Mumat Khayl and Tūrī Khayl, clans of the Utmānzāʾī Wazīrīs.

The Land and District of Sham Which Is [Also] Considered Part of the Wazīrī Tribe's Land

This piece of land inclines towards Zarmak. There is not a lot of verdancy or trees in it but its climate is very clean, pure, and excellent. The tribes and clans—Mumīt Khayl and Barhīm Khayl—who live here are branches /**74**/**76**/ of the Utmānzāʾī.

The Khaysūr Valley Which Is [Another] One of the Places of the Wazīrī Tribe

This land from east to west is lengthy and not so productive. On its south side Dūr is located. Its water is very sweet. At the head of this district the clan of the Mumīt Khayl have their homes. In the middle of it the Tūrī Khayl tribe has its residences. And at the foot (bottom) of it lives the Wardakī clan.

Shahranah, [Another] One of the Homelands of the Wazīrī Tribe

The area of this piece of land is six *kurūhs* [in length] to the west of Dūr and its width is one *kurūh*. In this wadi, Shahranah is quite small. In its center is the Madā Khayl clan. Lower down is the Khiżr Khayl. Adjoining the west of Dūr lives the Mandir Khayl tribe which is one of the Utmān Khayl Wazīrī tribes.

Sharakī, Which is Also One of the Wazīrī Lands

One should know that at the head of the Shakand Valley there is a very extensive but inaccessible area. This is the home of the Nūrī Khayl and Masʿūd Wazīrī tribes. In the middle of the Sharakī territory live the ʿUmarzāʾī Wazīrī tribe. They earn their living in agriculture and by the breeding of horses.

Shayrah [sic—Shayr, see below] *Talah and Other Places Which Are the Northern Locales of the Wazīrī*

The lands of the northern locales belonging to the Wazīrīs are in ruins, desolate, and without any resources, that is, it is not governed and ordered under the laws of nature. Originally it was a small mountain region and a hot place without even some wild trees and rain on it. In the southern part of this mountain region, there is Shayr Talah, an attractive and extensive area. Nature has created flat and level ground but unfortunately there is no water, which is the basis of life for plants, animals, and man. For this reason the land is sterile and is left uncultivated. The Mumīt Khayl and Tūrī Khayl have this land and the Mumīt Khayl have their homes there. In Nālah and on both sides of the Kītū River, the /75/77/ Ḥasan Khayl, Madr Khayl and Tūrī Khayl are established. In the river of Kurram District, which is situated lower down, is the place of residence of the Bangash people where various clans such as the Kabul Khayl, the Charkhānī clan of the Malikshī, the Kindā'ī, Zangarah of the Gangī Khayl, and the Zalī Khayl all live. The Shahīdān of the Tūjiyā Khayl, Asparah Lakarī, Sarūghā Bar Ghantū, Kūzh, Sim, Kharsīnah, and the Hātī Khayls—all these are reckoned to belong to the great Wazīrī tribe. The hill (*tal*, i.e. Shayr Talah?) with other lands occupied [by the Wazīrī] is the territory of Banūn which used to belong to this tribe as will be written later.

The Land of Wānah District Which is Reckoned as Part of the Territory of the Wazīrī Tribe

This district is in the southern part of Wazīrī territory and is located in the northern foothills of the Gūmal Valley. The southern part of this district rises on a steep diagonal to the Gūmal Valley. It is fifteen *kurūh*s from north to south and the same distance across. In the valley bottom there is some water in a river which flows to the south and is incorporated in Gūmal. Along both sides of this river are the principal lands. The entire valley is arable but [only] one-quarter of it is irrigated land while three-quarters is dependent on rainfall. In the midst of this land, the Dawtānī clan of the Lūdī tribe lives and is self-reliant. They have built a fort for themselves. The Wazīrīs have their homeland in the neighborhood and around [that fort]. The Zalī Khayl of the Aḥmadzā'ī Wazīrīs live there. The men of the Gūmal Valley are notorious for their evildoing, thievery, murder, plundering, and so on. Spring and winter its residents stay there but others like the Gangī Khayl, Khajal Khayl, Tūjiyā Khayl, Hātī Khayl, Bīzan Khayl, Pāyandah Khayl, and Jūniyā Khayl, all of whom are Aḥmadzā'ī Wazīrīs, make their winter quarters in Wānah District. Then in summer they head for summer pastures. The Hātī Khayl [goes for summer pastures] to the lands of Dab and Hindī and this is to the east, behind the Bīzan Khayl and the Khajal Khayl. The middle part of this district has been under the control of the Dūtanīs.

The Badr District, One of the Places Forming the Homeland of the Wazīrīs

This district from north to south, inclining towards the east as far as the town of Kān-i Gūrum, is five *kurūh*s long and one *kurūh* wide. At the head of this land lives the Shingī clan of the Bahlūlzā'ī tribe of the Mas'ūd Wazīrīs as well as a few of the Pāyandah Khayl of the Aḥmadzā'ī [Wazīrīs] and all the Bīzan Khayl of the Aḥmadzā'ī. At the bottom of the district live the Madan Khayl of the Isparakī [Aḥmadzā'ī Wazīrīs]. Still lower down live [other] Mas'ūd Wazīrīs. /76/78/

The Districts Forming the Homelands of the Masʿūd Wazīrī Tribe

A portion of this tribe, as was just recorded, have their homes in Badr District. The rest of them live in Shahr-i Makīn, Khūrah, Maydān, the Tūy Valley, the Tāk Valley, Kūh-i Bābar or Būbar, Zangarah, Shahīr, Shakand, and Karshtū in various hamlets. The total population of the great Wazīrī tribe comprising the Utmānzāʾī, Aḥmadzāʾī, Masʿūd, and the other sub-tribes that have been duly recorded one after another, according to the census of 1281 Hijrī[13] these were the number of fighting men from each of the Utmānzāʾī clans: from the Mumīt Khayl living in Khaysūr, 3,500 men; from the Manẓar Khayl who live in various places, 600 men; the Madah Khayl living in Kūh-i Gūr situated in Bālā Sardūr, 10,500 men; the Tūrī Khayl living in Shayr Talah and the Khaysūr Valley, 3,000 men; from the Kabul Khayl along the Kurram River, 3,200 men; from the Malikshī of Tahānah Mīrbān District situated on the skirts of Kūh-i Gabr, 300 men; from the Jānī clan living in the aforementioned Tahānah district [Tahānah Mīrbān], 1,000 men; from the Sardī Khayl living in Warghar of the aforementioned district [Tahānah Mīrbān], 400 men; from Takhtī Khayl in the aforementioned Warghar, 600 men; and from Zamī Khayl of Bāzāz of the Warghar district, 500 men, making a total of 15,700 fighting men from the Utmānzāʾī sub-tribe of the Wazīrī.

From the Aḥmadzāʾī subtribe of the Wazīrī the number of fighting men were: from the Sīn [or Sīnī] Khayl living in Tal adjoining the borders of Khatak tribal lands, 1,200; from Sarakī Khayl who are scattered, 800 men; from the ʿUmarzāʾī living in Tal and Kūmatī, 800 men; from the Būmī Khayl living in various places, 2,500 men; from the Khāyinah Khayl living in Turb adjacent to Kurram, 300 men; from Khūjal Khayl living in Tal-i Buland Khayl and Hangū of Kūhāt District 1,200; from the Badīn Khayl living in Tal, 50 men; from Bizan (Bīzan?) Khayl in Sadrāwan, Banūn District, and some from the mountains [of Banūn], 800 men; from Pāyandah Khayl living in Tal, 200 men; from Sadan Khayl living in the abovementioned Sadrāwan, 600 men; from Muḥammad Khayl living on the edge of Kurram District on the mountains slopes, 600 men; and from the Sadī Khayl living in the depths of the mountains, 600 men; the total therefore being 9,750 armed fighting men.

From the clans of the Masʿūd [the number of fighting men were]: from Shahānī Khayl in Kūh-i Bābar and various other places, 1,200 men; from the Manzāʾī living in and across Kūh-i Nā 2,300 men; /77/79/ from the Jabbār Khayl living in Shahīr and Maydān, 600 men, from the Khaylī Khayl from various places, 500 men; from the Badīnzāʾī from various places, 800 men; from the Gūl Shāhī living in Ghūr-i Lāmah of Kān-i Gūrum 1,000 fighting men; from the ʿAbdālī, both settled and muhājirs, 2,500; from the Malik Shabī living in the mountains on the far side of Kān-i Gūrum, 800 men; from the Naẓar Khayl scattered in various places, 900 men; from the Buland Khayl in Makīn, 300 men; from the Haybat Khayl living in various places, 1,300; from the ʿUmar Khayl also living in Makīn, 200 men; from the Kūkarī clan whose places are scattered, 600 men; from the Warmar Khayl who are also scattered, 200 men; and from the Shingī clan most of

[13] 1281/1864 marked the first India-wide census conducted by the British.

whom live in Tahānah Valley, 1,200 men. Thus the total from this sub-tribe [the Mas'ūd] is 13,500 sword-wielding warriors ready when needed. For these three sub-tribes of the Wazīrī the total number of fighting men according to the figures given in 1281/1864 which is now close to sixty years ago was 39,950. Now, the total population, men and women, young and old, amounts to 120,000 males and females in the census count. Of the total, a small number, i.e. a little before the war of 1337/1919[14] some 600 households of these tribes emigrated and were given arable lands by the government in Ghaznīn and the district of Shāh Jūy located in the southwest of Muqur District.

Also, some people of the Kākar tribe emigrated and went to those areas and made their homes there. Three thousand people from various tribes set forth and went to the Hazārahjāt and there the government gave them arable lands and pastures and they have taken up farming.

The Tribes and Clans Which Were the Offspring of Gurbaz, A Grandson of Khiẓrī, the First Son of Wazīrī[15]

Gurbaz, the son of Mubārak, whom we previously promised to mention, had two sons—Naṣr al-Dīn and Kharī Khayl.

Thus, Sarkalī, Shayr Khayl, Mānī Khayl, and Gadāy Khayl were the offspring of Naṣr al-Dīn.

Zūdīn, Bīkī Khayl, Landī Khayl, Pagah Gundah, Pīrī Gundah, Birī Gundah, Ḥusayn, Būryah Khayl, and Barīt (Parīt) Khayl were the offspring of Kharī Khayl. All /78/80/ are called Gurbaz. This tribe was in fact one of the sub-tribes of the Wazīrī but because their ways and culture were contrary to those of the Wazīrīs, they separated themselves and so they have been written about as being outside the Wazīrī. Originally this tribe was included in the Mas'ūd Wazīrīs and lived in the northern part of the mountains that were the Mas'ūdīs' homeland. Thus in Kūh-i Bābar, and the Shaktū Valley some people of advanced age can point out the water channels and traces of the houses of the Gurbaz tribe. It's been some 200 years since the Gurbaz tribe left. The reason for their leaving is the following: the Wargārī sub-tribe of the Bītanī tribe first lived in Kūh-i Gabr. The Gurbaz attacked them and subjected the Wargārī to a general massacre and took possession of Kūh-i Gabr. After a while the Bītanī tribe learned about this, informed others, and cinched the belt of revenge with the Kajīn sub-tribe of the offspring of Shaykh Bīt. They conducted a fierce war against the Gurbaz, defeated them, and took control of Kūh-i Gabr. At that time, the Gurbaz, when they were whipped and defeated, left and sought refuge and a place to live in the mountain region northwest of Dūr located south-east of Khūst, in a northwest corner of Wazīrī territory. The Gurbaz have been living in those mountains up to now. There, winter brings two months of snow and the mountaineers and mountain dwellers of the Gurbaz tribe make rush and reed mats for their own homes. They are very poor

14 The author is referring to the Third Afghan War, the Afghan War for Independence.

15 Murray, *A Dictionary*, p. 71, distinguishes them from the Gurbuz and describes them as, "Originally a clan of Wazīr origin but which have since lost all connection with the parent tribe."

and without means. Despite that, they are extremely brave and courageous and have taken control of a bit of the corner of the southeastern part of the *maydān* (plain) of the city of Khūst. They produce 1,500 fighting men and in conflict and strife they always side with the White Faction (*Qawm-i Aspīn*) with whom they are united.

The Lālī or Laylī Tribe Which is Counted as One of the Wazīrī Sub-Tribes

This tribe has 7,500 fighting men and has its homeland and place of residence northwest of Sapīd Kūh between Jalālābād and Kurram. As was earlier noted, Lālī, son of Wazīr, because of his killing someone from the Shītak tribe, was forced to flee from Kūh-i Shawāl. He went among the Khūgyānī tribe and made his home there. The Khūgyānī were living in the environs of Jalālābād and there he took a wife and separated himself from the Wazīrī. Some say that he made Laylī, his beloved, flee with him. While travelling /79/81/ he encountered a gang of Shinwārī bandits and he overpowered all of them. Later, some sons emerged from the womb of Laylī and after her the offspring came to be named as the Lālī or Laylī tribe.

The Tribes and Clans From the Lineage of Shītak, the Fourth Son of Kakī, Son of Karrān

The time has come for the account of the clans descended from Shītak which was promised earlier. The Lord bestowed six sons on Shītak, the son of Kakī, son of Karrān, two sons from each of his wives—Dūr, Tanī, Kīwī, Sūrānī, Zīlam or Jīlam, Huwayd or Ūd/Awd. The first son [Dūr] had two sons—Mawlī and Ibrāhīm.

Thus Arghūnd, Bī Bakī, Bahār Khayl, Sarakī Khayl, Ambārakshā, Ḥakīm Khayl, Katah Khayl, Mumal Khayl, Būbī, Shujā Dil, Nagrīz, Bārī Khayl, Tār Khayl, Khadī or Khadīw Khayl, Tīghāsī, Utmān Khayl, Mārī Khayl, Zabarakī, ʿAjab Khayl, Darzāʾī, Gulīwālah, Tūr, Hurmuz, Ḥasan Khayl, Karī Khayl, Sulaymān Khayl, Land, ʿĪsū or Sū Khayl, Dawlat Khayl, Zīrakī Khayl, Mamadī, Shamal, Sīrūsh Khayl, Wazī Khayl, Mītā Khayl, ʿUmrakī, Naṣrī, Bībakī, Mūsākī, Tūlar Khayl, Guliyah Khayl, Walīdī Khayl, Shānī Khayl, Dūr Khayl, Qāsim Khayl, Pīrakī Khayl, Shingī Khayl, Chār Gul Khayl, Sīnī Khayl, Īsūrī, Tūl Khayl, Shaniyā Khayl, Bānī or Būnī Khayl, Shānī or Shūnī Khayl, Mīnā Khayl, Ibrāhīm Khayl, Zanī Khayl, Ḥaydar Khayl, ʿAlī Khayl, Bāqī or Būkī Khayl, Qadam Khayl, Bābar or Būbar Khayl, Tarūnī (and this one is not related by blood), Jars Khayl, Parī Khayl, Naṣr Khayl, Kafshī or Kūshī Khayl, ʿĀlam Khān Khayl, Ṣāḥib Khayl, Tūz Khayl, Qiyāmat or Kīmat Khayl, Shar Khayl, Būlah Khayl, Makhal Khayl, Sapūkī Khayl, Mīr Khayl, Ayūbī, Bahlūl or Balīl Khayl, Zūkī Khayl, Khalī Khayl, Parl Khayl, Makhlī, Babah Khayl, and Barū Khayl. These are all offspring of Mawlī (Mūlī?), the son of Dūr, son of Shītak, son of Kakī, son of Karrān. Because of him they are called Shītak and Karrān.

Similarly, Patsī, Zhū Khayl, Batah Khayl, Rūzī Khayl, Marat Khayl, Fīrūz Khayl, Tūrī Khayl, Spahīn (Spīn) Khayl, Kibr Khayl, Palāpī Khayl, Mand Khayl, Rajī Khayl, Ẓafar Khayl, Samī Khayl, Bangash Khayl, Dawlat Khayl, Mīrām Shāh, Hūtī Khayl, Nūr Khayl, Tūrī Khayl, and Lashgarī, all offspring of Ibrāhīm, son of Dūr, son of Shītak, son of Kakī and so they are called Dūr, Shītak, and Karrān.

This tribe lives and makes its homeland along both sides of the Tūchī River and by way of metonymy /80/82/ (the region) is called Dūr and is best known by that name. It is not known whether this region was prosperous when the Dūr tribe occupied it or they developed it after they took possession of it. No date is indicated that relates to the taking of this district and its being improved by the Dūr tribe nor for what reason except for the fact that it is known that in 1112 Hijrī equivalent to 1696 A.D. (*sic*—1700), 228 years ago, in that same year Prince Bahādur Shāh, at the order of Awrangzīb, son of Shāh Jahān, the pādshāh of Hindūstān, conquered the territory of Banūn and taxed the residents of Dūr 12,000 rupees leaving a certain Sayyid Ḥusayn as governor. He governed with extreme severity until the thread of good order of Banūn District was broken and he also abandoned the district of Dūr to save his life. The Dūrīs now governed themselves as they wished without being subject to any government until Nādir Shāh Afshār took Afghanistan and made them obey by force of arms. Until the time of Shāh Zamān Sadūzā'ī, they paid those former 12,000 rupees that had been levied on them by Awrangzīb and at no time was any governor appointed over them. Every one or two years one of the leaders of the Durrānī tribe would go there with a contingent of soldiers for those 12,000 rupees and collect them. At the time of the incidents involving Wazīr Fatḥ Khān Bārakzā'ī concerning his relations with Shāh Zamān all of which is recorded in [my] history, Shāh Zamān, at the request of the sayyid and shaykh who was the spiritual mentor and leader of the Dūr tribe, did not collect the 12,000 rupees from them and [moreover] he exempted them from paying it. In compensation for this gift and bestowal, every year they would give the offspring of this shaykh some grain and other things until the English government gained control of Sind and Panjāb. Gradually, its influence spread to the far corners [of the region] and the Dūr tribe who had been brought to the brink of extinction by the [constant] attacks, raiding, and plundering of the Wazīrīs and were in dire straits requested protection from English officials and accepted the law of that government. The English government, which had witnessed heavy losses from its incursions onto Afghan soil and from 1255 until 1258 Hijrī [1839–1842], as has been recorded in the pages of this royal book, had suffered terrific and heavy blows, /81/83/ did not agree to extending its protection [to the Dūr tribe]. Believing the troublemaking of the Afghans to be the cause of the corruption of Hindūstān, it wound its foot in the skirt of evasion and retreated to the sea of contemplation until in 1280 (1863) when Amīr Shayr ʿAlī Khān acceded to [the throne of] sovereignty over Afghanistan, his brother, Muḥammad Aʿẓam, entered Kurram from Herat on the path of opposition to him. Word spread that the English government had given the Dūr District and the land of Banūn to the amir of Kabul. With the spread of this news the leaders of some of the Dūr clans, despite the fact of being Muslims and free came under the authority and protection of the English government and as this false news spread, they withdrew from obedience to an Islamic government. This is what Deputy Ḥayāt Khān, who himself is also an Afghan, writes. There is [also] what the esteemed scholar Mullā Fayż Muḥammad Khān Kātib wrote copied from the book of Ḥayāt Khān and the writings of that late one [Deputy Ḥayāt Khān] editorializing on the immorality of the Dūrī tribe and the rest of the Afghans. The [present] author of these lines, following the approach and style that he [I] have adopted in the writing of the seven volumes of *Amān al-tawārīkh*, is not going to include those lines [i.e., Deputy Ḥayāt Khān's, repeated by Fayż Muḥammad] because I believe that even in all those governments, nations, tribes, and clans of the world and among all classes and types of mankind that are famous for good morals and for having lofty attributes, one will still find people who are immoral and ill-natured. The purification of the soul and the rectification of morals is linked to proper education, to studying books of ethics, and to higher education. That in turn is tied to the proliferation of colleges and schools.

To sum up, the Dūr had at most 16,000 fighting men.

The Tribes and Clans of the Lineage of Tanī, the Second Son of Shītak, Great-Grandson of Karrān

The Lord favored Tanī, son of Shītak, with three sons—Aryūy known as Aryūzāʾī, Marī known as Marīzāʾī, and Sīnkī.

Thus Machī Khayl, Sīt Khayl, Gawhar Khayl, and Ḥīnkī Khayl were the offspring of Aryūzāʾī and related to the Tanī tribe.

Similarly, Khībī Khayl, Bandah Khayl, Dalak Khayl, Dabrī, Bīrān, Zarak, Dakhī, Barīm Khayl, Arkand Khayl, Kāmil Khayl, Rawshān Khayl, Utmānzāʾī, Khabarzāʾī, Darī Nāmī, Anī Khayl, Ḥiṣārakī, Andī Khayl, Shādzī Khayl, Shahdād Khayl, Lājmīr Khayl, Sipāhī, Shāhjahān Gundah, Jalītī Gundah, Wanchī, Ūshah Khayl, Bakr Khayl, Khūjī Khayl, Tarīn Khayl, Rashīd Khayl, Brāham Khayl, Chīrī Khayl, Mūsā Khayl, Isparakī, /82/84/ Tūr Khayl, Chīchkī, Garī, Lajī Khayl, Dagal Kūl, Aydal Khayl, Shādzī Khayl, Bārīk Khayl, Kūlī, and Landī were all offspring of Zālī and called Tanī and all of them are remembered by this name.

For the most part, this tribe lives in the mountains in the southwest corner of the territory of Khūst. A smaller number of them have made places for themselves on the skirts of those mountains. One hundred and fifty households live in the Darakī plain. They can raise 1,250 fighting men. The rest of the greater part of them other than those in Darakī live in Ḥiṣārak, Kūkhah, and Narkhī.

Additionally, the ʿĪsā Khayl, Niʿmatī, Shūbah Khayl, and Bīnah Khayl, are also the offspring of Sīnkī, the third son of Tanī. The whole tribe, men and women, numbers 12,500 persons.

The Four Tribes and Clans of Balakh, ʿAbdak, Dariyah Khayl, and Amzūnī or Amkhānī Which Are Connected to the Dūr Tribe

These four tribes are really not the offspring of Dūr but in the course of the passing of time they became incorporated in the Dūr tribe as Dūrī.

Thus Nuṣrat Khayl, Pāʾī Khayl, Mumī Khayl, Sīnī Khayl, Bālī Khayl, Tarkah Khayl, Īdal Khayl, Muḥammad Khayl, Katah Khayl, Miyāmī Khayl, ʿAbd al-Raḥmān Khayl, Kakah Khayl, Sīkī, Ṭāwūs Khayl, Land, Shādī Khayl, Nālī Khayl, Gadāy, Malik Khayl, ʿUmar Khān Khayl, Walī Khayl, Char Khayl, ʿUmarzāʾī, Darī Palārī, Sīnī Khayl, and Jān Khān Khayl are the offspring of *Balakh* and joined to the Dūr tribe. Their population numbers 1,250 individuals.

Similarly, Yalī Khayl, Mamad Khayl, Mandūrī, Katah Khayl, Fīrūz Khayl, Masʿūd Khayl, Karī Khayl, Ṣadr Khayl, Ibrāhīm Khayl, Tarūnī (this one is not blood-related but is affiliated, *waṣlī*) and the clans and offspring of his [Tarūnī's] like Aḥmad Khayl, Asadī Khayl, Raybah Khayl, and Tangūshī, are both *aṣlī* and *waṣlī* offspring of ʿAbdak and incorporated in the Dūr tribe. They number 1,250 individuals.

The Kūbīzāʾī, Hūzī Khayl, Tamr Khayl, ʿAlīzāʾī, Nālī Khayl, Tūr Bakī, Maryam Khayl, Char Khayl, and Samilzāʾī are the offspring of Darpah Khayl and included in the Dūr tribe. They have 1,250 fighting men.

The Zabarah Khayl, ʿAlīzāʾī Bilāl Khayl, ʿAbdal Khayl, Aḥmad Khayl, Tāyib Khayl, Nawāz Khayl, Lar, Ghulām Khayl, Rasīn Khayl, Bar, and Naṣrakī were the offspring of Amzūnī or Amkhānī and included in the Dūr tribe. They number 1,250 people. All these together total 5,000 and some people. /83/85/

The Five Tribes Linked to the Afghans Who Say They Themselves In Their Hearts Are Sayyids and These Five Are Bakhtiyār, Gandah Pūr, Mushwānī, Wardak, and Hunī

It has been said about the situation of the clans of the Bakhtiyār (this is not the same as the Bakhtiyārī tribe that came from Iran at the time of Nādir Shāh and has been written about already) that Alḥaq a youthful sayyid from the town of Ūsh, a dependency of Baghdād arrived in Kūh-i Sulaymān as a foreigner, settled among the Shayrānī tribe, and took a Shayrānī woman as his wife. From her a son was produced and he named him Abū Saʿīd. Because of the fortunate horoscope of that son, he was nicknamed "Bakhtiyār." Gradually, his line became known as the Bakhtiyār tribe and so they also called themselves. But people consider more correct the story that someone from the Bakhtiyārī tribe in Iran came to Afghanistan and established a line of descent. In short, there are now 750 households of this tribe and they live in Marghah among the Kākar people. There are not many clans (of this tribe) and all of them simply use the name Bakhtiyār. In the Bakhtiyār line the names of Kūrnī, Akū, Atū, Sayyid Muḥammad, Khwājah Ilyās, Khwājah Aḥmad Kabīr, Parī, Tūrī, Muqrī, Naẓarzāʾī, and Marghchī are written and attributed to him [the sayyid from Baghdād].

The (other) four tribes mentioned above are described in the following way: In the genealogy of Ūsturānī or Usturānī the name Gundah Pūr is also listed and found as it will soon be recorded but Gundah Pūr along with the Mushwānī, Wardak, and Hunī consider themselves sayyids and connect their lineage to Sayyid Muḥammad Gīsūdarāz.[16] They say that during the life of Shayrāni he came to Kūh-i Sulaymān and was taken in by the Afghans. Because of the miracles and wonders he performed, the Karrānī, Shayrānī, and Kākar all submitted to him and believed in him.

In the invasion of Amīr Tīmūr Gūrgān, after his arrival in Kabul, he wanted to go via this route to Hindūstān [i.e. via the Kūh-i Sulaymān]. As he himself has written, the Afghans fired arrows at him from the top of a fort and so he issued an order for a general massacre of all the people along the route. They killed all but three people who were saved by praying to the sayyid. The three brought their daughters to the sayyid as thanks for providing them with security from the evil

[16] On this important 14th–15th century South Asian Ṣūfī figure see Richard M. Eaton, "Gīsū-darāz," *Encyclopedia Iranica*, vol. 11, pp. 1–3.

of Amīr Tīmūr. He contracted marriage with all three girls and from the daughter of Shayrānī, Usturānī was born; from the daughter of Kākar, Mushwānī was brought forth; and from the daughter of Karrān, came Wardak and Hunī. After this, Sayyid Muḥammad Gīsūdarāz with his sons spent his time /84/86/ with the forebears of their mothers and [later] went to Hindūstān. In volume two of this royal book, the author of these lines has fully described the arrival of Amīr Tīmūr Kūrkānī [Gūrgānī] in Kabul and the reason for his killing and plundering from which horrific event few people escaped with their lives. Thus the bloodstained, murderous amir on baseless grounds destroyed cities and sent lakhs of people to the hereafter.

In short, when Sayyid Muḥammad Gīsūdarāz went to Hindūstān his sons grew up among the families of their mothers. They took wives from the Afghans and intermingled with them. These accounts that they offer [to establish their relationship to Sayyid Muḥammad Gīsūdarāz] are not sufficient evidence to establish their relationship because Sayyid Muḥammad Gīsūdarāz in 800 A.H. (1397–98 A.D.) went to Hindūstān. The author of *Makhzan-i Afghānī* wrote that Shayrānī was one of the sons of Qays, nicknamed ʿAbd al-Rashīd, and considered him to be a contemporary of Hażrat-i Payghambar (the Prophet Muḥammad) then this does not correspond with what is correct because the Afghan tribe was in the mountains northwest of Hindūstān many years before the mission of the Most Noble Prophet. Thus Zāl-i Zābulī fought them and moreover Shayrānī was the grandson of Sarban who goes back to the loins of ʿAbd al-Rashīd by three degrees. In fact, he (Shayrānī) was the son of Sharkhbūn, son of Sarban, son of ʿAbd al-Rashīd. Then this means that he must have lived almost 800 years so that Sayyid Muhammad could marry his daughter while he was still alive, as was mentioned above.

The *Tārīkh-i Firishtah* mentions that Sayyid Muḥammad Gīsūdarāz went to Dihlī and the Deccan in 810 A.H. during the reign of the Bahmanīd, Fīrūz Shāh (r. 800–825 A.H.) and he built a khanaqah in Ḥasanābād, adjacent to Gulbargah where he was buried and where his tomb has become a pilgrimage site. After Fīrūz Shāh, Aḥmād Shāh Bahmanī, who came to the throne in 825 A.H. also extended the hand of discipleship to the skirt of the sayyid who was still alive and right up until today, the descendants of that sayyid are still in the Deccan.

Another thing is that in 910 A.H., when Muḥammad Bābur Pādshāh had already come to Afghanistan, at that time the Wardak tribe and the Gundah Pūr were so numerous that it is impossible that over the course of the hundred years that had passed since the time of Sayyid Gīsūdarāz that this number of people could have been created from the lineage of one person. Now each Wardak, Gundah Pūr, Mushwānī, and Huni would have had to have a whole tribe of their own to approach the numbers that exist today of those groups.

Another point is that the section of Hunī and Mangal lived together on the territory of Banūn District for 150 years. /85/87/ They then fell out with each other but then abandoned the dispute and cut off the ten percent of the grain and the official stipend which they gave to the pīr, Shaykh Shāh Muḥammad Rūḥānī, who was living among them. He was hurt and left there with his son, Shāh Nīk Bīn, and found a place in Kūh-i Shawāl among the offspring of Shītak of the lineage of Kīsūy and Sūrānī and a branch of the Banūzāʾī. He gave them permission to drive the section of the Mangal and Hunī out of Banūn District which then was known as "Dand" [but] the offspring of Shītak were defeated and subdued.

The Wazīrī tribe considered this order of Shaykh Shāh Muḥammad to be a godsend and they set out for Banūn with all their people and possessions. At first they camped at Warghar [on the] Tūchī River on the southern skirts of the mountain and north of Gabr and then with the approval of the eldest son of the noble shaykh who was their commander they sent a message to the Hunī and Mangal saying "either hand over the district of Dand or prepare to be plundered and killed." Because of the dispute that they had had with each other and the curse of the shaykh, (the Hunī and Mangal) were forced to abandon their homeland. Most of the Huni tribe turned in the direction of Hindūstān and the rest left with the Mangals for the mountain region south of Sapīd Kūh. Up until now they have not gone beyond that area but have remained there. The Banūnzā'ī tribe, one of the offspring of Shītak, went to the district of Dand and took possession of it. Although this episode is not recorded in any history except that the Banūnzā'ī taking of Marān Malik [happened] during the life of Shāh Muḥammad Rūḥānī, a contemporary of Shāh Rukn-i 'Ālam and Rukn-i 'Ālam died at the age of 88 in 705 A.H. These historical facts about his death and about the shaykh being a contemporary of his have come to light and thus the Wardak, Hunī, Mushwānī, and Gundah Pūr tribes cannot consider themselves to be the offspring of Sayyid Muḥammad Gīsūdarāz because 100 years before the birth of this great sayyid, the Hunī tribe, which was the offspring of the brother of Wardak, Gundah Pūr, and Mushwānī made its home in the district of Dand which is now known as Banūn, as previously noted. More astonishing of all is that the Wardak tribe say that the properties of Khawād, Shanīr, and Gīrū-yi Rashīd which are located west of and adjoining the dependencies of Kabul and north of and adjacent to the dependencies of Ghaznīn, were granted to them by Sulṭān Maḥmūd Ghaznawī whose death took place in 421 A.H. (1030 A.D.). Their claim is that he gave these possessions to them so that they would develop and improve them. Well, of course, if a group within the lineage or outside the lineage or Hindūs, who before the conquests of Sulṭān Maḥmūd-i Sabuktagīn in India were called Bud'ī and believed in /86/88/ the creed of the Hindūs, had their homeland in the district of Dand and had possession of the city of Maturām named Akrār and fought against Sulṭān Maḥmūd and were defeated, destroyed, and exterminated, this is not our affair for as the Noble Verse says "We have created you from male and female and made you into nations and tribes, that you may know one another. Verily, the most noble of you with God is the most godfearing." (Qur'ān 49:13). Now they are called Muslims and Afghans and they behave as Afghans and Muslims. The traces of Islamic nobility are evident in their form and appearance, their character, and their nature.

The Tribes and Clans of the Ūstaryānī or Sataryānī Belonging to the Shayrānī Tribe Who Inwardly Consider Themselves Sayyids and Outwardly Afghans

The Lord bestowed five sons on Ūstarānī better known as Sataryānī—Shaykhī, Marīrī, Tarī nicknamed Gundah Pūr, Amr Khayl, and Hamraṭ.

Thus, Brāhīm Khayl and Pahbī Khayl were the offspring of Shaykhī, the first son.

Brāhīmzā'ī, Bāzak Khayl, Darī Palārah, Sayyidāl Khayl, Ḥawlat Khayl, 'Abdalzā'ī, Fatū Khayl, Qandū Khayl, Mandāwak Khayl, Aḥmad Khayl, Jubayl Khān,

Nuṣrat Khayl, Nuṣrat Khān, Bītā Khayl, Alahdād Khayl, Shaykh Ḥaydar Khayl, Tatūzāʾī, Utmānzāʾī, Khayrī Khayl (this one was "born of the house [*khānazād*])," Ḥusaynzāʾī, ʿUmar Khayl, Zāwulī Khayl, Mānī Khayl, ʿĀlī Khayl, Jalī Khayl, Tājīzāʾī, Dūd Khayl, Sikandar Khayl, Shahū Khān Khayl, Niẓām Khayl, and Bāzīd Khayl were the offspring of Tarī, nicknamed Gundah Pūr (but Murray, *A Dictionary* lists only a Gandahpur tribe), the third son of Ustarānī [*sic*], and these are all remembered as Gundah Pūrī.

The second and fourth sons of Sataryānī had no offspring.

The clans of the line of Hamr [or Humar],[17] the fifth son, will be mentioned after the listing of the clans of the Yaʿqūbzāʾī, ʿImrānzāʾī, Khūbīzāʾī, and Darī Palārah, which were also of the line of Gundah Pūr.

Thus Shāh Khayl, Dānah Khayl, Sarwān Khayl, Sulaymān Khayl, Mihtar Khayl, Ikhtiyār Khayl, Shabī Khayl, Bahādur Khayl, Muḥammad Khayl, Adīn Khayl, Barā Khayl, Aḥmad Khayl, Khwājah Khayl, Akhtī Khayl, Dāwī Khayl, Ḥayāt Khayl, and Qadam Khayl were the progeny of Yaʿqūb, known as Yaʿqūbzāʾī, son of Gundah Pūr.

Similarly, ʿĪsā Khayl, Sayyidāl Khayl, Sulṭān Khayl, ʿUṣmān Khayl, Mīrā Khayl, Pāmak Khayl, Dawlat Khayl, Shihāb al-Dīn Khayl, Barah Khayl, Bangī Khayl, Shahdād Khayl, Malank Khayl, Būjar Khayl, Banī Khayl, Yaḥyā Khayl, Gund Khayl, Ḥaydar Khayl, Gadāy Khayl, Āzād Khayl, Saʿīd Khayl, Nuṣrat Khayl, Zarnī Khayl, Rashīd Khayl, and Alahdād Khayl were all offspring of ʿImrān, known as ʿImrānzāʾī son of Gundah Pūr.

Also Żaḥḥāk, Shaddād /87/89/ Khayl, ʿAlīzāʾī, Mīdād Khayl, ʿĪsaf Khayl, Bahāʾī Khān Khayl, Abdak Khayl, Bāqir Khayl, Sikandar Khayl, Khalīl Khayl, ʿAbdal Khayl, Kamāl Khayl, Ḥayāt Khayl, Bābar Khayl, Jamak Khayl, and Mullā Khayl were also of the offspring and womb of Khūbī known as Khūbīzāʾī, daughter of Gundah Pūr.

Shaykhī, Khadrzāʾī, Marīrī, Nikandarzāʾī, Nīkāl Khayl, Khāzin Khayl, Bāzīd Khayl, Safrzāʾī, Ḥājjī Khayl, and Jaʿfarzāʾī were all the offspring of Darī Palārah who after Bārak Khayl, grandson of Gundah Pūr, bear the name [Gundah Pūrī]. Up to this point everything that has been written has been about the Gundah Pūrī tribe.

Regarding the lines of the Shaykhī and Marīrī clans, brothers of the abovementioned Gundah Pūr—the second of the clans mentioned above (ʿImrānzāʾī?) was without any offspring—they were incorporated in the Darī Palārah and it, Safarzāʾī, and Khadrzāʾī were included in the Shayrānī clans as *waṣlī*. Besides that, the Ibrāhīmzāʾī clan of the Gundah Pūrī was included in the Anzāʾi line of the Shayrānī lineage.

Similarly, Shaykhī Khayl, Sīn Khayl, Khuwaydādzāʾī, Naẓar Khayl, Ghurghushtī or Ḥusaynzāʾī were included in the offspring of Gundah Pūr.

ʿAlī Khān Khayl, Mālī Khayl, Malī Khayl, and Katī Khayl of the Yūsufzāʾī tribe were separate and joined and mixed with the Gundah Pūrī Yaʿqūbzāʾī so that one might say these clans are considered as related to Gundah Pūr not by blood

[17] Hamraṭ on first appearance (above). "Homar" is the way Bernhard Dorn, the translator of *Makhzan-i Afghānī* transliterates the name.

(i.e. *waṣlī* not *aṣlī*) yet all their habits and customs were the same so that no one could tell them apart.

Originally, Ustarānī with his progeny like Gundah Pūr and others whose names have already been recorded had their residences in a place called Sataryānī Chāh, situated seven manzils to the northeast of Qandahar. Of Ustaryānī's sons, Tarī, known as Gundah Pūr, was a handsome young man, with a good physique. Thus during the life of Ūstaryānī [*sic*] the daughter of the chief of the Shayrānī tribe was captivated by his good looks and, without the approval and permission of the parents, the girl entered the home of Gundah Pūr. Gundah Pūr also found that girl beautiful and seductive and those two hearts joined and they intended to marry. But Ūstaryānī with the other sons forbade Gundah Pūr from forming this attachment. But he was so enamored of the girl he paid no heed to their advice and, since they saw that he was stubborn, they stopped talking to him. So he left that place and with his family and relatives moved from the locale of Ustaryānī [*sic*] Chāh and settled in Tarwī, two short manzils from Sataryānī Chāh. Ustaryānī, the father of Gundah Pūr, because of his forbidding Gundah Pūr's moving to another place and Gundah Pūr's going anyway, he (the father) addressed him as "Gandah Pūr" (meaning "bad smell, stench"). The Hindīs append an 'h' to the end of his name./**88/90**/ The word is with the Persian 'k' and heavy 'd' and they say it expresses a smell. (This writer has written whatever the esteemed scholar Mullā Fayż Muḥammad Khān Kātib has written in (his) linguistic research on local usages, in particular on the word *gundah* but one should know that in the usage of Persian linguists, *gandah* with an 'a' on the Persian 'k' (the 'g') is from the verb *gandīdan* and *gandah* does not mean [exclusively] "bad smell, putrefaction." On the other hand, *gundah* with a 'u' on the Persian 'k' ('g') means a large fat person or an animal of strong physique. In the lexical meaning in Persian, in the languages of Iran, when *gandah* is used it describes the spoiling or rotting of something eaten or drunk which produces a stench from the rotting. *Gandah* therefore does not mean only a noxious odor. As the poet says, "If something is rotten, salt will revive it / Alas for the time when salt spoils." This is because salt is a preservative and an enhancer and draws out the evil microbes.

After the progeny of Gundah Pūr built aqueducts (*qanāt*s), improved Tar, and became known for their wealth and influence, other offspring of Ustaryānī) also moved from Sataryānī Chāh and joined up with the Gundah Pūrīs (in Tarwī). All of them then became known as Gundah Pūr. Some chose to be nomadic and some to be landlords and property owners. Thus their nomadic members would go to Dāman in winter and in summer come to Afghanistan. In the mountains of Ghūr in western Afghanistan during the events of one year, at the time when they were nomadizing, one individual named Khadal, from the Lahūn Ghurghusht tribe approached and stared at their (the Gundah Pūrīs) women. The jealousy of the Gundah Pūrīs was aroused by that person's gazing at their women and they killed him. When the news reached the Ghurghusht Lahūn, they set out to take revenge and commenced fighting and killing. Some from both sides were killed and wounded because of this incident. The result was that the Kākar tribe rose up to defend the Lahūn and boldly began to oppose [the Gundah Pūrīs] and to shed their blood until the Gundah Pūrīs were defeated. One of the groups of 'Imrānzā'ī crossed the Indus River and made a place for themselves in Chāh-i Gadāy in the

Tal Desert. Others also left their winter quarters in Dāman and abandoned their properties in Tarwī District out of fear of attack by the Kākars and in the north of that location [Tarwī] pitched their tents for their summer quarters and thus became helpless and homeless. They now all chose the nomadic way of life.

Consequently, they would spend a six-month period in the mountains of western Afghanistan and six months in Nālah Takwārah located east of Dāman and south of Kūh-i Sulaymān /89/91/ up to the eastern skirts of that mountain. Then with the help of Khān Zamān, who was the chief of the Katī Khayl clan established in Tāk Wālah and asked the Gundah Pūr to settle in Tāk so that they would be safe from the assaults of Marwatis who were their enemies, half of them chose Rūrī located in Dāman and went there for half the winter and then in the summer would come to Afghanistan. Later, a dispute broke out between Miyān Khayl and the Gundah Pūrs which led to much killing and wounding. At the end of the fighting to make peace it was agreed that the Gundah Pūrī men would leave the territory of Rūrī and would make their winter quarters in the direction of Tāk, the homeland of the Marwat tribe. It was also agreed that the Miyān Khayl would go for the winter to Nūḥānī, a place in Rūrī and so peace was reached in this fashion and up to now, things have remained in accordance with this agreement. The Gundah Pūrs returned and developed Rūrī. Out of fear of the English they stopped their fighting and contention and tended [to live] in friendship and brotherhood.

The Gundah Pūr tribe, both men and women, comprise some 40,000 people. They live in Dīrā (*sic*—Dīrah) Ismāʿīl District. Their homeland is bordered to the south by the land of the Miyān Khayl, to the north by the Dawlat Khayl lands, to the west, by the skirts of the Kūh-i Takht-i Sulaymān, and to the east by Dīrah Ismāʿīl Khān.

Peoples, Tribes, and Clans of Humar, the Fifth Son of Ustarānī

Humar, the fifth son of Ūstaryānī [*sic*] had two sons—Amanzāʾī and Gugalzāʾī.

Brāhīmzāʾī, Khānzāʾī, Naẓarzāʾī, Mashtīzāʾī, Ghūrnīzāʾī, Ḥasanzāʾī, and Kārīzāʾī were the offspring of Aman, who was known as Amanzāʾī, and were all known as the Humar-Ustarānī tribe.

Similarly, Akhūzāʾī, Shabīzāʾī, Aḥmadzāʾī, Shamūzāʾī, Alahdādzāʾī, Darzāʾī, Aldūzāʾī, Mūsāzāʾī, Jārūzāʾī, Lālakzāʾī, Madīdzāʾī, Pāyandahzāʾī, and Charmshāy were all offspring of Gugal, known as Gugalzāʾī.

All these clans were called Humar, being of the line of Humar, the son of Ustarānī, while all the others were recalled by the name Gundah Pūryā. A few of the clans of the Humar tribe had their residences in the plains south of the homeland of the Babar tribe and another group in the mountain region. On the southern side of the mountain, their homeland /90/92/ adjoined the territory of the Kasrānī Balūch tribe and on the west it adjoins the mountain lands of the Amrzāʾī. They have in their possession the locales of Amak, Pīwar Kūy, Dachah Kūy, Mangal, and Gundī. Including their clients (*hamsāyagān*) they number 4,500 households.

The Clans and Tribes of the Line of Hunī. Inwardly They Believe They Are Sayyids. Earlier They Were Mentioned in the Mamlan (?)[18] *Genealogy of the Clans and Offspring of Karrān. Then They Were Mentioned as Being of the Tūzā'ī By Virtue of a* Waṣlī *Relationship*

The Hunī were *waṣlī* offspring of Karrān and Hunī had five sons and two grandsons—Dawlat, Būgharī, Rūmusht or Dūmusht, Khūst, Rūdan, Khuwaydād Khayl, and Hūtīzā'ī. All of them call themselves Karrānī. Hunī in the beginning included the Mangal tribe. Thus up to now they are known as the Hunī-Mangalī tribe. They have places in Banūn where they are known by this name. It's been approximately 269 years since Banūnzā'ī, one of the offspring of Shītak, expelled the Mangal tribe from Banūn. A contingent of the Hunī tribe hurried off to Hindūstān and some, including the Mangal tribe, settled in the mountains west of Banūn as was already recorded. Presently, of the Hunī tribes, the Dūmusht, who are called [either] Dūmusht or Dumukhtī are living between the Bangash, Arūkzā'ī, and Kurram in the mountains southeast of the Sapīd Kūh. They are divided into two branches and count 12,000 fighting men.

The Tribes and Clans from the Line of Wardak, the Brother of Hunī Formerly in the Lineage of Karrān, then of Huni, and They Are Recorded as Waṣlī

Wardak, one of the *waṣlī* progeny of Karrān had six sons—Mamak, Mi'yār, Mīr Khayl, Nūrī, Larm, and Gadāy. He had four grandsons from the loins of Mi'yār—Malikyār Khayl, Khurram Khayl, Adīn Khayl, and Miṣrī Khayl. The size of the Wardak clan is reckoned at 12,500 households. Wardak territory takes the form of a valley, its length running from north to south. To the west and east of it are chains of mountains and between the valleys of Khwāt and Shinīz there is also a chain of hills. Each (valley) has separate rivers which rise in the south **/91/93/** and flow north to the Lūgard [Logar, i.e., Lahūgard] River and irrigate the two valleys.

The waters irrigate the locale of Dāy Mīrdād, the property and territory of the Hazārahs, which the Wardak took control of, along with the village of Shaykhābād and the gorge of the aforementioned river (the Lūgar) whose source is the village of Shaykhābād and Kajāb and other places within the mountains of Hazārah Bihsūd. This river (the Lūgar) goes through the narrow gorge of the Wardak and enters Lahūgard District, one of the dependencies of Kabul and flows northeast. By this river are irrigated the fertile lands of Lahūgard and Mūsā (?), the villages of Bīnī Ḥiṣār, Shīwakī, and Sahākān, adjoining the city of Kabul. At a distance of three miles farther down from the city it joins the Kabul River whose source is in Hazarah Sar Chashmah, Sādat Sanglākh, and Nirkh Maydān and originates in the Pamqān mountain range. Three miles farther down, it passes through Tangī Ghārū (Ghārū Gorge) six *kurūhs* from Kabul and then joins the Nīlāb River of Panjshayr, the Ghūrband River, and the many waters of Tagāb and Nijrāb District, all of which originate in the Hindū Kush mountains. At the terminus of the land of Lamqān, it joins with the Lamqān River which also originates in the Hindū

[18] There is no obvious meaning for this word. Nor have referrals back to the Karrān genealogies shed any light.

Kush mountains and the mountains of the homeland of Kāfiristān. A little farther on [the Kabul River] is united with the waters of the Surkh Rūd which originates in the eastern mountains of Lahūgard and the western Sapīd Kūh. Below the city of Jalālābād the Gaz River which also originates in the Hindū Kush mountains joins with all the abovementioned waters. All of them are then called the Kabul River. It passes to the north of the city of Peshawar and with the waters from the mountain homelands of the Muhmand tribe, from Bājāwur, from Yūsufzāʾī, and Sawād (Swat) District, it joins the Atak (Attock) River. It is then counted as one of the [five] rivers of the Panjāb. Near the port of Karachi, the name Sind (Indus) River is given to it and it then empties into the Arabian Sea.

The Mushwānī Tribes and Clans Who Also Consider Themselves Sayyids

The Lūdīn, Mitkānī, Samlānī, Rawghānī, Tafaż, Kayūr, Muhmand, Badūr, Tarak, Yūsuf Khayl, Mūsā, Ādam Khayl, Sanjar, Kazbūnī, Gharīb, Kharbārī, and Yāghan clans all being progeny of Mushwānī are all called Mushwānī. The Afghans of the Kākar tribe consider themselves to have the same origin [as the Mushwānī]. They count themselves as sayyids. In any case, this tribe is small in numbers. There are 550 households of this tribe who reside in Kūh Dāman, located twenty-five miles north of Kabul. They live (mainly) as agriculturalists though some are traders. A few households of this tribe reside in Qandahar and some in Sarī, in the district of Hazārah Chach (India) situated in the northern part of Kūh-i Gandagar. **/92/94/** In the locale of Kharbārah, Gandagar they have a shrine, whose name is unknown. Of this tribe, some of the Būdīn branch has been dispersed among the Ghiljāʾī. One of them, Muḥammad Rafīq Khān, the son of Mullā Bīdū, son of Mullā Nasū reached a high point by the end of his career during the time of Amīr Shayr ʿAlī Khān. Now Colonel Aḥmad ʿAlī Khān, son of ʿAbd al-Wāḥid Khān, son of the aforementioned Muḥammad Rafīq, is the border guard and in charge of the customs post of Dakkah [on the road between Peshawar and Jalālābād].

The Khūndī Tribe and Clans Whose Names Were mentioned Among the Clans of the Line of Dāwī, of the Clans of Ghurghusht

Since the Khūndī tribe says that they are sayyids, although they were recorded as belonging to the Ghurghushtī clans, here, because they consider themselves sayyids [in order to explain this claim], it is recorded that Dāwī, the son of Dāʾī (?) one of the grandsons of Ghurghusht married a widow, the daughter of a sayyid who had come from Khujand to Multān to visit her sister. That female sayyid who was pregnant by her [late] husband and had married him before giving birth, [she] gave the name Sayyid Ḥusayn to [the child]. As Deputy Ḥayāt Khān on page 444 of his book [*Ḥayāt-i Afghānī*] wrote, "Naturally such a marriage in the refined Hanafi doctrine is permissible." Or perhaps [he considered] the waiting period (*ʿiddah*) of four months, ten days before the birth to have been fulfilled.

Anyway, Sayyid Ḥusayn had four sons—Balīl, Sikandar, Mūsā, and ʿAlī. Because of the fact that the father of these sayyids had traveled in the womb of his mother from Khujand, the Afghans called them "Khūndī" [a corruption of "Khujandī"]. In any event, they were included in the Ghurghusht tribe and presently they have become separate and distinct and pursue their lives in the environs of Qandahar and are an insignificant (*kamī*) tribe.

The Sipandzāʾī Tribe Whose Members Also Consider Themselves To Be Sayyids

This tribe is included among the clans of the Tarīn tribe and lives on the territory of Fūshanj. They provide for themselves and satisfy their material needs through agriculture. Their numbers and importance are both quite insignificant and they have no power to speak of.

The Gharshīn Tribe Whose Members Consider Themselves the Offspring of Bilāl

This tribe was mentioned among the tribes in the genealogy of the Miyānah Afghans. Aside from Qandahar and its environs, 65 households of this **/93/95/** tribe reside on the northwest part of the territory of Dūr. Their ancestry to Ḥażrat Bilāl, the muezzin of the Most Noble Prophet—peace be upon him—comes only from what they say themselves. There is no source or evidence for it. The word "Gharshīn" presently has become corrupted and is now recognized as "Kharfīn."

The Kūtī Tribe Who Are Also Afghan Sayyids

They say that a certain Ibrāhīm, a grandson of Shaykh Bīt, whose descendant clans, as has been noted already, are known as Bītanī, studied at Shaykh Bīt's feet and when he had reached the age of maturity took a wife from the Bītanī family. Two sons named Ḥasan Shāh and Muḥsin Shāh were produced by that woman. They went to Banūn and settled there. Ḥasan Shāh chose to live in the mountains. From Muḥsin Shāh came two sons named Jang Shāh and Fīrūz Shāh. From Jang came three sons—Sīrī Khayl, Dawlat Khayl, and Sīnī Khayl. Eventually, Fīrūz Shāh became frightened and fled towards Tāk. His brother, Jang Shāh, was killed in Banūn. Presently his tomb is in his *khānaqāh* located in Dahāwah. Of his offspring, some are found among the Khāndū Khayl and the Sūrānī in Kūtī Khāndān Abādān.

The Kūtī tribe numbers 70 households in the district of Banūn.

The Tribe of Sayyids From the Offspring of Ḥażrat Ḥusayn, On Him Be Peace

The sayyids from the Banī Fāṭimah are numerous and one to two households live in some places while ten, twenty, thirty, forty, fifty, sixty or more households dwell in places in Afghanistan. The people of Afghanistan address them as *āqā, sayyid, mīr,* and *shāh* except for the sayyids who live in the Hazārahjāt whom they call "Hazārah sayyid." The Hazārah people are all of the Twelver Shīʿah sect. The Hazārah people have enormous respect for their own sayyids and give them lands and estates as votive offerings, the *khums* (one-fifth) tax, and "the sayyid's share" so that they all are owners of properties, estates, forts, etc. They enjoy the positions of chiefs and lords over the Hazārah people. The reason for the honor and esteem which the Hazarah people accord them is that those same sayyids with their wives and children were exterminated at the time of the rebellion of the [Hazārah] tribes of Uruzgān and Ḥajaristān by order of Amīr ʿAbd al-Raḥmān Khān. The explanation, according to what Mullā Fayż Muḥammad Khān **/94/96/**

Kātib writes, who himself is Shīʿah and of the Hazārah people, is that the late Amīr ʿAbd al-Raḥmān Khān inferred that the Hazārah mīrs and mīrzādahs at the instigation of the Hazārah people who were wont to travel back and forth to Karbalā and the sublime thresholds [holy sanctuaries of Iraq in Najaf, Karbalā, and Kāẓimayn] had raised their heads in rebellion. When these people went to Karbalā, scholars there would incite them and encourage them to side with the interests of the Iranian government. Amīr ʿAbd al-Raḥmān Khān ordered them to come to Kabul and when they came he gave the order for them to be executed. Nearly 300,000 Hazārahs were killed or made prisoner, all of which has been recorded in *Sirāj al-tawārīkh.* Since the labels of "evildoing" and "rebelling" have been borne by the Hazārah people it is incumbent to record the reasons for their mutiny and rebellion.

At the time when Amīr ʿAbd al-Raḥman Khān was returning from Balkh where he had gone because of the sedition of Muḥammad Isḥāq Khān, the son of his paternal uncle, who was governor of the part of Lesser Turkistān that belonged to Afghanistan, he dispatched Sardār ʿAbd al-Quddūs Khān with an army and the tribal militia of the Hazārahs of Wāy [*sic*—Day] Zangī and Bāmyān with orders to win over and bring to obedience the Hazārahs of Uruzgān—whose historical name is Arkatah Qūn—and (those of) Ḥajaristān, Zāwulī, and Sulṭān Aḥmad which are all part of the Hazārahjāt and, after Nādir Shāh Afshār, would not submit to anyone and were utterly free. The Hazārahs, by means of letters and messages, and without unsheathing the sword, accepted submission to the government. At the order of the government, they razed their forts and surrendered their weapons. At the time of the surrender of weapons, the soldiers, using as a pretext the claim that they might be hiding their weapons, oppressed them and put a cat under the clothes of the women, securely bound its feet, and beat it with sticks, until the feet and legs of the women were scratched and wounded from its teeth and claws. They [also] boiled eggs and placed them in the armpits and elbows of the women and men. They heated skewers until they were red-hot and burned them and by beating and torturing them they demanded to know the places where weapons had been hidden. Moreover, they stripped the wives and daughters and paraded them before their own men sparing them no indecency and nothing forbidden. Every army officer and leader took possession of two, three, or four wives and daughters and carried on like this for one year until in Ramażan 1309/April 1892, the Hazārahs of Uruzgān, because of these perverted violations of their honor, which were contrary to the Sharīʿah and all norms of dignity, preferring death to life (with dishonor), rose up against the royal army. When news of their uprising and rebellion spread to Kabul, the ulema /95/97/ of Kabul considered this obstinacy to constitute sedition and issued a fatwa pronouncing the Hazārahs to be infidels and their killing and enslaving [to be permissible]. By this decree, nearly two lakhs of men and women, sons and daughters of the Hazārahs, were taken prisoner, besides those who were killed, and the government gave all the property of two-thirds of the Hazārahs to Afghans. Many Hazārahs abandoned their homelands and Afghanistan and went to Iranian Khurāsān, Turkistān, and Hindūstān. Those who stayed faced oppression and hardship.

The powers that be in Afghanistan could not have cared less about them. As a result, in 1337/1919 when a call for jihad against the English was given, fearful that the people of Afghanistan would kill them, the Hazārahs did not answer the call but gave seven lakhs (700,000 rupees) in cash and 100 horses to support the government. [In return] promises were made on behalf of the government that were not fulfilled. Over and above all that, Sayyid Nūr Muḥammad Shāh Khān Qandahārī, in view of the directive given by the Prophet Muḥammad and the announcement of jihad on behalf of the *pādshāh* of Islām [Amīr Amān Allāh Khān] that all tribes and peoples of Afghanistan put the business of jihad above all else (had organized) 900 Qizilbāsh who are Shiʿah and provided weapons, tents, supplies, transport, and travel expenses for the jihad. He departed Qandahar and had not yet gone one manzil away from the city when Afghans who had come to Qandahar to join the jihad and knew that Sayyid Nūr Muḥammad Khān had left fell upon the (Qizilbāsh) quarter and attacked their homes from eight o'clock in the morning until sunset and killed and looted at will. When women tried to use the Qurʾān as intercession for their children, the Afghans shot holes in it. They killed many [Qizilbāsh] in a variety of ways and slaughtered nearly 150 men and women, young and old, and they looted twenty-one lakhs (2,100,000 rupees worth) of cash and goods of theirs. This is an amount which the Kūtwālī Court of Qandahar officially accounted for of which seven lakhs, fifty thousand rupees was the personal property of Sayyid Nūr Muḥammad Shāh Khān. For several days, the bodies of the murdered lay on the ground until finally Khūshdil Khān Lūynāb, the governor of Qandahar, who was the brother of the mother of His Majesty Amīr Amān Allāh Khān Ghāzī and was the instigator of this trouble, when he learned of the approach of Sardār ʿAbd al-Quddūs Khān, the prime minister, who had been sent to Qandahar from Kabul with an army to fight the English, threw the bodies onto carts, had them taken out of the city, and thrown on the dump trash pile. Miscellaneous bones were thrown on top of them and after that at a sign from Lūynāb, the cause of the trouble, they arrested five or six sayyids and barbers 96/98/ and sent them to Kabul, Lūynāb being afraid lest he be held responsible. After a while, the Amīr-ghāzī obtained a letter of satisfaction from the Qizilbāsh of Kabul that there would be no revenge killing or demanding of blood money [for the slain people] and the imprisoned men were sent back to Qandahar with a reward for Khūshdil.

This issue became the cause of oppression and emboldened the Afghans and thus many Hazārahs fled to Shālkūt and others to Iran. Of them, Sayyid Nūr Muḥammad Shāh Khān came to Kabul in Ramażān 1339 Hijrī (May-June 1921) equivalent to 1299 Shamsī and several times was honored [with an audience] where he repeated his complaints of the injustice done him but did not seek compensation for what he had lost. He only asked permission to move so that as a result such a thing would never happen again nor such a wrong ever be inflicted on him and other Qizilbāsh again. However, up until now his wishes have resulted in nothing and no one knows what will happen. This sentence which the esteemed scholar Mullā Fayż Muḥammad Khān Kātib adduced at the end of his remarks about the "sayyid tribe" this author also cites as a warning and writes it down though not relevant to this place (in the book). With regards to the oppression done to Nūr Muḥammad Shāh during the time that he intended to fight the enemy, this writer heard this story in numerous places while traveling in Hindūstān. I am certain [however] that because of his superior qualities and his intelligence and subject-loving nature, the Amīr-ghāzī by now has managed to satisfy Sayyid Nūr Muḥammad Shāh. In fact, this will be one of the events of the years of the reign and sovereignty of His Majesty the peerless amir, Amīr Amān Allāh Ghāzī, that will be recorded in volume seven of this excellent book (*Amān al-tawārīkh*).

The Quraysh Tribe Which Is One of the Large ʿArab Tribes

Besides the sayyids who are from the Banī Hāshim Quraysh, there are also one or two households of other Quraysh in a variety of places in Afghanistan. They make a living by serving as imams and prayer leaders in mosques, as professors, as landlords, and by collecting charitable gifts and income from charitable foundations. With respect to Qurayshī sayyids, there are few in Afghanistan. The people of Afghanistan hold them [the non-sayyid Quraysh] in high esteem because they are of the same tribe as the Prophet Muḥammad.

The Tribe Known As ʿArab

Besides the Quraysh, there are other ʿArabs in Afghanistan who perhaps in the past came from Iran and Khurāsān of western Afghanistan because during the reign of the Sāmānids, who ruled in Bukhārā, the ʿArab tribes of what is now eastern Iran /97/99/ were many and afterwards they came to Afghanistan. In Afghanistan, 2,500 households of this tribe have been counted. Also in Lesser Turkistān, which belongs to Afghanistan, there are a number of people of this tribe. They live as herders and all of them are thought of as ʿArabs. Of all the ʿArabs of Afghanistan, the largest number used to reside in Kabul in the Bālā Ḥiṣār and all of them are Shīʿah. At one time they served the government in different ranks, civil and military. Later, due to the killing of the Englishman Cavagnari which will be described in detail in this very volume, the English captured Kabul and immediately destroyed the Bālā Ḥiṣār which was one of the great constructions of the Mughal Shāh Jahān and a description of its construction will also be recorded. The ʿArabs living in the Bālā Ḥiṣār were made homeless and so scattered. Some who had the means took up residence in Chandāwul quarter of Kabul, which was the Qizilbāshes' quarter who were of the Shīʿah sect and in other quarters of Kabul. Of all the ʿArabs, there was the family of Yaʿqūb ʿAlī Khān whom Amīr Shayr ʿAlī Khān had singled out and distinguished with the high ranks of brigadier and colonel. But Amīr Abd al-Raḥmān Khān confiscated his properties and estates and exiled him to Iran with 80 men and women and boys and girls, under the worst conditions. During the reign of Amīr Ḥabīb Allāh Khān, they petitioned to return and he brought them back. But currently the family faces great hardship and suffering.

The ʿArabs who live in Jalālābād are Sunnis. Aḥmad Shāh Sadūzāʾī took in marriage the daughter of the chief of the ʿArabs of Jalālābād and (Aḥmad Shāh) had a son, Tīmūr Shāh, by her.

The ʿArabs by now have forgotten their original Arabic and speak Persian and Afghānī. They are rural peasants and work as tillers of the soil. In summer they come to Kabul. In the very last days of Amīr Ḥabīb Allāh Khān, he bought all their properties [in Jalālābād] by a compulsory sale and built on them the palace complex of Sirāj al-ʿImārah and a golf course. Ultimately, the golf course which was turned into a polo ground became his burial place. This will be recorded in volume five and volume six of *Amān al-tawārīkh*.

The Clans of the Bangash Tribe Who Consider Themselves To Be Quraysh

This tribe says Ismāʿīl, whose genealogy goes back in ten generations to the loins of ʿAbd Allah, son of Khālid, son of Walīd, had two sons—Gārah /**98**/**100**/ and Sā'il from the womb of a woman who had come from the Farbulī tribe. These two brothers grew to hate each other and there was much killing and bloodshed and so they were known as Bin Kush (Killer Sons). In colloquial utterance that became Bangash. Their progeny, whose homeland was the territory of Gardayz in Zurmat District, fought internally and the result was that they divided into two sections—Gārah and Samil. The genealogy of both was known to be to the Bangash tribe until, due to great conflict and a fight over the khan-ship, and the dominance and power of the Ghiljā'ī, in 959/1552, they left their original homeland and by way of Kurram, Paywār, and Shaldūzān settled and made their homes in the southern part of the Sapīd Kūh. Then, after the passage of 100 years, they fought with the Arūkzā'ī tribe and the Khatak tribe rose up in aid of the Bangash. After heavy fighting, they drove the Arūkzā'ī out of Kūhāt and took it over themselves. After many battles and the passage of a great deal of time, those two tribes, the Bangash and the Arūkzā'ī, as had previously been indicated above when mentioning the Arūkzā'ī tribe, reached a peace agreement together and affirmed that the Bangashīs should make their place in a valley plain and presently they are scattered in several places [in the valley]. In the mountain region to the north of that place, the Arūkzā'īs were to make their homes. Presently, the Bangash are mostly in Kūhāt District, the western part of Kurram District [read Kurram for Garm] and Shakūzān and have made their homelands in the locales of Sarī Ūbah, Tal, Samand, Hangū, Ūstarzī, Kasāy, Tūghah, Nūrah, Watī, Kanī, and Madkhūzah. The wadi-home of the Bangash is lengthy on the west and east, flat, and surrounded by mountains. The east and southeast are homelands of this tribe. The mountains (surrounding the valley) are the homelands of the Khatak. To the north are the Arūkzā'ī and to the southwest, the Wazīrīs have their place. To the west of that is Kurram District. The majority of the Bangash are of the Shīʿah sect; a minority are Sunni. Together they all total 24,000 households. Other than Afghanistan, some households also went to Māzandarān, Iran. Likewise, they went to other areas, especially to Farrukhābād, where there are many people of this tribe. The nawwāb of Farrukhābād, Hind, one of the Bangash zamindars, lives there. He had an annual salary as ruler of Lucknow of four lakhs, fifty thousand rupees until 1801 A.D. when the English occupied Lucknow. He collected that same amount from the English until 1803 when the English reduced his salary and a [new] annual salary of one lakh eight thousand rupees was fixed for the esteemed Nawwāb Ḥusayn Khān Nāṣir Jung. In 1857 A.D. /**99**/**101**/ because of something which the honorable Nawwāb Ḥusayn Khān instigated, the English kicked him out.[19] He went to Mecca and his income was cut off and was not given to anyone else. This trait and manner is inborn in the English that in order to get what they want they spread money around and after getting what they want, they get rid of the other party no matter who it is.

The Genealogy of the Clans of the Bangash Tribe

As was mentioned, Ismāʿīl, the grandson of ʿAbd Allah, son of Khālid-i Walīd, had two sons, Gārah and Sāʾil. Now the clans of the Miyānzāʾī, Ḥasanzāʾī, Badah Khayl, Ḥasan Khayl, Lābī Khayl, ʿAlīkhān Khayl, Mandarah Khayl, Yūsuf or Alīp Khayl, ʿUmar, Mīr Aḥmad Khayl, ʿAlī Shayrzāʾī, Mardū Khayl, Azī or Jāzī Khayl, Shāhī Khayl, Lūrī Khayl, Amīr, Bāʾīzāʾī, Nīsī, Mīrūrī, Shī Khayl, Gulkhān Khayl, Kamāl Khayl, Shādī Khayl, Dūdā Khayl, Shughlī Khayl, Mastū Khayl, Fatḥ Khayl, Mandar Khayl, ʿIzzat Khayl, Dawlat Khayl, Gulshāh, Jamshīdī, Dar Samand, Buland Khayl, and Anakzāʾī are the offspring of Gārī (*sic*—Gārah) and through him are related to the Bangash tribe.

Similarly, Mamāzāʾī, Bar Sitūrīzāʾī, Bāy, Khūqī, Kūz Sitūrīzāʾī, Mūzū Khayl, Nasū Khayl, Kalah, Sūr Khayl, Tānā Khayl, and Khwājah Aḥmad Khayl were all offspring of Sāʾil and related through Sāʾilzāʾī to the Bangash tribe.

The Tribe of the Tājiks, a Contracted Form of Tājīk, Residing in Afghanistan and (Afghan) Turkistān

This tribe is commonly known only by the name 'Tājīk.' It has no clans with distinct names. They are all referred to by the word Tājik prefixed to their homeland or place of residence such as Tajik of Ghaznīn, of Kabul, of Turkistān, or of Badakhshān, etc. Originally, they all came from ʿArab tribes. Since from the very beginning right up to the present Persians call the ʿArabs 'Tāzī,' their name has been written in history books as 'Tāzīk' with the diminutive letter 'k' suffixed. Due to the 'heaviness' of the letter 'z' it changed to the ʿArab letter 'j' and now people say 'Tājik' as a contraction of 'Tājīk'. This meaning can be demonstrated from books of history because the meaning of 'Tājik' as ʿArabs [comes] when, at the very beginning of Islām the Arabs conquered the kingdoms of Iran which were Fārs and Ūzbakīyah and brought them into Islam. The kingdom of Pārs, Iran, western Afghanistan, /**100**/**102**/ and Uzbekistan, which at that time were one, were occupied. [The ʿArabs] intermingled with the newly obedient who mostly spoke Persian and so they gave up Arabic and adopted Persian and conversed in it.

At this time, all the residents of the city of Ghaznīn and its surroundings are Tājiks. Similarly, they occupy most of Kabul; the region of Kūhistān south of the Hindū Kush, east of the Hazārahjāt, and north of Kūh Dāman; and west [*sic*—east] of the farthest extent of the aforementioned mountain (Hindū Kush) namely Nijrāb, Panj Shayr, Ghūrband, Dur Nāmah, Parwān, and other places. Also

[19] Lucknow plays a major role in both the English and South Asian mythology of the great but futile uprising against British rule in 1857.

the majority of this people have made their homeland in Badakhshān, Darwāz, Bāmyān, and Ghūrband. Also, the locales of Chūrah and Gīzāb in the Hazārahjāt, which were taken away from Tājiks who are of the Shīʿah sect, at the order of Amīr ʿAbd al-Raḥmān Khān, and with the property of 300,000 households of the Hazārah people, were given to 15,000 Achakzāʾī, Nūrzāʾī, Hūtakī, Tūkhī, Andarī, and ʿAlī Khayl Ghiljāʾīs and others. Dūst Muḥammad Khān *nāẓim*, who was in charge of Afghan muhājirs, stated that there were 60,000 muhājirs but all that property was handed over to [just] 15,000 Afghan men and women, girls and boys. Furthermore, the government provided rations and interest-free loans to that same supposed 60,000 people. At this time Sardār Muḥammad ʿUs̱mān Khān, the governor of Qandahar,[20] obtained information and verified that the (actual) number of muhājirs was 15,000 and the additional rations and interest-free loans for 45,000 (non-existent) people amounting to 90 lakhs, or in European calculations nine million rupees, that were allotted and sent to the government daftar, that the excess properties should be retrieved and restored to the Hazārahs and the (loan) funds to the government. But it is difficult to get at the truth of the matter because of religious fanaticism.

The Tajik people in all of Afghanistan and Afghānī Turkistān are counted as 60,000 households (*sic*—see below). Of that total most of those residing in Bāmyān have been Shiʿi. In the Khinjān Valley there are 12,500 households of Tajiks. Likewise, they live in (locales in) Lahūgard—Butkhāk, Charkh, Kulangār, Zarghūn Shahr, and other villages of Lahūgard and in Urgūn, Parmal, Sardah, Kulāl Gū, Lamqān, Sīstān, and Qāʾin [Iran], where the Tajiks are called "dirty Sunnis," and in Harāt and its environs. Nineteen lakhs of households equates to 1,900,000 by European calculations.

The Tribes and Clans of the Hazārahs and the Uymāq Between Whom There Is a Great Difference in Ethnicity (*Qawmīyat*) */101/103/*

These two large ethnic groups live in the mountains of Ghūr and its dependencies. The mountains that are their homelands are bordered to the north by the lands of the Uzbeks such as Balkh and Maymanah, to the south by the homeland of the Durrānī tribe and the Ghiljāʾī Afghans, to the east by Kabul and Ghaznīn, and to the west by Harāt. [The Hazārah and Ūymāq homeland] is 300 miles long from east to west and 200 miles wide from north to south. Although these people somewhat resemble and correspond to the Turks to the north of their homeland, it is unknown what lineage of people they originally come from. Most of their language, accent, and vocabulary is Zābulī. In their physiques, facial features, and natural dispositions they resemble Turk-Tātārs. Some, nay even most, people consider them to be, and call them, Mongols. Abu'l-Fażl, writing that they were from the army of Mangū Qāʾān says, "offspring of his army happen to be in this mountain region and they think some of them are Circassians, a large tribe of

[20] Sardār Muḥammad ʿUs̱mān Khān was governor of Qandahar from 1904–1913 and there is no evidence so far that he was governor again, notably in 1922 when ʿAbd al-Muḥammad "Muʾaddib al-Sulṭān" visited Kabul. This indicates the "presently" or "today" referred to a much earlier time and the information came from Fayż Muḥammad Kātib.

Turks living in the Caucasus." Bābur Shāh wrote in his book that "the Hazārahs speak Mongol which they don't know very well."

The Ūymāq tribe is Sunni while the Hazārahs are Shiʿi. On this factor alone they are thoroughly distinct from each other. We will write separately about these two tribes because they are different from each other.

The Ūymāq Tribe[21]

This tribe lives in the mountain region (*kuhsār*) to the west and somewhat to the south of the mountain region of the Hazārahs. In the northwest part of the homeland of this tribe the Jamshīdīs have their homes and safe havens. The Markas River and the Murghāb flow through the valley of the Jamshīdī homeland. They have had homes in Bālā Murghāb, Mārūchāq, Kūshk, Qarūmāch, and Tannūr Sangī. Now (the lands of) those Jamshīdī people who wound up in territory occupied by the Russians after the demarcation of the border have been much improved while the lands of those who wound up in territory on the Afghan side of the border remain desolate and in a state of ruin. As a consequence, Muḥammad Sarwar Khān,[22] the governor of Harāt, in 1299 Hijrī Shamsī equivalent to 1339 Hijrī Qamarī/1920–21 removed 1,000 households of Jamshīdīs belonging to Afghanistan from their homeland and sent them to Qaṭaghan and Badakhshān.

The Taymanī Tribe of the Ūymāq People

This tribe has its homeland in Kūh-i Siyāh Band in Ghūr. Their lands and farms, in the southern part of their homeland, are fine rich ones and are in the hands of the Zūrī clan, a section of this tribe. To the east of these verdant and well-managed farms and pastures of this section of the tribe is located in Sabzawār **/102/104/** or Isfizār and Maydān. Farther down from the hilly region is a vast desert on the edge of which Farāh is found. The Qandahar-Harāt road is also found there. Presently, the Durrānī Nūrzāʾī, ʿAlīzāʾī, and Isḥāqzāʾī tribes have forcibly taken over most of the homeland of the Zūrīs in their district.

The word *ūymāq* in the terminology of the Tātārs means a section of a tribe or a clan. The author of *Tārīkh-i Sir John Malcolm* has said that a large tribe of Ūymāq made their home in Syria and a branch of it has settled in Luristān. Atabek, who emerged from this people, is a well-known figure in the history of Iran. He ruled Shīrāz and Shaykh Saʿdī Shīrāzī composed an ode (*qaṣīdah*) in praise of him. (There were several atabaks (atabegs) during Saʿdī's time and also atabegs of Kirmān and Luristān.) Ordinary people also refer to them as "the four *ūymāq*s" (Chār Ūymāq) because they connected (the word) to four tribes but now the *ūymāq* clans/tribes are numerous. Originally there were four tribes—Taymanī, Hazārī, Taymūrī, and Zūrī, a branch of the Taymanī. Now, the Qibchāq, Durzī known as Durzāʾī—this tribe now said to be one of the clans of the Kākar line—the Jamshīdī, Fīrūz Kūhī, Chār Ṣadah, Khūk Rū, Gāl Kundī, Qāqchī, Zayngar, Zulfī,

[21] Despite the heading, this segment is about the Jamshīdī tribe, considered one of the Ūymāqs.

[22] See Adamec 1975, p. 227 (third "Sarwar Khān, Muhammad" on the page).

Amghalīdī (Amfalīdī), Juwālī, Khayr, Qirk, Dāh Rīzī, and others all belong to the Jamshīdī and all are referred to as "Ūymāq." The Jamshīdīs live in Fīrūz Kūh and by metonymy are called "Fīrūz Kūhī." The Karay [section] of the tribe has made its home to the south of Holy Mashhad and have an undying enmity for the Sālūr, Sāriq, Takkah (Tekke), and Yumūt (Yomut) Turkmens from the environs of Marw and Sarakhs. In 1336, Taymūrī and Hazāri of the environs of Mashhad raided the Hazārahs of Afghanistan and butchered many of them. The cause of this was Afghānī Hazārahs' transgressions perpetrated against the Taymūrīs over women.

The number of members of this tribe (the Tāymanī) is reckoned to be 600,000.

The Hazārah People Whom the Iranians Call Barbarīs

Since they apply this name (Barbarī) to that tribe by way of denigration without thought or reflection, it is necessary that we distinguish "Barbarī" and "Hazārah" from each other so that people know that the genealogy of "Barbar" goes back to Jām and Barbaristān, which is the homeland of the lineal offspring of Barbar, includes all of the borderlands of Africa and extends from the Atlantic Ocean to the kingdom of Egypt. The people of that region are called "Barbarī" [i.e. the Berbers]. They are all dark-skinned like the people of Ethiopia, Nubia, and Zangibār; moreover, like the dark-skinned people of Balūchistān, **/103/105/** Iran. Besides the Barbarīs, the Moors and the Bedouin ʿArabs have their residences there (in Barbaristān).

The Hazārahs, who in Iran are called Barbarīs were originally attributed to two sources—namely the Sīqdārs who were Zābulī and at the time of the march of Alexander of Macedonia towards Panjāb fought against him. The second source to which they were attributed are the Turks and Mongols—the genealogy of all three of whom goes back to Turk, the son of Yapheth, the son of Noah as follows: Alanjah Khān, the son of Guyūk Khān, the son of Dīb Bāyqū Khān, son of Abū Lajah Khān, son of Yapheth, son of Noah had twin sons, one (Alanjah) named Tātār, the other Mughul (Mongol). Turk was the first pādshāh and sat on the throne of sovereignty in Turkistān. He was the heir-apparent of Yāfit (Yapheth) and was established in Saylūk which they also called Salgārī, Salānīk, and Liyūlīk. The Turks of Salānīk who settled to the west of Islāmbūl are connected to this same place where the Ottoman sultanate was established. During his reign Abu Lajah, the son of Turk, conquered all the lands of the Dasht-i Qipchāq, places like Balās, Jīram, and Kūlang and occupied them as far as Bukhārā. Twenty thousand households of the tribe of Hazārah Shīrah and Būbāsh, whose homeland was in the northern part of Qandahar [Province] and whose lands Amīr ʿAbd al-Raḥmān gave to the Afghans, fled towards Khurāsān and other places. Yakah Awlang, located west of Bāmyān, which had nearly 8,000 households was related to these three places in Dasht-i Qipchāq. Band-i Amīr and the source of the Hijdah Nahr [canal system] of Balkh are in Yakah Awlang. Possibly because of the meadows found there and because *awlang* means 'meadow' they call it Yakah Awlang. Otherwise Kūlang in the Dasht-i Qipchāq is unknown to the people whose homes are in Yakah Awlang because they are from the Hazārah Dāy Zangī. If Kūlang were not the name of a place in Dasht-i Qipchāq then it should be understood in its normal meaning of *hīz* (effeminate[23]) and not the name of a tribe. Then the author of the treatise *Mukhtaṣar al-manqūl fī tārīkh-i Hazārah wa Mughul* who draws this connection [of Yakah Awlang to Kūlang in Dasht-i Qipchāq] has made a mistake.

In short, Tātār and Mughūl, after reaching maturity, divided the patrimonial kingdom into two parts. The kingdom was located in northeast Asia bordered on the east by Khitāy presently Manchuria, on the west by the land of Khutan, Turkistān, Uighūr, and Badakhshān, on the north by Salangārī or Salūnīk and Siberia, and on the south by the lands of China and Tibet. This is the land of Kūlang. In length and breadth it is ninety manzils by ninety manzils.

Of the two parts into which it was divided, Tātār chose one-half and Mongol one-half. Besides the territory with the borders given above, they occupied the lands of Badakhshān and Uighūr, the *ulūs* of the Nayqūr Dāy Zangī Hazārahs and connected and united them with the borderlands of Khitāy and Georgia which was the *ayl wa ulūs* of the Chūrah (clan) of the Dāy **/104/106/** Khitāy Hazārahs. Mongol formed four branches out of Merkīt, which also has the name Aduwīt and Tikrīt—Ūhar Tikrīt, Mūdān Tikrīt, Nūdāfīn Tikrīt, and Jīlūn or Jabalyūn Tikrīt. After this numerous tribes formed, each one with a name like Karluwūt, Tamghālīq, Tarqūt, Uyrāt, Barghūt, Qūramī, Nawālās, Tūnāt, etc., etc.

Thus, the Dastah Karī of the Hazarahs of Jāghūrī, who number 5,000 households, are descended from the tribes forming the Karātī. In brief, 122 tribes and clans gradually appeared whose names are found in history books.

The descendants of Tātār lived in the lands of Būyūz Nādir and also had wealth and power. Little by little numerous tribes appeared. Thus the Ūyrāt Ankūt, Garī, Nāymān, Tankqūt, Uighūr, Qibchāq, Turkmān, Qarlūq, Khalaj, and others who were of (Tātār's) line or Mongol's and others like Nakīnās (?) and Jūrjah from whom [Jūrjah] the Chūrah Hazārahs are descended. In view of the Tātārīyah conquest they [the Chūrah Hazārahs] relate to Tātār both by blood and otherwise.

From the abovementioned tribes, nine men of the Chūrah, whose name (Chūrah) was mentioned, one after another held sovereignty over China whom people called Altān Khān Turks.

Another tribe is the Jalāyir to which the people of Jaldīz, who separated themselves from the Asūs Bīsūk or Bihsūd Hazārahs, trace their genealogy. The Jalāyir tribe which originally inhabited the land of Ūtan branched out into ten tribes—Jās, Tū Farāʾūn, Qangqasāt, Kūmsāwut, Ūyāt, Nīlqān, Kūrkīn, Tūlānkqīt, Tūzanī, and Shankqūt. Besides that, the Sūnj people also merged with (joined) them (the ten tribes).

The line of Tātār proceeded father to son until eight had held sovereignty and their rule reached the eighth one, Sūyij Khān. After that (the line of Tātār) came to an end. Afterwards whoever came to rule from the Mongol or Tātār tribes, it's unnecessary to list their names here because our purpose in bringing up the subject is the genealogy and lineage of the Hazarah (Barbarī) people of Afghanistan,

[23] The modern meaning of *hīz* is of a man who ogles women rather than one with effeminate attributes.

since the Mongol and Tātār rulers, their names, their lives and reigns, and their deaths have [already] been dealt with in volume two of *Amān al-tawārīkh* which deals, year by year, with the period from the beginning of Islām until the year 1161 Hijrī/1747 A.D. and which I, the writer of these lines, Ḥājjī Mīrzā ʿAbd al-Muḥammad Khān Īrānī of Iṣfahān, Mu'addib al-Sulṭan, publisher of the journal *Chihrah Numā* of Egypt, have [myself] written. Here our purpose was to make known the genealogy of the Hazārah people. They are the offspring of Mongol and some from the line of Tātār, both sons of Turk.

Histories show that 4,400 years after the descent of Adam, Tūr ibn-i Farīdūn at the head of a vast host of Tātārs defeated the large Mongol army of Qayān, son of Īlkhān, along with his cousin Takūz Khān **/105/107/** and their wives and routed them and they fled towards Tibet and the mountains of Zābulistān where they sought refuge. This took place in the locale of Nāwur, located two manzils west of Ghaznīn and three manzils from Argunah Qūn today named Uzurgūn which people call Uruzgān. Nāwur is now the name of a flat level plain which is used as pasture and has lots of water. On its four sides are natural fortifications [read *ʿamūd-hā* for *ʿamū-hā*] located at a distance of ten *kurūhs* from each other. Each one has strong walls, thick and long, located on top of a motte with glacis.

The plain is twenty *kurūhs* long from south to north and ten *kurūhs* wide from east to west. For six months of summer, the grass of that plain suffices as fodder for more than 200,000 heads of livestock belonging to the Afghan government, and nomads and Hazārah tribes residing west of the plain [bring their herds to] pasture in this plain and in the mountains (around it).

Qayān, the son of Īlkhān, and Takūz, after the defeat of the Mongols, went to Arkinah Qūn which like the plain of Nāwur was vast and was surrounded with mountains and took refuge there. The difference between Nāhwur and Uruzgān is that Nāhwur has water and meadow while Arginah Ghūn [*sic*] is farmland and sown fields (*kalātah*). As a result from 12,000 to 15,000 households of Hazārahs live in that valley (of Uruzgān) and in the (adjoining) narrow mountain valleys. At the order of Amīr ʿAbd al-Raḥmān Khān, they were all killed and that region was given to the people of Afghanistan.

After 1,100 years when the offspring of Qayān and Takūz had proliferated and that plain and those mountains and mountain valleys had become too constrained for them, 5,500 years after the descent of Adam, they returned to Mughūlistān (Mongolia) and they took back the homeland of their forefathers from Tātar control by dint of the sword. Those (Mongols) who had fled having heard this news returned to their original home from Zābulistān and Tibet. From that day forward, thirteen rulers, one after the other until the time of Chingīz Khān, reigned in order. The first of them was Yaldūz Khān, the son of Sīgalī Khwājah and the last was Bīsūgā Bahādur to whom the Bihsūd Hazārahs trace their lineage.

When Chingīz Khān came into the world and became a person of repute among his tribe and the Mongols had proliferated, the offspring and line of Bīsūk now known as "Hazārah-i Bihsūd" and the tribe of Jirqah, which today is also known as the Jirghī Hazārahs, with the offspring of Yazū are from the womb of Alan Quwā, the daughter of Jūniyah, the daughter of Yaldūz Khān. They are divided into ... branches. They are Wūqūn Qīqī now known as the Ūqī Hazarahs of Jāghūrī, the Yūsufīn Sāljī, now known as the Shālī tribe or Shā ʿAlī and they live north of Uruzgān, and /**106/108**/ Nūranjah, who was the founder of the Mongol line of sultans. They chose enmity with Yazū's offspring and fought and won.

After some time, Jāmūqah, to whom is related the Jabā Mubāghah tribe and to whom the chief of the Ḥājīrāt, which is the Ḥājjī tribe living in Ḥajaristān [Afghanistan] traces his lineage, wanted to create trouble between Chingīz Khān and Ūng Khān but could not make any progress. Frustrated he then went to Sangūn, the son of Rūmag, the homeland of the tribe of Sangūn being Ḥajaristān, who was of his lineage. With Sangūn's support he instigated the father of Sangūn to encourage his son (Sangūn) to fight against Chingīz Khān until there was blood shed between them but Chingīz prevailed. After gaining the victory, Chingīz in 599/1202–03, at the age of forty, sat on the khanate throne. In 600/1203–04, he set out to fight Tābāng Khān, the ruler of the Khitāy or of the Nāymān, to whom is connected the lineage of the Dāyah Sākitah of Hazār(ah) Ḥajaristān. He (Chingīz Khān) prevailed and Tābāng Khān, was wounded and all of his army routed. From this we learn that the tribes of Dāyah and Jāmbāghah and Jāghūrī are from the Khitāy and are called Dāy Khitāy. The victorious Chingīz Khān returned to Qarāqurum.

The forces which rode with him (Chingīz Khān) in his fight with Ūng Khān were formed into groups of ten thousand, one thousand, one hundred, four hundred and ten men all of whom now live in the mountains of Ghūr known as the Hazārahjāt. Most were dispersed by the violence unleashed against them by Amīr ʿAbd al-Raḥmān Khān [in the 1890s].

Fifteen of the offspring of Chingīz Khān, according to what the history books record, ruled in Mongolia and China. Of all the Hazārah tribes, the Nīlaktū *ulūs*, were of the lineage of Tāyizī, the son of Tūlak, nicknamed Bīlaktū. Likewise, the Isak Timūr *ulūs* were of the line of Tūftūr son of Tīmūr Qāʾān.

The Tribes of the Hazārahs Living in Afghanistan Who Were Mongols and Tātārs and Are Known as Barbarīs

All these people (the Hazārahs) who are in Afghanistan form ten tribes and clans—Dāy Zangī, Dāy Kundī, Dāy Mīrdād, Dāy Mīr Kushtah, Dāy Mīrak, Dāy Chūpān, Dāy Khitāy, Dāy Lūrī, Dāy Mīrī, and Dāyah). The first five tribes are known as Sādah Suwaykah and the latter five as Sādah Fīr [*sic*-Qabr]. The Hazarah people call the tribe *dāy dar* in their dialect (meaning) a collectivity, a heap, a store, used metaphorically for the great tribes which comprise a large number of clans. Every tribe (*qawm*) is called *day* [*sic*] *dar* and sometimes they simply say *day*. Every *day* includes several clans like Jāghūrī, Fūlādah, Muḥammad Khwājah, Chahār Dastah, etc. If all the clans of the Hazārahs of Afghanistan /**107/109**/ were named in the manner of the Afghan clans then more than 1,500 clans would be counted.

The length and breadth of the homeland of this large tribe extends 200 miles from north to south and from east to west. In the east it adjoins Kabul, Ghaznīn, Qalāt-i Tūkhī, and the (territory of the) Hūtak tribe. In the west it adjoins the homeland of the Dawlatyār, Ghūr, and the Ūymaq, dependencies of Harāt. In the north it adjoins Balkh, Bāmyān, Ghūrī, and Baghlān and in the south Naghal (?) and Bāghrāl (Bāghrān?), dependencies of Farāh, and Qandahar and its environs. In fact, Darrah-i Ṣūf of Balkh and other places such as Qarābāgh of Ghaznīn, Sar

Chashmah, the Hindū Kush mountains touching Panj Shayr-i Kabul, Kāfiristān, Dāy Mīrdād, Gīzāb, Tamazān, and Tīmrān are included among the dependencies of Kabul, Ghaznīn, and Qandahar. (The Hazārahs) occupied a vast land with towering mountains, large flowing rivers, valleys, farmlands, and meadows. Now, two-thirds of that country has been given to Afghans by Amīr ʿAbd al-Raḥmān and Amīr Ḥabīb Allāh Khān and one-third remains to the Hazārahs who will be recorded below together. Their total numbers reached as high as twelve hundred and fifty thousand (1,250,000) people. Now the numbers [within Afghanistan] reach 450,000 adults, men and women, not counting minors and infants. The rest have either been killed or fled.

The Dāy Zangī Tribe Which Resides to the Northwest of the Other [Hazārah] Tribes

The places inhabited by the Dāy Zangī tribe are Sar Jangal, Yakah Awlang, Laʿl, Kirmān, Tarah Bulāq, Talkhak, Akhżarast [*sic*—Akhżarāt], Zaksar, Panjāb and places like Takāb-i Barg, Surkh Kūhak, Takhak, Miyādarah, Surkh Jūy, Zard Sang, Waraṣ, Khūrdak-i Takhtah, Sulṭān Ribāṭ, Jūy-i Timūr, Kāl Qūl, Takht, Chinār, Askān, Qawm-i Sulṭān, Ashkārābād, Bargar, Alqān, Chahār Ṣad Khānah, and other places. They number 40,000 people.

The Dāy Kundī Tribe Most of Whom Live to the West and South of the Dāy Zangī

The places inhabited by the Dāy Kundī are: Shaykh Mīrān, Takhak, Qunchqah Tū, Kūrakah, Talkhak, Shīnah Takht, Jūy Mīr Hazārah, Naydar, Nīlī, Dasht, Tamazān, Uzmah Tū, Shash Qūl-i Qadīr, and others. Their total population numbers 30,000 /**108/110**/.

The Bihsūd Tribe Which Branches Into Several Sub-Tribes

These sub-tribes of the Barbarī Hazārahs, explained below, are of the Bihsūd tribe and their branches named. They inhabit Karūn-i Dīwār, Kaj Āb, Khawāt, ʿUlyā, Tū, Surkh Sang, Maksak, Rāh Qūl, Bādalūm, Bīr Yak (?), Dīwār-i Qūl, Waqtak, Mūshak (or Mūshk?), Katah Khāk, Band Shūy, Gurk Ram, Sang Shāndah, and other places. Their population both young and old is reckoned at 200,000 people.

The Tribes of Jirghī [Jirghay], Būrjagī, and Bahādur Which Are in the South and Southwest of the Bihsūd Hazarahs and a Small Part of Whose Land Has Been Taken by the Mullā Khayl

The Jirghī, Būrjagī, and Bahādur tribes altogether are no more than 1,000 households whose place is south and southwest of the Bihsūd Hazārahs. The Mullā Khayl has forcibly taken from them a small part of their land.

The Jīghatū Tribe Which Is Descended from Chaghatāy and Lives In Ghaznīn District

The places inhabited by this tribe are Jū-yi Amīn Julghā-yi Ilyās, Qariyah Yūsuf, Khūsh Abdāl, Jarm Tū, Nargis, Gulrak, and other places. These people live with the Bayāt people who are in Qiyāq and Gul Būrī. They number 3,000 households.

The Muḥammad Khwājah and Chahār Dastah Tribe

They inhabit Qarābāgh, Chāwah, Shākī, Qūlbā Qūl, Nakhtiyah, Aṣghar, Qalūj, Talkhak, Khūshʿalī, Sarāb, Nāhwur, Gul Kūh, Bayram, Bīdarrah, Shākū, Tamkī, and Zard Ālūʾī. All of them are from villages that are dependencies of Ghaznīn. In the past, they numbered 8,000 households but presently the Chahār Dastah number 3,000 households and the Muḥammad Khwājah 1,250. All the rest have been scattered.

The Jāghūrī Tribe Which Has Seven Dastah and Used To Be 20,000 Households

The homeland of this tribe is situated west of Ghaznīn, north of Muqur and Qalāt, and south of Māltān (*sic*—Mālistān) and those places are known by these names: **/109/111/** Lūmān, Bū Saʿīd, Nīrān, Daskmāshah [Sang-i Māshah?], Gumruk, Surkh Jūy, Amalī Tū, Shūghalah, Bārīk, Shash Par, Fātū, Ghūjūr, Chihil Bāghtū, Tabar Namānak, Jawdarī, Tabqūs, Gulzār, and others. Now Afghans have seized the properties of the Chahār Dastah named Maskah, Qalandarī, and Dūrī. They (the Chahar Dastah) are 5,000 households.

The Tribe of Mālistān Which Is From the Fūlādah and The Descendants of Fūlād Bahādur

This tribe totals 2,000 households who are located south of Nāhwur, east of Ḥajaristān, west of Jāghūrī, and north of Zāwulī and Sulṭān Aḥmad. Their villages are Kandarlī, Ulūm Yalkhān, Hillah, Sabtark, Julgā, Qachanqah Tū, Ghūjūr, Sar-i Julgā, Ūrdah, and Mīr Ādīnah.

The Dāyah, Ḥājjī, Askah, and Satgūn Tribe(s) Who Live in Ḥajaristān

This tribe has been counted as having 12,000 households. It lives in Ḥajaristān District which is a broad plain with a large river flowing through it and high mountains serving as a stout wall. On the north side (Ḥajaristān) adjoins the land of the Jūrghi and Burjakī tribes. On the south it touches Shayr Qulū, Zāwulī, and Sulṭān Aḥmad and to the east Mālistān, and to the west to Kūh-i Shāh Ṭūs and the Sih Pāy Hazārahs of Dāy Zangī. [Ḥajaristān] is now occupied by the nomad Mullā Khayl Afghans.

The Zāwulī and Sulṭān Aḥmad Tribes Both of Whom Are From the Lineage of the Mongol Sulṭāns

These two tribes total 6,000 households with the Payk and Siyāh Baghal who are 1,000 households. They are at the mercy of migrant Afghans. Their homeland is situated to the south of Mālistān and Ḥajaristān, north of Uruzgān, and west of Zardak, Pashah, and Shayr Dāgh.

The Qalandar Tribe Which is One Dastah of the Jāghūrī

This tribe has 6,000 households. Now their homeland which used to be the territory of Īrān, Ūlūm Lālā, Āb Qūl, and other places, has come into the possession of the Afghan Khwājak [tribe].

The Uruzgān Tribe of the Hazārahs /**110**/**112**/

The Uruzgān tribe has 12,000 households. Now its territory is in the hands of the people of Afghanistan. That territory is west of Jāghūrī, north of Hazārah Dāy Chūpān, east of Gurgābah, the homeland of the Muḥammad Khwājah Hazārahs, and south of Zāwulī and Sulṭān Aḥmad.

The Hazarah Dāy Chūpān Tribe

The place of this tribe is south of the Qalandar, west of Arghandāb, north of Qandahar, and east of Gīzāb and Tamazān. Their population is reckoned at 15,000 households. Their territory is presently occupied by Afghans.

The Hazārah Dāy Khitāy Tribe Which Was Located In Qūl Khār, Chinār, Chahār Shanbah, and Tīrīn

The size of this tribe is calculated as being between 20,000–25,000 households. Its place is in Qūl Khār, Chinār, Chahār Shanbah, Tīrīn, Dihrāwud, Chūrah, and Bābulī. It is well-known now that their properties are controlled by Afghans and that this tribe has made *hijrat* to Iran because the eminent scholar Mullā Fayż Muḥammad Khān Kātib explains that their properties have been taken over by Afghans. He doesn't say though where they live now.

The Tribe of Gīzāb and Others

This tribe is counted as having 15,000 households. Their residences are north of Qandahar, east of Bāghrān and Bātṣīl (?), south of Gurgābah, and west of Hazārah Dāy Chūpan. Now all of this is occupied by Afghans.

The Chūrah Hazārah Tribe

Chūrah is located between Gīzāb, Hazārah Dāy Kundī, Shīrīn, Dihrāwud, and Qandahar. It has 2,000 households but now (Chūrah) is in the hands of the Afghans.

The Tamazān Tribe

The tribe of Tamazān is part of the Hazārah Dāy Kundī tribe. They number 2,000 households. This district is south of Nīlī and Dasht, north of Khalaj, east of Tīmrān, and west of the Mīrhind (Hīrmand?) River. The Afghans have taken two-thirds of their property /**111**/**113**/ and left the Hazārahs one-third.

The Sih Pāy Tribe of the Dāyangī (sic—*Day Zangī*) *Hazārahs*

The Sih Pāy Dāy Zangī place of residence is east of the homeland of the Dāy Zangī and Dāy Kundī Hazārahs, west of Ḥajaristān, north of Gīzāb and Uruzgān, and south of some Hazārahs of Bihsūd. They total 10,000 households and now except for Ashkārābād, the rest of their properties like Tākah, Miyāmī, Chahār Shīnah, and other places are in the possession of Afghans. Similarly, Kabsiyār, and many mountains valleys are the homelands of many Hazārahs but now are occupied by Afghans. The rivers of Harāt, Balkh, Kabul, Arghandāb, Hīrmand, and Qandahar all flow out of the Hazārahjāt and now of all the large Hazarah tribes other than the people of Bihsūd, Dāy Zāngī [*sic*], Dāy Kundī and only a few of the people of Jāghūrī, Fūlādah, Majd Khūdah (?), Chahār Dastah, and Jīghatū no one else still remains and the Afghans have taken their property.

The Kayānī Tribe

The Kayānī tribe has about 750 households, which are near Harāt and Qandahar. Most of them are of the Shīʿah sect and a minority are Sunni.

The Chaghatāy Mongol Tribe

The Chaghatay Mongols altogether have 1,250 households and their residences are located in the environs of Harāt. The Jīghatū [Hazārah] tribe, as has already been said, lives around Ghaznīn. The Mongols of Harāt are Sunnis and the Mongols of Ghaznīn are of the Shīʿah sect.

The Qizilbāsh, Who were Originally Turks and from the Kingdom of Iran

The Qizilbāsh moved to Afghanistan from Iran. They have their residences in Harāt, Qandahar, Kabul, and the dependencies of Ghaznīn. Nādir Shāh Afshār moved this tribe to Afghanistan. During the reign of that great pādshāh and during the time of Aḥmad Shāh Durrānī, there were many of them and they were esteemed and honored. After that, under Tīmūr Shāh, Shāh Zamān, Shāh Maḥmūd, Shāh Shujāʿ **/112/114/** Amīr Dūst Muḥammad Khān, Amīr Muḥammad Afżal Khān, Amīr [Muḥammad] Aʿẓam Khān, Amīr Shayr ʿAlī Khān and during the first part of the reign of Amīr ʿAbd al-Raḥmān Khān they were also esteemed and honored. They were *mustawfī*s (chief financial officers of the realm), munshis (clerks), and *dabīr*s (secretaries) of the government. In the army they held the ranks of field marshal, brigadier, general, and colonel. All civil and military affairs were entrusted to the Qizilbāsh but gradually religious bigotry interposed, especially at two times when the English invaded, as will be recorded in the pages of this same volume of *Amān al-tawārīkh*. In volumes one and two of *Amān al-tawārīkh* it was also recorded that at the time the English invaded the Qizilbāsh and Hazārahs had aided them. This assistance to the English was, according to what Mullā Fayż Muḥammad Khān Kātib wrote, because of the persecution they experienced from the Afghans. In short, violent hostility arose and the outcome was frustration [for the Qizilbāsh] and today the Qizilbāsh are being driven to misery and despair. The Hazārah people had many *mīr*s, *āqā*s, and leaders from among themselves, and the Qizilbāsh people, all of whom were ministers, secretaries, and counsellors in the machinery of government, were appointed as governors to some of the provinces and all served the government faithfully and honestly. But now they are without employment and spend their time at home. They cannot stay [in Afghanistan] and they cannot go anywhere else. Here the esteemed scholar Fayż Muḥammad Khān Kātib has written a full account that will be copied here.

In short, in the year 1281 (Hijrī)/1864 [the year of the first full British census in India] there were 20,000 households of Qizilbāsh counted in Harāt, Qandahar, Farāh, Ghaznīn, and Kabul. Now, there are 1,500 households in Kabul, 1,000 households in the dependencies of Ghaznīn, 500 in Qandahar, and 2,000 in Harāt. Those in Harāt work in agriculture and trade. Those in Qandahar work as craftsmen in the bazaar, as shopkeepers, as accountants, and as farmers and this is how they spend their days and earn their livings. Because of the episode in 1337/1919,[24] the Qizilbāsh in Qandahar now are under great duress. Those who are in Ghaznīn have their own land and pursue agriculture. Of those who live in Kabul, one group has land in Wazīrābād and the rest spend their time in low-level government employment, as shopkeepers, and two or three are merchants. Now they have lots of difficulty making a living. Of them, the Afshār tribe owned forts and property. Amīr ʿAbd al-Raḥmān Khān gave their forts to the Durrānī who were serving in the army. They left their property without making any improvements and dispersed. **/113/115/** At the order of Amīr ʿAbd al-Raḥmān Khān, they were expelled to Iran and to other places. Now the most important [Qizilbāsh] clans—Karlū, Kacharlū, Nimrlū, ʿUṣmānlū, Jawānshayr, Sipāh-i Manṣūr, Shāh Sawand and some called Shīrāzī, Khwāfī, Qart or Kurd, and others—have homes in Chandāwul, one of Kabul's quarters and in Murād Khānī [another Kabul quarter]. In the quarters of ʿAlī Rizā Khān, Qalʿah-i Ḥaydar Khān, and Chūbfurūshī (Woodsellers' Quarter) all the Qizilbāsh were originally from Iṣfahān and Shīrāz. The affairs of ministry and emirate used to be in their hands and in one fell swoop they were scattered, ruined, and deprived of food and drink. One of them, Ḥājjī Mīrzā Muḥammad Mahdī Khān who was a wealthy merchant and leased [out] some properties, because of the World War suffered losses and the Afghan government seized twelve lakhs of Kābulī rupees (the Afghan Kābulī rupee is two Iranian *qirāns*) from him and from his guarantors and a whole group of people was consequently ruined.

The Ūzbak Tribe

The original homeland of this tribe was Turkistān. In Balkh, Badakhshān, Maymanah, Andkhūd, Shirghān (*sic*—Shibarghān), Tāshqurkhān (*sic*—Tāshqurghān), Ay Bīk, Sar-i Pul, Khānābād, Qunduz, Tāluqān, Rustāq, Ḥażrat Imām, and the dependencies of all these places, there are 400,000 households of Uzbeks. Before the campaigning of Amīr Dūst Muḥammad Khān and the (Afghan) occupation of these urban centers, each (of these towns) was independent and had its own chief and this has been written about in the volumes of *Amān al-tawārīkh*. Nearly 150 Ūzbak households in Muqur, south of Ghaznīn, and a small number in other places spend their lives as farmers.

The Dīgān Tribe

The original place of the Dīgān tribe was in the northeast of Afghanistan. Now they reside in Gaz [Jalālābād], Bājāwur, and Lamqān. Their language is a hybrid of Sanskrit, Persian, and Afghānī. Because of this we know that this tribe is of Hindū descent. The Afghans, who consider the Dīgān and the Tajiks to be one

[24] See above pp. 77–78.

and the same, are mistaken because the Tajiks are a completely distinct people, a description of whom has already been given. This tribe [the Dīgān] has more than 5,000 households.

The Hindīs Living in Afghanistan

At first the people of India lived in eastern Afghanistan. They also occupied the area to the east of Sind /114/116/. The Jat tribe, known as Qawwāl, inhabited most places in Sind and Panjāb and their occupation was farming. There were also some of these people in Banūn District and Peshawar and there still are. The Balūch call them Jakdāl. A large group of this tribe lives in Sīstān, Iran. In recent times, the Jat tribe of Indians have entered Afghanistan among whom is the tribe of Parāchī, known as Parānchah, who have come to Kabul from east of the Indus River and work and earn their livings as traders and shopkeepers. Some 50 households of Jats reside in Murād Khānī Quarter in Kabul. The women work as phlebotomists and sell foodstuffs and the men earn their livings as brokers and horse dealers. They are Shiʿis. Another group of them from Gujarāt call themseles Rājpūts and they live in Bājāwur, Nangarhār, and Yūsufzāʾī District. The total number of Indians—Jats, Parāchīs, and Gūjars—in Afghanistan comes to between 4,000–5,000 households dispersed throughout the country. Because they don't congregate in one place, they have no importance.

The Katrī, Arūrah, and Sikh Hindūs Who Are in Afghanistan

The Hind(ū) tribe which is idol-worshiping is to be distinguished from the Hindīs (Indians) for technically a Hindī is a Musulmān and Hindū is an idol-worshipper. Hindūs form societies and live in Jalālābād, Kabul, Qandahar, and Ghaznīn as well as in the outlying areas. Most work in the banking and moneychanging business (*ṣarrāfī*), as goldsmiths, cloth merchants, brokers, farmers, and in government service. One of them, Naranjan Dās, was distinguished with the rank of honorary brigadier. He was a man of power and wealth and for years he was head of the chancellery and collected vast sums.

All the Hindūs of Kabul and Jalālābād have their own places of worship and idol houses. They are always firm adherents of their religion and faith and devoted to it. They pay *jizyah* annually to the government of Afghanistan. They are calculated to number 5,000 households.

In these times due to the unity and cooperation of the Muslim Hindīs with the idol-worshipping Hindūs, [in India] they unanimously demand their right of freedom from the English government. The Hindūs living in Afghanistan are honored and esteemed to the point that they serve in the military and are distinguished with the ranks of aide-de-camp (*yāwarī*), commander (*sālār*) and other ranks. In the War College (Madrasah-i Ḥarbīyah), the boys and young men of the Hindūs /115/117/ and Musulmāns associate with each other. They [also] have a seminary and their own priest. The government of Afghanistan has strictly prohibited the slaughter of cows and the sale of beef because in (their) doctrine the consumption of meat from an herbivore or from a winged creature is forbidden.

The Sawādī (Swātī) Tribe Which Calls Itself Dīgān and Originally Was Of Hindī Descent

The Dīgān tribe originally inhabited the region from Jahlam-i Panjāb [the Jhelum River] to Jalālābād. Then a group of Afghans little by little scattered them and so they went to the mountains of Sawād (Swat) and Bunīr for refuge. Now some of them live in Pakalī District in the region (*żalʿ*) of Hazārah in the back of the mountains. The people of Swat call themselves *faqīr*s (dervishes). All of them together are calculated to number 500 households.

The Shalmānī Tribe Whose Place Originally Was On the Edge of Kurram District

The Shalmānī tribe: The Shalmān made hijrat to Tīrāh from their original homeland. A group of them settled in Hasht Nagar. In the year 1500 A.D. the Yūsufzāʾī drove them out of Hasht Nagar and Sulṭan Uways Sawādī extended his protection to them and settled them in the locale of Ilah Dand and gave it to them as a refuge and safe haven. Once again, the Yūsufzāʾī occupied Sawād, conquered the Shalmānī people and scattered them so that now they have gradually come to live as clients of the Yūsufzāʾī. They are so few in number that they are not counted.

The Tīrāhī Tribe

The Tīrāhī tribe until the year 600 A.H. / 1203–04 A.D. was very large, powerful, and wealthy. In that year Sulṭān Shihāb al-Dīn Ghūrī set out with an army of horseman to deal with them. Many passed beneath the sword's sharp edge, and their property was cast to the winds of destruction and vengeance and he forced them to convert to Islam. Subsequently, from this great *zunnār*[25]-wearing tribe some settled in the territory of the Shinwār in Tīrāh. From the beginning they became known by the name of that place. Their language is Sanskrit but in their vocabulary are found Pashtū words, which is the Afghānī language. As a group they are quite small.

The Kashmīrī People Who Are In Kabul and Qandahar

A long time ago, because of injustice and oppression from the governors of Kashmīr, Kashmīrī people took the road to Kabul and settled there. **/116/118//** Most of them work as cooks, clothes washers, tailors, embroiderers, weavers, brokers, draftsmen, and at other trades. They are both Sunnis and Shiʿis but the Shiʿis work at the first trade (cooking) and the Sunnis have entered government service in the finance department (*dīwān*). One of them, Mīrzā Muḥammad Khān was the court secretary of Sardār Naṣr Allāh Khān. During the reign of His Majesty Amīr Amān Allāh Khān he was banished for some minor offense and his possessions were confiscated for the *dīwān*. After a while they were given back to him and he returned to Kabul. Also with regards to Mīr Aḥmad Shāh Khān, a

25 The *zunnār* was an item of clothing required of non-Muslims to identify them. It is not clear why, after being converted to Islam they were compelled to wear the *zunnār*. Perhaps it was a sign of their forced rather than voluntary conversion.

Sunni sayyid from Kashmīr and designated as "chief merchant," people say that on his behalf in 1306/1889 a sepoy in Mazār [-i Sharīf] Turkistān took a shot at Amīr ʿAbd al-Raḥmān Khān. Mīr Aḥmad Shāh at that time sent a memorandum from there and from Kabul to Sayyid Dūst ʿAlī Shāh Kashmīrī, a man from his own tribe, who was a merchant in Bukhārā. He published it in newspapers [and it said] that because he had sent a likeness of the horse Ẕū'l-Janāḥ from Turkistān to Kabul to the Qizilbāsh people there for the ten days of ʿĀshūrā and also had appointed Mīrzā Muḥammad Khān Qizilbāsh, as his own private secretary (*dabīr*), and had placed the registers of the diwan in the capable hands of the Qizilbāsh, men like Mīr Muḥammad Ḥusayn Khān *mustawfī*, Dabīr Abū'l-Qāsim Khān, his (Mīr Muḥammad Ḥusayn Khān's) brother, Mīrzā Muḥammad Muḥsin Khān Qandahārī, Mīrzā Muḥammad Ṭāhir Khān and other Sunnīs were jealous and so they fired upon their own amir. The dissemination of news about this incident turned Amīr ʿAbd al-Raḥmān Khān against the Shiʿis and little by little the foundation of their destruction was laid and they disappeared. The good behavior of that amir at the time [towards Shiʿis] when Sardār Muhammad Ayyub Khān was in Iran was so that Nāṣir al-Dīn Shāh not act against the wishes of the English and give (the sardār) assistance and send him back to Afghanistan. Otherwise (the amir) would not have treated Shiʿis well from the beginning.

This Mīr Aḥmad Shāh during the time of Amīr ʿAbd al-Raḥmān Khān stole several gold coins while he was counting them and hid them in his stockings. Khānjī Khān a *khānsāmān* (custodian) witnessed this, told the amir, and (Mīr Aḥmad Shāh) was imprisoned.

Also, in the time of Amīr Ḥabīb Allāh Khān, (Mīr Aḥmad Shāh) forged the signature of Amīr ʿAbd al-Raḥmān khān, defrauded the government treasury of 75,000 rupees, was again imprisoned, and the government confiscated everything that he owned. Ultimately, he was forgiven by the queen (ʿUlyā Ḥażrat Sarwar Sulṭān). His son, Ghulām Muḥyī al-Dīn Khān, and his brother, Mīr Muḥammad Ḥusayn Khān, are close companions (*muṣāḥib*s) of His Majesty Amīr Amān Allāh Khān and are held in high esteem.

Like Mīr Aḥmad Shāh is Mīr ʿAbd al-Wāḥid Khān, one of the sons of Mīr Wāʿiẓ who (Mīr Wāʿiẓ) during the time of Shāh Maḥmūd issued a decree calling for the killing of Shiʿis. Sardār Bakhtiyāri Khān, Hazārah of Ghaznīn, came to assist the Shiʿis of Kabul with 1,000 cavalrymen. Just as all the [Sunni] people of Kūhistān, Kūh Dāman, Lahūgard, and other places /117/119/ and the residents of Kabul had besieged the Qizilbāsh, [Sardār Bakhtiyārī] arrived in the nick of time and launched an assault, raised a mound of the slain, dispersed the Sunnis, and made the Shiʿis feel secure.

The story [from the time] of Amīr Ḥabīb Allāh Khān is recorded in the first volume of *Amān al-tawārīkh*. The story of the killing of the Hazārahs of Qarābāgh and Kadah, Sīstān where the Afghans had deceived them with promises and a covenant (of personal safety) on a Qurʾān and then killed, looted, and took (the survivors) captive, which was erased from the second volume of *Sirāj al-tawārīkh* but was given in the correct first draft of that which bears the signature of Amīr Ḥabīb Allāh Khān, is available. It was given to the great *ustād* (professor) and philosopher the most noble Ḥājjī Mīrzā ʿAbd al-Muḥammad Khān Ṣāḥib, "Muʾaddib al-Sulṭān," the expert author of the seven volumes of *Amān al-tawārikh*, so that he could record it in his own book.

To sum up, Mīr ʿAbd al-Wāḥid is exactly like Mīr Aḥmad Shāh. He is the companion (*muṣāḥib*) of the holy warrior king and so [we will have to wait and see] what will happen to Shiʾis. [However] as far as the writer of these lines, ʿAbd al-Muḥammad Īrānī, is concerned, [because of] the capable policies, the guilelessness, and the decisive intellect of His Auspicious Majesty Amīr Amān Allāh Khān Ghāzī, the *pādshāh* of Afghanistan, in whom religion takes refuge, in contrast to his predecessors, he views all the various subjects of the government, Sunni, Shiʿah, Hindī, Hindū, and others with a paternal gaze and [so] all dwellers in Afghanistan, without exception, come under the most illumined gaze of their sovereign equally. These writings of this insignificant one are based on signs and manifestations from the year 1160/1747 which I heard repeated about the kingly orders and the caesarean proclamations. "The early signs of dawn/ are indicative of a bright morning." [The best is yet to come.]

The Mukrī and Rīkā Tribes of the Kurds of Afghanistan

The Mukrī and Rīkā are two tribes descended from the Kurds living around Kirmānshāh, Iran who a long time also left Iran for the land of Afghanistan. [Some of] the Rīkā people settled in the Lahore Gate Quarter and [others], their name transposed to Yukrī, settled in the Qart Quarter of Chandāwul, Kabul. The commander of the Qart tribe, ʿAlī ʿAskar Khān, was the grandson of Bahmān (Bahman?) and Mīrā-yi Khān. Presently, his descendants are degraded, anxious, and impoverished. The total number of Mukrī and Rīkā is calculated at 300 households.

The Lakzī (Lagzī) Tribe Which Came to Afghanistan from the Caucasus

The Lakzī tribe was originally from Caucasian Dāghistān. At the order of the mighty *pādshāh*, Nādir Shāh Afshār, they were removed from the Caucasus and sent to Afghanistan where they were settled in Farāh. The number of them in cities and villages is presently **/118/120/** calculated at 300 households. Most of them, in recent times, have fled to Sīstān and Mashhad in Iran. A small number remain in place.

The Armenian Tribe in Afghanistan

There have been very few Armenians in Afghanistan. In the past, there were two households in Peshawar and three in Kabul. They read the Gospel in Greek. During the time of Amīr Muḥammad Aʿẓam Khān [r. 1867], he married the daughter of an Armenian, Tīmūr Khān. She was a peerless beauty and Sardār Muḥammad Isḥāq Khān was born [to her]. Later on this Sardār Muḥammad Isḥāq Khān rebelled against Amīr ʿAbd al-Raḥmān Khān and raised the head of insurgency, [an account of which] will be recorded in this volume, and because of that Amīr ʿAbd al-Raḥmān Khān ordered Armenians to be expelled from Kabul and they went to Peshawar where they joined their coreligionists.

The Qalmāq Tribe Which was From the Tātār Tribe

The Qalmāq tribe, originally descended from the Tātār tribe, are idol-worshippers. Tīmūr Shāh Sadūzāʾī gave them a place to live in Balkh and they served in the government bureaucracy. But with the passing of time, since they were originally few in number, they disappeared and presently only a few households of them remain.

The Ḥabashī (Ethiopian) People in Afghanistan

The Ḥabashī are black-skinned. In former times they were brought [as slaves] from Ḥabashistān to Masqat which is located on the coast of the Bay of Oman and the Persian Gulf, where they were sold. During the Sadūzāʾī period they were brought to Afghanistan and at that time were in government service. A group of them lives in Harāt while other groups are found in Kabul and in various cities of Afghanistan. Most of them are of the Shiʿah sect and they consider themselves to be the slaves [worshippers] of Ḥażrat Qanbar.[26] Their total numbers in all of Afghanistan approach 250 households. All of them are free and make their own decisions.

The Jews in Afghanistan Descended from the Banū Isrāʾīl

The Jews of Afghanistan are a small tribe. It's not known when they came to Afghanistan. In all there are five families **/121/**[27] in Kabul and presently no others are to be found in Kabul. But there are a few families of them in Harāt. They hold strongly to their religion. They read the Torah and the Psalms in Hebrew. Their occupation is making, selling, and drinking alcoholic beverages. They greet Muslims with *salām ʿalayk* in the same way Muslims do.

The Balūch Tribe Which Came from the Dependencies of Sīstān, Bam, and Narmāshīr

The Baluch tribe comprises nearly 9,000 households and resides in the mountains of the Hazārahjāt north of Qandahar and some in the Hazārah Dāy Kundī district. They are all of the Shīʿah sect. The rest of the Balūch people who used to be attached to Afghanistan have come under the jurisdiction of the English government. There are a small number in Kabul and Qandahar as well. They spend their time in business and in low-level government service. Approximately 1,500 households of them live in Chakhānsūr District adjacent to Sīstān. These Balūch are of the Sunni sect and earn their living as tillers of the soil. They also reside in the dependencies of Dīrah Ghāzī Khān.

[26] Ḥażrat Qanbar was a slave of the Fourth Caliph and First Imām, ʿAlī b. Abī Ṭālib.

[27] The print edition omits two pages here, pages 121 and 122 of the manuscript.

Miscellaneous Tribes and Clans Living in Afghanistan

There are miscellaneous tribes and clans who are known by the name of their place of origin for example, Sīstānī, Kirmānī, Qā'inī, Birjandī, Mashhadī, etc., and who are also called Persian speakers. Most are of the Shī'ah sect. Then there are the Kāshgharī, Andarābī, and Salghurī, known as Lāghurī, but these tribes are small and don't have many households, maybe just one or two households. One person from one of these small tribes, Muẓaffar al-Din, the son of Mawdūd, during the time of the second generation of Atabegs from 543 A.H./1148 A.D. adorned the throne of Shīrāz.[28] Aysh Khātūn was the grandfather [*sic*] of Muẓaffar al-Dīn and her father was the atabeg Sa'd, chief of the Salghurīyah. Mankū Tīmūr Khān, son of Hulāgū, asked for her (Aysh Khātūn) in marriage and that was the founding of the Salghurīyah dynasty. [According to] the esteemed scholar Mullā Fayż Muḥammad Khān Kātib, the implied meaning of this sentence is that Salghurī family known as Lāghurī in Afghanistan is from the Salghurī atabegs who ruled Shīrāz and that these (the Lāghurī) are from those.

The Dawlat Shāhī Tribe in Afghanistan /122/

The Dawlat Shāhī tribe has always been esteemed and honored and has held the office of *qāżī* during the time of the Sadūzā'ī sultans like Qāżī Fayż Allāh Khān and others. There were several households of them in Kabul and Peshawar. The (Dawlat Shāhī) residents of Kabul hold the office of *qāżī* no longer for the *qāżī*-ship of Kabul after Qāżī Muḥammad Sa'īd Khān, a contemporary of Shāh Maḥmūd, was fixed on his offspring and grandchildren, who were Bārakzā'ī Durrānī, as an inheritable office. Now it is held by 'Abd al-Shakūr, the son of Sa'd al-Dīn Khān, the chief *qāżī* (*qāżī al-qużāt*). But in 1299 A.H. Shamsī/1920 A.D. when nine ministries were formed in Kabul, the capital of Afghanistan—Justice, Foreign Affairs, War, Interior, Agriculture, Commerce, Security, Finance, and Transport—at the order of His Majesty Amīr Amān Allāh Khān an associate to the minister of justice was appointed.

Of the Dawlat Shāhī people, who in reality were mamluks (military slaves) and bondsmen and it was Aḥmad Shāh who gave them the name "Dawlat Shāhī" ("of the Royal Government"), it is calculated that there are 100 households in Kabul, Peshawar, and Qandahar combined.

The Siyāh Pūsh Kāfirs Living in the Valleys Deep in the Hindū Kush

In 1310/1892–93, at the order of Amīr 'Abd al-Raḥmān Khān, this tribe became Musulmān and entered the bonds of obedience and subjecthood. They make their homes and safe havens in the mountain range of the Hindū Kush. Their homeland is bounded by Badakhshān to the north; to the east by Kāshghar or Qāshqār; to the west by Khūst, Andarāb, Qaṭaghan, and Kūhistān-i Kabul; and to the south by the districts of Bājāwur, Kunar, and Lamghān [*sic*]. Their homes are snowbound and in fact some of their locales are always covered by, and hidden

[28] Muẓaffar al-Dīn b. Mawdūd was the first in a line of atabegs that formed the Salghurīd dynasty of Fārs. See Bosworth, *The New Islamic Dynasties*, p. 207.

under, snow. They call themselves Kūrāshī and Qurayshī Musulmāns. Originally there were four tribes—Kāmūz, Halār, Salār, and Kāmūj. Presently there are several tribes and clans for the three original tribes in past times, entered the religion of Islām over the course of time, the last tribe [Kāmūj] choosing to stay in the mountains.

Other people consider some of them the offspring of Żaḥḥāk-i Tāzī and others to be Greek. They say that when Alexander of Macedon marched through Asia he appointed one of the Greeks as governor and this tribe is his line. In form and likeness they resemble the Greeks and it is possible they are Greeks. Anyway, with their intermarriage with Hindūs a hybrid people came into existence. They are not one tribe with a genealogy that goes back to a [single source]. Each one is remembered by a separate name and all are either Siyāh (Black) or Surkh (Red) Kafirs. This [former] name derives from the color of their clothing and so they are known as "Black-clothed Kāfirs" **/119/123/** Muslims call the others "Red Kāfirs" because of their skin being red and white. Presently, fifteen clans are known with the names of Sū Kūy, Tarī, Gūmā, Kabīr, Katār, Bīrah Gal, Chanīsh, Damdū, Waylī Way, Kāsah, Kūshtah, Nīkū Wāy, Kāmūjī, Kāmūzī, Kātūz or Katūr. Besides these, there are [another] fifteen [sic—seventeen?] clans namely Ashī, Satū, Nashī, Jamkah, Āshkāmak, Bīrūnī, Patūnī, Pūtūz, Dīmash, Khulm, Ayrat, Haran Sapah, Amā, Chūniyābā, Chūmiyā, Anīshwar, Pishāgarī, and others. There are others who are known by the names Kāmdīsh, Dāygal, Kambīr, Kalāy Gal, Rājgal, Dawī Gal, Jamāmīsh, Nahach Gal, and Walī Gal, which are the names of the villages, towns, and locales where they reside.

All of these were idol-worshipping and are counted in the census as 12,000 households, even as many as 20,000 households.

At the time of his passing through on his way to Hindūstān, Amīr Tīmūr Gūrgānī killed and pillaged these people but he did not try to convert them to Islam. He passed through quickly as he records in his memoirs (*tuzuk*), which were translated into Persian.[29]

Amīr ʿAbd al-Raḥmān Khān made them Musulmans. Amīr Ḥabīb Allāh Khān, who had a great liking for women—and the girls of [the Kāfirs] were lovely and attractive—took many of them. One regiment of cavalry named Dasht-i [Dastah-i] Rikābī was formed from this tribe and Amīr Ḥabīb Allāh Khān made them ride beside him as his attendants. He greatly honored them until he was killed. All the women whom he had had sex with, whether Hazārahs, Kāfirī, or Afghan, amounting to 300, after his death were married to men of the lowest class—scoundrels, ruffians, the lowest of the low with whom they shared bed and livelihood. This did not include the twenty-four women who were his daughters.

29 This is the obviously influential but now believed to be spurious *Tuzuk-i Tīmūrī*, an appendix to the equally dubious *Malfūẓāt-i Tīmūrī* or *Wāqiʿāt-i Tīmūrī*. There was a single edition of the *Tuzukāt* published in Oxford 1783 and reprinted in Bombay in 1890. See Storey, *Persian Literature*, pp. 280–82.

The Tribes and Clans Whose Homelands and Dwelling Places Came Under the Control of the English Government

Of those tribes which have already been written about—Kākar, Wazīrī, Saʿūdī (*sic*—Masʿūdī), and most of the Aḥmadzāʾī, Dūrī, Khatak, Shītak, most of Khūsāk, some of the Jadrān, the Arūkzāʾī, Khalīl, most of the Muhmand, the Afrīdī, the Tūrī, the Bangash, the Khalīl [*sic*], Yūsufzāʾī, Bājāwurdī [*sic*], and others, each one of which was a large tribe and possessed numerous sub-tribes, after the demarcation of the border and the separation of the frontier lands between the territory of Afghanistan and the country of Hindūstān and its separation by arbitration in 1310 A.H./1893 A.D., because of the inability of people to get along, the lack of conscience, the [lack of] Islamic societal unity, the loss of enlightenment, and [the lack of] most human virtues, **/120/124/** were all separated from present-day Afghanistan and all of them came into the hands of officials of England and under the protection of the English government. Tribes which earlier [before 1893] had fallen into English hands included the progeny of Shāh Farīd known as Shītak, namely Samyī, ʿĪsagī, Sīnā, Dur, Patī, Sūrānī, Gharżzāʾī, Mandā Khayl, Haybak and similarly the tribes of Marwat all of whom will be organized and written about below. From what has already been written and what is to come, we know that presently four-fifths of the Afghan tribes are under the protection of, and subject to, the English government. One-fifth of them are subject to Afghanistan along with the other tribes of Turks and Tajiks, etc., whose homelands [in Afghanistan] have been described as well as those in [Afghan] Turkistān. Perhaps some Afghan leaders are fully aware of this matter but do not have detailed information about their own tribes and clans. Here again I have decided not to include the description of the researcher-scholar Mullā Fayż Muḥammad Ṣāḥib Kātib, who, by [writing] in support of Islām and speaking truthfully, has described the decline of Islamic countries and the advance of Christian countries, all of which he depicts as due to conflict and discord among Muslims and their lack of knowledge, their ignorance, and their bigotry.

The Clans of Shāh Farīd Known as Shītak, An Account of Which Was Promised Earlier

This Shītak was the fourth son of Kakī, son of Karrān. He was named earlier with the other sons and it was promised there to mention him. He produced five sons from three wives—Kīway, Sūrānī, Dūr, Zīlam, Huwayd.

The clans of Mīrī and Samī that are descendants of this one[30] will be mentioned later. The Bārakzāʾī, Nuqrah Dīn, Brāhīm Khayl, Sarakī Khayl, Dalah Khayl, Qalandar Khayl, ʿĀlam Gul Khayl, Khiżr Khān Khayl, Mand Bū Dapūtī (Deputy?), Ghāzī Khayl, Khwājak Khayl, Sindī Khayl, Shīshī Khayl, Mamah Khayl, Zargar Khayl, Būrā Khayl, Mūsā Khayl, Sap Khayl, Ghaznī Khayl, Fatḥ Khayl, Allāh Khayl, Līwān, Kakī, Maḥbūb, Ṭayyib, Ḥasan, Jaʿfar Khayl, Tūjak Khayl, Bālī, Aḥmad Khayl, Ibrāhīm, Mamū Khayl, Mīr Tabar, Jūnsham Khayl, Barat Khayl, Fatḥ

30 There seems to be something missing here from the text.

Khān Khayl, Darmur Khayl, Nīrī, Pīlā Khayl, ʿAbar Khayl, Khwājah Hūkar, Karak, Bartah, Katarī, ʿUmar Khayl, Pīrā Khayl, Shūbak Khayl, Shakhl, Shādī Khayl, Kāyir, Yarkhān Khayl, Kīdī, Mughul Khayl, Baḥī Khayl, Nūrar, Ṣad Yū, Māndī, Mālī Khayl, Dāwud Khayl, Būmal Khayl, Milyū, Kalā Khayl, Būqī Khayl, Darīb Khayl, Sīlāgān, Patī, Akhūnd Khayl, Targulī, Mīr Gul Khayl, and Īshim Khayl **/121/125/** were the offspring of Kīway, son of Shītak. Through these clans are all called Shītak.

Similarly Tūtalī, Ḥasan Khayli, and Ghūnd are the line of Zīlam, fourth son of Shītak.

Ismāʿīl Khayl, Tībī Randān, and Īsap are the lineage of Huwayd, the fifth son of Shītak and carry the name of the Shītak tribe.

The Clans That Are the Line of Samī, Second Son of Kīway, First Son of Shītak

Samī, son of Kiwāy, son of Shāh Farīd [*sic*], son of Shītak had four sons—Mandān, ʿĪsākī, Sīnāwar known as Ṣanūbar, and Patī.

Thus Bāzīd Khayl, Bālīd Khayl, Fatḥ Khayl, Khūbī Khayl, Afżal Khayl, Mītā Khayl, Bahāwun Khayl, Shahwār Khayl, Lāchī Khayl, Miyāndār Khayl, Qāsim Khayl, Malik Dīn Khayl, Kangar, Ḥaydar Khayl, Jīt, Sikandar Khayl, Mātak Khayl, Bahār Khayl, Kilk, Dīdān, Bashar Khayl, Miyān Khayl, Bārak Khayl, Parī Khayl, Kaftī Khayl, Kamāl Khayl, Dād Khayl, Andas Khayl, Muḥibbat Khayl, Karā Khayl, Mangar Shāh Khayl, Līdī, Khūjah Mad, Adrī Khayl, Darāz Khayl, Katī Khayl, Bāyak Khayl, ʿAqīb Khayl, ʿAbbās Khayl, Khān Khayl, Shighāl Khayl, Shujāʿ Khayl, Gulistān Khayl, Madī, Bahrām Khayl, Shābī Khayl, Kalān Khayl, Bād Bū, Bangash Khayl, Khatak Khayl, Khānī, Zakūy, Walī Khayl, Gandā Khayl, Mīr ʿAlī Khayl, Mumīt Khayl, Ṣābū Khayl, Jīgah Khayl, ʿAbī Khayl, and Pāy Khayl, were all of the line of Mandān, the first son of Samī, second son of Kīway, son of Shītak, and all were called Shītak.

Also Ḥasan Khayl, Langar Khayl, Ghaznī Khayl, Shash Pul Khayl, Khānā Khayl, Mātak Khayl, Haybat Khayl, Samil Khayl, Sikandar Khayl, Hānī Khān Khayl, Shahbāz Khayl, Salīmah Khayl, Muḥibbat Khayl, Shakī, Shujāʿ, Nuqrah Dīn, Bāyir Khayl, Chandū Khayl, Sarmast Khayl, ʿAbīt Khayl, Malik Khayl, Aʿẓam Khayl, Gilah Khayl, Ismāʿīl Khānī, Kabīr Khayl, Khānān Khayl, Badal, Sīlū, Sarū, Maysīrū, Badā Khayl, Salāmat Khayl, and Bahlūlī were the progeny of ʿĪsākī, the second son of Samī, son of Kīway, son of Shītak. These too are called Shītak.

Similarly, Anjīl, Rashtī Khayl, Mastī Khayl, Haybat Khayl, Miṣrī Khayl, Sūgarī, Walī Khayl, Bahādur Khayl, Shūẓī Khayl, Wazīr Khayl, Yaʿqūb Khayl, Ḥasan Khayl, Kamāl Khayl, Khūjarī Khayl, Saʿīd Khayl, Shāmah Khayl, Zība Khayl, and Sar Qawmī were all offspring of Sīnāwar known as Ṣanūbar, the third son of Samī, son of Kīway, son of Shītak. These are also called the tribe of Shītak.

Also Mīrā Khayl, Rasūl Khayl, Dawlat Khayl, Tājī Khayl, Būr Khayl, Ghazūr Khayl, Kūbar Khayl, Jandan Khayl, Tamī Khayl, Ighlāṭ Khayl, **/122/126/** Khūjah Khayl, Maywah Khayl, Niẓām Khayl, Ismāʿīl Khayl, Būmah Khayl, Farīd Khayl, Matah Khayl, Yāsīn Khayl, Bahār Khayl, Khwājah Ajram Khayl, Garī, Taghl Khayl, Hātī Khayl, Kalān Khayl, Ghalīl Khān, Sīghāl, Malīk Khayl, Darū Khayl, Bajal Khayl, Mandarah Khayl, Dūrī Khayl, and Nakhl Khayl are all offspring of Patī, the fourth son of Samī, son of Kiway, son of Shītak and they are reckoned as the Shītak tribe.

APPENDIX 1

The Tribes and Clans of the Line of Sūrānī, Second Son of Shītak

Sūrānī, the second son of Shītak and the grandson of Karrān had four sons—Bik, Ghūrzā'ī, Mandā Khayl, and Haybak.

Thus Khūzak, Mīr Shāh, Sayr Khūj Mishr, Būzī Khayl, Makhal Khayl, Mashgī Khayl, 'Irāq Khayl, Pul Khayl, Kamāl Khayl, Ashraf Khayl, Jājī Khayl, Aksīt Khayl, Samāl Tabār, Aḥmad Khān Kaṣar, Laday Khayl, Ẓafar Khayl, Mawsim Khayl, Sarmast Khayl, Khiẑr Khān, Ghaybī Khayl, Brāhīm Khayl, Shāl Khayl, 'Uṣmān Khayl, Galah Khayl, Ṣāhib Khayl, Mumīt Khayl, Khatak Khayl, 'Ambīr Khayl, Khujā Khayl, 'Azīz Khayl, Mumash Khayl, Ḥayāt Khayl, Dawlat Khayl, Ghayrat Khayl, Sa'īd Khayl, Rīmī Khayl, Bājī Khayl, Khwājah Khayl, 'Anbarak Khayl, Arīn Khayl, Khadī Khayl, Sūrānkī, Brāhīm Khayl, Barmandī, Kīway Khayl, Shūb Khayl, Utmān Khayl, Jānī Khayl, Ḥasan Khayl, Jundī Khayl, Kūlīzā'ī, 'Īsakī, Mas'ūdī Khayl, Sulṭān Khayl, Mullā Khayl, Qad Rāst Rū (?), 'Ālam Gul Tīr, Ḥājjī Tīr, 'Ālam Khān Tīr, Malīzā'ī, Dalah Khayl, Khadī, Būbak Khayl, Zūzī Khayl, Sangī Khayl, Nūrī Khayl, Naṣr Ādīn, Aḥmad Khayl, Maysū Khayl, Ādam Khayl, Fażl Khayl, Makhal Khayl, and Mītagān were all descendants of Bik, the first son of Sūrānī son of Shītak and they also were called Shītak.

Likewise, Wālah Dīn, Ṭuṭah Khayl, 'Āyid Khayl, Dadā Khayl, Balsh Khayl, Kīkal, Khūtī, Ḥasanī, Chināb Khayl, Abrūt Khayl, Pandā Khān Niṣār, Kach or Kaṣchīzā'ī, Mashgī Khayl, Amīr Allāh Khayl, and Rūbiyā Khayl were all the offspring of Ghūrzā'ī, the second son of Sūrāni, son of Shītak. These people were known by the tribal name Sūrānī of the Shītak tribe.

Also, La'lzā'ī, Mamar Khayl, Mīr Qalam Tabā (*sic*—Tabār), Bahrām Tabār, 'Ābid Khayl, Basyā Khayl, 'Īsak Khayl, Bangī Khayl, Kam Kīkī, Jūnī (Khūbī?) Khayl, Shūmī Khayl, Mālyū, Mandīzā'ī, Tūraki, Bālā Khān, Smā'īl Khān, Baẕr Tabār, Bahādur Khān Tabār, Nandar Tabār, 'Alizā'ī, Kūpā, Dand Khayl, Bāzīdī, Kamāl Khayl, Dūrī Khayl, Kūkal Khayl, Malīzā'ī, Bājī Khayl, Ibrāhīm Khayl, Adam, Chādzā'ī, Mīs Khayl, Brāhīm Khayl, Aymal Khayl, Ḥamzah Khayl, **/123/127/** Nawkar Khayl, and Bū Bakr Khayl are of the line of ...[31] Bālā Khayl, Salīmī Khayl, Nānī Khayl, Ismā'īl Khayl, [ms. has blank space for a tribal name] –zā'ī, Naẓar Khayl, 'Abdāl Khayl, Sarakī, Bārak Khayl, and Kī Bī, the line of Haybak, the fourth son of Sūrānī. All of them call themselves Sūrānī.

All the tribes of Shītak and Sūrmānī (*sic*—Sūrānī) whose names have been mentioned had their birthplace in Kūh-i Shawāl, part of the Kūh-i Sulaymān range. Shāh Farīd, known as Shītak, lost his mother when he was a baby. His father, Kakī, had him raised on donkey's milk and for this reason he was known as Shīrtak. After much use (of the name) and because of the Afghānī tendency to contract words, in the spoken language his name was shortened to Shītak. Then when he grew up, he married a woman named Bānū and with her produced Kīway and Sūrānī. Those two took their mother's name as Banūzā'ī which in Afghānī terminology became Banūchī, in contrast to the Hindī language, where it was

[31] It appears that the copyist made an error, not completing his list of clans stemming from the line probably of Mandā Khayl, the fourth son of Shītak, before inserting the phrase "of the line or progeny of" and then returning to the list of clans from Haybak.

pronounced as Bih Nūjī. The district of Banūn, originally called Dand, became known as Banūn because this tribe chose to make it their homeland.

Thus in past centuries, Hindūs lived there and later it became the homeland of the Greeks [and this is known] because of what was inscribed on the ancient coins found in the ruins there. These coins were in circulation among the Greeks and Hindūs.

The land of Banūn is bordered on the west by the mountain homeland of the Wazīrī tribe; on the east by the district of Shāh Pūr, the district of Manah Tawānah, and a little to the north [on the east side], by Talah Kang of Jahlam district; to the northwest by the banks of the Indus River as far as the mountain homeland of the Khatak tribe adjoining Kūhāt District and a bit of the district of Makad, one of the dependencies of Rawalpindi; and to the south by Dīrah Ismāʿīl Khān. The length from west to east up to the border with Shāh Pūr district is ninety miles. The width in the middle from north to south is a little more than forty miles. The residents of this territory (Banūn) are from the Marwat Shītak and ʿAlī Khayl Niyāzī and the population of it numbers 331,468 people from different tribes such as the Dīgān, Fāṭimah Khayl, Wazīrī, Dāwud Shāhgī, Shaykhān, Quraysh, Tīr Khayl, Jat, and Hindūs.

The Tribes and Clans of Marwat Who Is Of the Progeny of Nūḥānī or Lūḥānī, Son of Ismāʿīl, Son of Sayānī, Son of Lūrī

It was promised in the account of the tribes of Ibrāhīm, known as Lūdī, son of Ghilzāʾī, son of Shāh Ḥusayn Ghūrī, and how the name Ghilzāʾī came to be, that mention of the Marwat tribe would come. Here it is. Marwat son of Lūḥānī **/124/128/** had four sons—Mūsā Khayl, Bītī, Nūnāh Khayl, and Salār. Tribes and clans have emerged from all four of these and all are called the Marwat tribe.

Thus Jānūzāʾī, Tājūrī, Zangī Khayl, Dūr Khayl (this one is *waṣlī* related), Mīrzā Khayl, Kīmat Khayl, Miyān Khayl, Matā Khayl, Smāʿīl Khayl, Adīn Khayl, Bāzīd Khayl, Darī Palārah, Bāqir Khayl, Būpū Khayl, Sānid Khayl, Malikzāʾī, Badanī Khayl, Shamshān Khayl, Ghāzī Khayl, Dawlat Khān Khayl, ʿĀlam Khayl, Khān Khayl, Chandū Khayl, Jalū Khayl, Aspāy Khayl, Karīm Khayl, Mir Ḥasan Khayl, Bānīzāʾī, Bahrām Khayl, Mahrām Khayl, Dankūzāʾī, Qatl Khayl, Ḥandar (Ḥaydar?) Khayl, Mamar Ṣīr Khayl, Wajabī Khayl, Aḥmad Khān Khayl, Fatak Khayl, Takhtī Khayl, ʿAlī Khān Khayl, Aspīdū Khayl, Nangar Khayl, Naṣrū Khayl, Bāzī Khayl, Shahbāz Khayl, Fatḥ Khān Khayl, ʿĀlim Khayl, Azar Khayl, Sadū Khayl, Badūsh Khayl, Chūdār Khayl, Pārsanī Khayl, Ṣūrat Khayl, Nīk Zan Khayl, Bāzik Khayl, Faqīr Mullā Khayl, [blank space in ms.] Khayl, Razakīzāʾī, Ismāʿīlzāʾī, Maskū Khayl, and Zinā Khayl were all of the line of Mūsā, the first son of Marwat and known as Mūsāzāʾī of the Marwat tribe.

Also, Sulaymān Khayl, Balīzāʾī, Muḥammadzāʾī, Tārū Khayl, Nuṣrat Khayl, Ismāʿīl Khayl, Gūrī Khayl, Ḥabīb Khayl, Kūkū Khayl, Nīk Khayl, Milī Khayl, Pāyandah Khayl, Shādī Khayl, Karīmdād Khayl, Qalandar Khayl, ʿAsak Khayl, Tatar Khayl, Mīrzā Khayl, Utmān Khayl, Adamzāʾī, Mālik Khayl, Khuwaydād Khayl, Khwajī Khayl, Khamār Khayl, Khatak Khayl, Bāyist Khayl, Daryā Khayl, Khayl, Mīrzā Khayl, Chūrī Khayl, Mastān Khayl, Akīzāʾī, Bānizāʾī, Shādat Khayl, Aḥmadzāʾī, ʿAbdal Khayl, Bibā Khayl, Rājū Khayl, Aʿẓam Khayl, Durust Khayl, Khwājī Khayl,

Jabat Khayl, Ẕalū Khān Khayl, ʿAẓamat Khayl, Mamatīzāʾī, Qatl Khayl, Kamāl Khayl, and Mughul Khayl all of whom were branches of the three tribes—Sulaymān Khayl, Utmān Khayl, and Aḥmadzāʾī—and of the line of Patī, the second son of Marwat, son of Lūḥānī, and are called the tribe of Marwat.

Similarly, Milīzāʾī, ʿUmar Khayl, ʿĪsā Khayl, Balū Khayl, Khiżr Khayl, Khwājī Khayl, Ḥājjī Khayl, Sulaymānzāʾī, Mīralzāʾī, Lakā Khayl, Banī Khayl, Mūtī Khayl, Sīn Khayl, Tarī Khayl, Kalā Khayl, ʿAyb Khayl, Jān Khān Khayl, Kūkū Khayl, Pāyandah Khayl, and Machī Khayl were all offspring of Nūnah or Nūnā, the third son of Marwat. The tribe was called Nūnāzāʾī of the Marwat tribe. **/125/129/**

Also Sandar, Achū Khayl, Khadū Khayl, Mastī Khayl, Darīzāʾī, Jānū Khayl, Mamā, Kashā Khayl, Mīrdād Khayl, Fīrūz Khayl, Dādī Khayl, Barat Khayl, Sikandar Khayl, Qulī Khayl, Dawlatkhān, ʿAlī Khān, Khānān Khayl, Hātī Khayl, Ḥājjī Khayl, Āzād Khayl, Jallat (?) Khayl, Bīlū Khayl, Dalīl Khān, Nawrang Khayl, Khwājah Khayl, ʿĀlam Shāh Khayl, Ṭayūrī Khayl, Shāh Ḥasan Khayl, Shāh Bīk Khayl, Bahādur Khayl, Fatḥ Khayl, ʿĪsak Khayl, Ṣābit Khayl, Jamāl Khayl, Sag Khayl, Gulī Khayl, Tājī Khayl, Langar Khayl, Shayr Bīk Khayl, Shahzādah Khayl, Shādī Bīk Khayl, Akbarī Khayl, Shāh Salīm Khān, Lālī Khayl, Madd Bīk Khayl, Jabbār Khayl, ʿUmar Khayl, Ẓafar Khayl, Aʿzaz (Iʿzāz?) Khayl, Badr Khayl, Azal Khayl, Ṣadr Khayl, Bahādur Khayl, Khānjī Khayl, Shayr Khān Khayl, Shālimī Khayl, Bāriz Khayl, Sulaymān Khayl, Mihr Gul Khayl, Zarīn, Bashru, Dilāwar Khayl, Jalāl Khayl, Ḥasanī Khayl, Murādī Khayl, Adam Khayl, Bahār Khayl, Saʿd Allāh Khayl, Ṣāḥibdād Khayl, Māʾil Khayl, Dawlat Khayl, Shaml Khayl, Sharak, ʿAbdul Khayl, Ramas Khān, Ḥayāt Khayl, Nādir Khayl, Ajal Khayl, Karī Khayl, Khān Dawrān Khayl, Amḥalā Khayl, Ẓafar Khayl, Māʾil Khayl, Mullā Khayl, Aḥmad Khayl, Bihdīn Khayl, Saml Khayl, ʿAlam Khānī Khayl, Zikrī Khayl, Jalāl Dīn Khayl, Jānī Khayl, Sikandar Khayl, Bar Mazīd Khayl, Rājū Khayl, Shihāb Khayl, Miyān Khayl, Muʿīb Khayl, ʿAẓamat Khayl, Ṣadr Khayl, Gulkhān Khayl, Sīrī Khayl, ʿAlī Khān Khayl, Walī Khayl, Muniyā Khayl, Tājā Khayl, Nūr Khān, Bīk Khayl, Khuwaydād Khayl, Shayrī Khayl, Mīrī Khayl, Saʿīd Khayl, Milī Khayl, ʿĀqil Khayl, Ṣāḥib Khayl, Tamar Khayl, Sālār Khayl, Ḥasan Khayl, Dāwī Khayl, Mamū Khayl, ʿAlī Khayl, Qalandar Khayl, Jalū Khayl, Pahār Khayl, Patūl Khayl, Būlah Khayl, Bahādur Khayl, Gul Aḥmad Khayl, Sulṭān Khayl, Mandir Khayl, Pīrūz Khayl, Lālī Khayl, Jānak Khayl, Lājmīr Khayl, ʿUmar Khayl, Asak Khayl, Alahdād Khayl, Shahbāz Khayl, Ṣūrat Khayl, Azār Khayl, Allāh Dād Khayl, Chūrī Khayl, Chār Gul Khayl, Hawas Khayl, Māʾīyat Khayl, Ẓarīf Khayl, Zangī Khayl, Dāwut Khayl, Shādī Khayl, Ḥasan Khayl, Bāriz Khayl, Madar Bāriz Khayl, Karach Khayl, Mānak Khayl, Ismāʿīl Khayl, Jalāl Khayl, Madū Khayl, ʿĀlam Khayl, Kakā Khayl, Khūjī Khayl, Niẓām Khayl, Mīnā, Bahrām, Yūsuf Khayl, Tājīzāʾī, Gūgī, Ḥasan Khayl, Ismāʿīl Khayl, Ḥamāl Khayl, Tabrīḥ Khayl, Bāyist Khayl, Sanzar Khayl, Sharīf Khayl, Daʿwat Khayl, Nuqrah Khayl, Zaytūn Khayl, Dawlatkhwāhzāʾī, Mamah Khayl, Kīmī Khayl, Wakīd Khayl, Khābū Khayl, Laghkū Khayl, Khalī Khayl, Naẓar Khayl, Shakhāl Khayl, Īsap Khayl, Sharīf Khayl, Panjū Khayl, Rārū Khayl, Smāʿīl Khayl, Khabā Khayl, Ẓafar Khayl, Khān Khayl, Khālū Khayl, Ẕikr Khayl, Shayr Khayl, Satlūl Khayl, Ṭūṭizāʾī, Ghaznī Khayl, Mamā Khayl, Lūnak Khayl, Salīm Khān Khayl, Lakah Khayl, Mand Khayl, Muqur Khayl, Buland Khayl, Kakā Khayl, Mīrzā Khayl, Handal Khayl, Pāl Khayl, Mīrī Khayl, Fatḥ Masʿūd, **/126/130/** ʿAzīz Khayl, Shayr Khān Khayl,

Gul Khān Khayl, Farāz Khayl, Ẕalik Khayl, ʿUmar Khayl, Raḥmān Khayl, Humyāy Khayl, Masʿūd Khayl, Khadr Khayl, Alīn Khayl, Hawas Khayl, Landūy Khayl, Pāyist Khayl, Mīrā Khayl, Fatḥ Khayl, Tatar Khayl, Naṣrū Khayl, Badī Khayl, Datū Khayl, Shāhū Khayl, Alahdād Khayl, Kaydā Khayl, Farīd Khayl, Jal Khayl, Landakī Khayl, Qamar Dīn Khayl, Badīn Khayl, Daʿwat Khayl, Katī Khayl, Ghūdil Khayl, Jang Khayl, ʿAlā Dil Khayl, Sulaymān, Farīd Khayl, ʿUmar Khān Khayl, Ghāzī Khayl, Shayr Pāy Khayl, Nangar Khayl, Khūr Khayl, Khawāṣ Khayl, Jābū Khayl, Shayr Khān, Mahābat, Miyāndād Khayl, Mīr Khān Khayl, Sipāhī Khayl, Aʿzar Khayl, Sikandar Khayl, Quṭb Khayl, Andād Khayl, Ḥasan Khayl, Sanjar Khayl, Darkhīm Khayl, Pahār Khayl, Ghazā Khayl, Khīrū Khayl, ʿUṣmān Khayl, Aḥmad, and Nuṣrat were all from the line of Salā(r), fourth son of Marwat, son of Lūḥānī. They are known as Sandar, Bahrām, and Khadū Khayl of the Marwat tribe.

Of the Marwat tribe, the subtribes of Mullā Khayl, Ḥamrīz Khayl, Malikzāʾī, Mīrzā Khayl, Sangū Khayl, Khān Khayl, and Machan Khayl have associated with it but are different from it and are from various other tribes which have joined and been included with the seed of Marwat.

Also, these five tribes—Mutūrī, Dalw Khayl, Zīrān, Abā Khayl, and Washar Khayl—of the offspring of Dawlat Shāh are known as Abā Shahīd. Also, three sections—Gūndī, Dabāy, and Ḥaydarān—of the Niyāzī tribe have affiliated with the Marwat. As well, 1,250 households of sections of Katarī (Khatri) and Arūrah [Hindūs] are scattered amongst the Marwat households. All these subtribes of the Marwat live along with their tribes and mixed in with other tribes in the province of Banūn with the Banūchī tribe named Shītak. This land (Banūn) was defined previously along with this population. These [more recently named] tribes are counted among them.

The Tribes and Clans From the Line of ʿĪsā, son of ʿUmar, of the Niyāzī and known as ʿĪsā Khayl

It was previously written about this ʿĪsā following ʿUmar in the tribal genealogy which stemmed from Niyāzī, the son of Lūdī, so here is a description of the line of ʿĪsā.

ʿĪsā, son of ʿUmar, of the seed of Niyāzī, son of Lūdī, son of Shāh Ḥusayn Ghūrī, had eight sons. Their names are as follows: Abū Khayl, Khwājah, Māmā, Muḥammad, Zakū Khayl, Mīrā, Dāwar Shāh, and Aḥmad. According to God's plan, Muḥammad and Zakū were powerful and the progenitors of numerous clans. **/127/131/** The other six had no sons and successors.

Thus, Mamūn Khayl, Shaykh Malī, Khiżr Khayl, Shaykh Farīd Khayl, Bahār Khayl, Barīm Khayl, Ghālī Khayl, Muṣṭafā, Dawlat, Sayyidū Khayl, Shamsī Khayl, ʿUmar Khānī, Shayr Khānī, Jalāl Khānī, Salīm Khānī, Bālī Khānī, Nawrang Khayl, Khān, Changī Khayl, Sālat Khayl, ʿUṣmān Khayl, Zamān Khayl, Māchī Khayl, ʿAbd al-Raḥmān, Langar, Dawlat, Sarwar Khayl, Ḥājjī Khayl, Jalāl Khānī, Aḥmad Khayl, Bādīnzāʾī, Jūriyah Khayl, Hazār Mīl, Multānī Khayl, ʿAlī Shayr, Nūr Malik, ʿUṣmān Khayl, Jatah Khānī, Aḥmad Khayl, ʿUṣmān, Darwīsh Khayl, Ṣābū Khayl, ʿUmar Khayl, Bahrām, Muḥammad, Lakhmad, Pīrāʾī Khayl, Pahār Khayl, Yaʿqūb Khayl, Saʿīd Khayl, Ghāzī, Sārang, Malik, Utmān, Fīrūz, and Maḥmūd were the sons of Muḥammad, the fourth son of ʿĪsā.

Mīrzū Khayl, Khwājah Khayl, Khānī Khayl, Dalw Khayl, Shahālim Khayl, Shayr Khān, Kālā, Dilāwar, Bīram Khayl, Fatḥ Khayl, Changī Khayl, Ṣāhibū Khayl, Sarmast, ʿAlī Khān, Karbūs Khayl, and Landū Khayl were the progeny of Zakū, the fifth son of ʿĪsā and were known as Zakū Khayl of the ʿĪsā Khayl.

The homeland of the ʿĪsā Khayl Niyāzī tribe was the locale of Tāk [Tank] abutting the locale of Tal of the Marwat tribe. To the north it adjoined the town (*qaṣabah*) of Lakī Kamīlah; to the south the Kurram River, recently known as the Tarnah. The population of this tribe is counted along with the Marwat tribe living in Banūn which was inscribed above.

The Tribe and Clans Which Were the Line of Mūsiyānī, the Grandson of Niyāzī, Son of Luḍī, Son of Shāh Ḥusayn Ghūrī

In assembling the [information about] the Lūdī tribal genealogy, Mūsiyānī, known as Mūshānī was listed after Miʿyār or Mihyār. Here we record his line.

Mūshānī, one of the sons of Khākwayn-i Niyāzī, had six sons—Allah Khayl, ʿUmar Khayl, Mandā Khayl, Tanūzāʾī, Agāhī, and Kamālzāʾī.

Thus Mūsā Marghah, Tānī Khayl, Zaʿfar Khayl, ʿAbdalī Khayl, Shāhū Khayl, ʿAlī Khayl, Salīmah Khayl, Kāsī Khayl, Mūndī Khayl, Nahaz Khayl, Rastān Khayl, Naṣīr Khayl, Sikandar, Naẕrī Khayl, Adamū Khayl, Gulshīr Khayl, Aḥmad Khayl, Khalū, Balū, Dādī Khān, Sarmast Khayl, Bar Mazīdī, Shādī Khayl, Yār Gul Khayl, Shaml Khayl, ʿUs̱mānī Khayl, Mūsā Khayl, Jabbār, Shahālim, Jalū Khayl, Mandī, Khitān Khayl, Pahlawān Khayl, Khajān, Mīrzā Khayl, Zamānī Khayl, Maḥmūd Khayl, Babū Khayl, Mīr Gul Khayl, Jahān Khān Khayl, Yār Gul Khayl, Khānjū Khayl, Pīrūz, Bāqī **/128/132/** Khayl, Ghāzī Khayl, Laʿl Bīk Khayl, Allahyār Khayl, Jaʿfar Khayl, Amīr, Ṣadrī Khayl, Pakhānī Khayl, Fatḥ Khān Khayl, Muḥammad Khān Khayl, Gul Bīk Khayl, Hunāy Khayl, Mānd Khayl, Lūḥān Khayl, Shamū Khayl, ʿĀlamshīr Khayl, Barikī Khayl, and Smāʿīlī Khayl were all the offspring of ʿUmar, son of Mūshānī. In the terminology of the people of Afghanistan, they would say it Mushwānī.

Similarly, Dāwar Khayl, Salār, Mushkah, Shaykhū, Jabū Khayl, Rawish, Kulākh, Subḥān Khān, Tāzah Khān, Kulshī Khayl, Jānah, Hatāy Khayl, Khūshḥāl, and Mīrī live on the eastern skirts of the Khatak tribe's mountain. There number is undetermined, that is it remains unknown to the author.

Conclusion of the Account of the Tribes

This was the account of the various tribes, clans, and peoples of Afghanistan which came to, and was written down by, the hand of the writer of these lines, Ḥājjī Mīrzā ʿAbd al-Muḥammad Iṣfahānī Īrānī, nicknamed "Muʾaddib al-Sulṭān," owner of the newspaper *Chihrah-numā*, thanks to the efforts of the unique scholar, the careful and learned researcher, Fayż Muḥammad Khān, author of *Sirāj al-tawārīkh*. Although in volume one of this royal book [*Amān al-tawārīkh*] we took considerable pains to succeed in collecting and recording the general geography of Afghanistan, nonetheless the project above accounts for all the tribes and clans of Afghanistan including the names of their homelands and places of residence, both winter and summer; and names many important places whether cities, towns, or villages, mountains, valleys, river and streams, and does it in 178 chapters, each with a title, all of which will provide additional information for readers.

APPENDIX 2

SAYYID MAHDĪ FARRUKH, *TĀRĪKH-I SIYĀSĪ-YI AFGHANISTAN*

/65/ *Afghan Clans and Tribes*

Afghans name their children and [in general] refer to descendants by the name of the founding father [eponym] with the addition of *–zāʾī* or *khayl*. For example, they call the progeny of ʿUmar, ʿUmarzāʾī, and the descendants of ʿAlī or Mūsā, ʿAlī Khayl or ʿAlīzāʾī or Mūsā Khayl or Mūsāzāʾī. As has already been mentioned [see pp. 60–62 of the edition, not included here] historians of Afghanistan present the Afghans as descended from Sāmī (Sam) and the Banī Isrāʾīl. Most Afghans, both those resident in other countries and those living in Afghanistan, are divided into six branches or six original tribes each of which is further subdivided into several clans (*qabīlah*) and subclans (*shaʿbah*) /66/ as follows:

The six original tribes: 1) the Sarbani, 2) the Ghurghushtī, 3) the Bītī [Bītanī], 4) the Ghilzāʾī, 5) the Sarrānī [Sarwānī], and 6) Karrānī.

The Sarbanī [*Tribes*]

The tribe of Sarban, the son of Qays ʿAbd al-Rashīd is subdivided into several subtribes; 1) Abdālī, 2) Zīrak which includes Pūpalzāʾī, ʿAlīkūzāʾī, and Bārakzāʾī, one branch of which is Muḥammadzāʾī (the emirate of Afghanistan is currently in the hands of this branch); 3) Musāzāʾī, 4) Achakzāʾī, 5) Nūrzāʾī and the Panj Pāy which includes 1) ʿAlīzāʾī, 2) Adawzāʾī [Adūzāʾī], 3) Isḥāqzāʾī, 4) Khūgyānī, 5) Mākū Khayl. A branch of the Pūpalzāʾī clan already mentioned is the Sadūzāʾī. Aḥmad Khān Abdālī came from this tribe [the Sadūzāʾī]. The Pūpalzāʾī reside [mostly] in Qandahar. A branch resides in Ludhiana on the banks of the Sutlej River in Panjāb. One hundred households of Pūpalzāʾī live in Lahore, Peshawar, Multan and Derajat. Several households are in Kirisk [i.e. Girishk] and on the west side of the Hīrmand River, in Arghandāb District. They say the approximate size of this tribe is 15,250 households.

ʿAlīkūzāʾī

They say this tribe has as many as 19,750 households. It resides in Halāk Region east of Qandahar, northwest and west of Arghandāb, in the mountain region [of Qandahar], northwest of Maymanah, in Chakah District, Sārbān Qalʿah, Nawzād District, Zamīn Dāwar, and scattered in Harāt, Ghaznīn, and Kabul. The Nasūzāʾī and Sarkānī branch of this tribe lives in Chahchahah District, a dependency of Rawalpindi, in Gaz District, a dependency of Jalālābād, and in Farākhānah, in Duābah, a dependency of Peshawar. A few households also live in Balūchistān.

 | DOI:10.1163/9789004392441_006

Bārakzāʾī

They say this tribe has as many as 45,250 households who dwell in the southern part of Qandahar, on the banks of the Hīrmand, and in Maḥallah-i Khushk Maydān. The current emirate [of Afghanistan] belongs to the Muḥammadzāʾī branch [of the Bārakzāʾī].

Mūsāzāʾī and *Āchakzāʾī*

This tribe also includes the Nuṣratzāʾī. The Āchakzāʾī which is a branch of the Bārakzāʾī is today separated from it and they say it has up to 5,750 households. They live in the Kūh-i Kūzhak and in the environs of Khwājah ʿImrān. They are mostly subject to the English. Only 1,000 households /67/ of this tribe emigrated to Afghanistan during the time of ʿAbd al-Raḥmān Khān and chose to settle in Chūrah, Bāyilī, Gazāb (*sic*—Gīzāb?), Khalaj, Karkābah, and Zāwulī districts. These places where they settled belonged to Hazārahs but are now in the hands of this tribe. The Hazārahs went to Turkistān and emigrated to Khurāsān and Balūchistān.

Nūrzāʾī

They say this tribe has as many as 45,250 households. They make their homelands in the northern mountains of Qandahar, Harāt, Farāh, Isfizār, Sapīd Rawān, and along the Arghandāb River.

ʿAlīzāʾī

They say this tribe has as many as 20,000 households. A few are in Panjāb and are settled in the environs of Rawalpindi, Nuzdah District in the locale of Chahchah.

Adūzāʾī/Adawzāʾī

They say this tribe has up to 6,260 households. They live in the eastern part of Qandahar and in two locales of the districts of Harāt. A few are settled in the districts of the Garmsīrāt south of Qandahar.

Isḥāqzāʾī

They say this tribe has up to 15,000 households. They live in the western part of Qandahar, along the Arghandāb River as far as Qalʿah Bust, Farah District, in Chakah District along the east bank of the Hīrmand River. In Farāh, Isfizār, and Lāsh Juwayn [*sic*], and in northern Sīstān, Iran they practice agriculture. Approximately 2,000 households also live in Balkh.

Mākū wa Khūgyānī

This tribe is said to have up to 300 households. Its place of residence is Ghaznīn. Also, 100 households of them are settled in Qandahar.

Tarīn

This tribe is divided into two branches whose names are Tūr Tarīn and Aspīn Tarīn. They say the *abdāl* [the eponym of the Abdālī tribe] was from this tribe. People say they number 12,300 households. They dwell in Fūshanj District and are under the jurisdiction of the English.

Shayrāni and *Bābar*

This tribe is said to number up to 5,000 households. They live in the Kūh-i Takht-i Sulaymān and in the Jūdwān District. A few households reside in Qandahar City, the environs of Kabul, Lūgar, and Surkh Rūd in Jalālābād. They say the Bābar branch numbers between 500 and 600 households. Bābar is a branch of Shirānī [*sic*—Shayrānī]. Harīpāl is also a branch of the Shirānī [*sic*]. The Jalwānī is also part of this same tribe. They say the Gharshīn and Miyānah Afghans are also of the Shayrānī tribe. /68/

Tarīch [sic—*Barīch*]

They say this tribe has as many as 3,600 households. They live on lands located between the Kūh-i Khwājah ʿImrān and the place of the Brāhū'i in the Rīgistān (sand desert). A few households live on the border of Sīstān and Hindūstān.

Ūrmur

They describe the 480 households of this tribe as follows: the Khīkanī has 75 households; the Khurramjāʾī has 50; Talātānī has 80 households; Bīganī has 250; and Jarrānī 25. They live in Garm which belongs to England. A few households live in Lahūgard.

Kamālzāʾī

They say this tribe has up to 2,000 households and is divided into two branches: Kazhānzāʾī and Mashrānzāʾī and lives in Ṭūr and Huṭī.

Āmāzāʾī

This tribe is said to have up 2,500 households. They live in the locale of Charwarī. The Pīr Khayl and Bām Khayl are from this tribe.

Utmānzāʾī

This tribe has three branches: Katāzāʾī, Ākāzāʾī, and ʿAlīzāʾī. They are said to number up to 30,000 households [in total]. Their main estates are in the locales of Tūpī, Kūtah of Karhārī District and their lesser lands are in Mahāban. The Ṭāhiri Khayl of the ʿAlīzāʾī branch are scattered and dwell in Kaskar District and Harī. A number of them live in Maḥall-i Kalāyat-i Sayyid Khānī of Rawalpindi. Most of them are subject to the English government.

Sadūzāʾī

They state that this tribe has up to 15,000 households. The branches of it are the Zālūzāʾī, ʿUmar Khayl, and Darīzāʾī. The Zālūzāʾī live in Zahdah and the ʿUmar Khayl in Hindūstān. The Biyād Khayl lives in Marghūz and Tandī and in Kār-i Manārah. The Bīzād Khayl in Kalāyat [Kalābat?] and the Khadū Khayl make their homes in Chaklī.

Razar

This tribe has three branches—Razarzāʾī, Khiżrzāʾī, and Māmūzāʾī. Each of these has several khayls. It is said this tribe has up to 20,000 households and they reside in Yūsufzāʾī District and Shīwah. The Mānūzāʾī dwell in Ādīnah Dākī and Tarlātadī [?], the Malikzāʾī in Yārḥīn [?], the Maḥmūdzāʾī in Asūtah [Sawāt?], Shaykh Jānah, and Nawūnah. All are in English hands and are part of the government of Hindūstān.

Yūsufzāʾī

This tribe has five branches: 1) ʿAlī Khayl, 2) Mūsā Khayl, 3) Ūryā /69/ Khayl, 4) Mānīzāʾī, and 5) Alkūzāʾī. They say this tribe has up to 294,000 households. Regarding the clans of this five-part tribe, the Ḥasanzāʾī, Madā Khayl, Akāzāʾī, Ilyāszāʾī, Dawlatzāʾī, Chagharzāʾī, Nūrzāʾī, Khwājūzāʾī, Abāzāʾī, and Rānīzāʾī live in the districts of Bunīr, Sawāt, Kūhistān-i Shūl, Dīrah District, and Panjkūrah. The Malīzāʾī, Yūsufzāʾī and most of this tribe are subject to the English. Other tribes also inhabit the lands of the Yūsufzāʾī, like the Khatak, Muḥammadzāʾī or Mūmandzāʾī, and Utmān Khayl who are scattered in Tālāsh District. A number live in Kūshah Landī and some in Lawand Khūrd. The Khattak tribe which dwells on the land of the Yūsufzāʾī is stated to number up to 17,700. The Maymahzāʾī [are said to] have 31,500 [households].

Kakyānī

They say this tribe has up to 7,500 households and lives in Dūābah between the Kabul and Swat Rivers.

Tarkalānī

This tribe is divided into four sub-tribes: 1) Sālāzāʾī (*sic*—Sālārzāʾī), whose homeland is the Chār Ming Valley and is said to number 15,000 [households], 2) Mamūnd, which has two branches—the Kakāzāʾī and the Dūr Mamūnd—and is said to number 25,000; 3) Yūsūzāʾī, said to be 7,500; 4) Ismīlzāʾī [*sic*—Ismāʿīlzāʾī] said also to number 7,500. Besides the Afghans, the Barāwulīs are said to be 12,500 households. The Tarkalānī tribes who live in Bājāwur number 15,000. Bājāwur, which is bounded by Kāfiristān, has 5,000 people from the Ṣāfī tribe dwelling there; 37,500 households of the Tājīk people residing along the Bājāwur River, and 500 Āfrīdī and a number of Hindūs living in the Bājāwur Plain.

Ṣāfī

This tribe, which considers itself Sarbanī, is divided into six branches: 1) Qandahārī, 2) Maswūd, 3) Gurbuz, 4) Wahmī, 5) Kākīzā'ī and 6) Khāwī Khayl. They live in Sūd Kamar, one of the environs of Bājāwur. A few households reside in Takāb [*sic*—Tagāb] north of Kabul, in Gaz District [Jalālābād], and Swāt. They say they number 15,000 households. The mother of ʿInāyat Allāh Khān Muʿīn al-Salṭanah, son of Amīr Ḥabīb Allāh Khān was from the family of Muʿāẕ Allāh Khān, a resident of Takāb [*sic*] and from this tribe. /**70**/

Ghūryā Khayl

This tribe is divided into four branches: 1) Dawlatbār [*sic*—Dawlatyār] of which the Muhmand and Dā'udzā'ī are branches, 2) Khalīl, 3) Chamkanī, and 4) Zīrānī. The Muhmand [are divided] into two branches—Muhmand Bālā and Muhmand Pāyīn (Upper and Lower Muhmand). This branch [the Muhmand] is said to have up to 15,000 households and lives in Peshawar District. There is a group of the Muhmand known as Dighrū Muhmand meaning Muhmands of the mountains. They live in the mountains of the west as far as the Kabul River and in the eastern mountains as far as the Gaz River. The Muhmand Pāyīn have 2,500 households and together they are said to number 26,500 households. Some of this tribe lives in Laʿlpūrah, Kāmah, and Kūshtah. The mother of Muḥammad Yaʿqūb Khān and Sardār Muhammad Ayyūb Khān, sons of Amīr Shayr ʿAlī Khān, was from this tribe [and the daughter] of Saʿādat Khān of Laʿlpūrah.

Dāwudzā'ī

They say this tribe has up to 12,500 households. They live south of the Kabul River near Peshawar and are subjects of the English government.

Khalīl Khayl of the lineage of Ghūryā Khayl

They say that this tribe has up to 7,500 households. It resides in Maydān-i Pīshāwar.

The Chakanī [Chamkanī) tribe from the Ghūryā Khayl lineage

They say this tribe has up to 10,250 [households] and resides in Peshawar District in Kūh-i Sapīd.

Zīrānī

This tribe is scattered. A small number live on the outskirts of Jalālābād and a few are connected to the Tājīk people.

Mullāgūrī

One of the tribes connected to Mayhmand [*sic*—Maymand]. This tribe numbers about 750 [households] and has four branches: 1) Bahār Khayl, 2) Tār Khayl, 3) Aḥmad Khayl, and 4) Dawlat Khayl. They live in Tātar.

Zamand or *Jamand*

They say this tribe has up to 1,000 households. They live in Multān, Ghūrband, and in Quṣūr, east of Lahore. A few households are in Fūshanj-i Qandahar; one estate of theirs is in Hasht Nagar; a few households live north of the Kabul River adjacent to the Muhmandzā'ī, offspring of Tazmand [*sic*]; and in Chārṣadah, Tangi Naw Shahr, Parāng, and other places. All of this tribe of the Muhmand is said to number as many as 10,000 households.

Kānsī

This tribe is said to be up to 700 households. They live in Quetta and Balūchistān. /71/ They are a part of the seven-part Shinwār who altogether amount to 12,000 households. They live in Kūh-i Sapīd south of Jalālābād and in the Khaybar [Valley] near the Afrīdī tribe.

The Ghurghushtī [*Tribe*]

They say this tribe is also from the Kākar. It is divided into six sections. Its place of residence is [adjoined] to the north by the Ghilzā'ī lands and to the northwest by the Arghastān-i Qandahar and Tūbah, part to the lands of the Achakzā'ī tribe. On the southwest [they are bounded by] Balūchistān, the district of Aspīn Tarīn and a ridge of the Kūh-i Sulaymān. Some have said this tribe has 1,200,000 members; others say 1,800,000. The truest and most accurate and acceptable number is 750,000.

Nāghrāz

This tribe is a branch of the Ghurghushtī and is mixed with the Kākarī tribe. The Panī tribe is [another] branch of the Ghurghushtī and lives in Bahwī District and is said to have up to 100,000 members.

Dāwī and *Bābī*

[Another] branch of the Ghurghushtī, this tribe lives in Qandahar and Qalāt-i Naṣīr, Balūchistān. They say they are about 3,750 [households].

Mandū Khayl

[Another] Ghurghushtī branch, this tribe is said to have up to 10,000 members. They live on both sides of the Zhūb Valley which is in the mountains of the frontier. Some say that [the tribe] has as many as 15,000 [souls].

Tāymanī

This tribe is divided into two branches—1) Qibchāq and 2) Darzā'ī. They live in the Ghūr region of Harāt and are said to number 12,000 households.

Kalāwun

This tribe is divided into two branches—1) Salād [*sic*-Salār?] and 2) Manṣūr. They reside in the mountains of the Chahchahah District, Hazārah [District], along the edge of the river as far as Ūrash District. The say they number as many as 15,000 individuals.

Kākarī or Ghurghushtī Afghans also live in Rawalpindi and the Deccan and are said to number some 3,750 individuals. Another 3,760 also live in other parts of Hindūstān. Also up to 5,000 individuals are mentioned as being in the town of Khūrjah, one of the dependencies of Buland Shahr, [and in] Bengal and the Deccan.

The Bītī [Bītanī] Afghans

The founder (*jadd-i aʿlā*) of this tribe was Shaykh Bīt and thus they call this tribe "Bītī." They live east of the Kūh-i Sulaymān called Kūmal [*sic*—Gūmal]. They say they number 3,760 households. A group from this tribe lives in Kūh-i Kapar. The Afghan tribe of Kajūn [Gajūn] is also of the Bītū tribe. Their homeland is Nabūn (*sic*—Banūn). Three tribes—Danā, Katā, and Datatā—are all from /72/ the Bītī and are part of the Kachīn. The Ratanzāʾī are also Bītī Afghans.

The Ghilzāʾī, Lūdī, and Sarwānī

These three tribes are descended from the lineage of amirs or sultans of Ghūr and afterwards became attached to the Afghans but originally were not Afghans.

Hūtak

This tribe is Ghilzāʾī. Its population is said to be as many as 10,250 households. Their places of residence are Marghah, two sides of Bārī Ghar (Kūh-i Barī) and Sūr Ghar (Kūh-i Surkh). The clan of ʿĪsakzāʾī is a branch of this tribe, dwelling in Marghah and on ʿAṭā Ghar. The Malīzāʾī are in Girdī and the forest of Ghābirlān. The Barītzāʾī (live) in Ghināy, the Ākāzāʾī in Khaznāy and Mandyār, the Tūnzāʾī in Sūri, the ʿUmarzāʾī in Mandāwar, and the Dāmīzāʾī in ʿAtā Ghar. The entire Hūtakī tribe lives in the northern part of Qandahar. The Hūtak tribe is Ghilzāʾī and should be better known (than other Ghilzāʾī) because Mīr Ways, Ashraf, and Maḥmūd were from this Ghilzāʾī tribe. We have indicated the way this tribe is named according to the way Afghanistan's own historians explain it.

Tūkhī

This tribe is said to have up to 18,250 households. They live in the environs of Qalāt-i Tūkhī such as Tarnak, Pul-i Sangī, and Shībār up to the northern part of the Arghandāb Valley, to the Nawagī Valley and Khākāk. The homelands of the Bābakrzāʾī, one of the branches of the Tūkhī, are in Changīr, Sar Asp, Shāh Mardān and Nāwah and in Shībār, Haltāgh, Mandān, and other places. In addition, a few households [of Tūkhīs] live in Dih Afghānān in Kabul.

Sulaymān Khayl

Of all the branches of the Ghilzā'ī tribe, this one is the largest and most important. It is said that it numbers 60,000 households though some say up to 100,000. In the middle of the twelfth century Hijrī, Mr. Elphinstone wrote that there were 30,000 households [of Sulayman Khayl]. With respect to their homeland, they are divided into two sections, a southern and a northern. Of the southern section, the Qayṣar Khayl and Samalzā'ī reside in Katawāz; and the Ādīnah Khayl, Nasū Khayl, Qalandar Khayl, Shakī Khayl, Shāh Tū Dil, Jalālzā'ī, Kalā Khayl, Maḥmūd Khayl, Maṣal Khayl and others [also] live [in Katawāz]. Half of Zurmat is owned by the Sulayman Khayl. The Sulayman Khayl also dwell in Nānī Ghund, a dependency of Katawāz and in Wazī Khwāh. In the northern section are the Sitānzā'ī, Sulṭan Khayl, and Aḥmadzā'ī, who live in Tāy Tīmūr located west of the La'l Valley in Kabul /73/ and in all of Maydān-i Kabul District, Tīzīn, Jagdalak, Surkh Rūd, Gandamak, and 'Alishang Valley, dependencies of Jalālābād and Lamqān. The Aḥmadzā'ī from the Sulaymān Khayl tribe make their homes in the eastern part of Lahūgard, Altimūr, Sapīkah, Surkhāb, located on the western skirts of Kūh-i Sulṭan Aḥmad-i Kabīr. During the Mangal episode of 1303/1924, Amīr Amān Allāh Khān seized the lands of this tribe in Altimūr, gave them to the Wardak tribe, and banished this tribe to Turkistān.

'Alī Khayl

They state that this tribe has as many as 10,000 households. Half of it lives in Zurmat and the rest in Muqur. Five hundred households are in Khūst, a few reside in Ūlūm Lālā, of the Hazārah lands of Jāghūrī, and some are scattered in other places.

Akā Khayl

Thus tribe is said to have 1,250 households. They live in Muqur and most of them work as kelim weavers while [others] make their living in a variety of other ways.

Andarāz [sic–*Andar, Andarī*]

This tribe is said to comprise as many as 22,500 households. For the most part they live in Ghaznīn, Jāmrād, and Zurmat. Some are in Shībā, the territory of the Tūkhīs and Wāghaz. In other places in Afghanistan one or two households of this tribe may be seen.

Ghilzā'ī Tarakī

This tribe is said to have as many as 19,750 households. Two-thirds of this tribe live in Muqur and Nāwah and one third are nomads.

Isḥāqzā'ī or Sahhākzā'ī

People say this tribe has 8,700 households. They live in Zurmat, Pamqān, Bīktūt, Takāb [Tagāb], and a few also in Lamqān and in the southern part of the Hindū Kush mountains. A number also are scattered in Balkh, Turkistān, Iran, in

Narmāshir, Kirmān and Ṭabas even as far as the environs of Iṣfahān, Hindūstān, and Dāghistān.

Nāṣir

This tribe, which considers itself part of the Ghilzā'ī Hūtak, is said to have as many as 19,700 households. They live in Kāh Darrah, Shakar Darrah, Ḥājjī Kak, and in Kūh Dāman District of Kabul. A number of the Nāṣir tribe are also nomads.

Kharūtī

They say this tribe has up to 7,500 households. [Most of them] reside in eastern Katawāz [part] of the Kūh-i Sulaymān up to the Kūh-i Barmal and 625 households in Sar Rawżah. The rest are nomads /74/ who also engage in commerce. In summer they move up to the environs of Ghaznīn.

Khadūzā'ī

They say this tribe has as many as 2,500 households. Two hundred fifty-five of them are in Muqur and are mixed with the ʿAlī Khayl tribe. The rest are settled in Dih Khwājah in northeast Qandahar.

Zhamryā'ī

In all Afghanistan they say there are 1,250 households of them. They live scattered on the lands of the Tūkhīs, in Qandahar, and in Kabul.

Lūdī

This tribe is divided into three sections—Sayānī, Niyāzī, and Daftānī. Sulṭān Bahlūl, Shayr Shāh, and Sulṭān Sikandar, whom according to Afghan historians like Sulṭān Muḥammad Bārakzā'ī, author of *Tārīkh-i Sulṭānī*, held the emirate and chieftainship in Hindūstān, were members of this tribe of the Ghilzā'ī.

Parangī

This tribe is from the Lūdī Ghilzā'ī but there are none of them in Afghanistan. They are found in the Deccan and in Hindūstān.

Lūḥānī

They say this tribe has about 13,145 households. It is divided into two factions: Tūr and Aspīn. They live on lands north of the Garm River and in the dependencies of Banūn.

Dawlat Khayl

They say this tribe has up to 10,000 households. It lives in Tak District, one of the regions colonized by the English.

Miyāyān Ma'ī Khayl

They say this tribe has up to 3,750 households. Mostly, they live as nomads. In summer they come to the environs of Ghaznīn. In winter, they live in India. Their occupation is commerce and most of them go to Russian Turkistān, Bukhārā, and Iran to trade.

Tannūr

They are descended from the Lūdī Ghilzā'ī lineage and are said to have 375 households. They are settled in western Tāk District, on English territory.

Niyāzī

Of Lūdī Ghilzā'ī lineage, they say this tribe has 200–300 households of nomads. Their total numbers are 1,000 households living near the Bangash lands, in the environs of Qandahar, Ghaznīn, Kūh-i Kar, the environs of Kabul, and the village of Shīwakī, Hindūstān. Mostly they engage in trade. /75/

Daftānī

They state this tribe has 250 households. Some nomadize and some live in Wānah, and northern Harīpāl [territory]. In Bandī Qarābāgh, Ghaznīn, forts and farmlands have been given to this tribe.

Khaysūr

Of the Lūdī Ghilzā'ī lineage, this tribe is said to have 370 households and they live in the southern ʿĪsā Khayl District and eastern Patyālah.

Malaj

This is one of the branches of the Dawlat Khayl or the Niyāzī. It is a small khayl and scattered. Some are in Dīrah Ismāʿīl Khān and one family in Pīlān.

Ṭā'ifah-i Sarwānī

This tribe is of the lineage of Ḥusayn Ghūrī. In the past it was relatively large but today it has virtually disappeared. A few households reside in Chahchahah, one of the dependencies of Rawalpindi. One relatively large clan remains in Mālīr, Kūtalah. All the rest have become scattered.

Kardānī

This tribe also used to be quite large but now they say there are not more than 2,000–3,000 households of them. They are the progeny of Lāzāk and they live in Chahchah, Rawalpindi, and Peshawar in Hindūstān. But there are tribes in Afghanistan that consider themselves related to the Kardānī and we will describe them separately.

Tribes and clans related to the Kardānī lineage

They say the Ardak clan has 20,000 individual members. They live in the mountains of the frontier, in Kūh-i Sapīd, and in the region of Tīrā [*sic*—Tīrāh].

Mangal

They say this tribe has up to 15,000 members. They lived in Khūst but as a consequence of the 1303/1924 rebellion, they vanished at the hands of Amān Allāh and went to the land of India.

Muqbil

They say this tribe has 700–1000 households. They live in Jājī and northern Mangal. A few households also live in Khūst.

Awlād-i Kakī:

The "Awlād-i Kakī" (offspring of Kakī) is an expression used for the Afrīdī, Khatak, Utmān Khayl, Khūgyānī, Wazīrī, and Sītak. They say these tribes total as many as 29,750 households. [The offspring of Kakī] divide into two parts: the abovementioned section and [?]. They live in northern Tīrā and in the mountains of Jalālābād, as far as the borders of Peshawar, Bangash, and Kūh-i Sapīd. /76/

Afrīdī

A section of this tribe and some others of the Bangash and Tūrī are Shīʿah. They live in Lūdyānā and Pānīpat in Hindūstān. The subdivision that is Shīʿah is always fighting with the tribes around it and is said to number as many as 23,000 households.

Khatak

They say this tribe numbers up to 52,500. Their homelands are Būghah, Tīrī, Chūtarah, Lāchī, Shakar Darrah as far as the Indus River, Rīsī, and Patyālah and are part of the territory of Hindūstān.

Jadrān

This tribe is said to have as many as 19,750 households and lives in a green and fertile mountain region located between Khūst and Zurmat.

Utmān Khayl

They say this tribe has up to 6,000 households. Its homeland is Arang District and a number also live in villages.

Khūgyānī

They say this tribe numbers up to 6,250 households and resides in western Nanganār (Nangarhār). The Tūrīs of this tribe along with the Afrīdī and Bangash are as many as 32,000 households. They live in Garm District, south of Kūh-i Safīd and north of Khūst. Fifteen thousand Tūrī households are Shīʿah and 250 households of the Ḥamzah Khayl clan are nomads. Of the Mullā Khayl, 250 households are thieves by profession and they plunder the property of Sunni tribes. This subdivision of Tūrīs, Afrīdīs and Bangash are for the most part Shīʿah.

Jājī

They say this tribe has as many as 2,200 households. They live to the northwest of the Tūrī and they are subjects of Afghanistan.

Parbah

This tribe is a branch of the Khūgyānī and is related to the Karrānī lineage. It is said to have up to 1,250 households. It is comprised of the Mardī Khayl, Miyā Khayl, Banī Khayl, Sardār Khayl, Maḥmūd Khayl, Narī Khayl, Zay Khayl, Malīzā'ī, Ashīzā'ī, Dadah Khayl, and Pūchī Khayl. The tribe resides in Khūst District.

ʿAbd al-Raḥmān or *Durmān*

This tribe is said to have up to 1,250 households and is made up of six clans: Ḥājjī Khān Khayl, Sūdī Khayl, Aḥmad Khayl, Kūndī Khayl, Mangī Khayl, [and a sixth one?]. They are also called Maymūrī and Matūn. They live and have their homelands in Khūst District. /77/

There are other tribes in Khūst District which are connected to the Karrānī lineage, for example the Ṣabarī of 1,250 households, the Malī–750 households, the Landar–365 households, and the Akībī–125 households which are included in the Aspīn Gūndī (White Faction) of Khūst; the Zakī Khayl, Nukat Khayl, and Shādīzā'ī and the Ayyūb Khayl of 125 households including the Tūr Gūnd (Black Faction) and living in Aspīn Kūh and in constant conflict with each other.

Wazīrī

This tribe is made up of several clans: for example, the Utmānzā'ī, Aḥmadzā'ī, Masʿūdī, Kurbaz [i.e. Gurbaz], Ibrāhīm Khayl, Manẓar Khayl, Madd Khayl, Tūrī Khayl, Walī Khayl, Malik Shāhī, Bakā Khayl, Jānī Khayl, Sīn Khayl, Kālū Khayl, ʿAlīzā'ī, and Bahlūlzā'ī. They say this tribe [the Wazīrī] has as many as 125,000 households. They inhabit the districts of Su'āl, Shakī, Zarmak, the Khaysūr Valley, Sharakī, Sīr Talah, Dānah, Badr, and others on the land of Hindūstān and are subject to England. A few households are in Barmal and are Afghan subjects, 1,250 households in Barmal, Afghanistan. The tribes [sic] of the Gurbaz mentioned above live in the southern part of Khūst and 6,250 households of the Lālī tribe reside in the northwestern part of Kūh-i Sapīd, a dependency of Jalālābād and are subjects of Afghanistan.

Shītak

This tribe is divided into two subdivisions: Dūr and Tanī. Each one includes several subtribes such as [read *az qabīl* for *az qabīlah*] Banī Aryūzā'ī and Marrī. The subtribe Sīngī has 652 households and resides in the western corner of Khūst. From this tribe [the Shītak] 125,000 individuals live in the villages of Ḥiṣārak, Kūkhah, Narfī, and Utmān. Of the lineage of Shītak there are approximately 7,500 households living in the mountains along both banks of the Tūkhī River on English territory [read *khāk* for *khān*].

Bānūzā'ī

They say this tribe has as many as 38,186 households. It includes the subtribes of Banūchī, Gīway, Sūrānī, Mīrī, Abū Khayl, Tūtalī, Ḥasan Khayl, Ghūndū, and Huwayd. They consider themselves of the Shītak [read Shītak for Satīk] and Karrānī lineage.

Gandah Pūr

Of the Usturānī lineage, they say this tribe has as many as 37,500 households. It is divided into four branches: Ya'qūbzā'ī, 'Imrānzā'ī, Khūbīzā'ī, and Darī Palār[ah]. They live in Lahore, Dihlī, Bombay, Karachi, and Quetta. Basically, the tribes of Gandah [Pūr] are from the dependencies of Dīrah Ismā'īl Khān. /78/

Other Tribes Living in Afghanistan

Hamrāz

Of the Usturānī lineage, they say this tribe has up to 3,750 households. They inhabit the mountainous locales of Amak, Paywar Kūy, Dachah Kūy, Mangal, and Gundī in the eastern mountain region of the Amrzā'ī.

Four Tribes that Consider Themselves Sayyids

The first are the abovementioned Gandah Pūr and Hamrāz. The second tribe is Hunī; the third is Wardak and the fourth is [Mu]shwānī. These four consider themselves offspring of Sayyid Muḥammad Kaysūd Zār [*sic*—Gīsūdarāz]. The Gandah Pūr and Hamrāz are mentioned above.

Hunī

This is said to have up to 10,250 households. Most live in Hindūstān and a small number are included among the Mangal.

Mushwānī

They say this tribe has up to 500 households. It inhabits Kūh Dāman-i Kabul. Some live in Qandahar and also in Rawalpindi.

Wardak

This tribe is said to have as many as 12,500 households. They reside between Kabul and Ghaznīn. Several households live within the boundaries of Lahūgard.

Sayyids of Sound Genealogy in Afghanistan

These sayyids are the descendants of Imām Ḥasan and Imām Ḥusayn (peace be upon them). They are scattered throughout all of Afghanistan and there is not a place without one or two households of them. Aside from the sayyids of the Hazārahjāt and Darrah [*sic*—Dīrah] Ismāʿīl Khān who are Shiʿah, all the rest are Sunnis.

Quraysh

This group is scattered and their numbers are few. They work in Afghanistan as prayer leaders and are the recipients of charitable donations.

ʿArabs

The total number of ʿArabs living in Afghanistan is 2,500 households. Of that total a number of them were in the Bālā Ḥiṣār in Kabul. They are [now] scattered and are Shīʿah. They work in Jalālābād as zamindars.

Bangash

They consider themselves ʿArabs and of Quraysh lineage. People say they total as many as 22,500 households. /79/ Mostly they are Shīʿah. Their homelands are in the districts of Garm [i.e. Kurram?] and Shalūzān.

Tājīk

They say this tribe numbers as many as 56,250 [households]. They reside in Kabul, Ghaznīn, Balkh, Harāt, Qandahar, Badakhshān, Khinjān, and Lahūgard. Except for the Tājīks of Bāmyān, Chūrah, and Gīzāb, the rest are Sunnis. Thus, the government of Afghanistan seized the lands of Chūrah and Gīzāb and gave them to Afghans. Since those dispossessed were fervent [in their faith], they became scattered.

Hazārah and Ūymāq

These are two [separate] tribes but in terms of lineage they are one and of Mongol or Circassian lineage. The Hazārahs are Shiʿah and the Ūymāq are Sunni. The Hazārahs residing in Shaykh ʿAlī and Panjshayr and those Hazārahs residing in Qaṭaghan are also Sunni and a number are also Ismāʿīlīs.

Ūymāq

They say this tribe also numbers as many as 575,000 [*sic*—57,500?] households. It is divided into four branches: Tāymanī, Hazārī, Taymūrī, and Zūrī and each of these is further subdivided into many subtribes. For example Tāymanī is divided into two branches: Qīmāq and Darzāʾī. They [the Tāymanī] consider themselves the descendants of Kākar-i Afghān. The Hazārī are also divided into two branches: the Jamshīdī and Fīrūzkūhī. The Jamshīdī in turn include the Khūkar, Kālkandī,

Qāqchī, Zaynkar, Zulfi, Muflīdī, Jiwālī, Khayr, Qirk, and Dāh Zabar. The Jamshīdī people live along the Murghāb [River] and in Bālā Murghāb, Mārūchāq, Kūshk, Qarū Qāch, and Tannūr Sangī. The Tāymanī live in Kūh-i Siyāh of Ghūr and most of the Taymūrī live in Iranian Khurāsān. The Chār Ṣadah and Dawlat Bār [i.e. Dawlatyār ?] of [the Tāymanī] reside in Fīrūz Kūh. The Jamshīdī live close to the Russian border.

Hazārah

They say this tribe is formed of five or ten *days*. Every one of the five or ten *days* has one name: 1) Day Zangī, 2) Day Kundi, 3) Day Mīr Dād, 4) Day Mīrakshah [*sic*], and 5) Day Mīrak. These five are descended from Sādah Sūngah. Also 1) Day Chūpān, 2) Day Khiṭāy, 3) Day Nūrī, 4) Day Mīrī, and 5) Day Dāyah, these five are descended from Sādah Qabr. In addition, Ghūrī is a large tribe [of Hazārahs] which is divided into twelve branches and is related to Day Mīrakshāh. In addition, the Pūlādah [Fūlādah] are a large group and includes the Dāyah tribe. Each *day* has several subdivisions and subtribes all of which total 1,250,000 people **/80/** they say. For the most part they are [all] Shīʿah. But today no more than 600,000 to 650,000 people of this tribe still remain in Afghanistan. After the conquest of ʿAbd al-Raḥmān Khān and the general massacres and sale of women and children, the Hazārahs have disappeared, either killed or as refugees. The place where this tribe resides is the central part of Afghanistan [bounded] on the west side by Ghūr, Dawlatyār, and Harāt; on the south by Qandahar, the region around Girishk, and the dependencies of Farāh and Isfizār; to the east by Ghaznīn, Kabul, and Qalāt; to the north by Qaṭaghan and Balkh. But after the campaign by Amīr ʿAbd al-Raḥmān Khān and the defeat of the Hazārahs, most of the lands where the Hazārahs lived were given to other Afghan tribes and those of the Sunni sect. The Hazārahs became *muhājir*s to Khurāsān, Turkistān, and English Balūchistān.

Kayānī

They say this tribe has up to 625 households. This tribe came from Sīstān in Iran to Afghanistan and most are Shīʿah except for a small number who live in Qandahar and Harāt. They consider themselves descendants of Rustam and Zāl. But what has been heard in Afghanistan [by the author] is that they are believed to be descendants of Qubād.

Jaghatāy

This tribe is truly Mongol and has some 2,000 households who are mostly Shīʿah and known as Hazārah Jighatū and live in the western part of Ghaznīn. Some 1,240 households of them live in the villages of districts of Harāt and the Jamshīdī mountains. This segment is Sunni and speaks Turkī. They are also called the "Mongols of Harāt." But the Jighatū Hazārahs converse in Persian. One family of Tīmūrī descent claims to be descendants of Amīr Tīmūr Gūrgān. They live in Kakrak, part of the Wāghaẓ District of Ghaznīn. The chief of this tribe is a Jighatū.

Qizilbāsh

According to the work of Deputy Ḥayāt Khān, there was a census in 1271/1854–55 and 20,000 households of them were counted living in Harāt, Ghaznīn, Kabul, and Peshawar. All administrative affairs of government, especially finance, accounting, and military administration, used to be in the hands of this tribe but from the time of Amīr ʿAbd al-Raḥmān Khān, by means of repression and harsh treatment, they fled to Russian Turkistān, Khurāsān, and other lands and disappeared. Today in all of Afghanistan there are no more than 10,000–12,000 households of Qizilbāsh. The place of residence of this tribe is Kabul in the Chandāwul, Chūbfurūshī (Woodsellers'), and ʿAlī ʿRiżā Khān Quarters and in Qalʿah Ḥaydar Khān, Qalʿah-i Murād Khānī, /**81**/ Wazīrābād, Afshār, and Nānakchī. Of the subdivisions there are the Shāhī Savan, Manṣūr, Jawānshayr, Khwāfī, and Shīrāzī who, if they were able to travel, would emigrate to Iran. In Qandahar [there are also Qizilbāsh] living in the Tūpkhānah and ʿAlīzāʾī Quarters and in Harāt in [Harāt] City and in surrounding villages.[1]

Ūzbak

[They say] some 125 households of this tribe reside in Muqur. But there are many more of this tribe in Qaṭaghan, Badakhshān, Balkh, and Maymanah. They say that they number 900,000 households.

Dīgān

It is said this tribe numbers around 3,000 households. They live in Gaz District, a dependency of Jalālābād; in Lamqān; and in Bājāwur, which is Indian territory. Some of them speak Sanskrit and also Persian and Pashto (Afghānī). They say their original lineage is Hindū. The Afghans consider the Dīgān and the Tājīks to be of the same tribe but that is not correct.

Hindakī or *Jat*

They say this people numbers as many as 100,000 households. They live on the eastern edge of Sind, the districts of the Panjab, Balūchistān, Peshawar, Kabul, and other places.

Hindū

The population of this tribe today does not exceed 5,000 households. However, according to Deputy Ḥayāt Khān, there used to be 125,000 households [in Afghanistan]. The greater part of [their territory] has been taken over by the English, namely the Dīrahjāt, Banūn, Sīwī, Dāmawar, Peshawar, etc. This group [is found] in Kabul, Ghaznīn, and Jalālābād. In all the cities of Afghanistan they follow the

---

[1] [It is uncertain who wrote the following footnote, Farrukh or the anonymous editor of the 1993 edition.] This tribe chose to settle in Afghanistan as a result of the campaigns by Nādir Shāh. There is a large group in Lahore and Hindūstān. There are even some Bakhtiyārīs who came as a result of the campaigns and settled in Afghanistan.

professions of trade, dealing in textiles, brokerage, goldsmithing, and some as munshis in administrative offices. A number of them are Sikhs. Their religion is idol-worship. Some monuments to their religion still remain in some places.[2]

Swātī

They say this tribe comprises some 200 households. Their lineage is Hindī. The Dīgān are also said to be of them. Some live in Yūsufzā'ī District and some in the dependencies of Rawalpindi. /82/

Shalmānī

This tribe numbers between 200–300 households. They live among the Yūsufzā'ī.

Tīrāhī

This tribe is very well known. Formerly they were idol worshippers. Shihāb al-Dīn Ghūrī forced them to become Muslim. They live amongst the Shinwārī.

Kashmīrī

The majority of this tribe is Shī'ah while a number are Sunni. They say they number about 200–300 households. Their profession is rice husking, cooking, embroidery, shawl weaving, brokerage, and logistics (working as bearers). They reside in Bājāwur, Lamqān, and Kabul. Most of them recite the passion of Ḥusayn (*rawżah-khwān*), and are fervent adherents of the Shi'ah sect. Notwithstanding the fact that they are harshly suppressed, they are still known as a quarrelsome people.

Kurds

They say this tribe numbers around 3,750 households. People say that they emigrated from Iran to Afghanistan. In Kabul they live at the Lahore Gate in the lane called Rīkākhānah. Mostly they are Sunni and very fervent. In Afghanistan they say that this tribe has two subtribes, the Mukrī and Rīkā.

Lazgī

During the time of Nādir Shāh this tribe came from the Caucasus with Nādir to Afghanistan and settled in the vicinity of Farāh. They are also mostly Shi'ah and are known by the names 'Persian' (*Fārsī*) and 'Qizilbāsh.'

Armanī [*Armenians*]

There are very few Armenians in Afghanistan. They came to trade and make a profit. There are two or three households in Kabul and ten in Harāt. Their religion is Christianity. They read the Gospels in Georgian and Greek. The amirs and elite of Afghanistan are friends with the Armenians. Thus, Amīr Muḥammad A'zam

[2] The author here is probably referring to the many Buddhist stupas still found scattered in eastern and southern Afghanistan.

Khān married the daughter of Tīmūr Khān, an Armenian, and she gave birth to Sardār Muḥammad Isḥāq Khān. In Kabul they mainly have retail shops. In 1305 Shamsī/1926, I became personally acquainted with an Armenian in Kabul. He was a good man and had much useful information.

Qalmāq

They say this tribe numbers about 500 households. They are idol worshippers. During the emirate of the Sadūzā'īs, they were brought to Afghanistan. They reside in Balkh. Because of repression during the reign of Amīr ʿAbd al-Raḥmān Khān, /83/ most of them emigrated. Now only a few households remain in Khuttalān, Qaṭaghan, and Balkh.

Ḥabashī [*Ethiopians*]

They brought the Ḥabashīs from port cities to Afghanistan, bringing them as slaves from the port of Band[ar]-i Masqat to sell. They say there are some 225 households of them living in Harāt. In other cities their numbers are very small.

Jews

There are very few of the Banī Isrā'īl in Afghanistan. There were seven households in Kabul and now there are none. There are about 50 households in Harāt and they engage in trade.

Balūch

They say this tribe has about 200 households. They reside in Kabul, Qandahar, and Pusht-i Rūd and are Shīʿah.

Dawlatshāhī

They say this tribe numbers about 220 households. During the Sadūzā'ī era, they worked as judges (*qāżīs*). In Kabul, Qāżī Lane is well known and has been the place of residence of the Dawlatshāhīs. Today they make their livings at various occupations and consider themselves to be Quraysh.

Kāfir-i Siyāh Pūsh

This tribe lives in the Hindū Kush which extends from Chitrār and Bājāwur to Badakhshān and Panjshayr. Its [Kāfiristān's] boundaries to the north are Badakhshān, to the east Qāshqār [*sic*], to the west Andarāb, Qaṭaghan, Khūst, and Kūhistān-i Kabul and to the south Bājāwur, Lamqān, and other places. The Afghans consider them to be from the lineage of Abū Jahl and the Quraysh but they are [actually] [descendants] from the Greeks who came with Alexander of Macedon. They consider Kūrāshī to be their founding father (*jadd-i aʿlā*). They comprise several subdivisions such as Sūgar, Tarī, Kumā, Kambīr, Katār, Pīrah Kalī, Chanīsh, Damdū, Dīlī Wāy, Kāmah, Kūshtah, Dīnak, Kāmūz, Kāntūr, etc. It is said that they number some 200,000 households. Amīr ʿAbd al-Raḥmān Khān conquered them by force in 1313 Hijrī/1895 and compelled them to become

Muslim. Amīr Ḥabīb Allāh Khān changed the name of this place [where they lived], which was Kāfiristān, to Nūristān. Their dialect is Sanskrit. We here mention some of their words just to provide additional information. /84/ [Farrukh then gives a table of fifty Kāfirī words with Persian translations. Beneath the table is the following in small type]:

Babānūzā'ī

This tribe is known as Banūchī and are the descendants of Shītak of the Karrāni Afghans. The tribes of the Banūchī like the Kīway, Sūranī, Mīrī, Samī, Dūrwābū [*sic*] Khaylī, Tutalī, Ḥasan Khaylī, Ghūndū, Huwayd, etc. are of the Shītak lineage which was described above and number 37,186 households.

'Īsā Khayl

They say this tribe has up to 6,192 households. It has four branches: 1) Mamūn Khayl, 2) Badīnzā'ī, 3) Zakū Khayl, 4) Apū Khayl and they live on the edge of Sind. The Sarhang, Bahrat, and Sunbul are of the lineage of Dunyāzī. They say they ['Īsā Khayl] number 2,947 households and /85/ they live in Miyān Wālī. The rest of the peoples of Afghanistan, people from Sīstān, Qā'in, Kirmān, Bīrjand, and Mashhad who are subjects of Iran, are very few. In all of Afghanistan their numbers don't exceed 150 households. There are a few households as well who are of the Salghurī tribe.

Approximately nine-tenths of the [Afghan] tribes that have been mentioned are subjects of the Government of Hindūstān and only one-tenth of the tribes are subjects of Afghanistan. In order to know all the tribes of Afghans and all [the other] tribes which live in Afghanistan, we have researched and ascertained them as far as we were able to do so reliably and have put those results here in this section [of the book].

GLOSSARY

GLOSSARY

bayʿat-nāmah: written vow of obedience, allegiance
darrah: valley
dasht: barren land, wasteland, desert
dastah: subsection of a tribe, small military unit
dih: village, hamlet
firqah: section, tribe, section of a tribe
jamʿīyat: group, society
kadkhudā: village elder
kāfir: unbeliever, infidel, non-Muslim
kalāntar: elder, chief of a city quarter
khānah: house, household, family
khāndān: family
kharwār: largest unit of weight, approximately 565 kilograms[1]
khayl: clan, tribe, section of a tribe
kūh: mountain
kūhistān: mountainous region
kūtal, kutal: mountain pass
manzil: stopping place, route stage
niz̲h̲ād: lineage, descent
pādshāh: king, monarch, sovereign
qabīlah: people, tribe, clan
qalʿah: fort, fortified village
qaṣabah: town, large village
qawm: people, tribe
ṭāʾifah: tribe, clan
waṭan/mawṭin: homeland
tabār: race, lineage, ethnicity
yasāwul: (military) mounted guard, bodyguard
yāwar: aide-de-camp

[1] According to *Kitābchah-i ḥukumatī*. (For a table of weights and measures see Fayż Muḥammad, *The History*, vol. 3, part 4, Appendix 4.

Amānī Administration and Foreign Legations at the end of 1928[2]

Aide-de Camp: Maḥmūd Khān Yāwar

Warden of the Arg (*qal'ah-bīgī*): Ghulām Dastagīr Khān

Minister of Court: Muḥammad Ya'qūb Khān

Governors
Afghan Turkistān: 'Abd al-'Azīz Khān, son of Field Marshal Ghulām Ḥaydar Khān Charkhī
Bihsūd, Dāy Zangī, Dāy Kundī: 'Abd al-Razzāq Khān Muḥammadzā'ī (n.d.) succeeded by Mīr Muḥammad Ḥusayn Khān
Ghaznīn: Jānbāz Khān
Qandahar: 'Abd al-Karīm Khān, son of Qāżī Sa'd al-Dīn Khān

Mayor of Kabul: Aḥmad 'Alī Khān Lūdī

Foreign Legations
Iran: Naṣr Allāh Khān Khil'atbarī "I'tilā al-Mulk" 1922
Sayyid Mahdī Farrukh ca. 1924

Kalakānī Administration 1929[3]

Aide-de-camp: Muḥammad Sa'īd (or Sa'īd Muḥammad)

Warden of the Arg: Muḥammad Sa'īd
'Aṭā Muḥammad, son of Malik Muḥammad Istālifī
'Abd al-Ghanī

Chief of Police, Kabul: Sayyid Āqā Khān

Minister of Court: Shayr Jān Khān

Minister of War: Sayyid Ḥusayn Chārīkārī succeeded by Field Marshal Purdil Khān

Minister of Interior: 'Abd al-Ghafūr Khān Tagābī, son of Muḥammad Shāh Tagābī Ṣāfī

Foreign Minister: 'Aṭā al-Ḥaqq

---

[2] As named by Fayż Muḥammad, *Tażakkur al-inqilāb* and supplementing Adamec, *Who's Who*, pp. 286–289.
[3] As named by Fayż Muḥammad, *Tażakkur al-inqilāb* and not included in Adamec, *Who's Who*.

High Governors:

Afghan Turkistān: Mīrzā Muḥammad Qāsim Khān
Khwājah Mīr ʿAlam

Ghaznīn: Muḥammad Karīm Khān

Kabul and Central Province: Malik Muḥsin

Qaṭaghan and Badakhshān: Mīr Bābā Ṣāhib Chārīkārī

High Commissioners (*ru'asā-i tanẓīmīyah*)

Afghan Turkistān: Mīrzā Muḥammad Qāsim Khān
Khwājah Mīr ʿAlam

Southern Province: General Muḥammad Ṣiddīq Khān

Eastern Province: ʿAbd al-Raḥmān, son of ʿIṣmat Allāh Khān

Hazārahjāt: Nādir ʿAlī Jāghūrī, son of Sulṭān ʿAlī, son of Sardār Shayr ʿAlī Khān

Governors:

Jalālābād: Malik Muḥammad ʿAlam Khān Shinwārī

Director of Central Customs: Malik Zayn al-ʿĀbidīn

INDEX OF PERSONS

INDEX OF PLACES

INDEX OF TRIBES, GROUPS AND PEOPLES

NB The symbol < is used to show the lineage of individual tribes, where known, back to the founder. Because a number of tribes share the same name it also helps to distinguish one Mullā Khayl, for example, from another.

INDEX OF TERMS AND MATTERS

Printed in the United States
By Bookmasters